MW01047390

A Tagalog English and English Tagalog Dictionary

A
TAGALOG ENGLISH

AND

ENGLISH TAGALOG

DICTIONARY

COMPILED AND PUBLISHED

BY

Charles Nigg

MANILA:

IMP. DE FAJARDO Y COMP.ᴬ

101—CARRIEDO—101

1904.

add.

Catalog for stacks
LPH

PAUNAWA

Ang dahilan nang pagsulat nitong libro,i, dili iba kun di ang maka abuloy nang pagpapakalat nang mahalagang wika nang Ingles na ngayo,i, lumalatag sa halos lahat nang manga naciones, kayâ ang nasa nang sumulat ay ang tumulong hindi lamang sa manga Americano at Inglés na may pitang matuto nang wicang Tagalog kundi lalonglalô na sa manga maginoong taga rito sa Filipinas na ngayo,i, nagsusumikap sa pagaaral nang wikang Inglés.

Pinagpilitan sa pamamagitan nang masiyasat at masinip na paghahalunkat ang pagtitipon nang lahat nang manga matatanda at manga batang salita at wikang Tagalog sampo nang manga kahulugan 'nang bawat isa upang mai-hulog sa wikang Inglés at gayon din naman ang wikang ito sa Tagalog at gayondin naman pinihit ang ibinigay sa bawat isang wika sa paghuhulog ang halaga at kahulugan sa iba at gayon din na man ang manga tinatauag na Frances baga, ay pinilit ang magkaroon nang tunay na kahulugan sa kaniyang tunay na halaga sa iba.

Ang librong ito, ay nakasulat sa bagong ugali nang pagsulat nang wikang Tagalog, Kaya ang titic na C ay naging K ang Gui ay naging gi. ang Qui ay naging ki, at ang U ay naging W At dahil dito kung may ha-hanaping salita na sa dati ay nasusulat sa C at hindi makita ay dapat ha-napin sa K. At gayon din naman ang manga dating nasa Qui ay dapat hanapin sa Ki; at ang dati sa U ay hahanapin sa W

.450

PREFACE

The author's object in compiling and publishing this book is to put before the public a work that will aid both the American and the Filipino in learning either English or Tagalog whichever the case might be.

It has taken about three years to compile it and each word has been thoroughly tested so that the definitions will be found correct.

It is written in what is called the New Tagalog which differs from the old in the following respects. The C has become K, Gui has been shortened to gi; qui has been changed to Ki and w is generally substituted for U. Therefore should a person look for a word that begins with C and fail to find it he should turn to K; should he be unable to find Qui he should turn to Ki; and in case of u he should turn to w.

The English and Tagalog Alphabets.

Ang Mañga Alfabetong Englis at Tagalog.

ENGLISH	TAGALOG		
A	A	N	N
B	B	O	O
C		P	P
D	D	Q	
E	E	R	R
F	F	S	S
G	G	T	T
H	H	U	U
I	I	V	V
J	J	W	W
K	K	X	
L	L	Y	Y
M	M	Z	

Ang mañga reglang sumusunod ay tunkol sa pagsasalitâ nğ wikang Englis.

1. Ang sumusunod ay ang mañga vocales na letra sa wikang Englis at ang kanilang mañga tunog.

Titik sa Englis	Tunog sa Tagalog.
A	ei
E	I
I	Ay
O	O
U	Iu

2. Pag nauna ang titik na W sa letrang R ang W mamatay sa pagsasalita.

3. Pag nauna ang titik na C sa mañga letrang E, I, at Y ang pagsasalita ay tutunog nğ S

4. Pag nauna ang titik na C sa mañga letrang A, O, at U ang pagsasalita ay tutunog nğ K.

5. Kung ang titik na vocal ay sinusundan nğ alinmang letrang consonante bukod lamang ang R at isang E, ang vocal sa una ay tutunog nğ mahaba at ang E ay patay. [Mañga halimbawa Cane. Ang pagsasalita ay keyn, home ang pagsasalita ay hom scene sin bile bail abuse-abins Mañga exception care, have, come, love, dove, done, prove at gone.

6. Pag nauna ang titik na A sa letrang R ay di mababago ang pagsasalita nğ letrang A

7. Kung nagkakalaban ang dalawang regla ay ilalagay sa gitna ang pagsasalita

8. Sa mañga salitang maikli ang titik na vocales ay tutunog nğ gaya nito Ang a ay mamamagitan sa A at e, ang E ay mamamagitan sa E at I, ang I magiging I; ang O magiging A; at ang U magiging U

9. Kung ang letrang a ay nauna sa mañga titik na ll, lk O sa W, ang A ay tutunog sa pamagitan nğ A at O.

10. Kung ang mañga letrang igh ay magkakasama ang pagbasa ay parang ay

11. Kung ang mañga titik na ough av magkakasama ang pagsasalita ay parang ao, datapua,t, maminsanminsan ay tutunog nğ parang U

12. Kung nagkakasama ang dalawang titik na ow ay tutunog nğ parang ao

13. Kung ang dalawang letrang na ou ay sinusundan nğ nd ay tutunog nang parang ao; nğunni,t, kung ang susunod ay ld ay wiwikain nğ parang U

14 Ang karaniwang tunog nġ dalawang letrang ch ay parang tsh, kung na sasama sa salita Tangi lamang ang manġa sumusunod· Machine, Chagrin, Chivalry, Mustache, at Chaise, ang sa ganito ay tutunog nang parang sh.
15 Kung ang dulo nġ salita ay tion, cian ó sion tutunog na parang shun
16 Kung ang dulo nġ salita ay tous ó teous ay tutunog na parang shus
17. Kapag ang dalawang letrang gh at ph ay nagkakasama ay tutunog nġ F.
18 Kun ang letrang G ay nauna sa A, O, at U, ay tutunog nġ matigas
19. Kun ang titik na G ay sa katapusan nġ ahninang salita ang pagwiwika ay matigas ding para nġ nauna
20. Kun ang dalawang letrang M at B ay nagkakasama sa dulo nġ isang salita, ang B ay mamamatay sa pagwiwika
21. Kun ang dalawang titik na B at T ay magkalasama sa dulo nġ isang salita, ang B ay mamatay sa pagsasabi
22 Kun ang letrang G ay nauna sa N at M ay patay ang G   ,
23. Ang titik na H ay patay sa manġa sahtang sumusunod Honest, herb, hour at honor
24 Ang letrang L ay patay kaylanma,t, nauuna sa manġa titik na D—K at M.
25 Kun' ang dalawang letrang M at N ay nagkakasama sa dulo nġ isang salita ay ang M lamang ang tutunog at ang N ay patay,
26 Ang letrang Q ay katimbang ó kaparis nġ K.
27. Kun ang letrang O ay nauuna sa ld ay dapat tumunog nġ mahaba paris nġ Tagalog.
28. Kun ang dalawang letrang ed ay malagay sa katapusan ñg salita at ang kaniyan sinusundan ay P at K ay ang ed ay tutunog na parang T.
29. Kun dalawang oo ay nagkakasama at nauna sa P at K ay tutunog nġ U.
30. Kun ang dalawang oo ay nagkakasama at nauuna sa l ay tutunog nġ U
31. Kun sa dulo nġ isang salita ang E ay naiipit nġ isang consonante at D sa katapusan ang E ay patay at ang D ay siyang tutunog.
32. Kun ang W ay nauuna sa letrang R ang W ay patay.

Rules for pronouncing Tagalog.

1. The vowels have but one sound. The a-ah, the e-a, the i-e, o-o, and u-u.
2. When the nġ is written with a wave over the n it has the sound of nġ in the termination ang, while without the wave it is pronounced as t is spelled
3 The c is always hard
4 The g is always hard as in gun
5 The h has the same sound as h in English
6 The accent in Tagalog should never be forgotten as it sometimes changes the meaning of the word as Kayo-cloth while Kayó you.
The abbreviations used in this dictionary are the following
Ang manġa tanda nġ ginagamit sa librong ito ay ang sumusunod

a-adjetive, adjetivo	Conj-Conjunction, conjuncion
Adv-adverb, adverbio	Pro-pronom, pronombie
n ncun, sustantivo	Inter-Interjection, Interjecion
prep.-preposition, preposicion	V Verb, Verbio

A

A-a-A.

Aba *inter* Alas

Aba-a Miserable, wretched, de jected

Aba Po *(ang)* Prayer to the Virgen Mary.

Abahin-v-To tell, say.

Abala *n* Obstacle, impediment, hindrance, obstruction, nuisance, clog, arrest.

Abalahin-v To obstruct, impede, hinder, block, bother, clog, arrest, baffle, vituperate

Abay-n-Companion, retinue.

Abo-n-Ashes.

Abogado-n-Lawyer.

Abot-*inter*-There, well, what.

Abuloy-n Help, assistance, aid, succor, favor.

Abuluyan-v-To help, assist, aid succor, furnish, provide

Abutan *(Abutin)-v-*To reach, overtake arrive, obtain, amount to, *(ang masid)* iscover, disclose, show

Adyangaw *n-*Pitch, rosin

Agad *adi* Soon, immediately, instantly, presently, right away, betime, betimes.

Agadagad *adi* -Immediately, instantly very soon, speedily; in a trice in an instant, without delay, in a moment.

Agagan *n-*Cloth sieve or strainer.

Agagin-v To sieve or strain through cloth.

Agahan-n-Breakfast

Agamagam-n-Foreboding, scruple, doubt

Agap-n-Activity, haste diligence, anticipation

Agawin-v To snatch, grab, take by force.

Agipo *n-*Charcoal, half burnt wood

Agiw-n-Soot.

Aglahi-n-Feast, festivity, rejoicing

Agnat-n-Space or distance of time

Agos *n* Current or course of a river

Agpang-a-Opportune, convenient, right.

Aha *n-*Imagination, conception, fancy, purpose, design.

Ahas *n-*Snake, serpent.

Ahit-n-Shaving.

Ahitin-v To shave

Akala-n-Opinion, idea, design, object intent, intention, mind, notion, end, plan, perception, outline, scheme, view, purpose.

Akalain-v-To think, scheme, plan, devise, consider, contrive, imagine.

Akay *n* Brood.

Akayin v-To lead, guide, teach, train; instruct, conduct

Akin-*pro*-My, mine.

Akma-a-Fit, proper, appropriate, convenient; suitable, opportune fair, just, apt, due

Akma-*adv,*-Properly, suitably, intentionally, purposely, designedly.

Ako-*pro,*-I.

Akoin-v-To promise, go bail, stand good.

Aksayahin-v-To Waste, mis-spend, lavish.

Akyat-n-Ascension, acclivity, rising, mounting

Alaala-n Remembrance, recollection, memory, momento, gratification

Alabok-n-Dust, powder

Aladalad-n-Echo, resonance

Alagaan-v-To watch, take care of, heed, keep, guard, protect.

Alahas-n Jewelry, ornament

Alak-n-Liquor, grog.

Alakin-v-To distil

Alalahanin-v-To remember, recollect; bethink, mention, remind

Alalayan *(alalayin)-v-*To sustain, maintain, assert; support, endure.

Alam n-Knowledge, publicity, vulgarity.

Alam nang madla-a-Public, vulgar, common, general

Alampay-n-Kerchief, large handkerchief

Alang-alang-n-Politeness, regard, respect veneration, kindness.

Alangan-a-Questionable, irresolute, undecided.

Alanganin ang loob-a-Neutral

Alapaap-n-Cloud

Alapaap nang loob-n-Jealousy, suspicion.

Alay-n-Offering, oblation, offer, gift, contribution, obligation, homage, present, gratification

Alayan-v-To offer one's love

Ale-n-Aunt

Ale sa pakinabang-n-Step mother.

Alibadbad-n-Nausea

Alibugha-n-Jealousy Decrial, slander.

Alikabok-n-Dust, powder,

Alila Scullion servant, page, valet.

Aßlang babayi-n-handmaid, handmaiden
Ahhsan n-Sugar mill.
Alihsin-r-To grind, mill
Ahmango-n-Sand crab. crab.
Ahmasag-n-Crab
Ahmurahin-r-To insult, abuse, outrage, offend, revile, curse
Alin-pro-Which.
Ahndog-n-Caress, petting, fondling
Ahndnguin-i-To caress, pet, fondle, humor, wheedle, coax, jollify
Ahngasugas-n-Dispute, noise, rumor
Ahngawngaw-n-Rumor, noise
Ahmman-pro-Which so ever, who so ever, anyone, someone each, every one
Ahntana-n-Disregard, disobeyance, gibe, disrespect
Ahntanahin-v-To disobey, disregard, gibe, look down upon
Ahpin-n-Slave, serf, bondman, thrall.
Ahpinin-i-To enslave, subject, oppress, overpower, crush, enthrall
Ahpunga-n-Chafe
Ahpusta-n Insult, injury, wound, obloquy, fleer
Ahpustam-v-To insult, offend, malign, flout, fleer, wound.
Ahsaga-a-Inconstant, fickle, idle, lazy, loitering
Ahsan-v-To take off, take away, remove
Ahsin-v-To take away remove, subtract, extract, lessen, scratch out, divest, abolish, oust
Ahtaptap-n-Fire fly.
Ahtiit-n-Squeak, creak
Ahtuad-n-Echo
Ahw-n-Delight, pastime, comfort, satisfaction.
Aliwalas-a-Open, clear, plain
Aliwan-n-Sporting place, sport, diversion, pastime
Ahwin-v-To console, comfort, cheer, amuse, entertain, solace
Alkagfiete-n-Ruffian
Ahnanake-n-Almanac, calendar
Ahnirol-n Starch
Ahinrolin-v-To starch
Alok-n-Presentation, offering, proffer, overture, proposition.
Alon-n-Wave
Alquetran-n-Tar, pitch.
Alulod-n-Eavestrough, conductor, gutter, Drain, spout
Alulong-n-Echo.
Alupong-n-Snake, serpent, viper
Aluyan-n-Cradle
Ama n Father
Amag-n-Mold, mildew
Amágin-r-To become moldy, mildew

Amagin-a-moldy, musty, mildewed
Amam-n-Uncle
Amain sa pakinabang-n-Step father
Amala-n-Delay, detention
AMA NAMIN n-THE LORD S PRAYER
Ama nang nuno-n-Great grand father
Ambag-n-Contribution, assistance, aid, subscription
Ambon-n-Mist, drizzle
Amihan-n-Breeze
Amil n Stuttering, stammering
Amo-n-Flattery, caress, love, liking
Amoin-v-To tame flatter, coax, wheedle
Amoy-n-Smell, scent, stink, stench
Amoyan-i-To smell, scent
Ampatin-r-To stop, check
Ampon-n-Support, protection, patronage, shelter, aid.
Amponin-i-To support, protect, aid, shelter, patronize, provide, defend, help, assist
Amuyan-i-To smell, scent
Anak-n-Child, descendent, off spring, progeny, posterity
Anak sa asawang lauh n-Stepchild.
Anak sa ligaw-n-Bastard, illegitimate child
Anak sa pagka dalaga-n-Bastard, illegitimate child
Anas-adv-Softly, gently
Anasin r-To talk softly or gently.
Anat n-Artery, ligament
Anayad a-Soft, delicate docile
Anayad adv-Softly, delicately
Andukha-n-Defence, protection, help, paid, assistance, patronage
Anim a-six
Anim n Six,
Anim na daan n Six hundred.
Anino n-Shade, shadow, spirit, ghest
Anis n-Anis
Anis mascado-n-Nutmeg.
Anitin r-To strop
Anito-n-Idol
Ankin n Usurpation fraud cheat
Ankinin v To usurp defraud cheat, arrogate.
Anlnague n-carpenter
Ano pro What
Ano-adv-How, as if
Ano ang dahilan Since when, why, what is the reason
Anoman-pro What so ever who soever
Anoman-n-Something, any thing.
Anoman,y, wala None, not one, neither
Ano pa-What else
Antak n Pain ache
Antala-n-Delay, deterence, retardation.
Antalahin r To defer, delay, retard, dally, obstruct onut,

Antok-n Sleepiness, drowsiness, som-
nambulance, somnambulancy

Anyahan-r-To invite, stand treat

Anyaya n Invitation

Anyo n-Civility, custom habit, outline;
plan, scheme, project, means, form;
manner, shape

Apad n-Colic cramps

Apat-n Four.

Apat na daan a-Four hundred

Apat na panulukan a Four cornered,
quadrangular

Apat na puo n Forty

Apawan-r To submerge inundate, over
flow

Apdo-n Bile, gall

Apellahan ang usap-n-To appeal

Apo-n-Grand child, descondent

Apog n-Lime

Aporo n-Lining

Apo sa talampakan n-Great grand
child.

Apoy-n-Fire, conflagration

Apuhapin v-To feel or grope one's
way

Apuyan n-Hearth, fire place stove

Aral-n-Doctrine, teaching, instruction,
exhortation

Aralan-v-To instruct, teach, advise,
educate, drill, inform, apprentice

Aral na patnugot n-Maxim axiom

Araro-n-Plow

Ararohin-t-To Plow, furio a

Araw-n-Day.

Aarawaraw-adv -Daily

Araw nang kapanganakan-n-Birthday,
day_of birth

Araw nang fiesta n-Holiday.

Araw sa langit-n-Sun

Ari-n-Fortune farm, state

Arin-v-To own-use

Arin ang di kaniya-v-To usurp.

Ari nang sarili-n Fortune, property,
estate.

Aropel-n-Tinsel, tinfoil.

Areglahin-v-To organize, arrange,
regulate

Arzobispo n-Archbishop

Arokin-v-To try, fathom, sound

Asa-n-Hope, expectancy.

Asahan-v-To hope for, expect, await

Asal n-Custom, habit, mode, style, action;
fashion

Asal bata-n-Actions of a child

Asamasain-n-Anxiety, hankering anguish longing

Asamasamin-r-To hanker, long for,
desire.

Asarol-n-Hoe.

Asawa-n-Spouse

Asawang babayi-n Wife, helpmeet.

Asawang lalaki n Husband

Asim n-Cruelty, crudeness, sourness.

Asin-n-Salt.

Asinan-r To salt; corn; pikcle, cure season, brine.

Aso n Dog.

Asó-n-Smoke, steam; vapor.

Asong ulol-n-Mad dog.

Asukal-n-Sugar

At-conj -And.

Ataho n-Partition wall

Ataul-n-Coffin, casket

Atay-n-Liver

Atimin-v-To bear with patience

Atip n-Thatching, thatch, roof.

Atipan-v-To thatch, roof cover

Atuhin-v-To weigh, poise

Auspicio-n-Asylum

Awa-n-Mercy, clemency, condolence,
leniency, ruth, generosity, pity.

Awak n Crow, raven

Awasan-v To deduce, subtract, take
away, lessen.

Awatan-v-To separate, part,

Awatin ang hayop v-To wean animals,

Away-n-Dispute, quarrel, fight, riot;
tumult, strife, affray

Awit-n-Song-legend, fiction

Ay ano-What else

Ayaw-a Loth-unwilling

Ayaw magbait-a Incorrigible

Ayon-prep-According to, about, per-
suant, coincident.

Ayos-a-Fit, proper, elaborate, to the
purpose

Ayos n Symmetry, aptitude, pertinence,
array, opportunity

Ayunan v-To restore friendship

Ayunan ang iba r-To second, suscribe
consent, promise

Ayup-n Sarcasm abuse

Ayupan-v-To abuse ridicule.

Ayusin-v-To conform, arrange proportion, array, police, marshall, methodize.

Azogue-n-Mercury

Azul-a-Blue

Azul ang mata a-Blue eyed

B

B B.

Baakin a-Fissile capable of being split.

Baakin-r-To split, break,

Baba-n-Chin

Babag-n-Tumult, strife; contest, riot, quarrel, fray, scuffle, fight, dispute, setto.

Babagin-v To scuffle, fight, dispute offend, irritate, hurt, injure

Babala-n-Admonition, omen, advice, alarm, threat

Babala sa madla n-Programe, announcement

Babalam (babalan)-v-To imitate, induce, request, require, investigate

Babasagin a-Weak, delicate, brittle, frail, fragile, thin

Babayi n-Woman female, lady, mistress. concubine

Babaying abay sa pagkakasal n-Bridesmaid.

Babaying alila sa bahay-n House keeper.

Babaying banal-n-Virgen

Babaying Guinoo-n-Lady, damsel.

Baboy-n Pig, hog, barrow.

aboy ramo n-Wild hog.

ilulusan-n-Bellows

adya-n-Mockery, mimcry, tease

Badyahin-v-To tease, mock; mimic, imitate

Baga-n-Lung.

Baga-n Live coal, ember

Baga n-Abcess, tumor.

Bagabag-n-Vexation, mortification, disgust, disturbance

Bagabagin v-To vex, mortify, afflict, disgust, disturb.

Bagal n-Tediousness, prolixity, delay, laziness, tardiness, sloth

Bagaman prep Yet, as yet, still, ever, never, the less, though, however, not with standing

Bagang n-Back tooth, grinder, molar.

Bagaso n Bruised sugar cane

Bagay-n-Object, thing, item, desig, end, circumstance.

Bagay a-Fit, proper, adequate, apt, competent, seasonable, appropriate, useful, deft, profitable, convenient, suitable, natural, punctual, exact, applicable.

Bagay lupa a-Earthly, worldly, terrene.

Bagbagin v-To farm, plow till

Bagkus prep and conj.-If not, but, except; -only, besides; excepting

Bago a-New, recent, modern, young novel first.

Bago-adv. before Immediately, presently, right away, here to fore, rather.

Bagongbago a-Very new

Bagong binyagan n Convert neophyte.

Bagong laba- sa Colegio n Graduate

Bagong nagaaral n Beginner novice learner tyro freshman

Bagong tawo n Single man, youth.

Bagong tawong may edad-n-Bachelor

Bagot n-Displeasure, disgust

Bagok-n-Mud hole

Bagsik n-Strictness, strenuousness, sternness, severity, rigidness rigor, narshness, tyranny

Baguhin i To renew, remodel, alter; change, modify, deviate, vary, amend reform, convert, make over, retract, take, back, recall, annul, revoke

Bagwis-n Quill, quill pen

Bagyo n-Storm, tempest

Baha-n-Flood, inundation

Bahag-n-Truss or bandage for ruptures gee string

Bahag hari-n-Rainbow

Bahagi-n-Piece, part, portion, share division, section segment, quota, fragment,

Bahagi ng isang hukbo-n-Squad

Bahagihin-v-To divide, part, share

Bahagya-adv -Scarcely, hardly

Bahang bigla at malaki n-Torrent

Bahawin-v To wound, sear, scar.

Bahay n House, habitation, edifice

Bahay bata n-Womb.

Bahay gagamba-n Cobweb, spiderweb.

Bahay ginikan-n Hayloft, strawloft

Bahay na pinagtitinaan-n-Dyeshop

Bahay ng hari-n-Palace

Bahay pukyutan-n-Beehive

Bahid n-mark, sing

Bahin-n sneeze

Baho-n Stench, stink, corruption, polution infection,

Bahog-n-Mixture, medley, mortar, compound

Bait n-Sense, prudence, intelligence, ability, mind, will, skill, knowledge, knack, circumspection, print, under standing, disposition, standard, judgement, continence, continency

Baiki-n-Mumps

Baitang-n-Step of a flight of stairs, Rung of a ladder

Baka n-Cow, kine

Bakal n Iron.

Bakal ng kabayo-n Horse shoe.

Bakam-n Groove, hack, mortise.

Bakas n Track, footprint, rut, sign, furrow; mark, blot, vestige

Bakat-adv not alike, unequal, rough.

Bakbakin v-To unglue

Bakia-n Wooden shoe pattin

Bakin (bakit) adv -Why, how

Baklad n Fish corral.

Bakman n Sheep fold

Bakod n Fence, inclosure, yard, play ground court.

Baktasan-n-Shortcut

Bakman n-To Fence, inclosure, court, playground, railing

Bakman v-To fence, inclose.

BalA-n Theart, surprise, fright

Bala-n Bullet.

Balabatohm-a stony.

Balahibo-n-Hair, fleece, feather,

Balahibo ñg tupa n-Wool.

Balaho n Mud, mire.

Balak n Proffer, proposition, estimate, computation, calculation, supputation, account

Balakang-n-Loin.

Balakilan n-Crosspiece, cross timber

balakin-v-To compute, profter, reckon calculate, count, estimate, notify

Balakubak-n Dandruff, scurf.

Balang-pro -Each, every, someone,

Balanga n Round earthen pot

Balangaw-n-Arc, bow

Balang buan-adv-Monthly.

Balang lingo-adv -Wee ly

Balang na adv -some what, in a manner,

Balang na pro -Some one, whichso ever

Balan-n-Piles

Balantok a-Arched bowed

Balat-n-Peel, rind, crust, s m, pelt, hull

Balat kayo n Fiction, falsehood, stratagem, strategy

Balawis-a-Hot headed, quick tempered

Balayi-n Marriage,

Baldokin-n-Canopy

Balbas n Beard, whiskers barb

Bali n Granary mow

Bah-n-Break, fracture, crack.

Bahbul-n-Auger, gimlet, bit

Bahbuhn-v-To perforate drill, bore

Bahm v-To break, fracture, crack, crash, shatter disrupt.

Bahkat n-Shoulder

Bahkatan a-Firm, fast, hard, resolute

Bahkatin v To shoulder, carry on the shoulders

Bahk a-reversed inside out

Bahkin-v To verthrow, reverse, overturn, crush.

BahkIad-a-Reverse, refractive,

Bahktarin v-To overthrow, overturn, reverse, crush

Bahhsin-v-To raise, lift.

Bahndang n-Canvas, sailcloth

Bahntuna-adv-Against, backward

Bahsa n-Restlesness, hankering, anxiety.

Bahsa a-Restless, anxious

Bahsahin-v To vex, disturb, perturb, harass

Bahsaksakin a-Strong, robust, corpulent

Balisunsong n Wrap, Stingy person.

Bahsunsongin v-To twist, wrap

Bahsuso-a Curly, curled

Bahsusum-v To ring curl encircle

Bahta n News, notice, message, omen, information, report

Balita a-Famous, celebrated, renowned, accredited distinguished.

Bahtang mainam n-Evangel

Bahw-a-Furious, frantic mad, crazy

Bahwm-v-To mope fool, be come demented

Balok h Pellicule, cuticle, inner skin of truits,

Balon-n-Well, Cistern

Balot n-Bundle, parcel, pack cover, covering

Balot ñg Kalawang a Rusty.

Balot ñg sulat-n-Envelope,

Baltak-n-Haul, pull, tug

Balubaluman-n Crop, maw,

Balukan-v-Clean, husk, strip off huks.

Baluktot-a-Curved, bent, bowed, curvate

Baluktutin-v-To bend, curve, turn, clinch rivet

Balufigoyñgoy n-Nosebleed Hemorrhage of the nose

Balutan-v-To wrap up

Balutan n-Parcel envelop

Balutan ñg papel-n-Pad of paper

Balutan ñg sapot v-To enshroud

Balntin-v-To wrap up, embale, cover, envelop, pack, screen

Baluti sa dibdib-n-Nightmare

Bambo-n-Gallows, bamboo cane

Bambohm-r-To cane

Banakal-n-The wood around the heart of a tree

Banal-a-Virtuous, pious, holy, pure; virgen simple, just, merciful,

Banat a tense, tight, stiff

Banatin-v-To stretch, lengthen, expand, haul tight, thwart, tug, unfold, adjust, enlarge

Banayad-a-Moderate, modest circumspect, cautious, slow; sluggish, tardy

Banday a-impious, irreligious, profane

Bandila-n-Flag, standard, banner, colors pennant, ensign

Bandeja-n-Tray, salver.

Bandejada-n-Platter,

Banga n-Narrow necked olla.

Banga n-Combat, fray, knock, collision clash, fight, encounter.

Bangam v-To fight, assail, attack, assault

Bangahn v-To cut off at the root, chop off, maim.

Bangan n Granary, mow.

Bangaw-n Horsefly.

Bangbang-n Canal drain

Bangbangin v To dig a canal or drain,

Bangang gatasan-n-Milk pail.
Bangin-a-Rough, corduroyed
Banginbangin a-Rough cragged rude, rugged
Bangis n-Tyranny severity, ferocity, wildness, cruelty
Bangis a-Tyran-nical, severe, cruel, wild, fierce.
Bangit n Record, reference
Bangitin-v-To mention, relate, refer, touch, treat of, record, report, direct.
Bangungot n-Nightmare.
Banguyngoy-n-Hemorrhage, flux of blood from the nose.
Bango n-Sweet smell, redolence
Bangos n-Shad.
Banham-v To frame, begin work
Banka-n-Boat canoe, shallop bar
Bankay-n Corpse
Bankero-n Boatman, ferryman
Banko n Bench Bank
Banhan-v-To scald
Banhi n Mud, mire, slime
Bansag-n-Nickname, alias.
Bansagin v-To nic name, ridicule
Bantay-n Guard, watch, sentry, vigil, sentinel, custody
Banta-n-Idea, notion, fancy, admonish, forward, premeditate, permonish, have a nntion
Bantain-n- To intend, design, fancy; admonish; forward; premeditate, permonish, have a notion
Bantayan n-Guard, watch, patrol
Bantayin-v-To watch, keep guard, keep protect; preserve
Bantog-a Celebrated, famous noted, renowned illustrious notorious, distinguished, accredited noble, honorable
Bantog sa kahambugan a-Blown, notorious.
Bantuan-v To assuage, tune pour cold water with warm
Bao-n-Widow, widower
Baog a Barren, sterile, unfruitful
Bao ñg Hari-n-Queen dowager
Bao ñg ulo-n The crown of the head
Bao sa buhay n Grass widow, grass widower
Bara-n-Yard stick, shaft
Baraha-n Playing cards, pack of cards
Barahin v To measure by yards.
Barak-a-pale
Baraka-n-Market, market, place
Barak sa takot-Pale with fright,
Barandillas n-Baluster
Barazo-n-Arm.
Barazo ñg dagat n Bay, gulf, sound arm of the ocean.

Baria-n-Coppers, pennies, cents
Bariles n-Barrel, keg, cask.
Baro n-Shirt, jacket.
Barongbarong-n-Hut, cottage shack
Barrena-n-Gimble, auger
Barrio n-Suburb
Basá-a Wet, damp, moist. (ñg hamog) dewy
Basabasahin-v-To read, peruse.
Basabasain-v-To dampen, moisten, wet
Basag-a-Broken- fractured destroyed
Basag-n-Break, fractered crack
Basagin-v-To break, fracture, bust, destroy, crack, crash, shatter.
Basag ulo-n-Puzzle, perplexity, dissent, dissention, quarrel dispute
Basahan-n-Rag fragment of cloth.
Basahin-r-To read
Basahin ñg patakbo-v-To peruse; read swiftly
Basahin muli-v-To reread, read again.
Basain-r-To wet, dampen, moisten, water, dabble, sprinkle
Batisan-n-Ford
Bastos-a-Coarse, rude, indecent, illbred, tough, rough, disreputable; fell, immoderate, contumelious, rustic, unbecoming, gross, unpolished, noisy, blowzy, boorish, clamorous
Bastos na ugah-a-Abusive, insulting, illbred
Bata-n Child boy, girl, lass, lad
Batahin-t To maintain, suffer, sustain, tolerate, endure, resist, abide, oppose, repel, comport
Batak-n-Tug, pill, haul (na bigla) Jerk.
Batakin t-To pull, tug, touse, lenghten, stretch (nang pahigla) jer
Batang maganda n Cherub, (malut) Infant, babe
Batasan n-Short cut
BATHALA n-GOD
Bati-n Salute, greeting, salutation, curtsy, observation; remark, note.
Batia-n-Wash-tub, tub, laver.
Batibatihan-v-To beat, knock.
Batibot a-Strong; robust, sound, stout, firm, solid, inflexible, hard, rigid, arduous, tight, entire, complete, stubborn, just, informed
Batiin-t To salute, greet, halloo, repri, mand, rebuke, chide
Batik-n-Stain- spot, blot, blemish
Batikbatik a Spotted, speckled, mottled, brindle.
Batikola-n Crupper
Bato n Stone, rock, clif.
Batobalani-n Magnetism, loadstone.
Batohin-v To stone.

Batong Marmol-n Marble

Batong Malut-n-Cobble, cobble stone

Bato ng katawan n Kidney

Batugan-a-Lazy, indolent, inatentive, indifferent, idle, slow, tardy

Batugan-adv Lazily, indolently, tardily,
inattentively, slowly.

Batulang n-Basket, hand-basket, pannier

Batya-n-Washing place, laundry

Batvag n Listening, hearing

Batyagin-v-To hear, listen, hearken,
understand, comprehend.

Baul n-Trunk, locker, coffer

Baunan-n-Place of burial, grave, sepulcher

Bawal a Furtive, clandestine, prohibited

Bawang-n-Garlic, cives

Bawas-n-reduction, subtraction, deduc,
tion

Bawasan-v-To subtract, reduce, lessen,
discount, deduct, deduce, pare, clip,
lighten, cut away.

Bawat a-Each, every (buan) adv-monthly

Bawiin-v To recover, win bac', regain

Bayad n Pay fee, stipend, salary, compensation, wages, retribution, payment, satisfaction, reward

Bayag n-Testicle, (nang campana)-bell,
clapper.

Bayakan-n Bat, vampire

Bayan-n-Town, city

Bayani-a-Valiant, courageous, brave, intrepid, audacious, strong, gallant,
vigorous, noble, famous, celebrated,
illustrious, renowed, distinguished,
noted.

Bayani-n-Champion, combatant

Bayang tinubuan n-Birth-place.

Baybay n-Shore; strand, limit, border,
edge, (dagat)-n-Shore, beach sea shore
sea-coast; sea-side.

Bayaran-v-To pay; recompence, com,
pensate, retribute, idemnify, reward,
fee, liquidate a debt, (muli)-v Repay,
pay again, (nglagpos) v Overpay

Bayaw-n-Brother-in-law

Bayawak n-Guana; large lizard

Bavawang-n-Waist, (ng damit)-Waist
band girdle

Bayong-n-Sack; bag; sac

Bayubuan-v-To turn the ground, weave
the edge of a tray or basket

Bayugo fig tuhod-n-Kneecap

Bavuhan-n-Place of flailing, mall, mallet,
flail

Bayuhin v-To pound, flail, mall, drive
with a mall or mallet

Bayumbo-n-Screen

Belis n-Half cent

Benditahan-n-Holy watering pot

Benditahin-r To consecrate

Biak n-Half, crack, fracture, piece.

Biakin-v to have, break, crack; fracture

Bianan-n-Father or Mother in law

Bibi-n Goose.

Bibig-n-Mouth, chaps, orifice

Bibinga-n-Tile, piece of burnt clay.

Bigas n Rice

Bigasan-n-Place where rice is threshed,
building in which rice is threshed
or hulled

Bigat-n-Weight, gravity, heaviness,
heft, importance, consequence, toil,
burden, trouble, cross moment.

Bigatan-r-To poise, load, oppress, mor-
tagage, try the heft.

Bigay-n-Gift, present, donation, grant,
gratuity; keepsake

Bigay lamang a-Gratis, free of cost,
for nothing

Bigkasin-b-To pronounce, express, name

Bigkis n-Bundle, parcel, pack, fagot,
sheaf

Bigkisan v-To bundle, parcel, bind, tiegird

Bigkisin-v-To bundle pack, bind, tiegird

Bigla-a Unexpected, unforseen, quic-,
sudden; rapid, cursory; injudicious;
indescreet.

Bigla-adv-Hurriedly, unexpectedly; ra-
pidly suddenly; quickly, hastily.

Bigla-n-Error, mistake, hurry; sud-
deness; quickness

Biglaan-a-Urgent; pressing, executive

Biglabigla-a Unexpected; sudden

Biglain-v-To precipitate, hurry, hasten;
press.

Biglangbigla a-Sudden, hurried; precipitate: unexpected

Bigti-n-Suicide; hanging,

Bigtihin-v-To hang, commit, suicide.

Bigyan v-To give; present

Bigyan ang kahulugan v-To signif,
mean, declare

Bigyan ang kailangan v-To give the
necessities, provide, aid; succor defray, supply; turnish; minister

Bigyan kapangyarihan-v-To autorize
empower commision

Bigyan katibayan-r To guarantee,
ratify.

Bigyang loob-v-To gratify, condescend,
indulge, submit, give way.

Bigvang pasiya-v-To judge, decide; determine, conclude; resolve

Bigyang sala-v-To blame; condemn,
accuse, criminate, unpeach; reproach,
aggravate

Bigyang sindak-r To frigten, scare,
dispirit, render dejected

Bigyan lakas i To strenghten, cheer, give strength, or force; reanimate.
Bihagin-i-To capture, spirit, kidnap.
Bihasa-a-Accustomed, used, capable, skilful, practical, dexterous, sly, prudent, knowing, able, experienced, clever, expert, astute, cunning, elegant, excellent, polite, civil, certeous, graceful, smart; learned.,
Bihasahin r-To guide; teach, train; educate
Bihasang lubha a-very learned, wise well educated
Bihasa sa pag-gawa-a-Accustomed, fit; proper convenient,
Bihira-a-Scarce-uncommon; rare, old, excellent
Bihira-adv-Few, seldom, rarely, uncommonly
Bilis n Change of clotaes
Bihasan-n-Change of clothes, dress.
Bihisin-i-To change clothes, dress.
Buk-n-Shoat
Biis-n-Reward, remuneration
Bikas-n Shape, form, statnre, size, as pect, measure, ostent, mode, guise, will disposition, manner
Biki-n.-Mumps
Bikik-Choking; small obstruction.
Biklarin-i-To unfold, enlarge; extend
Bilang-u Count; computation, numeration
Bilangin v To count, ennumarate; calculate; compute, estimate, suppute
Bilang ng panahon n-Date,
Bilango n Jail, prison; calabose
Bilanguan-n-Jail, prison, calabose,
Bilaran-n-Drying place; place where anything is dried.
Bilas-n-Two people who marip two sisters, sister and brother, or two brothers
Bili-n-Cost price, buying price, value.
Bilibirin ng suga r-To fasten with a rope
Bilig sa mata n Catarat of the eye
Bilin n Message, errand, mission, charge, commission, request, mandate, injunction, order.
Bilingbilingan-n-Windlass
Bilis n-Vivacity; roidness, excessiveness, rapidity.
Billar n Billiards
Billete-n-Ticket
Bilog-n Roundness; circle; spahere; orb, globe, rotundity; disc, disk; total
Bilog-a Circular round; whole; total; universal, entire.
Bilugin v-To round, sum, add complete.
Bimbingin r To retard, delay, defer.

with hold; stop, check, dally, monopolize; preserve; suspend
Binat-n-Relapse second fall
Binata-a Young, youthful, juvenile
Binata n-Juvenile, youth
Bingas n-Gap or notch in a tool
Bingaw-n-Gap or notch in a tool.
Bingi a-Deaf, hard of hearing
Binghin-r-To deafent make deaf.
Binhi-n-Seed, grain, germ, bud
Binithay a & p p-Sifted
Bintang n False charge; imputation, presumption, suspicion, imposture,
Bintangin i To accuse falsely; inculpate indict.
Binti n-Calf of the leg, shang.
Binubukalan n Source; spring, origen
Binwit-n-Fishing tackle
Binuh-a & p p Polished.
Binutas ng tanga a-Moth-eaten
Binyagan-n-Christian, convert, baptism
Binyagin-i-To christen, baptize.
Biradoi n-Wrench,
Birang n-Handkerchief.
Biro-n-Joke, jest, pun, trick, buffoonry, hoa, flirt, drollery, grimace
Biroan-n-Carousol revelry, romping, jocularity, jocoseness, jollity, scuffle, (masaklap)-sarcasm.
Birnin-r-To Goke, jolly, fool, revel, laugh at, ridicule, flirt
Bisa-n-Activity, valor, force, fortitude vigor, courage, power authority, ability, possitivilty
Bisaklatin i-To spread or extend the feet
Biscotso-n-Toast
Biscuit n-Biscuit
Bisto-adr Perhaps
Bitag-n-Snare, trap
Bitak-n Crevice, chink, cleft, crack, fissure
Bitakbitak-a-Full of cracks or fissures.
Bitakin-r-To fissure; chink; crack.
Bitang-n Springe, Deer-net.
Bitay-n-Gallows.
Bitayin-r hang, execute by hanging
Bitbitayan-n-Scaffold gallows; place of execution
Bitbitin-r-To carry suspended; grasp, catch.
Bithay-n-Sieve, riddle, crib, cribble
Bithayin-i To sift, bolt.
Bitik-n-Garter.
Bitiwan-r-To let go, forsake, yield untie, loosen, discharge, slacken, selve, permit, forego, set at liberty
Bitiwan ang dala-r-To lay down a burden.
Birling-n-Ring
Bito n Feast, festivity, rejoicing, holiday

Bituin-*n*-Star.

Bituka-*n*-Intestine, tripe, gut

Biwas-*n*-Tug, pull, haul, wave, move

Biwasin-*i*-To tug, pull, haul, move, wave

Biwiin-*i*-To untwist

Biyaya-*n*-Gift, present, grant, favor, keepsake, gratification, compliments, pleasure.

Biyaya ng DIOS-*n*-Unction devotion anointing

Bokot-*a*-Rongh, rumpled, snarled

Bola-*n*-Ball

Bolinga-*n*-An obscure thought

Bomba *n*-Fire engine.

Boogin-*i*-To rot, remove

Buan-*n*-Month

Buan darating-*n* Proximo

Buan sa langit-*n*-Moon.

Buaya-*n*-Alligator, crocodile, cayman, caiman

Bubas-*n*-Small tumor

Bubo-*n*-Clown buffoon.

Bubog-*n*-Hall, crystal glass

Bubong-*n* Roof, thatching

Bubong ng paa-*n*-Instep, tarsus

Bubuan-*n*-Mold

Bubungan-*n*-Root shed

Bubuyog-*n* qumble-bee

Buchebuche-*n*-Fritter

Budbuin-*v*-To sow, scatter, powder

Budlongin-*i* To punch, bore

Buga-*n*-Pumice

Buba *n* Spit

Bugain-*i*-To burnish, glaze polish

Bugawin-*r*-To scare away frighten

Buglog *n* Contusion, bruise, hurt wound injury, blow

Bugbugin *i*-To contuse, bruise, hurt, injure; mongle, wound; maim cripple, pound crash

Bugnos-*a*-Loose, surplus

Bugnusin-*i*-To loosen, untie

Bugok-*a*-Addle, rotten, empty, void

Bugsok-*n*-Basket, hamper, hand basket

Bugtong *a*-only, single, particular, individual, unique, rare, singular

Bugtong-*ad*-alone

Bugtong-*n*-Enigma, puzzle, riddle, conundrum, poser, rebus, quiz

Bugtong na anak-*n*-Only begotten child

Buhaghag-*a*-Spongy porous fungus soft, blended; thin

Buhaghag-*n*-An idle talker

Buhaghagin-*v*-To thin rarify, dilute

Buhalhal-*n*-Fool, madman, idiot

Buhalhal-*a*-frank-open

Buhangin-*n*-Sand

Buhat *ade*-Since; after from.

Buhat *a* Originated, derived

Buhatan ang kasalanan-*i*-To accuse; impeach, criminate, incriminate

Buhatin-*r*-To raise lift, elevate, heave, get up.

Buhat ngayon-*adv*-Hereafter

Buhawi-*n*-Whirlwind

Buhay-*n*-Life.

Buhay-*a*-Active, lively, spirited, high; spirited

Buhayin-*r*-To vivify, enliven, spirit, electrify, inspirit, resuscitate

Buhayin muli-*i* To resusticate, restore, to life revive acquire new life.

Buhay na loob-*a*-Awake, lively impetous, vivacious, active, fervent.

Buhok-*n* Hair

Buhong-*a*-Haughty, lofty, rude, insolent, shameless impudent

Buig-*n*-Bunch, racenne.

Buis-*n*-Taxes impost, excise, duty, levy, contribution

Buisit-*a*-Ungrateful bad, unlucky, unfortunate

Buisitin-*i*-To cause to be unfortunate

Bukal-*n*-Origen, source spring, jet, fountain first cause

Bucalan-*n*-Head spring, spieng foun-tain.

Bukal sa loob-*a*-Spontaneous, voluntary

Bucas-*adi*-To morrow *n*-Morow

Bukas *adi*, open -*a*-clear, open

Bukbok-*n*-Grub, weevil, rotted tooth

Bukbukin-*a*-full of grubs or weevils

Bukid-*n*-Field, country, farm, soil, land, ground, region

Bukid na sinasaka-*n*-Cultivated ground, or land

Bukiran-*n*-Field, farm

Bukinin-*n*-To farm cultivate

Buklaw *n* Tumor, extuberance.

Buklod-*n*-Ring.

Buko-*n*-Joint knuckle

Buko *n* Green cocoanut.

Bukod-*adv*-more over, besides, except.

Bukod-*ang*-The rest, others.

Bukod-*a*-Special, particular

Bukod pa sa-*adi*-besides, moreover.

Bukod sa-*adv*-Let, besides, more-over except, away from, more than

Bukod sa iba-*a*-Strange, feroign, rare.

Bukod tangi-*a*-Distinct, particular

Bukol-*n*-Abcess, tumor, lump

Bukot-*a*-Crooked, hump-bac ed

Buksan-*i*-To open show, disclose, dis-cover, display

Bula-*n*-Froth, foam, spume scum

Bulaan *n* Liar, imposter

Bulaan *a*-Lying, erroneous.

Bulag-*a*-Blindman

Bulag-*a*-Blind

Bulagaw-*a*-Blue or gray eyed

Bulagin-r-To blind, darken cheat

Bulaklak-n-Flower blossom, posy

Bulaklakan-n-Place of many flowers, flower garden,

Bulanglang-n-Vegetable soup.

Bulaos n-Path, trail

Bulaw-n-Young wilb boar

Bulaw-a-Faded; withered

Bulati-n-Worm.

Bulaybulay-n-Meditation contemplation

Bulaybulayin i-To meditate, muse, consider, contemplate

Buli-n-Polish.

Bùli-n-Small tree snake

Bulihin-i-To polish, burnish, finish, smooth

Bulihin muli-v To repolish

Bulinaw-n-Short or near sighted

Bulo-n-Calf, suckling

Bulok-a rotten, corrupt, putrid

Bulong-n-Whisper

Bulong-adv -Softly.

Bulongbulongan-n-Whisper, rumor, report, murmur

Buló ng baka-n Calf, heifer, veal

Bulos-n A roll of cloth

Bulsa-n-Pocket, pouch

Bulukan n-Rotting place

Bulukin-n-To rot, corrupt, make putrid disrupt

Bululos-n-Diarrhea

Bumaba-v-To lessen, lower, descend, go down, flow, slump, let down

Bumabag-i-To fight, contend, dispute struggle

Bumaba ang loob-i-To humble, tame

Bumahasa-n-Beader.

Bumaho-v To stink, smell, bad, get or

Bumaka-i-To war, fight, oppose, contend, struggle

Bumala-i-To threaten, menace, proclaim announce

Bumago i-To renew, alter, change, disturb

Bumalak-i -To propose, offer, announce, proclaim

Bumahk-i To return, go back, fall back, retrograde, retrocede

Bumal kuas i To over-turn, double, duplicate; turn over

Bumalong-i To spring from, spring issue or proceed from, begin grow, have its beginning in.

Bumalong ang dugo-i-To bleed

Bumaluktot-i -To curve bend.

Bumanat-v-To extend,enlarge,grow large

Bumanga i-To attack, assault, attempt fight, collide

Bumangis i To become or grow fierce or wild

Bumangou-v To arise, rise, get up.

Bumasa-v-To read, peruse.

Bumati-v-To salute, hail, greet curtsy, halloo.

Bumatis i-To ford, wade

Bumautot-v-To stink

Bumawas-v-To slump, dwindle, lessen

Bumawi-i-To retrieve a loss, regain.

Bumbuan n-Grown of the head

Bumigat-v-To grow heavy, increase in heft

Bumigat ang damdan-i -To grow worse impair, deteriorate

Bumigti-v-To hang

Bumihag-i-To captivate, kidnap, capture, charm

Bumilang-r To count, enumerate, reckon, calculate

Bumili-i-To buy, purchase

Buminyag-i-To christen, baptize

Bumithay i To sift, separate

Bumuay-v To be unstable

Bumubuga ng-i-To vomit, spit.

Bumubukal-n-Springing

Bumuga v To vomit, spit, expectorate.

Bumugbog-i-To injure, hurt, wound, bruise, harm, cause pain, irritate

Bumuhat-r-To raise, lift up, erect

Bumus-r-To pay taxes, contribute, promote

Bumukal-v-To proceed from issue or sprink from, bubble, emanate

Bumukas-i-To open, dilate

Bumukod-r-To sort, separate, remove, dissuade

Bumukol-i-To lump

Bumula-v-To foam, froth, spume effervesce

Bumulok-r-To rot, addle, debauch, decompose

Bumulong-r To whisper, murmur, purl

Bumulongbulong-i -To whisper, mutter, murmur, grumble, growl

Bumulubok-v-To bubble

Bumuno-n-To wrestle, contend, struggle

Bumuti-n-To better, thrive, prosper

Bumutil v-To grain

Bundok n-Mountain, hill, mount, knoll

Bundok na bato n-Chill, rock, mountain of rock

Bundok na napuputok-n-Volcano.

Bunga n-Fruit, fruitage.

Bunga ng bayabas-n Guava

Bungang araw-n Prickly heat

Bungi a-Toothless

Bungin-r-To corrupt, rot make putrid

Bungin a Rough, coarse

Bungo n Skull, cranium.

Bungo n Clash, collision, knock, blow,

encounter, shock; push; fight, confusion, suddden meeting

Buni-n-Scurf, tetter; scurvy.

Bunihin-a-Scurvy

Buno-n-Wiestle, wrestling, tussle; struggle, strife.

Buntal n-Slap, blow with the open hand.

Buntalin-v-To slap, strike with the open hand

Bunton-n-Heap, pile; stack, crowd

Buntonbunton-a Piled, Having many piles

Buntong hininga n-Tail, tiain cue, caudal

Buntot n-Tail; train cue, caudal appendage.

dal appendage

Buntutan-v-To follow, pursue, persecute; dog; impoitune; implore, dun.

Bununhan-n-Fish corral, place of wrestling

Bunot n Pull, tug.

Bunutin-v-To pull up, eradicate; extract, abstract

Bunyi a-Illustrious, noble; famous, celebiated; noted, conspicuous, notorious

Buo-a entiie, whole, complete, full, perfect; integral, chock, intact, utter; sound, just, infoimed, candid.

Buo ang loob-a-Valiant, brave, bold, courageous, whole hearted

Buo at paikpik-a-Solid, firm; sound, consistent

Buoin-v To sum, add, fill up; fill, integrate, complete

Burahin-i-To blot, blur; erase; raze, efface; abolish, expunge, cloud.

Burak n-Mud, mire, slime.

Burakburak-a-Mudy, miry; slimy

Burol-n-Diy bed of a river, corpse

Buruhin v-To salt, season; sprinkle

Busilak-n Snow, frost

Buslo-n-Basket, hamper.

Busog a Full, satiated; satished

Busugin-v-To satiate, fill with food, satisfy

Butas n-Hole, aperture, eye, puncture.

Butasan-v-To perforate, puncture, bore

Butasin-i-To perforate, puncture, bore

Buti-n-Kindness, goodness, improvement; generosity, beniticence, benignity; clemency, good will

Butihan-n-Kindness, goodness; generosity, grace; gallantry, spruceness; smartness; pertection, delicacy; gayety, finery

Butihin-v-To better, make good or better

Butiki-n-Eft, small lizard.

Butiktik n-Reptile

Butil-n Fram, grain of corn

Butlig n-Pimple, pustle.

Buto-n-Bone, seed; kernel.

Buto nğ balakang-n-Haunch bone.

Buto nğ paypay n-Scapula, shoulder blade

Butong malambot-n-Gristle

Butones n Button.

Butuhan-a-Reward, premium, satisfaction gratification

Buya-n-Re'ard; premium, satisfaction; gratification

Buyain-i To Rewaid, satisfy; satiate, gratify.

C

Cabellería n-Cavalry.

Cabelleriza n-Barn, estable.

Cajon-n-Box, casing,

Cay-prep of, with, from; on, for; by, to

Camison-n-Smock.

Canta n-Choious, song.

Cantador-n Chorister.

Capital-n-metropolis, capital

Carbon-n-Coal, charcoal

Cuco n-Circus, Hippodrome

China n-Climate

Cosmetico n-Cosmetic

Cornetin-n-Cornet.

Cuartel-n Barrack.

Catolico Romano

D

Daan-n-Road, street, lane, gangway, place, spot, time, ocasion; leisure, itinerary

Daan nğ araro-n-Furiow

Dagá n-Rat, mouse

Daganan v-To cover, put below.

Dagat n-Ocean, sea. gulf, bay

Dagatdagatan-n-Lake

Dagdag-n-Addition, inciease, increment;

amendment; patch, repair, fringe; porder, binding

Dagdagan-v-To add to, increase; augment, add, enlarge, exaggerate amend. aggrandize. (ang bigat)—overload

Dagdagan nğ malabis-i To superadd

Dagdagin v-To augment, add, increase, enlarge; amend

3

Dagison n-Assistance; aid, help

Dagh adv -Soon, speedily, quickly; hurriedly, swiftly

Dagok-n Blow, cuff, knock.

Dagta-n-Sap, gum, juice

Dagukan-i-Te punch, strike, beat, knock

Dahak n-Cough

Dahandahan adv -Slowly, softly, gently; by degree

Dahas-n-Courage, boldness, strength of heart, vigor, force,

Dahasan-i To ferce, urge, give force-invigorate, strengtben

Dahidahilan n-Excuse, pretence, reason pretext

Dahilan-n-Excuse, pretence, reason; pretext, motive; cause; plea, right, occasion, allowance, forte; sake probability

Dahil dito-adv Therefore, thus; so also, for this reason, in this manner

Dahilig a-Sloping, inclined, slanting

Dahilig na lupa n Declevity, slope, incline

Dahil sa prep -For, be cause, about, as, by, through, on account

Dahon n Leaf.

Dahunan a Leafy

Daigin v-To overpower, overcome, surpass, excell surmount

Daing n-Lamentation, lament, complaint, petition, plaint, dole, wail, suplication, request, remonstrance, grievance, mormur, groan, entreaty, dolor prayer, evening prayer.

Dakila-a-Grand, noble; illustration magestic, splendid; honorable, magarfi cent, eminent: protent; famous; sublime, solemn, exalted, palatial, gorgeous, lofty, high; elevated, great, powerful, wealty; patrician, transcien dent; tremendous

Dakip n-Cappure, spoils, prize

Dako prep -Towards, about near, in the direction of.

Dakong kahwa-To the left side

Dakong lanan-To the right side

Dako rito-adv -Nearer, hither.

Dako roon adv.-Farther; forward, on the other side

Dako saan-prep Towards; about, near, in the direction of

Dakot-n Hand full.

Dakot a Few

Dakpin v-To capture; seize,' catch, imprison.

Dala a-Cautious, wary; suspicious

Daladalawang taon-adv Bi-ennial

Dalaga v Young lady, Single lady. Lass Maiden: nn

Dalagang may edad n-Old maid

Dalahan-n-Hand basket

Dalain-v-To frighten, scare, cause to be wary or cautious

Dalamhati-n-Trouble, pique; displeasure cross, pain; hardship, toil, ache, fatigue; grief, sorrow, concern, uneasiness

Dalang-n-Petition, prayer

Dálangan v-To rarity, dilute, thin

Dalangin-v-To petition, entreat, pray

Dalas n-Frequency

Dalaw-n-Visit.

Dalawa a-Two both

Dalawa-n-Two

Dalawa ang kulay-a-Bi-colored

Dalawdhin-v-To duplicate, repeat, halve

Dalawahin-a-double

Dalawin-v-To visit

Dalhin v-To carry, convey, conduct, transport

Dalhin dito-v-To fetch

Dali-n-Moment, instant

Dáli-n-Width of a finger

Dalidahan (dalidahin)-v-To hasten, precipitate, pispose of, alleviate, dispatch

Dalin-n-Finger, digit

Dalisay-a-Clean, pure, neat, clear, chaste, untouched, innocent, simple, cordial, perfect; unmingled, simple; cordial, delicate, genuine, smart, mere; tree, glad,

Dalisayin-v-To cleanse, purify; refine, perfect.

Dalishis-a-Sloping, slanting, inclined

Dalishis na lupa-n-Declevity

Dalishisin-i To cut away the edge

Dalit n Song, ditty dirge

Dalita n Misery, poverty, torment; pain; anguish; torture; patience, tolerance

Dalitaan-i-To suffe, bear, tolerate, abide, comport, torment, torture

Dalitain v To suffer, bear; abide, com poort, deign, condesend, pain

Dalit na malumbay-n Lamentation

Dalosdalos a Impetuous, hasty unexpected; precipitate, sudden, violent; fierce

Dalosdalos n Idiot, madman, fool

Dalubay n-Interpreter, translator

Daluhong n-Assault attack

Daluhungin v To assail, attack, assault

Dalumat n-Sufferance, suffering, tole ration

Dalumatin-v-To suffer, tolerate, abide, comport

Daluyong n Wave, surf, swell of the sea

Damag adv all night

Damahin v To feel, touch, grope, ex amine: investigate, prove, procure;

experiment, treat of, move, inspire, tempt.

Damara n Shade, tent

Damasko n-Damask

Damdam-n-Affliction, disease, suffering, sufferance, grievance, feeling

Damdamin r-To suffer, grieve, feel, perceive

Dami n-Maltitude, crowd

Damihan-n-To ongment, increase, sum; enlarge

Damit-n Clothes, dress; robe; costume garb, habilament, vesture

Damit na pang ibaba -n Loose garment; worn over the shoulders, overcoat

Damot-a Stingy, miserly, closefisted, scant, short, avaricious

Damot n Stinginess, closefistedness

Damotin-r To suffer, abide, telerate; comport, grasp, seize

Dampot n-Grasp, hold

Damputin-r-To grasp, hold, seize, pilfer, receive, hold up, heave, get up, raise

Damtan-i-To turnish, provide, sopply, hive

Damuhan-n-Hay-field, Meadow

Danaw-n Small lake, pond; loch lough

Danay-n-Boundary, limit, district

Dangal-n-Honor, reputation fame, glory excellent, kindness, excellency, triumph, esteem.

Dankal-n-Palm, hand breadth

Daong n-Ship, vessel, schooner, coaster

Dapat-a Worthv, deserving, adequate, competent, fit, apt, condign, convenient, exact, punctual, meritorius

Dapat-r a -Must, ought

Dapat akma a-Fit, seasonable, apt.

Dapat batin a-One who should be saluted

Dapat damdamin a Sensible, perceptible, feeling

Dapat a Reputable, estimable

Dapat gilwin-a-Adorable, lovable, amiable, affectionate

Dapat ibigin a Amiable, lovable, adorable, pleasing,affectionate,kind,loving

Dapat igalang-a Respectable, hanorable

Dapat ilagan a Avoidable, n-That which should be avoided

Dapat ipag-dangal-a-Illustrious, noble, honorable

Dapat ipag-tagubilin-a Commendable, laudahle, praiseworthy, deserving

Dapat isumbong a-Accusable, blamable

Dapat katakutin-a-A ful; trightful, dreadful, terrible, fearful terocious

Dapat matapos-a Terminable

Dapat inagalingin-a-Preterable, nepectable, praiseworthy.

Dapat mahalin-a-Preferable, commendable; appreciable, laudable, praiseworthy

Dapat pangusapin a Reprehensible

Dapat pamwalaan,-a Creditable' worthy of credit or belief

Dapat parusahan a Culpable, puushable

Dapat patawarin a-Pardonable, justifiable, excusable, venial.

Dapat purihin-a-Praise orthy, laudable, plauditory, eulogistic, laudatory, estimable

Dapat sisihin-a-Reprehensible, sufferable,

Dapat tangapin-a-Receivable, admissible, proper, fit

Dapit-n-The accompanying from one place to another, meeting and conveying from one place to another,

Dapitin-i-To take from one place to another, call, summon, meet and convey

Dapit sa prep -Towards, about, near, in the direction of

Dapog-n-Oven, fireside, hearth

Dapugan na labasan ng asó-n-Chimney, smoke-stack, stack

Darak-n-Bran, shorts, chaff.

Darating panahon-n-Future time

Dasal n-Prayer, oration.

Dasal na sumangpalataya n-Creed, articles of faith

Dasal sa umaga n-Matin

Datapua-prep -Except, yet, besides,more over, however, now be it

Datapwa-conj -But

Dati-n Original.

Dati a Original, quondani

Datihan-a-Accustomed, used, excellent; dexterous, original

Datnan-v-To overtake, reach, meet encounter

Dawag-n-Perplexity, impassible place

Dawis-n-Anguish, anxiety, grief, sorrov.

Daya n Cheat, deceit, delusion, imposition; fallacy; fraudulence, dodge; deceitfulness,trap,affectation,sham,trick, canard, claptrap, sleight, gull guile

Daya a false, deceitful, delusive, sham, claptrap, fraudulent, not real

Dayain-i-To cheat, delude, defraud; deceive, counterfeit; falsify; impose upon, default, sham, fleece, gull, jockey, coven, allure

Dayami n Straw

Dayap-n-Lime, lemon.

Dayu n Visit, challenge

Dayuhin i-To challenge, visit

Dayukdok-n-Glutton, hungry person

Demonio n-Devil, satan, the evil one
Di akma a-Unfit, improper, inconvenient, inexpedient.
Di bagay-a-Unfit, unbecoming, improper, mal apropos; inexpedient, unseemly, inconvenient
Di bagay sa anak a-Unfilial
Di binyagan-n Pagan, heathen; savage, idolater.
Dibdib-n Breast,
Di buo ang loob a-Half-hearted
Diciembre-n-December
Diccionario n-Dictionary
Didal-n-Thimble
Di dapat patawarin-a-Inexcusable.
Dighal n-Belch
Digma n-War, combat; fray, fight,
Di hikayat sa masama-a-Incorruptable
Di hinihintay a-Unexpected, unforseen, sudden
Di kaimukha a-Unlike, dissimilar, different,
Di karampatan a-Unworthy, unjust; inconvenient, perverse; improper, unbecoming
Di karaniwan-a Old, queer, non descript not general
Dikdikin-v-To crash, powder, pulverize, triturate, bray, pound.
Dikit-n-Beauty, fairness; comeliness, godliness
Dila-n-Tongue, tang
Dilaan-v-To lick, lap
Dilag-n-Splendor, brillancy; beauty, glory, greatness; granduer, finery; lustie, luster, magnitude
Dila ng compana-n Bell-clapper
Dila ,t, dila-One and all
Dilaw a-Yellow, yellowish.
Dilhay-n-Belch
Dili-n-Reflection, thought.
Dili-adv-Perhaps, maybe, perchance
Dilidili n-Imagination, fancy, conception
Dilig n-Sprinkling, watering
Diligin-v-To sprinle, water, spray
Dilim-n-Dar ness, obscurity; gloom, gloominess, opacify
Di maaninag-a Opaque, not transparent
Di maari-a impossible, impracticable
Di mababago-a Immutable, stable, stapla, unchangable, permanent, fixed, lasting
Di maaninaw a-Imperceptible, opaque
Di mababawas a-Irreducible
Di mabait a Restless, incorrigible.
Di mabasa a Illegible
Di mabubura n Indelible
Di magagaling n-Irremediable, incurable.

Di magka-kaila-a-Irrefutable, indisputable.
Di mahigpit a insecure unstaple
Di makababawi-a Irrecoverable.
Di maka-kilala-a-Incog, incognito
Di maka kita-a Blind, Latent
Di maka-raraan-a-Impassible
Di maka-sisira a Harmless, pure
Di maka-titiis-a Insufferable
Di maka-tulog-a-Sleepless
Di malapatan-a-Unh e, unequa
Di mahirap-a-Imperceptible
Di mahirip a-Iuscrutable, fathomless
Di malupo-a-impalpable, intangible
Di mapakali a Impatient, restless, fidgety, peevish-
Di mapalagay a Impatient, restless, fidgety peevish
Di mapasok ang hatol-a-Inflexible, In variable
Di maiamdaman-a-Imperceptible, im passive.
Di marating a Inaccessible
Dimarim-n Reluctance, aversion, repugnance
Dimarin ng sikmura na tila ibig magsuka-n Nausea
Di maiinig-a-Imperceptible
Di marunong mag-sinnugding-n-Veracios, truth teller
Di marunong mapagod-a-indefatigable unwearied
Di marunong tumanaw ng utang na loob a Ungrateful
Di masalat a-Impalpable, untangible.
Di masasaktan-a-Invulnerable
Di masaysay a Unspeakable
Di masupil a Invincible, unconquerable.
Di matagos-a Impenetiable.
Di matarok-a Unfathonable, incompre hensible, fathomless, impenetrable
Di matibay-a-Shaky, instaple, frail
Di matiis a-Intolerable, insufferable.
Di matingkala-a-Incomprehensible
Di mawawala a-Indestructible.
Din adv. also, a same, similar, like, seltsame
Di nagdadalita a Insensible, impassible
Di nahahati-a-Undivided
Di naka-tutulog a Sleepless
Di nal ikilala a Unknown, not known
Di Naka-sulat-a-Nuncupatory, nuncupative, un written, oral
Di namumunga a-Sterile, unfiutful, barren
Di nararapat a-Unworthy, undeserving; unfit; unjust, unseemly
Di nasasalang a-Untouched, numingled; pure, clean
Di nawiwih-a-Unfavorable.

Dinaya-a &p p -Deluded, deceived, cheated, swindled

Dinding n-Partition wall, wall

Dingin i-To hear, listen, understand, comprehend

Dini-adv -Here, hither, this way.

Dinig-n-Hearing, listening, understanding, comprehension-

DIOS n-GOD, THE LORD

Dios ng alak-n-Bachus, the god of wine.

Dipa-n Brace, spread of the arms

Di pagka-lalagay n-Restlessness, uneasiness

Di pagka-palagay a Inconstanty, fickleness

Di pagod-a Refreshed, unwearied, rested.

Di pagka-tunaw ng pagkain sa sikmura-n-Indigestion.

Di pa nasusupil-a-Untamed, wild

Di paniniwalain-a-Incredulous, unbelievable

Di pa panahon-a-Unseasonable undue, out of season

Di pa siguro-a-Comparative, not very certain

Dirain-a-Blear-eyed.

Diri-n Despicability, loathing

Di sapat a Insufficient, inadequaty, lacking

Discipulo-n-Disciple, scholar

Di sinasaysay a-Non' descript

Dispunte-n-Back-stich

Di sukat nangyari-a Impossible, impracticable

Di susuko-a-Indomnitable

Di tatalonin-a-Insurmountable.

Dito-adv -Here, hither

Dito at doon-a-Passim.

Diwara n-Curiosity, conversation.

Diwara-a-Curious, inquisitive

Diwin Spirit, soul

Diyan-adv -There, yonder

Di yari a-Imperfect, incomplete, faulty, defective

Doon-adv -There, yonder, thither, opposite, on the other side.

Doongan n-anchorage, place of anchoring, harbor, port; landing

Dowahagi-n-Persecution, harass, dun persuit

Dowahaginin-i To harass, persue, dun, importune, persecute, aid, sustain

Duag-n-Coward

Duag-a Cowardly, craven, chickenhearted, pusillaninous, timorous, timid, faint-hearted, fearful.

Duble-a-Double, duplicate

Dublihin-v-To double, duplicate

Dublihin ng tatlo-v To treble, triplicate.

Duda-n-Doubt, mis trust.

Duende n-Fairy, sprite, fray, elf, goblin.

Dugo n-Blood

Dugodugoan a-Bloody, sanguinary.

Dugtong-n Addition, splice, affix

Dukha-a-Helpless, destitute, poor, penurions, mean, niggardly, paltry, niggard

Dukuangin v-To overtake, reach, obtain

Dula sa kapwa n-Resentment, grudge, anger

Dulang-n-Table

Duling a-Cross-eyed torvous.

Dulo n Point, end extreme, extremity, sumit, headland, 'upshot, pinnacle

Dulo a-Last, end, latest, late, latter, final, extreme

Dulot n-Present, gratification

Dumaan-v-To pass by a place, go by, pass

Dumabog-v To growl, snarl, grumble, murmur

Dumadalaw n-Visitor

Dumahak-v-To spit, expectorate, cough

Dumahing laruin-v-To frisk, romp, sport.

Dumaing-v-To lament, bewail, remonstrate, wail, crave, complain, resent, reprimand, expostulate.

Dumakip-v-To apprehend, capture.

Dumakip-n-Apprehender

Dumal-n-Aversion, abhorence.

Dumalagang manok n-Pullet

Dumalagang-i-To thin, rarify

Dumalangin-v-To implore, beg, entreat, solicit, crave, pray

Dumalas-v-To frequant, repeat often.

Dumalaw-v-To visit

Dumalisay-v-To refine, purify, cleanse.

Dumalo-v-assist, support, produce, visit.

Dumalulong-v-To attack, assail, assault, undertake, attempt

Dumalusong-v-To assail, assault, attack.

Dumami v-To thicken, swell, increase, grow, thrive, improve, grow rich

Dumampot v To pick up

Dumapit-v-To meet at one place and escort to another

Dumapo v-To perch, roost

Dumating-v-To arrive, come, approach, reach,

Dumhan-v-To stain, polute, soil, dirty, daub, dab, bespatter, darken, corrupt; profane

Dumi n-Dirt, dross, slags, filthiness, nastiness, feaces, grime

Dumhan-a To dirty, soil, dab, daub, darken, obscure, cloud, confuse

Dumi fig tinta-n-Blot of ink

Dumikit-v-To stick, cling, cohere, paste.

Dumilhay-i To belch.

Duminig i-To hear, listen, understand, comprehend; overhear.

Dumoon-*i*-To lodge, rest, reside, dwell
Dumoong *r*-To anchor
Dumoong sa gawa-*i*-To complete one's work
Dumoon sa-*i*-To be at.
Dumpolin-*i*-To tinge, dye, stain
Dumudugo-*i*-Bo bleed
Dumudugo-*a*-Bleeding, bloody, sanguinary
Dumugo-*i*-To bleed
Dumulas *i*-To slip; slide.
Dumulas sa kamay-*r*-To slip from the hand
Dumulang-*i*-To wash gold
Dumulog-*v*-To present, arrive, reach, apppoximate
Dumunong-*v*-To illustrate, experience gro or become wise
Dumupo *r* To become weak or infirm
Dumusta-*i*-To become low or abject
Dumusta ng masama sa kapwa-*n*-Offender, delinquent
Dunğuis-*n*-Stain, blot, filthiness, dirty, daub, grime, nastiness
Dunğisin-*v*-To stain, blot daub, dirty, darken, corrupt

Dunğis sa puri-*n*-Stain or spot on one's character
Dunğut-*n*-Point, extremity, end, summit, headland.
Dunğo *a*-Pusillamımous, timid, dull, cowardly, timorous, rude, obscene torpid
Dunğol-*n*-Blow with the fist.
Dungot-*n* Summit, apex, top, point extremity, end, edge
Dupok-*a*-Brittle, weak, frail, fragile
Dunong-*n*-Sience, knowledge, accuracy, wisdom, understanding, excellence, excellency
Dupong *n*-Half burnt wood, charcoal
Duraduhin-*v* To gilt, gild, adorn
Dmo-*n*-Stitch
Duiog-*a*-Po dered, broken, ushed
Durugın *v*-To powder, crash, pound, shatter, pulverize
Durum-*i* To stitch, penetrate
Dusa-*n* Chastizement, punishment
Dusta *a* Bad, low, object, miserable,
Duyan-*n*-Cradle, hammock
Duyan ng lubid *n*-Swing
Duyo ng bilanguan-*n*-Dungeon

E

Edad-*n*-Age
Empatso *n* Indigestion
Enero-*n*-January,

Escandalo-*x*-Scandal
Espada *n* Sword
Europa-*n*-Europe.

F

Favor-*n*-Favor, boon
Febrero-*n*-February
Fecha *n*-Date; epoch
Filipino *n*-Philippino.

Formal *a* Formal, serious, solemn, important
Freno-*n* Bridle
Frenohan-*i* To bridle, curb

G

Gaan-*n*-Lightness, levity, celerity
Gaanan-*v*-To lighten, alleviate.
Gaano-How many, how much
Gabay *n*-Balustrade, banister
Gabok-*n*-Dust, powder.
Gabokin *i* To powder
Gabo na ginto *n* Flake gold, dust
Gabukin-*r*-So powder.
Gagad *n* Imitation, counterfeit, copy
Gagahin *i* To usurp
Gagarin *i*-To imitate, counterfeit, forge mimic, copy, mock, feont, ape.
Gahasa *a* Impetuous, violent, fierce
Galu-*n*-Tear laceration, mark
Galum-*i* To tear, lacerate, rend mark.

Gahısın-*i*-To force, allure
Gahısın and dalaga-*i*-To rape force ravish
Gala-*a*-Errant wandering, erring
Gala-*n* Walk
Galak *n*-Pleasure, glee, content, merriment, rejoicing, festivity, joy, happiness, satisfaction
Galakgak-*n*-Loud laugh.
Galang-*n*-Courtesy, civility, respect regard veneration, esteem, politeness, good manners, purity, reverence urbanity, breeding, education, manners, gentility, genteelness, homage-
Galang *n*-Small hand-basket, book clasp, hand cuff.

Galapong-n-Flour.

Galaw-n-Agitation; move.

Galawin-v-To agitate; move.

Galawing muli-v-To alter, dismiss change; remove.

Galing-n-Goodness; benefit, sutility, kindness, health, welfare, prosperity. salvation; generosity.

Galing sa-a-Originated derived from.

Galis-n-Itch; mange.

Galisin-a-Itchy mangy.

Galisin-v-To have the itch ormange.

Galit-n-Anger rage, animosity; indignation spite, madness, odium, annoy. annoyance, rancor enmity; discomposure, choler dudgeon.

Galit-a-Angray; mad, firetful. peevish-irate, ireful, wroth, indignant. at variance with another.

Galit na bigla n-Anger; rage; passion.

Galit na galit-a Mery angry; furious; enraged.

Galit na labis-n-Spite; hatred.

Gallera-n Cockpit.

Galletas-n Hardtack; crac ers

Galos-n-Scratch; scrape; scar.

Galosan-v-To scratch; scrape.

Gamit-a-Used; experienced, skilful, practical.

Gamit-n-Use; disposition, practice, experience.

Gamitin-v-To use; serve, wear, practice, accustom; adopt, employ, make use of, allay, espouse, yield, affiliate; (na lagi a ldict.

Gamitin-a-Useful; employed.

Gamot-n-Medicine; physic; portion.

Gamot na may halong apian-n-Opiate.

Gamutin-v-To dotor-cure; heal, mend; remedy.

Gamogamo-n-Horsefly dragon fly.

Ganap-a-Perfect; complete, exact, right, finished, punctual, clever integral, whole, candid, just, entire, faultless. critical.

Ganapin-v-To complete; perfect, finish.

Ganda-n-Beauty; godliness, fairness, beneficence, kindness.

Ganda ng tikas-n-Gentility; elegance, easiness; freedom.

Ganid-a-Cruel; hard-hearted; severe.

Ganiri-adv.-So; thus, also, therefore; vedileeit.

Ganito-adv.-So thus; also, therefore, in this manner.

Gansal-a-Odd. unequal-uneven,

Gansal-n-That which is left over.

Ganti-n-Revenge; reward, recompence. gratification. satisfaction, triumph. remuneration, compensation, retribution, premium, honor, amends, fee, wages, stipend, salary, payment glory, requital, meed expiation.

Gantihin-v To revenge; re ard, recompence, gratify, indulge, remunerate, retribute, requit, expiate; disgorge.

Gantihin ang loob-v-To reward recompence.

Ganting loob-n-Premium; reward, prize.

Ganting palad-n-Re ard; premium, prize; bounty.

Ganza-n-Goose.

Gaód;n-Paddle; scull.

Gapasan-n-Harvest place of harvesting.

Gapasin-v-To harvest; reap; mow.

Gapusin-v-To manacle; hand-cuff; trammel; gyue.

Gapusin ang paa ng hayop-v-To hopple.

Garabanso-n-Pen.

Garing-n-Ivory.

Gasa-n-Border; edge, brim; margin.

Gasaan-v-To chide; scold.

Gasgas-n-Waste; expenditure.

Gasgas-a-Used; worn.

Gasgasin-v-To waste; expend, wear by use.

Gasta-n-Charge; expense; cost.

Gastos-n-Charges; expenses, costs; outlay.

Gata-n-Juice, sap.

Gatas-n-Milk.

Gatasan v-To milk.

Gatasan-a-Milch.

Gatasan-n-Milk cellar.

Gatong-n-Tinder; kindlings, fire-wood.

Gawa-n-Work; means, toil, occupation, task, business, pursuit, labor, husbandry, operation, deed, action, act, conduct, management, procedure, cut, fashion, shape, figure; make.

Gawaan-n-Manufactury; factory.

Gawaang hunhang-n-Foppery; imprudence, folly; foolishness.

Gawa na marangal-n-Masterpiece.

Gawaan ng katad n-Tannery.

Gawaan ng libro-n-Book binder.

Gawang bastos n-Meanness, malice.

Gawang bata-n-Childish doings.

Gawang dapat tularan n-Example, precedent copy; pattern.

Gawang hamak-n Malice; meanness, navery; injustice.

Gawa ng kamay-a-Hand-made.

Gawang labas sa matwid-n-Wrong; injustice.

Gawang mabuti-a Remedy; good.

Gawang mahalay-v Knavery; malice; wantonness.

Gawang marangal-n-Glorious deed, masterpiece

Gawang masama-n-Wic edness, iniquity, guiltness, criminality, ugliness, rudeness, impurity, dulness, lewdness

Gawang pangit n Moral depravity; turpitude, ughness

Gawang ulol-n Frenzy, folly, silliness; foolishness

Gawgawin-v-To stir, revert, return

Gawi-a-Common, frequent' inclined

Gawi-n-Inclination; frequence, frequency, style, use, custom

Gawin-v-To do, work, operate, make, perform, execute, manufacture, produce, construct, form, realize

Gawi fig loob-n-Tendency, propensity, inclination

Gawing ginto-v-Ts convert into gold,

Gawing kalunuran-a-Occidental, western

Gawing kalunuran-adi -Westerly.

Gawing kanan-a-Right.

Gawing labas ng panulukan-n-Angle, corner

Gawing lagi-v-To practice

Gawing likod-n-Group, back-side

Gawing muli-v-To iterate, do again, reproduce, reconstruct.

Gawing panibago-i-To renew, repair, regenerate

Gawing parisukat-i-To square

Gawing tabas-v To shape; give shape, form.

Gawing tatlong duble-i-To treble, triple, triplicate.

Gawin ng pasulipat-i-To do or place anything obliquely,

Gayak-n-Preparation, pomp, show, decoration, adornment, embellishment, ornament, preparative, dress

Gayak a-Preperative, providefit, ornamental, pomptious

Gayakan-i -To embellish adoin, ornament, piepare, provide

Gayakin-r To prepare; ornament, adorn, embellish

Gayak na malaki-n Splendor, pomp, gayety

Gayat-n-Piece, slice.

Gayatin-r-To pick to pieces, cut, slice, divide.

Gayon-adv -So also, as, such, therefore, as much, as great, in this manner, similarly.

Gayondin-adi -Equally, uniformly, evenly, also, likewise, moreover, such, like, eke, straightway, ditto.

Gayon ·man-adr -Yet, notwith, standing, still, nevertheless, however, although

Gayon nawa-Amen

Gayon nga-a-Right, adr -that way

Gayuma-n-Fascination; hypnotism, enchantment

Giba-n-Destruction, ruin

Gibain-v-To destroy, demolish, ruin, plunder lerbel

Gibang n-Reel, stagger.

Gibang-a-Reeling, staggering

Gikan-n-Threshing place, threshing.

Gikkin-i-To thresh

Gilagid n-The gums.

Gilalas n-Temerity bashfulness

Gilalasin-a-Timdi; bashful, coward.

Gilalasin-v To frighten, make bashful

Guilid n-Edge, border, margin, brim, verge, fringe, limit, sire

Gilid ng kayo-n- Edge of cloth, selvage.

Gilig-n-Chaff

Gilik-n-Dust, powdei.

Gikban-i-To help aid, assiat

Gikban ako-inter -Help me

Gilingan-n-Mill, grinder

Gilingang munti-n-Hand-mill.

Gilingin v-To grindi mill

Gilit-n-Cut, slice

Gilitan-v-To cut slice.

Gilitan ang lug-v-To behead

Gihtin-v-To cut, slice.

Gihw-a-Beloved; dear, estimable.

Gihw-n-Esteem, love' delicacy

Gihwin-v To love, esteem, amuse, make happy.

Gimbal-n Kettle-drum

Ginagawa ng taontaon-adv.-Yearly.

Ginaw-n Cold, frigidness, frigidity.

Ginawa sabay-a-Simultaneous

Ginday-n-Affected gait or walk.

Ginawa-a-Easy, light, convenient, fit.

Ginbanggibang-a-Oscillating, vibrating.

Ginikan-n-Straw

Ginisa-n-Stew

Ginoo-n-Mister, gentleman, master, sir

Ginoo-a-Gentlemanly); polite.

Ginto-n Gold

Gintoin v To convert into gold

Giray n-Wabble, affected air or gait

Giray-a-Reeling, staggering

Gisahin-v-To stew.

Gisi n-Small piece, fragment, tear

Gisiin-v-To tear, rend, lacerate

Gising a-Watchful, lively, wakeful.

Gising-adv Awake, alive

Gisingin-v-To wake, awaken; waken,

Gitla n-Surprise; astonishment, fright amazement.

Gitlahiu-r To surpiise, astonish, amaze

Gitna-n-Center; middle, midst, medium

Giyon-n Hyphen

Gobierno-n-Government.

Gobiernador-n-Governor; prefect.

Goma-n-Gum; rubber.

Gorra-n-Cap.

Grifo-n-Faucet; hydrant.

Guang-n-A hollow spot; in wood.

Gubat-n-Woods; forest; backwoods.

Gubatin-v-To pillage; plunder; lay waste; desolate.

Gugol-n-Expenses; charges; costs.

Guhit-n-Line; mark; design; plan; sketch; vestige.

Guhitin-v-To line.

Guitara-n-Guitar.

Gukgok-n-Grunt.

Guk-gok-a-Disheveled.

Gulagulanit-a-Ragged.

Gulang-n-Age.

Gulang ñg isip-n-Solidity; firmness or integrity of thought.

Gulanit-n-Rag hanging from clothes.

Gulanit-a-Ragged; wornout.

Gulat-n-Fright; consternation; astonishment; alarm.

Gulatan-v-To frighten; astonish; surprise.

Gulatin-v-To frighten; alarm; startle make tremble.

Gulat na gulat-a-Fearful; awful; scared.

Gulay-n-Vegetables; herbs; verdure.

Gulili-n-Trifle.

Gulo-n-Perplexity; confusion; disturbance; turmoil; tangle; chaos; chayos; discord; dissention; din; revolution; sedition; scrape; agitation; shindy; ciscomposure; disquietude; disquietness; entanglement; ado; pother.

Gulo-a-Reverse; intricate; tangled; confused; chaotic.

Gulod-n-Hillock; barrow; slope.

Gulok-n-Bolo; large knife; corn-knife.

Gulo ñg isip-n-Bewilderment.

Gulong-n-Wheel; circle.

Gulonggulongan-n-Windpipe; gullet.

Gulugod-n-Spine; backbone; chine.

Guluhin v-To disturb; entangle; tangle; perturb; ensnare; row; subvert; perplex; disconcert; alarm; disquiet; discompose, confound, reverse, overturn, overthrow; stir; agitate.

Guluhin ang isip-v-To bewilder; confound; perplex.

Gulungin-r-To wheel; roll.

Gumaan-r-To lighten; alleviate.

Gumabi-v-To grow dark; benight; grow late.

Gumagad-r-To imitate; minic; ape; flout,

Gumagunti-a-Retributive; vengeful; retributing.

Gumagatas-n-Miller.

Gumagawa-n-Workman; doer; laborer; worker; journeyman.

Gumalaw-v-To move; stir.

Gumaling-v-To recover; get or grow well; convalesce.

Gumanap-v-To execute; perform; discharge.

Gumanda-v-To beautify; embellish; adorn; decorate.

Gumaod-v-To row; paddle; scull.

Gumapang-v-To crawl; creep; go on all fours, Sec. Rob or steal at night.

Gumapas-v-To mow; cut, reap; harvest.

Gumasta-v-To spend; waste; wear away.

Gumatas-v-To milk.

Gumanting loob-v-To correspond; suit; agree.

Gumawa-r-To do; make, manufacture; execute, labor; construct; build; perform; form; produce; practice; operate; cause; act.

Gumawa ñg antos-v-To digest; consider assist; produce.

Gumawa ñg hatol-v-To judge; make zudgement.

Gumawa ñg kautusan-v-To make or enact laws.

Gumawa ñg salitaan-v-To contract; stipulate.

Gumayak-v-To prepare; adorn; get ready; caparison; clean.

Gumayak agad-v-To prepare hastily.

Gumayongayon-v-To idle loiter; lounge-be careless.

Gumibik-v-To Aid; assist; help; save; succor; support.

Gumugiti-a-Growing.

Gumiik-v-To thresh.

Gumiit-v-Lo meddle; interfere.

Gumiliw-v-To love; like adore; esteem.

Guminday-v-To walk with an affected air or gait.

Guminhawa-v-To thrive; prosper; ease-become easier.

Guminhawa ang sakit-v-To recover trom sickness.

Gumiraygiray-v-To swagger; wabble; stagger.

Gumiri-v-To clamor; howl.

Gumisa-v-To irritate; smart.

Gumiti-v-To bud; grow; shoot; begin to appear.

Gumugol-v-To expend; spend; waste.

Gumuhit-v-To draw; line.

Gumukgok-v-To grunt.

Gumulo-v-To disturb; perturb; riot; destroy; be noisy; perplex.

Gumulong-v-To roll.

Gumulong sa lupa-v-To tumble.

Gumumon-r-To roll.

4

Gunamgunam-*n*-Memory; memorial; memoirs; reflexion.

Guniguni-*n*-Fancy; imagination; presumption; pantom, hallucination.

Guniguni-*a*-Fantastical; fantastic; whimsical; imaginary; fanciful; chemerical.

Gunignnihin-*e*-To imagine; fancy; suppose.

Gunting-*n* Shears; scissors; snips.

Guntiñgin-*e*-To shear; cut with shears or scissors.

Gupitin-*e*-To cut shear.

Gupitin ang buhok-*e*-To cut hair

Gupo-*n*-Fall.

Gurlis-*n*-Scratch.

Gusarin ang lupa-*e*-To clean ground.

Gusi-*n*-Large china jar.

Gusot-*a*-Tangled; intricate; difficult; snarled.

Gusutin-*e*-To entangle; snarl.

Gutom-*n*-Hunger.

Gutom-*a*-Hungry;

Gutumin-*e*-To make hungry; starve.

H

Haba-*n*-Length.

Habaan-*e*-To lenghten; prolong; protract; distend; extend; amplify; enlarge; stretch out.

Habag-*n*-Clemency; compasion; pity, condolence; mercy.

Habagat-*n*-North wind.

Habagin-*e*-To pity; have compasion; commiserate; condole; afflict; torment, pain; grieve.

Habagin-*a*-Compassionate; commisserate.

Habi-*n*-Weaving; plat.

Habihan-*n*-Loom.

Habihan-*e*-To weave.

Habihin *e*-To weave.

Habulin-*n*-To pursue; vex; persecute; chase; catch.

Hadhad-*n*-Abrasure; scratch; wound.

Hadlang-*n*-Stall; cell; obstacle; impediment; obstruction.

Hadlañgin-*e*-To stall; partition; obstruct; impede, hinder; restrain.

Hagdan-*n*-Stairs; staircase; steps; stairway.

Hagdanan-*n*-Staircase; stairway, steps, ladder; stile.

Haging-*n*-Whistle; whistling; hum; whir; whir; hiss.

Hagkan-*n*-Hug kiss.

Hagkan-*e*-To hug; kiss.

Hagulgol-*n*-Flood of tears; mourning.

Hagurin-*v*-To soften; pummel.

Hahalili-*n*-Substitute.

Haka-*n*-Thought; meditation; idea; design; supposition.

Hakain-*e*-To suppose; meditate; think; design.

Hakam-*n*-Presupposition.

Halaan-*n*-Bivalve; shellfish.

Halaga-*n*-Cost; price; charge; value; amount; worth; moment; valuation; appraisal; estimate, estimation; expense.

Halagahan-*e*-To appraise; value, estimate, assess; prize.

Halagahang muli-*e*-To reassess.

Halagahin-*v*-To value; prize; esteem, estimate.

Halak-*n*-Horselaugh; loud or boisterous; laugh.

Halakhak-*n*-Horse-laugh; loud or boisterous laugh.

Halamanan-*n*-Garden; orchard.

Halap-*n*-Alarm; notice of danger.

Halas-*n*-Ulcer.

Halata-*a*-Sensible; noticable; notable; plain.

Halatain-*e*-To notice; feel; note; scent; recognize.

Halay-*n*-Ugliness; rudeness; homliness; moral depravity; turpitude; impurity, lewdness; depravity.

Halayin-*e*-To ridicule; censure; decry; slight; disregard; laugh at.

Haligi-*n*-Post; pillar; support.

Halik-*n*-Kiss; osculation.

Halikin-*e*-To kiss; osculate.

Halikuatin-*e* To raise on edge; pry.

Halimbawa-*n*-Example; pattern; copy; precedent; exemplar; instance.

Halinghing-*n*-Sigh; moan; groan.

Halinhan-*e*-To change; exchange; substitute, succeed, surrogate.

Halo-*n*-Mixture; compound; medley; mortar; admixture.

Halobaybay-*n*-Anchovy.

Halohalo-*a*-Mixed; promiscuous; confused

Haloin-*e*-To mix; stir.

Halomignig-*a*-Luke-warm; neither hot nor cold; slippery.

Halomigmig-*n*-A small mixture.

Halos-*adv*.-Almost; nearly, well-nigh.

Halos wala-*adv*.-Scarcely; hardly.

Halubid; Stroke; with a whip or rope.

Haluin-*e*-To stir; mix; revert; derange; conufse; break the thread of intercourse.

Halumigmig a-Damp, humid, moist

Hamak-a-Low, abject, contemptible, vulgar; despicable infamous, unbecoming, vile, mean, base, knavish, unworthy, contumelious, cursed, undeserving, discreditable, clamorous, menial, servile, sneaking, slavish, petit; plebian

Hamakin-v-To underrate, undervalue, depreciate. disobey, lower the standard

Hambal n-Grief, anguish, affliction

Hambog n-Pride, haughtiness

Hambog-a-Haughty, supercilious arrogant, proud, vain. presumptuous, preposterous, disdainful, ostentatious.

Hamog-n-Dew

Hamon-n Challenge impeachment threat, fight.

Hampas-n-Stroke, scourge, blow.

Hampasin ng tungkod v-To came

Hampas lupa-n-Vagabond, vagrant tramp

Hamunin-r To challenge, rival, Fight threaten

Hanapbuhay-n-Occupation; situation, employment, employ, profession, vocation, work

Hanapin v-To search, look for, find, hunt

Hanay-n Row, file, line; arrangement, order

Hanayin-v-To put in line, order file, arrange.

Handa-n-Preparation, pomp, show, provision

Handa-a Preparative, prepared; provident, cautious

Handa na malaki-n-Splendor, pomp large feast

Handog n Offer, gift, grant, homage, tribute, gratification, pleasme, compliance

Handuka n-Tolerance, patience, forbearance

Handulungin v-To assault assail, attack.

Hanga-n-Limit, boundary, border, goal, district, milestone, bound, butt, confine, contour, term, milepost, landmark, end, edge, crisis, margin, period, frontier, condition.

Hangahan-n-Boundary, limit, landmark, border, frontier

Hangad-n-Concern, interest, desire.

Hangal-a-Foolish, stupid, ignorant, indecent, rude, coarse, clownish

Hangalin-v To astonish, stupefy, infatuate, fool, be rude, deceive, surprise, cheat.

Hangan-n-Extreme. extremity.

Hangan-adv.-even, till, as far as also;

Hanganan-n-Boundary, limit, end, termination; goal, milestone, district, period, term

Hangang di-a Provisional

Hangang ngayon-adv.-Here to, here tofore, here unto, till now.

Hanghang-n-Pungency acrimony, pique

Hangin-n-Wind; air

Hangin hilaga-n-North-wind

Hangin sa araw-n East wind.

Hangin sa bulas-n-North-wind

Hangin sa kalunuran-n West wind

Hangin-v-To extract; take out, take from- remove; bring out, extort, deduce, ransom, release, liberate, redeem free, set at liberty, acquit

Hangin sa sakit-v-To heal, cure

Hantungan-n-Halting place, stay so journ, habitation

Hanip-n-Louse; flea. small thing

Hapak-n-Cutlass.

Hapdi-n-Pain, prickling, smarting

Hapdi ng kalooban-n-Wound ;affliction, anguish

Hapis-n Gloom; sadness, grief, pain, ache, anxiety, hardship, disgust, sorrow grievance

Hapis-a-Grievous, sad, dejected, disgusted, dispirited, painful, pained; peevish.

Hapisin-v-To vex, mortify; afflict, pain, sadden, pain; torment, grieve; disgust, render dejected

Hapitan-v-To press

Hapitin v To press

Hapo-a-Exhausted, weary worn out

Hapo-n Fatigue, hardship, anguish, pain

Hapon n Afternoon

Hapunan-n Supper

Hapunán-n-Perch; roost

Harang-n-Hold-up, ambuscade. robbery, stop

Harangin v-To hold up, ambuscade, rob, plunder, beset- waylay, stop, restrain

Harap-adv -Forward; lead before.

Harap-a Front

Harapan n-Front; Face; fore-end, forepart, lead.

Harapan ng bahay-n-Facade, face of a house.

Harapin v-To present, ones self

Hari n-Monarch, king severign, ruler autocrat

Harina-n-Flour (Sp)

Hari nga inter.-Would to GOD, GOD grant

Harumpak-n-Waste, expense

Harumpak a-Active, wasteful.

Harumpakin-v To expend; waste.

Hasikan-n-Place of sowing.

Hasikan-v-To drill, sow

Hatdan ng viatico ang may sakit-v-to administer sacraments

Hati--a mid; half

Hatid-n Conveyance, conduction

Hatin-v-To divide; halve, part; share, compart; cut apart.

Hating gabi-n-Mid-night,

Hatol-n-Decision judgement, sentence, verdict, issue, advice, opinion, reso lution, proceedure, council

Hatulan-i To sentence; judge; decide, resolve, determine

Hawak-n-Clasp, clutch grasp.

Hawakan-i-To grasp, clutch, catch, hold

Hawan-a-Free, clean, neat, pure, clear-disengagad

Hawanan-i-To free, dissengage, facil-litate make easy, ease, expedite.

Haya n-Sheaf

Hayag-a-Manifest, plain; clear, public, general, open, vulgar, perceptible

Haym n Gift, oblation, offering.

Hayop-n-Animal, brute, beast

Hayop na apat ang paa-n Quadruped

Hayop na walang gulugod-n-Inverte-brate

Hayuma n-Patch.

Hayumahin-v-To patch, mend fix

Hibaybay-n-Boundary, district, limit, territory

Hibik-n-Lament, lamentation, groan, sob

Hibla-n Fiber; yarn,

Hibo-n-Cheat; fraud, deceit, delusion, decoy, sham; claptrap dodge, trick, guile.

Hiboin-v-To cheat, decoy,deceive,seduce; sham, guile, jockey, cozen

Hibuin v-To cheat, cozen, deceive, de-coy, sham, victimize, jockey seduce.

Hibuin sa pag ibig-v To jilt

Hielo n Ice.

Higanti n Vengence.

Higitin-i-To enlarge, stretch, lengthen, surpass,

Higo-n-Fig

Higop n-Swallow; draught; sip, absorp-tion

Higuit n Tenacity, pertinacity; contu-macy, asperity; closeness, tightness, narrowness, straightness

Higpitan-r To compel; press, oblige, oppress, squeeze tighten, restrain, bind, compact.

Higpitin uli-r To retighten; repress.

Higtan ang bahcak-i-To shrug the shoulders

Higupin-v-To swallow, sip

Hihigan-n-Conch, bed.

Hihigan ng hayop sa damo-n Lair,

Hika n Asthma

Hikaw-n-Earring

Hikayat n Attraction; invitation, faci-nation.

Hikayatin-v-To attract; facinate, invite.

Hiknatin-r-To pry up.

Ihla n-Draw, pull, tug, drag

Hilaga-n North, North-wind.

Hilaga-a-Northern, boreal.

Ihlagaan-n-North.

Hilagaan-a-Northern boreal

Hilagaan-adv -Northerly

Hilahin-v-To haul, tug, drag, pull, draw,; hale.

Hilakbot-n Horror, dread, fear

Hilamusan-n-Lavatory, wash-stand.

Hilatsa n-Thread ot cloth

Hilaw-a-Crude, green, rare, raw, unripe untinished

Hilawan-i-To separate, pick

Hilawin-v-To make crude

Hilbana n-Basting

Hilera-n Row, file, line

Hilig-n-Inclination, propensity, tenden cy; disposition

Hilig-a-inclined, disposed.

Hilig ng loob n-Inclination, fancy, pro-pensity.

Hiligan-n-Anything to lean on

Hilik-n-Snore; harsh sound

Hilo-a-Drunk, intoxicated, dizzy

Hilongo-n-Drunkard

Hilot-n-Mid,wife.

Hilurin-v-To soften, rub, stroke, act as mid-wife

Hilutin-i-To rub, act as mid wife, stroke.

Himagas-n-Dessert

Himala n-Miracle, wonder.

Himanhiman-n-Flatery, cajolery.

Himanhiman a-Prudent.

Himinlay-v-To rest; repose

Himatay-n-Fainting, swoon, faint

Himatayin-a-Subject to fainting

Himawa n-Blasphemy.

Himawain-v-To Blaspheme

Himpakhimpakan n-Loins of an animal

Himpakhimpakan-n Bashfulness

Himulhol-n-Small knot in cloth.

Himulmol-a Ragged; tattered

Himulmol-n-Small knot in cloth

Himulmulan-r-To pluck.

Himutok-n Complaint, murmur,

Hina n Weakness, prostration.

Hinabi p. p.-Woven.

Hinabi-*n*-That which has been woven.

Hinabing lino-*n*-Linen.

Hinagap-*n*-Suspicion; jealousy.

Hinagap-*v*-To beleive; credit; give faith.

Hinagpis-*n*-Tribulation; anguish; affliction; anxiety; envy; compasion; pity.

Hinahon-*n*-Moderation; forbearance; prudence; continence; continency.

Hinala-*n*-Dread; fear; suspicion; jealousy; presumption; supposition, malice; conjecture.

Hinalili-*p, p.*-Changed.

Hinanakit-*n*-Complaint: murmur; disgust

Hinang-*n*-Solder.

Hinangin-*n*-To solder.

Hinapang-*n*-Courage; valor; mind; intention.

Hinawan ng kamay *n*-Wash-stand.

Hinay-*n*-Delay; detention; lingering; slowness.

Hinayang-*n*-Grief; pity; compassion; condolence.

Hinayhinay *adv.*-Little by little.

Hindi-*adv.*-No; not.

Hindi Ayos-*a*-Disheveled; irregular.

Hindi ayos-*adv.*-Unlike; disorderly.

Hindi binyagan-*n*-Pagan; heathen.

Hindi dapat-*a*-Unbecoming; unworthy; unlawful, illicit; undeserving.

Hindi gamit-*a*-Disused; obsolete.

Hindi ganap-*a*-Imperfect; faulty; defective.

Hindi gumagalaw-*a*-Quiet; undisturbed.

Hindi kaayon-*a*-Contrary; unlike.

Hindi kailangan-*a*-Unnecessary; superfluous; dispensible.

Hindi kamu ha-*a*-Strange; foreign; unlike; dissimilar.

Hindi kaofficio-*a*-Foreigu; different vocations.

Hindi kaparis-*a*-Unlike; dissimilar; contrary; different. *parijo (Jb)*

Hindi kangalian-*a*-Strange; unknown, foreign.

Hindi quilala-*a*-Strange; unl nown; foreign.

Hindi mabahagi-*a*-Invisible.

Hindi mabuti-*a*-Bad; false; faulty; untrue.

Hindi mabuti ang lasa-*a*-Sour; bad-tasting; pungent.

Hindi magkaayos-*a*-Confused; disorderly; perverse; intricate; difficult; contrary.

Hindi mahalata-*a*-Imperceptible; hidden; unseen.

Hindi makamalay tawo-*a*-Spiritless weak; feeble.

Hindi malayo-*adv.*-Near; not far.

Hindi man-*adv.*-Though; notwithstanding.

Hindi mangyaring mabahagi-*a*-Indivisible.

Hindi mauso-*a*-Obsolete; disused; passed; gone by. *uso*

Hindi mapawi-*a*-Indelible.

Hindi marunong-*a*-Stupid; ignorant.

Hindi marunong sumunod *a*-Obstinate; disobedient.

Hindi masaysay-*a*-Indefinite; indetermined.

Hindi matangap-*a*-Inacceptable; inadmissible.

Hindi matarok-*a*-Unfathomable.

Hindi alipin-*a*-Free.

Hindi nababago-*a*-Constant; firm; loyal; permanent; durable; lasting; manifest.

Hindi nabubulok-*a* Incorruptible; imperishable.

Hindi nagagalaw-*a*-Untouched; pure; unmingled.

Hindi nagagayak-*a*-Informal; indisposed.

Hindi nagbuhat sa iba-*a*-Ooriginal; primitive; first.

Hindi nagpapaamo-*a*-Free; frank; liberal.

Hindi nakaalam-*a*-Stupid; ignorant; unknown.

Hindi nalulupo-*a*-Pure; untouched; unmingled; chaste.

Hindi mapaamo-*a*-Untamable; inflexible.

Hindi napaguusapan-*a*-Pure; clean (pertaining to conversation.)

Hindi pa nalalaman-*a*-Unknown.

Hindi pa nangyari-*a*-Unfinished; incomplete; lacking.

Hindi pa napaamo-*a*-Untamed; wild.

Hindi paris-*a*-Unlike; unequal; different.

Hindi patag-*a*-Rough; cragged; craggy.

Hindi payag-*a*-Inadmissible.

Hindi rin-*a* & *conj.*-Neither; nor.

Hindi sagrado-*a*-Profane; not sacred. *Sp*

Hindi sinasadya-*a*-Accidental; casual; unintentional.

Hindi tama-*a*-Amiss; false; not true; untrue, wrong.

Hindi tapat na loob-*a*-Unfathful; false; feigned; infidel; disloyal; instable; fickle; uncertain.

Hindi tinatalaga-*a*-Casual; unintentional, unexpected; accidental.

Hindi tinatangap-*a*-Unacceptable; inadmissible.

Hindi totoo-*a*-Fictitious; untrue; false; fabulous; feigned; uncertain; spurious.

Hindi tumupad sa ipinanumpa-*a*-Perjured; forsworn.

Hindi tunay *a*-False; untrue, feigned count erfeit, imitated

Hingal *n*-Pant, palpitation, difficult breathing.

Hingalo-*n* Agony, gasp; last breaths, of a dying person

Hingbubuh *n* Lizard

Hingil *a*-Propensity, inclination, desire

Hingil *a*-Disposed; inclined

Hingil sa *adv*.-Moreover besides; over, above, according to; relating to concerning

Hingkod-*a* Lame; hipshot

Hinhin-*n*-Urbanity, civility, calmness tranquility, politeness, kindness, frugality, bashfulness.

Hinkod-*a* Lame, hipshot

Hinlalaki-*n* Thumb

Hinlog-*n* Lineage, race, forfathers, off spring, class, parents, relatives; kindred, pedigree.

Hinog *a*-Ripe mature

Hintay-*n*-Stay, stop; hope.

Hintayin-*v*-To await; hope, expect.

Hinto-*n*-Stop, halt, pause

Hintuan-*n* Stopping place, halting place

Hinubahin-*t*-To collect deduce, infer

Hipag-*t*-Sister in-law.

Hipan-*t* To blow, play on a musical instrument

Hipo *n* Touch, blind man's stick

Hipoin-*t*-To feel, touch, grope.

Hipon-*n*-Shrimp

Hipon sa dagat-*n*-Lobster

Hipuin-*v*-To feel; touch, grope.

Hiram *a*-Lent,

Hiram-*n* The thing which is lent

Hiramin-*t* To borrow, loan, tax

Hirang *a*-Selected, chosen, select, choice

Huang-*n*-Selection, choice

Huangin *t*-To select, choce pick

Harap-*n*-Hardship, pain, torture, grief, toil, torment, misery, poverty, distress, affliction, anguish, cross, trouble, anxiety, fatigue, ado, dolor

Hirap ng kalooban *n* Wound, affliction injury.

Hiraran *n*-Example, instance.

Hirati *a*-Accustomed, used

Hiratihin *t*-To accustom, use.

Hiraya-*n* Illusion; apprehension

Hiringa-*n*-Syringe.

Hiringahin-*t*-To syringe.

Historia-*n*-History

Hita *n*-Thigh

Hitad *n*-Whore, harlot, prostitute

Hitit *n*-Suck, smoke.

Hititin-*v*-To smoke, such.

Hitsura-*n*-Shape, form, mode, appearance; phase, likeness, mien, garb; guise, ostent, cut, fashion, face

Hiwa *n*-Slice, cut, incision

Hiwaga-*n*-Mystery.

Hiwain-*v*-To cut, slice, carve.

Hiwalay-*n*-Separation

Hiwalayin-*v*-To separate, assort, sort compart, renounce, divorce, divide part.

Hiwas *n*-A cut on a bias.

Hiwas-*a* Slanting, squint-eyed, incorrect

Hiwasan-*v* To cut en a bias or slant

Hiwid-*a*-Hipshot, lame

Hiya-*n*-Shame, bashfulness' modesty; embarrasment, compunction

Hiyain-*v*-To shame, embarrass, affront, insult

Hiyas *n*-Ornament, adornment, trimming, furniture

Hiyasan-*v*-To ornament, adorn, embellish

Hiyaw-*n* Shout; cry, scream' howl, outcry, clamor, hoot.

Hiyawan-*v*-Outcry, clamor, shout, cry, hoot; howl

Hiyawin-*v*-To shout, cry out, howl; huzza, clamor, hoot.

Hodyat *n*-Countersign, watchword passport

Hodyatan-*n*-Countersign; wartchword, rendezvous, appointment.

Hogyat-*n* Alarm, notice of danger, watchword

Holhol-*n*-Howl, cry of horror

Howad-*n*-Counterfeit, imitation; copy, forgery

Howaran *v*-To counterfeit, copy, imitate, forge, mimic, pirate

Huad-*n* Counterfeit, copy, forgery, imitation, likeness, transcript.

Huag-*inter* -Shan't, do not, don't; stop

Huaggawin *v*-To neglect, quit, relinquish, forsake, leave, yield, let, omit, refuse to do.

Huag gumanting palad *v* To be disagreeable uncompromising

Huag ipakaloob-*t*-To refuse, deny.

Huag ipatuloy-*v*-To desist, discontinue, supercede, stop

Huag isaina-*v*-To exclude, shut out, ' eep separate

Huag lalingñayin *t*-To slight, disregard

Huag kumilala *v*- To disown, disclaim ignore, refuse to recognize.

Huag kumilala nğ utang na loob-*v* To be disagreeable, ungrateful

Huag kupkupin-*v*-To leave in danger, refuse to help, aid, shelter or protect

Huag magalnğin *t* To reject, condemn lower refuse to approve

Huag magsalita-*v*-To refuse to talk hush; remain silent

Huag mahalata-v-To hide; conceal; keep secret.

Huag mahalin-v-To slight; disregard.

Huag makipag-usap-v-To stand mute; remain silent.

Huag makilala-v-To disown; disavow; refuse to recognize.

Huag malaman-v To disown; disavow; be ignorant of.

Huag bilañgin-v-To exclude; shut out; refuse to count.

Huag mapanabi-v-To restrain; refuse to tell or say; bind.

Huag matanto-v-To be ignorant of; not to know.

Huag pahintulutin-v-To disapprove; disfavor; discountenance; refuse to permit.

Huag pamanahin-v-To disinherit.

Huag pumayag-v-To refuse; object; disfavor; veto.

Hung sabin-v-To refuse to tell or say keep secret or silent; seal; secrete.

Huag samantalahin-v To fail to take advantage of; fail to gain advantage; fail to procure.

Huag tamaan-v-To err; misjudge; mistake.

Huag tangapin-v-To reject; refuse; object to.

Huag tumupad-v To shirk fail to do.

Huag uminik-v-To remain silent; hush keep still.

Hubad-a Naked; nude.

Hubaran-v-To denude; underss; empoverish; make poor.

Hubaran ang luksa-v-To leave off mourning.

Hubdan-v-To undress; deude; disrobe.

Hubog-a Curver; bent; crooked.

Hubog-a-Bent; curved; crooked.

Hubog-n-Bend curve; arch; crook.

Hubog-p. p.-Bent; curved; arched.

Hubugan-v-To bend; arch; curve.

Hubugin-v-To bend; arch; curve.

Hudyatan d-Passport; countersign; watchword.

Hugasing-v-To wash; lave bath.

Hugos ñg compana-n Bell-clapper.

Hugutin-v-To extract; remove; take out; deduce; draw out; abstract; extort.

Hukay-n-Excavation; hole; pit; hollow; cavity.

Hukayin-v-To dig; excavate; hollow.

Hukayin muli-v-To exhume.

Hukbo-n-Army.

Hukom-n Governor; judge; arbiter.

Hukluban-n-Place of covering any thing; rotting place.

Hukuman-v-To Judge.

Hukuman n-Province; governor's house.

Hula-n-Prediction; prophecy; conjecture; surmise; omen; divination; augury; precursor.

Hulaan-v-To predict; foretell; prophecy; soothsay; prognosticate; divine.

Hulhol d-Howl; yelp; yelping.

Huli-adv.-Late; yelp; yelping.

Húli-n-Capture; spoils; prize.

Huli ñg sasakyan-d Stern.

Hulihan-n-The pack part; stern.

Hulihan ñg hokbo-n-Rear-guard.

Hulihin-v-To capture; seize; catch; get; apprehend.

Huli sa lahat-a-Last.

Hulma-n-Mold; mitrice.

Hulo-a-Upper.

Hulo ñg ilog-n-Source of a river.

Hulog-n-Fall; tumble.

Hulugin-v-To throw down; cast.

Hulugin ñg gracia ñg DIOS-v-To srnctify; bless.

Humaba-v-To lengthen; protroct; prolong.

Humabi-v-To weave; plat.

Humabol-v-To catch; run after.

Humagkan-v-So hug; kiss.

Humaging-v-To whir; whur, whistle, whiz; hum.

Humagpos-v-To slip; slide, skulk; escape from danger.

Humahalo n-Rocker; one who stirs.

Humakbang-v-To step; stirs.

Humal a-Nasal.

Humalaw-v To choose; select; elect.

Humalay-v To consume decry.

Humalik v-To kiss; osculate.

Humalili-v-To exchange; change, alternate, reciprocrate; supercede.

Humalimhim-v-To set; hatch. (per to fowls).

Humalinghing-v-To sigh; groan; moan; lament.

Humamak-v-Grovel; lower; degenerate.

Humamok-v-To bedew fog.

Humamok-v-To fight; struggle; contend.

Humamon-v-To anger; provoke; fight; irritate; offend; excite; contend; struggle.

Humanap-v-To find; search for; hunt; search; look for.

Humanda-v To prepare; get ready.

Humanga-v-To limit; finish; end; close.

Humañgitin-v-To gnaw; molest.

Humañgos-v-To pant; palpitate.

Humantong-v-To stop; halt; desist.

Humapdi-v-To smart; irritate; hurt; prickle.

Humapis-v-To oppress; grieve; mourn.

Humapon-v-To eat supper.

Humapon-v-To perch.

Humarap-*v*-To present; appaer; confront; witness.

Humatol-*v*-To judge; give sentence; sentence, decide; condemn.

Humawak-*v*-To clasp; clutch; hold; have.

Humbak-*n*-Concavity; hollowness.

Humibik-*v*-To sob; lament; groan.

Humigit *v*-To exceed; surpass; excell.

Humigit-*a*-More.

Humigit-*adv*.-More; over.

Humigop-*v*-To sip; suck; absorb; imbibe.

Humihip-*v*-To blow.

Humikayat-*v*-To attract; draw; invite.

Humilig-*v*-To incline; tend; lean; recline.

Humilik-*v*-To snore.

Humimalay-*v*-To take what is left.

Humimawa-*v*-To blaspheme; curse.

Humimig-*v*-To bubble; appear; answer.

Humimpay-*v*-To cease, forbear; desist; stop.

Humimpil-*v*-To appease; calm; pacify; becalm; rest; repose; stop.

Humina-*v*-To grow weak; debilitate, impair; weaken; pall; enfeeble; languish.

Humindusay-*v*-To weaken; give up an intention; dispirit.

Huminga-*v*-To respire; breathe, exhale; expire.

Humingal-*v*-To pant; palpitate.

Humingi-*v*-To ask; request; petition; beg; entreat; implore; demand; claim; exact.

Huminkod-*v*-To limp; deviate.

Huminkodhinkod-*v*-To limp.

Huminto-*v*-To stop; halt; desist; rest; repose

Huninit-*v*-To smoke; suck.

Humiwalay-*v*-To separate; diverge; deviate.

Humiyaw-*v*-To oyell; shout; exclaim.

Humpay-*n*-Intermission; interrudtion.

Humpayin-*v*-To interrupt, intermit; discontinue.

Humuad-*v*-To counterfeit; falsify; copy; imitate; mimic.

Humubad-*v*-To undress; denude.

Humubo-*v*-To undress; denude.

Humubog-*v*-To undress; denude.

Humukay-*v*-To dig; excavate; hollow; delve; enter.

Humula-*v*-To foretell; prophesy; perdict; portend; prognosticate; announce conjecture.

Humula-*n*-Predictor; prophet.

Humuni-*v*-To neigh.

Humupa-*v*-To rest; calm; grow quiet; become thin or weak.

Humutok-*v*-To arch; bend; curve.

Hunhang-*a*-Foolish; silly; ignorant; stupid.

Huni-*n*-Neigh.

Hurno-*n*-Oven.

Husay-*n*-Order; regulation array.

Busay-*a*-Regulated; arrayed; elaborate; orderly.

Husayin-*v*-To arrange; perfect; regulate; array; adjust class; order; correct; set off; put in order; rectify; repair; patch; conform; improve; mend; modify.

Husaying muli-*v*-To rearrange; rearray;

Husto-*a*-Enough; complete; complete. perfect; exact; right; sufficient effectual. equitable; upright honest; clever.

Hustuhin *v*-To complete; perfect; finish; execute, perform.

Hutukin-*v*-To arch; bend; curve.

Huwarin-*v*-To imitate; copy; simulate

I

Iabang-*v*-To wait for; watch for; await.

Iabot-*v*-To proffer; hand; offer: reach.

Iaga-*v*-To foresee; anticipate; preoccupy; prepare.

Ialay-*v* To offer; dedicate; present; give

Ialis-*v*-To to take away; discard; move; obviate.

Ialok-*v*-To offer; hold out; proffer; offer for sale; entrust; propose.

Iayos-*v*-To regulate; arrange; array; busk; put in order.

Iba-*a*-dissimilar; different; diverse; unlike; other.

Iba-*pro*.-Other.

Ibabá-*v*-To lower; put down.

Iba,t, iba *v*-Various.

Ibabala-*v*-To explain; announce; anticipate; foretell; signify.

Ibabao-*n*-Topside; outside; cover; surface.

Ibadbad-*v*-To soak; steep; imbue.

Ibagay-*v*-To make convenient; conform.

Ibago-*n*-To renew; make over; change.

Ibahin-*v*-To change; transform; alter; deviate; remove; vary; convert; reform; transfigure; transmute; modify.

Ibahin ang hitsura-*v*-To change the shape; disguise.

Ibahog-*v*-To mix; mingle; unite; incorporate.

Ibalabag *v* To throw; cast.

Ibalibag-*v*-To throw.

Ibalik *v* To return; restore; devolve.

Ibalita-*v* To relate: report; tell; announce;

say, mention, notify, apprise; make known, narrate, proclaim

Ibalot-r-To envelop

Ibangon-r-To raise, stand up, elevate, heave

Ibang tawo-n Stranger, foreigner

Ibanting-r-To tie, fasten

Ibaon-v-To bury, inter, submerge, conceal

Ibaon-i-To preoare or fix for a journey

Ibarka-i-To load or freight a ship

Ibatay-i-To prop, build, upon, be supported

Ibawal-r-To prohibit

Ibhan-v-To change, diversify

Ibig n-Love, friendship

Ibigay-i To give present, bestow, donate, cede, afford

Ibigav nawa ng Dios-inter —GOD grant, would to GOD

Ibigin-v-Lo love, like.

Ibilad-v-Todiy; sun, put in the sun.

Ibilango-i-To imprison, arrest, confine; shut up

Ibitin-i-To suspend, hang up

Ibon-n-Bird

Ibsan t-To lower, take away, forgive

Ibual-i-To overbalance, tip over, turn over, discomfit

Ibubo-i-To mold, cast, founder

Ibudbod-v-To sprinkle, scatter, sow, distribute

Ibuho-v-To empty, clear, induce; prompt

Ibuhol-v To tie, knot, join or unite by knotting

Ibuhos-v-To pour, spill, empty, effuse

Ibulod-v-To separate divide, except, exclude, preclude, set apart, blink, segregate, keep out, discriminate

Ibukod ang tuhapes sa palay-i To winnow

Ibuhid-i-To precipitate; expose to ruin

Ibuluak i-To pour; spill, leak.

Ibulusok-v-To precipitate; expose to ruin

Ibungo-i -To collide

Ibunton-i-To heap, pile up, put together

Ibunyi-r To extoll, praise, magnify

Ibusa r-To parch, roast

Ibuyo-i To induce, inspire, incite, rouse, stimulate, imbue, persuade

Idagdag-v-To add to, increase, accrue, aggrandize, aggregate, superadd

Idaing-i To implore, complain, beg, petition, appeal; entreat

Idaiti-v-To unite, join, touch

Idalangin i-To intercede, mediate

Idamay-r-To implicate, effect

Idaraing v-To complain

Idarang i To scotch, singe, heat

Idaos r-To dispatch, dispose of, complete, verificate

Idatay-i-To stretch; unfold, expand

Idatig-v-To unite join, put together.

Ideposito-v-To deposit

Idikit-v-To stick; paste, glue.

Idikta-v-To dictate.

Idukit r-To sculpture engrave.

Igalang-v To esteem, respect, venerate reverence, regard, appreciate, have regards for, notice

Igawgaw-v-To mix, mingle, unite, join coalesce, consolidate, copulate, incorporate; conjoin

Igayak-v-To prepare, get ready, adjust arrange

Igi-n Ease, goodness, kindness

Igiba-r-To destroy, demonish, obliterate

Iganagayak-v-To prepare.

Iguhit i To draw, trace, line

Iguho n-To demolish, obliterate, destroy

Igumon.v-To roll, wallow, humble

Ihabilin-v-To comission give charge

Ihagis-v-To throw, cast.

Ihagis ng pabigla-v-To jerk

Ihalabos-v-To boil, cook-in water

Ihalal-v-To elect, choose.

Ihalang-v-To put cross-wise

Ihalih-v-To substitute, change, exchange, surrogate.

Ihalo-v-To mix, mingle, alloy, join, unite, coalesce, admix, intermix, intermingle, blend

Ihampas-v-To strike, beat, whip

Ihanda-v-To prepare, get ready, supply, provide, arrange, adjust

Ihapay v-To incline, lean

Iharang-i-To stop, check, hold up

Iharap-n-To present, exhibit, confront, compare

Ihasa-v-To sharpen.

Ihatid v-To convoy, accompany, convoy conduct, carry, transport

Ihawin-v-To roast, toast, bake, grill

Ihayag-v-To publish, disclose, show, expose, apprise; divulge, lay open, reveal

Ihayin v-To offer, present, give

Ihi-n-Urine.

Ihian-n-Retreat

Ihiga-v To lay, down, stretch, unfold, expand

Ihilabos-v-To boil, cook in water, strike sweepingly.

Ihilbana-i-To baste

Ihilig-v-To incline, recline, lean back, influence, imbue, persuade, induce.

Ihimang v To solder, mend with solder

Ihinday-v-To move to a distance.

Ihingil-v-To incline, influence induce, persuade

5

Ihiwalay-*t*-To separate, divide, set apart, subtract, lay aside, revoke, with-draw; sunder, sort, remove, discriminate, divorce, segregate

Ihiwas-*r*-To slant, sling, diagonally

Ihuli-*n* To put last or at the end

Ihulog-*t* To throw down, translate, interpret

Ihulog ang kapwa sa infierno-*v*-To damn, condemn to eternal tormenst

Ihulog sa ibang wika-*v*-To translate, interpret

Iihan-*n* Chamber pot

Iinit-*v*-To heat, kindle

Iisa,t,isa-*adv*-One by one.

Iit-*n*-Nickname

Ikaanim-*n* Sixth

Ikaanim-*a* Sixth

Ikaanim na puo-*n* Sixtieth

Ikaanim na puo-*a*-Sixtieth.

Ikaapat-*n*-Fourth.

Ikaapat-*a*-Fourth.

Ikababayad-*n*-Payment, that which is paid, pay, reward, satisfaction

Ikabit-*v*-To fasten, stick, join, tie, paste, add to

Ikadalawang puo-*a*-Twentieth.

Ikadalawang puo-*n*-Twentieth, vigesimal

Ikadkad *v*-To unfurl, unroll, unfold stretch; expand.

Ikahon-*v*-To box, embale, pack

Ikaila *v*-To deny, he, negative, gainsay, refuse to tell

Ikaisang libo *a*-Thousandth.

Ikaisang-libo-*n* Thousandth

Ikait-*v* To deny, reject, refuse

Ikalabing apat-*n*-Fourteenth

Ikalabing apat-*a* Fourteenth

Ikalabing dalawa-*n*-Twelvth

Ikalabing dalawa-*a*-Twelvth

Ikalabing isa-*n*-Eleventh.

Ikalabing isa-*a*-Eleventh

Ikalabing pito-*n*-Seventeenth

Ikalabing pito-*a*-Sevententh

Ikalabing tatlo *n*-Thirteenth

Ikalabing tatlo-*a*-Thirteenth

Ikalabing walo-*n*-Eighteenth

Ikalabing walo-*a*-Eighteenth.

Ikalat-*v*-To scatter, distribute, disperse, diffuse, extend, publish

Ikalawa-*n*-Second

Ikalawa-*a*-Second.

Ikaling-*v*-To unite, join

Ikama *v*-To adapt, apply; adjudge consolidate, copulate, join,conjoin, unite, collect

Ikama ang isang bagay *v* To intervene insert

Ikanlong *v* To hide, conceal, defend excuse, disguise, keep secret.

Ikao *pro*-You, thou

Ikapit-*v*-To apply, adapt, adjudge.

Ikapito-*n*-Seventh

Ikapito-*a*-Seventh

Ikasampuo-*n*-Tenth

Ikasampuo *a*-Tenth

Ikasal-*v* To marry, betroth, match

Ikating-*v*-To incorporate, join, conjoin consolidate, unite

Ikatlo-*n*-Third

Ikatlo-*a*-Third

Ikawalo *n*-Eighth

Ikawalo-*a*-Eighth

Ikawalong *adv*-Eighthly

Ikawalong puo-*a*-Eightieth

Ikawing-*v*-To fasten, add, paste, tie, stick

Ikiling-*v* To incline, induce, persuade

Ikinabubuhay-*n*-Nourishment, food, maintainence, sustenence, ration, lıvlıhood

Ikintal *v*-To stamp, print, imprint

Ikiran *n*-Spindle, pivot, axle, bobbin

Ikiran-*v*-To wind, convolve.

Ikiskis-*v*-To scratch, smooth polish, rub, burnish.

Ikit-*n*-Turn

Ikhan-*v*-To shorten, abridge, reduce confine, restrain, pare, chip

Ikmo-*n*-Betel nut leaf

Ikog-*n*-Turn

Ikumpas-*v*-To beat time

Ikuskos-*v*-To scratch, scour, rub

Ikusot-*v*-To wrinkle, rumple

Ilabas-*v*-To remove put out; exclude extract, extort, reject, eject, effuse shut out

Ilabas sa katawan-*v*-To excrete

Iladlad-*v*-To unfurl, untold, expand, stretch.

Ilag-*n*-Shyness, fright, scare, avoidance, evasion

Ilag-*inter*-Begone keepoff

Ihgak-*v*-To deposit, entrust leave with another

Ilagan-*v*-To evade, shun, avoid, parry stave off,blink, obviate, escape

Ilagay-*v*-To put, place, set, lay, arrange, appoint, situate, wager, pledge, mortgage

Ilagay ng manga dingding *v*-To partition

Ilagay sa araw-*v* To to put or place in the sun

Ilagay sa grado-*v* To grade, class, classify

Ilagay sa hulihan *v* To put or place last

Ilagay a ibang wika *v* To interpret, transslate.

Ilagay sa kasukatan *v*-To appraise, value

Ilagay sa codigo-*v*-To codefy.

Ilagom-*v*-To congregate, unite, join, meet.

Ilagpak *v* To tumble or throw down, everturn

Ilahok-*v*-To mix, brew, comprise, intermingle

Ilak-*v*-To solicit, collect.

Ilak-*n* Collection, solicitation

Ilakip-*v*-To Reconcile, unite, join, league, congregate, coalesce, conjoin, tie, bind, alloy, copulate.

Ilalim-*adv* Underneath, below under

Ilalim nang-*prep*.-Under, below.

Ilang-*adv* -Deserted, lonely, barren

Ilang-*n*-Lonely place, desert

Ilang *a*-Sundry; several, various.

Ilang How many

Ilangkap *v*-To unite, join; conjoin, incorporate, knit, coalesce; comprise, contain include

Ilap-*n*-Wildness, shyness, coldness; temerity, avoidance, bashfulness

Ilapat-*v*-To unite, join, inclose

Ilapit-*v*-To approach, bring near approximate.

Ilarawan sa papel-*v*-To portrait, photograph, take pictures

Ilatag-*v*-To unfold, stretch, out, evolve, expand

Ilatag ang bato-*v*-To pave

Ilathala-*v* To declare, manifest, expound, explain, divulge, publish, present

Ilaw-*n*-Lamp, light; clarity, clearness

Ilawan-*n* Light lamp

Ilawit-*v*-To hang up, reach

Ilaylay-*v*-To hang up, hoist, reach

Ilayo-*v*-To remove, separate, divorce, distance, retire, withdraw, retract, lay aside

Ilibing-*v*-To inter, bury, intomb, sepulcher

Ilibad-*v* Te to take turns, cause to disappear

Iligaw *v*-To lose, err, commit a mistake, go astray, cause to misjudge

Iligin *v*-To move to and fro, handle much

Iligpit-*v*-To gather; collect, hide; hoard, conceal

Iligtas-*v*-To rescue, redeem, ransom, succor, save, free, exempt, acquit, excuse, liberate, pardon, relieve, remit

Ililim-*v*-To conceal, keep secret, hide, disguise, reserve

Ilihis-*v*-To separate; obviate; misguide, remove.

Ilikmo-*v* To become fit, suit, establish; smooth

Ilimbag-*v*-To stamp, print, emboss, seal

Ilimbang-*v*-To take a round about way.

Ilingid *v*-To hide, conceal; bury, keep secret, diminish.

Ilipat-*v*-To transform; remove; move, cross passover, transpose; transport

Ilipat ang tanim-*v*-To transplant

Ilitan-*v*-To envy, pay less than one should for anything, underpay.

Ilitaw-*v* To disclose, show, adduce, discover.

Ilog-*n*-River, creek, stream

Ilog na munti-*n*-Rivulet, creek

Ilong-*n*-Nose, snout

Ilual-*v*-To advance money

Ilubog-*v* To sink, submerge; immerse, dip, put under water, douse; duck, merge.

Ilugmok *v*-To wallow, roll

Iluhog-*v*-To beseech, appeal, ask, pray, implore, harangue

Ilulan-*v*-To load, ship; lade; freight

Ilunod-*v*-To sink, submerge; immerse

Imah-*v*-To err, misjudge, equivocate, mistake

Imang-ha-*v*-To stupefy, surprise.

Imarka-*v*-To mark, stamp

Imbak-*a*-Old, cured

Imbot-*n*-Concern, interest

Imot *n* Economy, frugality

Imot-*a*-Economic, frugal, close

Impas-*adv* -Equal, even

Impis *v*-To thin; diminish, lower

Impitin-*v*-To press, prolong the appearance

Impukin-*v*-To keep guard, watch, observe.

Imukha-*v* To resemble; conform; favor; assimilate

Ina *n*-Mother, mamma.

Inaakala-*v*-To intend, mean, design

Inaalon-*a* Wavy, undulatory.

Ina-ama *n*-God-father

Ina-anak-*n*-God-son, God daughter

Inaaralan-*v*-To counsel, advise; teach; correct

Inahin-*n*-Hen; Female *(per to animal)*

Inahit-*p* *p* -Shaved

Ina-ina-*n*-God-mother

Inam *n*-Beauty, goodliness, fairness; delight; pleasure

Inam ng kilos-*n*-Gentility, elegance, good breeding

Inam ng tikas-*n*-Genteelness; elegance, bravery

Inamoy-*p* *p* -Smeleed; scented

Inang *n*-Mamma.

Inanyaya-*p.p.-& imp* Bade, bad.

apo-*n*-Grandchild; descendant, posterity.

Inawak-*n*-Veil, cover

Incenso *n*-Incense

Indahin *v*-To feel; perceive, grieve

Infierno-*n*-Hell, purgatory.

Ingat-*n*-Care, solicitude, caution; guard, precaution, pains; attention, watch, observation; circumspection, protection

Ingatan-*v*-To guard, protect, observe, watch, care for; look after, heed, keep

Ingay-*n*-Noise; carousal, revelry, romping, scuffle, racket

Ingles *n*-English

Ingles-*a*-English

Inig-*n*-Tremble, sha' e, quake, quiver, quaver.

Iniging *n*-Shake, tremble, oscillation

Inihalili-*n*-Substitute, delegate

Ini-ibig-*p p* & *a.*-Loved, beloved

Ini-ibig-*a*-Dear, estimable

Ini-ibig-*n* Dear

Ini-irog-*p p* -Loved, beloved

Ini-irog *a* Beloved, dear

Iningat-*n*-Reserve, secret, exception

Ingit-*n*-Envy, jealousy

Inimot-*adv* -Gently, softly, little by little

Inip-*n*-Envy, impatience, eagerness, hastiness

Inis-*n*-Choking, suffocation, smother, oppression

Inisin-*v*-To smother, oppress, choke; suffocate.

Init *n*-Heat; warmth' zeal, fervor, chafe

Inomin-*n*-Beverage; drink.

Inomin *v*-To drink.

Inotinot-*adv.*-Gently, softly, little by little

Inpo-*v*-To become, smooth, suit, establish.

Insik *n*-Chinaman, chino

Insik-*a*-Chino, chinese

Instrumento-*n*-Instrument

Interes-*n* Interest, behalf

Inugin-*v* To go round, encompass encircle

Inumin-*n* Drink, beverage

Inumin-*v*-To drink.

Inuman-*n*-Afterbirth

Inunos *a*-Worm eaten.

Inupahan *a*-Hackney, hack.

Inutog-*v*-To grow large, enlarge, harden (*not used*)

Inutos-*p p* -Ordered; sent, bade

Inumit *n*-Theft.

Inumit *p p* Stolen

Inuyat *n* Treacle, sorghum.

Ipaala-ala-*v*-To remind; hint; suggest; prompt; mention.

Ipaalam *v*-To ask permission, bid adieu

Ipabigay alam-*v* To encourage, entice, reward, induce.

Ipabuya-*v*-To encourage, entice; reward; induce.

Ipadala-*v*-To send, dispatch; remit; transmit' expedite, convey.

Ipagayak *v*-To provide get ready

Ipag-awit-*v*-To sing, chant

Ipagbala *v*-To threaten, menace

Ipagbalobalo-*v* To feign, pretend; affect

Ipagbanda-*v*-To Proclaim, announce

Ipagbawal *v*-To prohibit, interdict forbid, refuse, deny, ban

Ipagbilin-*v* -To charge, enjoin, recommend

Ipagdiwag *v*-To shout, huzza, applaud

Ipagdiwang-*v* To celebrate, feast, solemnize praise, verify

Ipaghabla-*v*-To accuse demand, inform

Ipagintindi *v* -To signify, intend, mean, declare annunce

Ipa-gitna-*v* To center, put in the center

Ipagkaila-*v*-To deny, contradict; refuse disown

Ipagkait-*v* -To deny, contradict, keep secret, disown

Ipag aloob *v*-To concede; cede, donate, bestow; confer, assign

Ipagkapuri-*v*-To honor, respect, dignify, credit

Ipagkilala-*v* -To introduce, present.

Ipag atiwala-*v*-To give credit, confide, deposit.

Ipaglaan *v*-To prepare, persist, maintain

Ipaglaban *v*-To defend; protect, maintain, argue, sustain, persist, hold, dispute.

Ipaglagay *v* -To put or place for another

Ipagmasa it-*v* To interest, concern; defend, protect, give share in, enjoin, charge

Ipagmatowid *v*-To argue; regulate-dispute, contend; straighten.

Ipagpag-*v*-To shake brandish

Ipagpahuli-*v*-To put behind, leave behind

Ipagpalagay-*v* To suppose

Ipagpalit-*v*-To permute, exchange; barter

Ipagpalumat-*v*-To remove, transport transfer, convey; hold anything until it increases in value

Ipagpasial-*v*-To take for a walk.

Ipagpista-*v* To feast, celebrate, solemnize praise.

Ipagpauna *v* To expect; anticipate

Ipag-angalang *v*-To defend, maintian, sustain, protect; support

Ipagsabi-*v*-To tell; publish; reveal; proclaim.

Ipagtaboy-*v*-To divorce; separate; dismiss.

Ipagtabuyan-*v*-To Divorce; separate; dismiss.

Ipagtangol-*v*-To defend; protect; aid; save; help; support; maintain; sustain.

Ipagtuloy-*v*-To protract; prolong; continue; hold.

Ipagtulakan-*v*-To push; impel; shove.

Ipagwisi -*v*-To sprinkle.

Ipahalang-*v*-To lay crossways or crosswise; thwart.

Ipahalata-*v*-To display; show; make known.

Ipahalay-*v*-To thwart.

Ipahatid-*v*-To send an escort; dispatch; send.

Ipahayag-*v*-To proclaim; publish; announce; reveal; herald; cite; make known; impart; declare. manifest; apprise; send; forth; communicate; emit; divulge.

Ipahayag muli-*v*-To republish; reannounce.

Ipahintulot-*v*-To leave; let; permit; give consent; consent; agree; condescend; sanction; privelege.

Ipaibabaw-*v*-To add; augment; put upon; boot.

Ipailalim-*v*-To put under; put below; bury; cover.

Ipainom-*v*-To give to drink; invite to drink.

Ipakilala *v*-To introduce; present; manifest; demonstrate.

Ipakilos-*v*-To actuate.

Ipakipagtalo-*v*-To dispute; controvert.

Ipakita-*v*-To show; exhibit; lay before; point out; explain; expound; present; display; evince; produce; bespeak.

Ipakiusap-*v*-To beseech; implore; appeal; intercede; entreat; harangue; ask; pray.

Ipako-*v*-To nail; spike; peg.

Ipako sa cruz-*v*-To crucify.

Ipakuskos-*v*-To order to clean or rub.

Ipalabas-*v*-To put out; effuse.

Ipalagay-*v*-To choose; elect; name.

Ipalagay sa loob-*v*-To put within.

Ipalaman-*v*-To put inside.

Ipaligid-*v*-To beset.

Ipalit-*v*-To change; barter; substitute; exchange.

Ipaloob-*v*-To put within; enter; sheathe.

Ipalubog-*v*-To sink; immerse; inundate; hide; conceal.

Ipamahagi-*v*-To apportion; distribute; part; dispart; divide.

Ipamalit-*v*-To exchange; permute; change.

Ipamudmod-*v*-To sprinkle; distribute; divide; part; apportion.

Ipamulsa-*v*-To imburse; put in the pocket; pocket; pouch.

Ipanabi-*v*-To tell; publish; reveal; proclaim; say.

Ipanagano-*v*-To dedicate; consecrate.

Ipangako-*v*-To promise; insure.

Ipanganak-*v*-To give birth; bear children.

Ipangat-*v*-To expose; lay open; boil.

Ipangayaw-*v*-To refuse; retrocede; retire; deny.

Ipangusap-*v*-To advice; counsel; fore; show.

Ipanhik-*v*-To go up; take up; invite up.

Ipanumpa-*v*-To swear in; adjure.

Iparis-*v*-To favor; pair resemble;

Ipasan-*v*-To loard; land, put on the shoulders.

Ipasial-*v*-To take for a wal't.

Ipasya-*v* To ordain; decide; enact; determine conform.

Ipasok-*v*-To place in; put in; enter; interject.

Ipaspas-*v* To shake.

Ipataas-*v*-To lift up; raise; emboss; aggrandize.

Ipatag-*v*-To level; make level.

Ipatalastas-*v*-To make known; manifest; explain; announce; declare; construe; impart.

Ipatalo-*v*-To lose; cause to lose; lose purposely; let lose.

Ipatanaw-*v*-To show exhibit; expose; lay before; point out.

Ipatawad-*v*-To forgive; pardon.

Ipatong-*v*-To add to; put on; load; boot.

Ipatnugot-*v*-To direct; teach; guide; show the right way; manage; conduct; show; rule; govern.

Ipatuad-*v*-To invert; turn upside down.

Ipatuloy-*v*-To continue finish; persue; follow; accomplish.

Ipaunawa-*v*-To expound; explain; point out; announce; teach; lay before.

Ipawis-*v*-To perspire; sweat.

Ipayag-*v*-To concede; allow; admit; grant; conform.

Ipilig-*v*-To shake.

Ipinanganak sa bundok-*n*-Mountaineer highlander.

Ipinahiram-*v*-Loan; that which has been lent.

Ipinta r-To paint
Ipinta ang tabas-t-To draw the outlines, trace.
Ipis n Cockroach.
Ipisan-v-To unite, join, congregate
Ipit-n-Tweezers, pincers
Ipitin-v-To pinch, press
Ipoipo-n-Whirlwind, vortex
Ipukol-r-To throw, cast
Ipunin-v-To gather, store, hoard, lay up
Ipunta-r-To point; direct.
Iraos r-To finish; complete
Ire-pro-This.
Iri-n-Groan
Irog a-Dear, beloved
Iungin-r To love esteem
Isa-a-One
Isa-n-Digit
Isabat v-To interrupt.
Isabit-v-To hang up, suspend
Isabog-t-To scatter, throw broadcast, bestrew, squander, lavish, misspend, (sa gulo)-discomfit; disperse
Isabong-v-To fight or pit cocks
Isadya-v-To do intentionally or purposely
Isagi-v-To use out of place or when one should not
Isa-isa-one by one, one at a time,-adv - singularly.
Isakay-v-To ride, embark.
Isalangsang-v To oppose; object, contradict, trespass cross, go through
Isalin-v-To copy, transcribe; transfer
Isaht r-To alternate, mix, mingle
Isalong ang sandata-v-To sheathe
Isaloob ang hindi totoo v-To suppose
Isama-v-To join, unite, conjoin, consolidate, associate, adjoin, include, accompany, incorporate, collect, alloy, mix, mingle, affiliate, knit
Isambulat-r-To scatter, squander lavish.
Isampav-v-To hang up, suspend
Isandig r-To recline, lean back
Isandok-r-To dish, stir with a spoon
Isangag-v-To toast, torrefy
Isang dah-n Instant, trice
Isang docena-n-Dozen
Isang kasuotang husto n-A complete suit
Isang laksa a-Ten thousand
Isang kisap mata-n-An instant
Isang pulutong-n-A platoon.
Isanla-v-To mortgage, pledge, pawn; plight, hypothecate,
Isara-v-To close; shut.
Isarin-v-To resemble, be alike
Isauli v-To return, restore. reestablish
Isawala-v-To cause to lose; make lose lose.

Isaw-a Gut, tripe, intestine, entrail
Isawsow-v-To dip
Isda-n-Fish
Isikad v To kick spurn
Isiksik v-To cram in, force, put in by force
Isihd-v-To put in, pack; place in
Isihd sa supot-v-To sack
Isinga-v-To blow the nose
Isingit-v To cram, put in by force
Isip n-Reason, thought, sense, will understanding, mind, idea, meditation judgement; notion, fancy
Isipin-v-To think, reason, meditate, conceive, contrive, fancy, suppose.
Isiping v-To put or place by the side, lay beside
Isipot-v-To cause to appear, show, disclose.
Isisid-v To duck, put under water, dip, douse
Isisin-r-To scrub, wash, mop
Isubo-v To eat with the fingers
Isuga-v-To tie to a rope, tether
Isugba r-To precipitate
Isulat-v-To write.
Isulat ang huhng kalooban-v-To write a will, bequeath.
Isulat ang ngalan sa isang libro v-To marticulate, register, enroll, record
Isulong-v-To propel, shove along
Isumbong-v-To accuse, inform
Isuot-v-To put on, wear.
Isurot-v-To indicate, point out
Isurot sa isip-v-To suggest, hint, prompt
Isusi-v-To lock
Itaan r To dedicate, consecrate, reserve
Itaas-v-To lift; raise up, heave up, elevate, upbear
Itaas-adv -above, over, high
Itaboy-v To divorce, remove, separate.
Itagal-v-To suffer; tolerate, abide, comport, prolong
Itagnilid r-To raise on edge
Itago-v To hide; conceal, guard, keep secret, reserve, adclose
Itagpu v-To patch, mend
Itagpos-v-To continue, hold, protract, lengthen, endure
Itahan r To Quiet, still, place, put
Itak-n Bolo, Gorn-knife
Itakad-v-To move by degrees
Italatag-v-To exhibit or show all
Italav v-To dedicate, consecrate
Itakwil r To reject, repel, gainsay, contradict
Itali-r To tie; fasten, bind, oblige

Itambal *t*-To strenghen, join or unite in order to strengthen

Itampok-*t* Toemboss, extoll; aggrandize

Itanda-*r*-To remember, note; record, register

Itangi *v*-To except, exclude, keep out, separate, divide, lay aside; refuse, deny, disown

Itanong *v*-To ask, question, quaere

Itanyang-*t* To present, extoll, manifest, magnify exhibit.

Itaob-*e*-To overbalance, put face down, overset

Itapal-*v* To poultice, put on, apply

Itapon *t*-To throw away cast, lavish, mis-spend, waste, discard

'tapon ang may sala sa ibang lugar-*v*-To banish, deport, exile.

Itapon sa labas *t*-To eject.

Itatag *v*-To establish, institute, found, ordain; fix, enact

Itatua-*r*-To deny; contradict; gainsay, disown; refuse

Itayo-*v*-To establish, build, situate; construct.

Itayong *t*-To delay, suspend

Itayo uli *t* To rebuild; reestablish, reconstruct.

Itigil-*v*-To discontinue, suspend, delay; stop

Itim-*a* Black; jetty; blackish, gloomy.

Itim *n* That which is black, blackness

Itimbuang *t*-To leave or let lay

Itirik-*t*-To set posts

Itiwalay *t*-To separate, sort, divide remove, divorce, withdraw, lay aside, dissuade

Itiwasay-*e*-To calm, tranquilize

Itlog *n*-Egg, testicle

Ito-*a* This.

Ito-*pro*-This

Itoon-*t* To join, unite, add; increase

Itowid-*v*-To straighten make right

Itudla-*v*-To point with the finger.

Itulag-*t*-To throw a spear.

Itulak *r*-To push, impel, shove, drive, press, forward.

Itulos-*t* To set on end, set posts

Itulot-*v*-To compare, dedicate, permit, give permission.

Itulay-*v* To continue, keep, on, persue

Itungo *v* To direct, conduct, incline; influence

Itungkol *t*-To destinate, pertain

Ituro *v* To teach, train, guide, direct, show, construe, point out, denote

Iudyok *r*-To induce, egg on, encourage, persuade, prejudice

Iugoy-*t*-To swing, rock, move

Iukol-*v*-To destinate, pertain

Iuli-*t* To restore, reform, reestablih mend; renew

Iuna *v*-To anticipate preceed, forego.

Iunat *v* To unfold, extend, stretch out

Iutos-*v*-To order, enact, ordain, send, command

Iwa-*n*-Cut, gash.

Iwaan *t*-To cut; slash, gash

Iwagwag-*t*-To shake wave

Iwaksi-*v*-To separate, reject, condemn, repel, preclude

Iwala *v*-To lose; miss

Iwan-*v*-To leave, let, abandon, forsake, omit; quit, relinquish

Iwayway-*v*-To wave; shake.

Iwisik *v* To sprinkle.

Iyak *n*-Cry, howl

Iyak ng tupa-*n* Bleat.

Ivan-*a*-That

Iyan-*pro*-That

Iyangyang *v*-To dry; put in the air, air

Ivang manga-*a* Those

Iyan manga-*pro*-Those

Iyan nga-*pro*-That

Iyo *pro* Thy; thine; your, yours

Iyon *a*-That

Ivon *pro*-That

Ivuko-*v*-To bow, incline or lower ones, head

Iyukod-*t*-To humble, lower.

J

Jelea-*n* Jelly, jam

Jesu Cristo-*n*-Jesus Christ, Messiah

Judio-*n*-Jew, Hebrew.

Judio-*a*-Jewish, Jew hebrew.

Jumento *n*-Jackass, ass

K

Ka *pro*-You, thee.

Ka *adv*-Very.

Kaabalahan-*n*-Obstacle, impediment

Kaagaw-*n* Rival, competitor, antagonist, opponent

Ka-agulo *n* Mistress concubine

Ka-agusan-n-Current, torrent

Ka-akma-a-Sympathetic

Ka-alaban ng loob-n Fervor, warmth, zeal ardor.

Ka-alakbay-n-Companion, chum; company, accomplice associate

Ka-alam-n-Accomplice associate, confederate

Ka-ahmurahan n Abuse, insult, contempt outrage

Ka-alisagaan-n-Inconstancy levity; fickleness

Ka-alit n-Enemy, antagonist

Ka-aliwan n-Solace, sport, consolation, happiness; relaxation

Ka-amoan-n-Tameness, kindness, humility, modesty.

Kaamuan n Tameness, meekness, gentleness, mildness.

Kaanayaran-n-Softness, gentleness, mildness, delicacy meekness

Kaang n-Dyer's copper

Kaapit bahay-n-Neighbor

Kaasalan-n Rite,ceremony,custom,habit

Kaawa-awa-a-Pathetic

Kaaway-n Enemy, opponent, antagonist; competitor

Kaaya-aya-a-Smiling, agreeable, peaceful, pleasing, delightful delicious

Kaayahan-n-Festivity' rejoicing, gayety; happiness

Kaayawan-n-Reluctance

Kaavawan gumawa-n-Idleness, laziness, reluctance to do work

Kaayon n-Unanimity.

Kaayon-a Unanimous

Kaayos a-Unanimous

Kaayupan n- Baseness, rudeness, insult, humiliation

Kaba-n-Fear,dread, suspicion; emotion.

Kababaan-n-Meekness, humility, mildness, interiority, modesty.

Kababaan ng kilos-n-Meanness, lowness, lewdness.

Kababaan ng loob n- Humility, mild ness; modesty, meekness.

Kababalaghan n-Impediment; obstacle, prevention, anything that can perturb the mind

Kabangisan-n Ferocity, wildness, cruelty; inhumanity

Kababayan n-Fellow-citizen, countryman

Kabag-n-Gust of wind from the stomach, colic.

Kabàg-n-Wave of the hand.

Kabagalan n Slowness, heaviness; dulness; turpitude, carelessness slovenliness minutiæ tediousness, ugliness

Kabagay-a Fit, appropriate; sympathetic, accomadating

Kabagayan-n Fitness, propriety, reliableness, reliability, adaptation, aptitude

Kabagkabág-n Small bat

Kabagsikan-n-Severity, harshness, rigor, asperity; cruelty, truculency, sharpness, inhumanity, force.

Kabagong tawohan-n-Youth, celebacy

Kabahagi-n-Part; piece, portion

Kabahayan-n-Place of many houses

Kabahoan-n-Fetidness, stench, stink

Kabaitan-n-Wisdom, knowledge, prudence; skill, moderation, judgement, learning, discretion, morality

Kabaitan sa pagpalapat-n-Equity, right, justice, impartiality, moderation; concientiousness.

Kabaitan sa pagtupad-n Equity, justice, impartiality, concientiousness, moderation

Kabalikan-n-Wrong side, back part, reverse

Kabalisahan n-Restlessness; unrest, commotion, disturbance

Kabaluktutan n-Crookedness, bend, curvation; curvature

Kaban-n Trunk, chest, coffer, locker

Kaban ng sombahlo-n Hat box

Kabanalan-n-Virtue, purity, sanctity, holiness; godliness.

Kaba ng dibdib-n-Palpitation, pant, heaving of the breast.

Kabanayaran-n-Prudence; equity, justice, right, mildness, impartiality, moderation

Kabáng n Coffer, bier

Kabangisan-n-Cruelty, inhumanity, truculency, asperity, ferocity.

Kabangnhan n Fragrance, fragracy

Kabantugan n-Fame, celebrity, glory, reputation, renown, name, excellence

Kabastusan-n Roughness; rudeness, coarseness, rowdyism contumely

Kabastusan-n Roughness; rudeness, coarseness, rudeness, vile conduct meanness, contumely, rowdyism.

Kabataan-n-Youth, girlhood, boyhood, childhood

Kabatuganan n Slowness slovenliness carelessness

Kabayanihan-n-Heroism; bravery, courage.

Kabayo n Horse, shelte, hackney, plug

Kabayong ginagamit nang sundalo n-charger, cavalry horse

Kabayong kaugban n-Pack-horse

Kabayong kulaklang n Spotted horse

Kabayong ñguso-n Peevish horse

Kabayong siklan-n-Stallion

Kabiak-n-Half, counterpart

Kabiawan n Sugar-mill; cane press

Kabigatan n Heaviness, heft; weight; gravity, enormity, seriousness

Kabigayan n Liberality, giving

Kabiglaan-n Speed; quickness, promptitude; rapidity, promptness, activity, haste.

Kabiglaanan-n-Haste; activity, speed, urgency, exigence, quickness, promptness, promptitude

Kabihasahan n-Habit; custom

Kabihasanan n-Learning, wisdom, knowledge; skill, ability, sagacity.

Kabihasnan-n-Revelation, illucidation; illustration, the forming of a habit

Kabilangan ñg tawo sa isang lugar n-census, population

Kabilugan-n-Whole, total; totality, roundness, account

Kabilugan ñg buan-n-Full moon

Kabingihan-n-Deafness.

Kabinian-n-Modesty, decency, chastity; gentility, genteelness, meekness

Kabinyagan-n-Day of baptism

Kabkab-n-Cavity in wood

Kable-a-Cable

Kabo-n Corporal

Kabog-n-Fall,hurt, contusion, blow, knock.

Kabubuhiran-n-Precipice, fall

Kabuisan-n-Revenue, tax, rent

Kabulaanan-n-Fictitiousness, falsity; uncertainty; lying, unreliability

Kabulagan-n-Blindness; error; stupidity, dulness

Kabuluhan-n-Weight, worth, consequence, importance, moment, use

Kabulukan-n-Corruption; pollution, putrefaction depravity rottenness

Kabulukan ñg sugat-n-Proudflesh, gangren, pus.

Kabundukan-n-Mountain system

Kabuntisan-n-Pregnancy

Kabunyian-n-Fame, glory, reputation, excellence, name

Kabuoan-n-Total, totality, entirety, sum, amount, roundness

Kabuoan ñg loob-n-Valor; bravery; boldness; courage, intrepidity.

Kabuoan ñg puso-n-Serenity, valor, in trepidity

Kaburakan-n Quagmire, slough, marsh, swamp, miry place

Kabusugan-n-Satiety, satiation; satisfaction.

Kabuthan n Goodness kindness good, benefit, utility benevolence

Kabutihan ñg isip n-Wisdom; knowledge, prudence

Kabutingtingan-n-Folly, tedium, useless work

Kabuyaan n Satiety,satiation,satisfaction

Kadaghan-n-Promptitude, activity.

Kadakilaan-n-Greatness, sublimity, magnitude, preeminence, superiority, royalty, grandness, dignity; loftiness, majesty, sumptuousness

Kadalagahan-n Maidenhood

Kadalamhatian-n-Grief, disgust; abhorrence

Kadalasan-n-Frequence, frequency

Kadali-n Instant

Kadalian-n Quickness, activity; speed, promptitude, rush' facility, ease, hurry; pressure, ready compliance

Kadahitaan n-Poverty, misery

Kadataan-n-Softness, delicacy, tenderness; suavity

Kadiliman n- Darkness, obscurity, density, opacity

Kadiñgatdiñgat a-Unexpected, unforseen, sudden

Kadiñgatdiñgat-adv Suddenly; unexpectedly

Kadiosan-n-Diety, divinity, sanctionary

Kadiwaraan-n-Curiosity; inquisitiveness

Kadlit-n-Small cut, incision

Kadlitan-v To incise, make a small cut

Kadoonñan-n-Harbor, anchorage

Kadowahagian-Affliction, humiliation, injury

Kadugo-n-Kindred, relation,-having the same blood, of the same blood

Kadugtong n Addition, continuation; end, postscript.

Kadukhaan n-Lowness, lewdness, vile ness, abjection, degradation.

Kaduluhan n-End, extremity

Kaduluhan-a-Last; end, extreme

Kadunñan n-Contiaction, humiliation, humility, backwardness.

Kadunñuan-n Bashfulness, backward ness, temerity, pertness

Kadustaan-n-Lowness, vileness; lewdness, abjection

Kadustadusta a Humiliating, ignoble, ignominous, disgraceful, low, abject, mean

Kagaanan-n-Levity, lightness.

Kagabi-n Last night

Kagagawan n-Action, doing, feat, event, tact

Kagalañg-n-Pair, the other

Kagalañgan n-Respect, reverence, regard; politeness, civility, homage; courtesy goodmanners,education breeding, manners, observance, obedience.

6

Kagalanggalang-*a*-Respectable, polite, respectful, courteous, reverend, civil

Kagalawan-*n*-Movement, disturbance, moving

Kagalingan-*n*-Goodness, kindness, gentility

Kagalit-*n*-Enemy, opponent, antagonist.

Kagálitan-*n*-Anger; indignation, vexation, passion, rage.

Kagalitan-*v* To anger; perturb vex

Kagamitan-*n* Use, custom, utility; profit.

Kagamitan *a*-Ordinary, usual, customary.

Kagampanan-*n* Compensation, value

Kagamutan-*n*-Remedy, reparation; cure, redemption; recourse

Kagandahan-*n*-Beauty, elegance, comeliness, kindness, gentility, amiability, genteelness

Kagandahan nang loob-*n*-Munificence, kindness; benignity, benificence, generosity, benevolence, liberality

Kagasohan *n* Noisiness, restlessness.

Kagaspangan-*n*-Rudeness; roughness, coarseness; illbreding, stupidity; rusticity

Kagat-*n*-Bite, mouthful

Kagatin-*v*-To bite, gnaw, nip

Kagawian-*n* Inclination;habit,use,custom

Kagayat *n*-Slice, Piece, cut

Kagilit-*n*-Companion

Kagilit *adv*-side by side

Kaginhawahan-*n*-Ease, facility, prosperity

Kaginsaginsa-*adv* Suddenly, unexpectedly

Kaginsaginsa *a*-Sudden, unforseen

Kagipitan *n*-Narrowness, closeness, straightness; hard straits

Kagulangan *n*-Maturity

Kagulanggulang *a* Mature.

Kagulatan *n* Fright, scare

Kagulatgulat *a*-Dreadful, frightful, shocking

Kaguluhan-*n*-Disturbance, confusion, commotion, carousal, tumult, revelry, scuffile, romping, quarrel, perturbation, overthrow, noise; fight

Kagungkong-*n*-Noise; clamor, bustle, dispute, tumult, rumor

Kagyat-*adv*-Hardly; with trouble, scarcely, almost

Kagyatin *v*-To prepare

Kahabaan *n*-Length, protraction

Kahabaang malabis *n*-Tediousness

Kahabaan ng buhay-*n*-Longetivy

Kahabagan-*n*-Wretched, misery.

Kahabaghaba_ *a* Wetched miserable downfallen.

Kahalagahan *n* Appraisement valuo or value, price worth

Kahalakhan *n*-Boisterous laughing

Kahalakhalak-*a*-Happy, joytul

Kahalayan-*n*-Lowness, lewdness, ughness, obscenity, impurity, unchastity, dishonor, dishonesty, rudeness, sordidness, turpitude, covetousness

Kahalili-*n*-Substitute, exchange substitution, relief, successor, alternate, delegate, successor

Kahalo-*n*-Mixture, accomplice

Kahamakan-*n*-Lowness, lewdness, baseness vice, contumely, infamy, dishonor, scoundrelism, accident

Kahambalhambal-*n*-Sad, deplorable, lamentable, dismal, doleful, horrible

Kahambugan *n*-Braggartism, haughtiness, arrogance, presumption, vanity, boast, pompuosity, disdain, vaunt, ostentation, pride

Kahanga-*n* Limit, bound

Kahangahanga-*a* Miraculous, wonderful, admirable, marvelous, astonishing

Kahanginan-*n*-Braggartism, brag, boast, presumption; ignorance; foolishness, clownishness, emptiness

Kahapisan-*n*-Suffering, hardship, suference, infelicity, calamity

Kahapishapis-*a* Doleful, sad, dismal, deplorable

Kahapon-*n*-Yesterday.

Kahapon-*adv* -Yesterday

Kaharian-*n*-Kingdom, crown, dynasty, realm

Kabayopan-*n* Brutality; inhumanity

Kahigpitan-*n* Tightness; tenacity, contumacy, pertenacity, severity, harshness

Kahigtan-*n*-Surplus, increase, augmentation, overplus, preterence, difference

Kahigtan sa iba-*n*-Superiority.

Kahihiyaan-*n*-Bashfulness, shame, confusion, humilation, compromise

Kahilawan-*n* Crudeness, crudity

Kahiman-*prep* -Though, notwithstanding

Kahinanawari-*inter*-Would to GOD-GOD grant

Kahimpak-*n*-Large slice

Kahinaan-*n*-Weakness, debility, feebleness, Prostration.

Kahinaan ng loob *n*-Effeminence, effeminency.

Kahingian-*n*-Petition; request, claim; prayer, demand

Kahinhinan *a*-Decorum; purity, honor, circumspection, modesty. chastity, keeney respect meekness, gravity, seriousness

Kahinugan-n-Maturity, ripeness
Kahirapan-n-Hardship, poverty, misery, sufferance, disaster, suffering, duress, yoke, disadvantage, calamity.
Kahit-adv -Though, notwithstanding
Kahitman prep -Though; notwithstanding.
Kahiwa-n-Slice, cut; piese; part
Kahiyahiya a-Disgraceful, shameful, inglorious, low, lewd
Kahon-n-Box, crate.
Kahoy-n-Timber, wood,tree,cudgel,stick
Kahoyan-n-Grove, woods, timber.
Kahuad n-Likeness; imitation, copy, counterfeit.
Kahubaran-n-Nakedness, nudity
Kahulihan n-Posteriority
Kahulhulihan-a Last, hindmost; latest mizzen, utmost, uttermost
Kahulhuhbang pasiya-n-Ultimatum.
Kahulhulihang salita-n Ultimatum
Kahulugan-n Signification, definition; prognostic; utility
Kahumalan-n-Nasality
Kahumbakan-n-Concavity; hollowness
Kahung-hangan-n-Foolishness, silliness, rusticity
Kahusayan-n-Decency, order, arrangement, propriety.
Kahustuhan n-Sufficiency, enough
Kaiba-a-Foreign, strange; rare
Kaiba-n-Difference' strangeness
Kaibahan-n-Difference, diversity, variety
Kaibhan ng lalaki sa babayi-n-Sex.
Kaibigan-n-Inclination, desire; mind; wish, intention
Kaibigan-n-Friend
Kaibuturan-n-Center; interior, inside
Kaidkuran-n-Scraper. cylinder, roller; meanness; avarice
Kaigutan n-Penury, avarice; meanness, paltriness poverty, difficulty.
Kaikhan-n-Shortness; brevity
Kaikhan ng isip-n-Dulness, stupidity, ignorance, turpitude.
Kaila-n-Negation, denial, refusal, re pulse.
Kailagan-n Wildness; bashfulnesss, shyness. backwardness
Kailangan-a Necessary, needful; requisite, stringent, esssential
Kailangan n-Necessity, need, want, requisition, essential, requisite
Kailangang malubha-n-Indespensible, needful.
Kailanganin-v-To require, need necessitate, want.
Kailanman adv. Never, always, at one time.

Kailanman hindi narinig-a-Unheard of; strange, foreign.
Kainaman-n-Neatness, beauty, elegance; prettiness; finery, nicety; goodness
Kainam manalita-n-Fluency or elegance of speech
Kainan n-Feast dinner, banquet.
Kaing-n Basket
Kaingatan n-Care, prudence; caution
Kaingayan n Noise, carousal, revelry, romping, clamor, scuffle, jargon, racket, bustle
Kainipan n-Envy, impatience, eagerness, hastiness
Kainitan-n Heat, fervor, warmth; zeal, ardor, zest
Kain aan-n-Proverb
Kaisa a-Identical, similar, equal uniform; like, unanimous; united
Kaisa-n-Unanimity, similarity.
Kaitaasan-n-Top, peak, summit
Kaitiman-n-Blackness, darkness
Kaiva n-Fish-basket
Kakaiba-a-Eccentric, strange, absurd ridiculous
Kakaibang umisip n-Paradox.
Kakailangan-n Stringency.
Kakal na may ngipin n-Curry comb
Kakanan ng hayop-n Manger, crib, rack
Kakapalan-n Thickness, density
Kakapusan-n-Lacking, shortcoming lack
Kakapusan ng isip-n-Incapability, incapacity, inability, dulness, stupidity, ignorance, folly
Kaunti-a-Scanty, scare, limited' small; little; slight
Kakaunti ang halaga a-Trifling, of little value, valueless, worthless.
Kakikita-adv -Recently, seen
Kakilakilabot-a-Horrible; awful, monstrous, terrible, horrid, dire, direful, grime, grisly, ghastly, horrific.
Kakilala n-Acquaintance, friend
Kakinangan-n Brightness, smoothness, terseness; purity
Kakinisan-n Brightness; delicacy, finery, cleanliness, beauty, terseness.
Kakiputan-n-Narrowness; straightness, closeness.
Kakitiran n-Narrowness, straightness, closeness
Kakubaan-n-Hump, curvature, Humpback
Kakubutan-n Curvature, hump-back
Kakulangan a-Lacking defect, deficiency, shortcoming; shortage, slight; discrepency, want, need; necessity

Kakulañgan ng̃ ayos-n Discord, disarrangement

Kakulañgan nang palad n-Misfortune, mishap; misery, unhappiness, disappointment

Kakulañgan ng̃ bait n-Folly, nonsense, indescretion absurdity.

Kakuparan n-Slowness, sloth, slothfulness; laziness, indolence

Kakupinan-n-Slowness, laziness indolence; slothfulness.

Kala-n-Shell of the turtle, turtleshell

Kalaban-n-Opponent, competitor, antagonist; rival, onemy

Kalabasa-n Squash

Kalabaw-n-Carabon

Kalabisan-n-Excess surplus, overplus, superfluity, profuseness, residue, remainder

Kalabnawan-n-Liquidity, thinness

Kalabog-n-Fall, tumble, noise, clamor; bustle

Kalabuan n-Muddiness, opacity, opaqueness, dulness, stupidness

Kalagayan-n-State, condition, aspect, situation, rank, attitude, disposition, mode, consistence; consistency; predicament; manner, quality

Kalagayang mahirap n-Peasantry

Kalagayang bata-n-Childhood, perulity

kalagayan ng̃ loob n Humor, mood

kalagin-v-To unhitch, unfasten, untie, loosen, absolve, pardon.

Kalagin sa sala-v-To pardon; acquit, forgive

Kalugitnaan-n-Middle; center, midst, medium, average, half, diameter

Kalagok-n-Swallow, draught

Kalagposan-n-Surplus, overplus; superfluity; excess, superabundance

Kalagpusan n-Surplus, overplus, superfluity, excess, superabundance

Kalaguan-n-Fertility, plenty, fruitfulness

Kalaguan ng̃ sanga-n-Thickness of foliage

Kalaguyo-n Companion, comrade, partner; friend.

Kalahatan n-Totality, total; entirety, whole

Kalahati a Half; semi, moiety.

Kalahatian n Half, middle, midst, average

Kalahati ng̃ bilog-n-Semicircle, half circle

Kalahok n-Ingredient, mixture, companion, associate

Kalaitlait a Nefarious; abominable, hideous; despicable, vile; reprehensible, low.

Kalakkal n-Merchandise, commodity

Kalakaran-n-The usual or ordinary custom or habit

Kalakasan-n-Strength, force vehemence, vehemency, hardness, robustness

Kalakhan-n-Size, amplitude, greatness

Kalakhan ng̃ katawan-n-Corpulence, corpuledcy

Kalakhan ng̃ puso-n Liberality, generosity, largeness of heart

Kalakihan-n-Size; largeness, amplitude, grandness

Kalakip-n-Annexation, joining, inclosure

Kalaliman-n-Depth, profundity.

Kalaluan-n-Surpassing, excess; surplus, superfluity

Kalamañgan n-Overplus, surplus, excess, residue

Kalambutan-n-Softness, delicacy, tenderness, mildness, suavity, pliability, phableness

Kalamigan n-Cold, coolness, frigidness

Kalamkam-n-Tickling

alamnan-n-Hip, buttock rump

Kalan-n-Fireplace, forge, hearth

Kalanda n-Bier, hearse

Kalang-n- edge; prop

Kalap-n-Timber, wood

Kalaparan-n-Width; space, capacity, interval

Kalapastañganan-n-Offense, injury, insolence, impudence, transgression

Kalapati-n-Pigeon, dove

Kalapit-a-Neigboring, next, proximate, mediate, contiguous, conjunct, united, near

Kalapitan-n-Proximity, closeness, vicinity, contiguity

Kalapsawin-v-To stir revert

Kalaputan-n Thickness, density

kalasag-n-Shield

Kalasin n-Chaise

Kalasin-v-To undo

Kalasing n Clatter, jingle, jangle

Kalat n-Distribution, scattering.

kalatis-n-Noise made in walking

halatog-n-Noise made by shaking anything, sound, report.

Kalaulin-v To torsee, know beforehand

Kalaunang panahon-n-Antiquity

kalawang-n Rust, stain

Kalawañgin-a-Rusty, moldy.

Kalawañgin-v-To rust

Kalawang ng̃ tanso n-Verdigris

kalawit-n-Hook

Kalawitin v To hook

kalayaan n Freedom, liberty, release

Kalayolayoan-a Farthest, farthermost; utmost; uttermost.

Kalendario *n* Calender

Kalesa-*n*-Chaise, gig

Kalibañgan *n*-Neglect, joy, pleasure, amusement.

Kalibugan-*n* Obscenity, immodesty, unchastity; lewdness, shamelessness; impudence impurity lust; ugliness, rudeness, turpitude, lowness

Kalidad-*n*-Quality.

Kaligayahan-*n*-Happiness; joy; gayaty; conviviality.

Kahgharan-*n*-Spitting, expectoration

Kahgharaan-*v*-To spit; expectorate

Kaligtaan-*n*-Forgetfulness, carelessness; neglect, omittance

Kalihim-*n*-Secretary detective, allay, confederate, emissary

Kaliitan-*n* Smallness, nicety, sutility

Kaliksihan-*n*-Quickness, activity, agility; promptness promptitude, acceleration; nimbleness, velocity, lightness; speed, accuracy

Kalikutan-*n*-Restlessness, mischievousness, trick, wile

Kalilohan-*n*-Treachery, perfidy, treason; disloyalty, felony, overthrow, overturning

Kaliluhan-*n*-Treachery, perfidy, Treason, disloyalty, overthrow, overturning.

Kalimutin *i*-To forget, neglect, overlook; miss

Kalinawan *n*-Clarity; purity.

Kalinawan ng isip-*v*-Illustration, saneness, sanity, clearness of thought; illucidation

Kaling-*n*-Door-knocker, crossbar

Kalingain-*v*-To favor, patronize protect.

Kalinisan-*n*-Cleanliness, chastity, purity, neatness, decency; decorum, excellence; frankness, modesty, cordiality, accuracy, honesty

Kalipulan-*n*-Destruction; havoc

Kalisan-*v*-To scrape

Kaliskis-*n*-Scales

Kalituhan *n*-Confusion: perplexity, perturbation, lightheadedness, overthow, overturning

Kaliwa-*a*-Left

Kaliwa *n*-Left

Kaliwagan-*n*-Delay, protraction, tardiness

Kaliwanagan-*n* Illustration, clearness, brightness, clarity.

Kaliwang kamay-The left hand

Kalo-*n*-Pulley

Kalog-*a* Emputy, hallow.

Kalóg-*n*-Clatter

Kaloob-*n* Gift; grant, present, gratification, keepsake, donation, boon, benefaction.

Kaloob-*n*-Will; mind, sense, understanding, sheathe, interior.

Kalooban *adi* -At will

Kalooblooban *a*-Most central; most inward, inmost

Kalaoblooban-*n*-Center

Kalos *n*-Strickle, level

Kaluagan *n*-Breadth, width, freedom liberty

Kalualhatian-*n* Glory; honor; sanctionary, fame, felicity

Kaluban-*n*-Implement shed, place for keeping implements.

Kalubayan *n*-Stop, compliance

Kalubayan ng loob *n*-Amiability, prudence; affability, serenity; meekness, mildness.

Kalubong-*n*-Cover, covering net

Kalugolugod-*a*-Delightfull, pleasing, acceptable, happy, delicious.

Kalugkog-*n*-Anything that serves to make a noise

Kaluguran-*n*-Happiness, gayety, conviviality; amusement.

Kalukuñgan-*n*-Convexity

Kaluluwa-*n*-Soul, spirit, ghost; spright

Kalunitan-*n*-Obscurity, closeness

Kalungkutan-*n*-Sadness, sorrow, grief; contrition, contriteness, infelicity.

Kalunitan-*n*-Obscurity, closeness

Kalunoslunos-*a*-Deplorable, lamentable, detestable, Wretched.

Kalunuran-*a*-West, Western

Kalunuran-*n*-West

Kalunya-*n*-Mistress, concubine

Kalupaan-*n*-Earthliness; sensuality, lewdness, moral depravity, ugliness, homliness, turpitude

Kalupitan-*n*-Cruelty, inhumanity, detestation, hatred

Kalutpit lupit-*a*-Detestable; hateful. loathesome, cruel, inhuman

Kalupkop-*n*-Noise; horse shoe; anything that serves to make a noise

Kalupkupan-*n*-Cover, spread.

Kalupkupan-*i*-To cover, overspread, screen

Kalusakan-*n*-Muddy place, rubbish

Kamaganak-*n*-Parent, relative; kindred, relation

Kamaganakan-*n*-Lineage, kindred, relatives; offspring

Kamahalan-*n*-Dignity, honor, rank; reputation, nobility; purity; respect, decency, decorum, valor, distinction; splendor, glory; lustre, generosity

Kamahalan po ninyo--Your Grace, Your worship

Kamakalawa-*n*-The day before yesterday.

Kanakalawa *adv* -Day before yesterday.

Kamalbasan-*n*-Mallow ground, place where mallows grow.

Kamalian-*n*-Wrong; error, mistake; blunder; fault, slip, injustice.

Kamalig *n*-Store house

Kamahin-*i*-To knead.

Kamanahan *n*-Inheritance, heirloom

Kamandag-*n*-Poison.

Kamandagan-*i*-To poison.

Kamanghamangha-*a*-Wonderful, stupendous, miraculous, extraordinary, fabulous

Kamangmangan-*n*-Stupidity, folly; foppery, ignorance; foolishness; nonsense, incapability, inability, dulness, ughness, rudeness, absurdity, incapacity.

Kamatayan-*n*-Death, mortality, fate, pest fatality

Kamaw-*n*-Wrist, earthen pan,

Kamay-*n*-Hand

Kamiyaw-*n*-Accomplice, associate

Kamiyawin *i*-To stir, associate, begin, move

Kamkaan-*n*-Proverb.

Kamkam-*n*-Avarice, envy

Kamote-*n*-Sweet-potatoe

Kampapalis-*n*-Swallow.

Kampit-*n*-Knife

Kamukha-*a*-Like; similar, uniform, equal, alike

Kamukha-*adv* -Alike, on a par

Kanitan-*v*-To attain, obtain, collect, gather, possess

Kamuluan-*v*-To hate, abhor, detest; deslike

Kamumno-*n*-Bee.

Kamunti-*n*-Mite, whit

Kamunti-*adv* -Very little, some what

Kamuntian *n*-Smallness

Kamuraan-*n* Immaturity, tenderness, sauvity, delicacy, softness

Kamurahan-*n*-Cheapness, insult, infamy, censure, affront, outrage, baseness; lowness, dishonor, humiliation

Kamutin *v*-To scratch; scrape

Kanan-*n*-Right

Kanan-*a*-Right.

Kanawin-*v*-To dilute, dissolve

Kandara-*n*-Latch.

Kandila-n*n*-Candle

Kandirit-*n*-Hop

Kanga-*n*-Wagon

Kanginong-*pro* -Whose

Kanila-*pro* -Their, theirs

Kaningasan *n*-Fervor, warmth zeal, ardor, flame, vehemence; vehemency

Kannong-*pro* Whose

Kanipisan *n*-Thinness, nicety, tenuity, subtileness, delicacy, acuteness

Kaniya-*pro* -His, hers.

Kaniyahin-*v*-To appropriate, usurp, defraud, cheat

Kanlungan-*n*-Conversation among many, group of talkers

Kanlungin-*v*-To shelter, protect, defend

Kanot-*a*-Bald

Kanta-*n* Song

Kantero-*n*-Mason; bricklayer

Kanugnog-*n*-Limit, bound.

Kanunuan-*n*-Ancestry, forefathers

Kanyon-*n*-Cannon.

Kapabayaan-*n* Neglligence, neglect, abandoment; carelessness; laziness, inadvertance, inadvertancy, lassitude, indolence, idleness, tardiness, inaccuracy

Kapag-*adv* -How, as; if, after, just as

Kapagalan-*n*-Service, work.

Kapahamakan-*n*-Calamity, disappointment, accident

Kapahingahan-*n*-Rest; quiet, tranquility, repose, quietude

Kapahintulutan-*n*-Permission, leave, liberty, freedom

Kapain-*v*-To search, grope; feel; touch

Kapaitan-*n*-Bitterness, asperity, poignancy.

Kapakinabangan-*n*-Utility, profit, gain, advantage, usefulness

Kapakumbabaan-*n*-Submission; compliance; modesty, meekness; density, multitude, creation

Kapal-*n*-Tickness; coarseness, density, multitude, creation

Kapalagayan-*n*-Tranquility, rest, repose' calmness

Kapalagayang loob-*n*-Confidence

Kapalagayang loob-*a* Confident

Kapalaluan-*n*-Pride; presumption; arogance; haughtiness; vanity, loftiness; pompuosity; pompuousness, inflation, swelling

Kapalan *i*-To thicken; strengthen, make thick

Kapalaran-*n*-Fortune, success, chance, luck, fortuity, doom, fate, hap, contingent, contingency; hazard, happiness

Kapalibhasaan-*n* Affront; outrage, infamy; dishonor

Kapalit-Exchange; sustitution, substitute, barter, delegate; commutation

Kapalit nang-*prep*,-For, by, about, as by, on account

Kapanaghilian-*n*-Envy, covetnousness

Kapanahon-*a* Contemporary, time

Kapanahuman *n* Maturity; season; time, term; age; epportunity.

Kapanatagan-*n*-Tranquility; rest; repose; peace; calmness; quiet; security.

Kapañgahasan-*n*-Zeal; valor; bravery; boldness; insolence; impudence; precociousness; precosity.

Kapañgana-an-*n*-Nativity; birth.

Kapañganakan-*a*-Natal; native.

Kapañganiban-*n*-Danger; risk; hazard.

Kapañgitan *n*-Ugliness; hideousness; homliness; sordidness; moral depravity; turpitude; covetousness.

Kapanglawun-*n*-Gloom; sadness, obscurity; darkness.

Kapañgyarihan-*n*-Power; authority; ability; jurisdiction; means; right; command; dominion; virtue; faculty.

Kapañgyarihan gumawa-*n*-Authority or power to do.

Kapañgyarihan ñg hukom-*n*-Jurisdiction.

Kapantay-*a*-Equal; similar; uniform; equable.

Kapantayan-*n*-Similarity; equivalence; uniformity; equinamity; equalization.

Kapara-*a*-Identical; equal; similar; alike.

Kaparis-*a*-Alike; similar; equal; identical; unifom; even; equable.

Kaparisan-*n*-Equality; uniformity; similarity likeness; comparison.

Kaparte-*n*-Participation; part.

Kapaslañgan-*n*-Impudence; insult; outrage; abuse; contempt.

Kapatagan-*n*-Evenness; levelness.

Kapatak-*n*-Drop; little.

Kapatawaran-*n*-Pardon; absolution; forgivenness; acquital.

Kapatid-*n*-Brother; sister.

Kapatid na lalaki-*n*-Brother.

Kapatid na babayi-*n*-Sister.

Kapatid ñg ama-*n*-Uncle.

Kapausan-*n*-Hoarseness.

Kapayapaan-*n*-Rest; repose; tranquility; calmness; quietness; quietude; peace; pacification.

Kapayatan-*n*-Feebleness; leanness; thinness.

Kape-*n*-Coffee.

Kapighatian-*n*-Disgust; vexation; antipathy; mortification; humiliation.

Kapilayan-*n*-Lameness.

Kapilipitan-*n*-Sinuosity.

Kapilitan-*n*-Force; perseverance; persistence; persistency; necessity; indispensibility; persuasion.

Kapinsalaan-*n*-Reunion; obstacle; impediment; herd; flock; drove.

Kapintasan-*n*-Fault; defect; censure.

Kapirañgot-*n*-Particle.

Kapiraso-*n*-Piece; slice; cut; fragment; scrap; part; portion; share.

Kapisanan-*n*-Reunion; congregation; meeting; facition; clique.

Kapisanan ñg bundok-*n*-Range of mountains.

Kapisanan ñg kalap-*n*-Raft of logs.

Kapisanan ñg mga utos ñg gobierno-*n*-Code of laws.

Kapisanan ñg mga hayop-*n*-Flock; herd; drove.

Kapisanan ñg mañga tawo-*n*-Society; partnership; corporation.

Kapisanan ñg mga utos-*n*-Digest.

Kapistahan-*n*-Feast; holiday; festivity; exhibition; presentaton.

Kapit baluy-*n*-Neighbor; fellow creature.

Kapootan-*n*- Anger; vexation; rage; hatred.

Kapormalan-*n*-Formality; seriousness; gravity; circumspection.

Kapos-*a*-Lacking; insufficient; wanting; inadequate; short; scanty; small.

Kapowa-*pro*-Both.

Kapowa tawo-*n*-Fellowcreature.

Kapulaan ñg sahing-*v*-Io paint or cover with pitch.

Kapurihan-*n*-Purity; chastity; excellency

Kapurulan-*n*-Dulness; turpitude ugliness; impurity; stupidity; rudeness; lewdness.

Kapuspusan-*n*- Roundness; fullness.

Kapusukan-*n*-heat; vivacity.

Kaputican-*n*-Marsh; slough miry place, Karagdagan-*n*-Addition; increase; improvement.

Karakaraka-*adv*- imidiately; instantly; suddenly.

Karakot-*n*-Handful; fewness.

Karakot-*a*-Few.

Karatula sa ibabaw ñg libiñg-*n*-Epitaph.

Karalañgan-*n*-Rarity; looseness.

Karamihan-*n*-Abundance; plenty; multitude; torrent.

Karamiramihan-*a*-Most.

Karampatan-*a*-Fit; proper; convenent; corresponding.

Karampot-*n*-Mite; whit.

Karamutan-*n*-Stinginess; penury; poverty; avarice; covetousness; paltriness; meanness; voracity; voraciousness; sordidness:

Karang-*n*-Cover; covering; awning.

Karañgalan-*n*-Glory; honor: dignity; royalty; fame; prestige; majesty; exellence; eminence; sublimity; elevation; loftiness; superiority.

Karaniwan-*a*-Usual; ordinary; familiar; customary; vulgar; common; epidemic; prevalent; prevailing; mediocre; plebian; hackney.

Karaniwan tawo *n* Plebian

Karapatan-*n*-Dignity, condignity; merit

Karapatan-*a*-Just, deserving, corresponding

Karatig-*adv*-Near, close, neighboring

Karatula sa ibabaw ng libing-*n* Epitaph

Karayom *n*-Needle.

Karayom na panahi ng supot-*n*-Packing, needle.

Kareton-*a*-Wagon, cart

Kargador *n*-Porter, packer

Kargahan *n*-Pack

Kargahan *i*-To pack, load

Karikitan-*n*-Neatness, beauty, elegance, prettiness; gentility

Karne-*n*-Meat

Karne ng baboy-*n* Bacon, pork

Karromata *n* Chaise; gig

Karuagan-*n*-Cowardice, dastardness, poltroonery, effeminence effeminency

Karugtong-*n*-Annex, addition, annexa, tion, sequence; sequel.

Karukhaan-*n*-Penury, poverty; misery, lowness; lewdness

Karumihan-*n*-Dirt; filthiness, obscenity, impurity, sordidness sloven] ness

Karunungan-*n*-Wisdom, knowledge, learning, science sagacity, ability, ken, erudition, discretion; art, illustration, sapience; virtue, culture, aptitude; cleverness, dexterity, excellence

Karupukan-*n*-Frailty, britleness, weadness, feebleness

Karyagan-*n*-Clearness, clarity, front or right side of anything

Kasabay-*n* Contemporary, companion, company

Kasabay-*adv*-Together; simultaneously, at the same time

Kasabihan-*n*-Proverb, maxim

Kasaganaan-*n*-Abundance, plenty; profuseness; profusion, fullness, amplitude; lavishness, multitude, excess

Kasaganaang inalabis *n*-Overabundance, superfluity, overplus, surplus, excess

Kasaganaan ng pagaari *n* Opulence, wealth; affluence

Kasagsagan-*n*-Trot, haste

Kasakiman-*n*-Avarice, stinginess, covetousness.

Kasakitan-*n*-Sickness, suffering; sufferance calamity, hardship, cross, toil, trouble, epidemic, anger; vexation

Kasakitsakit-*a*-Painful, sensitive

Kasaklapan *n* Detestation. acerbity asperity, sharpness, roughness or severity of taste.

Kasaksaan *a* Time season, opportunity

Kasal-*n*-Marriage, wedding, esponsal; betrothal, betrothment, espousal

Kasalanan *n*-Fault, crime, guilt, transgression, offence defect, slight infringement, failure, deficiency, infraction

Kasalatan *n*-Want, need; necessity, penury, poverty. meanness, paltriness, narrowness, misery, bereavement blight, misadventure

Kasalaulaan-*n*-Filth, dirt, sordidness, filthiness, obscenity, impurity, lust, immodesty, unchastity, rudeness, lewdness, squalor, squalidness, squalidity, ughnesss, impudence

Kasalbahian-*n*-Savagery; savgaeness, truculence, truculency

Kasaliwaan-*n*-Misfortune, mishap, misery, stubbornness, contrariness

Kasaliwaang loob-*n*-Inconstency, fickleness, contrariness

Kasaliwaang palad-*n* Calamity, misfortune, mishap, disaster, illiluck, bad luck, fatality; unhappiness.

Kasalukuyan-*a*-Actual, present, real, effective.

Kasama-*n*-Companion; colleague, company, partner, comrade, helpmate

Kasama-*a*-Inclusive, united

Kasama-*adv*-Near, close, near at hand

Kasamaan *n* Malice, wickedness, iniquity, lowness, vileness; infamy, baseness; dishonor; profligacy, evil, banevice criminality,

Kasamaan ng lasa *n* Bitterness, asperity, want or lack of taste

Kasamahan-*n* Companion, accomplice, colleague.

Kasamasamaan-*a* Worst

Kasama sa paggawa-*n*-Cooperator, accomplice

Kasanayan-*n*-Practice, ability, aptitude

Kasandok-*n* Spoonful, ladle

Kasangkapan-*n*-Instrument, tool, furniture, appliance, apparatus

Kasangkapan panugat ng araw-*n* Heliometer

Kasangulan-*n*-Infancy, childhood, beginning

Kasantosan-*n*-Sanctity, holiness, god, liness

Kasantosantosan-*a*-Most holy

Kasapatan-*n*-Sufficiency

Kasarapan-*n*-Sweetness, delicacy

Kasariwaan-*n*-Freshness, coolness

Kasayahan-*n*-Happiness, jocularity, gayety, mirth, glee joy, festivity, rejoicing; content. pleasure; comedy, comicality, conviviality, vivacity, vivaciousness; jocoseness, comicality, comicalness

Kasaysayan n-Signification, explanation, interpretation account, comment; declaration, definition, affirmative, narration; relation

Kasia-a-Sufficient, apt, fit, proper, enough .

Kasiba n-Splinter.

Kasibaan-n-Glottony

Kasiguruhan-n Security, certainty, bail, sponser, probability

Kasutan-n-Grove of bamboo

Kasikian-n-Impediment, obstruction, obstacle, difficulty, nuisance

Kasikipan-n-Narrowness, closeness; intimacy.

Kasikpan n-Narrowness, intimacy; closeness

Kasindakan-n Fright, scare, horror

Kasindaksindak-a-Awful, horrible, terrible, dreadful, horrific, tremendous

Kasing-adv-So as much as, so much; as much, as well

Kasing buti-adv-As good as

Kasing halaga-a-Equivalent, of the same value

Kasinsinan-n-Density, thickness, solidity, closeness, compactness

Kasinungalingan-n-Lying, untruth, false hood, fib, fiction, fallacy, delusion; deceit

Kasipagan-n-Industry, diligence, activity, promptness, promptitude, lightness, quickness

Kasiping-adv Beside, near, mediate

Kasiraan n Destruction fault, defect, death, error, mistak, disadvantage, rotting

Kasiraan malaki n-Calamity; havoc, disappointment

Kasiraan ng bait-n-Madness, insanity derangement of the mind

Kasiraan ng loob n-Dementea.

Kasiraan ng puri n-Shame, disgrace, dishonor, tall, baseness, degeneracy, degredation, discredit; stain or spot on one's character

Kasiraang tinatangap n-Prejudice, injury, detriment, damage, dishonor

Kasiyahan-n-Sufficiency frugality, commensuration, sobriety, proportion; competence, moderation, temperateness abstinence, justice; temperance, thrift, method

Kaskasan n-Grater, scraper, raker, roller cylinder

Kas asan-v To grate, scrape, rake

Kasko n Casco; barge

Kasowayan-n-Rebelliousness, stubornness, disobedience

Kastila-n Spaniard

Kastila-a-Spanish

Kasubha n-Saffron

Kasuitikan n-Theft, thieving, rascality; fraudulence, cheating

Kasukaban-n Treachery, disloyalty; perfidy, felony, crime

Kasukalan-n-Dirt; filth; sordidness, filthiness, rubbish, dumping-ground.

Kasukalan ng loob-n-Mortification, vexation .

Kasukasuan-n-Joint.

Kasukatan n-Measure, dimension measurement, justice, right, enough, sobriety; equality.

Kasuklaman-n-Hate, disgust; abhorrence; detestation, repugnance, dislike, antipathy; revulsion, curse, execration,

Kasuklamsuklam-a-Detestable, hateful, loathesome, dreadful, awful, horrible.

Kasulatan-n-Writing, deed, contract, treatise, document, maxim, abstract; accord, accordance, schedule

Kasulatan ng isang puno-n-Attestation, disposition, or command in writing

Kasunod-n-Successor, follower, one who follows

Kasunod-a-Successive following, consecutive, next.

Kasunod-adv -Then following

Kataasan-n-Height, eminence; eminency, superiority, preeminence, arrogance, haughtiness

Kataastaasan a Supreme, paramount, tallest, most high, highest, omnipotent, most powerful; almighty

Kataastaasan lugar-n-Highest place; acme.

Katabaan-n-Corpulence, corpulency, obesity, fat.

Katabaan ng lupa-n-Fertility, fruitfulness

Katabi-adv -Beside, conjunct, near

Katad-n-Skin, leather, hide

Katagan-n-Conveniency

Katahimikan-n-Peace, tranquility; pacification, quietness, quietude, restcalmness, serenity, composure, silence repose, selfpossession, continencecontinency; dispassion, lull, heartsease; quiescence.

Katakataka-a-Strange, rare, -scarce, stupendous, wonderful' marvelous, astonishing, miraculous, fabulous, ad; mirable, unheard of; excellent, foolish, silly, egregious, awful, dire; dreadful; extraordinary

7

Katakawan-*n* Glutton.

Katakottakot-*a*-Awful, dreadful, terrible, horrible, dire, fearful; monstrous, direful, tremendous, formidable ghastly, grim, grisly; grand

Kataksilan-*n*-Treason, perfidy, treachery, instability, criminality

Katalasan-*n*-Sagacity, sharpness, cunning, craft; wisdom, sagaciousness, ability; prudence, skill, learning, sapience, handiness;

Katalinuhan-*n*-Learning, wisdom, ability, sagacity, sagaciousness, prudence, skill, handiness, sharpness, quickness

Katalo-*n*-Rival, antagonist, opponent, adversary, competitor.

Katám *n*-Plane

Katamanan-*n* Constancy, perseverance, persistence, loyalty, persistency,

Katamaran-*n*-Laziness, idleness, indolence, slovenliness, negligence, tardiness, lassitude, neglect, carelessness

Katamasan-*n*-Advantage, gain.

Katamin-*i*-To plane

Katamisan-*n*-Sweetness, fineness

Katamisan ng dila-*n*-Eloquence

Katamlayan-*n*-Sadness, indisposition, gloominess, coolness toward a friend.

Katampalasanan-*n*-Insolence, impudence incivility, insult, disrespect, disregard, flippancy, petulence; haughtiness, inhumanity

Katampatan-*n*-Justification, justice, right, conscientiousness, reason, moderation; impartiality, uprightness, exactitude, righteousness

Katampatan-*a*-Equitable, just, honorable, impartial

Katamtaman-*n*-Sufficiency, enough

Katamtaman-*a* Sufficient, fit; proprotional

Katamtaman-*adv*-Middling, so so

Katandaan-*n* Antiquity, longlevity, age; old-age, anteriority, decrepitude

Katanghalian-*n*-Noon, lateness, dinner, lunch

Katangihan-*n*-Refusal, denial, negation, exception, difference

Katapangan-*n*-Boldness, bravery; sauciness

Katapatan-*n* Opposition, convenience, reason, sufficiency; equality, confidence

Katapatang loob *n*-Loyalty, sincerity, frankness, cordiality, fidelity; honesty, fealty, candor; troth

Katapusan *a* Last, latest, final; hind most, extreme, conclusive, determinative, end

Katapusan *n End* final, finish, extreme ity, conclusion, goal, result, boundary; termination.

Katas-*n*-Juice, sap, substance, essence.

Katasahan-*n*-Valuation, appraisal, approximation, appraisement, calculation-

Katasin-*v*-To draw out the sap; sap

Katas ng katawan-*n* Humor, mood

Katatagaan-*n*-Medium, middling sufficient.

Katatagaan-*adv* -So so, middling, even

Katawan *n*-Body

Katha-*n*-Fiction, fabulosity, invention of the minde

Kathain-*t*-To bring forth, produce, generate

Kati-*n*-Ebb

Kati-*n*-Itch

Katibayan-*n*-Guarantee, plight, bail, document, firmness, solidity, steadiness stability

Katibayan ng loob-*n*-Inflexibility, perseverance' constancy, loyalty, firmness, candor, proof reliance

Katig-*n*-Out-riggers, balance

Katigasan-*n*-Hardness, stiffness; firmness, stubbornness

Katigasang makipagusap-*n*-Harshness or severity of speech

Katinsan-*n*-Forbearance, suffering, patience' respite, indulgence, penance-

Katimtiman-*n*-Prudence; moderation, modesty

Katimtiman ng loob-*n*-Constanck, loyalty, fidelity, fealty, firmness.

Katingan-*n*-Boiler, cauldron

Katinig-*n*-Unison, two things which have the same sound.

Katipunan-*n*-Meeting, congregation, reunion, society, secret society

Katiwala-*n*-Agent

Katiwasayan-*n*-Tranquility, repose, quietude, serenity, peace

Katiyagaan-*n*-Constancy, loyalty, perseverance, persistance

Katog-*n*-Blow, knock

Katotohanan-*n*-Truth, veracity, truism, reliableness, reliability, criterion, proof, reality, equity, testimony certification; witness, reason, indication

Katowiran *n* Right, justice, loyalty lawfulness, reason, cause uprightness, exactitude, straightness, prerogative, consideration, argument forte, moderation

Katugon *n*-Response, reply, answer aid; help

Katulad *n* Similarity; uniformity, likeness resemblance; simile; facsimile equality,

Katulad na lubos-a Like similar; equal, even, on a par.

Katulinan-n-Swiftness, agility, activity; rapidity; promptitude, speed; quickness; celerity, acceleration

Katulsan-n-Sharpness, keenness

Katulong n-Co-operator; accomplice, helper, helpmate

Katulungin-i-To associate, cause to help or aid

Katunayan-n-Reality, truth, fact; certainty, legitimacy, legitimateness, security, truthfulness

Katungkulan n-Position, occupation, duty, employment, obligation, work, profession; situation, business; trade, engagement, employ, contract, command, power, authority, prefecture

Katunugan-n-Sonorousness.

Katuparan-n-Compliance, exention, discharge

Katusuhan-n-Craft, cunning, astuteness, sagacity, sagacousness, ability

Katutubo a-proper, fit

Katutubong hilig-a-Natural

Katuwaan-n-Joy; gladness, drollery, mirth, merriment, diversion, gayety, happiness, comicality comedy, comicalness, joytulnes

Kaugalian-n-Custom, habit, use, usage, style; fashion, mode, manner; rite, skill

Kaugaliang sarili-n-Natural custom

Kaugoygoyan-n Underbrush, copse, shrubbery

Kaukol-n-Coreespondent

Kaukulan-n Correspondence, relevance-relevancy, pertinence

Kaululan-n-Non-sense, foolery; foolishness, bosh, madness, insanity

Kaunahan-n-Pretorence, preceedence

Kaunannahan-a First.

Kaunaunahan-adv First

Kaunaunahan martir n-Protomartyr

Kaungasan-n-Nonsense, ignorance, stupidity, foolishness, turpitude

Kaunti-a-Some; few; little, scanty not much

Kauntian-n-Smallness, scantiness paucity

Kauntian ng pagmamahal-n-Lack of respect, scorn, contempt

Kauntiuntian-a-Minimum, least.

Kauntiuntian-n-Minimum

Kanunuan-n-Ancestry, fore fathers, ancestors

Kaunuran-n-Dulness, stupidity, non sense, ignorance, foolishness

Kaunuran-n-Confidante, crony

Kaupahan-n-Wages,payment,fee,salary.

Kaupasalaan-n-Threachery, perfidy, inconstancy, treason

Kausap-n Companion in conversation, the person with which one converses or speaks

Kausutin v-To move, touch; manage, direct.

Kautulan-n Stammering, stuttering

Kautusan-n-Proclamation, order, command, errand, message. edict, precept; rule, law, mundate

Kawa-n-Caldron; boiler.

Kawad-n-Wire

Kawalaan n Loss; deficiency, lack, absence

Kawalang hiya-n Shamelessness, impudence, insolence, immodesty

Kawalan magampon-n-Lack of support, destitution

Kawalan ng awa n-Inhumanity, cruelty, inclemency, rigor; severity

Kawalan ng ayos-n-Slovenliness, carelessness, disarrangement

Kawalan ng bait-n-Impudence, indescretion

Kawalan ng damdam-n-Health, welfare, prosperity, apathy

Kawalan ng damit-n Nakedness, nudity.

Kawalan ng dunong-n-Inaptitude; inability, ignorance, lack of know-ledge

Kawalan ng galang-n-Incivility impudence, disrespect, inattention, lack of beauty

Kawalan nang ganda-n-Awkwardness, lack of beauty

Kawalan ng gawa-n-Liesure, lack of work, idleness.

Kawalan ng gusto n-Displeasuse; lack, of taste, disssatisfaction

Kawalan ng hiya-n-Impudence, shamefilippancy.

Kawalan ng interes-n Sangfroid.

Kawalan ng kailangan-n-Necessity want, need, lacking

Kawalan ng kailangan-n-Inattention, abandonmant, carelessness

Kawalan ng kaya-n-Incapability, incapacity; inability, inaptitude

Kawalan ng laman-n-Vacancy, vacuity, emptiness

Kaawlan ng lasa-n-Want or lack of taste; bad taste, disgust.

Kawalan ng pag-ibig-n-Lack of love, unconcern.

Kawalan ,ng pagmamahal-n Scorn, contempt

Kawalan ng pananampalataya-n Incredulity; unbelief, disquisition.

Kawalan ng̃ paniniwala-n-Incredulity, unbelief, disquisition

Kawalan ng̃ puno-n-Anarchy

kawalan ng̃ tikas-n-Awkwardness

Kawalan ng̃ tuto-n-Ignorance, stupidity, error; blindness, lack of knowledge

Kawalan ng̃ ugah-n Disrespect, incivility, lack of manners

Kawalan ng̃ wasto-n-Uncleanliness, filthiness, carelessness; lack of care

Kawali-n-Griddle, skillet.

kawan-n-Herd, flock; bunch, multitude.

Kawang̃is-a Like, similar, alike

Kawang̃is-n-Li eness, simile, similarity

Kawangki-a-Like, similar; alike, equal

Kawanki-n-Similarity, likeness, equality, resemblance; simile.

Kaway-n Brandish, flourish.

Kawayan-n-Bamboo; cane.

Kawayan-v-To call or summon by signs; signal, brandish

Kawikaan n-Proverb

Kawihwili-a-Agreeable, pleasing, amusing, attractive, delightful

Kawit-n-Hook, gaff, drag-hook

Kaya-n Ability, power, aptitude, capacity, authority, possibility

Kaya-adv -Since, perhaps, then, by what way.

Kaya ng̃a prep -Therefore

Kayabang̃an-n-Braggartism, brag, boast, vaunt, pompuosity, pompuosness

Kayabung̃an ng̃ sang̃a-n-Thickness of foliage

Kayamanan-n-Riches, wealth treasure, fortune, property, pelf, potency affluence, opulence, mamon

Kayamoan n-Gluttony, excess, superfuity

Kayarian-n-Cut, shape, make, fashion, figure termination, completion, perpection; faultlessness

Kayariang lubos-n-Completion, perfection, faultlessness.

Kayasan-v-To scrape, clean, polish

Kayas n-Scrape

Kayayari pa lamang a-Recent, modern, new

Káyo-n Cloth, texture

Kayó-pro -You

Káyong panluksa-n Crape

Káyong sutla n Silk, silk cloth

Kayó po-pro -You.—Your honor, your worship, you sir

Kayong sutla at makintab n Satin.

Kay sa conj -Than

Kayumangi-a Brown, swarthy, drab

Kayumangi a Drab, brown

Kayumanging mura a Brownish

Keloo} n Mire, mud; quagmire

Kiba-n-Fish hook

Kibal-n-Bend, curve

Kibit n-Grimace, wry face

kibitin-t To make a grimace or wry face, shrug, hook

Kibitin ang isda-v-To hook a fish.

Kibot-n-Pant, palpitation, nervous movement

Kidkirin-t-To unwind, wind

Kidlat n Flash

hikil-n-File, rasp.

Kikilin v-To file, rasp

Kikio-n-Desire

kilabot-n-Pore, Horror, fright, scare

Kilala-n-Acquaintance

Kilalanin-t-To acquaint, know

Kilalanin maaga-t-To anticipate; forsee.

Kilalanin mabuti-t-To ascertain, consider, recognize, know well

Kilap-n-Splendor, brilliancy gloss, lustre

Kilay -n-Eyebrow

Kilig-n-Shrug

Kibkih-n Armpit '

kihkin-t-To take in ones arms

kiling-n-Inclanation, sidp motion, declevity

Kiling-n-Mane

Kihñgan sa masama-t To defend any one who is bad

Kihti-n-Tickling, tickle.

Kilitiin-v-To tickle

Kilkilin t To, file, rasp

Kilos-n Act, action, move, movement, manner, form, deportment, civility, antic todo

Kilna-n-Mustard

Kilusin t-To move act, excite, inspire, touch.

Kimi n-Temerity, shyness bashfulness

Kimpot n-Temerity shyness, bashfulness; pant, palpitation

Kinagatan-p p -Bitten

kinakabagan a-Windy, indigestible, colıky

kinalong ng̃ abogado n-Client.

Kinamtan-p p -Gotten

Kinampan-n-Unition, joint, addition.

Kinang-n-Gloss, polish, finish, brightness; splendor, terseness

Kindat n-Wink

kindatin-t-To wink

Kinch n-An affected air or walk

Kinikita-n-Wages, salary, earnings, pay.

kinis-n Polish, finish, brightness, lustre, gloss, fineness; terseness

Kinsay n Celery

Kintab n Gloss; polish; shine; finish, brightness, sheen, shimmer, twinkle, glimmer; glitter; coruscation

Kintal-n-Seal, signet, sign, crucible, melting pot
Kintalan-v-To purify, cleanse, clean
Kintalin-v-To smelt; melt
Kinukulungan-n-Place where anything or anyone is confined
Kinulty n-Tanning
kinusa-adv Intentionally; purposely, designedly, knowingly
Kipot-n-Narrowness
Kiputan-v-To borrow; contract, curtail, restrain, constrain, tighten
Kirot-n-Pain; ach
Kisap-n-Flash, wink, brilliance; sheen, shimmer corruscation twinkle
Kisap mata n Instant wink of the eye, moment, jiffy
Kiskis-n-Polish, file; scarf
Kiskisin-v-To file, polish, smooth, rub
Kita-n-Appearance, face, looks, likeness.
kitang-n-Roundfish
Kitáng n-Fish-net
Kitid-n Narrowness
Kitid-n-Fish-net trawlnet, trawl
kituran-v-To narrow
Komediahan-n-Theatre; theatricals
Komediante-n-Actor, player, comedian.
Komerciante n-Merchant, dealer
Konowa-a-False; apparent, deceitful, hypocritical
Konowari-a-False, hypocritical, deceitful; apparent but not real
Konvento-n-Convent; priory .
Kopa-n-Cup, goblet, wine-glass
Kosina-n-Kitchen.
Kosina ng sasakyan-n-Galley
Kosinero-n-Cook
Korona-n-Crown, diadem
Koronahan-v-To crown
Kotsero-n Coachman
Kreosote n-Kreosote
Kruz-n-Cross, intersection
Kuago-n-Owl
Kuako-n-Pipe.
Kuarta-n-Money, coinage
Kuarto-n-Room, chamber.
Kuarto ng babayi sa Turkia-n Harem.
Kúba-a-Humpback, deformed, crooked.
Kubo-n-Cabin, hut; barrack; shed, shanty
Kubkob-n-Defense; protection.
Kubkubin-v-To defend, protect; sustain
Kudkuran n-Grater, scraper.
Kuenta-n-Calculation; example; problem.
kuentahin v-To calculate, reckon, figure, compute, estimate.
Kuetis-n-Skyrocket
Kugon-n-Straw; mountain-grass
Kuha inter -There, well, what
kuintas n-Rosary.

Kintib-n-Blackant
Kókak-u-Toad
Kuko-n Nail; claw; hoof, talon
Kukob-a Convex, convexed.
Kulam-n-Fascination, enchantment,
Kulambo-n-Mosquito net
Kulamin-v-To fascinate, charm, enchant,
Kulamos-n A furrow made by a plane
Kulandong-n-Cover, covering; awning, curtain
Kulang-a Defective, lacking; deficient, faulty, incomplete, wanting, insufficient, inadequate, scrimp; scant; less
Kulangan ng anoman-v-To discount, deduct; curtail
Kulang ng ngipin-a-Toothless
Kulang palad-a-Unlucky, unhappy misfortunate, miserable, wretched dejected
Kulang sa pagkain-a-Hungry.
Kulapulan-v-To besmear, smear.
Kulay-n-Color; hue.
Kulay dalanghita-n-Xanthia.
Kulay dugo-a-Bloodcolored.
Kulay ginto-a Gold colored.
Kulay kapis-a-Pearl colored.
Kulay lila-a-Lilac colored, mauve.
Kulay pula-a-Red, ruby, ruddy
Kulay pulot-a Honey colored
Kulay rosas-a-Rose colored
Kulay suha-a-Orange colored. ,
Kulay tabaco-a-Tobacco colored.*
Kulay talon-a-Livid.
Kulay trigo-a-Brownish.
Kuliglig-n-Katydid, cricket, locust
Kulkulin-v-To scrap; scratch.
Kulo-n-Boil; boiling·
Kulog-n-Thunder·
Kulos-n Rústle, rustling, noise
Kulot-n-Curl, ringlet.
Kulot-a-Curly, crisp
Kuluban-n Sweater, sweating, place
Kulubot-n-Wrinkle.
Kulubot-a-Wrinkly, rugose
Kulungan-n Coral, pen, inclosure,'place of confinement
Kulungan ng tupa-n-Sheepfuld.
Kulungin-v-To shut up, pen up; lock up, seclude, circumscribe, immune
Kulutin-v-To twist, curl
Kumaba ang dibdib-v To pant, palpitate
Kumabila-v-To cross go over.
Kumagat-v-To bite, gnaw, nip.
Kumagungkong-v-To make a noise
Kumain-v-To eat, dine
kumain ang agahan-v-To breakfast, eat, breakfast
Kumakaw-v-To bark, howl
Kumalasing-v-To jingle, jangle, sound, rattle
Kumalat-v-To scatter throw broadcast.

Kumalinga-v-To care for, protect, look out for administer; govern serve.

Kumalog-v To clatter, make a noise from within

Kumapal-v-To thicken, grow, increase, swell, augment, enlargo

Kumapit i-To grasp, sieze

Kumasal-i-To espóuse

Kumaskas v-To rub

Kumatas i-To extract the sap or juice

Kumatha-v-To think, plan, invent, create, appoint.

Kamati-v-To itch, smart

Kumati ang tubig-i-To ebb, recede.

Kumatig-i-To take hold of anything to keep it from falling

Kumatog-v-To knock

Kumausap v-To talk, speak

Kumavod v-To grate

Kumidlat-v-To flash, lighten

Kumilap v-To glitter; glow, shine, glisten

Kumilig-v-To shrug

Kumiling-v-To incline, lean

Kumilos-v To move, act

Kumimot-v-To economize, save, hoard

Kumindat v-To wink

Kumindi i-To assume an affected air or walk.

Kuminig-i-To tremble, vibrate

Kumintal-i-To glitter, glow, shine; glisten, coruscate, twinkle, glimmer.

Kumipot-v-To narrow, contract

Kumirap-v-To move the eyelids, wink

Kumisap-v To shine, glisten; glitter, glow, corruscate, twinkle

Kumislot-v-Make a sudden move, move suddenly, act quickly

Kumita-i To gain, earn, see.

Kumitid i-To narrow; contract

Kumitil-v-To pinch, cut, gather one by one

Kumyaw-v-To brag, threaten

Kumon-n-Toilet; closet.

Kumot-n Blanket, Comforter; counterpane

Kumot na linso-n Bed sheet

Kumpari-n-God-father

Kumpisal-n-Confession

Kumpisalin-i To confess, hear confession, ascertain

Kumpunihin-r-To recompose, mend; make over

Kumudkod-v-To grate

Kumuha-n-Taker

Kumulang sa-adv -Nearly, almost in sufficient; less than, scrimp

Kumulo i To boil seethe, simmer et fervesce

Kumulog i To thunder.

Kumunpuni-v-To repair; patch, mend fix,

Kumumtrato-v-To contráct

Kumunti v-To lessen decrease, grow, smaller.

Kumupas-i-To fade

Kumurot-v-To pinch; nip

Kumusta-i To greet

Kumusta-n-Compliments, greeting.

Kumuto i-To be lousy, have lice

Kunnutog-v-To palpitate, pant, flutter

Kundi-conj -But

Kundi adv -Yet; besides, moreover, if not, except

Kundol-n-Citron.

Kung prep -It, though, when

Kung gayon-adv -Then, at that time

Kung hindi-adv It not, on the contrary.

Kung sacali-If perhaps; provided, if it should happen.

Kunin v-To get, take; fetch; extract, remove; subtract, seize, grasp, receive

Kuning ilabas-i-To extract, draw out.

Kunotin-v-To corrugate

Kunotkunot-a-Rugose, wrinkly.

Kunowa-a Fictitious, fabulous; hypocritál, deceitful, illusive, delusive.

Kupas-a Faded, discolored, colorless withered, decayed, pale

Kupitin-i-To steal rob; theive

Kupkupin-i To aid, help, succor, protect, defend, assist, champion shelter, advocate, preserve

Kural-n-Coral

Kurap-n-Movment of the eyelids

Kuripot-a Stingy, petit, close, miserly

Kurlit n-Comma

Kuro n-Imagination, fancy, conception.

Kurot-n-Pinch, scratch, nip, flip; tweak

Kuiso n-Diarrhea.

Kuruin-v-To imagine; fancy, calculate, concept

Kurus-n Cross

Kuiusan v-To cross.

Kurutin i-To pinch, tweak, scratch

Kusá n-Spontaneousness, spontaneity, voluntariness; voluntariness

Kusina n-Kitchen

Kuskusin-i -To scrub; rub, polish.

Kusot-n-Shavings, sawdust.

Kusutin-v-To rub, scrub clean

Kuta-n-Rampart; fort, wall, castle

Kutab n Groove, hack; mortise

Kuting-n-Kitten, kit

Kutkutin i To excavate, hollow, investigate

Kuto n Louse

Kutod a-Short.

Kutod ang buntot-a-Shorttailed
Kutog ng puso n Foreboding, movement of the heart.
Kutong aso-n-Flea.
Kutsara-n-Spoon
Kutuhin-a-Lousy
Kutuhin-i-To become lousy

Kutuhin-i To plait, fold; double crimple.
Kutuhin ang kayo f-To fold cloth
Kutyam-v-To censure, decry; criticise, defame, deride
Kuyumpis-a Wrinkled, denied, timid, pusillanimous
Kuyusin-v-To rub against

L

Laan-n-Secret; reserve
Laba n-Wash, Washing
Labag-n-Contradiction, resistance
Labahin-v-To contradict, gainsay, oppose, resist
Labahin-v-To wash, laundry
Labak n-Puddle, rut, pit, pond
Laban-a-Adverse, contrary, opposite.
Labanán-n-War, fight, setto, assault, attack
Labánan-v-To war, fight, resist, assault, assail attack
Labangan-n-Crib, rack manger, trough, hog-trough
Laban cay prep-Against, by favor of
Labanos-n-Radish.
Laban sa prep-Against; counter
Laban sa katowiran-a-Illegal, unlawful
Laban sa pagkabulok a-Antiseptic
Laban sa pinuno-a-Against the goverment; insurrectionary
Labas prep Besides; except that, without, excepting. over and above.
Labasa n-Razor
Labasan-n Outlet, result.
Labasan ng ilog-n-The mouth of a river
Labas ng bayan-adv Abroad, in public.
Labas sa hirap at sakit-a Healthy; sound, well
Labas sa katowiran-a Illegal, unlawful, unjust, unrighteous
Labas sa matowid-a-Wrong, faulty.
Labas sa panahon-a-Unseasonable, abortive; untimely
Labas sa pangamb-a-Safe' unhurt, undamaged
Labay n-Skein
Labayan-n-Reel.
Labhan-v-To wash, laundry
Labi-n-Lip.
Labing apat-a- Fourteen
Labing apat n-Fourteen
Labing dalawa-a-Twelve
Labing dalawa-n-Twelve.
Labing isa-a-Eleven.
Labing isa-n Eleven.
Labing lima a-Fifteen
Labing makapal-n-Thick lip.
Labing tatlo-a-Thirteen

Labing tatlo-n-Thirteen.
Labis-n-Excess; surplus, superfluity, remainder, residue, overplus, refuse, debauch
Lablab-n-Quagmire, mud; mire, marsh
Labnutin v-To pluck out, pull out
Labo-n-Obscurity, darkness.
Labuan-v-To cloud, obscure, darken, delay make muddy
Labúlan-v-To feed by scattering,
Laceta-n-Knife, skean
Lagablab-n-Flame, blaze, fire light.
Lagak-n That which is left with another
Lagálag-n-Tramp, vagabond; bum.
Lagánap-a-Universal, general, public
Lagápac-n Sound or report made by the falling of anything.
Lagari-n-Saw
Lagariin-v-To saw.
Lagasan-n-To strip, draw
Lagasan ng dahon-v To strip off leaves
Lagasan ng ngipin-v-To draw teeth.
Lagay-n-State, condition, rank, status, category; form, shape, appearance, look; likeness, face aspect.
Lagay na loob a Frank, outspoken, clear
Lagay ng loob-n-State or condition of the mind
Lagi-adv.-Always.
Lagi-a-Perpetual, everlasting, habitual permanent, durable, stable, firm, steady, continuous
Lágim-n Sadness; gloom gloominess, gathering-
Lági na-adv Always, frequently.
Lági na a-Perpetual, everlasting, habitual, frequent
Laging madilim-n-Perpetual darkness
Laglag-n-Fall,
Lagnat-n-Fever.
Lagot-n-Draught, swallow, tragus, potion
Lagot n-Break.
Lagpak n-Fall, collapse
Lagpos n-Excess; surplus, remainder, overplus; overtime
Lagpos-a Excessive; superfluous, exhorbitant, extravagant, lavish, enormous.

Lagpos *adv* -Too much

Lagpos sa pag-gasta-*n* Lavishness, extravagance

Lagpus-*a* Superfluous, excessive, lavish

Lagpusan ang karampatan-*v*-To transgress, exceed

Lagúmin-*v*-To Gather; collect, hoard

Lagúsaw-*n*-Noise made by the rustliny of paper or the shaking of water, movement

Lagusaw-*adv*.-Spread out.

Lagutin-*v*-To break, pull apart

Lagutok-*n* Crack, crackling, clash.

Lagyan-*v*-To put, place

Lagyan nḡ asin-*v*-To salt

Lagyan nḡ bubong-*v*-To roof

Lagyan nḡ butas *v*-To perforate

Lagyan nḡ halaga-*v*-To estimate, value, appraise

Lagyan nḡ ribete *v*-To hem

Lagyan nḡ sangka-*v*-To construct canals or drains

Lagyan nḡ sello *v*-To stamp

Lagyan nḡ siya sa kabayo-*v*-To saddle a horse

Lagyan nḡ sopas *v*-To put soup

Lagyan nḡ tanda-*v*-To seal, sing

Lagyan nḡ tandang krus-*v* To make the sign of the cross

Lahang-*n*-Crack, cleft; fracture, chink

Lahangin-*v*-To crack, cleave; split, fracture

Lahangin-*a*-Brittle, frail; fissile, fragile.

Lahat-*a*-All; whole; entire; each, every, total, gross, universal

Lahat-lahat-*adv* Wholly, entirely, quite,

Lahat-lahat-*a*-Entire, all, whole, every, total.

Lahi *n* Progeny, race, clan, lineage, sept; faction; class, offspring.

Lahi nḡ hari-*n* Dynasty

Lahok-*n*-Admixture, mixture

Lait-*n*-Insult, abuse; execration; curse

Laitin *v* To insult, abuse, curse revile, execrate

Lakad *n* Walk, step, pace, passage, excursion, journey

Lakad nḡ paa-*n*-Pedestrian

Lakad nḡ panahon *n* Course or space of time.

Lakas *n*-Strength, hardiness, vigor force, fortitude, valor; brawn, might, thew, impetus violence, robustness; activity, ability

Lakas nḡ loob *n* Resolution, courage, decision, fortitude, will, power, strength of mind, promptitude

Laki *n*-Size, largeness

Laki at lapad-*n*-Dimensions, extent, capacity, bulk

Laki nḡ anoman *n* Magnitude, greatness, granduer.

Laknip *n*-Cream

Laksa-*a*-Ten thousand

Laksa-*n*-Ten thousand

Laksi-*n*-Confidence, aid; help

Laktaw-*n*-Omission, skip.

Lalagin-*v*-To Undo, gather; collect

Lalagyan-*n*-Place of putting.

Lalagyan nḡ asin-*n*-Salt-cellar.

Lalagyan nḡ ginikan-*n*-Hay or straw loft

Lalagyan nḡ labasa-*n*-Razorcase

Lalagyan nḡ manḡa kopa-*n*-Cupboard

Lalagyan nḡ palaso-*n* Quiver

Lalagyan nḡ salapi-*n*-Till.

Lalagyan nḡ salsa *n*-Saucer

Lalagyan nḡ sombrero-*n*-Hatbox

Lalagyan nḡ tabaco-*n* Tobacco-pouch

Lalaki-*n*-Man, male

Lalaking bagong kasal-*n*-Groom

Lalamin-*v*-To reserve, retain, restrain; with-hold, suspend

Lalamunan-*n*-Throat, gullet, windpipe, esophagus, gorge

Lalang-*n*-Strategy stratagem, snare, industry, trick, wile, cunning, craft, slyness, skill, creation, invention; handiness; handicraft, work; toil; labor, employment

Lalangin-*v* To produce, create, generate make, institute bring forth

Lalas-*n*-Banishment, extermination.

Lalasin-*v*-To banish; exterminate, halve.

Lalawigan-*n*-Province, county, shire

Lalikan *n*-Axletree, wheel

Lalikin *v* To turn, wind around

Lalim *n*-Depth, profundity, profoundness

Lalo-*adv*.-More

Lalo-*a*-More

Lalong-*adv*-More

Lalong dakila *a*-Superior, paramount

Lalonglalo *adv*.-Principally

Lalong mabuti-*a*-Better.

Lalong magaling *a* Better

Lalong malaki *a*-Bigger, larger; more grand; superior, paramount

Lalong maliit-*a* Smaller

Lalong masamá *a*-Worse

Lalong mataas-*a*-Higher; loftier, superior.

Laman *n*-Substance, essence.

Laman nḡ tiyan,*n*-Viscera

Lamang *adv* Alone, solely; sole

Lamang *a* Sole; singular

Lamasin *v* To knead, pummel, handell

Lamat-*n* Crack, chink

Lambanog-n-Sling
Lambat n-Net, snare
Lambo n-Tassel, tuft
Lambong n-Black veil,
Lambot-n-Softness, delicacy tenderness
Lambutin-v-To soften, mollify
Lamig n-Cold, freshness, coolness, frigidness, damp, frigidity.
Lamok-n-Mosquito, gnat
Lampara-n-Lamp, light.
Lampas n-More; exssive; exhorbitant
Lampas-n-Excess; surplus, remainder, residue, superfluity, overplus·
Lampas sa panahon-a-Overdue
Lamugin-v-To pumel; make soft, soften
Lamunin-v-To swallow, glut, eat hurriedly, stuff ones self, imbibe; engulf, gorge, gobble, gormandize, gulp devour, consume, absorb.
Lamuymoy-a-Threadbare; shabby; ragged
Lamuyot-n-Deceit, fraud, imposition
Lamuyutin-v To deceive, delude; seduce, impose upon; pick to pieces
Lamuyutin ang isang dalaga v-To seduce a young lady
Landas n-Path, trail, defile, pathway, way
Langam-n-Ant
Langaw n-Fly
Langaylangayan-n-Swallow *(bird)*
Langib-n-Scab, scurf;
Langis-n-Oil
Langislangis-a-Oily, unctous; greasy.
Langit-n-Sky, heavens
Langitngit-n Creaking, crackling, creak, squea .
Langkumin-v-To fold, gather, unite, collect, hoard
Lango-a-Drunk, intoxicated, inebriated
Lango-n-Drunkenness
Lango-n-Drunkard
Langotse-n-Gunny.
Langoy-n-Swim, swimming
Languay-n-Beetlenut box
Languhin-v-To inebriate, intoxicate; make drunk.
Lansa-n-Stench, fetor, bad smell
Lansag a-Ruined, broken.
Lansag-n Destruction, ruin
Lansagin v-To destroy; ruin; tear to pieces
Lansakin-v-To congregate at a certain place to do a piece of work
Lansangan-n-Street; road; lane, avenue.
Lansetang panagra-n-Lancet, small knife or lacne.
Lansi-n-Trick, stratagem, wile, craft, thrust in fencing, throwing of a lance
Lanta-n Fading, withering
Lanta-a-Faded, withered, parched.

Lantahin-a-Perishable.
Lantahin v-To perish, fade, wither
Lantot-n-Stench, fetor stale water.
Laon-a Old, stale, musty.
Laon n Duration, age, preservation; prolixity, prolixness, oldness, time; continuance.
Laot-n-Middle, center
Laoya-n-Stew
Lapad-n-Width
Lapak-n-Break, fracture.
Lapakin-v-To break, slice, part.
Lapang-n-Piece; slice; part
Laparan-v To widen; extend, outspread, expand; enlarge; amplify.
Lampastanganan-n-Insult, offense, outrage, abuse
Lampastanganin-v-To insult, offend, abuse, outrage, depreciate
Lapat-a-Exact, even, punctual apt; proper; fit.
Lapok-a-Weak; feeble, forceless, frail.
Lapukin-v-To enfeeble; make weak, rot; make brittle
Larak-n-Proof, review
Lakarán-v-To review, prove; observe
Larawan-n-Effigy, image, figure copy, portrait
Larawan ng Jesu Cristo-n-Crucifix
Larga vista-n-Telescope
Lario-n-Brick
Laro-n-Play, sport, game, jest; amusement.
Laroan-n-Plaything.
Larong karat-n-Lottery
Larong rifa-n Raffle; lottery
Larong tanga-n-Play that resembles pitching.
Laiot-a Leaky, ragged, broken; destroyed
Lasa-n-Taste; palate; relish; flavor, essence, smack, gust, aesthetics, delight, pleasure, satisfaction, substance
Lasang matapang-n-Tang, taste.
Lasap-n-Taste, smack, relish, palate, gust, aesthetics, pleasure, delight.
Lasapin-v-To taste, relish, smack; like, sip, enjoy. try.
Lasa sa pananalita-n-Wit
Laseta-n Knife
Lasing-a-Inebriated, intoxicated, drunk
Lasing-n Drunkard
Lason-n-Poison, venom.
Lasunin-v-To poison, envenom
Latá n-Weakness; feebleness, debility.
Lata-n-Can
Latag a-Flat, extended; outspaead.
Latag-n-Extension paving
Latagán v-To unfold, expand, stretch.
Látak-n-Sediment, silt

8

Laták ng alak-*n* Lee
Latigo-*n*-Whip, scourge
Latok *a*-Rotten; putrid
Lawá *n*-Pool, pond, lake, reservoir
Lawak *n*-Width, extension, size
Láway-*n*-Spit; saliva
Lawin *n* Hawk, castrel, falcon
Laya *a*-Ungoverned, free, exempt, independent, unencumbered, unrestrained
Laya-*n*-Freedom, independence, exemp, tion.
Layag *n*-Sail
Layás-*n*-Tramp, fugitive
Layaw *i*-Caress, favorite.
Layawin *i*-To caress; favor, free
Layo-*inter*-Keep off; begone
Láyo-*n*-Distance.
Layog-*n*-Distance
Layolayo Rather far
Layolayo ang pagkalagay-At certain distances.
Layuan-*v*-To distance, put at a distance
Lecion-*n* Lesson
Letra-*n*-Letter
Ley-*n*-Law.
Liad-*a* bent back
Libag-*n*-Filth, dirt, nastiness
Libagan *v*-To dirty, make filthy or nasty
Labágan-*n*-Gossip
Libak-*n*-Mockery, ridicule, sneer; scoff, derision, jeer, moc
Libakin-*v*-To deride, ridicule; scoff; mock, sneer at, laughat, reprimand.
Liban-*adv* -Less, except
Liban-*n* Happiness, gayety
Libangin-*v*-To make happy, distract
Liban sa-*adv* -Away from, except, without, excepting
Libing *n* Funeral, burial
Libingan *n*-Grave, sepulchre, vault; tomb.
Libingang marilag-*n*-Mausoleum.
Libis-*n* Declevity, low land
Libo *n*-Thousand.
Libo-*a*-Thousand
Libro-*n*-Book, volume
Ligalig *n*-Perturbation; vexation, confusion, laziness, riot
Ligaligin-*v*-To perturb, vex; disturb, molest, confuse
Ligas-*n*-Garter.
Ligaw *a*-False, erroneous, medacious, lost.
Ligaw-*n*-Fugitive.
Ligawan-*v*-To love, court, pretend
Ligaw na balita-*n* Silliness, false news.
Ligaw sa akala-*a*-Deluded, deceived
Ligaw sa daan-*a* Misguided, illadvised.
Ligaya *a* Mirth, merriment pleasure, happiness, felicity; delight, comfort; satisfaction, caprice.

Ligisin-*i*-To mill, pound, break into, bits, powder.
Ligtaan-*i*-To neglect, forget, omit
Ligtas *a*-Free; saved, exempt, ungoverned.
Liguan-*n*-Bathing place
Liha-*n*-Emery.
Liha-*n* Ginger.
Lihim-*n*-Secret, termination, secrecy; clandestination, caution, silence.
Lihim-*adv* -Secretly, suddenly
Lihim-*a*-Hidden, secret, clandestine, reserved, private, silent.
Lihis-*n*-Avoidance, shunning, escape
Lihisan-*v* To evoid, shun, escape.
Lihis sa daan-*a*-Misguided lost,
Lahis sa matowid-*a* Wrong; illicit, unlawful, unjust
Lig-*n*-Neck
Lig ng pantong *n*-Urethra
Liit *n* Smallness, littleness
Liitan-*v*-To decrease, curtail; chip, abridge, impair, reduce, lessen
Lija-*n*-Fruits.
Lija-*n*-Joint of bamboo
Likat-*n*-Intermission, interruption
Lako-*a* Illegal; unlawful, illicit, wrong
Liko-*n*-Angle, turn, salient, ply.
Likod-*n*-Back reverse
Likod ng hukbo-*n*-Rear guard.
Liksi-*a*-Activity lightness, speed, quickness, promptness, nimbleness
Likuran-*n*-Back part, croup, back
Lila-*n*-Toaster; toaster
Lilik *n*-Scythe, sickle, reaping hook
Lilim-*n*-Shade.
Lilis-*n*-Raising of the pantleg
Lilis ang binti-*a* Barelegged
Lilo-*a*-Unfaithful, treacherous, disloyal, perfideous; infidel
Lilukan-*v* To engrave, cut in metal
Lima-*n* Five
Lima *a*-Five
Limangpuo-*n*-Fifty
Limangpuo-*a* Fifty.
Limbag *a*-Print, printing; edition
Limbagin-*v*-To print, stamp
Limbagin muli-*e* To reprint, republish
Limonada-*n* Lemonade, sode water, pop
Limos-*n*-Charity, alms
Limutin-*v*-To forget omit
Linab-*a* Greasy, fatty
Linangin ang lupa-*v*-To cultivate; farm
Linaw-*n*-Clarity, clearness
Linawan-*v*-To clarify, clear, illuminate, lighten.
Lindol *n* Earthquake
Lingap *n* Notice; appreciation, regard, observation.

Ingapin-r-To regard, notice; appreciate, watch, observe, behold
Linkod-n-Servant
Linkod sa isang dalaga-n-Woer, lover.
Lingo n-Sunday, week
Linguhan-adv.-Weekly
Linis-n-Cleanliness, neatness
Linis-a-Clean, neat, pure
Linisin-i-To clean, clear; purify, cleanse, scour
Linisin ng walis-v To brush sweep
Linkaw-n Sickle
Linso-n-Linen
Linta n Leach, blood-sucker
Lintik-n-Electricity, lightning.
Lintos n Blister.
Lipa-n-Nettle
Lipak n-Callous.
Lipas-a-Old, stale, gone by, musty, obsolete, disused, passed
Lipay-n-Vine
Lipi-n-Offspring, descendent, race
Lipos a-Full, replete, complete
Lipolin-r-To destroy, abolish, obliterate, annihilate, exterminate, suppress, raze, rase efface
Lisa n-Egg of a louse
Listahan-n List, dock, bill, catalogue, role; file, register, schedule
Listahan ng manga bagay sa isang lugar-n-Invoice
Listahan ng mga salita n-Vocabulary
Listahan ng mga tawong tumatahan sa isang lugar-n-Census, poll, voice, register
Listahin-v-To list, schedule, invoice, register.
Liston-n-Ribbon
Litak-n-Crevice, fissure, chink, cut, clett, crack
Litang-n-The spreading of a ladder so that the rounds fall out.
Litaw-a-Vulgar; apparent, public; general, notable, sensitive, sencible perceptible
Litaw n-Upshot, apearance
Litid-n-Nerve, ligament
Litiran-a-Nervous, strong robust
Lisanin-v-To choose, select
Litiran-i-To cut the cord or ligament of the ankle
Litohin-v-To amuse, entertain
Lituhin-i-To amuse, entertain.
Liwag n-Delay
Liwanag-n-Clarity, clearness, brightness, splendor, refulgence, refulgency, illumination explanation
Liwanagan-v-To clear, clarify, illuminate, lighten; illustrate, explain, involve.

Liwanagan ang isip v To enlighten the mind
Liwanag na malaki-n-Splendor, great light
Liwanag nang isip-n-Illustration, illucidation, revelation, clearness of thought
Liwayway n-Dawn; twilight
Lobo n-Wolf
Loco-a Crazy, daft, delerious
Longib-n Cave, grot; cellar
Loob-n Interior; inside
Loob-a-Interior
Loob ng bulaklak-n-Corol, corollo
Loob ng bubungan-n-Ceiling
Loob ng dibdib-n Breast busom
Loob ng simbahan n-Nave
Look-n Bay, gulf
Lotería-n-Lottery
Luad-n-Mud, mire
Luag-n-Width.
Luagan-i-To widen, loosen, free, ease, slacken
Lualhati-n Glory honor, fame.
Lualhati-a-God-like famous, glorious holy
Luang-n-Width.
Luagin-v- To widen, free; extend, enlarge
Luat-n-Delay, protraction, length of time, prolixity, prolixnees
Luatan-i-To delay; prolong, protect; extend, lengthen, postpone
Luat ng isang panahon-n-Era, age, length of time.
Lubag-a-Toose, free
Lubagin v-To loosen free slacken, ease
Lubak-n Hollow, hole.
Lubha-adv-More, greatly, very
Lubhang-a-Exhorbitant, enormous, excessive
Lubhang dakila-a Superior, supreme
Lubhang duag-a-Timorous
Lubhang gahit-a- Furious, frantic
Lubhang hambog-a-Presumptious
Lubhang hunghang-a-Savage, barbarous, very ignorant
Lubhang mabaho-a-Fetid, stinking.
Lubhan mahalaga a-Inestimable; invaluable
Lubhang mahigpit-a-Austere, strict, rigorous
Lubhang mainam-a Exquisite, superfine, excellent
Lubbang tago-a-Hidden,secret,abstruse.
Lubid-a Rope, cord
Lubid na may silo-n Halter
Lubirin i-To twist, make rope
Lubluban-n-Wallowing place
Lubog n-Dip, souse, douse.

Lubos *a* Complete; full; perfect; utter, quite, plenary, absolute, plentiful.

Lubos ang inam *a*-Beautiful, fair, handsome, fine.

Lubugin *v* To sink, submerge, put under watar, dip, souse; douse

Lubukin-*v*-To aid; assist, preserve

Lubunutan *v*-To pluck

Lubusin-*i*-To complete, perfect, finish, crown.

Lugal *n*-Place, position, spot, region, time; occasion, leisure, stead lien

Lugal na ahwan-*n*-Place of recreation, play ground

Lugal na doongan-*n*-Place of anchoring, port; harbor

Lugal na gawaan ng̃ larlo-*n*-Brickyard.

Lugal na gawaan ng̃ lubid-*n* Ropewalk, ropery, ropefactory.

Lugal na gawaan ng̃ tisa-*n* Tileworks

Lugal ng̃ ilang-*n*-Desert

Lugal na labahan *n*-Washing place.

Lugal na madulas *n* Slippery place

Lugal ng̃ ling-*n*-Throttle

Lugal na patakbuhan ng̃ cabayo-*n*-Racetrack.

Lugal ng̃ parusahan *n*-Place of punishment

Lugal na patuyuan-*n* Place of dryiug.

Lugal na pinagaalakan-*n*-Distillery, still, brewery

Lugal na pinagpapatayan ng̃ hayop-*n*-Slaughterhouse.

Lugal na pinagtuturuan *n*-School, collega, studio, place of study.

Lugal na tago *n*-Place of privacy.

Lugal na yangyang̃an *n*-Drying place.

Lugi-*n*-Loss; perdition, disadvantage

Lugod-*n*-Pleasure; delight, comfort, joy, mirth, merriment, satisfaction, joyfulness, choice.

Luha-*n*-Tear

Luhaan-*n*-Place where the tears come from

Luhaluhaan-*adv.*-Weepingly

Luhog-*n*-Request; entreaty; petition, suplication, oration, demand

Lukba-*n*-Bulb

Lukob-*n*-Gouge, round chisel

Lukubin-*v* To gouge.

Luksa-*n*-Mourning, sorrow.

Lukso-*n*-Jump; leap; bound

Lula-*n*-Seasickness, dizziness.

Lulan *n*-Load; baggage.

Lulod-*n*-Tibia, shinbone.

Lulon-*n*-Swallow; draught

Luluan *v*-To gain, profit

Lulunin *v* To roll up, swallow.

Luma-*n*-Old, stale; rank, antique, musty, archaic; worn out.

Lumabag-*v*-To disobey; oppose

Lumabag sa kautusan-*v*-To violate, oppose

Lumaban-*v* To fight, war, oppose, defend, protect, attack, combat; contend, resist, repel, conflict; cope, advocate, antagonize, champion, tilt, rival, undertake, attempt, defy

Lumaban sa utos-*v*-To violate

Lumaban sa utos *n*-Violator.

Lumabas-*i* To go out, sally, depart, proceed forth

Lumabis *v*-To exceed, overflow, surpass

Lumabis na lubha *v*-To superabound

Lumabnaw-*i*-To thin; rarify.

Lumabo *i*-To grow dim, darken, bedim

Lumaganap *v*-To extend in all parts.

Lumagay *v*-To put, place

Lumagi-*v*-To endure, last, persist

Lumagitig-*v*-To crack, crackle

Lumago-*v*-To grow; thrive, improve; increase, swell, become fruitful or fertile, fertilize.

Lumago muli-*v*-To resprout

Lumagpak-*i*-To fall, collapse, plumpbod

Lumagpos-*v*-To exceed, superabound

Lumagutok-*v*-To crack, crackle.

Lumahang-*i*-To split, crack, splinter, chink flaw

Lumahok-*v*-To mix; mingle

Lumalait *n*-Insulting person

Lumakad-*v*-To walk, go away, depart, amble, march

Lumakad ang hukbo-*v*-To decamp march

Lumakas *v*-To strengthen become or grow strong.

Lumaki-*v*-To swell, increase, aggrandize, ascend, eke; grow large; accrue, dilate, plumpbod

Lumalo *v*-To increase; aggrandize

Lumalakad-*n*-Pedestrian, passenger

Lumalak-*n*-One who grows

Lumalang-*v*-To create, found, institute invent

Lumalik-*v*-To wind about, turn, increase; aggrandize, outvie

Lumalo *r* To exceed, surpass, excel, increase, aggrandize, outvie

Lumambot-*n* To soften, emolliate, grow or become soft; limber

Lumampas *v*-To exceed; surpass, excel.

Lumang̃itng̃it *v*-To squeak, creak, grate

Lumang̃oy-*n*-To swim.

Lumapit-*v*-To draw near, approach, abut, advance, join, arrive.

Lumapot-*i*-To thicken, condense, curdle, grow; thick

Lumata-*i*-To become or grow weak, enfeeble.

Lumayag v To sail
Lumayo-v-To separate, quit, absent go away, abandon, forsake, leave; evade
Lumbay-n-Sorrow, grief; concern, gloom, anguish, affliction; melancholy.
Lumbayin t To render dejected, dispirited, sad, gloomy or melancholy.
Lumbo n-Drinking gourd
Lumibak v-To ridicule;roast; make fun of
Lumibat-t-To repéat, try again
Lumibis-v-To descend,let or go down,flow
Lumigalig-v-To perturb, disturb,terrupt, harrow
Lumigpit-v To collect; gather, hide, conceal
Lumihis v-To separate, remove, sort, escape, lose ones way.
Lumiit v-To grow smaller; descend, fall, decrease, lessen.
Lumiklik-v-To go round, encompass
Lumikmo-v-To sit
Lumiko-v-To sheer, digress, turn.
Lumiko sa kanan-v-To turn to the right
Lumiksi-v-To be active,accelerate
Lumilim-t-To be came or grow shady
Luminbutod-t-To put out
Lumindol-v-To quake
Luminaw-t-To clear up, grow or become clear, clarify.
Lumipad-v-To fit, transfer
Lumipad na magpasikosiko-v-To flutter
Lumipana v To extend to a certain print-
Lumipas-t-To pass, grow stale, elapse.
Lumipat-v-To transfer; transport; remove, convey.
Lumitak-v-To creack, split; splinter
Lumitaw-v-To appear, come out, occur, result, come into view, seem, resemble
Lumiwanag-v-To clear up, clear, illuminate, lighten, explain, be come serene, clarify
Lumkahn-t-To inspect, survey, investigate, register; record
Lumpo-n-Dingue, inability to walk, weakness of the lower limbs.
Lumpon-n-Crowd, group, bunch
Lumnag-v-To loosen, free, ease; slacken
Lumuag ang loob-t-To appease grow calm, be come pleasant or generour
Lumuang-v-To broaden, widen, extend, loosen; free, ease
Lumubog v-To sink;submerge, inundate, put, under water
Lumuha-v-To weep, mourn, lament be wail
Lumuhod-v To kneel.
Lumuhod-v imp -Knelt
Lumuhog-t-To beg, petition, crave, implore; pray, solicit, entreat, demand, claim, covet.

Lumukso-v-To leap, jump, rebound
Lumulan-v-To load, ship, freight, embark
Lumulutang sa tubig-a-Natatory
Lumundag-t-To leap, jump, rebound.
Lumura-v-To expectorate, spit
Lumusob-t-To fight; combat; attack assail; assault
Lumusong-t-To descend, flow, go down, help another do work
Lumusot-v-To fall through; pass in a running match
Lumutang-v-To float, be on the surface of the water.
Lunas-n-Antidote.
Lunas ng ilog-n-Bed of a river
Lundag n-Jump, leap, bound
Lunga-n Cave, grotto; grot, cellar
Lunga ng daga-n-Rathole
Luningning-n-Splendor,finery,brillance, brilliancy, glory
Lunit-n-Frequence, frequency
Lunusin-v-To affect: move, touch
Lupa-n-Ground, soil, land, earth, globe universe
Lupain-n-Large tract of land
Lupang alatan-n Salt marsh, land that is reached by the tide.
Lupang asinan-n-Saltmarsh
Lupang maluag at patag-n-Plain, prairie, champaign
Lupang may tanim na mansanas-n-Apple-orchard
Lupang panagulan-n Riceland
Lupang patag-n-Prairie, plain, level ground.
Lupang puti-n Chalk
Lupang sinasaka-n-Farm;estate, grange, plantation
Lupang tuyot at mahina-n-Barren-ground,sterile ground
Lupang walang damo-n-Desert
Lupaypay-n-Weakness, debility
Lupaypay na loob-a-Languid, downfallen; feeble.
Lupian-n-Place of doubling or turning, folding, turning.
Lupigin-v-To usurp, aproprate by force
Lupit-n-Sternness; harshness; cruelty, inhumanity, rigor; moral depravity; inclemency
Lupon-n-Reunion, meeting; congregation
Lupong-n-Reunion, meeting, congregation, gathering
Lura n-Spit, saliva
Luraan-n-Spittoon.
Lusak-n-Mud, mire
Lusaw-n-Liquid, fluid.
Lusaw-a-Liquid; fluid,

Lusawm-i-To liquefy, dilute, dissolve, melt, cosume, mis-spend

Luslos n-The unwinding, giving out, freedom.

Luslosan-v-To unwind, give more rope; free give more freedom, increase.

Lula n-Profit, advantage, improvement, proficiency; progress, utility.

Lutasan-v-Finish, termination, conclusion, end

Lutasin v-To terminate, finish, conclude, close, end, dispatch, dispose of

Luto-n-Cooking, manner of cooking

Lutos-n-Rottenness.

Lutusin-v-To rot on the inside

Lutuin-i-To cook, boil.

Lutuin sa mantika v-To fly

M

Maaaring ipahintulot-a Permissible; admissible, allowable

Maaaring mabiak a-Fissile

Maabala-v-To be embarrassed

Maabot-a-Attainable, obtainable

Maabot ng isip-a Comprehensible, conceivable.

Maabot ng isip v-To comprehend, understand.

Maaboy-v-To be led, taken to

Maaga adv -Early, soon.

Maagap-a-Active, smart, quick, alert, diligent, ready

Maagap adv. Early, soon, quickly, diligently.

Maagasan-v-To miscarry; menstruate

Maagaw-v-To be stolen

Maagaw tulog v-To doze, nap; be drowsy

Maakma-a Proper; fit, suitable, agreeable

Maakma-v-To be proper, fit, correspond, suit, be ready, fit

Maaksayá-i To be spent foolishly, misspend

Maakyat-v-To ascend, go up.

Maalaala-a Memorable, memorial.

Maalab-a-Fervent, ardent

Maalaga-a-Diligent, active, officious, careful, obsequious

Maalam na loob-a Gentle, mild, mee', quiet, prudent.

Maalam ng lahat-a-General; omniscient, omnipotent

Maalas v-To note.

Maalat a-Salty; salted, briny, husky; brakish; saltish.

Maalikabok a-Dusty

Maalindog a-Facetious, happy

Maalis ang galit v-To become appeased, appease.

Maalis ang puit-v-To lose the bottom

Maalisan ang atip-v-To unroof

Maaliw v-To rest, sport, live at ease.

Maaliw a-Diverting, free, happy.

Maaliwalas-a-Spacious, capacious wide, commodious; free.

Maaluningning a-Brilhant, sparkling

Maaluningning-a-Brilliant, sparkling, magnificent

Mainag-a-Musty, mouldy

Maamo-a Tame, meek; gentle, mild, benign, benignent

Maamong loob-a Soft affable, meek, placid, jovial; gay, merry, cheerful

Maamoy a-Sented, oderous; oderiterous

Maanghang-a peppery, sharp

Maangihn-v-To growl, demand in a loud voice.

Maangihn-a-Growling snarling

Maaninag a-Transparent.

Maanta-a-Rank, stale, strong scented

Maantala-v-To retard, defer, delay, detain

Maasahan-a-Sanguine, hopeful, expectant

Maasim-a-Sour, acrid, sharp salty; crude, briny, salted-

Maaso-a-Smoky, fumy, full of smoke.

Maáwa a-Clement, compassionate

Maawa-v-'o pity be clement, be sorry for another

Maawain-a-Clement, humane, compassionate, commiserate, magnanamious, generous, merciful, touching, noble, godly.

Maawain sa mahirap-a-Charitable, generous, liberal

Maaya-a-Eloquent, pleasant, pleasing.

Maayos a-Honest, pure, arranged, clean, convenient, decent; reasonable modest, suitable

Mabaak-v To be cleaved, quartered taken to pieces.

Mababa-a-Low, abject, ordinary, vulgar; plebian, dull

Mababa ang halaga-a-Cheap, inferior.

Mababakla-v-To be disturbed, perturbed or vexed.

Mababa sa iba a-Inferior, lower.

Mababang loob-a Humble, meek, submissive, gentle, quiet, mild, tame, simple; plain. resigned, respectful.

Mababasa a-Legible.

Mababaw-*a*-Low, shallow, superficial

Mabagal-*a*-Slow, dull, tardy, lazy, indolent, dilatory, sluggish

Mabagay-*a*-Fit; proper, suitable convenient, becoming, adaptable, agreeable

Mabagbag ang sasakyan-*v*-To be shipwrecked

Mabago-*v*-To be altered, changed or renewed.

Mabagsik-*a* Rigid, severe, rigorous austere, cruel, truculent, fell, stern, arbitrary; fierce; terrible, grim, tyrannical, hard-hearted, despotic, rough; ugly

Mabahagi *v* To be divided or parted.

Mabahaw ang sugat-*v*-To heal or cure a wound

Mabaho-*a*-Stinking, bad-smelling

Mabait-*a* Prudent, judicious, modest, discreet; just, fair, honest, honorable, reasonable; skillfull; capable, smart, clever, candid; wise, sensible, circumspect; decent, sharp; mature, continent, becoming, suitable, considerate

Mabait ang ugali-*a*-Decorous, decent

Mabakbak-*v*-To unglue.

Mabalahibo-*a*-Wooly; fleecy; hairy

Mabalaho-*a*-Swampy, marshy, muddy,

Mabalakubak-*a*-Scurvy; scurry

Mabalat-*a*-Unpolished, unfinished, rustic, skinny

Mabalatong *v*-To be intercepted, deviate

Mabalda *v*-To be interrupted

Mabali-*v*-To break

Mabalian ang buto-*v*-Break a bone

Mabalisa-*a*-To be restless, disturbed, perturb

Mabaliw *v*-To mope, fool, be mopish.

Mabaliwag *a*-Deep.

Mabalot *v*-To be embaled, packed

Mabalot—Having many wraps.

Mabaanagan-*v*-To have an idea

Mabanga-*v*-To bump against, collide

Mabangis-*a*-Severe, cruel, hard-hearted, tyrannical, despotic, sanguinary, ugly; wild, fierce, savage, ferocious, arbitrary, truculent grisly grim, intolerable.

Mabango-*a*-Fragrant, arromatic; redolent, oderiferous, oderous.

Mabantog-*a*-Famous, noble, honorable, great; grand, celebrated, renowned.

Mabao-*v*-To become a widow or widower.

Mabasa-*v*-To become wet or moist

Mabasa-*a*-Wet, moist.

Mabasag-*a* Broken

Mabasag-*v*-To become broken

Mabatbat-*v* To be scratched or scraped

Mabatid-*v*-To understand, hear

Mabato-*a*-Stony, rocky.

Mabawasan-*v*-To diminish, lessen, waste.

Mabawi-*v*-To recover, gain back

Mabiak *v*-To crack; cleave

Mabigat-*a*-Heavy, burdensome, weighty, important, grievous, offensive, serious, cumbrous, ponderous; grave; onerous

Mabigat gawin *a*-Laborious, tiresome, painful

Mabigla-*v*-To surprised or astonished, do without thinking or in a hurry.

Mabihasa-*v*-To be accustomed or trained

Mabihasa *a*-Wise

Mabilango-*v*-To be confined or imprisoned

Mabilis *a*-Rapid, quick, precipitate, swift, light

Mabilog-*a*-Round; circular, spherical

Mabilog na haba-*a* Oval, plump, egg-shaped, oblong

Mabilog ang katawan-*a*-Plump, plumb

Mabinat-*v*-To relapse, devolve

Mabingbing *v*-To be impeded, checked, or stopped.

Mabingi *v*-To become or grow deaf, deafen.

Mabini-*a* Quiet; peaceful; modest, chaste decent, unassuming

Mabisa-*a*-Stout; strong, fervent, ardent, active, effective, diligence, vigorous

Mabitin-*v*-To suspend, be suspended.

Mabood-*v*-To be obstructed; impeded

Mabnal-*v*-To tumble; fall, topple

Mabubo-*v*-To overflow, run over

Mabudbod-*v*-To be distributed, divided

Mabugnos-*v*-To come untied, open.

Mabuhaghag-*v*-To become loose, free

Mabuhangin-*a*-Sandy.

Mabuhay-*v*-To live, be alive

Mabuhay-*a*-Lively, active, alive

Mabuhay sa gugol ng iba-*v*-To live on another, live on another's salary.

Mabuhay na mahaba sa iba-*v*-To outlive, survive

Mabuhay uli-*v*-To restore to life, revive, resusticate, live again

Mabuhok-*a*-Hairy.

Mabukid-*a*-landed

Mabula-*a*-Frothy, foamy

Mabulalas-*v*-To be frank, open or indiscreet

Mabulalas-*a* Talkative, generous, spendthrift

Mabuhel-*v*-To fall tumble topple

Mabulo-a-Wooly, fleecy

Mauulok-a-Rotten, spoiled, damaged, putrid

Mabulok-i-To rot, spoil, decay, corrupt, putrefy

Mabulungin-a-Grumbung

Mabunga-a-Fruitful; fertile,

Mabuni-a-Scurvy

Mabunot v-To be pulled up

Mabunton-v-To be heaped up; piled

Mabunyi-a-Celebrated, famous, renowmed, noble, extolled, excellent, magnificent.

Mabura a-Erasable.

Mabura v-To blot, be effaced or clouded

Maburak a-Muddy; miry, s ampy

Mabusog-i-To be satisfied, filled, satiate

Mabuti a-Good, wholesome, suitable; healthiul, salutary, useful, fit, proper, profitable covemeut

Mabat -adi.-Well

Mabuti ang gayak a-Elegant

Mabutihin-v-To make good, justify, accept.

Mabutil-a-Seedy, granulous, granular.

Mabuting kapalaran-n-Good-luck; success, prosperity

Mabuting loob-n-Kindness, generosity, benevolence, magnanimity

Mabuting ngalan-n-Fame, good name; reputation

Mabuting paguugali-n-Urbanity, good; manners; civility.

Mabuti sa katawan a-Healthful salutary.

Mabuto-a-Bony, seedy.

Mabuya-v-To stuff or glut one's self

Mabuyo-v-To be induced or persuade

Madagdagan-v-To be augmented

Madagi-i-To wear away by friction gall, chafe

Madahakin-v-To spit phlegm

Madahon-a-Leafy

Madaig-v-To lose, be conquered

Madakila a-Grand; superior; paramount, excellent, glorious, noble; honorable

Madala-i-To avoid, be scared or frightened; become timid, evade, shun

Madala-v-To be carried or conveyed

Madálang a-Rare, scarce, wide, spare

Madalang adv -Seldom.

Madalas and Frequently, often

Madalas-a-Frequent habitual

Madah-adv -Quickly, promptly, briskly, urgently, actively; swiftly, soon.

Madali-a-Quick; urgent, pressing, brisk, brief, prompt, ready; nimble; concise active swift; cursory

Madahan i To be in a hury. be in haste; be quick or active.

Madaling araw-n-Day-light, dawn

Madaling galawin-a-Movable, variable, unsteady, shifting

Madaling gawin-a-Practicable, feasible; easily done

Madaling gumalaw-a-Unsteady, movable, variable, shifting

Madaling gumulong-Easily rolled

Madaling hubugin a-Eithe.

Madaling humalata-Easily noted or distinguished

Madaling intindihin-a-Intelligible, conceivable, easily understood

Madaling kalagin-a-Soluble, solvable

Madaling kurum-a-Intelligible, conceivable; easily, understood

Madaling macaraan-a-Transitory

Madaling mamuo-a-Congealable

Madaling maniwala-a Believable credible, trustworthy

Madaling masira-a-Brittle

Madaling matunaw-a-Soluble.

Madaling matunaw sa sikmura-a-Digestible

Madaling ulohn-a-Simple, artless

Madahta a-Poor, penurious, suffering

Madapat-v-To become, behoobe; concern, belong to

Madapat-a-Proper, fit, corresponding, convenient

Madapilas-v-To slip, slide

Madatay-v-To be laid smoothly

Madawag a-Thorny, shiny

Madaya-a-Deceiving, delusive

Madidikit-a-Vicid, viscous, sticky

Madilaw-a Yellow, xanthia

Madilim-a-Dark, gloomy, hazy, shady, opaque; murky, obscure, unintelligible

Madiwara-a-Curious, troublesome prying, cautious

Madla n Public, multitude

Madla a Much, abundant, plentiful, many.

Maduag-a Cowardly, dastardly

Madugo-a Bloody, sanguine, gory.

Madulas-a-smooth, slippery

Madulas v To slip, slide

Madumhan i-To besmear, be covered with dirt or filth

Madungis a-Nasty; dirty, filthy

Madungo-a-Silent, dumb, repellent.

Madurog v To break, powder.

Maestro-it-Master; teacher, pedagogue

Maestra-n-Lady teacher.

Mag v-To grow; do

Magaan a Light, gay, nimble, swift; agile, spry; buoyant, jaunty, janty, giddy, trifling

Ma gaan ang dugo a Sympathetic.

Ma gaang basahin a-Legible, easily read
Mag aarawn Day laborer; journeyman; laborer
Mag abot v-To reach, amount to.
Magagalitin-a-Hot-headed, cross-grained intractable, seasily enraged, grumbling, snarling
Magagamit-a-Usual, customary; ordinary, profitable, useful, fit; servicible, helpful.
Magagapas—Fit to be harvested
Magagawa-a-Possible, feasible, practicable
Mag akala i-To think plan, wish, design, invent fancy, imagine, try, intend, desire, discuss
Mag alaala-v-To remember; remind.
Mag alab-v-To burn, blaze, glow
Mag alaga-i-To breed, bring up, care for, heed, nurse, educate
Mag alak-v-To distill, still
Magalang-a-Urbane, polite; respectful kind, obliging, decorous; decent, courteous
Magalang-adi -Respectfully, courteously, kindly; obligingly, politely
Magalangin-a-Courteous, polite; civil, wellbred.
Magalaw-a Lively, noisy, boisterous, restless, mischievous
Mag alay-v-To dedicate; consecrate, sacrifice, offer, pay homage.
Magaling a Gallant, gay, smart; elegant, noble, genteel, polite, fine, perfect, delicate civil; good, precious; valuable, magnanamous, generous, liberal, attentive, heedful
Magalingin-v To respect; appreciate; have regard for, honor, be polite; credit, dignify, approve, prefer, like, enjoy; adorn, be pleased with
Magaling kay sa iba-a-Better.
Magaling na lubha-a-Wonderful, astonishing, miraculous, marvelous.
Mag alipusta-v-To blackguard, defame, run down
Mag alis v-To leave off, take away.
Mag alis ang luksa-i-To leave off mourning
Mag alisaga-i To loiter, idle, lounge
Mag alisan v-To take off or away.
Magaht-a-Angry, mad
Magaht-v-To be angry, irritated offended, enraged; exasperated, provoked, displeased, disgusted
Mag aliw-v-To intertain, keep in hope, amuse, delight, comfort; rest, gratify; recreate; sport, live at ease
Magámit-a-Usual, customary, ordinary, useful

Mag ampon-v-To shelter, aid, help, protect, assist
Maganda-a Beautiful, pretty. handsome: fine, fair; delicate, smart, neat, exquisite; gorgeous, winsome, comely
Magandang kalooban-n-Gentility, magnanimity- generosity, liberality, benevolence; nobility
Magandang loob-a-Generous, magnanamous, benignant, liberal, bounteous, benevolent, benign, gracious, noble
Magandang tikas-a-Elegant graceful, exquisite; gallant; gay; gentle; polite. excellent, brave, strong; robust.
Maganit-a-Tough, glutinous.
Mag aral-i-To study, learn, pore
Mag araro-v-To plow; plough
Mag asawa-Man and wife.
Magaslaw a-Rompish; boisterous, noisy, fidgety; restless
Mag asawa-v-To betroth, espouse, wive, marry, match.
Mag aso-v-To smoke.
Magaspang-a Coarse, rough, rude; illbred, incident, blowzy, gross
Magasta-a Expensive, costly.
Magawa-v-To do, be done.
Mag away v-To fight, wrangle, war, quarrel; dispute, struggle, oppose
Magagawi-a-Inclined
Mag-ayos-v-To arrange, put in order, place.
Mababag-v-To struggle, fight
Magbabahwag-n Haberdasher.
Mag bago-v-To be eformed, reform, renew, correct, mend, change, alter, transfer.
Magbahala-v-To care for, take carn of, man, manage, run, take charge of
Magbahin-v-To sneeze.
Magbakod-v-To build fence, make a fance.
Magbala-v-To threaten, menace
Magbalak-v-To proffer; announce.
Magbalatkayo-v-To go incognito, delude, deceive.
Magbalita-v-To inform, report, relate, proclaim, announce; give notice, herald; warn, tell
Magbalwag-v-To traffic trade
Magbaliwas-v-To pull up a pole and line
Magbalobalo-i-To feign, pretend; delude
Magbanalbanalan-v-To feign, pretend, be a hypocrite
Megbangay-v To combat, fight; attack.
Magbangit-v-To allude, mention
Magbankat-v To reinforce; tie, bind, fagot.

9

Magbangon-v-To arise, rise, get up, edify, build; erect.
Magbanhay-v-To frame
Magbanli-v-To scald
Magbansag-v To nickname, dub
Magbantay-v-To patrol, guard, watch
Magbasabasa-v-To moisten, dampen, wet.
Magbasag-ulo v-To dispute, fight quarrel, wrangle
Magbatikbatik-v-Spotted; speckled
Magbawal-v-To prohibit, divest
Magbawas-v-To lessen, reduce; decay, sink, decline, abridge, grow smaller
Magbayad v-To pay; recompence, retribute, disburse, liquidate a debt
Magbayaran-v-To pay, recompence, retribute
Magbeberso n Poet, Author
Magbigay-v-To give, grant, concede; allow; admit, donate
Magbigay alam-v-To inform, warn, tell; give notice, participate, advise
Magbigay daan-v To allow, give way, admit, give a reason, assign amotive
Magbigay galang-v To salute, hail greet, pay one's regards or respect
Magbigay loob-v-To condescend, sub-
Magbigay lugod-v To please, gratify; humor, content, satisfy.
mit, comply, allow
Magbigay ñg fianza-v-To bail, give security
Magbigay ñg katibayan-v-To bail, give security
Magbigay pagkain-v To give food, feed, nourish, maintain
Magbigay pakinabang-v-To give or yield a profit
Magbigay parte-v-To give notice, participate
Magbigay puri-v-To purify honor, respect, credit, dignify, adorn.
Magbigay sala-v-To criminate, accuse, impeach
Magbigti-v To commit suicide by hanging
Magbihis-v-To dress, change clothes.
Magbinata-v-To act like a child
Magbiñgibiñgihan-v-Ta grow deaf, act like a deaf person.
Magbintang v-To accuse falsely, impute, attribute; suspect, criminate
Magbinyag-v-To christen, baptize.
Magbiro v-To play, joke; palter pun, jest
Magbithay-v To sift, sieve
Magbitin-v-To hang up, suspend.
Magbuho v-To found, cast
Magbubong v To roof.
Magbugbugin v To contuse, bruise
Magbugnos v To loosen; untie free extricate.

Magbuhat-v-To originate, arise from, commence, begin, descend from, occur, happen
Magbuhat kailan-Since, when.
Magbuhol v-To knot, tie in a knot
Magbukid v-To farm, plow, plough, cultivate; till
Magbukod-v-To separate, remove, sort, dissuade
Magbulaan-v To lie, falsify, deceive.
Magbulaybulayan-v-To cogitate, muse; think, meditate
Magbuno-v-To wrestle, struggle, tussle
Magbuntod-v-To pile up heap, accumulate
Magbuntong hiniñga-v-To sigh, draw a deep breath.
Magburil-v-To engrave, polish
Magcompisal v-To confess.
Magdaan-v-To go by, pass, walk
Magdagta-v-To gather sap.
Magdalilan v-To feign, give a reason, give an excuse.
Magdala-v To carry, wear, bring, bear
Magdahit-v-To sing, cant, hum.
Magdahta v-To suffer
Magdamdam-v-To feel, be sensible of, suffer; grieve, resent, be sorry, be affected or moved, deplore, lament, bewail, smart, irritate
Magdaragat-n-Mariner, seafaring man, sailor, seafarer
Magdaragat-v-To sail the seas
Magdaraya-a-Knavish, counterfeit, cheating, false, untrue, fraudulent; sham; deceitful, guileful, vile
Magdaraya n-Impostor, defaulter; sharper swindler; cheat, detrauder
Magdasal-v-To pray, beseech
Magdenuncia-v-To denounce, blame, accuse
Magdibuho-v-To draw, lithograph
Magdiladila v-To flatter, coax, delight, please
Magdilig-v-To sprinkle, spray, water, moisten
Magdilim-v-To grow dark, daze
Magdilim ang buan ó araw-v-To eclipse.
Magdiwang v-To celebrate
Magdiwara-v-To pry, be inquisitive
Magduda-v To doubt, mistrust
Magdugtong-v-To add, exaggerate, at-
Magdulas--v-To slip, slide.
Magduhng-v-To look crosseyed,
Maggalaw-v-To move, traverse
Maggalawin-v-To stir begin; move
Maggamot v To doctor
Maggantilhan v-To revenge, retribute, recompence

Maggasta-v-To spend, disburse.

Maggihwan v To amuse one another; love one another.

Maggisa-i-To cook.

Maggrado i-To grade, class, reach a certain class or grade.

Magguhit-v-To draw

Maggunigum i-To imagine, cogitate, muse

Maghahalaman-n Gardener; horticulturist.

Maghain-v-To offer, present, sacrifice.

Maghaka-v-To deliberate; reflect, consider, imagine, fancy

Maghakbang-v-To step.

Maghalaman-v-To garden

Maghalimbawa-i To give or set an example, instance

Maghahnhinan-i-To take turns, alternate, exchange.

Maghalo-v-To mix, mingle.

Maghambog-v-To brag, boast, blow, bully, swagger, vaunt; infatuate.

Maghampas-i-To chastize, punish; strike, whip

Maghampas lupa i-To tramp, loiter, lounge, lead a licentious life

Maghamunan-v-To defy, rival; challenge

Maghanda-v-To prepare, get ready, provide; furnish, cater, busk, dispose, dispatch.

Maghandog-v-To present; offer, sacrifice, dedicate, pay homage.

Maghangad-v-To desire, wish; long for; require, demand

Maghangin-v-To boast; brag, blow; swagger

Maghaplit-v-To hustle, hurry; rush; bustle

Magharang-i-To hold up; rob on the public highway

Maghari-v-To govern, reign, command, predominate, be king

Maghasik-v-To plant by drilling, sow.

Maghatid v-To conduct; accompany

Maghigab-i To yawn, gape

Maghikab-v-To yawn, gape.

Maghilatsa-v To ravel

Maghilik-v-To snore

Maghimatay-i-To faint. swoon

Maghimutok-v-To lament, complain, resent; murmur.

Maghinagap-v-To believe, credit, give faith.

Maghinakdal-v-To receive, protect, give shelter

Maghinala-v-To presume, suppose, conjecture, suspect.

Maghingalo-v-To gasp expire.

Maghingutuhan-v To criticize one another.

Maghinto v-To stop; pause; halt, cease

Maghirap-v-To grow or become difficult.

Maghubad-v-To denude, undress, doff

Maghubo v-To denude, undress, doff.

Maghugas-i-To wash; bathe.

Maghusay-v-To arrange, put in order, adjust

Mag iba-v-To alter, change, reform

Mág iba-v-To fall, tip over, topple

Mag ihaw v-To roast, bake.

Mag ikit-v-To turn

Mag ilaw-v-To enlighten, illuminate

Magihw-a Tender, loving, affectionate, amorous, friendly

Maginaw-a-Cold, frigid.

Maginawin-a-Chilly

Maging-v-To become; be; be current, exist, belong to, behoove; concern, beseem; worth.

Maging alak-v-To ferment.

Maging asawa v Future wife

Mag ingat-v-To care, heed, watch, be on one's guard; reck; beware

Mag ingay v-To make a noise, be noisy; be boisterous

Maging bagay-v-To beseem.

Maging bastos v-To become coarse

Maging buto-v-To ossify.

Maging bubog v-To vitrify.

Maging paano ay hindi—in no degree, by no means

Maging para sa isa-v To become like

Maginhawa-a-Prosperous; successful; fortunate, happy, easy, eminent, potent, wealthy

Mag inis-i-To smother, oppress.

Mag init-v To heat

Maginoo-a Principal, honorable.

Maginoo-n Sir, mister miss, master, madam, gentleman, lady.

Mag isda-v To fish

Magising v-To wake, awake.

Mag isip-v-To think, reason, meditate; muse, contemplate, consider, pore, deem

Mag isip isip-v-To meditate, muse, deliberate, reflect, consider, con, cogitate; ponder

Mag isis-i-To scrub

Magitla-v-To be surprised or startled.

Magitlahin-a-Timid, fearful, skittish

Magitna-i-To be between.

Mag iwan v To leave, forsake, abandon.

Mag iwi-v-To nurse, breed, bring up, care for.

Maglaakma-v-To sympathize, be sympathetic

Magka amag-t-To moss; cover with moss

Magkaanohan-justly or unjustly, by all means

Magkabungo-t-To bump against, collide

Magkabutasbutas t-To be perforated.

Magkagalit-v To displease, anger, offend

Magkagusto-v-To be pleased, like; enjoy; relish

Magkahalaga-t-To amount to

Magkahiang-r-To sympathize, be sympathetic

Magkaiba-v-To dissent.

Magkaibigan-v-To be friends

Magkaibigan-t-Friends

Magkaila-v-To negative, disclaim, contravene, abjure, recant

Magkailangan-v-To want, need, necessitate; be in need

Magkailangang mahigpit-t-To be urgent or absolutely necessary.

Magkailanman-adv.-Always,perpetually

Magkainkil-v-To wear or waste away by friction, collide

Magkaisa-t-To resemble; be equal, agree, coincide, be of the same opinion

Magkaisa ang layo-Equally distant; of an equal distance

Magkaisaisa v To agree, concert, be united.

Magkakaayon-a-Accordant.

Magkakahoy-n-Woodsman; woodcutter

Magkakalakal-n-Merchant, trader, shopkeeper, dealer

Magkakalap n-Wooddealer, timber-merchant

Magkalabog v-To fall and make an noise

Magkalagot-v-To pull, apart, break.

Magkalakal-v-trade, buy and sell.

Magkalaman-v-To grow fleshy; be of the same flesh and blood

Magkalawas-v To tie, bind, fagot.

Magkahlim-v-To be shady.

Magkaloob v-To allow, give, bestow, grant, concede, admit

Magkalugat-v-To contain

Magkalunatlunat-v-To defer, delay differ.

Magkamali-v-To err; make a mistake, mistake, commit an error.

Magkamatayan a-Mortal; fatal.

Magkamit-t To reach; overtake; come up; obtain; attain

Mag amtan r To acquire, get beget, win

Magkanlalahis-t To overflow.

Magkandili t-To bing up; breed; care for, watch.

Magkanlong-t-To protect, hide, shield, conceal

Magkano-How much

Magkanta-t-To sing

Magkaparis-t-To resemble; be alike

Magkapuri-t-To honor, respect, dignify, credit.

Magkarinigan-t-To misunderstand, confound, confuse

Magkaroon-t-To have, get, beget, contain, possess; attain, obtain; procure, take, hold fast

Magkaroon ng karampatan-t-To deserve; merit.

Magkaroon ng pag-asa-t-To hope

Magkaroon ng ugah-t-To have habits

Magkasakit-t-To be sick, feel indisposed, ail

Magkasakitan r-To pester, annoy.

Magkasala-v-To sin, infract, commit a misdeed

Magkasalot-t -To pester; annoy.

Magkasalungat-v-To oppose

Magkasamá ang loob-t To displease, offend

Magkasiksikan-t-To stuff, ram, jam

Magkasunduan-v-To agree, accord

Magkatam-v-To plane

Magkataon-t-To happen; befall; bechance, hap, be casual, take place.

Magkatipon t-To assemble, meet, congregate.

Magkatiwala-v-To be an agent

Magkathat v-To cast a net, unfold

Magcatulad-t-To assimilate, resemble, favor, be equal

Magkaumpog-t-To collide

Magkayayat v-To extenuate, debilitate, waste away; emaciate.

Magkidkid-t-To wrap up, reel, wind

Magkidlat-v-To flash; lighten.

Magkita-v-To meet; see, encounter

Magkonowa-t-To counterfeit, pretend, forge, mimic; pirate

Magkonowa i-t-To counterfeit, pretend, mimic, pirate, feint, dissemble

Magkontrato-t-To contract.

Magkrus-v-To cross, intersect· make the sign of the cross

Magkuako-t-To smoke a pipe

Magkulang-t-To fall short; lack, be deficient, fail, lessen, diminish, decline, decay, sink, waste shrink.

Magkulang sa kautusan-t-To sin; offend

Magkulung-r To imprison, shut up

Magkulimlim t-To darken, become dark.

Magkumot-*v*-To blanket use a blanket
Magkumpuni-*v*-To repair; fix, mend, adjust
Magkunot-*v*-Ta wrinkle, plait; knit
Magkupkupan-*v*-To help one another.
Magkural-*v*-To pen up, corral
Magkuro-*v*-To muse meditate; reason, contemplate, provide, get ready, furnish, conceal
Maglaan-*v*-To reserve, restrain, separate; provide, get ready, furnish, conceal
Maglaban-*v*-To fight; contend, war, invest; wager, sustain, defend
Maglabatiba-*v*-To syringe
Maglagay-*v*-To put, place, set, lay, appoint, wager, arrange
Maglagay ñg iit-*i*-To nickname, give an alias.
Maglagay ñg nota-*v*-To make note of, note, mark. -
Maglagay ñg tanda-*v* To note, mark.
Maglagay sa loob *i*-To put in.
Maglagda-*v* To legislate, enact laws
Maglagos-*v*-To omit, exeed, overlook.
Maglaitan-*v*-To insult; scoff, deride, ridicule, criticize in an insulting manner, execrate; curse
Maglakad-*v*-To walk; march journey.
Maglakbaybayan-*v* To go from place to place, travel.
Maglalabra ñg bato-*n*-Stonecutter
Maglalario-*n*-Brickmaker.
Maglaman-*v*-To contain, comprise-
Maglamas-*v* To knead
Maglámas-*v* To handle
Maglampaso-*i*-To play, gambol
Maglaro-*v*-To play, gamblo
Maglaro ñg rifa *v*-To raffle
Maglasing-*v*-To get drunk, inebriate, intoxicate, besot, tope.
Maglatag-*v*-To unfold, stretch out
Maglatag ñg bato-*i*-To pave.
Maglaway-*v*-To spit, expectorate.
Maglhab-*i*-To blaze, glow, burn
Maglibakan-*v*-To scoff, ridicule, insult, laugh at, criticize
Maglibang-*i*-To sport, rest, live at ease, amuse one's self.
Magligaw-*v*-To become lost,lose one's way
Maglignak-*v*-To spill
Maglhit-*v*-To shorten, become smaller.
Maglhit ñg gastos-*v*-To reduce expenses
Maglikot-*v*-To caper, frolic, frisk, jest; joke, be restless; be mischievous
Maglihingo-*adv*-Weekly
Maglihingo-*a*-Weekly.
Maglimas-*d*-To bail.
Maglingas-*v*-To blaze, burn, glow
Maglingkod-*v*-To court, wait upon, woo, love

Maglinis-*v*-To clean; scour; purify
Maglipat-*v*-To transfer, alter the position, transmit
Maglipat ñg pananim-*v*-To transplant
Maglitak-*v*-To crack, split
Magliwanag-*v*-To glitter, shine, glow, gleam, become clear illuminate
Magluat-*v*-To prolong, extend; protract; retard, lengthen, defer, delay, dally, remain.
Magluha-*i*-To weep, cry
Magluksa-*v*-To be in mourning
Magluluat-*a* Perpetual, tedious tardy.
Maglunas *v*-To build the bottom of a canal
Maglunas-*v*-To massage
Maglundag-*v*-To jump, caper, frolic; spring, bound
Maglungkot-*v*-To mourn, pine; lament be sorrowful
Maglura-*v*-To spit, expectorate.
Magluraan-*v*-To spit at one another.
Magluto-*v*-To coo .
Magmadalas-*v*-To frequent, haunt.
Magmadali-*v*-Tohurry, be in haste bestir, bustle, hustle; hie, rustle
Magmagahng *v*-To make good, become good or agreeable.
Magmahalan-*v*-To value, prize, love, respect.
Magmalikmata-*i*-To change appearance assume different aspects, be trans. figured
Magmamana-*n*-Interior, heir
Magmana-*v*-To inherit
Magmamarmot-*v* To be stingy, penurious, closefisted or cordid; act the miser; act miserly
Magmasa-*v* To knead
Magmasid-*v*-To observe, watch, notice, heed, behold, look, mind; scrutinize
Magmasiran-*v*-To spy; watch; closely; scrutinize
Magmatigas-*i*-To become hard, harden, persist; persevere, be obstinate.
Magmatuid *v*-To argue, reason, correct, remonstrate, set aright, make right, object, oppose, protect, assist.
Magminindal-*v*-To lunch
Magmithi-*v*-To resent, fail, begin to give way.
Magmuang-*i* To cast; throw.
Magmukha *v*-To resemble.
Mamgukhang angel-*i*-To resemble an angel
Magmula-*i*-To begin, commence, arise orignate, proceed from, issue, spring from came from, occur, happen
Magmuh *v*-To repeat
Magmúra-*v*-To sprout, bud.

Magmurá-*i*-To curse; slander, insult, blakguard; censure

Magmurahan-*v*-To blackguard, insult abuse, revile

Magnakaw-*v* To steal; rob; plunder, purloin.

Magnana-*v*-To suppurate

Magnanakaw-*n*-Thief, robber, freebooter, pickpocket

Magnangis-*i*-To whine, whimper, sniffle, cry.

Magnasa-*v*-To wish; desire, long for, covet, claim, demand

Magngasab-*v*-To smack, masticate

Magningas-*v*-To burn, blaze glow

Magningning-*v*-To glitter; glow, shine; glisten, gleam, radiate, sparkle, twinkle.

Magnutnot-*v*-To ravel.

Magpaalaala *v*-To remember, record; mention.

Magpaaraw-*v*-To put oa dry in the sun

Magpabaya-*v*-To neglect, forget, overlook, lounge

Magpabuis-*i*-To loan money on interest rent to another

Magpabuya-*v*-To recompence, reward, gratify.

Magpadala-*v*-To dispatch, send, transmit; carry.

Magpagal-*v*-To tire, work until tired.

Magpagalit *v* To exasperate, irritate, anger, offend

Magpahalata-*v*-To cause to feel.

Magpahamak-*i*-To damage, injure, hurt; lower; make worthless

Magpahayag-*v*-To say, tell; announce, declare. manifest, expound, express, explain.

Magpahid-*v*-To wipe; smear

Magpahinga-*v*-To rest; stop, repose. cease, live at ease.

Magpahingalay-*v* To rest, repose, live, at ease; stop work.

Magpahiram-*v* To lend.

Magpahirap-*v*-To oppress, make poor; everpower, crush; squeeze, press

Magpakahirap *i*-To hurt one's self by work.

Magpakailanman *adv* -Never, for ever and ever.

Magpakain-*v*-To feed, nourish, maintain.

Magpakainom-*v*-To drink often

Magpakalaon-*v*-To prolong, delay, retard, defer.

Magpakalnat-*v*-To prolong, defer, delay; retard; detain.

Magpakasakit *i*-To work until one become sick.

Magpakilala-*v*-To make known, introduce, lay before; expound.

Magpakita-*v*-To show, exhibit

Magpako *v*-To nail, spike

Magpakumpisal-*v*-To confess, receive confession

Magpalagay *v* To adduce, suppose.

Magpalagi-*i*-To accustom, frequent

Magpalago-*v*-To make fruitful, maintain or nourish plants

Magpalahaw-*i*-To exclaim shriek

Magpalakas-*v*-To strengthen, make, stronger, cheer, reanimate, give stregnth

Magpalaki-*i*-To increase, aggrandize, make larger

Magpalalo-*v*-To boast, drag, bully, be proud or haughty

Magpalamig *i*-To cool, refresh,

Magpalibhasa-*v*-Lo insult, revile, abuse, revile

Magmaligid-*v* To encompass, go round, encircle

Mapaliit-*v*-To lessen, diminish, make smaller

Magpalimos *i*-To beg, ask alms

Magpalipas-*v*-To pass, cause to pass, leave or let become stale

Magpalipathpat-*i*-To fly across.

Magpalit-*v*-To change, exchange, trade, barter, transfer.

Magpalitan-*v* To barter, exchange

Magpamana-*v*-To bequeath demtze

Magpamangha-*v*-To astonish; amaze

Magpamula-*v*-To commence, begin

Magpamulsa-*v*-To reimburse put in the pocket

Magpanayán-*v*-To continue, mal e equal

Magpangako-*v*-To promise, plight.

Magpangalan-*v*-To call, name, summon by name.

Magpangkat-*i*-To chapter, divide into chapters or paragraphs, paragraph.

Magpapalayok-*n* Potter

Magpapari-*v*-To admonish, correct, advise

Magpapaupa sa maghapon-*n*-Workman; journeyman; laborer.

Magpaputok-*v*-To have shot, cause to shoot

Magparaan-*v*-To leave or let pass, resort.

Magparátang-*v* To accuse; charge, impute, attribute

Magpari *v*-To be ordained, be a priest

Magparis *v*-To compare, make alie or equal.

Magparusa *v*-To chastize, punish, remonstrate, sentence

Magpasakit-*r* To cause or give pain feel.

Magpasalamat *r*-To thank.

Magpasalubi-_v_-To except; exclude; keep out.

Magpasandali-_ı_-To lend.

Magpasawatan-_ı_-To compromise without advantage

Magpasial-_v_-To take a walk, stroll, saunter.

Magpasinmuno-_v_-To begin, commence.

Magpasiya-_ı_-To sentence, resolve, determine, give sentence.

Magpasok-_ı_-To put in

Magpastol-_v_-To herd; watch cattle

Magpasuso-_ı_-To nurse; give suck

Magpataba-_v_ To fatten

Magpatahimik-_ı_-To calm, pacify, appease

Magpatama-_v_-To hit the right thing

Magpatawa-_v_-To cause to laugh, make laugh

Magpatawad-_v_-To pardon, forgive.

Magpatotoo-_v_ To assure, approve, prove; credit.

Magpatubo-_ı_-To loan money on interest, cause to grow

Magpatuloy-_ı_-To shelter, protect, continue, protract.

Magpatupat-_r_-To smoke a pipe

Magpatutot-_v_ To be lewd, prostitute.

Magpatutot-_n_-Harlot prostitute, strumpit, whore.

Magpaugap-_ı_-To counterfeit, forge, mimic, feign affect, pretend

Magpauna-_ı_-To advance, go first

Magpaunawa-_ı_-To announce, proclaim, advertise

Magpaunti-_ı_-To diminish, lessen, shorten make smaller

Magpaupa-_ı_-To rent, hire, let

Magpayo-_ı_-To reconcile, council.

Magpighati-_ı_-To grieve, disgust, detest, feel; consume with rage.

Magpilapil-_v_-To embank, terrace

Magpilipit _ı_-To distort; twist

Magpinta-_v_-To paint, delineate, picture.

Magpisan-_ı_-To join, associate, adhere; be united, unite, assemble; congregate, meet, abut, adjoin

Magprisk-_v_-To sputter

Magpita-_ı_-To desire, wish, long for, require

Magpugad-_v_-To nestle, dwell.

Magpugay-_v_-To salute, hail, greet.

Magpugot-_ı_-To behead, decapitate

Magpuhkat-_ı_-To cramp, convulse

Magpumilit-_ı_-To persist, exert, enforce, contend, force, urge, persevere

Magpunas-_v_-To wash the hands and face

Magpunla- -To propagate, make a nursery, sow broadcast.

Magpuno-_ı_-To direct, preside; command; govern.

Magpurol-_ı_-To become dull, get dull.

Magpustahan-_v_-To bet, wager.

Magputok _ı_-To shoot, fire, break, burst, split, crack

Magputok sa towards-To burst with, laughter.

Magpuyat _v_-To stay up all night

Mag rabo-_ı_-To mortise.

Magrenuncia-_ı_-To renounce; resign; give up; abjure

Magsabi-_ı_-To tell, say, speak; express

Magsabi ng̃ cahang̃inan-_ı_-To brag, boast.

Magsabi ng̃ mabuti-_v_ To expound, explain, interpret, translate

Magsabog-_ı_-To scatter; propagate, sow broadcast; throw broadcast

Magsabog ang ari-_ı_-To misspend squander, lavish, dissipate

Magsabong _v_ To pit cocks

Magsagsag-_v_-To trot; be in haste

Magsaka-_ı_-To till, cultivate

Magsakdal-_ı_-To go to another and ask a favor, petition.

Magsalaghati-_v_-To resent

Magsalamangka-_ı_-To juggle.

Magsalangsang-_v_-To oppose, contradict, confute

Magsalansang̃an-_ı_-To impugn; contradict; confute

Magsalat-_v_-To Hunger, want, need; lack; famish, starve; be hungry or in need

Magsalita-_ı_-To talk, speak reason address, harangue, converse

Magsahtaan-_ı_-To converse, talk together, condition, convenant, parley

Magsalung̃atan-_ı_-To contradict, gainsay

Magsamasama-_v_-To unite put together, bind; alloy, mix, league, coalesce, collect, gather

Magsanay-_ı_-To practice; exercise

Magsangalang-_ı_ To defend, protect, assist' prohibit

Magsang̃ayon-_ı_-To associate, join, unite, be united.

Magsanklletas-_ı_-To wear toe slippers

Magsapantaha-_ı_-To suppose, suspect, conjecture; presume

Magsasabon-_n_-Soapmaker.

Magsasaka-_n_-Farmer; agriculturist

Magsaulian-_ı_-To return, restore, give, back.

Magsaya-_ı_-To be happy, enjoy one's self, be comforted, sport

Magsayaw-_ı_-To dance

Magsaysay-_ı_-To to relate, report, explain, announce, tell, characterize

Magsikad _ı_-To kick

Magsil ap-v To economize, save
Magsilbe-v-To serve, be useful
Magsinok t-To hiccough.
Magsingkaw-i-To hitch up, harness; yoke
Magsinungaling-v-To lie, fib, deceive, falsify
Magsira-v-To break, rot, degrade.
Magsiraan ng puri-i-To tarnish or darken one's reputation
Magsirain-i-To blacken or dar en.
Magsisi-v-To repent, rue, bemoan
Magsiste-r-To assist, make or cause to laugh
Magsubsob-v-To fall down, crawl under anything
Magsubukan-v-To trig spig, watch, rival.
Magsugal-v-To play cards, gamble
Magsuhol-v-To bribe.
Magsuntik-v-To rob, plunder
Magsuka-v-To vomit, disgorge
Magsulsol-v-To provoke, induce, excite, arouse
Magsumakit-v-To economize, lay up, lay away, hoard
Magsumbong-v-To Accuse, blame, tell, denounce
Magsumikap v-To economize, lay away
Magsungad-v-To pit two animals
Magsuot-v-To put on; wear, cover, screen, put in
Magsuot sa gubat-v To hide in the woods
Magsupling-v-To sprout, shoot, bud, germinate.
Magsuri v To fold; plait; double, crimple, probe, investigate, eaxmine
Magsusutla-n-Silkmercer.
Magtaan-v-To reserve, defer, exempt, conceal, separate, restrain, leave
Magtabil-v-To gossip
• Magtaglay-v-To fetch, carry; wear
Magtago-v-To hide; conceal, disguise; hoard, collect, protect, shelter
Magtahan-v-To cease, desist, forbear.
Magtaka-v-To marvel, wonder
Magtakapan-v-To insult.
Magtacbo t-To run, caper, frolic, frisk
Magtali-v-To tie, bind, fagot
Magtalo-i-To dispute, contend, rival, fight, struggle, antagonize; cope
Magtaman-i To suffer, tolerate
Magtamasa-v-To gain, succeed, procure, acquire
Magtamo-t-To follow, pursue, reach, overtake, come up, obtain
Magtampo-i-To pout, be sulky.
Magtanan i-To run away, leave secret ly, skip out.
Magtanan ng sundalo-r To desert
Magtanka i To be motheaten

Magtanga-a-Motheaten
Magtangal-v-To take apart, take to pieces, discompose
Magtangkal-t-To lump
Magtangol-v To defend, protect, help, assist, resist, oppose; repel.
Magtanim-v-To sow, plant
Magtanong-v-To ask, question, enquire, consult
Magtapon-v-To throw away, mis-spend.
Magtapon ang ari-v To mis-spend
Magtatag-v-To found, institute, build, set up, establish, construct, edify
Magtatagal-a-Lasting, durable
Magtatapayan-n-Potter, earthen ware maker
Magtayo-v-To build; found; institute, edify, construct, form.
Magtihaya-v-To fall on the back, lay face up
Magtiis-v-To suffer, endure, abstain, refrain, tolerate; submit; resign, undergo.
Magtuka-v-To determine, decide
Magtimbang-i-To weigh.
Magtinda-i-To sell, vend; cater
Magtipid-i-To economize, lessen expenses
Magtipiran-v To economize, curtail or clip expenses
Magtipon-i-To accumulate, gather, lay up, store; save, lay away, cumulate
Magtira-i-To reserve, defer, exempt, conceal, separate, restrain, leave.
Magtirik-v-To set on end
Magtitinapay i-To Baker, breadmaker
Magtitisa-n-Tilemaker
Magtrabaho-i-To work, labor.
Magtubo-i-To gain, profit, grow; increase
Magtulak-i-To push; impel; press for ward
Magtulakan v-To push; shove.
Magtuli-v oT circumsize
Magtuloy-i-To continue, proceed, advance; stay, sojourn
Magtulungan-v-To favor, protect; help, assist, aid
Magtunaw-v-To dissolve; liquefy; melt
Magtungayaw-v-To curse, swear, blaspheme, execrate
Magturing-r To propose, guess; haggle, higgle, offer a certain price
Maturo i To teach, educate, breed, instruct drill, discipline, coach, edify.
Magturuan-i-To discipline, drill, punish.

Magtuos-v To balance an account; close an account; redeem a pledge.

Mag ubo-v-To cough.

Mag ugat ang halamanan v-To take root; sprout.

Magugol-a-Expensive; costly; highpriced.

Mag ugnay v-To add to; exaggerate; recompose; put in order.

Mag ugoy-v-To swing; rock; move to and fro.

Maguhit-a-Full of lines.

Maguho-v-To fall; collapse.

Mag ukol-v-To pertain; belong to.

Mag ukol parang may ari-v-To master; domineer.

Mag ulak-v-To reel; wind; wrap up·

Magulang-a-Ripe; mature; parent; aged.

Magulang-n-Parent.

Mag ulap-v-To cloud; darken, obscure.

Magulat-v-To be astonished, startled, surprised; astonish, surprise.

Magulatin-a-Timid; skittish; easily frightened.

Mag uliuli-k-To whirl; eddy.

Magulo-a-Noisy; troubled; disorderly; troublesome; chaotic; clangorous; blatant.

Magulo-v-To put heads together.

Magulo ang kalooban-a-Turbulent; unquite; dissatisfied; perturbed.

Magulungin-a-Rolling; wheeling; easily rolled.

Mag umpok-v-To converse; hold or carry on a conversation.

Magunigunihin-v-Apprehensive; fanciful; visionary; fearful; timid; sensitive.

Mag usap-v-To talk; converse; litigate; contend; dispute.

Mag usbong-v-To sprout; shoot up; bud; germinate.

Mag usisa-v-Investigate; pry; reconnoiter; espy; reconnoitre.

Magustuhan-v-To like; enjoy; be pceased with; be delighted.

Magutom-a-Hungry; ravenous; starved.

Magutom-v-To hanger; starve; famish; be hungry.

Mag utos-v-To order; send; command; ordain; enact.

Mag utos parang may ari-v-To master domineer.

Magviage-v-To travel, journey; make a journey.

Magvisita-v-To visit.

Magvoto-v-To vote.

Magwagi-v-To wave; brandish.

Magwalis-v-To sweep; brush.

Magwangki-v-To appear; see; hypocricize.

Magwari v-To think; meditate; muse contemplate; consider. reason; reflect, cogitate; ponder; theorize.

Magwariwari-v-To think; meditate; muse; consider; contemplate; reflect; cogitate; con; deem; reason.

Magyabang-v-To boast; brag; vaunt.

Magyari-v-To complete; finish.

Magyari ng salitaan-v-To contract.

Mahaba-a-Long; lengthy.

Mahabag-a-Compassionate, clement; sympathetic.

Mahabag-v-To sympathize; pity; have compassion; grieve; be sorry.

Mahabagin-a-Compassionate; merciful pious; piebald; holy; godly.

Mahabang lubha-a-Prolix; tedious; very long; troublesome.

Mahal-a-Costly; dear; highpriced; magnificent; grand: splendid.

Mahalaga-a-Precious; dear; costly; expensive; valuable.

Mahalal-v-To be elected; elect; choose; declare; decree.

Mahalata-v-To feel; note; percieve.

Mahalata-a-Notable; percievable.

Mahalay-a-Indecent; immodest; obscene; shameless; lewd; impure; mean; homely; ugly; bad; depraved; licentious; sordid; rude; imprudent; unbecoming; malicious; dirty; dishonest; slow; dull; torpid.

Mahalan-v-To grow dear; overvalue; raise the price.

Mahalin-v-To have regard; overvalue; value; profer; endear; enshrine; praise appreciate; love.

Mahal kay sa iba-a-Superior; paramount; dearer; more dear.

Mahal na ugali-a-Noble; honorable; gentlemanly; ladylaike; prudent.

Mahambal-a-Mournful; sad.

Mahangal-a-Stupid; dull; mean; low; abject.

Mahapdi-a-Sensitive; painful; smarting; prickly; pungent.

Mahapdian v-To irritate; smart; cause a sharp pain.

Mahapis a-Sad; mournful; grievous.

Mahapis-v-To sadden; afflict; be mournful.

Mahapishapis-a-Woebegone.

Mahawig-v-To incline; be disposed.

Mahibang-v-To rave; dote; become mad; go crazy; become demented.

Mahiga-v-To lie down; lay down.

Mahigit a-More.

Mahigpit-a-Tight; tenacious; exact; severe; harsh; strict; taut: rigid; close; inflexible; narrow.

10

Mahigpit kumapit-a Tenacious, firm, obstinate

Mahigpit na nasa-n-Eagerness; violent desire

Mahikayat-v-To excite, rouse, stimulate; be attracted

Mahilig-v-To incline, be inclined

Mahilig a-Liable, subject

Mahilig sa pakikipagtalo-a-Peevish, touchy

Mahilig sa basagulo-a-Ensnaring, quarrelsome.

Mahilig sa kasiyahan-a-Temperate, regulated, quiet

Mahilig sa pakikipagsama a-Sociable, corteous, social

Mahiman a-Prudent; slow; moderate

Mahina a-Weak, languid, infirm, feeble, rickety, delicate; frail, thin, imbecile; insecure, withered

Mahina ang tainga a-Hard of hearing

Mahinahon-a-Moderate, prudent, temperate, circumspect, abstemious, affable, peaceful, courtious, confidential, quiet, frugal, continent, reserved

Mahinahon-adv -Moderately, calmly, quietly, peacefully

Mahinang loob-a-Coward, languid, weak, forceless.

Mahinang umintindi a-Stupid, slow to comprehend, dull minded

Mahingil a Liable, subject, inclined

Mahinhin a-Chaste, pure, modest, decorous, polite, kind, obliging; honest, moderate, attentive, circumspect, decent; virtuous, heedful, unassuming

Mahinog v-To ripen mature, mellow

Mahinto v-To stop

Mahinto muna v-To stop before

Mahipohipo a Tactile, frequently handled.

Mahirap-a-Poor, hard, difficult, burdensome, needy, grievous, important; dissatrous, dolorous, weary, anxious, painful, decrepid, tiresome, onerous: arduous, profound, disadvantageous, abstract, inaccessible, faint

Mahirap gawin-a-Laborious; difficult, tiresome, painful, hard to accomplish.

Mahirati a-Usual, ordinary, used, accustomed

Mahiya-v To be ashamed; blush

Mahiya-a-Shameful, timid, backward

Mahiyain-a-Timid, shameful, backward, bashful, shy

Mahiyang-v-To be acclimated, united, or accustomed.

Mahiyawin a Clamorous, vociferous, boisterous, loud voiced

Mahubdan v To denude disrobe.

Mahubog-a-Phant; easily bent

Mahubog sa lambot-v-To bend because of the softness.

Mahukay-a-Pitted, full of holes

Mahulaan-v-To foretell, prophesy

Mahulagpos v-To avoid, escape liberate, avoid punishment

Mahulog-v-To fall, yield under a difficulty

Mahulog sa ibang wica-v-To interpret, translate

Mahulog sa iba v-To relapse; fall back.

Mahusay a Sound, healthy, wholesome, arranged, secure, discreet, generous noble, safe, sincere, just

Mahusayin-v To arrange; justify, make good, classify

Maibigan-v-To like have regard for, appreciate

Maibigan-a Friendly, beloved, temperate.

Maibigan sa kasiyahan a-Loving, friendly, beloved

Maibsan-v-To throw off

Maigot-a Paltry, niggard, niggardly

Maigot-v-To be bound tightly

Maihaw-v-To be roasted, roast

Mainom-a Potable, drinkable

Maikli-a Short, brief, concise, small limited, diminished, compendious, summary

Maikli ang isip a Dull minded

Mailag-v-To avoid, be bashful or shy be afraid of

Mailagan-a-Avoidable, evitable, eludible, that which may be avoided

Mailap a-Wild, unsocial, intractable

Maimot a-Close, chary

Maimot at masakim-a-Avaricious

Mainam a-Handsome, fair, pretty, fine, genteel, dainty, tasty, cheerful; neat, entertaining beautiful, exquisite, gorgeous, janty, jaunty

Mainam na lubos-a-Elegant, exquisite, excellent; graceful, dexterous

Maingat a-Careful prudent, moderate, modest, circumspect, vigilant, mindful, solicitous, cautious, chary, confidential, aware, precautionary, precautional, reserved

Maingat a Carefully, moderately, prudently

Mainipi-v To be impatient, restless, fidgety or jealous, vex, irritate.

Mainipan-a-Restless, impatient, fidgety, jealous

Mainis-v-To smother

Mainit a Hot, warm, fiery, sultry.

Mainit ang ulo a Quick tempered, hot headed.

Maintindihan v To understand; comprehend

Maipagkakaila-a-Deniable

Maipahihintulot-a-Permissible

Mupapalit a-Changeable, permutable

Manog a Loving, lovable, fine, tender, affectionate, delicate mild; kind, pleasing, perfect

Mairogin-a-Lovable; amiable, pleasing

Mais-n Coin.

Maisan-n Cornfield

Maisasabit-a Fit to be hung up -n-that which may be hung up

Maisipan-v To remember remind, think, meditate

Maisipan a-Pensive, thoughtful

Maitatago-a-Concealable

Maitatangi a Deniable.

Maitim-a-Black, blackish, jetty, obscure, gloomy, dark, raven; ebony; dark brown

Maiwan-i To leave, forego, quit.

Máka v-Can, could, having the power.

Makabubuhay a Nutrimental, nourishing

Makagagahng a-Sanative, sanable, healthful

Magkagupilit-n Cutter

Makahalin ang loob-v-To call or court the love of another

Makahapis-a-Painful, sad piteous

Makahawa-v-To contage, be contagious, infect, corrupt, pervert

Makahawig a Propitious

Makahinga sa harap-i-To breathe audibly; perspire.

Makahihiwa-a-Sectile

Makahilagpos v-To pull apart; elude, slip away, get away

Makahon v-To embale, be packed or boxed up

Makahulubog a Phable.

Makaisa ang halaga-v-To be equivalent, be of equal value.

Makaisa ang layo-v-To be of an equal distance

Makaiyak-a-Crying

Makakaiba-a-Alterable alterant

Makakain-a Eatable, edible, comestible

Makakamtan a-Attainable, obtainable.

Makakita-v-To see

Makalat-v To scatter, extend

Makalawang a Rusty

Makaligtas-v-To liberate, save from danger.

Makahlin a Shady.

Makahlimot-a Omissible

Makahhwanag a-Illuminative; illuminating

Makalimot-i-To forget; omit miss, neglect

Makahnga a-Careful; solicitous, vigilant: mindful, assiduous, attentive, diligent, anxious, obsequeous, compliant

Mekalugod v-To be pleasing, gratifying or humorous

Makahulugi-a-Disadvantageous losing

Makalulugod a Agreeable, pleasing, smiling; humorous

Makalunos-i-To cause sadness

Makalunos a-Painful; sad; piteous.

Makamamatay-a Deadly, mortal

Makamandag-a-Poisonous; venemous

Makamandagan-i To be poisonous, be attected by poison

Makanaw-i-To dilute, dissolve

Makapagbigay lihim i-To make shady, produce shade

Makapal-a-Thick, large, corpulent, compact, numerous, serried, stocky, gross.

Makapal ang buhok a-Hairy

Makapainahala-n-Jurisdiction;authority.

Makapamala v-To heed, watch, manage.

Makapangyarihan a Powerful, potent, omnipotent, most powerful, almighty, eminent, wealthy

Makapangyavari a-Powerful potent, mighty; wealthy

Makapangyayari sa lahat-a Omnipotent, almighty, most powerful

Makapasok-v-To contain, be able to enter

Makapitong doble-a-Sevenfold

Makapulas-v- o escape; avoid danger.

Makapupurga n Cathartic

Makaraan-i-To elapse, go by, pass.

Makasalanan n Sinner, offender, delinquent

Makasama-i-To hurt, injure, cause pain,

Makasapat-v-To be just or sufficient satisty, gratify

Makasasama-a-Injurious, harmful

Makasasawa-a-Tiresome

Makasilaw-r To dazzle

Makasilingit-i To crowd in, slip intake part aiter the proper time.

Ma asing layo—Of an equal distance

Makasira v To be able to break or destroy

Makasistra-a Harmful, injurious, not healthful, deleterious, disadvantageous, noxious

Makatanaw i To see, look view

Makatas a-Juicy, sappy, succulent.

Makatatawa a Laughable, ludicrous, smiling, agreeable, droll, absurd.

Makatawan-a-Vast, massive, corpulent; tat; large

Makatekas i To cheat, deceive, swindle.

Makatimbang-*v*-To balance, counterpoise, weigh.

Makatitis-*a*-Bearable; forbearing, patient

Makatulad *v*-To be lake, resemble

Makatulog-*v*-To sleep

Makaulimig-*v*-To misunderstand; hear imperfectly

Makawala-*v*-To escape; avoid

Makawangis *a*-Alike, equal, similar, as similated

Makaya-*v*-To be able, have the power or ability

Makayamutan-*v*-To displease, offend, disgust

Makialam-*v*-To interfere, meddle, intermeddle.

Makiapid-*v*-To seduce, fornicate adulterate.

Makiayon-*v*-To coincide, acquiese, yield have the same idea

Makibagay-*v*-To sympatize, accomodate

Makihalubilo-*v*-To be one of a multitude

Makusa *v* To yield, coincide, agree, attest; comform, prove.

Makusa sa pasiya-*v*-To feel or grieve for another.

Makilala-*v*-To know, understand; detect, meet, ascertain, discover, recognize, judge

Makiling-*a*-Leaning, inclined

Makihtiin-*a*-Ticklish

Makimatyag-*v*-To look after, care for, attend to pay attention

Mákina *n*-Machine

Makinabang-*v*-To gain; profit, interest

Makinang-*a*-Bright, shiny, polished, glossy, brilliant; lustrous

Mákinang pangapas-*n* Harvester; mower, reaper

Makinig-*v*-To hear; listen

Makinis-*a*-Glossy, elegant, fine, shiny, nice, gay; graceful, lucid, shining, plain, neat, natty; terse, slick.

Makintab-*a*- Showy, shiny; lambent, lucient; glossy

Makintal-*v*-To print, stamp, emboss

Makipagaway-*v*-To dispute, litigate, contend; fight, rival, quarrel opposse pick; a quarrel

Makipagbabag-*v*-To fight, rival contend, quarrel

Makipagbaka *v* To war; fight, attack, combat, oppose.

Makipagdamdam-*v*-To feel, grieve.

Makipaghamon-*v* To fight oppose, combat defy challenge

Makipagapowa *v* To be cordial, kind, social or corteous.

Makipagcasundo-*v*-To reconcile, comply, be friends or congenial

Makipaglamas-*v*-To attack, assault, fight, combat

Makipaglikutin-*v*-To be boisterous, be, rompish or noisy

Makipagmook-*v*-To fight, war; oppose combat

Makipagpasiya-*v*-To feel, grieve

Makipagsalitaan-*v*-To converse, talk, enter into a conversation

Makipagtalo-*v*-To dispute, argue, litigate, contend, quarrel, resist, oppose, repel, murmur, snarl.

Makipagusap-*v*-To litigate, dispute, study, talk, discuss, contend, converse, speak, reason, confer, harangue

Makipagyari-*v*-To complete, finish

Makipot-*a*-Narrow, close, tight.

Makiskis-*v*-To scratch, waste by friction.

Makisama-*v*-To be friends; be with

Makisap-*a*-Brilliant, shiny, bright, lucid, lucient, glossy

Makita-*v* -To see, look, meet, ken.

Makitalamitam-*v*-To meddle, interfere

Makitang muh-*v*-To review, see or meet again

Makitid-*a*-Narrow, close; tight; rigid, exact

Makiusap-*v*-To entreat, speak, harangue, reason, implore, crave; beg pray; request, petition.

Makiugali-*v* To sympathize, be congenial.

Makuha-*v*-To get, take

Makulot-*a*-Curly

Makulot-*v* -To curl

Makunan-*v*-To miscarry, menstruate very strongly.

Makupad-*a*-Dilatory, lazy, dull, indolent, late, slow.

Makupitin-*v*-To purloin; pinch, knock down

Makuro *v*-To know, understand

Makuto-*a*-Lousy.

Malában-*a*-Opposite

Malabas-*v*-To be excluded or kept out, be exempt

Malabis *a*-Excessive, exhorbitant, enormous, profuse, abundant, lavish, extreme

Malabis *adv* -Abundantly, lavishly, excessively, profusely.

Malabis *n*-Rest, remainder, residue.

Malabis na kasamaan *n*-Perversity, wickedness

Malabis na luat *n*-Tedium, tediousness, prolixity

Malabis na pagmamahal-n-Predilection, excessive love

Malabis ng tipid a Miserable, mean; miserly, stingy

Malabnaw-a-Thin, rare, diluted

Malabo-a-Muddy; obscure, murky, dark, gloomy, dubious, indistinct, unintelligible, enigmatic, thick

Malagak-v-To put in charge of another,

Malagamgamgam-a-Tepid, lukewarm

Malagas ang dahon-a-To fall off (per to leaves)

Malaglag-v-To fall

Malagkit-a-Sticky, unctious; greasy-mucous, gluttinous, soft.

Malago-a-Leafy, fertile; luxuriant, fruitful, copious.

Malago ang buhok-a-Hairy

Malagot-v-To break, pull apart

Malagot ang hininga-v-To expire, die

Malagpos-a-Exxcessive, overabundant

Malagpos-adv -Excessively, abundantly, profusely.

Malagpos-n-Residue, remainder, over-plus

Malagpos ang dami-a-Overabundant, exuberant; too many

Malagpos ang kababaan a-Obese, too fat

Malait-a-Contemptible, despicable, low, abject

Malakad ang paa i-To go afort, walk.

Malakas-a Strong; stout, firm, husky, vigorous, mighty, drawny, burly, hale; corpulent robust, rigid, perfect, sound, solid, stocky, inflexible, hard, coarse, brave, valiant; active, effective, bouncing, vehement

Malakas ang katawan-a-Healthy, sound.

Malakas kumain n-Glutton, healthy eater

Malakas uminom-n-Tippler, drunkard

Malakhin-v-To honor, respect, dignify, adorn

Malaki-a-Large, great, vast, huge, burly; gigantic; heavy, weighty, important, compact, strong, lofty, corpulent, circumspect, arduous, stout; grievous

Malaking lakas n-Power, might

Malakingmalaki-a-Very great or large, chief, principal

Malaking pag-ibig n-Deep love

Malaking tawo-n-Largeman, gentleman

Malaki pa-a-Larger, greater

Malakuko-a-Warm; lukewarm; tepid

Malalaluan-a-Superable, conquerable

Malalim a-Deep, profound

Malaman-a-Fleshy, full of meat.

Malaman-v-To know, wit, ken, understand, comprehend, cognize.

Malambot-a-Soft, spongy, pliable, limber; bland, mellow, tender, lithe, flexible, delicate, docile plaint; weak, mild.

Malambot ang ugali a Submissive, humble, resigned, affable, meek; gentle, placid solft tempered; lenient

Malamig-a Cold, frigid; cool, bleak, retrigerant.

Malangib-a- Scabby, scurvy, scurry; mangy

Malangis a-Oily, oleagneous, fine.

Malanta-v-To pine or fall away wither; dry up

Malaon-n-Time, tide, term, season, age, duration

Malaon-a-Prolix, old

Malapad-a-Wide, open, spacious, capacious.

Malapad-n-One cent

Malapit-adv.-Near, close

Malapit a-Proximity, next; negbhboring; contiguous, mediate, impending.

Malapít na malapit-adv -Very near, nearly, almost

Malapot-a-Thick, dense, close

Malasa a-Palatable, tasty, mellow

Malasin-v-To run over, peruse, survey review, revise, observe, notice, heed, mind

Malason-v-To be poiasn.

Malason-a-Poisonous, venemos

Malata-a-Tender, weak, delicate, languid faint, soft, heartless, withered

Malawak-a-Large, extensive, ample, wide, capacious, spacious; champaign.

Malaway a-Salivous; salivary.

Malawig-v-To explain in a round about way.

Malayo-a-Distant, remote, outlying, far, retired, solitary

Malayo sa kaguluhan-a-Quiet calm

Malayo sa kapowa-a Shy, diffident.

Malayo pa sa-adv.-Beyond, farther, on the other side.

Mali-n-Mistake; error, fault; defect, oversight, blunder

Mali a-False, mendacious, erroneous, bad, incorrect, faulty

Mali sa sulat o limbag-n-Erratum

Malibag-a-Dirty, greasy, filty

Malibog-a-Lewd, lustful; immodest, indecent, obscene, impure, shameless

Maligaw v-To mistake; commit an error lose one's way, err.

Maligaya-a-Joyful, pleasant, merry, happy, fortunate; prosperous, convivial, holiday.

Mahgo-z-To bathe, take a bath

Mahgtus r-To be saved

Malhhim a-Secret reserved, cautious, confidential, silent

Malhhis-z-To err, mistake, misjudge, become lost

Malut-a-Lettle small, short, scanty

Malut na kuta n Bulwark, defence

Malut na malut-a-Very small, very litle.

Malut pa sa-a Smaller, less

Mali ot-a-Restless, boisterous, mischievous, hvely, noisy, turbulent

Maliksi-a-Active. quick speedy, expeditious, smart, nimble, light, hee, prompt, lithesome, highspirited, swift, ready, spry, dihgent, loose, mercurial

Malihm-a Shady, umbrageous

Malihmutin-a Fo'getful, oblivious, neglectful

Malmbag z-To stamp, ·print

Mahmit-a-Close dense, thick, compact; condensed

Malimutan-v-To forget; neglect, omit, mistake, unlean

Malinamnam-a-Delicious, select, mellow, buttery

Mahnaw a-Clear, bright plain, distinct, open, evident, manifest, public transparent, sheer; obvious

Mahnaw dingin-a Intelligible, concievable, pronounced

Malingatin-z-To neglect, forget; overlook, skip.

Malingat a Forgetful, neglectful

Malinis-a-Clean, pure, clear, decent, unmixed, tree, neat, plain, immaculate, unadulterated, virtuous, devout, tidy, honest, modest, refined, mere

Malinis na loob a-Sincere, clear, frank, cordial, pure

Malinsad z-To disjoint.

Malipo v-To extinguish; become exterminated or destroyed

Malipos-a-Pustly, fnll of pustles.

Malipos-z-To be full of.

Mahrot-a-Unsavory; having a bad taste

Mahted-a-Strong, robust, nervous, vigorous

Malito v To mistake, err, embarrass; be uneasy or discomposed

Mahwag-a-Slow, tardy, slothful, indolent, lazy

Maliwag mangyari-a-Difficult, hard

Maliwanag-a-Clear, bright, evident, obvious, luminous; lucid, distinct, refulgent, overt, ostensible, express, notable; quite, pronounced, point blan'\ sheer.

Mahwanag na malabis a-Glistening, too shiny or bright

Malowag-a-Wide, hee, open, loose

Malowag-a-Loose, free, open, wide.

Maluag ang kamay-a-Spendtrhift, prodigal

Maluag ang loob-a-Free hearted, generous calm, free, good natured

Mahialhati-a Blessed, glorious, happy, beloved

Maluag-a-Wide diffuse, ample, open; spacious, champaign diffusive, capacious, slow

Malnang mangusap-a-Eloquent

Maluat-a-Slow, tardy, protracted, prolix, tedious

Malubay-a Easy, pliant, amiable, pleasing, slow, easy of success

Malubay ang asal-a Amiable, pleasing, good natured

Malnbay makipagusap-a-Mild or speech

Malubay na loob-a Meck, gentle, tamequiet, mild

Malubha-a-Excessive, extreme

Malubha-adv Too; very

Malubog-z-To sink, submerge

Malugas-v-To fall out, shed hair.

Malugod-a Amiable, pleasing, happy; merry, convivial, good natured

Malugod-v-To be happy, contented, pleased, satisfied, delighted or convivial

Malukong-n-Concave, concavity, hollow; hollowness

Malulan v-To contain, hold, have, comprise, be held.

Malulutang a-Bouyant

Maluma-z-To become old, stale or musty

Malumanay-v-To Docile, gentle, slow; meek, tame.

Malumbak-a-Pitted, full of holes

Malumbay-a-Gloiny, sad, sorrowful, mournful, plaintive, mean.

Malumbay-v-To be afflicted or sad

Malumbay na loob-a Sad; mournful.

Malumot-a-Mossy, oozy, shmy

Malumpo v To have the dingue, give way in the knees

Malundo a-Sagged

Malungkot-a Sad, sorrowful, gloomy, unhappy mournful, melancholy, mean, rueful, bleak, hapless, downcast, crestfallen, chapfallen, contrite plaintive pensive, disconsolate

Maluningning a-Bright shining; brilliant, glistening glittering

Malunusan-r To be sad or mournful.

Malupa-a Earthy, having much land, territorial

Malupaypay n To grow or become weak or languid

Malupavpay -a-Languid, weak

Malusaw -a-Liquid

Malusaw v-To dilute, dissolve

Ialuto-i-To boil, cook.

Ialutong a Brittle, fragile

Iamaang i-To wonder, stare

Iamaga v-To swell, become swollen, tumefy

Iamagitan-v-To intercede, interpose, mediate, bespeak

Iamahal-v-To grow or become dear, raise the price

Iamahala-v-To manage, look after, heed, take care, keep, govern, command, direct, administer, man, wield, reek, boss.

Iamagpag v-To shake, wag

Iamalagi-v To continue, endure, habituate, subsist, protract

Iamalago-i-To become fruitful, be abundant

Iamali-i-To err, mistake, equivocate, blunder; misjudge; commit a mistake

Iamali ang diñg-v-To misunderstand

Iamalo-v-To falsify, be false

Iamalso-n-Falsifier, falsificator

Iamamayapa n-Pacificator; pacifier

Iamana-v-To inherit.

Iamauas-i-To swell, tumefy

Iamangha-i-To wonder, marvel, stare

Iamanhid-v-To numb, benumb, cramp, become torpid or senseless

Iamanhik v-To intercede interpose, mediate, go up

Iamansa-i To brag, glory, boast

Iamansag-v To spot

Iamantal-i-To be flea biten

Iamantika-a-Puttery, mellow, fat, corpulent, coarse, obese

Iamantog-v-To inflate, fill with wind, blow full of wind.

Iamaos v To become hoarse

Iamaos a-Hoarse.

Iamasdan-v-To see, watch; detect, find, discover, meet with; hit upon

Iamaslang v To be rude or disrespectful

amatay-v-To die, perish, end, go out; stop, terminate or conclude life

Iamaulo-v-To fill, be filled or stuffed

Iamaya-adv.-Presently; soon immediately, right away, at once; then, before long, in a moment, after

Iamili-i-To choose, buy, purchase, go shopping, prefer.

Maminsanminsan-adt Now and then sometimes, from time to time

Mamintas v To find fault; censure; ridicule, crrticize

Maminsa-v-To iron

Mamohaghag-v To ranify, become thin.

Mamook-v-To war; fight, oppose

Mamualan-v To fill; stuff, satisfy.

Mamuhi-i-To disgust, displease, offend, vex; molest, loathe, excite.

Mamuhunan-i-To found, furnish capital

Mamuisan-i-To loan on interest, rent for cash

Mamukha v-To resemble, be like, favor,

Mamukod-v To separate, divide, be distinct, except, distinguish

Mamukod sa lahat-i-To surpass; outvie, exceed, excel

Mamula-v-To redden, blush, dye red

Mamulaklak-v-To flower, bloom, flourish, thrive.

Mamulamula a Reddish

Mamulañgos-v-To slip or run through the fingers

Mamulayan-i-To have knowledge

Mamulayan-a-Wise, knowing

Mamuñga-i-To bear fruit, produce, bring forth, flower, be fruitful

Mamumula-That which will become red

Mamulubi-i To beg, be poor, impoverish, hunger, starve, famish

Mamuno-v-To command, lead, head, marshal

Mamumuhunan n Capitalist

Mamuti-v-To whiten.

Mamutik-i To become muddy

Mana-n-Inheritance, heirloom, rheum, patrimony.

Manabako v-To smoke cigars

Manada-n-Flock, herd

Managal-i-To last, continue, subsist; endure, persist.

Managhoy-v-To lament mourn; grieve, cry, bewail

Managot-i-To bail, answer

Manahan-v-To inhabit, reside dwell

Manaig-i-To conquer, predominate, excel, outdo, surpass

Managing i-To lament, bewail, tell one's misfortuness.

Manainga-v-To listen, hear en, hear, attend

Manakanaka-adi.-Sometimes, now and then, from time to time

Manakit-v-To hurt, wound, offend

Mana ot-i-To frighten, terrify, daunt, intimidate, scare

Manalangin-i To petition, harangue, beseech pray, plead invocate invoke_

Manalig-v-To have faith
Manalo-v-To win, gain; conquer, exult, triumph
Manamanahan a-Hereditary
Manambitan-v-To lament, mourn, cry; grieve, bewail
Manampalasan-v-To insult, offend; make, angry; revile, abuse, injure
Mananagot-n-Bondsman
Mananagpi-n-Cobbler, one who patches.
Mananagwan-n-Rower, paddler
Mananakop-n-Savior, rescuer, redeemer.
Manananim-n-Planter, one who plants
Mananayaw-n Dancer
Manangis-v To cry, mourn; snivel, sob, grieve, lament, bewail
Manaog-v-To descend; go down
Manariwa v-To grow or become green
Manatili-v-To continue. protract, endure, subsist, last, fix, fasten persist
Manbabayo n Mallet
Mandala-n-Stack, rick
Mandaya-v-To deceive, cheat.
Manduduit-n-Thief, robber, freebooter, pillager, plunderer
Mandudurog-n-Pounder; one who flails
Manekas-v-To cheat, defraud, swindle, gull, impose upon
Manenegosio-a Negotiable.
Manenekas-n-Swindler, defaulter
Mangaahit n Barber
Manga anak-n Children
Manga bagaybagayan n Chattels, fixtures, furniture
Manga bagay nakasamsam sa kaaway-n-spoils, capture, prizes
Manga bituka n-Entrails, intestines.
Mangabayo-v-To ride a horse
Manga damit-n-Apparel
Mangagamot-n-Doctor, physician
Mangagamot na hindi nag-aral-n-Quack-doctor
Mangagamot ng hayop-n-Vetrinarian, terrier, horse doctor
Mangagaod-n-Rower, paddler
Mangagapas-n Reaper, harvester; mower, one who reaps or harvests
Manga gastos-n-Expenses, charges
Mangagaw n-Robber, plunderer; thief.
Mangagawa-n-Doer, maker, author.
Mangagawa ng bariles-n Cooper
Mangagawa ng kutsilo n-Cutler
Mangagat-v-To bite
Mangagkayonkayon-v-To agree, consent, decide
Mangahas-a-Agressive, saucy, bold, plucky, intrepid, forward, stalwart, stalworth; spunky, precocious; high-spirited
Mangahas v To dare; defy, venture try.

Mangahgkig-v-To shiver or tremble with cold.
Mangaling-v-To come from, issue from, arise, proceed or spring, from, originate in
Mangaling sa-v-To descend or come from
Manga manok-n-Poultry.
Mang amba-v-To pretend to threaten.
- Mangangahoy-n-Woodsman, woodcutter, timber merchant
Mangangalakal-n-Merchant, dealer, trader, shopkeeper.
Manganib-v-To be in danger
Manganinag v-To be transparent
Manga pagkain-n-Victuals, provisions
Mangapit v To grasp; seize, catch; snatch
Mangas-n-Sleeve
Mangas na maluag-n-Poke
Mangaso-v-To hunt, chase; go hunting, course, gun, go on a chase
Manga sundalong bantay-n-Guard.
Mangatal-v-To oscillate, vibrate, shiver; tremble
Mangangatal a-Tremulous, quivering.
Mangangayat-v-To become or grow thin, weak or poor.
Mangati-v-To attract by deceit
Mangatowiran-v To argue; reason, discuss, discourse, affirm, give a reason
Manga upang bato-n-Judge's fees
Mangayayat-v-To become weak, thin or languid, debilitate
Mangbabasag-n-Breaker, one who breaks
Mangbadya-v-To imitate, scoff, mock; ridicule, copy.
Mangbansag v-To nickname,
Mangbihag-v-To capture; captivate.
Mangbihag ng sasakyan-v-To pirate
Mangbububo n-Founder
Mangdirigma-n-Warrior, soldier
Mangubat-v-To go to the woods, work in the woods, become or grow woody
Mangugupit-n Barber
Mangha n-Wonder, admiration, amazement
Manghahabi n-Weaver.
Manghahabi nang sutla n Silkweaver
Manghahalo-n-Mixer, roller
Manghaharang-n Highwayman, bandit; robber.
Manghahayuma-n-Patcher; cobbler
Mangharang-v To hold; up, rob, plunder; assault
Manghawak v-To attach; hold up, catch, hold of
Manghihinang-n Soldering iron.

Manghimasok-ı-To interfere, interrup, meddle

Manghimatav-v-To faint, swoon

Manghina T-To weaken, pine, away, debilitate, extenuate waste away

Manghina ang loob-v-To dishearten, become, discouraged, grow dejected, become weak

Manghinapang-v-To become courageous, strengthen; invigorate, enforce, exert, reinforce, gather farce, make strong or brave.

Manghinguto v-To louse, clean from, lice or fleas

Manghiniksik-v-To louse, clean from lice or fleas

Manghinuha-v-To collect; gather

Manghiya-v-To shame, make ashamed, cause to be ashamed

Manghuhula-n Prophet

Mang iba-ı-To alter, change

Mang iba sa capowa-v-To distinguish one's self

Mang iit-v-To nickname, ridicule scoff, censure.

Mangilabot-ı-To terrify, frighten, scare

Mangilalás-v-To marvel, wonder

Mangilid-v-To approach the edge or shore

Mang imay v-To shell

Mangimig-ı-To tremble, sparkle, oscillate, vibrate

Mángiti-v To smile look pleased or happy

Mangitlog v-To lay eggs

Mang iyaw-ı-To mew

Mangkok-n-Crock, bowl, porringer

Mangkulam-v-To bewitch

Mang-laban ı-To struggle, fight, war; oppose; strive, contend; resist

Manglahik-n-Turner

Manghbak-v-To deride, scoff, jeer; mock.

Manghligis-n Miller, grinder

Manghlinag n-Cultivator, gardener, horticulturist

Mangloob v-To plunder, assault, pillage, rob

Mangluhsog-n-Plunderer, destroyer, pillager, consumer

Mangmang a-Folish, idiotic, stupid, dull, cowardly, ignorant, rude, silly

Mangnang-n-Brute, idiot

Mangmumuli n Grinder; miller.

Mangulo-v To wrangle, fight, perturb, disturb, harrow.

Mang ulo ı-To head, command, be chief, govern.

Mangulam-v-To eat nothing but meat.

Mangulo-v-T ourl

Mang umit-v-To steal, pilfer, rob; seize, grasp.

Mang unay-ı-To benumb

Mang undot-ı-To wrinkle, become wrinkly.

Mang urong-v-To revoke; retract, retreat, retire, go back

Mang nsap v-To talk, utter, converse speak; reason; harangue

Mangusap na hindi mawatasan-ı-To mumble, mutter

Mangyari n-Result, consequences

Mangyari-v-To happen, be done, have, may, can, be possible, be able or feasible, possess

Mangyari-conj -Because

Mangyaring bigla-v-To do in a hurry

Manyayari-a-Feasible practicable, possible, easy

Mangyayari sa arawaraw-a-Quotidian

Mangyayariring ihiwalay-a-Separable

Mangyayaring mabusog a Satiable

Mangyayaring mamah-a-Fallible

Mangyayaring mapagaling-a Curable, healable

Mangyayaring matapos-a-Terminable.

Mangyayaring matawa a-Laughable, ludicrous

Mangyayaring tusin-a-Sufferable, endurable.

Manhnd-n-Numbness, ache.

Mahilakbot-v-To terrify, scare, frighten.

Manhinayang v-To pity, have compassion, grieve for, be sorry for

Mambasib-ı-To attack, assault, undertake, attempt

Manibay-ı-To strengthen, secure, make fast, prop, affirm

Manigarrillo-u To smoke cigarettes

Mamihasa-ı-To accustom, inure.

Manin v-To prop up, build upon, raise on the hands, support on anything.

Manika-n-Wrist

Manikad-v-To kick, fling out.

Maniklnhod-v-To ask, beseech, petition, beg

Maniko v To elbow

Mamlbihan ı-To serve, favor, make use of

Manindal-v-To be added or supported by another.

Maningas-a-Fervent, ardent; vehement

Manigid n-Trowel

Maningil-v-To collect

Maningming-a-Bright, sparking, radiant, shining, luminous, lucid, refulgent, grittering, lucient, quivering

Maningning-ı-To sparkle, shine, glitter, radiate scintillate

Maniningil-n-Collector. taxgatherer.

Manininta-*n*-Lover

Maninna-*n*-Breaker, destroyer, misdealer, corruptor

Maninra ang ari ng may ari-*n*-Defaulter, defrauder

Maninra ng pagaari-*n*-Spendthrift, squanderer

Maninra ng puri-*n*-Defamer, slanderer

Maninirahan sa isang lugar-*n*-Inhabitant.

Manipis-*a*-Thin, slender, fine, sleazy.

Manirahan-*t*-To dwell; live, lodge, reside, inhabit

Manirintas *v*-To braid

Maniwala-*t*-To believe trow, credit, trust; have faith.

Maniwalain-*a*-Trustful

Manlalabra-*n*-Stonecutter

Manlalagari-*n*-Sawyer

Manlalahk *n*-Turner

Man lamang-*adv* -Though; at least, scarcely, hardly, otherwise.

Manliso-*n* Cramp, spasm

Manlulupig-*n*-Usurper

Manok-*n*-Rooster, cock; chanticleer

Mano na-*inter*-Would to GOD, for heaven's sake

Manong-*inter*-At least

Manong *adv*-Though, at least, scarcely, hardly; otherwise.

Manotnot-*v*-To ravel

Mansa-*n*-Spot, stain, blot, blur, blotch, blemish; faeces, dirt

Mansahan-*v*-To stain, spoil, blur, blot, tarnish; bespatter, daub, contaminate, blotch.

Mansuhin-*v*-To tame, domesticate.

Mantel-*n*-Mantel; tablecloth, altarcloth

Mantika-*n* Grease, lard, fat

Mantinilin-*t*-To maintain; support, sustain, hold up

Mantiquilla-*n*-Butter

Manuag-*t*-To hook with the horns, butt

Manuba-*t*-To deceive, cheat, defraud, swindle, impose upon

Manuba-*a*-Deceitful, cheating.

Manubig-*v*-To urinate, emit urine

Manubok-*t*-To spy, espy, watch; test, try.

Manuka-*v*-To peck

Manukod-*v*-To jut out, surpass, excel·

Manuluyan-*t*-To lodge, board, repose; entertain in one's home

Manumpa-*t*-To swear, mal e oath, curse, blaspheme

Manumpa ng kasinungalingan *v*-To perjure, swear falsely.

Manunula *n* Swindler, cheat

Manunubok *n* spy; hangdog

Manunula *n* Poet

Manunulid-*n*-Spinner of thread, examiner

Manunulong-*n*-Helper, aid, assistance, one who aids or assists.

Manunulsa-*n*-Raper, papist.

Manununog-*n*-Incendiary, burner

Manuya-*v*-To flatter, coax, delight, please

Maohngan-*v*-To bespatter with soot

Maowi-*v*-To return, devolve, become

Mapa-*n*-Map.

Mapag aglahi-*a*-Joking, funny happy

Mapag aksaya-*a*-Spendthrift, prodigal.

Mapag aksaya ang pag aari-*n*-Spendthrift, squanderer, prodigal

Mapagal-*v*-To fatigue, tire

Mapag ampon-*a*-Generous, noble, liberal, magnanimous; kind.

Mapagnumpa *a*-Cursing

Mapagbalbas-*n*-Flatterer

Mapagbanalbanalan-*a*-Hypocritical, insincere.

Mapagbasagulo-*a*-Quarrelsome, entangling, ensnaring; contious, bellicose, controvertible.

Mapagbata-*a*-Childish

Mapagbigay galang *a*-Respectful, polite

Mapagbigay loob-*a* Obedient, attentive, compliant

Mapagbiyaya-*a*-Extravagant, generous; wasteful, magnificent, grand, splendid

Mapagbuhos-*a*-Effusive

Mapagdasal-*a*-Prayerful, pious

Mapagmagaling-*a*-Curable, healable

Mapaghamon-*a*-Provocative, imitative, provocating, provoking

Mapaghangin-*a* Boastful, arrogant

Mapaghihk *a*-Snoring

Mapaghinala-*a* Fearful, distrustful, suspicious, suspective, jealous

Mapag isip-*a*-Thoughtful, imaginative, fanciful, contemplative

Mapagkit-*a*-Viscid viscous, sticky

Mapagkonowari-*a*-Hypocritical, deceitful, false, untrue; counterfeit

Mapaglantunay-*a*-Slothful, tardy, slouchy

Mapaglaro-*a*-Playful; jesting; rompish, wanton

Mapaglaway-*a* Salivous.

Mapaghnkod *a*-Compliant; loving, kind, obliging, obsequeous

Mapag lura *a*-Salivous

Mapagmarikit *a*-Spruce, proud, haughty, blown

Mapagmarunong-*n*-Pretender, sciolist

Mapagmasid-*a*-Observing, careful; cautious.

Mapagmayabang *a* Conceited, proud; haughty

MAP 83 MAP

Mapaginnra-a-Vile, slandering, low, slanderous

Mapagnasa-a-Desirous, eager; greedy, longing; lewd

Mapagod-r-To be or become tired; be fatigued or worn not

Mapagimbabaw-a Feigned, false

Mapagpalaro-a Playful

Mapagpanaginip-a-Dreamy

Magpagpasial-a Strolling, walking

Mapagpasiya a- Abstinent.

Mapagpatawa a-Laughable, happy, gay; joyful, ludicrous

Mapagpatubo a Fertile, profitable

Mapagpigil a-Temperate, frugal moderate; abstemious, prudent, sober

Mapagpita a-Respectfully, kind, generous

Mapagpitagan-a-Polite, respectful, kind, obliging, generous

Mapagpasinufigaling-a Lying, deceitful, erroneous.

Mapagsiste-a-Joyful, gay, festive, happy, graceful

Mapagsngal-n-Gambler

Mapagsumbong-n-Telltale.

Mapagsumbong-n-Informer, telltale, talebearer

Mapagtago-a-Secret, underhanded

Mapagtago ang galit-a Rancorous, spiteful

Mapagtamasa-a-Profuse; lavish; showy, abundant

Mapagtanim sa loob-a-Rancorous, spiteful

Mapagtapon-a-Spendthrift; prodigal

Mapagtawa-a-Laughable

Mapagtuis-a-Patient, forbearing, accomodating, abstinent.

Mapagtumpak-a-Prudish, fastidious.

Mapagtungayaw-a-Cursing, slanderous, vile, foulmouthed

Mapagupasala-a-Critical, slandering, insulting

Mapagwari-a Prudent; considerate, maditating, contemplative

Mapaghamak-v-To injure, hurt.

Mapahinga-v-To rest, repose, be calm, breathe, respire

Mapaigatan-a-To interpose, intercede

Mapaikpik v-To compress, press

Mapainom-v-To invite to drink

Mapait-a-Mordant, bitter, poignant, pungent, rough to the taste

Mapakaila-v-To deny, retract

Mapakaila-a-Deniable

Mapakaluma-r To be old or stale

Mapakatanda-r To be very old.

Mapakialam-a-Maddlesome, interfering.

Mapakikinabañgan-a-Profitable; servicible; utseful; beneficial

Mapalad a-Happy, lucky; fortunate, blessed, prosperous; successful; thriving

Mapalagay-i-To elect; chose, nominate.

Mapalaran-v-To be lucky, happy; or fortunate

Mapamanhin a-Superstitous

Mapamansa-a-Spotted; dirty, proud, arrogant

Mapamula-v-To commence, begin

Mapanaog-v To go down, descend, let or send down

Mapang agad-a-Quick, early

Mapang agad adv -Early, quiclkv

Mapangaw ang gulong v-To stick in the mud.

Mapangbabayi-a-Lewd, lustful

Mapanghibe a-Deceitful, cheating

Mapanglibka-a-Scoffing, ridiculous

Mapanglibak n-Scoffer; scorner, censor.

Mapanghicayat a-Attractive, exciting.

Mapanhinayang a-Attractive

Mapangiba-n-Gainsayer.

Mapanglaw-a-Gloomy dark; obscure, sorrowful, sad, mournful; sullen; somber, cheerless, rueful mean, murky, hazy.

Mapanggulo-a-Turbulent, seditious, malcontent, discontented; noisy; boisterous

Mapanhik-i-To mount, ascend, go up, increase.

Mapanira-n-Destroyer, breaker

Mapanirang puri-n-Defamer

Mapansin v-To feel, note, understand; hit upon.

Mapantay-v-To become equal or matched.

Mapanumpa-a-Foulmouthed, vile.

Mapannya-a-Flattering

Mapaos-a-Hoarse, husky.

Mapalitan a-Changeable

Maparañgalan-a Boastful, arrogant; proud, haughty

Mapasa iba i-To fall to another, devolve, relapse

Maparis-i-To be like or equal, resemble, match

Mapasal-v To meddle, interfere.

Mapasalan-v-To be obstructed or choked up

Mapasigaw-v-To exclaim, cry out.

Mapasok-v-To enter, go in

Mapatawa-a-Comic, comical

Mapatong-r-To put on, add to, augment.

Mapatpat-r-To go to a place without any difinite object in view.

Mapatulala-a astonishing, stufeying, wondefull
Mapawis-v-To be sweaty or sweated
Mapawis-a-Sweaty, perspiring
Mapeka-v-To feel angry or hurt
Mapekas a-Angry; disgusted, hurt
Mapiga-v-To squeeze, press
Mapaghati-a-Antiphatethic, irritated
Mapigil-v-To be bound or restrained
Mapilay v-To become lame, limp, sprain.
Mapilpit-v-To be twisted or twined, twist; twine about
Mapilit a Urgent, compulsory
Mapilitin-v-To press, urge, compel, oblige.
Mapintasae-a-Censorious Particular
Mapoot v-To be exasperated, irritated, offended or provoked
Mapoot a-sulky, testy
Mapootin-a-Touchy, moody, fretful, irrascible.
Mapudpod a-Blunt, dull, stupid
Mapula-a Red, reddish, ruddy.
Mapula ang mukha-a Redfaced
Mapulang mukha-n-Blush
Mapulapula-a-Pink, reddish
Mapúlot-v-To find, pick up, detect, hit upon; meet
Mapúlot-a-Full of honey; having much honey
Mapungay ang mata-a-Squinteyed, sleepy.
Mapuno-v-To fill, stuff.
Mapurol-a-Dull, obtuse, blunt, spiritless
Mapurol ang isip a Dull, torpid. stupid, inert; slow.
Maputi-a-White.
Maputik-a-Muddy; miry
Maputiputi-a-Whitish.
Maputla-a-Pallid; pale, discolored, colorless, sallow, ghastly.
Marabilis n-Maravedi.
Marahan-adv -Slowly; little by little, by degrees
Marahas a-Brave, valiant, bold, audacious; forward.
Marahil-adv-Probably; perhaps, maybe; can be; haply.
Maralita-a-Needy, poor, poverty-stricken, in want
Maramay v-To effect; inculpate
Maramdaman-v-To feel, grieve, perceive, note
Maramdamin-a-Sensible; tender, notable; sensitive, tender, hearted, affectionate
Marami n Many. numerous copious, abundant; plentiful, manifold, several.
Maraming buto a Bony
Maraming dahon a-Leafy, full of leaves.

Maraming nabasa sa libro a-Learned
Maraming pagaaring lupa-n-Land holder, planter
Maraming panulukan-a-Angular, cornered
Maraming taba-a-Greasy, fatty, corpulent, obese.
Maraming sanga-a-Branchy, ramous, ramose: having many branches
-Maramot a Stingy; miserly, paltry, niggardly, petit, close, mean, closefisted, penurious, tight, grasping, frugal, voracious, selfseeking, miserable, churlish narrow
Marangal-a-Eminent, honorable, noble, illustrious, solemn, exellent, sublime, grand great, fine splendid, sumptuous, surpassing, potent, just, fair, honest, patrician, transcendant, exalted, powerful, wealthy, large, huge, lofty, important.
Marapat-i -To deserve, merit, have due appertain, belong to
Marapatin-v-To incur, merit, have due
Marapatang tangapin a- Acceptable
Marapat nasain-a-Desirable
Marapat pagpalain a-Meritable;deserving
Marapat parnsahan-a Punishable; that which should, be punished
Maratihan-v-To accustom, be experienced, able or accustomed to
Marawal-a-Unworthy, undeserving, unmeritable
Marawal ang ugali a-Impolite, rude, false; bad mannered
Marawasan-i -To know, experience, be able
Margen-n-Margin, edge
Marikit-a-Beautiful, graceful, pretty gen seel, elegant, excellent, nice neat, fair, handtome, gay, gallant, fine, exquisite, dexterous
Marilag a Eminent, grand, tamous, illustrious, magnificent, noble, honorable: splendid, graceful, gay, shining,lucid.
Marinero-a-Sailor, marine, seafaring man.
Maring-v To hear, understand; pay attention, perceive, overhear
Marka-n-Mark, stamp
Markáhan-i -To stamp, mark, brand
Marques n-Marquis
Martillo-n-Hammer
Marumhan-i -To dirty, soil; bedpattei
Marumi-a-Dirty, soiled, nasty, filthy; foul, sordid; indecent; dingy; grtmy, dowdy; droosy; obscene, licentious, obscure, jetty, gloomy, unbecoming.
Marungis-a Dirty, soiled; filthy, foul, nasty, dowdy; droosy, sordid, dingy;

unmindtece, becoming, lewd, licen
tious; obscene

Marunong-a-Wise, learned, knowing,
discreet; prudent, judicious, sage,
erudite, shrewd, proficient; prudential, conversant; able, civilized, sapient, reserved

Marunong-n-Sage, wise man.

Marunong magingat ng lihim-a Secret;
silent, reserved.

Marunong makipagkapwa tawo-a polite,
urbane, courteous, wellbred.

Marupok-a Brittle, frail, feeble, fragile;
delicate, forceless, frangible, weak

Marzo-n-March.

Masabi a Loquacious, talkative

Masadhan-i-To be obstructed or choked
up

Masagana a-Abundant, excessive, plentiful, wealthy, rich

Masagana-adv-Abundantly, excessively,
plentifully.

Masagana sa dugo a Sanguine

Masagana sa pagaari a-Rich, opulent,
affluent, wealthy

Masagi-i-Gall, wear away by friction

Masagutin a-Answerable, responsive,
respondent

Masahin v-To knead

Masakim-a-Avaricious, greedy, miserly

Masakit-a Sick, painful, dolorous, la-
borious

Masaklad a-Sour, mordant, rough to
the taste, unpleasant, disagreeable;

Masakop-v-To protect, defend, be an-
nexed, be included, impend

Masaktan-i-To cripple, hurt, injure,
main, wound; affend, grieve

Masaktin-a-Unhealthy, painful, sickly

Masakuna-a-Disastrous

Masalab-i-To scortch, singe.

Masalanta-i-To be of no use.

Masalita a-Loquacious, talkative; conversant, garrulous, voluble

Masalubong-v-To encounter, meet join;
hit upon

Masalungat-i-To oppose, repugn, contradict.

Masama-a-Bad, evil; wicked; vile, perverse vicious, pernicious, unbecoming, indecent; baneful, deleterious,
harmful, abusive, profligate, arrant,
despicable depraved, infamous, omi-
nous; destructive, dreadful, false,
ferocious, terrible, fatal

Masama-adv-Perversely, viciously, per-
niciously, banefully

Masama-n Evil, bad harm, faul, hurt,
injury, mischief

Masama at hilig-a-Sinister, inauspicious,
vicious

Masamang hitsura a-Illshaped, deformed

Masamain-v-To disapprove, censure,
dislike reprove; make or cause to
be bad; hate; adhor, detest; loathe

Masamang kaugalian-a-Illbred, rude

Masamang ugali a-Illmannerred, impo-
lite, illbred.

Masama pa-a Worse

Masama sa lahat-a-Worst.

Masambulat-i-To scatter, sow broadcast

Masanay-v-To practice, know, experience; be accustomed or able

Masandat-v-To fill, stuff, satisfy, glut

Masanga-a-Branchy, ramose

Masansang-a-Strong scented.

Masapantaha-v-To presume, suppose,

Masapong v-To meet; encounter, collide, hit upon.

Masarap-a Palatable, sweet, savory, delicious, rich, dainty, tasty, nice,
select; delicate

Masarapan v-To be sweet, sweeten,
make palatable or savoiy

Masaya-a-happy, joyful, cheerful, jocose,
jocular, entertaining, merry, halcyon,
facetious, pleasant; affable; convivial, bouyant, gleeful, jaunty, vivacious, winsome; comical, comic, good
natured, cavalier, festive, amusing,
tasty

Masáyang-v-To throw away, fail of
success, do in vain.

Masaya ang loob-v-Happy, gay, jovial,
merry, cheerful, compliant

Masaya ang mukha-a-Smiling; agreeable

Masculino a-Masculine

Masdan-n-Exploration, watching; examination, study, observation; notice,
spying

Masebo-a-Greasy fatty, rat.

Maselang-n-Clean; neat, tidy, fastidious,
cleanly; particular cleanly

Masiba-a-Gluttinous, fond of dainties

Masid n-Observation, glance, gaze,
look

Masidhi-a-Active, affective

Masigla-a-Diligect, active, merry, amusing

Masikap a Officious, diligent, industrious,
solicitous; anxious, assiduous

Masiki-a-Shy, bashful, embarrassed.

Masikip-a-Narrow, close, tight

Masiksik-i-To fill up, stuff

Masilaw-v-To be dazzled, daze

Masindak v-To be startled, surprised,
or astonished

Masinop-a-Curious, inquisitive

Masinsay r To be clear, evident or known

Masinsay-a-Clear, evident.

Masinsin-a-Close, thick, compact, firm, solid, consistent, gross, tight; strong; massive

Masintahin-a-Affectionate, kind, loving, pleasing.

Masintahin sa Dios-a-Pious, holy, merciful

Masipag a-Diligent, industrious; thrifty, sedulous, officious, ready, prompt, quick, active, smart

Masipag magaral a Studious.

Masipak-v-To break (per to, the jaws)

Masira-v To break; damage, rot, spoil, impair.

Masna ang isip v-To go crazy, become demented or crazy.

Masiyasat-a Curious, inquisitive.

Maso n-Nave; hub

Masobasob-v-To full down

Masowail a Stubborn, rebellious, contradictory; disobedient

Masawayin a-Disobedient, contradictory, stubborn, obstinate, rebellious, conceited

Masubok-v To try, experiment, attempt, experience

Masubucan v To wound; hurt, cause pain.

Masuhin-v-To drive or pound with a mallet

Masucal-a-Dirty; filthy; slattern

Masucal ang loob a-Malcontent, discontented

Masuklam-a-Acrid, detestable, loathesome; execrated, antipathetic.

Masuclam ang loob-a-Angry, irritated

Masulat-v-To be written or composed.

Masulong v-To swell increase, continue, be brave or bold

Masumpong-v-To run against, meet by chance; strike or butt against.

Masundo-v-To be called or sent arter

Masunduan-a-Reconcilable.

Masungit-a-Cross; intractable, severe; harsh, arduous; crampy; cynic, fell, rigid, arbitrary, combative, cynical, pugnacious; vixenish; vixenly; crabbed.

Masunod-v-To Follow, come next

Masunog-v-To burn, blaze; inflame

Masunurin a-Docile, convenient, gentle, moderate, obedient, attentive, compliant submissive; humble; dutiful; amiable, resigned duteous, indulgent

Masupok v-To be on sumed.

Masustancia a-Succulent, juicy, nourishing

Masusuklam-a-Repulsive.

Masuwayin-a-Obstinate, obdurate, stubborn, conceited

Masuyo-a Obedient, attentive, compliant, civil; polite, courteous

Mataas a Tall, high; elevated, lofty transcendant; majestic.

Mataas ang gitna-a-Convex, convexed

Mataas magsalita-a Grandiloquent

Mataas ang halaga-a-Dear, costly, high priced

Mataas pa a-Higher, taller, superior

Mataba-a Fat, obese; greasy chubby chunky; plump, thickset; corpulent unctious, fertille; fruitful, copious

Matabang a-Tasteless; insipid, dull; heavy

Matabil-a-Talkative, loquacious

Mataboy-v-To be divorced or separated.

Matagal-a Staple permanent, firm, steady, lasting, durable, prolix, indefatigable, unwearied

Matagid-v-To be obstructed, take the clear and leave the muddy

Matagilid-adv -Sidewise.

Mataginting-a Sonoreus, pleasing, harmonious

Matago-v-To be hidden or concealed

Matago-a-Hidden, concealed

Matagpos-a-To be deficient, fail

Matagpuan-a-To find detect, meet' encounter, discover; hit on.

Matagumpay-v-To triumph exult;

Matahimik-v-To become calm peaceful; serene or quiet

Matahimik adv -Quietly, calmly

Mataho-v To know; be able, experience.

Matacaw a Gluttonous, greedy; sharpset; ravening, hoggish

Matakot-a-Afraid, terrified, intimidated tremulous, timid; fearful.

Matakutin-a-Tremulous, timid, fearful, cowardly, apprehensive, sensitive; coward, chickenhearted

Matalas a-Cute, cunning, sly, sagacious; fine, smart, lively; knowing, crafty, diligent; adroit, shrewd, discerning, ready, delicate; perfect

Matalas ang isip-a-Learned, sharp, intelligent; skillful; skillful; awake, knew, ing; ingenious, able, sagacious, keen, sapient; sage, watchful, lively

Matalas ang mata-a-Sharp eyed

Matalas magmasid a-Cunning, sagacious

Matalastas-v To know, understand, comprehend, prove, demonstrate, manifest; experience.

Matalim-a-Sharp; pointed, edged

Matalino-a Clear, circumspect; witty, prudent, judicious, wise; knowing; sharp, sensible, light, acute, discreet, learned, smart, intelligent, skillful, sagacious; sage, sapient; mature.

Matalo v-To lose

Matambog-v-To throw to another.

Matambok-a-Swollen

Matamis-n-Sugar sweets

Matamis a-Sweet dulcet.

Matampuhin-a-Sulky, touchy, pouting

Matanda a-Old, aged, decrepid, ancient; antiquated; antique

Matandang galit-n-Rancor, grudge

Matandaan-a-Mindful, retentive

Matanga-v To astonish, stupefy.

Matangisin-a-Touchy, snivelling

Matankad a Tall; straight.

Matanto v-To understand, hear

Matapang-a-Brave, valiant, bold, intrepid, spirited; vigorous, gritty redoubtable, courageous, stong, firm, gallant, doughty, graceful; stalwart, stalworth, spunky, plucky, agressive; saucy; pungent, poignant

Matapos-v-To finish, terminate, end, perish, die, conclude.

Matarok-v-To enter, penetrate remark, sound, be understood, judge.

Matastas-v-To rip, ravel

Matatag-a-Strong, robust vigorous firm, fast, resolute, consistent inflexible, solid, stubborn, tight

Matatag-v To be established, ordained or enacted.

Matatahanan-a-Inhabitable.

Matatakutin-a-Fearful, timorous, timid, coward

Matatangap-a-Admissible, acceptable, fit, proper, recievable

Matatawanin-a-Smiling, agreeable

Matayog-a-High, tall, elevated

Matayong-v-To obstruct, check stop

Matibay-a-Firm, storng, staple, compact, stout; sound, permament, perfect, fast, steady resolute, secure, entire; constant; coarse, complete; solid, vigorous ,hard, rigid, informed, close

Matibay na loob-a-Constant, loyal, manifest, steadfast, firm

Matigas-a-Hard; solid, stubborn, firm, inflexible, vigorous, tight

Matigas ang buhok ó balahibo-a-Bristly

Matigas ang ugali a Stubborn, pertinaceous, obstinate

Matigas ang ulo-a-Stubborn, pertina-

ceous, obstinate, contumelious; dogged, tenaceous

Matigmak-v-To impregnate; be impregnated, soak

Matiis-a-Tolorable, sufferable; constant, abstaining; obstinent, firm, loyal, manifest

Matikman v-To try; attempt, experience; taste, experiment.

Matilh n-Shrill

Matimbang-v-To balance, counterpoise, be weighed

Matindi a-Heavy, weighty; cumbrous, strong; cumbersome

Matinik-a-Thorny, spiny

Matining-v-To resound, tingle

Matining na kalooban a-Brave, strong; valiant

Matining na loob-a-Moderate, forbearing, temperate, kind; obliging, polite, constant, manifest, brave; valiant, firm, loyal

Matinkal a-Cloddy

Matipi a-To compress, be compressed

Matipip-a- Economic; frugal, economical, close, stingy

Matira-v-To remain; stay, stop over, reside.

Matisod-v-To stumble, stub.

Matisuran-a-Stumbling; tripping.

Matitiis-a-Tolerating, abstemious, sufferable, abstaining

Matitirahan-a-Inhabitable, habitable

Matiyaga-a-Constant, loyal, firm, diligent tolerating; sufferable

Matong-n-Hamper, basket

Matowa-v-To be happy, gay, merry, delighted, rejoiced

Matowid-a-Right, legal, la ful, just, constitutional, honest; upright, straight, direct, pointblank

Matowid adv.-Rationally; justly, honestly, ighteously

Matsing-n-Monkey.

Maturan-v-To debate, discuss, dispute, controvert, reason

Matúbo-a Lucrative, profitable; flourishing, thriving, increasing, growing

Matuklasan-v-Te discover, detect, find, search.

Matulin-a-Swift, quick, fast, nimble, rapid, prompt, hasty, precipitate, spry

Matulin-adv -Rapidly; lightly, quickly, ready, promptly, precipitately

Matulad-v To resemble, be similar

Matulis-a-Sharp pointed, marked.

Matulog-v To sleep, doze, slumber

Matuloy v To continue, proceed, effect accomplish.

Matumal-*a*-Dull, depiessive,

Matumbakan *v*-To conjecture, assert, guess, hit upon, stamp

Matunaw-*v*-To dissolve, liquefy; melt

Matunaw ang kinain-*v*-To digest

Matungkol-*v*-To respect, belong or pertain, to apportain, concern, relate, iefer, behoove, correspond

Matunog-*a* Sonoious, resounding; loud.

Matuto-*v*-To learn, experience comprehend

Matutol-*n*-Respondent, replier

Matuto *a* Ready, having the last word.

Matutol-*v*-To iespond

Matutuhan-*v*-To leain

Matuwa-*a* Happy; joiful, content, satisfied; fain, gleeiul. good humored, joyous.

Matuyo-*v*-To dry up, dessicate, fall, pine away, become lean or thin

Mauban-*a*-Hoary, grey headed old, hoai-

Maubos-*v*-To give out, expend, run out of, use up.

Maubo-*a*-Hoarse with a cold

Maubuhin *a*-Subject to colds oi hoarseness

Maugat-*a*-Nervous, robust lithe, vigorous

Mauhaw-*a*-Thristy, dry

Maukol-*v*-To pertain, belong to, appertain

Maukol sa *v*-To belong, pertain, concern, behoove

Maukol sa amoy-*a*-Olfactory; pertaining to the sense of smell

Maulan-*a*-Rainy, showery, pluvious, pluvial

Maulap-*a*-Cloudy, hazy, foggy, misty

Mauliningan-*v*-To hear impeifectly; hear indistinctly

Maulol-*v*-To dement, become ciazy oi demented

Maumid *a*-Mute, short.

Maumid-*v*-To stand mute or silent; shorten

Maumpog-*v* To bump against, run against

Mauna *v*-To go before, anticipate, go ahead, preceed

Mauntog *v*-To bump against, collide, strike against

Maupo *v*-To sit down

Mausisa-*v*-To inquire, investigate, be cuiious.

Mausisain-*a* Inquisitive, curious.

Mautak-*a*-Brainy.

Mautak at mahinahon *a* Prudent sedate.

Mautal-*v* To stutter, stammer

Mautas-*v*-To finish, terminate en l con clude

Maujam-*a*-Critical, scoffing, sarcastic, sardonic

Mawanki *v*-To be similar or like, iesemble, be alike

Mawala *v*-To lose, be lost

Mawalan-*v*-To lose, be lost

Mawalan ang hiya-*v*-To become shameless, lose one's sense of same

Mawala ang dili-*v*-To lose one's sense of honor,

Mawalan ang pitagan-*v* To lose one's selfrespect, become rude or imprudent, be disrespectful

Mawatasan-*v*-To understand, comprehend, know.

May-*v*-To have; possess, contain, hold

Mayabang-*a*-Boasting, bragging, boast, ful, vaunting, conceited, blown, vain proud, haughty, whimsical

Mayabang (*ang*)-*n*-Boaster, biaggei

Mayabong *a*-Leafy, luxuriant, branchy, sprightly

Mayaman-*a*-Rich; potent, wealthy, opulent, powerful, eminent, affluent

Mayamot-*v*-To disgust, vex, displease, molest, loathe, iiritate lose patience-

Mayamutin-*a*-Tedious, tiresome; disgusting irksome, loathe some irrita ble; vexatious

May anim na panulukan *a*-Sixcornered,

May apat na mukha-*a*-Four faced, quadrilateral, having four faces

May apat na paa-*a*-Fourfooted, quadruped

May ari *n*-Owner, propietor, loid, master

May ari ng daong-*n*-Shipownei

May ari ng gilingin-*n*-Miller; millowner

May asin-*a* Salty, briny, saline

May bait-*a*-Judicious, prudent, discieet.

May buig-*a*-Bunchy, full of bunches

May buto-*a*-Bony

May damdam-*a*-Suffering, sick, indisposed, feeling; patient

Mav dangal-*a* Honorable illustrious, noble, gentlemanly, honest.

May daya-*a*-Counterfeit; false, cheating

May duda *a*-Doubtful, mistrustful.

Mav dunong-*a*-Wise, intelligent; apt erudite, knowing, fit, learned

Mav galit *a*-Angry. mad

May gawa-*n*-Authoi, maker.

May gawa-*a*-Busy

May guhit *a* Striped, full of lines

May gusto-*a*-Voluntaiy

May gusto-*adv*-Voluntarily

May haligi-*a* Columnai.

May balong lupa *a*-Terrene, earthy.

May hanga *a* Limited finite, bounded

May isip a-Rational, prudent, judicious, sensible

May kamandag-a Baneful; poisonous.

May kapal-n-Creator

May kasalanan-a-Culprit, delinquent.

May katawan-a-Corporeal, corpulent plump, fat, obese.

May katowiran-a-Justificable

Mav katungculan-n-Officeholder, One who has a trade or vocation

May katungculan magbayad-n-Paymaster

May kaya-a Competent, fit; able; apt, proper, sufficient, enough

May lalang n-Creator

May lañgib a Scabby.

May lipak-a-Callous

May luha a-Weeping

May malaking nasa-a-Greedy; ravenous, very desirous.

May mansa-a-Stained, spotted, dirty.

May masamang kalooban-a-Malevolent, malignant, malicious, angry

May maraming butas-a Cellular

May maraming hitsura-a-Multiform

May nana-a Purulent

May ñgipin-a-Toothed

Mayo n-May

May pañgintindi-a-Intelligent, skillful, learned, knowing, wise

May pagitan-adv.-At intervals, by intervals

May pagcaulolulol a Foolish; silly, half-witted

May pagsala-a Fallable.

May pakinabang-a-Profitable useful, gainful, profitious.

May pahid na sebo-a Greasy; greased

May pakpak-a Pennate

Mav pañgako-a-Votary

May pañganib-a-Dangerous, perilous, hazardous

May pañganib mahulog a-Wevering; unsteady, unstable

May pañganib mahulog-adv.-Waveringly

May pawis-a-Sweaty, perspiring

May pitagan-a-Respectful, honorable, noble, gentlemanly

May puri a-Honorable, honest, pure, just, fair, virgen

May putik-a-Muddy; miry

May oon-v To have, possess, contain

May sakit a-Sick; ill, unwell, infirm, patient

May sakit n-Patient, sufferer, sick person

May sala a- Faulty; guilty, dilinquent, amiss

May sala-n-Dilinquent; offender, criminal.

May salapi-a-Rich wealthy

May sugat-a Wounded

May sungay-a-Horned

May supil sa kamatayan a-Mortal, fatal, deadly

May sutla-a-Silken

May tali-a-Subject, tied, knotted, bound.

May tañgan-Motheaten

May tanim sa loob-a-Angry, wroth, odious

May tatlong ñgipin-a-Trident

May tatlong ñgipin n Trident.

May tatlong panulukan a-Triangular

May tatlong panulukan-n-Triangle

May tatlong wika-a-Trilenguar

May timik-a-Thorny, spiny

May tubo-a-Profitable, gainful

May tuka-a-Beaked.

May tuhis a-Pointed, sharp

May uban - a - Hoary, white headed, chaffy.

Mayuñgib-a-Pitted, full of holes

May uod-a-Wormeaten.

May usap-n-Latigant

Mayúscula-n-Capital letter.

May utang-n-Debtor.

May walong silaba-a-Octosyllabic

Melon-n-Melon

Mercurio-n-Mercury

Mey-v-To have, possess, contain.

Microbe-n-Microbe.

Mina-n-Mine

Minamahal - v - Beloved, dear, favorite; darling

Minana-a-Inherited.

Mina ng asin-n-Salt mine

Minindal-n-Lucheon, lunch

Mitsa n-Lamp-which which

Mo-pro-Thy, thine, your, yours.

Molinette n-Windlass.

Monja-n-Nun

Monje n-Monk

Muang-a-Foolish, ignorant, artless; simple

Mugmog-n-Gargle

Mugmogin-v-To gargle

Mahi-n-Molestation xexation, disgust, abhorence, hardship, detestation; grievance

Muhiin-a Disgusting, tedious, irritable; impatient, loathesome

Mukha-n-Face, aspect, surface, shape; outside, countenance, looks; front, cover, side

Mukhaan-v-To face, make a face.

Mukha ng dahon ng libro n-Page of a book.

Mukhang angel a Seraphic angelic.

Mula-n-Beginning, origination, origin.

Múla-prep -Since, after

12

Mula-*adv* -Since, after.

Mulaan-*v*-To commence, begin, undertake, attempt

Mulain-*v*-To commence, begin, attempt, undertake, examine, investigate

Muli-*adv* -Again

Mulihin-*v*-To grind.

Muling-*a*-Foolish

Muling bumalik *v*-To return, come back again

Muling gawin-*v*-To reproduce, do again, do over

Muling ibigkis-*v*-To rebundle, rebind

Muling ipatnugot-*v*-To renew a lease or contract

Muling katham *v*-To reproduce

Muling mubuhay-*v*-To acquire new life, revive

Muling magsisui *v*-To resprout

Muling magsupling-*v*-To resprout.

Muling tingnan-*v*-To review, revise

Multa-*v*-Mulct, fine, forfeit

Multahan-*v*-To fine, mulct, make pay a forfeit

Multiplicando-*n*-Multiplicand

Muna-*adv* -Before, prior

Mundo-*n*-World

Muni-*n*-Peanut.

Munika-*n*-Doll

Munti-*a* Small, little

Munti ang halaga-*a*-Trifling, light, of no consequence

Munting duende-*n*-Elfin.

Munting damdam-*n*-Indisposition

Munting trabaho-*n*-Chore

Muog-*n*-Rampart, wall.

Munting piraso ag lupa-*n*-Plot, plat.

Mura-*a*-Cheap, valueless, tender, young, modern, new, recent

Mura-*n*-Curse· imprecation

Mura ang halaga-*a*-Cheap, valueless, trifling

Murahin-*v*-To insult, revile, abuse; affront, accuse, curse; detract, vilify, vituperate

Muselina-*n*-Muslin

Música-*n* Music.

Músico-*n*-Musician

Muson-*n*-Landmark.

Mustasa *n*-Mustard, mustard greens

Mutain-*a*-Soreeyed

Mutya *n*-Love,

Mutyang-*a*-Beloved, dear, darling

N

Na-*prop* -Who, which, that, whom

Naagaw tulog *a*-Sleepy; drowsy

Naayon sa matowid-*a*-Just; fair, equitable, honorable; according to right

Naayos-*a*-Shipshape; arranged

Naayos sa mabuting caugahan-*a* Just, simple; sacred, honorable, noble, virtuous

Naayos sa matowid-*a* Lawful, just, according to law.

Nababagay-*a*-Convenient, fit, proper, suitable, proportional, corresponding

Nabangit-*a*-Said, aforesaid, aforementioned, abovementioned

Nabibitin *a*-Pendant, hanging, unpaid.

Nabubuhay sa limos-*n*-Beggar

Nabubukod-*a* Solitary, separated, lone; extra, especial, special, extraordinary, exceptional, rare uncommon.

Nabubulok-*a* Corrupting

Nabulok-*a*-Corrupt

Nadadapat-*a*-Proper; fit, merited, corresponding

Nadadaya *a*-Delusive, cheating, deceiving.

Nadarapat-*a*-Proper fit, corresponding, merited

Nadarapat sa ilong *a* Nasal pertaining, to the nose

Nagaabot *n*-Giver, donator, donor

Nagalay-*n*-Dedicaton, giver, donator, donor

Nag-aalon alon *a*-Wavy, undulatory

Nag aampon-*a*-Tutelary, helpful, tutelar, protecting

Nag aantok-*a* Sleepy, drowsy, somnambulent.

Nagaaral-*n* Student, Scholar, pupil, disciple.

Nagaaraw-*n*-Laborer; journeyman, mercinary

Nagaasahan-*a* Expectant

Nagaaso *a*-Smoky, full of Smoke

Nagagalit-*a*-Angry, mad, hostile,

Nagagatid,-*v*-To be speechless, unable to explain

Nagagayak-*a*-Prepared; provident; ready

Nagbabalita *n* Narraton, relater, reporter, herald

Nagbabalita *a* Monitory, newsy, admonitory

Nagbabanalbanalan-*n*-Hypocrite

Nagbabanalbanalan-*a* - Hypocritical; false, demur

Nagbabayad-*a*-Retributive, retributing; paying

Nagbabayad *n* Payer he who pays

Nagbibigay-*n* Giver; donor.

Nagbibili *n*-Buyer, seller.

Nagbibili ng̃ asin *n* Salt dealer

Nagbibintang-*n* Imputor accuser

Nagbibinsita-*n*-Visitor.

Nagbigti-*n*-Suicide

Nagbubung-*a*-Bunchy, full of bunches or clusters

Nagbubung̃a-*n*-Fertilizer

Nagdadakop-*a* Needy, in want

Nagdadalit-*n*-Vocalist

Nagdadalamhati-*n*-Sorrowful, low spirited; dejected

Nadaindam-*a*-Sorrowful, low spirited, dejected.

Nagdaraan-*a*-Transitory

Nagdidiwang-*n*-Celebrator, one who celebrates

Naghabilin *n*-Repositor

Naghahalal *n*-Elector, chooser

Naghahalaman-*n*-Gardener, horticulturist.

Naghahandog-*n*-Donater, giver, donor.

Naghahatid *n*-Convoy.

Naghahayag *n*-Herald; reporter

Naghihiman-*v*-To exist; cause, make, form, practice; produce.

Naghihing̃alo-*a*-Dying, near death

Nag nibig-*a*-Loving, desirous, longing, eager.

Nag hinainalon-*a*-Wavy, undulatory

Nag iisa *a* Solitary, lone; only, sole; singular, single, individual, particular, especial; solus, lonely

Nag iisa-*adv*-Alone, purely, simply

Nag iisipin *a*-Pensive, thoughtful

Nagising-*a*-Awake, watchful; lively

Nagkakaakma-*a*-Uniform, agreeing; fit; proper; convenient.

Nagka kadugtong-ductong-*a*-Continuos, lasting, asiduous

Nagkakahati-*a*-Halved

Nagkakaisa-*a*-Attesting, unanimous, uniform, confirming.

Nagka-kaloob-*n*-Donor giver.

Nagka kapisan-*adv*-Unanimously, uniformly, joinedly, conjointly

Nagka-kataon-*t*-Accident, casualty, happening

Nagkaroon-*v*-*Imp*-Had

Nagkasala-*n*-Violater, sinner delinquent, malefactor

Nagkataon-*a*-Accidental; casual, unexpected, fortuitous, haphazard

Nagkataon-*n* Contingent, accident

Naglalakad-*n*-Pedestrian, traveler, walker

Naglalako ng̃ asin-*n* Saltdealer

Naglalaro-*n*-Player

Naghhgaw-*n* Lover, wooer, one who courts

Naglalaman-*a*-Increasing; thriving, or growing

Naglliwanag *a* Radiant, resplendent, shining; glittering

Naglululan-*a* Containing, having

Nagmana-*n*-Heir, legatee

Nagnakaw-*n*-Robber; peculator, thief

Nagnanasa-*a* Desirous, longing, eager, greedy

Nagniningning *a*-Resplendent; glittering, shining.

Nagpang̃ako *n* Votarist, votaress, votary

Nagpapabung̃a *n* Fruit grower.

Nagpapadala-*n* Sender, remitee, remittor

Nagpapahina *a*-Extenuating.

Nagpapayayat-*a*-Extenuating

Nagpapagayongayon-*n*-Tramp, hobo, bum

Nagpapakati *a*-Diminutive

Nagpapakonowari-*a*-False, feigned.

Nagpapala as *a*-Strengthening

Nagpapalambot-*a* Softening, mollifying.

Nagpapalit *a*-Diminutive

Nagpapalimbag-*n*-Editor

Nagpapalimos-*n*-Beggar

Nagpapaluang-*a* Laxative.

Nagpapamana-*n*-Legator

Nagpapastol-*n*-Herder, cowboy, herdsmen, herdman

Nagpapasulsol-*n*-Agitator

Nagpapaupa sa araw-*n*-Laborer, journeyman, worman.

Nagpipigil-*n*-Detainer, one who stops.

Nagpipita *a*-Desirous, longing, eager

Nagsasalawahan-*n*-Irresolute undecided; flirting.

Nagsaysay-*n* Narrator, relator, reporter, analyst

Nagsisisi *n* Penitent.

Nagsusumbong-*n*-Accuser, informer, denouncer

Nagsusugal-*n*-Gambler

Nagtatangi-*v*-To deny; refuse

Nagtatakbo-*n*-Runner

Nagtatanim-*n*-Planter, farmer

Nagtitiis-*n* Sufferer, patient.

Nagtitinda-*n*-Seller, vender.

Nagtitinda ng̃ binhi-*n*-Seedsman

Nagtitinda ng̃ bung̃ang kahoy *n* Fruit vender

Nagtitinda ng̃ mg̃a pagkain-*n*-Grocer

Nagtitira sa bundok *n*-Mountaineer

Nagtuturo *n* Teacher, educator.

Naguas-*n*-Petticoat.

Nag utos *v*. *Imp*-Bade

Naghahalal sa katungkulan-*n*-Elect, the chosen.

Náhahanga-*a* Bordering, neighboring.

Nahahapis-*a*-Grievous, pitiful.

Nahibo-*n*-Victim.

Nahihiya-*a* Ashamed, shy, coy, crestfallen, mortified

Nahuhuli-*a*-Last, hindmost, posterior

Naibigan *a*-Lovable

Nais *n* Wish, desire, will; want, longing, eagerness, hankering, lust; mind, aspiration, cupidity, whim anxiety.

Nais ng sarili *n*-Selfwill

Naka-aakit-*a*-Attractive, inductive.

Naka-aalibadbad-*a*-Nauseous

Naka-aalimura-*a*-Outrageous; dishonorable

Naka-aaliw-*a*-Loving, recreative, diverting, comfortable

Naka-aanyaya sa katamaran-*a*-Lazy; Indolent, inattentive

Naka-aaral-*a*-Wise, learned, sage

Nakaahon sa mga utang-*a*-Solvent

Nababagot *a*-Sharp; rough, mordant; disagreeable

Nakababawas-*a*Diminutive

Nakabibigkis-*a*-Bundled

Nakabitin *a*-Pensile, suspended.

Nakabubulok-*a*-Curruptive; putrifying

Nakabubuti-*a*-Wholesome, heathful, salutary

Nakabukod-*a*-Distinct,discrete,exclusive

Nakadadaya-*a* Delusive, illusive; deceitful, affected, claptrap, sham.

Nakadayti-*a*-Touching, adjacent

Nakadudulit-*a*-Terrifying, frightful

Nakadudusta-*a*-Ignominious, disgraceful, dishonorable; reproachful, shameful

Nakadugtong-*a*-Adjunct

Nakadugtong-*n*-Appendix.

Nakagagaling-*a*-Sanative

Nakagagalin sa katawan-*a*-Healthful; wholesome

Nakagagalit-*a*-Offensive, onerous, disagreeable, unpleasant; vexatious, ugly, immodest, homely; fastidious, grievous

Nakagayak-*a*-Prepared, ready, prompt.

Nakahahalina-*a*-Alluring, attractive, instructive.

Nakahalo-*a*-Mixed, mingled.

Nakahanda-*a*-Prepared, prompt, ready, fit

Nakahanga *a*-Bordering

Nakaharap-*a*-Present

Nakaharap *adv* -Present, in front of

Nakahiga *a* Laid down, horizontal

Nakahigpit-*a*-Tight, close, contracted

Nakahihibo-*a* Cheating, deceiving, illusive; alluring, claptrap, guileful, sham, simulate.

Nakahihikayat-*a* Provorative, exeiting, quarrelsome, inciting.

Nakahihila-*a* Attractive, inductive.

Nakhihinayang-*a* Pitiful, sad, doleful, sorrowful

Nakahihiya-*a* Shameful, nefarious,abomnible hienous, shameless

Nakahilig *a*-Minded, inclined.

Nakahiwalay-*adv* -Apart, asunder

Nakansip *a*-Abstracted

Nakakain-*a*-Eatable, nutritous, nutritive.

Nakakalakip-*adv* -Jointly, unitedly, - conjointly

Nakakalat *a*-Scattered, wide, open.

Nakakalat-*adv* -Broadcast; wide

Nakalabas *a*-Free, unencumbered, independent, exempt unrestrained

Nakalagay-*a* Situate, situate

Nakalaman-*a*-Full of meat; having sustinence.

Nakahibang-*a*-Recreative, diverting

Nakalilnis *a*-Cleansing, purifying

Nakahliwanag *a* Luminous, luminary; light giving

Nakaluhod-*v* *p* *p* -Knelt

Nakalulugod-*a*-Affable, recreative; pleasing, agreeable, comfortable, happy, placid, gentle

Nakalulumbay-*a*-Mournful, sad, melancholy, saddening

Nakamamangha-*a*-Marvelous,wonderful, astonishing, awe inspiring

Nakamamatay-*a* Fatal, deadly

Nakamatay-*n*-Murderer, cutthroat

Nakamumuli-*a*-Disagreeable, disgusting, vexatious, agravating

Nakangiti-*a* Smiling, agreeable, pleasant.

Nakapagaantok-*a* Sleepy, drowsy

Nakapagkakasakit *a*-Morbid, unhealthful, sickening

Nakapagpapalakas-*a* Healthful, wholesome, salutary

Nakapagpapalambot *a* Softening; mollifying

Nakapanginginlabot-*a*-Hideous; frightful, shocking, disgraceful, awful

Nakapanginginbubo-*a*-Enviable

Nakapapagod-*a* Tiresome; tedious, anxious, painful

Nakapapangit-*a*-Ugly, disfiguring

Nakapipiht-*a*-Provocative, exciting persistent, inciting

Nakapilipit-*a*- Twisted

Napapawis-*a*-Sudorific

Nakaraan na *a* Preterit, past, gone by, past

Nakaririmarim-*a*-Nasty; filthy; dirty, ugly, homely, immodest

Nakasabit-*a*-Pensile, suspended.

Nakasadsad-*a*-Anchored

Nakasasaklaw sa lahat *a*-Universalgeneral

Nakasasama *a*-Harmful, bad, evil, prejudicial: pernicious, vicious; wicked.

Nakasisindak *a*-Terrifying, terrible, awful, terrific, dreadful.
Nakasisira-*a*-Corruptive; pernicious,
Nakasisira ng̃ katawan *a*-Unhealthful, sickening.
Nakasisira ng̃ malaki *a* Destructive.
Nakasisira ng̃ puri-*a*-Ignominous, disgraceful, blighting, ugly, homely, immodest.
Nakasusuka-*a*-Nanseous
Nakasusuklam-*a* Disgusting; ugly, homely, immodest
Nakasusunok-*a*-Sweet but not palatable, sickening sweet
Nakasusuya-*a* Sweet but not palatable, sickening sweet
Nakataan sa DIOS *a*-Sacred, holy
Nakatagihd-*adp* Sidewise
Nakatataho *a*-Learned
Nakatatakot *a*-Timorous, timid, fearful
Nakatatalastas-*a*-Learned, wise.
Nakatatawa-*a*-Laughable, ludricous, facetious, jocose, good natured
Nakatatawag sa iba *a*-Attractive, alluring, inductive
Nakatayo *a*-Perpendicular
Nakatitibay-*a*-Strengthening, corroborative
Nakatotowa-*a*-Cheerful, entertaining happy, joyful.
Nakatutulong *a*-Co-operative
Nakatuñgo-*a*-Directory.
Nakatutuwa-*a*-Pleasing, happy; entertaining, cheering, cheerful; joyous
Nakatutuyo-*a* Dessicated
Nakaupo-*a*-Sitting.
Nakaupo-*v p p*-Sat
Nakaw-*n* Theft, robbery
Nakawala-*a*-Astray.
Nakawin-*v*-To steal, rob, plunder; peculate, filch, thieve.
Nakayamot *a*-Grievous, vexatious
Nakayayamot-*a*-Fastidious, disagreeable; tedious; unpleasant, offensive
Nakita-*n* That which was seen
Nakita *v-imp* Saw.
Nakita-*n* Wages; salary, earnings
Nalaban-*a*-Opposite, adverse, contrary.
Nalalabok-*a* Mixed, mingled.
Nalalayo-*a*-Distant, far, remote.
Nalaman-*v-imp* -Knew
Naliligaya-*a*-Glad, content, joyful
Nalilihim-*a*-Secret; confidential
Nalilimutan-*a*-Forgetful
Nalimutan-*v imp*-Forgotten, forsaken
Nalulugod-*a*-Happy, glad, gay; cheerful; content
Namaga *a* Turgid
Namamagitan-*a*-Intervening, intermediate, mediating

Namamanhid-*a*-Numb.
Namamaos *a*-Husky
Namamang̃inoon-*b*-To hunt a superior, recognize one's superiors
Naman *adv* -Also, likewise, moreover, even, still, yet, as yet, nevertheless, equally; evenly.
Namatay-*v imp* -Died, dead
Namimili ng̃ asin *n*-Saltbuyer.
Naminami-*a*-Naseous, loathesome' despicable
Naminami-*n*-Nausea, despicableness
Namnam-*n*-Taste, relish, pleasure; delight, choice, caprice, mind.
Namnamin-*v*-To taste relish, like,enjoy
Namumukod-*a*-Singular, single; individual, particular, surpassing; excellent.
Namumuho ang dugo-*v*-To contuse
Namumula-*a*-Reddish
Namumula-*v*-To become red
Namumung̃a *v*-Te bear fruit
Namumuti-*v*-To whiten, become white.
Namamutla-*a*-Discolored, pale, pallid, colorless
Namumutla-*v*-To grow or become pale or pallid
Nana *n*-Pus, gleet.
Nanalo-*v imp* -Won.
Nanalo-*n*-Victor, winner
Nananaing̃a-*n*-Hearer; listener, auditor
Nang-*prep*-For, about, to, in; on, with if, as by, on account
Nang̃agaw ng̃ isang babayi-*n*-Rapist; ravisher
Nang̃ang̃alakal ng̃ puri ng̃ isang babayi-*n*-Pimp.
Nang̃ang̃aninag-*v*-To be transparent.
Nang̃ang̃aral-*n*-Preacher, orator, speaker
Nang̃ang̃atal-*a* Tremulous, quivering
Nang hindi-*v*-To refuse
Nagi-inter -Meaning disgust.
Nang̃ing̃ibig-*n*-Lover
Nang̃ing̃inig-*a* Tremulous, quivering
Nang̃ing̃itim-*v*-To blacken, become black, dark, or brown.
Nang̃is-*n*-Whimper,crys,obsnivel, whine
Nang panahong yaon-*adv* -Then, at that time
Nangyari na-*p p* -done.
Nangyari na-*v. imp*,-Did
Nangyari na *a*-Preterit; past.
Nangyaring sabay-*a*-Simultaneous
Nayayari-*n*-Event, issue, success.
Naningas-*v*-To become hard, harden
Naninigid-*a* Prickling,piquant,acrid, hot.
Nanininta-*a*-Lover sweetheart
Nanonood-*n*-Spectator, looker on, bystander, gazer
Nanugat-*n*-Wounder.
Nanunuod-*n*-Spectator.

Nanumpa ng̃ di totoo-*n*-Perjurer, forswearer

Nanunuluyan-*n*-Lodger, boarder guest

Napahiya-*v*-To be ashamed

Napakadakila-*a*-Excellent, magnificent, potent, fine, grand

Napakatulis-*a*-Very sharp

Napakatuyo-*a*-Very dry.

Napapagal-*a*-Tiresome, fatiguing; grievous

Napapaloob-*adv* Within

Nararamdaman *a*-Sensitiva, feeling, sensible, perceptible, painful

Nararapat-*a*-Worthy, meritable, suitable, serving

Nasunog *v imp* Burned, burnt

Nasusuklam ang loob-*a* Disgusted, restless, sorrowful

Nasusulok-*i*-To be in the corner.

Natakpan-*a*-Covered.

Natatago *a*-Secret, hidden, dark confidential.

Natatalaga-*a* -Intentional, disposed, ready

Natatalaga-*adi*-Purposely, intentionally, always

Natatangi-*a*-To be retired, refuse, separate, divide

Natatapat-*a* Proper; fit; convenient

Natatapat-*adv* Opposite, in front

Natatapos-*a*-Terminable, transitory transient

Natay-*n*-Cutthroat, murderer

Natay sa ama-*n*-Patricide

Natay sa hari-*n* Regicide

Natay sa ina-*n*-Matricide

Natay sa kapwa-*n*-Homicide, murder

Natay sa sarili-*n* Suicide

Natimawa-*a*-Free, unencumbered, independent, exempt, unrestrained

Natotowa-*a*-Glad, pleased, happy; gay, merry, cheerful, joyous, entertaining

Naturan na-*a*-Aforesaid,abovementioned.

Natutungcol-*a* According, belonging, pertaining

Natutungcol sa regla-*a*-Regular, according to rules or regulations

Natutwa *a* Glad; happy free; pleased, joyous; merry, content, contentted

Nauna *a* Foremost; first, previous, primeval.

Nauuhaw-*a*-Thirsty, dry

Nauukol *a*-To pertain or belong to

Nauukol *a*-Fit, apt

Nauukol sa *a* Revelant

Nauukol sa alipin-*a* Servile, slavish; menial.

Nauukol sa alon *a*-Tidal, wavy.

Nauukol sa ama *a* Patrimonial, paternal; fatherly.

Nauukol sa anak-*a*-Filial, childish, pertaining, to children

Nauukol sa araw-*a*-Solar.

Nauukol sa aso-*a* Canine, doggish

Nauukol sa awit-*a*-Legendary

Nauukol sa babayi *a*-Feminine, womanly; womanish

Nauukol sa baboy-*a*-Porcine

Nauukol sa bakang lalaki-*a*-Taurine

Nauukol sa bata-*a*-Perule, childish

Nauukol sa Bathala-*a*-Sacred, godly, holy

Nauukol sa bubog-*a* Vitreous

Nauukol sa buto *a*-Bony.

Nauukol sa kristal-*a*-Vitreous

Nauukol sa dati-*a*-Primeval

Nauukol sa dugo-*a*-Sanguine, sanguinary

Nauukol sa gatas-*a* Milky, lacteal

Nauukol sa gawa-*a*-Pertaining to work

Nauukol sa gobierno *a* Administrative; gobernatorial

Nauukol sa halamanan-*a*-Horticultural

Nauukol sa hilagaan-*a*-Polar, pertaining to the north

Nauukol sa historia-*a*-Historical, historic

Nauukol sa hukom-*a* Juridic; juridical

Nauukol sa ilog-*a*-Fluvial

Nauukol sa ilong-*a*-Nasal

Nauukol sa infierno-*a*-Hellish, infernal

Nauukol sa itim-*a*-Ethiopic, ethiopian, pertaining to black.

Nanucol sa kaluluwa *a*-Spiritual; ghostly

Nauukol sa kalunuran-*a*-Occidental, western

Nanucol sa kapang̃anacan-*a*-Natal, native

Nauukol sa karunungan-*a*-Scientific

Nauukol sa kasal-*a*-Nuptial, connubial; conjugal

Nauukol sa katawan-*a*-Bodily

Nauukol sa konvento *a*-Monastic

Nauukol sa kosina-*a*-Culinary

Nauukol sa lalaki-*a*-Male, virile

Nauukol sa lamesa-*a*-Tabular

Nauukol sa laway-*a*-Salivous

Nauukol sa lug-*a*-Jugular

Nauukol sa likod-*a*-Dorsal.

Nauukol sa limbag-*a*-Editoial

Nauukol sa lingo-*a*-Weekly

Nauukol sa lulod *a*-Tibial

Nouukol sa lupa-*a* Eartly, terrene, worldly; earthy.

Nauukol sa lupang tinubuan-*a*-Vernacular

Nauukol sa pagkakasama-*a*-Social, companionable, sociable

Nauukol sa mana-*a*-Hereditary

Nauukol sa mg̃a kulay-*a* Chromatis.

Nauukol sa pag iisip-*a*-Intellectual; mental; ideal.
Nauukolsa pagkain-*a*-Nutritious; nutrive
Nauukool sa pagkakapatid-*a*-Brotherly; fraternal.
Nauukol sa pagsasaysay *a*-Narrative.
Nauukol sa pagtangi-*a*-Negative; negatory.
Nauukol sa pagtatawa-*a*-Laughable.
Nauukol sa panahon-*a* Chronic; primeval.
Nauukol sa parang-*a*-Rural; rustic.
Nauukol sa paskong mahaba-*a*-Quadrigesimal.
Nauukol sa patay-*a*-Obituary.
Nauukol sa puso-*a*-Cordial; sincere.
Nauukol sa religion-*a*-Sacred; holy.
Nauukol sa sacramento *a*-Sacramental.
Nauukol sa salapi-*a*-Pecuniary.
Nauukol sa katawohan-*a*-National.
Nauukol sa serafin-*a*-Seraphic; angelic.
Nauukol sa sulat-*a*-Graphic.
Nauukol sa tingin-*a*-Visual.
Nauukol sa tiyan-*a*-Ventrial.
Nauukol sa umaga-*a*-Matin.
Nauukol sa voces-*a*-Vocal.
Nauukol sa volcan-*a*-Volcanic.
Nauna-*a*-Primitive; former; anterior; preceeding.
Nauuso-*a*-Customary; fashionable; frequent.
Nanutal-*a*-Tongue-tied; stuttering; stammering.
Nauutas-*v*-To finish; terminate.
Nawala ang diwa-*n*-Spiritless; languid; weak; down-hearted.
Nayon-*n*-Suburb; district; territory; hamlet; burg; small village.
Negro-*n*-Negro; ethiopian; ethiop.
Naetro-*a*-Neuter.
Ñga-*adv.*-Well; then, since; therefore.
Ñgalan-*n*-Name; vocable; denomination.
Ñgalanan-*v*-To name; denominate; give a name; nickname.
Ñgala-ñgala-*n*-The roof of the mouth; pharnyx.
Ñgasab-*n*-Munching; crunching.
Ñgatñgat-*n*-Gnaw; gnawing.
Ñgatñgatin-*v*-To gnaw.
Ñgayon-*adv.*-Now; at the present time.
Ñgayon araw-*adv.*-To-day.
Ñgayon din-*adv.*-Now; immediately; instantly; plumb.
Ñgiaw-*n*-Mew.

Ñgiba-*a*-Singular; individual; particular.
Ñgibit-*n*-Grimace; wry face.
Ñgiki-*n*-Chill.
Ñgimi-*n* emerity; scare; fright.
Ñgiñgi-*n*-The edge of the eyelids or lips.
Ñgipin-*n*-Tooth.
Ñgipinin at paglapatin-*v*-To mortise.
Ñgiti-*n*-Smile.
Ñgiwi-*n*-Grimace.
Ñgumasab-*v*-To crunch; munch.
Ñgumiaw-*v*-To Mew.
Ñgumiki-*v* To chill.
Ñgumiti-*v*-To smile.
Ñgumuso-*v*-To pout; pucker.
Ñgumuya-*v*-To masticate; chew.
Ñguni-*conj.*-But; nevertheless; except; yet.
Ñguso-*n*-Upper-lip.
Ñguso ñg baboy ó hayop-*n* Snout; nose.
Ñgusuan-*a*-Longsnouted.
Ñgusuyan-*v*-To point with the nose.
Ñguyain-*v*-To chew; masticate.
Ni-*prep.*-To; of; from; wit; on; by; for.
Nila-*pro.*-Their; theirs.
Nilay-*n*-Thought; meditation; idea.
Nilayin-*v*-To think; muse; moditate; contemplate; consider.
Nilimbag-*n*-Pamphlet; printed matter; edition.
Ninakaw-*n*-Theft; robbery; that which has been stolen.
Niñgas-*n*-Fervency; flame; ferventness; ardency.
Niñgning-*n*-Lusteo, glitter; brilliancy; brightness; shine; refulgency; refulgence; scintilla; shimmer; gleen.
Niog-*n*-Cocoanut.
Nipis *n*-Thinness.
Nipisan-*v*-To thin; make thin.
Niya-*pro.*-His; her; it's; hers.
Niyon-*adv.*-Then; at that time.
Noo-*n*-Forehead.
Noon-*adv.*-Then; at that time; when.
Nunal-*n*-Mole.
Nuno-*n* Grandfather;grandmother;spectre; specter; spight; pantom.
Nuno sa talampakan-*n*-Great; great-grandfather.
Nutnut-*n*-Ravellings.
Nutnotin-*v*-To unravell.
Nuynoy *n*-Exploration; examination.
Nuynoyin-*v*-To explore; examine; name, specify.

O

Octubre-*n*-October.
Onza-*n*-Ounce.

Oo-*adv.*-Yes; sure; aye; yea; indeed.
O-opo-*adv.*-Yes-sir; yes-ma'am.

Oras-*n*-Hour, time

Orasion-*n* Orison, even, eve

Oras ñg camatayan *n*-The hour of death.

Orason-*n*-Clock; watch, timepiece

Ordenanza-*n* Ordenance by law.

Oropel-*n*-Tinsel

Oroy-*inter*. Begone, gitout, hum

Owang-*n*-Horned bug which rembles the june bug

Oyam *n*-Mockery, scoffery, jeer, sneer, scoff, hoax.

Oyamin *i*-To riducule; scoff, jeer

P

Pa-*adv*-Yet, still, notwith standing

Paa *n* Foot.

Paalam-*n*-Goodbye, adieu; valediction; valedictory.

Paalisin *v*-To dismiss, send away, pnt out, dispel.

Paamoin-*i*-To tame, domesticate.

Paamuin-*v*-To tame; domesticate

Paa ñg ibon ó hayop na matilis ang kuko-*n*-Talon, claw

Paanayarin-*v*-To soften, mollify, mitigate

Paano-*adv* How, as, why, in what manner.

Paano iyan-How is that.

Paano na ay hindi-By no means; in no degree.

Paasahan *v*-To give hope

Paaasohan-*v*-To make or cause to smoke

Pa asohan-*n*-Smoke stack, chimney.

Paasohin-*v*-To smoke; fumigate

Pababain-*v*-To lower.

Pababain ang loob-*i*-To humble, humiliate; tame, dishearten.

Pabalik-*a*-Reverse, backward

Pabalikan-*v*-To reverse, rebut

Pabaliktad *a* Contrary, reversed

Pabañgisin-*i*-To make wild or fierce.

Pabañgo-*n*-Perfume, odor

Pabañgohan-*v*-To perfume

Pabaya-*a*-Indolent, neglectful, lazy, negligent; careless, heedless, injudicious, indescreet, inert, forgetful, indifferent, devious, inadvertent, improvident, slovenly, slouchy

Pabayaan-*i*-To neglect; omit, forget; overlook abandon, countenance, quit, leave, let, relinquish, forsake

Pabalungan-*n*-Spring

Pabigat-*n*-Weight, burden, ballast

Pabiglabigla-*adv*.-Hastily, hurriedly, precipitately

Pabilin *n*-Compliments, message, errand, commission.

Pabuis-*n*-Interest; profit; gain.

Pabulabukin sa lalamunan *v*-To gargle.

Pabuya *n*-Premiun, prize, reward, bounty, encouragement, inducement, stimulant

Padakilain-*v*-To extol, exalt, sublimate, elevate, magnify

Padaluyan ñg tubig *n* Canal, gutter; drain.

Padapa-*a*-Prone, facedown

Pader na lupa-*n*-Mud-wall

Padilagin-*v*-To embellish; aggrandize, beautify, adorn; emboss, raise,elevate; illustrate

Padilimin-*v*-To blacken, darken, blind; obscure

Padparan-*v*-To pare, shorten, cut away, delineate.

Padparin-*i*-To equalize; match; make, equal

Padron *n*-Census

Pag aagawan-*n*-Scrambling; snatching, scrambling match.

Pag aalaala-*n*-Remembrance, reflexion, thought; thinking; meditation; contemplation

Pag aalab ñg loob *n*-Passion, rage, anger, strong love

Pag aalaga *n*-Tutelage education,breeding, taking care of; bringing up

Pag aalay-*v*-Dedication, consecration, present; offer, gift

Pag aalis *n*-Going, leaving; evacuation.

Pag aaliw-*n*-Diversion, sport; merrymaking, liesure, recreation, consolation, comfort, entertainment, amusement, pastime

Pag aalsa-*n*-Rebellion, uprising, insurrection; mutiny, riot

Pag aampon-*n* Protection support, maintainance kindness; favor, patronage, help, aid, tutelage

Pa gaanin-*v*-To lighten; aleviate, make lighter

Pag aanito-*n*-Idolatry, inordinate love.

Pag aanyaya-*n* Invitation.

Pag aapoy-*n*-Kindling; ignition, setting on fire

Pag aaral-*n* Study, learning, instruction, apprenticeship

Pag aari-*n*-Fortune, wealth, estate farm

Pag aari sa salaping buisan-*n* Mortgage, pledge, security.

Pag aasawa sa dalawa-*n* Bigamy.

Pag aaway-*n*-Fight; war; combat; dispute; quarrel; conflict; contest; disagreement.

Pag abuloy-*n*-Aid; help; succor; assistance.

Pag agap-*n*-Activity; lacrity; quickness; prevention.

Pag agaw - *n* - Scrambling; snatching; rape; pillage; plundering; marauding

Pag ahit-*n*-Shave; shaving.

Pag ahon-*n*-Going up; ascendency. mounting.

Pag akay-*n*-Leading; teaching; drawing.

Pag agkyat-*n*-Ascension; ascendency.

Pagal-*n*-Fatigue; hardship; weariness; molestation; work.

Pagal-*c*-Wearisome; tiresome; fatiging; painful.

Pagálá *n*-Pelican.

Pag alañgan ñg loob-*n*-Uncertainty; perplexity; irresolution; wavering; hesitation; suspicion; suspense.

Pag alimura-*n*-Insult; abuse; reproach; slander; denunciation.

Pag alalay-*n*-Support; help; assistance.

Pagalingin-*v*-To cure; heal; mend; heighten; extol.

Pagalingin-*r*-To clean or clear land; prepare brush land for planting.

Pag alispusta-*n*-Insult; abuse; offence; effontry; contempt; denunciation; vituperotion; vilification; injury; abusiveness.

Pagalis-*n*-Start; departure; egress; agression; exodus.

Pagalitan-*v*-To anger; make angry.

Pag alitan-*n*-Cause of a quarrel.

Pag ambag-*n*-Contribution; subscription; tax.

Pagandahin-*v*-To beautify; embellish; adorn; decorate; emboss.

Pag añgil-*n*-Growling; snarling; grumbling.

Pag ani *n*-Crop; harvest.

Pagano-*n*-Pagan.

Pagapan-*adv*.-Creepingly.

Pag apaw *n*-Inundation; overflow.

Pag api-*n*-Grievance.

Pag apid-*n*-Adultery.

Pag aguhap-*n* Groping; hunting for anything by feeling; blind man's stick.

Pag asa-*n* Hope; expectancy.

Pag asiste-*n*-Help; assistance; aid.

Pag ato-*j*-Poise.

Pag ayaw-*n*-Refusal denial; quitting.

Pagayongayon-*a*-Lazy; indolent; idle; careless; negligent; wandering; slipshod; harumscarum.

Pagayongayon-*adv*-Indolently; carelessly, lazily; negligently.

Pag ayusin-*v*-To arrange; regulate; set in order.

Pagbaba-*n*-Descent; descencion.

Pagbabadbad-*n*-Steeping; soaking; wetting.

Pagbabag-*n*-Fight; mutiny; riot.

Pagbabaga-*n*-Kindling; ignition setting on fire.

Pagbabago-*n*-Renewing; change; alteration; transfiguration; metamorphosis.

Pagbabagong lakas-*n*-Convalescence; recovery.

Pagbabahagi-*n*-Partition division.

Pagbabahin-*n*-Sneezing; sneeze.

Pagbabahog-*n*-Incorporation.

Pagbabaka-*n*-War; fight; conflict; fray combat; dispute.

Pagbabala-*a*-Threat; menace; intention.

Pagbabalbas-*n*-Flattery.

Pagbabalayi-*n*-Wedding; nuptials.

Pagbabalibag-*n*-Throw; cast; casualty.

Pagbabalintuna-*n* Doing of anything by another, that should be done by one's self; reverse; perpersity; perverseness.

Pagbabalita-*n*-Narration; relation; notification reference; telling of news.

Pagbabaliwas-*n* Traffic; trading; commerce.

Pagbabalot-*n*-Package; wrapping; baling.

Pagbabaluktot-*n*-The bending; clinching.

Pagbabanal *n*-Virtue; sanctification; virtuousness; purity; chastity.

Pagbabasta ñg kalakal-*n*-Packing; package; baling.

Pagbabawas-*n*-Diminution; decline; fall.

Pagbabayad-*n*-Payment; pay; retribution-reward; disbursement; quittance.

Pagbabayad ñg lubos-*n*-Satisfaction; gratification; recompence.

Pagbabayad ñg upa-*n*-Payment; recompence.

Pagbagayin *v*-To adjust; adapt; fit; make proper or convenient.

Pagbago-*n*-Renewal; alteration; renewing; transition.

Pagbaha-*n*-Overflow; inundation.

Pagbala-*n*-Threat; challenge; impeachment.

Pagbalak-*n*-Intention; innouncement.

Pagbalik-*n*-Return; devolution.

Pagbanalbanalan-*n*-Hypocricy.

Pagbangit-*n*-Mention; allusion.

Pagbása-*n*-Wetting; moistening.

Pagbása-*n*-Reading.

Pagbatak-*n* Pull; haul; tug; draw; pulling; tugging; regress.

Pagbati-*n* Salutation; greeting; salute.

Pagbatiin-*v*-To saluteg reet; reconcile.

Pagbawalan-*n*-Prohibition; prohibiting.

13

Pagbawalan-v-To prohibit; deprive, suspend

Pagbawan ñg kahoy-n-The felling of trees

Pagbawas-n Dwindle.

Pagbawi-n-Recovery, redemtion, redeeming; retaliation

Pagbayaran-n-Payment; recompence

Pagbibigay-n-Giving, offer, gift; bequest; legacy, present, presentation, gratuity.

Pagbibigay ñg upa-n-Payment.

Pagbibigay parte-n-Notification; participation.

Pagbibigla-n-Haste, hurry, confusion, tumult, speed

Pagbibilang-n-Count, counting; enumeration

Pagbibilango e-Imprisomment imprisoning

Pagbibilin n - Commission, command, errand; charge, request, recommendation

Pagbibilog-n-Rotation, rounding sum

Pagbibintang-n-Impotation, accusation, indiction indictment

Pagbibintañgan-v-To accuse, blame, impeach

Pagbibithay-n-Sifting; bolting

Pagbigat-n Gravity, weight, importance

Pagbigkas-n-Pronunciation; publication, saying of anything without thinking.

Pagbigyang lingkod n-Courtship, lovemaking

Pagbigyang loob-n-Indulgence, compliance

Pagbitakan-n Cracking, sphtting

Pagbitakin-v-To crack, split .

Pagbual-n-Tumbling, tumble, demolition.

Pagbubulbo-n-Founding, casting, fusion, smelting

Pagbubugbog-n-Bruise, contusion

Pagbubuhat n-Origin, beginning, raising; lifting.

Pagbubucod-n-Separation, segregation, preclusion.

Pagbubula n-Effervescence; effervescency

Pagbubulaybulay n-Meditation, contemplation, musing thought idea

Pagbubulungbuluñgan-n-Whisper, whispering, gossip gossiping

Pagbubuno-n Wrestling; wrestle, scuffling.

Pagbugaw-n-Scaring, fright

Pagbugbog-n-Contusion, bruise

Pagbuhat-n-Lift; raising

Pagbuhos n Effusion, pouring

Pagbukal-n-Springing up, dawing, emination

Pagbuli n Polish

Pagbulok-n-Rottening, pus, corruption, decomposition

Pagbunot-n Eradication, pulling up

Pagbutasbutasin parang bithay-n-Perforation

Pagbuti-n-Improvement, improving, progress, advancement, growth, addition

Pagdabog n-Grumbling, growling, murmuring

Pagdadala n-Carrying; carriage, transportation, transporting.

Pagdadahilan-n Excuse; plea, allowance, apology

Pagdadalawahin-n-Bi section

Pagdadaop-n-Dispute, disagreement, the closing of two things

Pagdahak n Hawk; hawking.

Pagdahas-n-Force, courage, vigor, fortitude, valor, violence, co-ersion

Pagdadalhin-n Transportation

Pagdaing-n-Lamentation, entreaty, imploration, expostulation

Pagdaka-adv. Soon; immediately, instantly; suddenly, right away, presently; speedily.

Pagdaka-a Sudden, unexpected, immediate; plumb

Pagdalakip-n Seizure, capture

Pagdalañgin-v-To request, eutreat; petition, pray

Pagdalaw-n-Visit, visitation

Pagdalo-n-Succor, assistance, aid, help

Pagdama n-Moistening

Pagdamay-n-Implication, inculpation

Pagdamdam n-Sentiment, perception, feeling sensation, indisposition

Pagdami-n-Increase, multiplication, proficiency.

Pagdaraan-n-Passing, review.

Pagdaragdag-n-Addition, increase.

Pagdaragdag ñg lakas-n-Reinforcement

Pagdaramdam-n-Suffering, feeling, sufferance, indisposition, sensation

Pagdarasal-n-Prayer

Pagdaraya-n Cheating, allurement, deceit, fiction.

Pagdatal n Arrival, coming

Pagdating-n-Arrival, coming.

Pagdayo-n-Visit; visitation, going to a place for a certain purpose

Pagdedeposito-n Depositing, deposition.

Pagdedesthero-n-Deportation, banishment, exile

Pagdidikit-n-Gluing; co-hesion, coherence, coherency

Pagdidilidili-n Meditation, musing, contemplation

Pagdidilig n Sprinkling, watering.

Pagdidilim ñg araw n Eclipse of the sun.

Pagdidilim ng buan-n-Eclipse of the moon

Pagdidiwang n Celebration

Pagdool-n-Perversion, perversity, perverseness. deprevation.

Pagdowahagi-n-Persecution; illtreatment, abuse

Pagdowahagun-v-To persecute, illtieat, abuse

Pagduduble-n-Doubling, duplication

Pagdudurog n Pulverization; powdering

Pagdulog-n Presentation, presenting

Pagduruin-i-To prick, perforate, punch through

Paggahis-n-Rape, ravishment, allurement

Paggala-n-Stioll; gadding, going

Paggalang-n-Respect; adornation; worship

Paggalaw nMovement, commotion.

Paggaling-n Recovery, growth advance, progress, advancement

Paggamit-n-Use, service, employment; custom, adoption, affiliation, style, espousal; fashion

Paggamot-n-Remedy, reparation, cure, healing, doctoring, recourse

Pagganti n-Remuneration; revenge; reward, retribution

Pagganti ng utang na loob-n-Gratification, satisfaction, gratitude.

Paggapas-n-Harvesting, harvest, reaping, gathering of a crop.

Paggasliw-n-Liking; affection, taste.

Paggasta-n-Expense, costs; charge, disbursement

Paggawa-n-Work, construction, operation, working

Paggawa uh-n-Iteration.

Paggiba-n-Destruction, overturning, desolution, devastation.

Paggibik-n Succor, assistance, aid, help.

Pagguik-n Threshing

Paggisi ng balat-n-Itch; itching.

Paggitti-n Sprouting

Pagguhit-n-Lining; line, drawing of lines

Paggulamos-n-Scratching, piuching

Paggulong-n The rolling

Paghahaba-n-Lengthening; prolongation

Paghahabilin-n-Trust; recommendation

Paghahalaga-n-Valuation, appraisal, appraisment

Paghahalaman-n-Horticulture

Paghahalili n-Change, substitution, rehel, exchange, succession, surrogation, remission.

Paghahamak-n-Depreciation, contempt, scorn; disregard, insult.

Paghahamok-n Dispute, dissagreement, fight, war, battle, conflict

Paghahandog-n-Preparation; preparing, pleasure, present, gratification

Paghahati-n-Division; partition; apportionment, compartment, distribution

Paghahatid-n-Conduction conducing, accompanying.

Paghahayin-n-Oblation; offering

Paghahalal-n-Election; choice, electing, choosing

Paghalay-n-Awkwardness, scorn, contempt; depreciation

Paghalo-n-Mixture, mixing.

Paghaluhalun-v-To mix; jumblé.

Paghaluin-v-To mix, mingle

Paghahanga-n Limitation, limit; distinct; bounds.

Paghamak-n-Depreciation, disregard, scorn, contempt, insult

Paghamog-n-The falling of the dew.

Paghamon-n-Challenge, threat, provocation

Paghanap-n-Search; hunt; searching, looking for

Paghandulong-n-Assault, attack.

Paghapis n-Excruciation.

Paghapit n-Pressure.

Pagharap-n Presence, presenting, presentation; exibition.

Paghátol-n-Sentence, judgement

Pahawan-n-The felling of trees

Paghibik-n Groan, sob.

Paghibo-n-Seduction; deceit; illusion, imposition, cheating

Paghigpit-n Tightening, oppression, cruelty, hardship

Paghihigop-n-Supping, sup; absorption; swallow

Paghihimagsik-n-Rebelliournes; severity; stubbornness.

Paghihimagsik ng bayan laban sa puno-n-Revolution; sedition; insurrection, rebellion

Paghihimpil-n-Alleviation

Paghihintay-n-Expectation, stop, stay, sojourn, pause, expectancy

Paghihip-n-Blow, blast, puff.

Paghihuap-n-Excruciation, pain

Paghihiwalay-n-Separation, disunion, segregation, divergence, devergency, compartment

Paghila n-Draw; drawing, haul, hauling, dragging, tug, tugging; towing, tow.

Paghilig-n-Inclination; fancy, propensity, reclining

Paghilo n-Dizziness

Paghilot-n Softening; mollifying.

Paghiluman ng sugat-n-The knitting together of a wound

Paghimangit-*n*-The tearing into small bits

Paghinapangin-*v*-To fortify, strengthen, give courage

Paghingal-*n*-Pant; palpitation, respiration; breathing.

Paghingi-*n*-Entreaty, request; petition, prayer, claim, demand, imploration.

Paghinto-*n*-Stop, pause, suspension, cessation, relay, delay.

Paghinuhod-*n*-Apology

Paghipo *n*-Touch

Paghiwa *n*-Cut, cuttings slicing

Paghiwa-hiwain-*c*-To cut into small pieces

Paghiwalay-*n*-Division, separation; sunder

Paghiwalayin-*v*-To separate, divide, part, sunder.

Paghuad-*n*-Counterfeit; imitation, copy.

Paghuhula-*n*-Prognostication, prophecy

Paghuhulog-*n*-Falling, fall, throwing down

Paghuhulog ng isang wika sa iba-*n*-translation, interpretation.

Paghukay-*n*-Excavation

Pgahukay muli-*n*-Exhumation

Paghupa-*n* Decay; decline, fall, declination extenuation

Pagi-*n*-Dog-fish

Pag ibig-*n*-Love, affection, esteem, attachment, desire, estimation; philanthropy, good nature

Pag ibig sa DIOS-*n*-Piety.

Pag ibig ng mahigpit-*n*-Fraternity, brotherhood.

Pag igi-*n*-Improvement, easing, alleviation

Pag igihin-*v*-To ease, alleviate.

Pag iba-*n* Alteration, transformation; change, metamorphosis.

Pag ikit-*n*-Giration, turning

Pag iilag-*n*-Wildness, evasion, scare

Pag ilagan-*n*-Wildness, temerity, evasion; scare

Pag iilagin-*n*-Diarrhea.

Pag iilagin-*a*-Wild; timid

Pag iingat-*n*-Care, caution. precaution, prudence, painstaking; safeguard watching, heed, reserve, security

Pag iinog-*n*-Gyration, turning

Pag iipon-*n* Hoarding, gathering, laying away, storing, putting away

Pag iisa-*n*-Solitude, unison; lonliness; agreement, conformity

Pag iisip-*n*-Thinking, thought; reason, talent, mind brain understanding; intention, justice, consideration, prudence; right, principle, ability

Pag iiwan *n*-Abandonment, quittance.

Pag ikit-*n*-Rotation, turn, turning.

Pag ilag-*n*-Avoidance, evasion

Pag iling-*n* Negation; denial, negative, refusal

Página-*n*-Page

Pag intindi-*n*-Intelligence, understanding, skill, ability, sense, spirit

Paging-*v*-To be, become, exist

Pagitan-*n*-Space, interval, interlude, distance, middle

Pagitan-*prep*-Among, between

Pagitna-*a*-Intermediate, intervening, mediate

Pag inis-*n* Smothering, hardship, oppression

Pagiwi-*n*-Nursing;tutelage, guardianship

Pag iyak-*n* Cry, weeping, act of corying; mourning.

Pagka *adv*-After, afterwards

Pagka aba *n* Misery, humiliation

Pagka agas *n*-Miscariage, strong menstruation

Pagka ahon-*n*-Ascencion, ascendency

Pagka ahon sa pagka alipin *n*-Freedom from slavery

Pagka akma-*n* Corespondence, fitness

Pagka alaala-*n*-Remembrance, recognition, memory

Pagka ahila-*n*-Servitude, state of being a servant

Pagka alipin *n*-Servitude, bondage; slavery, thralldom, thrall, yoke, oppression

Pagka antala-*n*-Detention, delay, obstacle

Pagka api-*n*-Degredation, fall, degeneracy, diminutive

Pagka ayos *n*-Arrangement, order

Pagka ayos sa matowid-*n*-Justification, equity, justice

Pagka baba-*n*-Degeneracy, declination, fall, decline

Pagkabagbag ng sasakyan-*n*-Shipwreck.

Pagkabalam-*n*-Detention, delay, slowness, lingering

Pagkabalatong-*n*-Accident, incident, delay caused by the breaking of an instrument or machine

Pagkabahsa-*n*-Restlessmess; perturbation, uneasiness

Pagkabantay-*n*-Guard, watch.

Pagkabasa-*n*-Wetting, moistening

Pagkabasag ng sasakyan-*n*-Ship-wreck

Pagkabata *n*-Child hood, perulity juvenility.

Pagkabawi-*n*-Recevery, regaining

Pagkabayani *n* Boldness, courage audacity

Pagkabigatan *n* Heaviness, overloading, surcharging.

Pagkabigla-*n*-Hurry, quikness, activity, promptitude, speed

Pagkabihag-*n*-Captivity, confinement

Pagkabili-*n*-Cost cost-price, price

Pagkabitin-*n*-Suspension, hanging

Pagkabawal *n*-Tumble, fall, overbalance; overturning

Pagkabuhay *n*-Maintainence; support, sustinence, subsistence, life.

Pahkabuhay na muli-*n*-Resurection revival

Pagkabuhos-*n*-Effusion, pouring

Pagkabuli-*n*-Polish; finish

Pagkabulok-*n*-Rottenness, putrefaction, pollution, corruption, infection, putridness, depravity; depravation.

Pagkabusog *n*-Satiety, fullnes of the stomach

Pagkadalaga-*n*-Virginity; girlhood

Pagkaduble-*n*-Duplication

Pagkadulas-*n*-Smoothness, slipping

Pagkagalit-*n*-Anger, rage

Pagkadios-*n*-Diety; divinity.

Pagkagawa-*n*-Work, cut, shape, fashion, make; doing.

Pagkagastahan-*n*-Expense, cost

Pagkagawgaw-*n*-Mixing

Pagkaginoo *n*-Rank, honor, decorum, honesty, decency. nobility, distinction, respect

Pagkagitla-*n*-Surprise, amazement

Pagkagulo *n*-Disturbance, fight, noise, war, insurrection, commotion, tumult, riot, confusion, perturbation

Pagkahamak-*n*-Infamy, dishonor, disgrace, humiliation, baseness

Pagkahanda-*n*-Preparation, pomp, show

Pagkahango-*n*-Redemption; taking out, ransom.

Pagkahapay-*n*-Inclination

Pagkahapo *n* Inability

Pagkahapon-*adv*-Afternoon; after dinner, in the afternoon

Pagkahawa-*n*-Infection, contagion

Pagkahibang-*n*-Delirim, dotage, rant

Pagkahilig-*n*-Inclination, inclining

Pagkahilig ng loob-*n*-Affection, inclination, fancy, liking, taste

Pagkahinog-*n*-Maturity, ripenness

Pagkahubo-*n*-Nakedness

Pagkahukluban-*n*-Decrepitude, old age

Pagkahuli-*n*-Posteriority,

Pagkahulog-*n* Fall

Pagkaiba-*n*-Dissimilarity, dissimilitude, inequality.

Pagkaibig-*n*-Love, liking; desire, choice; caprice

Pagkain-*n*-Food, victuals, viand, ration, fare, sustenance

Pagkaina-*n* Maternity, motherhool.

Pagkaing tkinabubuhay-*n* Food, maintenance, subsistance

Pagkaisa-*n* Uniformity, unison, unity, conformity

Pagkaitan-*n*-Refusal, denial, negation

Pagkaa akgpang ng mga tawo *n*-Fraternity; brotherhood

Pagkaka alit-*n*-Dispute, disunion; difference; controversy, discord, disagreement, misunderstanding, variance.

Pagkaka ayaw *n*-Refusal, denial

Pagkaka ayon-*n*-Accord, accordance; conformity, uniformity, unity, coincidence.

Pagkaka ayos *n*-Arrangement, equality, alliance, unity

Pagkakagalit *n*-Discord, anger, dispute, rage, passion

Pagkakagalitan-*n*-Qurreling, misunderstanding, disagreement, dispute

Pagkakagulo-*n*-Revolution, insurrection, disturbance, sedition

Pagkakahalo-*n*-Mixture, mixing

Pagkakahiwalay-*n*-Separation, disunion, division

Pagkakaiba-*n*-Alteration, difference

Pagkakaila-*n*-Denial; contravention.

Pagkakailangan *n*-Necessity, want, need, urgency, exigence

Pagkakaisa-*n*-Unity, agreement, unanimity.

Pagkakakuha *n*-Seizure, capture, taking, getting

Pagkakalagay-*n* State, condition

Pagkakalakip-*n*-Juncture, joint, unity, state of being together.

Pagkakalapat-*n*-Juncture, union, connection, uniting, combination, joining, unity; coalition, contiguity

Pagkakalapit-*n*-Froximity, vicinity, proximation, approximation.

Pagkakaling *n* Reference, relation

Pagkakalinga-*n* Heed, care, attention; colicitude, caution, watching.

Pagkakaloy-*n*-Timbrel maker or seller; stamp maker.

Pagkakamag anakan-*n* Relation, relatives, kindred

Pagkakamali-*n* Error; mistake, blunder, oversight.

Pagkakamatay-*n*-Mortality; death

Pagkakamit-*n*-Attainment

Pagkakamtan-*n*-Attainment, acquisition

Pagkakamukha-*n*-Resemblance similarity, likiness, equity, equaelity, similitude, simile

Pagkakapantay-*n*-Equality, similitude

Pagkakaparis-*n*-Equality, similitude, similarity, simile, equivalence; equity, likeness.

Pagkakapisan-n-Unity, union, combination, meeting, congregation, alliance.

Pagkakapatid-n Fraternity, brotherhood.

Pagkakasal n-Espousal; nuptials, wedding.

Pagkakasahmoot-n-Density, closeness, compactness

Pagkakasahngsalng-n-Tradition

Pagkakasalot-n- overty, badluck, pestilence.

Pagbakasama-n-Juncture, joining, union.

Pagkakasangayon n Unity of time.

Pagkakasua-n-Discord, variance, misunderstanding, disunion, corruption, pollution

Pagkakasunduan-n Reconciliation, concord.

Pagkakasunod-n-Succession, series

Pagkakasunodsunod-n-Row, file

Pagkakatalaga-n-Intention, appropriation, propriety, manner, mode

Pagkakatah-n-Tie, tying, binding.

Pagkakatalo-n-Dispute; opposition, argument, contradiction

Pagkakataon-n-Accident; occurence, occasion, happening, hap; opportunity

Pagkakatimbang-n Equilibrium; balance.

Pagkakatipon n-Meeting; gathering, congregation, hoarding, laving up

Pagkakatipon ng madla-n-Multitude, crowd, meeting, congregation.

Pagkakatotoo-n-Proof; realization, truth

Pagkakatulad-n-Resemblance; similitude, likeness, similarity.

Pagkakaumpog n-Company; meeting

Pagkakatapat-n-Equality; equivalence.

Pagkakawanag-n-Reference; relation

Pagkakawangis-n-Comformity, likeness, resemblance, similarity, simile, similitude

Pagkakawanki-n-Similitude; resemblance, likeness, simile

Pag akwasto-n-Order, likeness; uniformity; regularity

Pagkakayas-n Whitling, shaving.

Pagkakikil n-Filings

Pagkakiskis-n-Scratching, friction.

Pagkakabahog-n-n Incorporation, combination, mixing

Pagkakilala n Amnesty, cognizance, intelligence; knowledge, skill, ability, friendship

Pagkakiling-n Inclination, declination

Pagkakintal-n Stamp, print, edition; impression.

Pagkakola n Gluing

Pagkaknha ng kabuntisan-n-Miscarriage, abortion.

Pagkakulo-n Effervescence, effervescency

Pagkalagay-n-Attitude, position, state, condition, rank.

Pagkalalaki-n-Virility

Pagkalanta-n-Withering, fading

Pagkalasa-n-Taste.

Pagkalat-n-Scattering; distribution, dispersion

Pagkaligpit-n Picking up, gathering; putting away; putting in order.

Pagkalimot-n-Forgetfulness, carelessness; heedlessness; oblivion

Pagkalipa-n-Leveling

Pagkalipol-n-Extermination, distruction, extinction

Pagkalis-n-Scraping; taking of the edge

Pagkalito n-Confusion; perplexity, perturbation, lightheadedness

Pagkalunok-n-State or condition of poverty

Pagkaloob n-Giving, gift, presentation, offering

Pagkalubog-n-Snbmersion, immersion

Pagkalugso-n Destruction.

Pagkalula-n-Swoon,dizziness,seasickness

Pagkalulo-n-S oon.

Pagkalusaw-n-Fluidity, liquescency, squandering of an inheritance

Pagkaluto-n-The manner of cooking; cookery, decoction

Pagkamaan-n-Amazement, charm.

Pagkamalahininga-n-Tepidity

Pagkamalakuko-n-Tepidity.

Pagkamapagpatawa-n Jollity, joyfulness

Pagkamaraindaman-n-Tenderness, delicacy

Pagkamasdan-n-Look, review, examination

Pagkamatay-n-Death, decease, mortality.

Pagkamot-n Scratch, scratching.

Pagkanlong-n-Hiding, protection concealment, shading, palliation, defense.

Pagkapa n Feel, touch

Pagkapalabunga-n-Fruitfulness, fertility.

Pagkapalagay-n-Adulation.

Pagkapaos-n Hoarseness

Pagkapatawad n-Acquittance, acquittal, forgiveness

Pagkapilay-n-Lameness, sprain, limpdisability, halt.

Pagkapilipit-n Twist, wreathing, contortion, twining

Pagkapoeta-n-Poet

Pagkapuno-n-Repletion.

Pagkaraka adv.-Suddenly, instantly, immediately.

Pagkasagi-n Broshing of one's clothes, against another, walking where one should not

Pagkasakit-n-Disability, sickness.

Pagkasaklaw-n-Universality.

Pagkasala-n-Violation

Pagkasalangasang n Contravention.

Pagkasalawahang loob n-Inconstancy, infidelity; uncertainty, suspicion, doubt, hesitation

Pagkasauli n Return, reintegration

Pagkasira-n-Ruin, downfall, pollution, corruption, putrefaction

Pagkasunduan-n-Accord, accordance, amenity, reconciliation, accommodation

Pagkasunodsunod n-Alteration, succession.

Pagkasupil-n-Subjection, submission

Pagkatagpo-n-Find discovery

Pagkatakid-n-Trip, stumble.

Pagkatangi-n-Singularity; separation re, moteness, solitude.

Pagkatangi n-Refusal, denial

Pagkatapos-adv -After, afterwards, then, next

Págkatápos-n-Termination, end.

Págkatapos nang-prep -After

Pagkáti-n-Ebb

Págkatí-n-Itching.

Pagkatina n-Dye, dying, act of dying

Pagkatingnan-n-Review, examination

Pagkatisod-n-Stumble, trip, impediment, obstacle, difficulty.

Pagkatulisan-n-Outlawry.

Pagkatunaw-n-Smelting, melting

Pagkatunaw ñg kinain-n-Digestion

Pagkaugnay-n-Reference, relation; unity union

Pagkaugpong-n-Juncture, union, connection

Pagkauhanin-n Decrepitude; old age, repitition.

Pagkauhila-n-Orphanage

Pagkauhit-n-Repitition, reiteration

Pagkaulol-n-Delirium, dotage, rant, craziness; insanity

Pagkautal-n-Hesitation; stammering, stuttering, haw.

Pagkautas-n-Finish; termination, end

Pagkawala-n-Loss

Pagkawala ñg diwa-n-Loss of sense

Pagkawalang dalita-n-Impassibility

Pagkawalan ñg loob-n-Perturbation; uneasiness.

Pagkawáy-n-Waving, motioning

Pagkawili-n Affection, liking taste; pleasure

Pagkikikil-n-The filing

Pagkilala ñg utang na loob-n Gratitude, gratefulness

Pagkipagkitaan n Meeting; visiting, encounter.

Pagkit-n Glue, mucilage, waxtaper.

Pagkubkob sa isang lugar-n-Siege

Pagkuenta-n-Summing, addition

Pagkuha-n-Taking; seizing; grasping; grasp, capture, seizure

Pagkuha ang di kaniya n-Usurpation

Pagkukulang-n-Lack; shortage; want

Pagkukulong n-Confinement, seclusion

Pagkukulong sa kusa-n-Hermit; recluse.

Pagkukunuwari-n-Affectation, deceit, hypocricy

Pagkukupkup-n-Shelter, protectios, safeguard

Pagkukuro n-Correction; regulation.

Pagkukuton-n Wrinkling, wrinkle; ruf, fling

Pagkulo-n-Boiling.

Pagkupas n Pading, withering

Pagkurot-n-Nip, pinch

Pagkuskus-n-Scrape; catching, friction

Pagkusot-n-Rumple, rumpling.

Paglabag-n-Resistence, stubbornness, rebelliousness, rebellion, insurrection.

Paglabag sa kautusan-n-Violation

Paglaban-n Resistence, fight, war, antagonism, opposition; assualt

Paglabas-n-Departure, start, exit, exodos, going ont

Paglabnot-n-Pluck, plucking

Paglagin-n-Prequence, frequency, permanency, duration

Paglago-n-Proficiency, profusion, improvement, addition.

Paglagom-n-Unision, uniting, joining, junciure, joint

Paglahang-n-Crack, cracking.

Paglahok-n-Inclusion, incorporation.

Paglahu in-c-To incoporate, include

Paglait-n-Abuse, contempt; outrage, insult

Paglakad-n-Walk, march

Paglaki-n- ncrease, growth, swelling; dilation.

Paglakip-n-Unision, joining, alloy, uniting, coalescense gathering.

Paglakasan-n-Strengthening, exertion, invigoration, enforcement

Paglaktaw n-Omission; skip, leaving, out

Paglaktaw ñg isang salita n Elipsis

Paglala-n-Weaving

Paglalaba-n-Washing; wash

Paglalagari-n-Sawing

Paglalahok -n- Inclusion, incorporation, mixture, mixing.

Paglalacbay-n-Travel, travelling, journey, passage

Paglalakip-*n*-Joining union, juncture, conjunction; coalition, combination, alliance

Paglalang *n*-Creation, creating

Paglalaro-*n*-Play, playing; romping, amusement, sport, game

Paglalatag ng̃ bato-*n*-Paving, pavement

Paglalaway *n*-Salivation; spitting

Paglamas-*n* Kneading

Paglamatin-*v*-To flaw, crack

Paglamutak-*n*-Kneading

Paglamuyot-*n*-Seduction

Paglang̃itng̃it *n* Creaking, squeaking

Paglapad *n*-Width, widening

Paglapastang̃anan-*n*-Outrage; insult, affront, abuse, contempt, injury, slight, injustice, wrong, offense

Paglapit-*n*-Approximation; approach, calculation

Paglasap-*n*-Tasting, taste, relish

Pagsalon-*n*-Poison, poisoning

Paglayo-*n*-Retreat, distance, privacy

Paghbak-*n*-Slander, defamation, ridicule

Pagligalig *n*-Laziness, indolence, depravity, carelessness, tramping about without any definity object

Paghgaw-*n*-Love making, courtship.

Paghgawhgaw-*n*-Subversion

Paghgpit-*n*-Gathering up, putting in order, putting away

Paghgtas *n*-Salvation; saving, preservation.

Paglut *n*-Diminution, declination, decline

Paghko-*n*-Sheer, digression.

Paghhbang-*n* Recreation, amusement, pastime, diversion, sport, play, jest, game; festivity, feast, vacation, rejoicing, liesure

Paghhbing-*n*-Funeral burial, sepulture

Paghhgaw-*n* Lovesuit, love, courtship

Paglilihim-*n* Secret, reserve, secrecy, exception

Paghhkot *n*-Restlessness, boisterousness; uneasiness

Paghhmbag-*n*-Stamping, printing, edition

Paghhnkod *n*-Service, courtship, attendance, compliance

Paghhnis-*n* Cleansing, cleaning

Paghhpat-*n*-Transition, transfer, transportation.

Paghmot-*n*-Neglect; forgetfulness negligence; disregard.

Paghnang-*n*-Harrowing

Paghnkuran *n* Service, courtship.

Paghpana *n* Extension; scattering, skin mishing

Paglipat *n* Passage, transition transfer.

Paghpol-*n*-Extinction, destruction, extermination, abolition.

Paghyasin-*n*-Try, attempt, examination, proof

Paghtakin-*n*-Cracking, crack; split, splitting

Paghwanag-*n*-Solution, illumination

Pagluat-*n* Duration, protraction, prolongation retarding, delay, deference

Paglubay-*n* Stop, cessation

Paglubo-*n*-Flattery; flattering, coaxing, decoy

Paglubog *n*-Inundation, sinking, overflow, immersion; occident; west, submersion

Paglubog ng̃ araw *n*-The setting of the sun

Pagluhog-*n* Request, suplication, entreaty, imploration; petition

Pagluluat-*n*-Slowness, delay, detention, lingering; prolongation

Palulubog-*n*-Submersion, immersion

Paglululan-*n*-Embarkation, sipping, loading

Paglupig-*n*-Usurpation

Paglupi-*n*-Fold

Paglupilupin-*n*-Redoubling, refolding

Paglura *n*-Spitting, expectoration.

Paglusob-*n*-Attack; assault.

Pagmamadalas-*n*-Frequence, frequency.

Pagmamadah-*n*-Haste, hurry, speed, exigence, hastiness, celerity, rush; promptitude

Pagmamagahng-*n*-Pride, selfesteem.

Pagmamahal *n*-Affection, estimation, esteem, endearment, value, price

Pagmamahal ng̃ tang̃i *n* Brotherhood, fraternity, predilection.

Pagmamaka ano-*n* Suplication, request, petition, doing in any way.

Pagmamalikmata *n* Transfiguration

Pagmamana *n*-Heirdom, inkeritance

Pagmamarati-*n*-Durability, permanency, stability, duration, durance, minute, ness.

Pagmamasid *n* Observance, observation, note, scrutiny, remark

Pagmamatowid-*n*-Reasoning; argument, discussion, correction, disquisition, dissentation, dispute

Pagmamatwiran *n*-Reasoning, argument, dispute, discussion, disquisitation, dissentation

Pagmumukha-*n*-Mode, face, aspect, countenance, look, appearance; front, outline, arrangement, manner.

Pagmumultiphcar *n* Multiplication

Pagmura *n* Slander, insult; abuse; vituperation, vilification slandering insulting.

Pagmura sa hindi kaharap-*n* Backbiting, gossiping

Pagnacaw *n*-Theft, robbery, larcency, peculation, pillage

Pagnanaknak ng sugat *n* Ulceration.

Pagngatngat-*n*-Gnawing

Pagngingiti-*n* Smiling

Pagngiti-*n*-Smile

Pagngiwi-*n*-Grimace, wry face

Pagnguso *n*-Pout.

Pagnitin-*n*-Unglueing

Pagod *n* Anguish, fatigue, weariness, anxiety

Pagod na malabis-*n*-Fatigue, hardship, anguish

Pagong-*n*-Turtle, tortoise, terrapin

Pagpaalis-*n* Expulsion

Pagpagalan-*n*-Work, fatigue

Pagpag-*n*-Shake, flourish, brandish

Pagpagpag-*n*-Shaking, brandishing, flourishing

Pagpakonowari-*n*-Sham, fiction, falsehood, stratagem, pretense, deceit.

Pagpalabas-*n*-Ejection, ejectment, expulsion.

Pagpalagay *n*-Ascription

Pagpalain-*i*-To help, support, shelter, protect; heed, take care of, do well improve, mend; meliorate

Pagpalaki-*n*-Increase, aggrandizement.

Pagpalayaw *n*-Cajolery, favoritism, caress

Pagpalitan-*n*-Change, barter, permutation

Pagpalitan ng ngalan *n* Misnaming, alias, taking of another name

Pagpalitpalitan-*n* Changing with frequency

Pagpalo-*n* Strike, beating- whipping, hit.

Pagpana-*n* Shooting of an arrow, archery.

Pagpanaog *n*-Descent, descension

Pagpanaw-*n*-Deportation, exile, banishment.

Pagpambaguhan-*n*- Renewal, mending; reiteration, reformation

Pagpaalaala-*n*-Remembrance, momento

Pagpapaalis-*n*-Expulsion, sending away, banishment

Pagpapabaya-*n*-Abandonment, neglect, negligence carelessness

Pagpapabunga-*n*-Fertility, fruitfulness

Pagpapabuti,*n*-Betterment.

Pagpapala-*n*-Remittance, remission, remittal, remitment.

Pagpapagayongayon-*n*-Idleness, indolence, laziness

Pagpapahangin-*n*-The airing.

Pagpapahayag-*n* Relation; notice, anunciation, manifestation, declaration, revelation, proclamtiaon

Pagpapahid-*n*-Smearing, wiping

Pagpapahinga-*n*-Rest, vacation, cessation, pastime, repose, diversion, intermission, liesure.

Pagpapahinga ng hokbo-*n*-Camp, encampment

Pagpapahinog-*n* Maturity; maturing; ripening

Pagpapahintulot-*n*-Permission, leave; permit

Pagpapahiram *n*-Lending, loaning

Pagpapahrap-*n*-Illtreatment, abuse, giving or causing of pain.

Pagpapakababa-*n*-Humility, submission, meekness, humiliation, self-contempt

Pagpapakabanal-*n*-Sanctification; virtue.

Pagpapakain-*n*-Maintenance; sustinence, feeding, giving of food

Pagpapaiwan-*n*-Leaving, abandonment

Pagpapakilala-*n*-Presentation, introduction, acquintance, explication, manifestation

Pagpapalagay-*n*-Supposition, putting.

Pagpapalago-*n* Fertilization

Pagpapalalo-*n* Bragging, pride, haughtiness

Pagpapaligo *n* Bathing.

Pagpapalimos-*n*-Beggary, mendicancy; begging

Pagpapalit-*n*-Changing, permutation

Pagpapalitan *n*-Commutation, change, exchange;

Pagpapaloob-*n* Insertion, putting in

Pagpapalumagak-*n*-The leaving of anything with another.

Pagpapamook-*n* Affray; scuffle, strife, struggle

Pagpapanaw *n* Deportation, banishment transportation

Pagpapanday-*n*-Blacksmithing.

Pagpapantay-*n* Equalization

Pagpaparatang-*n*-Imputation, accusation charge

Pagpaparusa-*n*-Punishment, chastizement

Pagpapasákit-*n*-Tortue, pain, torment, anguish.

Pagpapasiyal-*n*-Stroll walk.

Pagpapasiya *n*-Sentence, judgment advice, determination.

Pagpapatalastas-*n*-Announcement,notice; declaration, annunciation.

Pagpapatawad-*n*-Pardon, relief, remission, absolution, liberation, forgiveness

Pagpapatawag *n*-Call, calling, notice, notification, summons, admonition

Pagpapatay-*n*-Murder, assasination

Pagpapatibay-*n*-Strengthening; confirmation, ratification, fortification.

14

Pagpapatigil-*n*-Suspension, cessation, stop

Pagpapatiwakil-*n* Exasperation, indignation

Pagpapatotoo-*n* Confirmation ratification, affirmation, certification, testimony, assertion.

Pagpapatuloy-*n* Continuation, continuance

Pagpapaupa-*n*-Hire

Pagpapaupa ng puri-*n*-Brothel, whoring

Pagpapautang-*n*-Giving credit, crediting, loaning

Pagpapawis-*n*-Perspiration, perspiring, sweating

Pagpapayo *n*-Advice, exhortation

Pagparoon-*n*-Going

Pagpasáin-*n*-Contusion, bruise, burn

Pagpasalamat-*n* Thanksgiving, thanks, thanking

Pagpaslang-*n* Illtreatment, abuse, offence, injury, insult, lack of respect; transgression

Pagpasok-*n*-Entrance, ingress, entree, entry, importation, beginning, interjection

Pagpasuko-*n* Repulsion

Pagpasulong-*n*-Propulsion, drive

Pagpasuso-*n*-Lactation, nursing

Pagpatalastas-*n*-Annunciation, proclamation, announcement.

Pagpatawad *n* Quittance, pardon

Pagpatay-*n* Murder

Pagpatay sa hari *n*-Regicide

Pagpatay sa kapwa-*n*-Homicide, murder

Pagpatay sa sarili-*n* Suicide

Pagpatay sa sariling ina-*n*-Matricide

Pagpatibay-*n* Confirmation, ratification, fortification strengthening

Pagpatotoo *n*-Affirmation, testimony, proof, attestation, evidence, indication, verification

Pagpaunawa-*n*-Annunciation, proclamation

Pagpatuad *n*-Inversion demolition

Pagpawala nang halaga *n* Depreciation in value

Pagpayapa *n*-Pacification, quietude, calmness, quietness; quiet, tranquility.

Pagpayohan *n* Advice; advising

Pagpayuhan-*n*-Advice, admonition, influence

Pagpiga-*n*-Pressure, squeeze

Pagpighatian *n*-Disgust, loathing.

Pagpigil-*n*-Suppression, suspension, stop, check, constraint

Pagpigilan-*n* Check, stopping

Pagpigilan ng kalooban *n* Moderation

Pagpili-*n*-Election; choice; choosing.

Pagpilipit-*n*-Twisting, twist, twining; wreating, contortion; winding

Pagpilit-*n*-Persistence, force, urgency, coersion, enforcement, compulsion, violence

Pagpilit sa babayi-*n*-Rape

Pagpipigil-*n*-Stopping, checking; stop; check

Pagpipiging-*n*-Festivity, feasting

Pagpipilit-*n*-Urging, persistence,

Pagpipinsan *n*-Cousinship

Pagpipisan-*n* Reunion; meeting, congregation.

Pagpipisik-*n*-Sputtering, sputter

Pagpipista-*n* Feasting, rejoicing, feast

Pagpiral-*n* The twisting of the ear

Pagpisan-*n* Accumulation, heaping, unision; uniting

Pagpitagan-*n*-Respect, regard, esteem, veneration

Pagpugot-*n* Beheading, decapitation

Pagpukol-*n* Thow, cast.

Pagpulandit-*n*-Spattering

Pagpupúlo-*n*-Congregation, meeting

Pagpupulong *n*-Meeting, congregation

Pagpupulong ng congreso *n*-A session of congress

Pagpupuri-*n*-Plaudit, eulogy.

Pagpuputong ng korona-*n*-Coronation.

Pagpuputukan ng baril-*n*-Shooting of a gun

Pagpupuyat-*n*-Night watching

Pagpuri-*n* Commendation, esteem, estimation, virtue, acclamation

Pagpuri ng kabutihan-*n* Praise

Pagpusta-*n*-Wager, bet

Pagputok-*n*-Shooting, shot; explosion, crack, report

Pagputol-*n*-Amputation, cutting cut.

Pagputol ng kahoy-*n* The felling of trees.

Pagsabog-*n*-Dispersion, scattering

Pagsabunot-*n* Plucking out

Pagsadsad *n*-Anchorage, anchoring, beaching

Pagsagot-*n* Answer, reply, repartee, contestation, response

Pagsagsag-*n*-Trot, trotting

Pagsaka-*n*-Cultivation, agriculture

Pagsakay-*n*-The riding, ride

Pagsakop-*n* - Redemption, salvation, ransom; taking under protection

Pagsalakay *n* Stealing, thieving, surprise

Pagsalangsang-*n* Resistance, opposition; contradiction, refutation, contrariness, violation

Pagsálat-*n* Touch, touching, notation; comprehension.

Pagsalat *n*-Misery, hardship; proverty, bad-luck

Pagsalin-*n*-Transcription; copying; empting from one vessel into another.

Pagsalsal-*n*-Flattening; riveting; clinching; expending; wasting.

Pagsalubong-*n* Reception; meeting; encounter; compromise.

Pagsalungit *n*-Contrariness; opposition; disobedience; stubbornness; contrariety; reverseness.

Pagsáma-*n*-Connection; meeting; company; retinue; corporation; affiliation; uniting; joining; aggregation; aggregate.

Pagsáma-*n*-Perversion; perversity; depravation; wickedness; disobedience.

Pagsamahin-*n*-The joining, collection; gathering; spoils; capture; of anything.

Pagsámasámahin-*n*-Collection; gathering.

Pagsamsam-*n*-Collection; capturing;gathering.

Pagsandig-*n*-Reclining; leaning; against.

Pagsapsap-*n*-Munching; crunching

Pagsasabi-*n*-Telling; report; narration; relation; predication.

Pagsasabon-*n*-Making of suds; soaping.

Pagsasagupa-*n*-Scuffle; strife; fight; affray.

Pagsasaka-*n*-Cultivation; farming.

Pagsasakdal-*n*-Recourse; appeal; petition; entreaty.

Pagsasalab-*n*-Scorching.

Pagsasalaysay-*n* Explanation; narration; signification; saying.

Pagsasalin-*n*-Putting from one vessel into another; copying transcribing.

Pagsasalita-*n*-Talking; saying; conversation.

Pagsasalitaan-*n*-Conversation chat; conference; talking.

Pagsasamba-*n*-Homage.

Pagsasandokan-*n*-The taking by spoonsful; ladling.

Pagsasangla-*n*-Hypothecation.

Pagsasauli-*n*-Devolution; returning; restitution; reintegration.

Pagsaway-*n*-Stopping checking,

Pagsasaysay-*n*-Relation; narration; report; explication; declaration; account; saying; telling.

Pagsauli-*n*-Devolution; restoration.

Pagsawa-*n*-Fullness.

Pagsasaya-*n*-Feasting; rejoicing; festivity; happiness; celebration.

Pagsayaw-*u*-Dance.

Pagsaysay-*n*-Narration; reference; relation; solution; predication; portrayal; analysis

Pagsesello-*n*-Stamping.

Pagsesermon-*n*-Preaching.

Pagsiyasat-*n*-Inquiry; investigation; examination;.

Pagsigaw-*n*-Cry; screaming; yell; yelling; calling; vociferation.

Pagsilangñgaraw-*n*-The rising of the sun.

Pagsilbihan-*n*-Serving; making use of.

Pagsimana-*n*-Turn; order; succession, vicissitude.

Pagsimba-*n*-Worship.

Pagsingâ-*n*-The blowing of ahe nose.

Pasingaw-*n* Steaming; exhalation.

Pagsinta-*n*-Love; loving; courtship.

Pagsipot-*n*-Appearance; apparition; emanation; birth.

Pagsira-*n*-Breaking; destruction; disruption; demolition; dilapidation; destroying; rotting.

Pagsirang puri-*n*-Slander; defamation.

Pagsilid-*n*-Putting in; sacking up.

Pagsisisi-*n*-Repentance; penitence; regret.

Pagsisiyasat-*n*-Examination; investigation; inquiry; inspection; survey.

Pagsoway-*n*-Disobedience; contrariness; contradiction; opposition.

Pagsuhol-*n*-Bribery; subordination.

Pagsukat-*n* Measurement; mensuration; measuring.

Pagsuko-*n*-Subjection; surrender; rendition; yielding.

Pagsukol-*n*-Prevention.

Pagsukot-*n*-Humilliation; self-contempt; shame; submission.

Pagsulat-*n*-Writing; contract; treatise;

Pagsulong-*n* Progress; advancement; growth; augmentation; improvement; proficiency; addition; increase.

Pagsuma-*n*-Sum; summing; up; total; addition; amount; conclusion.

Pagsungab-*n*-Wrestling; wrestle.

Pagsunod-*n*-Obedience; submission; observance; following; succession.

Pagsunod -*n*- Burning; conflagration; combustion; burn.

Pagsuob *n*-Fumigation; smoking; fumigating.

Pagsupil-*n*-Domination; control; governing.

Pagsusulatan-*n*-Correspondence; writing; intercourse.

Pagsusulsol -*n*- Instigation; infusion; domination.

Pagsusumakit-*n*-Work;working with care.

Pagsusumbong-*n*-Accusation; impeachment; accusing.

Pagsusupling-*n*-Sprouting; germination.

Pagtábas-*n* Shape; shaping; cut; outline.

Pagtabas-*n*-Cutting; delineation.

Pagtagupak-*n* Slap,sound;made by a slap.

Pagtahol-*n* Bark; Barking.

Pagtakal-n-Measurement; measuring

Pagtakas-n-Migration, escape, elope ment; secret leaving

Pagtakbo-n-Run, running, flight.

Patakpan-n-Cover, covering

Pagtalikod-n-Denial, negation,

Pagtalop-n-Paring, peeling

Pagtangan-n-Hold; holding

Pagtangap-n-Receipt; acceptance, reception, acceptation; receiving

Pagtangi-n-Denial, refusal, negation

Pagtangis-n-Crying, weeping; bewailing; snivelling

Pagtapak-n-Tread, tramp

Pagtapakan-n-Treading; trampling

Pagtarok-n-Sounding, sound

Pagtatae na may halong dugo-n-Dysentery

Pagtatagal-n-Duration, continuance; stability; continuation, subsistence, prolongation, tardiness; slowness.

Pagtatagpi-n-Mending, patching

Pagtataguinpay-n-Defense, protection; support

Pagtataka-n-Wonder, amazement, charm, admiration; amaze.

Pagtatakapan-n-Dispute, fight with words; argument in which bad words are used

Pagtakip-n Cover, covering hiding, concealment; concealing

Pagtatakpanan-n-Covering, concealment hiding

Pagtataktak-n-Branding; marking; sealing.

Pagtatali-n-Tying

Pagtatalo-n-Dispute, quarrel, strife fight; contest; conflict, rivalry, competition, antagonism; argument, difference, litigation; lawsuit, controversy

Pagtatalunan-n-Cause of a dispute or argument, argument, quarreling

Pagtatamo-n Sufference; suffering, tolerance; toleration.

Pagtataman-n-Elopement

Pagtatanan ng sundalo n-Desertion; deserting

Pagtatanaw-n-Dicernment; view.

Pagtatanda-n-Memorization, remembering, marking; branding, sign

Pagtatangal-n-Solution, disintegration, taking to pieces

Pagtatangap n-Receiving; acceptance, acceptation, taking

Pagtatangol-n Shelter, protection, defence

Pagtatanim-n-Planting, sowing.

Pagtatanim galit n Hatred; aversion, rancor; grudge

Pagtatanim sa kapwa n-Hatred; aversion.

Pagtatanim sa loob-n-Anger, passion; rage

Pagtatankilik n-Protection, support; maintenance

Pagtatanod-n-Guard, watch; sentinel

Pagtatapat-n Fidelity, constancy. the telling of the truth, comparison of two things

Pagtatapon-n-Throwing away, wasting, cast; scattering

Pagtatapos n-Conclusion finish, finishing, ending.

Pagtatatag-n-Institution, founding; establishment, edification

Pagtatayo-n-Edification, building, founding establishment, establishing, institution

Pagtatlong bahagi-n-The dividing into three parts

Pagtawad n-Bartering; haggling, offering of a certain price for anything

Pagtawag-n Calling, announcement; announcing; summons

Pagtayo ng bigat-n-Weighing.

Pagtibayan-n-Ratification, affirmation, fortification, strengthening, corroboration, making, fast, security.

Pagtigil-n-Stop, check; pause, delay; suspension, suspence, sojourn

Pagtigpas-n-The act of cutting or shoing.

Pagtilhim-n-Taste, tasting

Pagtiklop-n-Fold, folding, doubling

Pagtikloptiklopin-n-Refolding

Pagtilansik-n-Splashing; splash.

Pagtimbangan-n-Weighing, balancing

Pagtingin-n-Sight, respect, regard, veneration

Pagtipirin n Economy

Pagtira-n Habitation, lodging, dwelling; living, inhabiting

Pagtitiis-n Patience, endurance, tolerance, toleration; sufferance, suffering

Pagtitina-n-The act of dyeing

Pagtitipan-n-Notification; agreement an nouncement

Pagtitipid-n-Economy, frugality.

Pagtitipon-n Gathering, hoarding, laying away, collection, collecting, congregation, meeting

Pagtubo-n-Increase, growth, augmentation, profit, gain

Pagtubos n-Redemption; ransom, remission.

Pagtudla-n-Throw, cast

Pagtugtog-n The playing of musical instruments

Pagtugtog ng kampana n The tolling of a bell.

Pagtuká-n-The pecking, peck
Pagtukso n Teasing joking; jesting temptation
Pagtutukin-n-The collision.
Pagtulad n-Imitation copying.
Paktulak-n Shove, push, propulsion
Pagtulong n Help, assistance, aid- co-operation, safe-guard
Pagtupad-n-Compliance, complying, observance, obedience
Pagturo n-Teaching, instruction, doctrine.
Pagtutukam-n-Peck or pecking of a fowl
Pagtutulangan-n-Cooperation, aid, assistance help
Pagtutunaw-n-Thawing, melting, smelting, loss, losing of money.
Pagtuturo-n-Teaching; instruction; edification
Pagdulot-n-Rebounding returning, bouncing, retrocession
Pag uga-n Rocking, moving, commotion, movement
Pag ugpungin-n-The joining at the ends
Pag ugtungan-n-The joining at the ends
Pag uli n Repetition, reiteration
Pag ulit n-Reiteration, repetition
Pagulogulo-adv -Disorderly, madly; sillily.
Pagulungin-v-To roll; run, on wheels
Pag umit-n-Peculation, stealing
Pag uno n-Hesitation, wavering, stammering, stuttering
Pag unti-n-Diminution, decline, fall, declination, dwindle, decay
Pag upak-n-Clap
Pag upak-n The husking
Pag upat-n-Instigation, flattery, persuasion, destitution; leaving of another in destitute circumstances.
Pag uraly-n Instigation, impulse, persuasion, opinion
Pagurin-v To tire, make tired.
Pag urong-n-Retrocession, taking back, return
Pag usad-n-Crawling, creeping, wooden rattle.
Pag usig-n-Persecution
Pag usisa-n-Examination, investigation; inquiry
Pag usisain-v-To inquire, investigate, review
Pag uugali-n Procedure, conduct manner, demeanor, use, custom, style, fashion, mode, form, method; deportment
Pag uugnay-n-Conformity, contiguity, combination, union, conjunction, order, unity, composition
Pag uugoy-n-Swinging, moving; rocking
Pag uukol n Destination pertamence.

Pag uuli-n-Restoration, restitution; devolution, renewing, reestablishment.
Pag uuhit-n-Iteration; reiteration; duplication
Pag uurong n-Recession; backing down.
Pag uusap-n-Dispute, litigation, lawsuit; contract
Pag uusapan n-Session, conference; conversation
Pag usbong n-Germination.
Paguusisa n-Examination, research; review, probation, inquiry.
Paguusisang muli-n-Revision, review
Paguuyam n-Ridicule
Pagvovoto n-Voting, vote, poll, ballot
Pagwawaksi-n Separation; division; culling, refusal, negation
Pag awari-n-Meditation, deliberation, reflection, cogitation, contemplation, reasoning
Pagwiwika-n-Talking, talk, saying.
Pawiwika ng masama-n-Backbiting, slander, gossip, bad talk.
Pagwiwika ng katampalasanan-n Insult; abuse, slander, libel, abusiveness; libeling
Pagwiwisik-n Sprinkling.
Pagyamanin-v-To enrich, make rich; make fruitful or fertile
Pagyaw-n Departure
Pagyari-n-Construction; termination, finish
Pagyasak-n-Trampling, treading
Pagyukod-n-Respect veneration, homage, reverence, backwardness
Pagyurak-n-Trampling, treading
Pahaba adv-Lengthwise, sidelong
Pahalang-n-Crosspiece, cross-timber.
Paham n-Learning, wisdom
Pahanginan-v-To air, dry in the air
Paharap-adv-Face forward
Pahayag n-Notice, proclamation, revelation, publication
Pahayag ng kasal-n-Banns
Pahayag ng patay-n Obituary
Pahid-n-Smear, wipe
Pahiga-adv-Horizontally.
Pahiga a-Horizontal
Pahigitin-v-To excell, exceed, surpass
Pahigtin-v-To tighten; press.
Pahimpihin-v-To ease, lighten, calm, cease
Pahinain v To weaken; make weak
Pahinain ng loob-v-To dishearten; discourage, dismay
Pahinayin-v-To prepare for cooking.
Pahindi n-Denial, refusal, negation, contradiction; disowning
Pahingahan n Resting place, place of rest

Pahintoin-v-To stop, check, detain, keep, retard

Pahintulot-n-Permission, assent, leave, license, ' privelege, approval, admittance, approbation, sanction, consent, indulgence, turlough; liberty, authority, right, power, good will

Pahintulotin v-To permit; leave, consent, approve, admit, give permission, let, sanction, assent, privelege, license

Pahinugin-v-To ripen, make ripe

Pahiran-v-To wipe, smear

Pahiran ng alkitran-v To tar

Pahiran ng cebo v-To grease

Pahirapan v-To chastize, punish, injure, abuse, aggrieve, agonize, distress

Pahiwalayan-v-To separate, divide

Pahiwas adv. -Slantingly, slopingly

Pahiwas-a-Sloping; slanting

Pahiyain v-To shame, disgrace, embarrass

Pahumal-a-Nasal

Pahupain-v-To diminish, make thin, weaken

Pahusayin v-To arrange, put in order

Paibabaw-a-Uppermost, top, superficial, shallow.

Paikit-adv -Gyratory

Pakipik-a-Tight, compressed, pressed, solid

Paikpikin-v-To press, tighten, make solid, tamp

Pailangilang Scatteringly

Paimbabaw-n-Hypocrisy, haughtiness

Paina-n-Shelf

Painainin v-To adorn, embellish, decorate; beautify, extol, exalt, honor, magnify

Painisin v-To overwhelm, smother

Painitin-v-To heat; warm.

Painog-adv -Gyratory

Painom-n-Drink, beverage

Painugin-v-To spin twirl

Painumin-v To invite to drink, give to drink

Faisipan-a-Thoughtful, meditating.

Paisipan-n-Puzzle, enigma

Pait-n Chisel

Pait n-Bitterness

Paitan-v-To chisel

Paituman-n-To blacken, darken; ebonize

Pagkaasahan-n Hope, expectancy.

Pagkabanal n-Purity, virtue

Pagkabanalin sa gracia ng P. Dios n Sanctification

Pakgamruan n Powdering, pulverizing

Pagkagiliwin. To love; make love

Pagkagiliwin-n Deep love, anxious desire.

Pakakaisa-n-Unity, agreement, unanimity. union

Pakakinisin v-To polish, smooth, finish

Pakalayaan-n-Liberation; giving of freedom, setting at liberty

Pakaligisin-v-Pulverization

Pakaliningin-n-Review, revision, inquiry, close observance, examination, investigation.

Pakalinisin-v-To clean, cleanse; purify.

Pakalog n Rattle

Pakamasdan-n-Look, observation, inquiry, review; revision, examination

Pakamusta n-Compliments, message

Pakana-n-Idea, notion, fancy, design

Pakanasain-a-Anxious, desirous

Pakanin-v-To feed, give to eat

Pakapilitin-n-Twisting, twining

Pakapilitin-n-Perseverance, persistence, inciting

Pakasalin v- o betroth. marry, match

Pakasamuin-v-To condemn

Pakasintahin v-To love

Pakasiyasatin-v-To ascertain, examine; investigate

Pakatinain-v-To dye

Pakatingnan-n-Review, revision, look; investigation; sight, watching

Pakaway-n-Movement of the hands, weight, balance

Pakay-n-Intention, desire, end; goal; object; design-

Pakikinpid-n-Adultery, seduction

Pakikinabangan-a-Profitable, useful

Pakikipag usap n-Style of address or conversation

Pakikisama n Partnership, company, society, treatment, behavior, gallantry, compact

Pakikitungo n-Compact, contract, traffic, trade

Pakinabang-n-Profit, revenue, gain, advantage, utility, benefit interest, benefaction, lucre, improvement, income, tax, usefulness, acquisition, rent.

Pakinabangan-v-To profit, benefit, gain

Pakinangin-v-To smooth, polish

Paking a-Distracted.

Pakingan-v-To listen, hear, heed, hark, hearken, comprehend, understand

Pakinisin-v-To smooth, polish, finish, brighten

Pakintabin-v-To brighten, polish, smooth, finish

Pakiramdam n-Feeling, sensibility, notability.

Pakita-n Appearance

Pakitang loob n-Gallantry, manners

Pakinsap-n-Request, entreaty, petition suplication; prayer.

Pakiusapan-v-To request; entreat; beg
or petition.
Pakli-n Intercalation; contestation; distant answer.
Pakó-n-Nail.
Pakong bakal na walang ulo-n-Brad;
tenon; spile.
Pakong kahoy-n-Wooden peg; peg trunnel.
Pakong maliit-n-Tack; shingle nail;
small nail.
Pakoug sabitan nğ papel-n-Paper file.
Pakpak-n-Wing; lean to; addition;
pennon.
Pakuan-n-Watermelon.
Pakuluin-v-To boil.
Pakumusta-n-Compliments; expressions
of kindness.
Pakupasin-v-To fade; wither; cause to
fade or wither.
Pakupkop-n-Protection; help; aid; assistance; favor.
Pakunutin-v-To wrinkle.
Pakunutin nğ noo-n-To wrinkle the
forehead.
Pakuyumpisin-v-To shrink; contract.
Pála-n-Shovel; spade.
Palá-n-Improvement; gain; reward; profit; compensation; triumph; gratification; glory.
Pala-inter.-So.
Palaanito-n-Idolater; pagan.
Palaantok-a-Lethargic; sleepy.
Palaaway-n-Quarreller.
Palaaway-a-Quarrelsome; noisy; touchy;
peevish.
Palabá-n-Wash; washing.
Palabahan-n-Place of washing; laundry.
Palabá nğ buan-n-The raining at night
when the moon shines.
Palabiro-a-Jocose; jocular; droll.
Palabiro-n-Joker; jester; wag; droll.
Palabisin-v-To exceed; excell; surpass;
overcome; give more than is necessary.
Palabuin-v-To darken; blur; blot; obscure; cloud; confuse; make muddy
or murky.
Palabunğa-a Fruitful; prolific.
Palacio-n-Palace.
Palad-n-Chance; fate, luck; doom hap;
happiness; prosperity; felicity.
Palagay-n-Supposition; election; appointment.
Palagay na loob-a-Calm; serene; tranquil; affable meek; plain.
Palaguin-v-To make leafy; unfold; unroll;
increase.
Palahanğin-v-To crack; split; cleave;
flaw; chink.

Palahanğin-a-Boastful; bragging.
Palaihi-a-Continually making water.
Palá isipan-n-Riddle; enigma; puzzle;
rebus.
Pala isipin-a-Thougtful; meditating.
Palak-a-Distant; remote; separated.
Palak-adv.-At a distance.
Palaka-n-Frog; toad.
Palakad-n-Proceedure; conduct; demeanor; management; manner; custom;
use; usage; mode; method.
Palakad lakad a-Wandering; vagabond;
erring; errant; excursive.
Palakain-n-Glutton.
Palakain-a-Gluttonous.
Palakang kakapsoy-n-Toad.
Palakasin-v-To invigorate; strengthen;
fortify; inspire or give courage; make
courageous; renove fear.
Palakhin-v-To enlarge; aggrandize; increase; heighten; augment; improve.
Palakihin-v-To augment; increase; enlarge; aggrandize; heighten.
Palakihin ang isip-v-To educate; instruct; breed; bring up; teach; broaden the mind.
Palakihin ang katawan-v-To make fat;
fatten.
Palakol-n-Axe; ax.
Palakolin-v-To chop; hew; cut with an
axe.
Palakpak-n-Slam; sound caused by the
fall of anything; wooden-rattle.
Palalasing-a-Intemperate; immoderate.
Palalimin-v-To deepen; profound.
Palalo-a-Proud; haughty; supercilious;
overbearing; arrogant; lofty; presumptuons; insolent; impudent boastful;
inflated.
Palaluin-c-To make proud or haughty;
exceed; excel; surpass; overcome;
overpower.
Palamara-n-Traitor.
Palamara-a-Infidel; inconstant; untrue;
traitorous; ungrateful; shameless.
Palambutin-v-To soften; mollify; make
soft, bland or tender.
Palampasin-v-To exeed, excel; surpass
go beyond; pass.
Palananğis-a-Snivelling.
Palananğis-n-Sniveler.
Palanas-n-Stony place; fiat rock.
Palangana-n-Washbasin; basin.
Palangoy-a-Floating; bouyant.
Palanğoyin-v-To make or cause to swim.
Palansikin-v-To bespatter; splash
dab.
Palamigin-v-To refresh; cool; refrigerate.
Palapala-n-Scaffold; shade.

Palaputin-v-To thicken, condense, cur
dle
Palapasial n-Walker, one who is on
the go all the time, gad-about
Palaso-n-Dart, arrow
Palasugal n-Gambler.
Palasumbong-n-Taleteller, telltale
Palatain-v-To cause to wither or fade
Palatak-n-Chick
Palatanong-n-Querist
Palatanong a Quizzical
Palataw-n-Hatchet, broad axe.
Palausap-a-Quarrelsome, touchy
Palawit n Anything that is hung up as
an adornment
Palay n-Rice that is still in the hull.
Palayan-n Rice-field
Palayasin-v-To send away, dismiss, oust
Palayaw-n-Caress, cajolery; dandle, pet-
ting, freedom
Palayawin-t-To caress, pet cajole, hu-
mor; cheer, coddle, dandle; free lib-
erate, give much freedom
Palayok na gatasan-n Milk-jar
Palayok-n-Jar, olla
Palayok na tanso-v-Copper kettle.
Palayuin-v-To distance, remove to a
distance; send away; separate part
Palibid-n-Circumference, circuit, enviro-
rons.
Palibhasain-t-To depreciate, insult, re.
vile; abuse
Palibot-n-Circumference, circuit' envi-
rons.
Paligid-n-Circumference, circuit, per-
imeter, periphery
Paligid-adv -About.
Paligid-prep. About
Paligiran-t-To circuit; skirt
Paligin-v-To bathe lave.
Paliban-n-Anvil
Palihim-adv.-Secretly; hiddenly, surrep-
tuously, treacherously
Palikid-n-Ball of string
Palikoliko-adv -Flutteringly
Palikoliko a-Fluttering, crooked, turn-
ing, tortuous.
Palikpik ng kayo n-Fringe of cloth
Palihgo n Bath
Paliling-adv Obliquely
Paliling-a Oblique
Palinamnamin-v To taste, relish, give
taste
Palinawin-t-To clear, make plain, ex-
plain, expound, demonstrate the
truth
Palinsarin ang buto r To disjoint pull
apart
Palinuhod a Humble, meek begging
kneeling

Paliparin-v-To cause to fly.
Palipisan-v-Temple.
Palis a-Clean
Palis-n Place
Paht-n-Change, barter, exchange, sur-
rogation, commutation.
Palikatin-t-To split, cleave, crack·
Pahtaw-n-Apparition, appearance, overt
Palitan-v-To change, exchange, barter;
- substitute, surrogate, commute, per-
mute, replace
Paliwanagin-v-To explain, clear, ex-
pound, lay open, evince; make plain
or clear, demonstrate
Paliwas a-transverse; oblique
Paliwas-n Evasion, avoidance
Palo-n-Pole, mast, stick, cudgel, blow
with anything
Palopalo ng danit-Clothes beater
Paloob-t-To put in enter, meddle, in-
terfere
Palso-a-False
Palsohin-t-To falsify, counterfeit.
Paltos-n Burn.
Paluagin-v-To loosen, free, liberate
Paluagin ang loob-v-To appease; calm,
tranquilize
Palubalub t-To wallow; roll in mud.
Palubalub sa bisio-v-To wallow in vice.
Palubayin-v-To mitigate, assuage, ap-
pease, calm, stop, check, soften
Palubugin-v-To submerge, inundate.
Palugit n-Advantage, start, handicap,
distance
Palugit ng panahon-n-Increase of time,
furlough.
Palun-t To beat, strike, belabor, pum-
mel; scourge.
Palumatlumatin-t To crack, split, defer;
delay, dally
Palumatin-v-To crack, split
Palundagin-t-To cause or make jump
Palungkutin-v-To make or cause to be
sorrowful or sad
Faluputan-v-To wrap up.
Paluputin-v-To wrap up.
Palutang-adv Floating, bouyant
Pamagain-t-To cause to or make swell.
Pamagat-n-Vow, promise
Pamagat-n Nickname, alias, denomina-
tion
Pamagatan v-To nickname, give an alias,
denominate, make a vow or promise.
Pamahalaan-t-To manage, heed, care
for, keep, guard, govern, direct, con-
duct, domineer.
Pamahi l n-Wiping rag, packers waste.
Pamahid ng pawis n Handkerchief
Pamalin n-Superstition
Pamakpak-n-Addition, lean to, wing.

Pamalimali-a-Erroneous; full of mistakes; inconsiderate

Pamamaga-n-Swelling, inflamation, tumidity, tumidness.

Pamamagpak-n-The waving of one's arms, cruse, beginning, appearance.

Pamamag itan-n-Intercession, intervention, mediation.

Pamamahagi n-Partition, distribution, division, dividing

Pamamahala-n-Care, cargo watch, guard; duty, management; government

Pamamahala na mabagsik-n-Tyranny, severity, rigidity of government

Pamamahay-n Habitation, abode, residence; lodging, mansion

Pamamalagi-n-Stability, lasting, habituation; subsistence

Pamamalat-n-Hoarseness.

Pamamahta n-Narration, speaking, revelation, speech, talk, talking.

Pamamanas-n-Beri beri, swelling caused by a cold

Pamamanglaw-n-Solitude, lonliness, gloominess

Pamamansag-n-Nickname, alias

Pamamantog-n-Inflation

Pamamaos-n-Hoarseness

Pamamarati n-Stability, duration; permanency, eternity

Pamamayad-n-Payment, compensation

Pamana-n-Legacy, inheritance.

Pamanahan-v-To legate, inherit

Pamanghain-v-To amaze, cause to stare or wonder, astonish.

Pamankin n-Nephew, neice

Pamankin na babayi-n-Niece

Pamankin na lalaki-n-Nephew

Pamankin sa pakinabang-n-Stepchild.

Pamansa-n Promise, denomination, determination

Pamantugin-v-To inflate, fill with wind

Pamaoy-n-Scare crow

Pamaratihin-v To accustom, inure, frequent

Pamagatan-n-Level, anything used for leveling

Pamatay ng ilay-n-Light extinguisher

Pamawis-n Handkerchief.

Pamaypay-n-Wag, fan, shaking

Pambigan-n-Talk, anything that is put in the mouth

Pamigkis-n-Belt, sash, girdle, band, ligature, scarf

Pamigkis ng balat-n-Leather belt

Pamihasanin-v-To abuse, inure, accustom

Pamimih-n-Purchase; buying, selection; choice, volition

Pamimintuho n Petition, prayer, asking, service, obedience, submission

Pamimintuho sa Dios-n-Prayer to God.

Paminghihin-n-To deafen.

Paminsan-adv -Once

Paminta-n-Pepper

Pamitpit-n-Instrument for cutting

Pamugaw-n-Scarecrow

Pamula n-Origin, source, beginning; root; entree, entry; element, principle, motive

Pamulaan-v To commence, begin, undertake, attempt.

Pamumubok-n-Crystalization

Pamnmukod-n-Separation, distinction, singularity

Pamumula ng mukha-n-Blush, bashfulness

Pamnmuno n-Government; commanding, commandment; leading; heading

Pamumutla ng balat-n-Pallor, wanness, paleness, ghastliness

Paniunas-n Washingcloth; dusting cloth, trifle

Pamungahin-v-To fertilize, make fruitful

Pamuti-n Adorment, adornation, or nament; embellishment.

Pamutihan-v-To adorn embellish, set-off, fit up, ornament, clean.

Pamutihin-v-To decorate, embellish, adorn; set off.

Pamutiin-v-To whiten, make white.

Pana-n-Arrow, dart.

Panabihan-n-Toilet, retreat

Panabing n-Curtain, covering, awning, screen

Panabing sa pinto-n-Screen

Panagano-n-Dedication, consecration, inscription

Panagap ng bula n-Skimmer

Panaghihng banal-n-Emulation; envy; jealousy.

Panaghoy-n-Lamentation, dole, dolor; lament, bewailing, wail, strong sentiment

Panaghoy na malumbay-n-Sad lamentation

Panaginip-n Dream.

Panagpi n-Patch

Panagutan-n-Guarantee; bail, response, responding, answering

Panahod-n-Receiver, small bucket.

Panahok-n-Spice.

Panahon-n-Time, era, age, term; tide; season, epoch, occasion; opportunity.

Panahon mabuting ipagtanim-n-Seedtime

Panahon na magkasing luat ang araw at gabi-n-Equinox.

15

Panahon nakaraan n-Past time, past tense.

Panahon na walang gawa-n-Rest, repose, recreation.

Panahon nang babaj i-n-Periodical indisposition of women menses

Panahon ñg gapasan n-Harvest time

Panahon ñg pagani n-Harvest time

Panahon ñg tatlong buan-n Quarter.

Panahon salat sa ulan-n-Drought

Panahunan n Turn, time, succession.

Panakip-n Cover, lid, stopper

Panakip ñg hihigan-n Coverlet, bedspread

Panakot-n-Scarecrow

Panaksak-n-Poniard, dagger; dirk, stilleto

Panaktak-n-Branding iron

Panalangin-n-Prayer, petition, invocation, oration; evening prayer

Panali-n-String, thong.

Panali ñg zapatos-n-Shoestring

Panaluyan bahay-n-Hotel; inn, boarding house

Panambil-n-Covering, screen, cover; inclination, vocation

Panambitan-n-Lamentation, lament, moan

Pananahan n-Habitation, abode, living at a certain place

Pananakot n-Fright; threat, surprise

Pananalig n-Hope, expectancy, firmness, constancy.

Pananalita-n-Talk, discourse, conversation, idiom, language

Pananalo-n-Victory, winning

Pananamit-n-Garb, wearing apparel, clothes; complete suit.

Pananampalataya-n-Credence, faith, creed, belief, troth; theory; credit

Pananamsam-n-Plunder, spoils, pillage

Pananatili-n-Stability, permanence, duration, tenacity, continuance, persistency.

Pananauli-n-Restoration; devolution

Pananda-n-Branding-iron; stencil, marker; marking iron.

Panangis-n-Weeping, crying, snivelling

Pananim n Seed, sowing, seed time, that which is planted

Panat-a-Tight, hard; firm, solid.

Panata-n-Promise, offer.

Panauhan-n Border, lodger, guest.

Panay-a-Even; equal, continuous, all

Panay adv. Evenly, equally, totally.

Panáva n Continuance, evenness, equality

Pandak a Short chubby; stocky; chunky

Pandampe-n-Blotter.

Pandareta-n-Tambourine

Panday-n-Blacksmith, ironsmith.

Pandayan-n-Blacksmith [shop, forge, iron works.

Pan de sal-n-Salt· bread, bun, bunn.

Pandilig-n Sprinkler, watering pot

Pandiñg-n-Ear trumpet, ear

Pandulo-n-Final, conclusion, acme finish, termination; crisis, goal.

Panduro-n-Punch.

Pangâ-n-Jawbone

Pangadya n-Anything used to defend something else

Pangahas-n-Daring, boldness, sauciness, forwardness, insolence, impudence, dissolution, audacity, intrepidity, fearlessness, spunk

Pang ahit-n-Razor

Pangako-n-Promise, guarantee, plight

Pangalág ñg tornillo-n-Screwdriver,

Pangalan-n-Name

Pangalawa-n-Second, assistant

Pangalawa buhat sa dulo n-Penultimate, the last but one.

Pangalawang ñgalan-n-Surname, nickname

Pangaling-n-Brush-hook; instrument for cutting away brush

Pangalos-n-Scraper, anything used as a craper.

Pangamba n-Doubt, suspicion, jealousy; fear, plight, indicision, dread suspence, hesitation

Pangambahin-a-Fearful, distrustful, jealous suspicious

Pangamoy n Nostril, nose

Pangañgalakal n-Traffic, trade; commerce

Pangañgalakal ñg katawan n-Brothel, whoring, prostitution.

Pangañgalan n The giving of a name, naming

Pangañganak-n Birth giving birth

Pangañgaral-n-Preaching, sermon, exhortation

Pangañgaso-n-Hunt- chase, gunning

Pangañgatawan n-Shape or form of the body

Pangañgayaw n Negation, unwillingness.

Pangañgayayat-n Extenuation, feebleness, weakness debility, wasting away

Pangañgayupapa-n-Submission, humilation, yielding, losing in a fight.

Panganib-n Danger, risk; peril, jeopardy, hazard

Pangapas-n-Siekle; scythe, reaping hook; gyue

Pangapon-n-Discard

Pangapos ñg paa n Shackles, hopple,

Pangapos ng kamay-n-Handcuffs.
Pangaral-n-Discourse; sermon; advice; preaching.
Pangaralan-v-To exhort; preach.
Pangaral kristiano-n-Sermon.
Pangarap-n-Dream.
Pangaso-n-Chase: hunt.
Pangati-n-Decoy; snare.
Pangating ibon-n-Decoy bird.
Pangatlo-n-The third.
Pangatngat-n-Bite; gnaw; nible.
Pangayayatin-v-To extenuate; debilitate; make weak or thin.
Pangayod-n-Grater; scraper.
Pangbatak-n-Pull; tug; haul; attraction.
Pangbatid-n-Dam.
Pangbayo-n-Mallet; mall.
Pangbulok-n-Anything that will make or cause another to rot.
Pangbutas-n-Auger; gimble; punch; weevil; puncheon.
Pangbuya-n-Incitement; spur; stimulous.
Pangdaindam-n-Sensibility; sense; sentiment; perception.
Panggapus-n-Trammel; handcuff; shackle.
Panggising-n-Alarm clock; alarmbell.
Panghahapdi-n-Smarting; stinging-smart pain.
Panghaharang-n-Highway robbery; holdup.
Panghahalili-n-Substitute; that which is put in place of another.
Panghalina-n-Attraction; magnet.
Panghalo-n-Mixer; rocker; mortar; anything that is used to mix with.
Panghapit-n-Pestle.
Panghihiganti-n-Vengeance, retaliation.
Panghihimagsik-n Sternness; rigor; strictness; severity.
Panghihimagsik laban sa puno n-Insurrection; rebellion; sedition.
Panghihina-n-Debility; weakness; extenuation; feebleness; wasting; away.
Panghihina ng loob-n-Lack or want of courage; temerity; weakness of heart; faintheartedness.
Panghihinang-n-Soldering.
Panghihip ng platero-n-Jeweler's blowpipe.
Panghihiwalay-n-Separator.
Panghikuat-Lever; fulcrum.
Panghila-n-Attraction; anything which serves to draw another.
Panghilamos-n-Towel; the washing of the face and hands.
Panghina-n-Anything which serves to weaken another.
Panghinang-n-Solder; soldering-iron.
Panghininga-n-Toothpick.

Panghinuli-n-Earphick.
Panghuhula-n-Prophecy; surmise; conjecture.
Panghuit-n-Lever; fulcrum.
Panghukay-n-Spade; hoe.
Panghuli ng isda-n-Fishtrap.
Panghuli-n-Trap.
Pangiki-n-Chill.
Pangil-n-Eyetooth; fang; tusk.
Pangimayin-v-To benumb; cause to be senseless.
Pangimbubo-n-Envy; jealousy.
Pangingiba-n-Singularity; distinction; novelty; strangeness.
Pangingilabot-n-Fright; terror.
Pangingilag-n-Avoidance; evasion.
Pangigilalas-n-Admiration; wonder; amazement; stupor.
Pangininig-n-Trembling;shaking;quaking; sparkling.
Pangingisda-n-Fishing.
Pangingitlog-n-The laying of eggs.
Pangingitlog ng isda-n-The spawning of fish.
Panginoon-n-Master; overseer; propietor; owner; mistress; lord.
Pangintindi-n-Sense; spirit; intelligence; knowledge; skill; ability.
Pangispiki-n-Lever; fulcrum; handspike.
Pangit-n-Ugly; homely; immodest; disfigured; dirty; deformed; sordid huge;
Pangitlugan-n-Hen's nest; haunt of a hen.
Pangkat-n-Chapter. part; clan.
Pangkat ng bayan-n-District; part.
Panglalata-n-Prostration; languidness; weakness.
Panglasap-n-Palate; taste; relish.
Panglaw-n-Gloom; sorrow; grief; sadness; lonliness; depression of spirits.
Panglilibak-n-Slander; insult; ridicule.
Panglingot ng tapon-n-Corkscrew.
Pangloloob-n-Robbery; robbing.
Pangnamnam-n-Taste; palate; relish.
Pangpahimpil-n Sedative; anything which serves to quiet; ease; or calm.
Pangiti-n-Smile; budding of blossoms.
Pangpakilos-n-Motor.
Pangpalakas-n-Corroborative; anything which serves to strengthen.
Pangpang-n-Shore; strand; bank.
Pangpawis-n-Sudorific.
Pangpasuka-n-Emetic.
Pangpasulong-n-Propeller; incitement; inducement.
Pangpatibay-n-Corroborative; guarantee; anything which serves to strengthen.
Pangpatulog-n-Marcotic; drug.

Pangpatuyo-*n*-Drier

Pangpiga-*n*-Press, pestle

Panpigil-*n*-Brake.

Pangpihit *n* Wrench

Pangsual-*n*-Handspike.

Pangsurong-*n*-Shovel, spade

Pangtala-*n*-Rule, marker, that which serves to govern.

Pangudngod-*n*-Grater; scraper

Pangulo-*n*-Leader, commander; chief, principal, head.

Pangunahan *n*-Head, leader

Pangungulili - *n* - Sordidness, filthiness, dirtiness

Pangungundot-*n*-Lance, blunt instrument used for purposes of defense.

Pangungurong-*n*-Contraction bucking; shortening, retraction, retirement; backing down

Pangungusap-*n*-Advice, talking, lecture, locution, speech

Pangusap-*n*-Correction, advice, charge, reprehension; reproach, censure, reprimand; reproof

Pangusapan-*v*-To advise, reprimand, censure, reprehend, admonish, lecture

Pangusap na masaklap-*n*-Reprimand, reproof, lecture

Pang uumit-*n*-Theft, peculation, steal ing, thieving

Pangwakas-*n*-Final, conclusion, deter mination; end, remembrance

Pangwakas-*a*-Final, conclusive; last

Pangyayari-*n*-Accomplishment, event; incident; issue, success, realization, casuality.

Pangyayaring bigla-*n* Sudden happening.

Pambago-*a*-New; renewed

Pambagong pagbabangon *n* Rebuilding reconstruction

Pambugho-*n* Jealousy, envy.

Panimbá-*n*-Bucket.

Panimba-*n*-Clothes used to go to church in

Panimbang-*n*-Weight, balance

Panimdim-*n* Meditation; anxiety, restlessness caused by thinking of another

Paningasin-*v*-To kindle, set afire.

Paningilan-*n*-Collection of debts; place of collection.

Panimigalan-*n*-Sideboard, dresser

Panimlaw-*n*-Pallor, ghastliness, wanness; pallidness

Panimlay *n*-Meditation, contemplation, musing

Panimilbihan-*n* Service; servitude

Panimilo at pagbabalat ng libro *n* the binding of books.

Paniningil-*n*-Collection of outstanding debts

Paniminta *n*-Courtship; love-making, love suit

Paninirang puri-*n*-Slander, gossip, backbiting

Paninira sa isang lugar-*n*-The living or lodging at a certain place.

Paniwala-*n* Belief; faith, credit; credence, confidence, testimony

Panipit-*n*-Tongs, princers, clamp

Panira ng puri *n*-Slander, defamation

Pani ala *n*-Belief, credence, credit.

Paniwalaan *i*-To believe; credit, have faith in

Paniwalaan *a* Credulous; simple.

Panlimas-*n*-Bail

Panot-*a*-Bald, hairless; baldheaded.

Pansimin-*a*-Notable, perceptible, sensible, sensitive, thoughtful.

Pantain-*i*-To level, make equal

Fantás-*n*-Sage wise man; writer

Pantay-*a*-Equal, uniform, level, even, similar, of the same height

Pantayin-*v*-To equalize, level, make equal, match, make similar

Panti-*n*-Net

Pantuyo *n*-Drier

Panual-*n*-Lever; push, shove

Panudlok-*n*-Stimulan, billiard cue

Panugtog ng kampana-*n*-Bell clapper.

Panukat-*n* Measure; tape line.

Panukat ng ulan *n*-Udometer.

Panukaba-*n*-Design, intention

Panulat-*n*-Penmanship

Panulukan-*n*-Angle, corner, nook

Panuluyanan-*n*-Inn, hotel; inn of a monastery

Panumpa *n*-Adjuration

Panumpaan-*v*-To make oath, swear, promise

Panungkit *n*-Hook, gaff, window pole, provocation.

Panunuan-*n*-Lodging, champion; friend

Panunúba-*n* Trick; deceit, trap, fraud.

Panunubok-*n*-Secret observation or watching, surprise

Panunumbalik-*n*-Restoration, devolution

Panunumpa *n*-Vow, oath, curse, imprecation.

Panunumpa ng hindi totoo *n*-Perjury, false oath.

Panuob-*n* Disinfectant.

Panutog-*n*-Prick.

Panutog ng pabete *n* Snuffers

Panutsot *n* Whistle, call

Panuyo *n* The asking of the father for the hand of his daughter in marriage, gallantry, service of love, congratulation.

Panuyuan-*v*-To court, love; woo

Panyito nğ damit-*n*-Gore of a skirt.

Panyo-*n*-Hankerchief

Panyo sa lug-*n*-Ketchief

Paos-*n*-Hoarseness.

Papa-*n*-Pope, pontiff

Papag aralin-*v*-To send to school, make or cause to study; teach.

Papag alsahin-*v*-To cause to raise

Papagbagahin-*v*-To rubify, make like a live coal

Papagdalitain-*v* To cause to suffer

Papaghirapin-*v*-To give or cause pain, impoverish, make poor.

Papag initin-*v*-To heat, make angry.

Papag asunduin-*v*-To reconcile, cause to become friends again

Papaglamatin-*i*-To crack.

Papagluatin-*v*-To prolong, stretch, lengthen (*per to time*)

Papagpasain-*v*-To bruise, burn, contuse.

Papagtakahin-*i*-To astonish, amaze cause to wonder or stare, surprise

Papanghimagsik *n* Vengeance, cruelty, tyranny

Papangilabutin-*v*-To terrify, scare

Papangilinin *v*-To observe, sanctify, respect, worship

Papangitan-*v*-To pollute, stain, make ugly or homely.

Papangitin-*v*-To pollute, stain, make homely or ugly

Papanglawin-*v*-To sadden, make or cause to be sad, gloomy, dark or mournful.

Papang undutin-*v*-To contract, wrinkle, shrink

Papang urungin-*v*-To contract, shrink

Papaniwalain-*v*-To persuade; imbue, induce, make or cause to believe

Papasok-*n*-Entering, manner of entering, entrance.

Papayo-*n*-Advice

Papal-*n*-Paper.

Papel na bastos-*n* Wrapping paper

Papilipit-*adv*.-Twistingly, on the contrary

Papulahin-*v*-To redden, rubify; stain; make or cause to blush

Papulanditin-*v*-To squirt.

Papurihan-*v*-To honor, respect, dignify

Paputihin-*i*-To pick

Paputiin-*v*-To whiten

Paputukin-*i*-To shoot, burst, break open

Paraan-*n* Path, mode, method, way, manner, form, course, gangway, disposition; will, aspect.

Paraan nğ isip-*n*-Theory

Paraanan nğ masid ang isang libro-*v*-To peruse, run over; read hurriedly.

Paraanin-*v* To pass, let pass, give way.

Paraanin sa-*v*-To make go a certain way, compel to go a certain way.

Paragala-*n*-Girt, reward, present.

Paragos-*n*-Harrow, drag

Paralis-*n*-Roller, rolling pin

Paralis nğ nagliligawan-*n*-Pimp

Paramihin-*v*-To multiply, increase, augment, dilate, diffuse, propagate

Parang-*n*-Country; field, meadow

Parangalin-*v*-To extol, exalt, elevate, sublimate, honor

Parang apoy *a* Fiery

Párang bato-*a*-Stony.

Párang hayop-*a*-Brutal

Párang hindi-*adv* -As if not, as if it were not

Párang langib-*a*-Scabby, scablike.

Parang nğ pastulan-*n*-Pasture

Párang nuno-*a*-Ghastly

Párang serafin-*a* Seraphic, angelic.

Párang sutla-*a*-Silky-

Párang uhog-*a*-Mucous; slimy

Parapara-*adv*.-Equally; uniformly, evenly

Para sa-*prep* -For, to, towards, in order to, to the end that.

Parátang *n*-Accusation, charge, imputation.

Paratangan-*v*-To accuse; charge, impute; criminate, impeach.

Parati *adv* -Always

Paraya-*n*-Deceit, fraud

Parayá-*n*-Suffering, patience, toleration.

Pareja-*n* Pair, brace, couple; match, doublet.

Pari-*n*-Priest, clergyman, divine, ecclesiastic.

Parikit *n*-Ornament, adornment.

Parikitin-*v*-To ornament beautify, embellish, adorn

Parinsa-*n*-Sadiron

Parinsahin-*v*-To iron.

Pares-*n*-Pair; brace, doublet

Parisán-*n*-Pattern, precedent, type, model, example

Parisan-*v*-To imitate, counterfeit, mimic, forge, pattern

Parisukat-*n*-Square; quadrate.

Parisukat *a*-Square, quadrate, quadratic.

Parisukatin *i*-To square; quadrate.

Parol *n* Lantern

Paroodin-*v*-To go after, send, after.

Paroparo-*n*-Butterfly

Parti-*n*-Quota; part.

Partihin-*v*-To part divide

Parusa n-Punishment; chastizement, penality, correction, requittal

Parusahin-v-To punish, chastize; correct, requit

Parusahin sa sahta-v-To rebuke, censure, scold.

Pasá n-Bruise, burn, contusion.

Pasabi n-Message; errand

Pasabugsabog-adv Helterskelter

Pasa ng̃ dugo-n Serous blood

Pasakabila ng̃ bundok-v-To go over the mountain

Pasak-n Plug; stopper, calk, peg

Pasakin-v-To calk, plug; stop; check

Pasakit-n Torment, torture; pain, anguish

Pasákitan-v-To pain, distress; torment, torture, afflict, chastize, mortify; disgust, disable.

Pasal-n-Oakum

Pasalan-v-To calk, stop a leak, block up

Pasalapsap-a-Shallow, superficial

Pasaliwa-adv -Backhanded.

Pasalung̃a adv -Reluctantly, contrarily, reverse, pepugnantly

Pasalung̃at-a-Contrary, reluctant, repugnant, reverse, against

Pasamahin-v-To unite, join, put together

Pasamain v-To deprave, corrupt; make or cause to be bad

Pasamain ang loob-i-To displease, disgust

Pasan-n-Load

Pasanin-i-To carry or put on the shoulders

Pasarapin-v-To relish, give zest.

Pasaulan-n-Devolution restoration

Pasayahin-n-To gladden, cheer, make happy

Pasial-n Stroll, walk, saunter.

Pasialan-n-Promenade, avenue; walk

Pasigan-n-Shore, strand, beach

Pasiglahin-v-To vivify, incite, excite, imbue, revive.

Pasimalaan-i-To commence, begin

Pasimulan-n-Beginning, commencement

Pasinung̃aling̃an v-To give the lie, contradict

Pasiya-n-Decision; verdict, judgement, sentence, resolution, determination, decree, rebuke

Pasko-n-Christmas

Paskong mahaba-n-Quadrigesima

Pasko ng̃ pagkabuhay n-Easter

Paslang̃in-a Skittish.

Paslangin r To surprise; make a sudden movement

Paslang-n Insolence, impudence; daring

Paslang̃in-v To insult, profane, dare, be impudent, violate, impute

Pasht-a-Mucous, mucky, low, abject, ignorant, despicable, depraved

Paso n-Burn

Páso n-Earthen pan or tub

Paso-n Pass

Pások-n Entrance

Pasolo-n Sharp point

Paspás-n Shaking, dusting, instigation

Paspasin-v-To dust, shake

Pastol ng̃ tupa n Shepherd

Pastor-n-Castor; divine, ecclesiastic

Pastulan-n Field, meadow; pasture

Pasubah-n-Exception, condition, conditional promise.

Pagsubah sa-n-On condition that

Pasúgo-n-Embassador, counsel

Pasúin-v-To burn, scortch

Pasukab asv.-Treacherously, underhanded

Pasukal-adv -Treacherously, underhanded, low, dirty

Pasukahin ang loob-i-To vex, disgust; disturb, molest, displease

Pasukain-i-To subdue quell, overcome conquer; subject worst, overwhelm, cause to surrender; captivate, charm.

Pasulat n-Dictation, order to write

Pasulung̃an-v-To drive, impel

Pasunod n-Example, precedent, copy, pattern

Pasupil-n-Triumph, subjection; conquering; overcoming, overwhelming

Pasupilin-v-To overcome, subdue, overwhelm

Pasuotsuot-adv -Twistingly, tortuously

Pasuotsuot-a-Twisted; crooked, winding;

Pasusuhin-v To nurse, give suck

Pasutsot-n-Whistle

Pataasin-i-To raise, elevate

Patabain-i-To fatten, batten; fertilize, maka fruitful

Patad-n-Rosin

Patag-a-Level, flat, even, plane, firm, equal, similar, uniform, contain, consistent; tranquil, smooth

Patagin r-To level; flatten

Patago adi -Hiddenly, secretly, clan, destinety,

Patahimikin-v-To calm, tranquilize, pacify; appease, settle, quiet

Patak n-Drop, blot, drip

Patakasin-i-To cause or help to escape, steal.

Patalim-n-Steel, cutting edge

Patalimin-r To sharpen, make keen

Patanaw n Sight, apparition, model, pattern.

Patangahin-r-To canse to be lazy or indolent.

Patani-n-Lima beans.

Patapangin-v-To encourage; strengthen; invigorate; enforce; make valiant. exert.

Patabanin-v-To quiet; pacify; appease; tranquilize.

Pátaw-n-Weight.

Patawad-n-Pardon, absolution; palliation; forgiveness.

Patawarin-v-To forgive; pardon; absolve; spare; acquit; condone; palliate.

Patawin-v-To weight.

Pataynn-n-Killing; slaughter; carnage; slaughter house.

Patayin-v-To kill; murder; assassinate; quenca: put out; extinguish.

Patayo-a-Perpendicular.

Patay sa kapatid-n-Fratricide.

Patay sa sariling ina-n-Matricide.

Patibong-n-Trap; deceit; fraud; cheat.

Patibong na panghuli ng daga-n-Rat. trap.

Patid-n-Break; cut.

Patigasin-v-To toughen; harden.

Patilansikin-v-To spatter: splash; dab; bespatter.

Patingkayad-a-Tiptoe; walking on the toes.

Patiningin-n-To clear up; settle; make ser ene.

Patirin-v-To cut asunder; break; fracture.

Patis-n-Brine.

Patitiin-v-To drain.

Pati tis-n-Lampblack.

Patiwasayin-v-To tranquilize; calm; pacify.

Patnugot-n-Maxim; adage motto.

Patong-n-Addition; boot; premium; augmentation.

Patos ng gulong-n-Clinch.

Patotohanan-v-To ratify; verify; prove; manifest; testify; confirm.

Patotohanin-v-To make true; prove rat; ify; verify; true.

Patuad-a-Inverted.

Patuad-adv.-Upside down.

Patubo-n-Interest; profit; gain.

Patuhin-v-To toss; pitch.

Patulinan-v-To accelerate; enliven.

Patuloy-n-Continuation; succession.

Patuluyan-v-To continue; lodge.

Patuluyan ang kapwa-v-To receive-lodge; entertain; protect; give shelter.

Patuluyin-v-To lodge; let lodgings.

Patungan-v-To add; augment; give boot; give a premium.

Patungot-n-Small addition; or premium·

Patunugin-v To whistle; make a noise or sound on anything.

Patúpat-n-Pipe.

Patutot-n-Whore poostitute; harlot.

Patuyo-adv.-Dryly; morosely.

Patuyuin-v-To dry; dessicate.

Patuyuin sa hangin-v-To dry in the air.

Paulól-adv.-Foolishly; sillily; madly; harumscarum.

Paúlol-n-Increase; addition.

Paulol ulol-adv. Foolishly; madly; sillily; precipitately; rashly.

Paulúlin-v-To make foolish.

Páululin-v-To fill; augment; add to.

Pantang-n Credit; trust; bill; note.

Páwa-a-All; each; every; all; whole.

Pawalaan-v-To loosen; slacken; free; liberate; set at liberty.

Pawalan ang alipin-v-To emancipate; liberate.

Pawalan ang halaga-v-To condemn; depreciate; diminish the value.

Pawalan ng kabuluhan-v-To condemn; depreciate; diminish.

Pawiin-v-To blot; erase; abolish; extinguish; efface; put out; suppress.

Pawiin ang antok-v-To wake.

Pawiin ang knlay-v To discolor; fade wash out.

Pawiin ang uhaw-v-To quench thirst.

Pawikan-n-Tortoise.

Pawis-n-Perspiration; sweat.

Payamanin-v-To enrich; make rich.

Payamoyin v-To chafe; disgust.

Payanigin-v-To make or cause to tremble.

Payaos-a-Husky; hoarse.

Payapa-a-Pacific; tranquill; calm; quiet; mild.

Payapain-v-To calm; pacify; tranquilize, quiet; allay; settle; appease.

Payat-a-Weak; lean; thin; poor; meagre; delicate; slender; gaunt; wizen; infirm; faint; barren.

Payatin-v-To prostrate; exhaust; debilitate; make thin or lean.

Páyo-n-Advice; admoniton.

Payong-n-Parasol; umbrella.

Payoug na munti-n-Parasol.

Paypay-n-Fan.

Paypayin-v-To fan.

Pekas ng mukha-n-Freckle.

Pepino-n-Cucumber.

Peras-n Pear.

Perdegones-n-Buckshot.

Pidpid-n-Stick; splinter.

Pidpirin ang kahoy-v-To chop wood.

Piga n-Squeeze; press; crush.

Pigain-v-To Squeeze; press; crush.

Pighati-*n*-Disgust, melancholy, annoy, annoyance, distaste; dudgeon; grievance; grief, sorrow,· gloom, sadness, affliction

Pigi-*n*-Breech, buttock, haunch, hip, rump, posteriors

Pigil-*n*-Curb, check; stop

Pigilan-*v*-To stop, curb, check, rein

Pigilin-*v*-To stem, constrain, check, curb, bridle, stop, obstruct, restrain, withhold

Piging-*n* Banquet, feast, fete

Pigingin-*v*-To banquet give, a feast in honor of another

Pigsa-*n*-Tumor, abcess,tumefaction, boil.

Pigtain-*v*-To drench, soak

Pihit-*n*-Turn, sinuation

Pihitin-*v*-To turn, tighten, sinuate.

Pikit-*n*-Wink, blink

Piklat-*n*-Scar

Piko-*n*-Pick

Pilak-*n*-Silver

Pilapil-*n*-Terrace; dike, dam, embankment; imbankment

Pilay-*a*-Lame.

Pilayin-*v*-To lame; disable, truncate, make lame

Pilduras-*n*-Pill.

Pilegas-*n*-Plait, ruff, ruffle

Pilegasan-*v*-To plait, ruffle crimple

Pili-*n*-Choice, volition; selection

Pilat-*n*-Scar

Palihin-*v*-To twist, warp, disort, turn, curl

Pilin-*v* To choose, select elect.

Pilikmata-*v*-Eyelash

Piling-*n*-Cluster; bunch.

Pilipit *a*-Sinous, twisted, contorted

Pilipit *a* Sinuation; twist

Pilipitin-*v*-To twist, curl, sinuate

Pilit *n*-Persuasion, obligation; enforcement, compulsion

Pilitin-*v*-To persuade, urge, enforce, oblige, extort, press, persist; beset, compel, ply, prevail; convince, drive, persevere

Pina-*n* Pine

Piña *n* Pineapple.

Pina aapuyan-*n* Hearth, fireplace, stove.

Pinag aaralan- *n* - Breeding, education, manners

Pinag bubuan *n* Foundry, casting house

Pina buhatan *n*-Cause, occasion, beginning; motive, source, origin, germ, inception, principle, ancestry, forefather

Pinag gagawan *nğ* sabon *n* Soap factory.

Pinag hugasan-*n* Dirty water left after washing.

Pinagkakautangan-*n*-Creditor.

Pinagkaratihan-*n*-Habit, custom

Pinagkaskasan-*n*-Filings; scrapings

Pinagkasunduan-*n*-Agreement; reconciliation.

Pinagkikilan-*n*-Filings.

Pinaglagarian-*n*-Sawdust

Pinaglihbangan-*n*-Place of recreation or amusement

-Pinaglihmbagan-*n*-Printing shop

Pinaglinisan-*n*-Cleanings, rubbish

Pinaglulutuan-*n*-Place of cooking

Pinagmulan-*n*-Source, origin, beginning, motive, cause, occasion; principle, inception.

Pinagpag-*v* *imp* -Shook

Pinagpagihan-*n*-Filings made by filing with the tail of the pagi

Pinagpilian-*n*-Remainder, residue, refuse, leavings, offal

Pinagpupugutan *n*-Place of beheading, garrote

Pinagputulan *n*-Residue or remainder of anything that has been cut.

Pinagsabunan-*n*-Soapsuds, suds, lather

Pinagsasabunan-*n*-Place of making suds

Pinagsugpungan *n*-Joint, juncture

Pinagtabasan-*n*-Chippings or leavings of a tailor

Pinagtatalan-*n*-Chips, fagots

Pinagtinghasan-*n*-Chips, fagots.

Pinag usapan-*n*-Contract, subject of conversation, argument; agreement.

Pinagtutunğuhan-*n*-Design; purpose, object.

Pinag uusapan-*n*-Object, design, purpose, subject, of conversation

Pinag utusan-*n*-Servant, agent; errand boy.

Pinagyagitan-*n*-Place of congregation, stolen articles

Pinakamatanda sa lahat-*n*-Senior

Pinamili-*n*-Purchases

Pinamili-*v imp*-Bought; purchased

Pinanğalinğan-*n*-Source, origin, headspring, beginning, cause, ancestry, ancestors, forefathers, root, germ.

Pindang-*n*-Jerked beef, dried beef

Pindanğin-*v*-To jerk or dry beef

Pindot-*n* Pinch, nip; press; squeeze; tweak.

Pindutin-*v*-To pinch, nip, squeeze, press, tweak

Pindutin-*v* To pinch; squeeze, press; tweak

Pinga-*n*-Level, carrying stick.

Pingan-*n* Plate

Pingan na malaki-*n* Platter

Pinğas-*n* Chip; notch, chink; gap.

Pingasan v-To notch, chip; chink

Pinsan-n-Cousin

Pinta-n-Paint.

Pintahin-v-To paint.

Pintakasi-n-Mediator, favor, patron, protector, intercessor, solicitor, one who does a favor

Pintas-n-Fault, defect, drawback, denial, disappointment; criticism, scorn; contempt; censure, aspersion.

Pintasan-v To criticize, censure, underrate, undervalue; dissapprove, reprove; find fault; asperse

Pintasin-v-To find fault, criticize, carp; censure, gibe; inculpate

Pinto-n-Door, gate, entry, gateway.

Pintuho-n-Veneration, reverence; respect; regard

Pintuhuin-v-To respect; venerate; reverence; esteem; obey, have regard for.

Pinuno na walang sinusunod, na utos -n Tyrant; despot

Pinya n-Pineapple

Pipi a-Dumb; mute, silent.

Piral-n-A pull or twist of the ear.

Piralin-v-To twist or pull the ear

Piraso-n-Piece, fragment, scrap, shred; sherd; morsel,

Pirasong manipis,n-Slice, thin piece

Pirasong munti n-Fragment; morsel; nip, pinch, small piece.

Pirito-a-Fried

Pirma-n-Signature.

Pirmahan-a-To sign, attach one's signature,

Pirmahin-v-To sign; attach one's signature

Pisak ang isang mata a- One eyed.

Pisanin-v To meet, congregate gather

Pisaw-n-Large knife, resembling a cornknife.

Pisi-n-Cord, string.

Pisigan-a-Strong, stout, vigorous, robust.

Pisik-n Sputter, flicker.

Pisngi-n-Cheek.

Pista-n-Feast, banquet; holiday.

Pistahin-v-To feast, banquet

Pisunin-v-To level, flatten, stamp, ram; drive down

Pita-n-Desire, wish, liking, lust; mind; ambition, aspiration; cupidity

Pitagan-n-Respect, politeness, veneration, reverence; homage; kindness

Pitahin-v-To wish; desire, like, aspire, have ambitions.

Pitik-n-Chalk line, snap.

Pitikin n To chalk line, snap.

Pitisin-v To squeeze; press; wind, tighten.

Pito-n-Whistle, picolo

Pitó a-Seven

Pitó-n-Seven

Patong daan-a-Seven hundred.

Pitong daan n-Seven hundred.

Pitpitin-v To mash

Piyaos a-Hoarse; husky

Platero-n-Jeweler; silversmith.

Plaza-n-Square; park

Polhia-n-Boiler, kettle, dyers copper, copper dipper

Pokyotan n-Honeybee.

Policia-n-Police.

Pook n-Corner, point, place

Poon-n-Lord, saint

Poot-n-Indignation, dislike; disgust; aversion

Porcelena-n-Porcelain

Pootin-v-To irritate, provoke, disgust; cause to be indignant or to dislike

Pormal a-Formal, serious; ritual, earnest, grave.

Potro-n-Colt.

Presidente-n-President, mayor; chairman.

Prituhin-v-To fry

Pronombre-n-Pronoun.

Provincia-n-Province, country.

Puang-n-Space, interval; distance, breech.

Pudpod-a Dull, blunt.

Pugad-n-Nest

Pugaran-n-Hen's nest, haunt of a hen.

Pugay-n-Salute, salutation, greeting

Pugo-n-Quail, bob white

Pugpog n-Knoll, low hill.

Pugot-a Headless; decapitated, beheaded, blunt, cut off.

Pugutan ng ulo v-To behead, decapitate.

Puhunan-n-Capital, fund

Puit-n-Bottom, breech, hinder.

Pukaw-n-Fright, surprise, scare

Pukawin-v-To surprise; excite; scare; frighten, rouse

Pukuhin-v-To throw cast

Pukuhin ng bato-v-To stone.

Puklin-v-To stone, throw; cast

Puklo-n-Udder, bag of a cow.

Pukol-n-Throw; cast

Pukot-n-Fishing boat or smack.

Pukpok-n-Hammer, stroke with a hammer

Pukpukin-v-To hammer

Pukpukin ng maso-v-To pound with a hammer.

Pula-n-Red; ruby, color of flesh.

Pula-n Criticism; censure

Púlaan-v-To criticise, censure.

Pula ng itlog n-Yolk; yelk.

Palgas-n-Flea

Púlikat-n Spasm, cramp, convulsion.

Pulo-n-Island

Pulong-n-Reunion, meeting, congregation

16

Pulos a-All; entire, whole, each; every; equal, uniform.

Pulot-n-Honey; molasses.

Pulpol-a-Blunt, dull, obtuse

Pulubi-n-Beggar

Puluhan-n-Handle

Pulutin-v-To pick up, gather.

Pulutong-n-Plattoon

Pumagod-v-To . tire, weary, fatigue, molest, irk

Pumagpag-v-To shake, flop.

Pumaibabaw-v-To be superior; put on.

Pumalatak-v-To click.

Pumalit v-To change, barter, alter.

Pumalo-v-To beat, strike, cudgel; drub

Pumalo-n-Gudgel, club

Pumana-v-To shoot a dart or an orrow

Pumanaw-v To absent one's self, go away, leave

Pumanday v-To blacksmith

Pumangit-v-To grow or become ugly or homely.

Pumanhik-v-To go up; ascend, mount.

Pumanhik sa kabayo-v-To mount a horse

Pumantay-v-To equalize, match, become equal or of the same height

Pumagaypay-v-To wave, undulate.

Pumaroon-v-To go, resort, wend

Pumasok-v-To enter, go in, interfere; meddle.

Pumatak v-To drop, drip, dribble

Pumatakpatak-v-To drip, drop, fall in drops.

Pumatáy v-To kill, murder, assassinate

Pumatnugot-v-To defend, guard, attend, accompany; go with

Pumáwidpawid-v-To Stagger, waver.

Pumawis-v To perspire; sweat

Pumayag v To concede; permit allow; cede, agree, acquiesce, grant, coincide, accord; countenance

Pumayapa-v-To calm, pacify, appease, tranquilize, allay, settle; rest

Pumayapa-n-Pacificator, pacifier

Pumiga-v-To squeeze, press out

Pumihit-v-To turn; go back, return

Pumikit-v-To blink; wink

Pumili-v-To choose, prefer, elect

Pumiling v-To cluster, bunch.

Pumilipit-v-To twist, twine

Pumilit-v-To urge, persist; force, oblige.

Pumipintas-n-Critic, faultfinder.

Pumirma-v-To sign, subscribe; underwrite.

Pumisan-v-To join, congregate; meet, collect; unite, aggregate; associate

Pumisik-v-To sputter, flicker.

Pumukpok-v-To hammer; trob.

Pumulaan-v-To commence, begin

Pumulot-v-To pick up; gather; acquire,

Pumunit-v-To tear, touse

Pumuno-v To fill, pod

Pumunta v-To go, wend.

Pumusta-v-To wager; bet

Pumutok-v-To burst, shoot, explode, break open; breach; fulminate

Pumutol-v To chop, cut down.

Pumuyat v-To stay up, keep awake at night.

Puñal n Dagger, poinard.

Punasan-v-To clean with a rag

Punduhan-n-Anchoring place, anchorage, harbor; port, place where people stop to rest

Pungke-n-Pannier; basket, dust pan

Pungusin-v-To slice, cut away, pare off, shorten

Punla-n Sprout, shoot, seedling.

Punlaan-v-Seed plot; nursery, hot-bed.

Punin-v-To fill, stuff

Punit-n-Tear, touse.

Punit-a-Torn; ragged

Punitin-v-To tear, touse.

Punitpunit a-Ragged, torn very ragged

Punó-a-Full, replete, chock; plenary, complete,

Puno-n Commander, chief, leader, principal, prefect, trunk

Puno-n-Beginning, principle, motive, cause

Puno ng ahkabok-a Dusty, full of dust

Puno ng banlik-a-Muddy, full of mud

Puno ng kasamáan a-Malicious, wicked-bad.

Puno ng lukban-n-Orange tree

Punong aral-n-Axiom, maxim, rule; standard. proverb

Punongpuno-a-Replete; full to the brim.

Púno sa catedral-n Dean

Puntahin-v To point, aim.

Puntas-n-Lace; edging, bobbinet

Punto-n-Point

Punto sa pagsasalita-n-Style or manner of speech

Punuin-v-To fill; replete, stuff, satisfy, satiate

Purga-n-Purge, cathartic

Purgahin-v To purge

Puri-n-Virtue, honor, reputation, rank, fame, glory; applause; dignity

Purihin-v-To praise, honor, respect; dignify; commend; plaudit; eulogize extol.

Pusa-n-Cat, pussy; puss

Púsak n-Movement, moving.

Pusakal-a-Accustomed

Pusali-n Mud, mire, slime, clay.

Púsalian-n-Place that is muddy, sink hole; sink.

Puso-*n*-Heart.
Puso nğ mais-*n*-Ear of corn.
Pusod-*n*-Center of anything.
Pusód-*n*-Chignon.
Pusod nğ tiyan-*n*-Novel.
Pusok-*a*-Proud; bragging; passionate.
Pusok na loob-*a*-Fervent; impetuous, fiery; lively.
Puson-*n*-Groin.
Pusot *n*-Bottom; bed of a stream or river.
Puspos-*a*-Full; replete; round; circular; complete.
Puspos nğ kalualhatian *a*-Glorious; excellent.
Pusta-*n*-Wager; bet.
Pustahan-*v*-To wager; bet.
Pustahan-*n*-Wager; bet.
Puta-*n*-Whore; harlot; prostitute.
Putakti-*n*-Hornet; wasp; yellow jacket.

Putik-*n*-Mud; mire; clays.
Putla-*n*-Paleness; wanners; pallor; ghastliness.
Putlain-*v*-To extenuate; grow pale.
Putlin-*v*-To cut; chop; amputate; truncate; resind.
Putlin nğ manğa sanğa-*v*-To prune.
Putok-*n*-Shot; burst; report; crack; cracking; sound.
Putol-*n*-Piece.
Putol ang kamay-*a*-Handless.
Putong-*n*-Crown; wreath; coronet.
Putulin-*v*-To chop; cut; resind; truncate; amputate.
Putunğan nğ corona-*v*-To crown.
Putusan-*v*-To fill.
Pututin-*v*-To rape; ravish; force.
Puyat-*n*-Vigil; nightwatch.
Puyat *a*-Sleepless.
Puyatin-*v*-To keep awake.

Queso-*n*-Cheese.

Quitá—You, by me.

Rabo-*n*-Mortise.
Regla-*n*-Rule; order; precept; method.
Religion *n*-Religion; faith; creed; belief.
Retaso-*n*-Remnant.

Retrato-*n*-Portrait; picture.
Rienda-*n*-Rein.
Rifa-*n*-Raffle; lottery.
Rigudon-*n*-Quadrille; cotillon.
Rin-*adv.*-Also; too; self same; similarly

S

Sa-*prep.*-To; of; from; with; at; for; on; or; about; through; towards; in.
Sa aba ko-*inter.*-Poor me; unlucky me; pity me.
Saan-*adv.*-Where; whither; to or at what place.
Saan banda-*adv.*-Where; whither; at what place; at which side.
Saan man-*adv.*-Whereever; everywhere; anywhere.
Sabado-*n*-Saturday.
Sabak-*n*-Crotch; joint; mortise; groove.
Sa balasan-*n*-Northwind.
Sabarin-*v*-To vex; harrow; perturb; disturb; interrupt; interfere; disgust.
Sabat-*n*-Wedge.
Sabatan-*v*-To Wedge; split with a wedge.
Sabatin-*v*-To ambush; ambuscade; lay in wait; meet; encounter.

Sabaw-*n*-Broth.
Sa bawat sandali-*adv.*-Momentarily; every moment.
Sabay-*adv.*-Together; at the same time.
Sabay-sabay-*adv.*-Simultaneously; together; at once; at the same time.
Sabi *n*-Talk; speech; citation; narration.
Sabihin-*v*-To say; tell; narrate; cite; speak; talk; predicate.
Sabihin ang nğalan-*v*-To name; call by name.
Sabihin uli-*v*-To reiterate; repeat; say or tell again.
Sabisabi-*n*-Rumor; report; gossip; foolish talk.
Sabisabing lihim-*n*-Secret; gossip.
Sabitan-*n*-Hook; hanger; peg; coat-rack; anything that is used to hang things on.
Sable-*n*-Sabre.

Sabon-n-Soap

Sabsában-n-Trough; hog trough.

Sabsabán-v-To scrape but leave the scrapings, clean but leave the cleanings.

Sabúgan-n-Scattering

Sabugán-v-To scatter, throw broadcast

Sabunin-v-To soap.

Sadhan-v-To obstruct; close, block up; seal.

Sadia-adv -Intentionally, purposely, avowedly, disignedly, deliberately

Sadja adv -Intentionally, purposely; avowedly, designedly, deliberately, knowingly; on purpose.

Sagad-a-Brim full, replete, exhausted

Sagad na sagad-a Brim full; replete

Sagana-a-Abundant, copious, plentiful, profuse, rich, numerous, much, many, lavish, bounteous, provident, fertile, fruitful large in quantity.

Sagana-adv.-Fully, completely, abundantly, copiously, plentifully, bounteously; magnificently.

Sagápan-n-Skimmer.

Sagapán ang bula v-To skim

Sagawing-adv -In the direction of; toward.

Sa gawing hilagaan-adv -Northerly, northward.

Sa gawing kalunuran-adv -Westerly, westward.

Sa gawing silanganan adv.-Easterly; eastward

Sa gawing timugan-adv -Southerly; southward.

Sagiok-n Crack, snap.

Sagipin v-To save, succor, deliver.

Saght-adv.-Shortly, briefly, in a short space of time

Sago n-Sago.

Sagot-n-Answer, reply, retort, response; repartee, contestation

Sagpangin-i-To snap, bite quickly

Sagsag-n-Trot

Saguan-n-Paddle, oar, scull

Saguing-n-Banana, plantain.

Saguingan-n-Banana grove or plantation.

Sagutan-v-To answer, respond; contest; guarantee.

Sagutan-n-Answer, debate, response, guarantee

Sa harap-adv.-In front, against, before; in presence of.

Sa hayag-adv -Abroad, in public, at sight, publicly.

Sahig-n-Floor.

Sahigan-v-To floor.

Sahing n-Pitch; rosin

Sa hipo-adi .-By the touch.

Sa huli-adv.-Lastly, after, behind, backwards.

Sa hulihan-adv -Lastly, after, behind; then.

Sa hulo adv At the upper part, at the source

Sahurin-v To receive; accept.

Sahurin ang upa-v-To receive one's pay or salary

Sa ibaba-adv.-Below, beneath, under.

Sa ibabaw-adv.-On, upon, above: on top.

Sa ibayo-adv -Beyond, on the other side

Sa ilalim-adv Under, beneath, below.

Sa ilalim a-Nether.

Sa isang dali adv.-In a moment, presently in a trice

Sa itaas-adv -Above, over, high up

Sa ito-adv -Here in; hereon, herewith.

Sa iyo—For, with, to, of, from you.

Saka-adv.-After, afterwards, next.

Saka-conj -And.

Sa kaduluhan-adv -Lastly, at the end.

Sakag-n-Fish net

Sakang-adv.-Open-legged

Sakang-a Bowlegged

Sakah adv -Perhaps, by chance, at least; should it come to pass

Sakasakali adv.-Perhaps, if by chance, should it come to pass.

Sa katapusan-adv -Lastly, at the end, then, at last

Sakdal-a-Full, replete; complete

Sakdalan-n-Protection, shelter.

Sakit n-Sickness, desease, torture, pain, hardship, anguish, torment, ail, distress, dolor malady, afliction, suffering, ache, trouble

Sakit ng himatay-n Fainting, swooning.

Sakit na nakahahawa na buhat sa gawaang kalupaan-n-Venerial descase

Sakit na pasma-n-Spasm; convulsion

Saklap-n-Bitterness; disgust; harshness, severity

Saklaw n-Hold up, heading off, turning

Saklawin-v-To head off; hold up; turn

Saklolo-n-Defense, help; protection; support, aid, suffrage.

Saklolohan-v-To help, aid, succor; provide, support; protect; defend

Sakong-n-Heel

Sakramento n Sacrament.

Saksak-n Stab, thrust

Saksakin-v-To stab; stick, dirk

Saksi-n-Witness

Saksi nakakita ng pinaguusapan-n-An eye witness.

Saktan r-To hurt, wound; pain; cripple, maim; lame, chastize, agrrieve, offend; irritate.

Sakuna-n-Disaster; calamity; misfortune; misadventure; mishap; misery; accident.

Saknpin-v-To take or put under the control of another; subdue; subject; subordinate; overcome-

Sala-n-Sin; fault; crime; culpability; infraction; infringement; violation; guilt; offense; transgression; defect; vice; deficiency; slight.

Salaan-n-Strainer; collander; sieve; filter; cullander.

Sa labas-adv.-Out side; abroad; in public; publicly; moreover.

Salabin-v-To scortch; singe.

Sálag-n-Man midwife.

Salág-n-Contradiction; opposition.

Salagin-v To stop anything that is thrown toward you.

Salaghati-n-Resentment: grudge; disgust; loathing; restlessness; inquietude.

Saláin-v-To strain; filter.

Salain muli-v-To restrain; refilter.

Salagubang-n-Junebug.

Salakuban-n-Leather bag or pouch.

Salahin v-To reject; condemn; find fault; criticize;

Sálahin-v-To weave.

Salahula-a-Sloppy; dirty; filthy; slattern; slatternly; slutish; squalid; dowdy.

Salamangka-n-Jugglery; leger de main.

Salamat-n-Thanks.

Salambaw-n-Fish net, snare, or trap.

Salamin-n-Looking glass; mirror; speculum.

Salamin sa mata-n-Eyeglasses; spectacles.

Salamin ng tainga-n-Eardrum.

Salangin-v-To touch.

Salang palad-n-Bad luck; misfortune.

Salang palad-a Unlucky; unfortunate; miserable.

Salangsang-n-Trespass; contravention.

Salangsangin-v-To contradict; confuse; oppose; resist; controvert; dispute; transgress; trespass; refute; reject; repel; contravene; object.

Salanta-n-Abuse; illtreatment; misuse; mistreatment.

Salanta-a-Illused; mistreated; abused.

Salantain-v-To misuse, illtreat; abuse.

Salapang-n-Fork; pitch fork; spear.

Salapi-n-Money; cash; pelf; specie.

Salaping katubusan sa anoman-n-Ransom.

Salapungan ng daan-n-Crossroad,

Salas-n-Salon; saloon; hall.

Salat-a-Poor; needy; helpless; destitute; disconsolate; poverty stricken; scarce; scanty; wanting; lacking; deficient; penurious; paltry; mean; short; close.

Salatin-v-To touch; feel; sound; probe; investigate; procure.

Salat sa bunga-a-Sterile; fruitless; barren; unfruitful.

Salaulain-v-To soil; make foul, nasty, or filthy.

Salawal-n-Pant; pantaloon; trouser.

Sálay-n-Nest; receiver; dripping pan.

Salaysay-n-Relation; narration; account; explication; declaration; proposal.

Salaysayin-v-To narrate; relate. declare; account; tell; explain; refer; propose.

Salbahi-n-Savage.

Salbahi-a-Savage; truculent; mean; rude bad.

Sa likod-adv.-Behind; after; at the back.

Sa likuran-adv.-Behind; at the back; after; following.

Salilongan-n-Redemption; ransom; assistance; defense; guard; shelter.

Salilungan-n-Vindication: defense; protection; shelter; guard.

Salin-n-Copy; transcript; likeness; counterpart; duplicate.

Salinan-n Place of copying or transcribing.

Salinsing-n-Wild growth of grain.

Salisalita-n-Foolish talk; rumor.

Salita-n-Discourse; speech; talk; word; conversation; converse; gab; locution; vocable; term.

Salitaan-n-Conversation; agreement; contract; discourse; colloquy; parley; chat; argument; conference; convention; convenant; pact; paction; parlance.

Salitaan ng dalawa-n-Dialogue.

Salita at kilos palalo-n-Braggartism.

Salitain-v-To speak; talk; reason; harangue; narrate; say; tell; relate.

Salita na may maraming silaba-n-Polysyllable.

Salita ng isang nacion ó kapulungan-n Language; idiom; dialect.

Salitang hunghang-n-Nonsense.

Salitang makaisa ang kahulugan-n-Synonym.

Salitang mahalay-n-Rude word, phrase, or speech.

Salitang malasa n-Wit; witty talk.

Salitang panininta-n-Love talk.

Salitin-v-To mix; mingle; alternate; jumble.

Salitsalit-a-Streaked or interlined with fat and lean; alternate.

Salawahang loob _n_ Fickleness; infidelity, indicision; inconstancy

Sahwahang loob-_n_-Inconstancy, infidelity, indicision; fickleness

Sahwang kapalaran-_n_-Bad or ill luck; misfortune

Sahwang loob _a_-Unhappy; unlucky; unfortunate

Salmon-_n_-Salmon

Salong-_n_-Cabin, barrack; hut.

Salongan-_n_-Place of concealment, protection, help.

Sa loob-_adv_-Within, inside, internal

Sa loob _a_-Nether.

Salopihn-_v_-To dam, obstruct; augment, exaggerate, add to.

Salpok-_n_-Blow, knock, encounter, clash, shock; fight; sudden meeting.

Salsal-_a_-Obtuse; blunt, dull, flat nosed.

Salsalin-_v_-To blunt, dull the point; rivet, clinch; squander or spend money foolishly

Salubsob _n_-Thorn on splinter that has been run into the foot slantwise

Salubong-_n_-Gift, present.

Salubungin _v_-To meet, encounter

Sa lugar ng _adv_-Instead.

Salukan-_v_-To skim; take off.

Salungahan-_n_-Ascension, acclivity.

Salungat-_a_-Opposed, contrary

Salungatin-_v_-To oppose, contradict, object, resist; brush back, turn back, impugn

Salungat sa-_a_-Opposite; contrary.

Salungat sa-_adv_-On the contrary.

Salungatin _v_-To raise with the point of a needle or pin; reach with a pole or stick

Saluysoy-_n_-Ravine, gully, brook, rill, rivulet

Samá _n_-Ugliness, wickedness, evil, badness, imperfection, fault, mischief, injury; hurt harm; moral depravity, homliness, turpitude, misfurtune.

Sa mabuting panahon _a_-Opportune

Sa magisang sarili-_adv_-Alone; only.

Samahan _n_-Society; company, partnership, assembly.

Samahan _v_-To accompany, unite; join

Sa maikling panahon-_adv_-Shortly, briefly, soon; in a short time

Samakalawa-_adv_-Day after to-morrow.

Samakalawa-_n_-The day after to-morrow

Samá ng loob _n_ Displeasure, disgust, uneasiness, resentment, grudge, anger, discontent, asperity, pique.

Samang palad-_n_-Bad luck, ill luck; misfortune.

Samantala-_adr_-While, in the meantime; meanwhile, interim.

Samantalahin-_v_-To whille away time; take advantage of, improve.

Samantalang-_a_-Provisional

Sa may-To him who has; in the direction of, near; near to

Sambahan-_n_-Church, temple, place of worship.

Sambahin-_v_-To worship; reverence; hallow, sanctify

Sambahin ang anito-_v_-To indolize, worship idols

Sambahlo-_n_-Hat.

Sambilatin-_v_-To scatter promiscuosly; throw about, tumble topsy-turvy.

Sampaguita-_n_ Small white flower

Sampal-_n_-Slap, blow whith the open hand

Sampalataya-_n_-Faith, creed; belief.

Sampalatayanin-_v_-To believe, credit; give faith

Sampalin-_v_-Slap

Sampalok-_n_-Tamarind, tamarac.

Sampayan-_n_-Clothes line; line used to hang things on

Sampayin-_v_-To hang up.

Sampong-_adv_-Till, until, also, even, as far as

Sampulong-_a_-Whole, entire, all

Sampuo-_n_-Ten

Sampuo-_a_-Ten.

Sampuong utos ng DIOS-_n_-The Ten commandments of GOD.

Samsaman-_n_-Collection, gathering

Samsamán-_v_-To collect, gather, take away, congest

Samsamán ng sandata-_v_-To disarm

Samsamin-_v_-To capture, collect, gather

Sanay-_n_-Practice; experience, exercise.

Sanay-_a_-Experienced, expert; able; skilful, capable, fit, adroit, graceful, deft, dexterous, practical

Sanayin _v_-To teach; instruct; practice, train, exercise, break in, learn by experience, accustom

Sandali _n_-Instant, moment, trice, jiffy short space of time.

Sandalias-_n_-Sandals.

Sandat-_a_ Full, replete; abundant, satiated, satisfied.

Sandata-_n_-Sword, weapon, arm.

Sandatin-_v_-To satiate, satisfy, replete; gratify

Sandig-_a_-Slanting, sloping, leaning.

Sandigan _n_-Couch, baluster, anything to lean on.

Sandigan-_v_-To put a rail or balustrade on the side of a stairway

Sandok _n_-Ladle; large spoon.

Sandok na malaki-_n_ Scoop.

Sandokin-v-To scoop; take out with a spoon; ladle.
Sang-a-A; an; one.
Sanga-n-Branch; sprig.
Sang daan-n-One hundred.
San daan-a-A hundred.
Sangdaig-digan-n-The universe.
Sanghaya-n-Dignity; rank.
Sang haya-n-Hand full.
Sangka-n-Canal; drain; sluice, ditch.
Sangkang patubigan-n-Canal; drain.
Sangkap-n-Jewel; ornament; part piece.
Sangla-n-Pledge; pawn; mortgage; attachment; plight; security.
Sanglang lupa-n-Mortgage.
Sanglibutan-n-The earth; globe; universe.
Sangol-n-Creature; babe; baby.
Sangtaon-n-One year.
Sanib-n-Juncture; joint.
Sanepa-n-Picture frame.
Sankalan-n-Butcher's block.
Sankap-n-Implement; tool.
Sankatawohan-n-Humanity; nation.
Sankleta-n-Slipper.
Sankutsahin-v-To parboil.
Sansalain-v-To impede; hinder; obstruct; restrain; detain.
Santa Biblia-n-Holy bible; evangel.
Santa escritura-n-Holy seripture.
Santo-n-Saint.
Sapa-n-Rivulet; brook; creek.
Sa paanomang paraan-adv.-Resolutely justly or unjustly; by all means; in any possible way; no matter what passes.
Sa pagitun-prep.-Between; betwixt;among.
Sa pagitan-adv.-Meanwhile; meantime.
Sapagka't-conj. Because; for; as; since.
Sapakin-v-To break.
Sapakin ang bibig-v-To break the jaws.
Sapal-n-Trash; crushed sugar cane.
Sa palibid-adv.-Round; about; around; round about; on every side.
Sa paligid-adv.-Round; about; around;
Sa palibot-adv.-Round; about; round about; around; on every side.
Sa pamagitan ng-adv.-By means of; by virtue of; by favor of.
Sa panahon-adv.-Timely; in time.
Sa panahon-a-Opportune;
Sapantaha-n-Supposition; hypothesis; conjecture; presumption; suspicion.
Sa paraan ito-adv.-Hereby; herewith; hereon.
Sapat-a-Sufficient; anough; full; complete; replete.
Sapatos-n-Shoes.
Sapatos na bakal-n-Horseshoe.
Sapilitan-adv. By force or persuasion.

Sa pilitan-a-Obligatory; binding, necessary; needful; precise; indespensible
Sapin-n-Shoe; shoes.
Sapol sa ngat-adv.-From the root; entirely.
Sápot-n-Shroud; Winding sheet.
Sapsapan-v-To husk; strip off husks; peel.
Sáputin-v-To enshroud.
Sara-n-Closing; sealing.
Saraguete-n-Truant; rascal.
Sara ng sulat-n-The sealing of a letter.
Saráp-n-Taste; relish; pleasure; sweetness; delight; gratification.
Sarili-a-Self.
Sarili-n-Self,
Sarih ng araw-a-Solar; belonging to the sun.
Sarili ng mga alipin ó alila-a-Servile; menial; slavish.
Sariling asawa ng isang babayi-n-Husband.
Sariling asawa ng isang lalaki-n-Wife.
Sarili nila-pro-Their; theirs,
Sarili niya-pro.-His; her; hers.
Sarisari-n-Notions.
Sarisari-a-Various; miscellaneous; multiple.
Sarisaring kulay-a-Motley.
Sariwa-n-Fresh; green; young; delicate.
Saro-n-Jar; pot.
Sasakyan-n-Ship; vessel.
Sa sarili-To him or her.
Sa silong-adv.-Down stairs; beneath; below; under.
Sastre-n-Tailor.
Satsat ng pari-n-Bald spot on a priest's head.
Sa tabi ng-adv.Beside; on the brim or edge.
Sa tanyag adv.-Abroad; in public visibly.
Sa tanyag-a-Visible; public.
Sa tapat-adv.-Opposite; facing; in front.
Sa towitowi na-adv. Always; momentarily; frequently; every moment.
Sanlan-v-To restore; give back; return.
Sa uli uli-adv.-Again; again and again.
Sawá-a-Enough; sufficient; full; complete.
Sawain-v-To prohibit; interdict; forbid.
Sawatain-v-To impede; hinder; obstruct; restrain; detain.
Sawi-adv.-Opposite; contrary.
Sawing kapalaran-n-Ill luck; bad luck; misfortune.
Sáya-n-Skirt.
Sayá.n-Joy; happiness; glee; festivity, mirth, merriment; gladness; pleasure; gayety; joyfulness; airiness.
Sayá na malabis-n-Ecstacy.

Sayang-n-Grief, pity, compassion, condolence, waste

Sayang *inter.*-Pity, what a pity

Sayangın v-To waste, squander, throw away

Sayaw-n-Dance

Sayawan-n-Ball, dance.

Sayasatın v-To examine, investigate.

Saysay-n-Explication, declaration; demonstration, signification, narration, account, proposal, precept, method; order,

Saysayan-v-To decide; distinguish, determine, give importance, explain, tell, narrate; account, expound

Saysayin v-To Explain, portray, say, tell, narrate, recite, translate, relate, cite, predicate, analyze interpret, signify. lay open, expound, manifest, report; rehearse, construe, declare, characterize, demonstrate, mean, denote

Saysayin ang kahulugan-v-To interpret, translate, tell the meaning

Saysayin mabuti-v-To explain

Saysayin malinaw v-To define describe, explain; delineate

Saysayin maliwanag v-To describe, explain; define, say or tell clearly.

Saysayin sa pintas v-To comment

Sebada-n-Barley.

Sebo-n-Grease; fat

Sebuyas-n-Onion.

Sentencia-n Sentence, decision, judge, ment

Sermon-n Sermon

Sermon sa paglilibing n-Obsequy

Servilleta-n-Doile, napkin.

Sesgo-n-Gore, plait

Sexo-n-Sex.

Siasatin-v-To investigate, examine, inspect, review, survey, study, probe, revise, register

Siap-n-Puling, chirping, chirp.

Sibá n-Gluttony

Sibad-n-Running like the wind.

Sibak-n-Split

Sibakın-v-To split

Sibat-n-Spear; lance pike; staff

Sibatın-v-To spear, lance.

Sicante-n-Blotter

Sidhi-n-Rigor; sternness; harshness, keenness, fullness; completeness.

Sigá-n-Bonfire

Sigén-i-To set afire; kindle, burn

Sigaw n-Cry, shriek; yell, loud call; scream, howl; shout; screak, scheech.

Sigawan-v-To shriek, call, cry out. gowl, shout, hoot,

Sigawin-v-To shout, howl, scream, cry, exclaim, hoot, clamor.

Sigáwin-a Vociferous, clamorous, noisy, howling

Sigirin-v-To prick, pierce

Sigla-u-Boldness, courage, activity, livliness, vivacity

Sigwa-n-Storm, tempest

Sihang-n-Jawbone.

Sikad-n-Kick; spurn; thrust with the foot

Sikang-n-Cross timber, long bolster of a bed

Sikap n-Diligence, industry, activity, afficiousness; assiduity.

Sikapat-n-Shilling, bit, 12½ cents

Sikapat labing dalawa-n-Twenty cents

Sikapat sikolo-n-Eighteen and three quarters cento inex

Sikaran v-To kick, spurn

Sikat-n-Appearance, rising.

Sikat ng araw-n-The rising of the sun.

Sikmura-n-Stomach.

Sikmura ng hayop-n Maw.

Siko-n-Elbow; hock.

Sikolo-n-Six and a quarter cents mex

Sikpinin-v-To Narrow; contract.

Siksik-a-Dense, close, thick, compact.

Siksikin v-To pack closely; cram; stuff, jam, force in

Sikulate-n-Chocolate.

Silab-n-Burn, parch, scortch

Silabin-v-To burn; scortch; parch.

Silanganan n-The east, orient

Silay n-Glance, glimpse.

Silid-n-Room, chamber, apartment

Silid na tulugan-n Bed chamber, bed room; sleeping apartment

Silip-n Glance, glimpse, blink, peep.

Silipin-v-To peep, glance, blink.

Silla-n-Chair

Silo-n-Snare

Silong-n-The first story

Silsilin v To clinch; rivet, secure

Sibangot n-Frown; displeasure; wryface.

Simaron-a-Intractible, wild; savage, cross grained.

Simbahan-n-Church; temple, house of worship

Simot-a-Exhausted, fatigued, tired; used up, totally drained

Simpan-n-Economy, guard, watch

Simpanin-v-To economize, keep, guard.

Sinabi i p p Said.

Sinadya-a-Intentional.

Sinadya-adv,-Intentionally, designedly, avowedly, purposely.

Sinandali-v-To borrow

Sinapete n Anchor.

Sinapupunan-n-Grons

Sinasamá-v To be unhappy, unlucky

Sinasapantaha-*a*-Putative; supposed; suppositional.

Sinasaysay-*a*-Affirmative.

Sinaysay sa libro-*v*-To quote; affirm.

Sindak-*n*.Fright; terror; dread; scare; surprise.

Sindakin-*r*.-To scare; frighten; surprise.

Sindi-*n*-Fire; light; burning.

Sindihan-*v*-To kindle; light; set fire to.

Sinelas-*n*-Slippers.

Singaw-*n*-Appearance; eruption.

Singaw na anoman sa balat-*n*-Eruption or outbreak of the skin.

Singhot-*n*-Snuff; snuffle.

Singilin-*v*-To collect; dun; request payment.

Singit-*n*-Groin; crack.

Singkad-*a*-Chief; principal; important; great; collective.

Singkaw-*n*-Yoking; hitch.

Singkawin-*r*-To hitch; yoke.

Singsing-*n*-Ring; finger ring.

Sinkad-*a*-Full; complete; replete.

Sinkamas-*n* Turnip.

Sino-*pro*.-Who; which.

Sinok-*n*-Hiccough.

Sinoman *pro*.-Anyone; anybody.

Sinoman-*n*-Somebody.

Sinoman ay hindi-*pro* Nobody; none

Sinop-*n*-Curiosity; inquisitiveness; inquisition.

Sinsay-*a*-Illegal; illicit; unlawful.

Sinsin-*n*-Solidity; thickness; closeness; compactness.

Sinsinan-*v*-To condense; thicken, confine; press; condense; put close together.

Sinsinin-*v*-To thicken; confine; press; condense; put close together.

Sinta-*n*-Love; courtship.

Sintahin-*r*-To love; court.

Sintas-*n*-Ribbon.

Sintaron-*n*-Belt; strap;

Sinulat ng nagpapalimbag-*n* Editorial.

Sinulid-*n*-Thread.

Sinungaling-*n*-Lie; cheat; imposter; liar; swindler; sharper.

Sinungaling-*a*-Lying; false; fraud; unfaithful; inconstant.

Sinusundan-*n*-Former antecedent.

Sipa-*n*-Kick; spurn.

Sipag-*n*-Diligence; attention; industry; thrift; officiousness.

Sipain-*v*-To kick; spurn.

Sipakin-*v*-To split; cleave.

Sipan-*n*-Toothbrush.

Siphayo-*n*-Insult; censure; reproach.

Sipiin-*v*-To compile; copy.

Sipit-*n*-Tweezers; pincer; tongs.

Sipon-*n*-Constipation; catarrh.

Sirá-*n*-Putrid; broken; disrupt; cracked;

used up; useless.

Sirá-*n*-Break; scath; breach: blight; putridness; putridity.

Sirá ang isang mata-*a*-One eyed.

Sirá ang isip-*a*-Crazy; insane; delirious; mad; frantic; furious.

Sirain-*v*-To break; destroy; ruin; injure; fracture; scathe: disrupt; blight; delapidate; hurt pervert; polute; corrupt; infect; deprave; shatter; stain; impair; waste; misspend; deteriorate.

Sirain-*a* Brittle; fragile; perishable.

Sirain ang loob-*v*-To dishearten; alienate.

Sirain ang mabuting kaugalian-*v*-To corrupt; viliate; mar; seduce; bribe.

Sirain ang puri-*v*-To: stain; viliate; degrade; deprave; detract; profane; stain or tarnish one's character.

Sisid-*n*-Dive; immersion; dip; plunge.

Sisi-*n*-Repentence.

Sisihin-*v*-To repent; scold; reprimand; admonish; blame.

Sisiw-*n*-Chick; small chicken.

Sisiwa-*n*-Wet nurse.

Sitaw-*n*-Beans.

Sitsit-*n*-Gossip; false rumor.

Siya-*pro*.-He; she; it.

Siyá-*inter*.-Enough; stop; halt.

Siya-*n*-Saddle.

Siya nawa-*n*-Amen.

Siya nawa *adv*.-Amen

Siya nga-*adv*.-Sure; surely; yes; yea.

Siyasat-*n*-Inquiry; investigation; examination; inquisition; survey curiosity.

Siyasatin-*n*-To inquire; investigate; examine; explore; search; try; prove; scrutinize; scan; survey; peruse; detect; find.

Siyasating maingat-*v*-To search; pry into; consult.

Siyasatin ang lihim-*r*-To scent; pry or peep into; discover secrets.

Sobre-*n*-Envelope.

Sombrero-*n*-Hat; castor.

Soriso *n* Sausage.

Sowail-*a*-Obstinate; disobedient; pertinaceous; rebellious; intractible; dogged.

Suabe-*a*-Soft; tender; delicate.

Suabe-*adv*.-Softly; tenderly; delicately.

Suag *n*-Butt; hook.

Suagin-*v*-To butt; hook.

Suatan-*v*-To fail to keep one's word because of an accident.

Suhiang-*n*-A thorn or sliver that is run into the foot slantingly.

Subo-*n*-Mouthful.

17

Subok-*n*-Proof; assay; trial; indication; sign; token; evidence; reason.

Subukin-*v*-To try; prove; assay; examine; try one's strengh.

Sudsod-*n*-Plow point; colter; coulter.

Sudsuran-*v*-To give the lie; contradict.

Sudlan-*n*-Spindle.

Sudya-*n* Gore; plait.

Suela ng̃ sapin-*n*-Sole; sole leather.

Sueldo-*n*-Pay; wages; salary; stipend; fee; payment.

Suga-*n*-Thether; stake line; stake rope; lariat.

Subukin-*v*-To spy; watch closely; lurk; surprise; overtake; astonish.

Sugal-*n*-Game; gambling; card-playing.

Sugahin-*v*-To tether; stake out.

Sugat-*n*-Wound; cut; incision; injury.

Sugatan-*a*-Ulcerous; easily hurt.

Sugatan-*v*-To wound: hurt; injure.

Sugat ng̃ pana-*n*-Arrow wound.

Sugat ng̃ saksak-*n*-Stab.

Sugpo-*n*-Large shrimp; Lobster.

Sugpong-*n*-Joint; juncture; union.

Suhay-*n*-Prop; fulcrum; support.

Suhol-*n*-Bride; bribery; subordination; incitement.

Suhulan-*v*-To bribe; suborn,

Suhulin-*v*-To bribe; suborn.

Sui-*n*-Shoot or sprout of a banana plant.

Suit *n*-Small bowl.

Suitik *n*-Thief; robber; higwayman.

Suitik-*a* Cheating; infidel; disloyal; inconstant; crafty.

Sukab-*a* Treacherous faithless; infidel; false. inconstant; traitorous; perfidous.

Sukal-*n*-Disgust; garbage; filth dirt.

Sukal ng̃ loob-*n*-Disgust; displeasure; discontent; anger.

Sukat-*n*-Measure; rule; dimension; extent; capacity; bulk.

Sukat-*inter*-Enough.

Sukat-*a*-Sufficient; enough; effectual; mete; apt; fit.

Sukatin *v*-To measure mete.

Sukatin ang lalim ng̃ tubig-*v*-To sound.

Sukatin muli-*v*-To remeasure.

Sukat kamtan-*a*-Obtainable; attainable.

Sukat mabusog-*a*-Satiable.

Sukat magasta-*a*-Expendable.

Sukat magawa-*a*-Feasible; practical; practicable.

Sukat manyari-*a*-Feasible; practical; practicable.

Sukat makadaya-*a*-Delusive; deceitful.

Sukat makaliwanag-*a*-Illuminative.

Sukat mamuo *n*-Congealable; that which may or can be melted.

Sukat matalastasin -*a* Comprehensible; conceivable.

Sukat na-*inter*.-Enough; halt; stop.

Sukat ng̃ anoman-*n*-Measurement; size; dimensions; measure.

Sukdan-*prep*.-Though; notwithstanding; never the less.

Suki-*n*-Customer; patron.

Suklam-*n*-Disgust; dislike; reluctance; repugnance; antipathy; nausea; loathing.

Suklam-*a*-Nauseous; dispicable; disgusting; loathesome.

Suklam ng̃ loob-*n*-Aversion; abhorence; displeasure; loathing.

Suklay-*n*-Comb.

Suko-*n* Defeat; surrender; subjection; vanquishment; cession; repulse.

Sukob-*n*-Buckram.

Suksukan ng̃ palaso-*n*-Quiver.

Suksukin-*v*-To shuffle.

Sulambi-*n*-Row; aisle; flank; brim.

Suklob-*n*-Cover; covering; lid.

Sulasurin-*v*-To fall headlong; stumble into errors.

Sulat-*n*-Writing; deed; letter; contract; treatise; inscription; epistle.

Sulat kasama sa testamento ó huling kalooban-*n*-Codicil.

Sulat kamay-*n*-Manuscript.

Sulat na bustos-*n*-Scribble.

Sulat ng̃ banhay-*n*-Rough draft.

Sulat na maikli-*n*-Summary.

Sulat na paninta-*n*-Billetdoux.

Sulat sa ibabaw ng̃ libing-*n*-Epitaph.

Suliap-*n*-Glance; peep; gaze; glimpse; ogle.

Suliaw-*n*-Cup; crock; bowl.

Suligi-*n* Dart; bamboo; lance.

Sulipat-*a*-Oblique, squint eyed.

Suliran-*v*-To spin; weave.

Sulirán-*n*-Spindle.

Sulit-*n*-Examination; investigation.

Sulitin-*v*-To investigate; examine; explore.

Suló-*n*-Torch; firebrand.

Sulok-*n*-Corner; angle.

Sulot-*n*-Shoot; sprout.

Sulong-*inter*.-Hurry up; continue; be gone; get away; get out; go on.

Sulsol-*n*-Agitation; excitement; incitement; instigation; temptation.

Sulsulan-*v*-To incite excite; agitate; tempt; urge; instigate; prompt; hint; suggest.

Sumaad-*v*-To inform; advise; admonish; warn.

Sumaba-*v*-To be at home or in mourning.

Sumabang-*v*-To fall headlong; remit.

Sumahit-*v*-To cling; hang; catch on.

Sumadsad-*v*-To anchor.

Sumagana-v-To Swell, grow, teem, increase, abound, grow abundantlv

Sumagana ng malabis-v To superabound.

Sumagiok-v-To smack the lips

Sumagot-v-To answer, reply, respond; acknowledge, guarantee

Sumagsag-v-To trot, be in haste.

Sumaguan-v-To row, paddle, scull.

Sumahod-v-To receive; accept

Sumakay-v-To ride; embark

Sumakay sa cabayo-v-To ride a horse.

Sumakit-t-To pain. hurt, smart.

Sumaklaw-v-To ambush, encounter, meet, he in wait, be bounded by

Sumakop-v-To join with another, be under the control of

Sumaksi-v-To testify, certify; be a witness; give evidence

Sumala-v-To miss, fail; violate, be deficient, be guilty

Sumalangsang-t-To oppose, go against; violate, resist, contradict

Sumalig-v-To recline; lean back, he back

Sumahlong-v-To be sheltered, protected, helped or favored

Sumalin-v-To copy, transcribe.

Sumalipad-lipad-t-To flutter

Sumaloysoy-v-To gully.

Sumaluhong v-To meet, join, encounter.

Sumalunga-v-To mount ascend

Sumáma-v-To accompany; attend, go with; join, associate; follow; adhere, unite, be united

Sumamá-t-To be bad, go to the bad, deprave, corrupt, become depraved.

Sumamba-v-To praise worship

Sumámo v-To implore, petiton, beg, pray; crave

Sumampa-v To mount, ascend, rise

Sumampalataya-v-To believe, trow, credit, have faith in

Sumampalataya sa Dios-v-To believe in God.

Sumamyo-v To smell

Sumandal-v-To recline, lean back

Sumandall adv Shortly, briefly, immediately, instantly.

Sumandig sa siko v-To lean on the elbow.

Sumangun t-To consult, take or receive, advice

Sumanib-v To join, unite; associate, adhere

Sumansala-v-To prohibit, interdict forbid, stop; check.

Sumapaw-v-To appear, sprout, shoot, overflow

Sumápit-v-To arrive, reach, fetch amount to, approach; join, end.

Sumariwa-v-To green, become green

Sumasagana-a-Luxuriant, abundant; superfluous, superabundant

Sumasaklaw sa lahat-a Universal, public, vulgar; general.

Sumasal-t-To irritate.

Sumasama ang loob-v-To disgust, displease

Sumasamba sa anito-n-Adolater.

Sumawa-v-To tire, loathe, disgust, grow tired of anything.

Sumaway-v-To stop, check; dissuade

Sumaya-v-To elate, exult, be happy.

Sumbang-n Headlong fall, dispute; quarrel contradiction.

Sumbangin-v-To fall headlong, dispute, quarrel, contradict; gainsay.

Sumbi-n-Slap, blow, cuff, box

Sumbong n-Accusation, complaint.

Sumentencia-v-To sentence, condemn

Sumiap-v-To pule, chirp, peep; pip

Sumibol-v-To sprout, bubble, spring, appear

Sumigaw-v-To cry, scream, shout, shriek, exclaim; clamor, vociferate, halloo, hoot, screech, screak.

Sumikat-t-To appear; rise, sally.

Sumikat ang araw v-To rise (per to the sun.)

Sumiki-v-To narrow, contract, mix, mingle.

Sumikip v-To narrow, contract, grow, less, lessen.

Sumilakbo ang tubig-v To bubble; spring; gush.

Sumilang-t-To appear, grow out, occur.

Sumilip-v To glance; peep; peek

Sumiphayo-v-To insult; slander, abuse.

Sumunangot-v-To pout, make a wry face.

Sumimba-v-To go to church, hear mass.

Sumingap-v-To draw a long breath after drinking.

Sumingasing-v-To sniff, blow one's nose

Sumunghot-t-To sniff, snuffle.

Suminsin-v-To grow thick, condense; become dense.

Sumiuta-t To love; woo, court

Sumisinta-n Lover, sweetheart.

Sumipot-v-To appear; begin, sprout, eminate, loom, grow out

Sumipot na walang abog abog-v-To surprise, overtake, astonish, come without notice, appear suddenly

Sumira-v-To break, impair, delapidate, ruin

Sumisi-v-To repent

Sumisi sa namamali-n-Reprehender.

Sumisid-v-To dive; plunge, dip

Sumisigaw-n-Shouter, clamorer, cryer.

Sumoway-v-To resist, disobey; oppose, violate

Sumpa-n-Curse; imprecation, oath

Sumpain v-To curse, detract, accurse; swear, make oath, imprecate

Sumuway-v To disobey, violate, oppose

Sumuway sa kautusan-n-Delinquent, offender

Sumubo-v-To eat with the fingers

Sumubsob-v-To crawl under, fall headlong

Sumugat-v-To hurt; wound, injure

Sumugat n-Wounder, striker

Sumuhol-v-To bribe, suborn

Sumukab-v-To be traitorous, unfaithful, inconstant, bad, infidel or evil

Sumuko-v-To Surrender, truckle; be defeated.

Sumukot-v-To crouch; stoop

Sumulat-v-To write, compose

Sumulat ng bastos-v-To scribble

Sumulat sa bato-v-To lithograph

Sumuhid-v-To spin

Sumulong-r To continue, advance, go ahead

Sumumpa-v-To swear imprecate, blaspheme, execrate, accurse, curse, make oath

Sumundo-v-To send for.

Sumungkal-v To loosen; rot, scatter about.

Sumuno-v-To board; lodge, live with another.

Sumunod-v-To follow, obey yield, comply, submit, ensue, be inherent

Sumunod sa mangyari-r-To happen, supervene

Sumunod sa iba v To follow another, comply; yield; yield to another's wish or desire.

Sumunodsunod-a-Following, ensueing

Sumunodsunod sa uso-v -To be in use

Sumunodsunod s a uso-a-Fashionable, customary.

Sumurot-v-To point.

Sumuso-v -To suck

Sumustento-r-To sustain; support, maintain

Sumusulat ng historia-n-Historian

Sumusunod-a Successive, following, consecutive

Sumusunod sa aral-a-Sectary

Sumususo-n Sucker one who sucks

Sumutsot v-To whistle, whiz

Sumuyo-r-To love, court

Sundalo n-Soldier.

Sundalong dagat n Marine marine soldier.

Sundalong lakad n-Grenadier infantryman.

Sundalong nagtanan-n-Deserter.

Sundan-v To persue, follow, go after; obey.

Sundang-n-Poinard, pointed knife.

Sunday-a-Inclined, leaned against; propped

Sundin-v To follow; obey, submit, comply, persue, persecute

Sundulin-v To punch

Sungaban-n-Wrestling, scrambling

Sungabán-v-To wrestle, (catch as catch can)

Sungay-n Horn

Sungayan-a Horned, horny.

Sungkal-n-Rooting (per to the hog)

Sungkal-n-Disorder

Sungkalin-v -To root

Sungoy-n-Gulch, gully.

Suno n Guest, lodger, boarder

Sunodsunod a Successive, following, alternative, consecutive, alterate

Sunodsunod-adv Successively, consecutively

Sunog-n-Fire, conflagration, burn, burning, combustion

Sunok-n Distaste, aversion to the taste

Suntok n-Blow, fistycuff, punch with the fist

Sunugin v -To burn, fire; scorch, set afire, kindle

Suob-n Fumigation, disinfection

Suobin v -To fumigate, disinfect, smoke

Supil n-Domination, subjection, repression, humiliation, reduction

Súpil n-Round or circular comb.

Supihn-v -To subject, dominate, subdue, conquer overcome, humble, curb, rein, subjugate, subordinate, repress, confine, humiliate

Supling-n-Sprout, shoot

Súpot-n-Sack, bag, pocket, pouch; poke

Supot ng dalawang itlog-n Scrotum

Supot ng sulat n-Mail bag

Súri-n-Ruff, ruffling, pleat.

Surin-v -To ruffle, pleat.

Súrot-n-Bedbug.

Surót n The pointing with the finger

Suuutin-v-To surprise by pointing with the finger

Susi-n-Key; cock

Suso n-Teat, dug, pap

Suson-n Layer.

Susuhan-a-Having large teats

Susuhan-v-To weave the corners of a bag or basket.

Sutla-n-Silk.

Sutsot-n-Distaste, aversion to the taste,

Suyo n Distaste, aversion of the taste

Suyo n -Courtship; courting, love making, loving.

Suyo-n Compliance; civility

Suyuin-v-To love; court; make love; comply; be civil or polite.

Suyod-n-Fine haircomb.
Suyurin-v-To comb with a fine comb.

T

Taan-n-Reserve, exception; secret; caution.
Taas-n-Height; highness.
Taas ng katawan-n-Stature; height of the body.
Taasan-v-To raise; heighten.
Taba-n-Grease; lard; fat; corpulancy.
Tabad-n-Scratch; call by whistling.
Tabagan-v-To increase; augment.
Tabak-n-Long knife; point; lack of spice or seasoning.
Tabak-a-Fresh.
Tabang-n-Lack of spice or seasoning; insipidity; insipidness.
Tabaran-v-To Scratch; cause to bleed.
Tabas-n-Cut; shape; fashion; appearance; aspect; look
Tabasan-v-To cut; delineate; pare off.
Tabasán-n-Tailors pattern; tailor's table.
Tabas pusod-a-Naval shaped.
Tabi-n-Side; edge; brim; limit; border; margen; fringe; verge; shore; bank; strand.
Tabig-n-Push; shove.
Tabing-n-Curtain; veil; screen.
Tabing ng pinto-n-Door-curtain.
Tabla-n-Board.
Tablang makapal-n-Plank.
Taboy-n-Divorce.
Tabsing-a-Saltish; brakish.
Tablado-n-Scaffold.
Tabunan-v-To cover anything with dirt, chaff, straw, grain or sand.
Tadhanaan-v-To determine, assign or give time; set a limit.
Tadhaanaan-n-Time; limit; duration; season.
Tadtarin-n-To chop fine; make into sausage.
Tadyak-n-Kick; tread.
Tadyang-n-Rib.
Tae-n-Flux; excrement; faeces.
Taeng bakal-n-Slags; dross.
Tae ng hayop-n-Dung; manure.
Taga-n-Fishhook.
Tagá-n-Cut; slash; gash.
Taga-prep.-From; of.
Taga bayad-n-Paymaster; paying-teller; payer.
Taga bilang-n-Acomptant.
Taga Filipinas-n-Filipino.
Taga gawa-n-Workman; artificer; maker; author; mechanic.

Taga gising-n-Alarm.
Taga ibang bayan-n-Stranger; foreigner.
Taga infierno-a-Hellish; infernal.
Tagak-n-Crane; heron; swan.
Taga kabila ng bundo.-n-Transmountaineer.
Taga kabila ng bundok-a-Transmountane; belonging to the other side of the mountains.
Taga kilala-n-Examiner.
Tagal-n-Duration; time; protraction; delay; prolixness; prolixity.
Tagalan-v-To protract; delay; prolong; lengthen postpone.
Taga langit-n-Saint
Taga langit-a-Heavenly; belonging to or from heaven.
Tagaan-a-Clear; neat; pure; clean.
Taga pag alaga-n-Breeder; trainer; nurse; janitor.
Taga pagdala-n-Conductor; carrier.
Taga pag inas-n-Transporter; carrier.
Taga pagkanlong-n-Defender; abettor; protector.
Taga pagkudkod-n-Scraper.
Taga pagluto-n-Cook.
Taga pagpasan-n-Porter; carrier.
Taga pagpasuso-n-Wet-nurse.
Taga pagsalin ang sulat-n-Copyist.
Taga pagsunog-n-Incendiary burner.
Taga pagtangol-n-Defender; protector; supporter.
Taga pag ugoy-n-Rocker; one who rocks.
Taga pamagitan-n-Intercessor; mediator; petitioner; solicitor; advocate.
Taga pangusap-n-Speaker; one who speaks.
Taga pigil-n-Brakeman.
Taga panubok-n-Examiner; scout; spy.
Taga pulo-n-Islander.
Taga Roma-n-Roman.
Taga sa-prep.-Belonging to; from.
Taga sa ibang bayan ó lupa-n-Foreigner; stranger.
Taga siyasat-n-Examiner; investigator; surveyor.
Taga sulat-n-Writer; secretary; notary; clerk.
Taga tangap ng buis-n-Tax collector.
Taga taktak-n-Sealer.
Taga tupad-n-Complier; one who complies; envoy.
Taga tawag-n-Call boy; bellboy; caller.

Tagdan-n-Handle

Taghoy-n-Lamentation, grief, complaint, story of hardship

Tagihran-n-Side, flank, margen, brim, edge

Tagihran kanan nğ sasakyan-n-Starboard

Tagihran kahwa nğ sasakyan-n-Larboard.

Taginting-n-Sonorousness

Taglay-n-Equivalent

Taglayin-v-To equalize, ietch; carry

Taghran-n-Side, illank, verge

Tago-a-Hidden; concealed, secret, clandestine, profound, deep, private

Tagóbana-n-Porosity, porousness

Tagobilin n-Recomendation, charge, injunction, praise, command

Tagpi-n-Patch

Tagpian-v-To patch

Taguan-n-Storehouse, repository, place of concealing anything

Taguan nğ damung tuyo-n-Hay loft.

Taguan nğ labasa n-Razorcase

Tagumpay-n-Defense, protection, support

Tagupak n-Report of a slap, clapping, clap

Tahanan-n-Habitation, abode, residence, lodging, mansion

Tahanan-v-To live, reside, lodge, inhabit

Tahid n-Spur (of a chicken).

Tahi-n-Sewing, stich

Tahiin-v-To sew, stitch

Tahian-n-Tailor shop, dressmaking establishment

Tahiin muli-v-To resew

Tahiin na bigla-n-To baste, sew quickly

Tahimik-a-Quiet, peaceful, calm, pacific, placid, noiseless, gentle, undisturbed, serene, tranquil, mild, tame, meek, self possessed, dispassionate, halcyon; quiescent, composed, continent, tacit, mature; judicious.

Tahong-n Bivalve, shellfish

Tahul-n Bark, howl

Tainan-n Tenacity, flexibility

Taintim a-Loving, affectionate, intimate.

Tainğa n-Ear

Tákal-n-Measure, extent, dimension, capacity, bulk mete, guage, contents

Takalan-v-To measure (for someone else)

Takalin-v To measure, mete guage

Takalin muli v To remeasure.

Takápan n-Quarrel, dispute, insult fight, affray.

Takapan v-To quarrel, dispute, insult.

Takaw-n Gluttony

Takaw na malabis-n-Greed

Talas-n-Cunning, craft, sharpness, wit, quickness of thought

Takbo-n Run, scamper, running, sprint, course

Takbo nğ panahon-n Lapse or space of time

Takbuhan-n-Race

Takdaan-v-To determine, distinguish, decide, resolve

Takip-n-Cover, lid, covering, casing

Takipan-v-To cover, case, put on the lid.

Takip nğ lamesa-n-Tablecover, tablecloth

Takot-n-Fright, terror, affright, temerity, timidity, cowardice, dread, consternation

Takot nğ marami-n-Panic

Takpan-v-To cover, overspread; hide, thatch, conceal stop up

Takotin v-To scare, frighten, overawe

Takpan muli v-To recover

Taksay-n-Fishing boat.

Taksil-a-Treacherous, perfidous, disloyal, false, unfaithful, infidel, inconstant, instable, seditious

Taktak-n-Seal, stamp, brand mark

Takutin-v-To scare, frighten, apall, cow, overawe

Tala-n-Star, sign, mark.

Taláan-v-To mark, assign; designate, brand, note

Talaan n-Clam, bivalve, cockle

Talabá-n Oyster.

Talagá-adv-Avowedly, disignedly intentionally.

Talagahan-v-To intend, do intentionally or avowedly

Talagahin-v-To do intentionally, or avowedly

Talahib-n-Reed grass; rushes.

Talaksan n-Measure of wood (64 X 64 X 32 inches (about 73 cu. ft)

Talampakan-n The sole of the foot

Talampakin-v-To tread; trample under foot

Talampakin-v-To speak clear, frankly, plainly or openly

Talas-n-Cunning, slyness, wit, skill, sharpness of wit; handiness; craft-

Talas-n-Drip, dripping.

Talas nğ isip-n-Talent, ability, genius, understanding, wit.

Talalasok n Wooden wedge.

Talata n Row file, line

Talbos n Vegetables such as the squash and sweet potatoe.

Tali-n-Garter; band; tie; litigation; string.
Talian-c-To tie; bind; hitch; chock.
Talián-n-Place of tying.
Taliba-n-Guard; watch.
Talibaan-c-To guard; watch.
Talibis na lupa-n-Ravine.
Talibugso-n-Knot.
Talikuran-v-To turn the back; retract; take back; renounce; reject; abjure; negative; disclaim; recant; disown.
Talim-n Sharpness; cutting edge; steel.
Talinhaga-n-Proverb; allegory; example; mystery.
Talino-n-Clearness of thought; wisdom; quickness of thought.
Talino ng isip-n-Talent; ability; wisdom; genius; clearness of thought.
Talipandas-a-Exempt; unrestrained; loose; dissolute; rude; insolent.
Talis-n-Sharp prickle; fork; point.
Talisuyo-n-Serf; slave; servant; lover; one who courts.
Talo-v-Setto; dispute; dissension; perdition; repulse.
Tálob-n-Cover; lid.
Talohaba-a-Oval; oblong.
Talohaba-n-Oval; oblong; elipse.
Taloktok-n-Top; apex.
Taloktok ng bundok-n-The top of a mountain.
Talon-n Jump.
Talonin-v To jump; overcome; overpower.
Talonin ang hari-v-To dethrone.
Talon ng tubig-n-Falls; cascade, cataract;
Talong-n-Eggplant.
Talop-n-Peeling; peel.
Táltálan-n-Dispute; quarrel; argument.
Taltalan-v-To dispute; quarrel; argue.
Taluban-v-To cover.
Taludtod-n-Row; file; line; lay.
Taludtod ng bundok na sunodsunod-n- A chain of mountains.
Taludtod ng haligi-n-Colonnade.
Talu ap ng mata-n-Order; method; rule; example; precept; following.
Taluntonin-v-To follow.
Talupan-v-To peel; shell; bark; husk; pare.
Tama-a-Right; exact; dogmatic; dogmatical; upright; faithful; honest.
Tamad-a-Lazy; indolent; idle; inattentive; neglectful; heedless; negligent; careless; slow; tardy; inert.
Tamad-adv.-Slowly; lazily; idly; tardily.
Taman-n-Firmness; steadiness; constancy; resolution.
Támanán-v-To be constant; firm; resolute or steady.
Tama sa katuiran-n-Reasonable; fair; just; right.

Tambak-a-Level; even.
Tambakan-v-To level; even.
Tambal-n-Joining; putting together; addition; exaggeration.
Tambalan-v-To join; put together; add to exaggerate.
Tamban-n-Anchovy.
Tambing-adv.-Immediately; instantly; hastily; right away; presently.
Tambingin-v-To do immediately; prepare hastily.
Tambol-n-Drum.
Tambubong-n-Granary; mow; place where traders stop or meet to buy and sell.
Tambuli-n-Hunter's horn; deerhorn.
Tamlay-n-Indisposition; sorrow; down heartedness.
Tamnan-c-To sow; plant.
Tamnan muli-v-To resow; replant.
Tamnan panibago-v-To resow; sow again; replant.
Tamuhin-v-To feel; bear; wear; suffer; forbear; lead; carry.
Tampa-n-Advance of money on anything.
Tampahan-v-To advance money on a crop.
Tampak-prep.-Against; opposite.
Tampal-n-Slap; cuff; blow with the open hand.
Tampalasan-n-Insolence; discourtesy; discourteousness; rudeness; abusiveness; insult; immodesty.
Tampalasan-a-Insolent; rude; discourteous; impudent; flippant; abusive, profligate disreputable; overbearing, immoderate; contumelious; lofty; inhuman; soulless; perverse; haughty;
Tampalasanin-v-To insult; abuse; injure. misuse; malign; illtreat; mistreat; maltreat.
Tampalin-v-To slap; cuff.
Tampi-n Blow; knock; cuff; slap.
Tampo-n-Pout; resentment; anger; pique.
Tampuhan-v-To sulk; pout; resent. quit; forsake; abandon.
Tamtam-n Compensation; idemnification;
Tamtaman-v-To indemnify; compensate; repair.
Tamuhiu-c To Reach; gain; feel; succeed; procure; obtain; attain; bear; suffer; forbear; lead; wear.
Tanaw-n-View; sight; prospect; look.
Tanawan-n-Place of watching; ken.
Tanawin-v-To view; behold; observe; watch; notice; discern,
Tanda-n-Mark; emblem; sign; standard; note; symptom; precursor; score, badge; significant; prognostic; note, brand, seal; banner; print; stamp.

Tandaan-n Catalogue, list, role,, file, memorandum.

Tandaán-v-To remember, mark, seal, record, note, stamp, name, score.

Tandaan ng nañgamatay-n-Necrology

Tandos n-Spear, lance, javelin

Tañga-a Stupid, slow, dull, ignorant, wondering; staring

Tañgá-n-Moth

Tanga-n-A game which resembles pitching

Tañgaan-v To cause to stare or wonder, scare

Tangal-n-Disconnection

Tangalin-v-To disconnect, take to pieces, disunite, disintegrate, take apart, disarm, disband

Tangapin-i-To reseive, take, accept

Tanghali-n-Noon, noontime, midday.

Tanghali-adv-Midday.

Tanghalian-n-Dinner

Tanghalan-n-Fair, exposition

Tañgi a-Singular, single, individual, particular, rare, strange, unequalled, special, foreign

Tañgi-adv-Solely, only, purely; alone

Tañgi-n-Refusal, denial, contravention.

Tañgihan i-To deny, refuse, contravene, resign, disown

Tañgi ng inam-a-Exquisite, excellent

Tañgi sa-prep.-Besides, without, above, over

Tañgi sa-adv.-Besides, moreover

Tañgis-n-Snivel, crying

Tangkakal-n-Defense, protection, vindication; aid, assistance

Tangkalag-n Block.

Tang ilik-n-Protection, defence, aid, shelter

Tangkilican-v To shelter, protect, assist, aid

Tanglaw-n-Light clearness, clarity.

Tangnan-n-Handle,

Tangnan-i-To take, hold, have, grasp, catch, obtain

Tangnan ng baldi n-Bail.

Tangnan ng palakol n Helve.

Tañgo-n-Nod of the head signifying yes, conformity.

Tanikala-n-Chain.

Tanim-n-Plant, seed, seedtime, planting

Tanim na loob-n-Rancor, anger, hatred, odium.

Taning-n-Term, end

Taningan-i-To determine, decide.

Taning na araw n Last day writ.

Taning na panahon n Crisis, end of time

Tankay-n-Stem handle, culm; hanlon.

Tankilik-n Shelter, protection, aid

Tanod-n-Custody, guard, watch, sentry; sentinel

Tanong-n-Question, inquiry, interogation

Tanso-n Brass, copper

Tansong dilaw-n-Brass

Tansong pula-n-Copper

Tantia n-Comprehension, understanding

Tantuin-v-To comprehend, understand, consider, try, ascertain, recognize

Tanyag a-Manifest, clear; open, plain

Taob adv.-Overset; up side down; face down

Taon-n-Year

Taontaon-adv -Annually; yearly.

Taontaon-n-Anniversary, annual

Taos-n Affection, liking

Taos na loob-a-Affectionate, intimate

Taos sa puso a-Cordial; sincere

Tapa-n-Driedbeef, jerked beef

Tapak-n-Footstep, foot print, tread, track.

Tapal n Cover, poultice; cataplasm

Tapal na pangtabay ng sikmura- i Abdominal bandage

Tapang-n-Courage, bravery, fortitude, intrepidity, boldness, valor, vigor, spunk, grit, mind, intention

Tapat-a Just, straight, upright, honest-lawful; perfect, strong; sound, complete, steadfast, evident, certain.

Tapatan-n-Short cut

Tapat ng loob-a-Loyal, confident, firm, faithful, honest, sincere, frank cordial, pure, gentle

Tapat sa matuid-adv.-Straightly; justly, honestly, frankly

Tapayan-n Ewer, large earthen pot or jar.

Tapiasan-i-To cut slantingly or on a slant

Tapik-n Slap, clap of the hands

Tapon n Cork, plug, bung.

Tapos n-Finish, end, final, close, termination; conclusion.

Tapsin-a-Brakish, saltish

Tapunan-n Dumping, ground

Tapunan ng yagit-n-Dunghill.

Tapusan-i-To Close; finish, terminate, end, conclude

Tapusin-i-To Close, finish, end; terminate

Tapusin v-To finish, end, terminate, close, conclude; complete, perfect, crown.

Tarak-n-Stake

Tarik-n Steep slope

Tarik-a-Steep.

Tarok-n-Depth, profoundity, skill, judgment, wisdom.

Taros-*n*-Prudence; knack; activity; skill; judgment.

Taruhin-*c*-To measure; compare; estimate

Tarukin-*r*-To try; fathom sound; probe; investigate; perforate; penetrate; sift.

Tarukin ng̃ isip-*c*-To comprehend understand; enter the mind.

Tarunahan-*v*-To board a floor.

Tasa-*n* Cup.

Tasahan-*v*-To appraise; value.

Tasahan-*c*-To sharpen; point.

Tasak-*n*-Plug; cork; bung.

Tasakán-*r*-To plug; cork; stop a crack.

Tasik-*n* Brine.

Tasok-*n*-Plug; wooden stopper; cork; wedge; stab.

Tastas-*n*-Rip.

Tastasin-*r*-To rip; unseam.

Tata-*n*-Papa.

Tatag-*n*-Equilibrium; solidity; integrity; firmness; establishment; founding.

Tatahan at muling babalik-*a*-Intermittent.

Tatak-*n*-Stamp; brand; sign; seal; mark.

Tatakan-*v* To seal; stamp; brand; mark.

Tatal-*n*-Splinter; chip,

Tatang-*n*-Papa.

Tatangnan-*n*-Handle.

Tatay-*n*-Papa; father.

Tatlo-*n*-Three.

Tatlo-*a*-Three.

Tatlo ang kulay-*a*-Tricolored three colored.

Tatlong kulay-*a*-Tricolored; three colored.

Taula ng̃ paggawa-*n*-Glorious deed; noble work.

Tawa-*u*-Laugh; laughter; giggle.

Tawad-*n*-Bid; immunity; pardon.

Tawag-*n*-Call; summons; announcement; proclamation.

Tawagin-*r*-To call; summon; name; announce; proclaim; evoke.

Tawag sa madla-*n*-Proclamation; publication; notice.

Tawas-*n*-Alum.

Tawiran-*n*-Ferry.

Tawirin-*v*-To ferry; cross on a ferry; ferry across.

Tawo-*n*-Person; man; individual; woman; people; nation.

Tawong bastos-*n*-Curmudgeon; carl; myrmidon; rude person.

Tawong bukid-*n*-Tike; farmer; person.

Tawong duag-*n*-Coward; poltroon.

Tawong gubat-*n*-Backwoodsman.

Tawong ginoo-*n*-Gentleman; lady.

Tawong hamak-*n*-Plebian; hangdog; varlet.

Tawong kumakain ang kapwa-*n*-Cannibal.

Tawong itim-*n*-Negro; ethiop; ethiopian.

Tawong mababa-*n*-Plebian.

Tawong malakas-*n*-Carl.

Tawong mahirap-*n*-Peasant.

Tawong maramot-*n* Codger; stingy person.

Tawong marung̃is-*n*-Dowdy person; slouch.

Tawong marunong-*n*-Sage; savant.

Tawong matakaw-*n*-Glutton; gormand; gourmand.

Tawong matalas-*n*-Wit; genius; witty person.

Tawong mayaman-*n* Potentate.

Tawong napakababa-*n*-Dwarf.

Tawong napakasuitik-*n*-Sharper; cheat; swindler.

Tawong natatanoha-*n* Overseer; foreman; inspector.

Tawong sinoman-*n*-Anybody; any person.

Tawong taksil-*n*-Traitor; turncoat.

Tawong ulol-*n*-Lunatic; crazy person; madman.

Taya-*n*-Bet; wager.

Tayaan-*v*-To bet wager.

Tayantang̃in-*v*-To be well or accustomed.

Tayantang̃in-*adv*-Little-by-little.

Tayo-*n*-Position; posture; attitude; form; situation; shape; size; mode.

Táyog-*n*-Height.

Tayom-*n*-Indigo: indigo plant.

Tayum-*n*-Suspense; uncertainty.

Teatro-*n*-Theatre.

Tekas-*n*-Pickpocket; cheat; swindler; gull.

Tekasin-*v*-To cheat; swindle; victimize; gull.

Tiaga-*n*-Sufferance; constancy; tolerance; tenacity.

Tiakad-*n*-Stilts; booth.

Tian-*n*-Abdomen; belly; paunch.

Tianak-*n*-Goblin; sprite; spirit.

Tibag-*n*-Bank; avalanche; cave in.

Tibagin-*v*-To cave; slide; down quarry.

Tibay-*n*-Solidity; firmness; fortitude; strength; integrity; force; vigor.

Tibayan-*v*-To strengthen; plight; man; fortify; support.

Tibay na loob-*n*-Fortitude; forbearance; strength of heart.

Tibo-*n*-Thorn; fishhook.

Tibok-*n*-Pant; palpitation.

Tibok ng̃ puso-*n*-Palpitation; forboding.

Tibyaya-*n*-Squash

Tigagal-*n*-Idler; loiterer, indolent person

Tigas-*n* Hardness; solidity stiffness, firmness, strength; force, fortitude; violence, inflexibility

Tigas ng loob-*n*-Resolution, decision, inflexibility, tenacity, hardness of heart

Tigdas-*n*-Measles, pimple.

Tigdasen-*v*-To break out with the measles or with pimples

Tighabol *n*-Augmentation, increase, addition.

Tigil-*n*-Stop, halt, lull; cessation

Tigil-*inter*.-Halt, stop; beware

Tigmak-*n*-Stain, drench,

Tigmakin-*v*-To wet, drench, stain, dampen.

Tigpas-*n*-Slice, cut

Tigpasin-*v*-To cut, slice, divide

Tihaya-*adv*.-Face up

Tihaya-*a*-Faced

Tiis-*n*-Toleration, sufferance, endurance, repentance, patience

Tiisin-*v*-To suffer, tolerate, endure, bear.

Tika-*n*-Intention, meaning, mind, view, design, purpose, intent

Tikas *n*-Form, shape; size, mode, design, manners, gentility

Tikim-*n*-Taste, palate, relish, proof, experiment

Tikis-*adv*-Intentionally, purposely, designedly, knowingly

Tiklop *n*-Fold; plait, ply

Tiklupin *v* To fold, plait, double.

Tiklupin muli-*v*-To refold, redouble

Tikman-*v* To try; taste, prove, experiment, probe, attempt, assay, grope, investigate.

Tiktik-*n*-Spy, hedger; scout, one who aids another to win at cards

Tiktikan-*v* To spy; watch secretly, lurk,

Tila-*adv*-Like. it seems, it appears

Tila patay-*a*-Ghastly.

Tili-*n* Shriek, loud cry

Tinain-*a*-Fusible.

Tinawa-*n*-Peace, tranquility, freedom

Timawa-*a*-Peaceful, calm, tranquil, quiet, free.

Timawain-*v*-To free; liberate; tranquilize, make tranquil

Timawain ang alipin-*v*-To emancipate; free a slave

Timbang-*n*-Weight, balance, poise

Timbangin-*v*-To weigh, balance, poise, counterpoise

Timog *n*-South, south wind.

Timpla-*n*-Temper

Timplahin *t*-To temper

Timplahin *v*-To temper.

. Timsim-*n*-Wicking.

Timtim-*n*-Modesty; decency, chastity; firmness.

Timtiman-*a*-Decent, chaste, unassuming, modest

Timtiman-*n*-Chastity; decency, modesty, firmness

Timtimin-*v*-To extract; remove, investigate, inquire

. Timug-*n*-South.

Tinugan-*n*-South; south wind

Tina-*n*-Dye, stain, indigo.

Tinaan-*v*-Dye shop; place of dyeing

Tinag-*n*-Touch

Tinagin *v*-To move, touch, direct, guide, manage use.

Tinago-*a*-Hidden, secret

Tinago-*v* *p* *p*-Hidden, secreted

Tinain-*v*-To dye, stain

Tinalaga-*adv*-Intentionally, designedly; knowingly, deliberately; purposely, avowedly

Tinali-*v*. *p*. *p*-Tied, bound

Tinapay-*n* Bread.

Tinuturuan-*n*-Scholar, pupil

Tinda-*n*-Notions, anything that is sold, fund

Tindahan-*n*-Store, shop, canteen

Tindahan ng gatas-*n*-Dairy.

Tindahan ng alak-*n*-Groggery, grogshop, saloon

Tindahan ng mga pagkain-*n* Grocery

Tindi-*n* Weight, gravity, importance, burden, guarantee.

Tindig-*n*-Stand, position

Tindigan-*v*-To stand; guarantee; be responsible.

Tindihan-*n*-Stretcher, place of stretching anything

Tinekus-*n*-Victim

Tinga *n*-Lead

Tingalan ng asin-*n*-Salt marsh

Tingang puti-*n*-Tin, tin-plate

Tinghas-*n*-Chip, splinter, sharp point

Tingin *n*-Sight, look, gaze, glance, prospect

Tingin sa labas-*n*-Appearance, face; likeness

Tingkal *n* Lump, clod

Tingkayad *adv* On tiptoe

Tingkayad-*a*-Squatted, stooped.

Tingnan-*v* To look, see.

Tingnan muli-*v*-To review, revise, look or see again.

Tingnan muna-*v*-To foresee, see before

Tinig-*n* Sound, tone, echo, tune.

Tinis *v*. *p* *p*-Underwent, undergone

Tinik *n* Thorn, fishbone, thistle

Tining-*n*-Settlings, residue; remainder.

Tiningal-n-Provision

Tiningal-adv.-Stored away, put away.

Tining ng̃ loob-n-Determination; resolution; intrepidity, bravery, valor, boldness, courage, moderation, forbearance

Timitingnan-n The object which is seen, that which one is looking at

Tinkal-n-Clod lump

Tinta-u-Ink

Tinutulugan n-Bed chamber, bed; place of sleeping.

Tinutungtungan-n-Route; ending, object, itinerary; goal

Tipa-n-Convention; appointment; contract

Tipan-n-Promise; vow, testament

Tipanan-n-Convention contract, agreement, utility, profit

Tipiaw-n-Trip, stub, stumble.

Tipid-a-Economical, frugal, close

Tipi-a-Compact; firm, close, solid, compressed

Tipiin-v-To press; compress

Tipirin-v-To enonomize, clip or curtail expenses, be frugal or saving.

Tipó-n-Gap or notch in a tool.

Tipó-a-Toothless.

Tipon-n-Gathering, meeting; assembly, congregation

Tipuin-v-To break; nick, notch

Tipunin-v-To gather; unite, compile, pouch, congregate, meet.

Tirá-n-Gleanings; residue, remainder, remains; residium; excess; refuse; overplus; remnant.

Tirahan-n-Habitation, abode, house, home, place of living

Tirahán-v-To save, leave over, reserve; set aside, keep for.

Tirik a-Steep, perpendicular

Tirikan ng̃ kandila n-Candlestick.

Tirikan-v To put a candle in a candlestick

Tirintas-n-Braid

Tirintasin-v-To braid,

Tisa-n-Tile

Tisain-v-To tile

Tisod-n-Stub, stumble, trip, slip, impediment, obstacle, difficulty

Tistisin-v-To sew, hem

Tisurin-a-Tripping, stumbling

Tisurin-v-To cause to stumble.

Titik-n-Letter, deed, writing

Titingkatingkayad-v-To walk on tiptoe or in a cowering manner.

Titulo-n-Title, diploma.

Tiwalag-a-Separated, distant, far, retired, divided

Tiwangwang-adv.-Wide, open.

Tiwasay a-Firm; secure; safe; clear.

Tiyan a-Abdomen, belly; paunch.

Tiyot-n Drought.

Toktok n-Top, crest, crown

Tono-n-Tone; tune; volume.

Toro n-Bull

Totohanin-v-To be serious, verify; accomplish, affect; make, true

Totoo-a-Certain, serious, evident, true; positive, sure, effectual; devout, downright, veritable, dogmatic, dogmatical, peremptory, reliable, catagorical

Totoong-adv -Very; greatly.

Towa-n Joy, pleasure, glee, mirth; merriment, gayety, delight, comfort, rejoicing; satisfaction

Towid n-Right, straightness

Towid-a-Right, straight; just.

Towi na adv -Always, often, frequently.

Towirin-v-To straighten, rectify, justify; make right, right, clarify

Trabajador-n-Worker, workman, laborer, journeyman; artificer, mechanic

Trabajo-n-Work, task, labor, husbandry.

Trangka-n-Gate, gateway.

Trangkahan-n-Gate, gateway

Trato-n Contract, agreement.

Tresagio-n-Matin.

Tresillas-n-Gimp.

Tresiete-n-Whist

Trono-n-Throne

Tropa-n-Troupe, company.

Tropang lakad n-Infantry.

Trote n-Trot.

Tsa-n-Tea

Tubig n-Water, lymph

Tubig na bumukal-n-Spring water.

Tubig na ulan-n-Rain water

Tubó-n Interest; profit, gain, lucre, revenue, emolument, acquisition, advantage, growth, increase

Tubó-n-Sugarcane

Tubo-n-Lamp chimney

Tubos n-Redemtion; ransom

Tubó sa ibang bayan-a Strange; foreign

Tubo sa ibang lupa-n-Stranger, foreigner.

Tubsin-v-To ransom, redeem

Tubsin ang sangla v To redeem a pledge.

Tubuan-n-Sprout growing; growth

Tubuan-v-To grow, sprout

Tubuan ng̃ ng̃ipin-v-To cut teeth

Tubusin-v-To redeem, ransom

Tudla-n-Aim, point

Tudlain-v-To aim, point

Tudling-n-Furrow

Tudling̃an v To furrow, plow.

Tudlok-n-Punch, point.

Tudlukin-v-To punch; poke, point, shoot with a cue.

Tugak-n-Frog

Tugatog-n-Hill, knoll, hillock, small, mountain; hommock

Tugno n-Brine

Tugon-n-Answer, repartee, reply, response, retort

Tugtog-n Play, piece of music, playing on musical instruments

Tugtog muna sa kanta-n Overture

Tugtog ng loob-n-Inspiration

Tugtog ng músico n-The playing of a band or an oschestra

Tugtugan-n-Piece of music, playing of musical instruments

Tugtugan na walang ayos-n-Dissonance, discord

Tugtugin v-To play on a musical instrument

Tuhod-n-Knee

Tuhog - n Stringer, that upon which anything is strung

Tuhuguin-v-To string, impale, pass through

Tuhuran-v-To push or shove with the knee.

Tuka-n Beak, bill, peck

Tukain-v-To peck, pick

Tukarol n-Cap, bonnet; turban.

Tukó n Small lizard

Tukod n-Post; prop, support, Protection

Tukso-n-Teasing, temptation, vexation; aggravation, enticement, instigation

Tuksuhin-v-To tease, vex, entice; tempt, instigate, worry, chaff, haggle, inveigle

Tuktok-n-Top, crest.

Tuktok ng manok n Comb of a chicken

Tuktok ng ulo-n-The crown of the head

Tulá-n-Poem.

Tulad-n-Copy, counterfeit, imitation

Tulag-n-Spear, lance, dart; javelin.

Tulagin-v-To throw a dart or spear, lance

Túlak-n-Push, shove, thrust, drive

Tulakin-v-To shove, push, thrust.

Tulala-a Stupid, lazy, ignorant, indolent, idle, weak, feeble, imbecile.

Tulalain-v-To-astonish, stupefy

Tularan-v-To imitate, copy; counterfeit; mimic

Tularan n Precedent, example, pattern

Tulatod a-Last, hindmost

Tulatod n-Rump, croup

Tulay n Bridge

Tuli-n Circumcision.

Tulig-n-Foolish, stupid, torpid, ignorant; idiotic, senseless

Tulig-n-Fool, idiot, madman

Tulin v-To circumcise

Tulin-n-Speed, velocity, quickness, activity, promptness, promptitude, nimbleness

Tulingad n-Fool, idiot, madman

Tulis-n Sharpness, point, acuteness, end

Tulisan n-Robber, highwayman, bandit

Tulisan v-To sharpen, point

Tulisan sa dagat-n-Pirate, corsican

Tulo n Leak.

Tulog-n-Sleep, slumber.

Talong n-Help, aid, assistance, support, succor, vindication

Tulongan n-To help, aid, assist, succor, defend, facilitate, protect

Tulos-n-Stake

Tulot-n Permission, license, furlough, leave, admittance.

Tuloy-a Continued, successive, continuous, lasting, following

Tuloytuloy a-Prompt; speedy, expeditious, continued without interruption.

Tulungan v To assist, defend, aid, help, protect, furnish, favor, minister, supply

Tulungin a To help, aid assist, defend, protect

Tulutan v To permit, license, give leave or permission

Tuluyan v To continue; keep going, terminate

Túluyan n-Hotel, boarding house.

Tumaan-v-To reserve, put away, keep separate

Tumaas-v To grow in height, ascend, mount, rise, raise

Tumaba-v To grow or become fat or fleshy, fatten.

Tumaba ang lupa-v-To fertilize, grow or become fruitful- (per to land).

Tumadiak-v-To kick

Tumae ang ibon-v To mute.

Tumagal v To last, prolong; endure, suffer, dally, subsist.

Tumagilid-v-To turn sideways, lay on the side

Tumaginting v To sound

Tumagistis ang luha-v-To cry, weep, run (per to tears).

Tumago-v-To hide, conceal, put away.

Tumagos v-To penetrate, leak, run through

Tumagupak v-To clap, make a noise by clapping the hands or stamping the feet

Tumahan-v To dwell, nestle, reside, lodge

Tumahan-v-To calm; appease; grow or become quiet or peaceful.

Tumahi-v-To sew; stitch.

Tumahol-v-To bark; yelp; yap; yaul; howl.

Tumahimik-v-To appease; become or grow peaceful or calm; calm; rest; repose; lull.

Tumakas-v-To decamp; escape; slip off; leave on the sly; sneak off; leave secretly.

Tumakbo-v-To run sprint; course; hasten; flow.

Tumakot-v-To intimidate; frighten; scare; terrify.

Tumal-n-Depression; scarcity; slowness; scantiness.

Tumal a-Slow; depressed; not salable.

Tumalas-v-To filter; strain; leak; trickle; trill; pour down; ooze.

Tumalas-v-To become or grow witty.

Tumali-v-To tie; bind.

Tumalikod-v-To turn one's back; take back; retract; recant.

Tumalikod sa kanyang bandila-v-To desert one's flag.

Tumalima-v-To yield; submit; obey.

Tumalima-v-To contradict; oppose; gainsay.

Tumalon-v-To jump down; precipitate.

Tumáma-v-To hit; guess; conjecture.

Tumanan-v-To run away; elope; sneak off; make off; leave secretly.

Tumánga-v To prohibit; interdict; forbid.

Tumangan-v-To have hold.

Tumangap-v-To receive; accept; take.

Tumangap-n-Receiver; taker; recipient.

Tumangi-v To refuse; renounce; deny; resign.

Tumangis-v-To weep; mourn; lament; bewail.

Tumango-v-To consent; agree; confirm; affirm; promise.

Tumaning-v-To give or prolong time; extend time; reprieve.

Tumankilik-v-To protect; defend; support; favor; corroborate; confirm; hold up; prop.

Tumanong-v-To ask; question; inquire; interrogate.

Tumantan-v-To rest; quiet; appease.

Tumaos-v-To penetrate; pierce.

Tumapang-v-To encourage; become brave, courageous, bold or valiant.

Tumarok-v-To sound; delve.

Tumatahan sa isang lugar ó bahay-n-Inhabitant; lodger.

Tumatakbo-n-Runner.

Tumatanaw-n-Spectator.

Tumatatua-n-Backslider; one who denies anything; gainsayer; contradictor.

Tumatawa-n-Laugher; one who; laughs.

Tumatua-v-To deny; contradict; gainsay.

Tumawa-v-To laugh; giggle.

Tumawag-v-To call; summon; name; term; send for; announce; evoke; hallo.

Tumaya-v-To bet; wager.

Tumayo-v-To establish; build; edify.

Tumba-n-Tower; grave stone.

Tumba ng patay-n-Tomb vault; sepulcher; tomb stone.

Tumbong-n-Anus; fundament.

Tumibay-v-To fortify; strengthen; affirm; guarantee.

Tumibok-v-To palpitate; flutter.

Tumigas-v-To harden; indurate.

Tumiguil-v-To stop; cease; stay; lull; remain; leave off; work.

Tumlin-v-To ooze; leak.

Tumika-v-To limp.

Tumikim-v-Taste; try; attempt; assay.

Tumikim-v-To cough; draw ones attention.

Tumila-v-To cease.

Tumili-v-To shriek; scream; cry in a high tone.

Tumimbang-v-To weigh.

Tumimbuang-v-To lay down; stretch one's self on a bed.

Tumindig-v-To arise; rise; stand up.

Tuminag-v-To be brisk or smart.

Tumingin v-To see; look; view; gaze; behold; observe; watch; notice; discern; vide.

Tuningkayad-v To stoop; squat; walk or stand on the toes.

Tumira-v-To dwell; live; reside; lodge; inhabit; nestle.

Tumira-v-To remain; be left over.

Tumita-v-To drain; let fall drop by drop.

Tumitig-v-To eye; glance; look.

Tumitis ang pawis-v-To sweat or perspire freely.

Tumiwalag-v-To separate; remove; sort; dissuade.

Tumpa-n-Last journey or trip; going.

Tumpa gawi-n-Inclination; tendency; fancy.

Tumpak-n- Skill; judgment; prudence; knac ; mischievousness; restlessness.

Tumpok-n-Small round heap; patty.

Tumubo-v-To grow; increase; swell.

Tumubo punatong sa ibabaw-v-To outgrow.

Tumugon-v-To answer; respond; reply; acknowledge.

Tumugtog-v-To play on a musical instrument, ring a bell

Tumuka-i-To peck, pick

Tumuktok-i-To beat, strike or knock with the knuckles.

Tumulad-v-To equalize, make equal, match.

Tumúlak-i -To push, shove, thrust.

Tumulo-i -To leak, drip, fall drop by drop.

Tumulong-i-To help aid assist cooperate, favor, succor, support, serve, defend; protect, corroborate, hold up, confirm, prop, minister.

Tumulotulo-v-To drip.

Tumumba i-To Tower

Tumumog na malakas-n-Resolution, courage, mind; promptitude, aid, determination.

Tumumok-i-To gather, crowd

Tumumpa-v-To carry down, have the last of anything

Tumunaw-v To melt, liquefy, dissolve.

Tumungo-i To wend, trend, bend, bow

Tumunog-i-To sound, clank, clang; ring

Tumuntong v To tread; trample, stamp put on, occupy.

Tumupad v-To execute, discharge, perform, comply, heed, do one's duty, dispense, observe

Tumurote-i-To trot.

Tumutul-v-To reply, answer, respond, affirm, allege; oppose, fight.

Tumutol sa pagtangol-v-To fight for another, defend, argue in another's favor.

Tunang-n-Outcry.

Tunang malaki-n-Tumult; out cry, riot

Tunaw-n-Liquid, fluid

Tunawin-v-To melt, liquefy, dissolve, smelt, consume, spend

Tunawin-a-Soluble, solvable, meltible liquefiable.

Tunawin ang kinain v-To digest

Tunay-a-True, cordial, sincere, loyal; constant, firm, manifest, solemn, dogmatic, dogmatical, certain, downright, reliable; legitimate, actual, candid confident, real, peremtory, important.

Tunay adv Really, truly, actually, loyally, candidly, certainly, seriously, surely, positively, evidently

Tunay nga a-True, serious, certain, positive

Tunga-a Slow, halt witted, ignorant; torpid, rude, foolish

Tungag-a Half witted, foolish, dull, torpid, slow, ignorant. rude wild, obscene

Tungaw-n-Tick; woodtick

Tungayaw-n-Curse, implecation, oath malediction, swearing, ban

Tung ayawin-i To curse, swear, imprecate; ban

Tungkay-n-Object, design, end; intent

Tungkod-n Cane, staff; prop, fulcrum, support, protection, truncheon

Tungkol-p a -According, pertaining, concerning.

Tungkol prep -About, over

Tungkol n-Duty; obligation, contract, agreement

Tungo-n-Bow, nod, object, behavior; trend

Tungo a-Inclined, disposed

Túngo n-Tuber

Tungó ng loob-n-Intent, design, purpose

Tungtong-n-Cover, lid, pot lid.

Tunod-n-Magnetic needle, the unrolled leaves of the palm or banana.

Tunog-n-Sound, noise; report, clank, clang, ring, resonance

Tunog na bagol n-Grating, harsh sound.

Tunog ng voces-n-Tune, tone

Tunsoy-n Shiner

Tuntungan n-Objective, place that one is heading for.

Tupa n-Sheep

Tupád n Compliance, doing of one's duty

Tupang babaye n-Ewe.

Tuparin-v-To comply, do one's duty

Turing-n-Bid, asking; price proposal, overture, proposition, guess.

Turo-n-Teaching, instruction, doctrine.

Turuan-i-To teach, instruct, educate, discipline, inform, civilize, point out.

Tuso a sly, cunning, crafty, sagacious; vulpine, keen, sapient, wily

Tusok-n-Stitch

Tustusin-v-To loosen, slacken

Tusukin-i To stitch, prick.

Tuto-n Skill; learning, knowledge, judgment, prudence, wisdom, sagacity; circumspection

Tutol n Answer, reply; response, repartee

Tutop-n Patch, cover

Tutos-n-Stitch, union.

Tutsang n-Bristle.

Tutugin v-To separate or take out the ashes, reduce to ashes.

Tutupan-v To patch, mend, splice

Tutusin v-To stitch, sew.

Tuwa-n-Happiness, mirth, merriment, joy, pleasure, content, solace, consolation; gladness, gayety, festivity; rejoicing

Tuwa a Glad, joyful, merry, happy.

Tuwi-a-Each; every; all, entire; whole.

Tuwituwina-*adv.*-Often; frequently.
Tuyá-*n*-Flattery; false praise,
Tuyáin-*v*-To flatter.
Tuyo-*a*-Dry; barren; withered; arid; scar; sere; wizen.
Tuyongtuyo-*a*-Very dry.
Tuyot-*a*-Dry; dessicated.
Tuyuin-*a*-To dry, dessicate.

U

Uban-*a*;Hoary; gray headed; white.
Uban-*n*-Gray hair; chaff.
Ubanin-*a*-Old; hoary; grayheaded.
Ubanin-*v*-To grow old or gray headed.
Ubas-*n*-Grapes; grape.
Ubo-*n*-Cough.
Ubod-*n*-Heart; center.
Ubod ng̃ hirap-*n*-Worst misery.
Ubong malakas-*n*-Whooping cough.
Ubos-*n*-Termination; consumation; ending.
Ubos-*a*-Terminated, consumed; used up.
Ubusin-*v*-To consume; use up; end; terminate; expend; waste.
Udiok-*n*-Stimulation; incitement; persuasion; inspiration; instigation.
Udiokan-*n*-To incite; stimulate; instigate; excite; persuade; induce; imbue.
Udiukan-*v*-To Persuade; incite; induce, prevail upon; inspire; move.
Udlok-*n*-Boman.
Udyok-*n*-Persuasion; incitement excitement; stimulation; inspiration; encouragement.
Udyukan-*v*-To inspire; persuade; induce; incite; ply; imbue.
Uga-*n*-Move; rock.
Ugain-*n*-To rock, move.
Ugali-*n*-Use; custom; habit; disposition; usage; wont; fancy; temper.
Ugaling parang-*a*-Rough; illbred; rustic.
Ugang̃in-*v*-To make foolish.
Ugat-*n*-Root; vein; blood vessel; bud; source; origen; spring.
Ugit-*n*-Plow beam; plow handle; helm.
Ugong-*n*-Noise; clamor; crack; clash; din.
Ugoy-*n*-Rocking; swinging.
Ugoyin-*v*-To rock; swing.
Uhalea-*n*-Buttonhole.
Uhaw-*n*-Thirst.
Uhaw na uhaw-*a*-Very thirsty; dry.
Uhaw-*n*-Head of grain.
Uhog-*n*-Mucous; slime; snot; muck.
Uhugin-*a*-Mucous; slimy; snotty.
Ukit-*n*-Dent.
Ukitin-*v*-To dent.
Ukol-*n*-Correspondent; trustee; agent.
Ukol sa-*a*-Pertaining to; concerning; apt; fit; ready.

Ukol sa sikmura-*a*-Gastric; pertaining to the stomach.
Ukol sa lupa-*a*-Terrestrial; belonging or pertaining to the earth.
Ulak-*n*-Spindle; reel; pinfeathers.
Ulakan-*n*-Wrapping frame; spindle; reel.
Ulakin-*v*-To wind; roll up; wind around.
Ulam-*n*-Meat.
Ulam-*n*-Rain; shower.
Ulang bigla at masasal-*n*-Heavy. shower of rain.
Ulap-*n*-Cloud.
Ulak na makapal at mababa-*n*-Mist;fog.
Ulapot-*n*-Rag hanging from the clothes.
Ulian-*a*-Wornout; decrepid.
Ulianin-*a*-Old; worn out; decrepid.
Uli-*adv.*-Again.
Uliin-*v*-To repeat; renew; patch; make; over.
Ulila-*n*-Orphan.
Ulilang lubos-*n*-Orphan; child who has neither father nor mother.
Uling-*n*-Coal; charcoal; soot; cinder; grime; lampblack.
Uliran-*n*-Type; pattern; example; model.
Ulit-*adv.*-Again; once more.
Ulitin-*v*-To repeat; duplicate; renew; double; iterate; reiterate; rehearse; do or try again.
Uliting madalas-*v*-To repeat frequently.
Ulinli-*n*-Whirlpool; eddy; vortex.
Uliyaw-*n*-Echo.
Ulo-*n*-Head; poll.
Ulog-*n*-Movement; management; direction.
Ulogin-*v*-To move; manage; direct.
Ulol-*n*-Lunatic; madman; idiot; dolt; gump; loggerhead; crazy man.
Ulol-*a*-Demented; crazy; insane; mad; daft; delirious; foolish; stupid; distracted; idiotic; ignorant; unlearned.
Ulong ulo-*a*-Baldheaded.
Ulong-*n*-Meeting; union; congregation.
Ulos ng̃ sandata-*n*-Slash or stab.
Ulug-*n*-Handling; moving.
Ulugin-*v*-To handle; move to and fro.
Ululan-*v*-To exaggarate; add to; increase.
Ululing-*v*-To infatuate; stupefy; make; or cause to be foolish; alienate.
Umabala-*v*-To interfere; oppose; prevent; molest. trouble; vex; prolong.

Umabot-v-To reach, overtake, catch up, approach, arrive, come up, get, obtain, abut

Umabuloy v-To assist, help, aid, support; serve, contribute, suffice; defray, succor, minister, promote

Umaga-n Morning, forenoon

Umaga-adv -Early, soon, betimes

Umagang umaga-adv -Very early

Umagang umaga-n-Dawn, break of day

Umagap-v-To preoccupy, foresee; anticipate; be quick or active

Umagaw-v-To steal; snatch

Umagaw sa isang babayi n-Rapist, ravisher

Umahon-v-To go up, ascend, land, mount; climb up disembark

Umakin-v-To tame, domesticate

Umakyat-v-To climb; ascend, mount, go up; increase

Umakyat na magukiabit-v-To climb with the use of the hands.

Umalalad-v-To resound, jingle, clink.

Umalalay-v-To support; help, assist; aid; maintain.

Umah-v-To succeed; happen

Umalimura-v-To insult, revile

Umalingasaw-v-To rise, extend, transcend.

Umalingasaw ang baho-v-To stink, smell, bad

Umalingawngaw-v-To echo, resound, rumble, rumor

Umalis-v-To go. leave, sally, retire, abandon; forsake, quit, emigrate, absent one's self

Umalitut-v-To grate, creak, scrape

Umalsa-v To rise, loosen, grow fluffy, uprise.

Umambag-v To contribute, give, promote

Umambon v-To mist; drizzle, mizzle

Umamo-v-To tame, domesticate, become domesticated.

Umampon v-To help, protect, aid, defend, support corroborate, favor conform

Umamoy v-To smell.

Umangil-v-To howl, snarl, growl, murmur, grumble.

Umangis-v -To stink, smell bad

Umani v To gather; harvest, reap

Umanit-v-To pull

Umankin-v-To appropriate, usurp

Umanod-v-To descend, flow with the current

Umanta v To grow rancid or stale

Umapaw-v -To overflow, inundate; over run.

Umapid v To seduce, abort

Umaral-v-To advise, warn; inform.

Umari-v-To own; have

Umari ng hindi kaniya-v-To usurp, appropriate anything that is not one's own

Umasa-v-To hope, await, desire; expect

Umasim-v-To sour, become salty or briny,

Umaso-v-To smoke, fume, reek

Umaso-a-Funy; smoky, fuming, smoking

Umasok v-To smoke, fume

Umaway-v-To fight, war oppose, dispute; rival, contest

Umayon-v-To conform, coincide, acquiesce, agree, accord

Unawit-v-To sing, carrol.

Umayaw-v-To resign, decline, quit, renounce, reject, stop

Umayos-v-To arrange, agree, put in order

Umbok ang gitna-a Convex, convexed

Umibig-v-To love; like, wish, desire, court; will

Umbis-v -To dismount, get off.

Umigi-v To ease; improve, appease, become less painful.

Umihi-v-To urinate

Umiki-v-To limp.

Umikit-v-To turn, revolve, roll, gyrate

Umiko-v-To limp.

Umilag v-To dodge, avoid, escape; shun, grow or become wild

Umimik-v-To murmur, mutter; mumble; reply, respond, answer.

Umindayog v-To oscillate, vibrate, move

Umingos-v-To grumble, snarl, growl

Uminis-v-To smother, oppress, overpower, crush; subject

Uminog-v-To turn, gyrate; roll, spin

Uminom-v-To drink; imbibe.

Umintindi-v-To understand, comprehend

Umisip-v-To think, invent; plan; plot, contrive, meditate.

Umitim v-To blacken, become black, darken.

Umitim-v-To steal, peculate; pilfer; cabbage, purloin, filch.

Umiyak v To cry; weep; bewail, lament; Umiyak ang hayop-v-To low; bleat howl; grunt.

Umpog n-Collision, encounter, clash, shock, push

Umpok-n Conversation, converse

Umudlot-v-To rebound, bounce, recoil

Umug-n Moth; the fouling of grain so that it lumps

Umuga-v-To move, shake; vibrate

Umugum-v To molder, lump because of dampness.

Umugit-*v*-To steer; pilot.
Umugit sa sasakyan-*n*-Pilot; steersman; helmsman.
Umugong-*v*-To make a noise.
Umugong parang kulog-*v*-To fulminate; make a noise like thunder.
Umugoy-*v*-To rock; swing.
Umukit-*v*-To dent.
Umayabit-*v*-To claw; scratch.
Umulayaw-*v*-To coax; wheedle; fondle; pet; humor.
Umulan-*v*-To rain; shower.
Umulan ñg busilak-*v*-To snow.
Umulan ñg bnbog-*v*-To hail.
Umuliaw-*v*-To echo; resound.
Umulit-*v*-To pilfer; steal; peculate; filch.
Umuna-*v*-To go before; go first; anticipate; forsee; expect.
Umunut-*v*-To stretch; lengthen; adjust; enlarge upon.
Umugot-*v*-To whisper.
Umunouno-*v*-To stutter; hesitate; stammer.
Umunti-*a*-To lessen; decline; fall; descend; dwindle; grow or become smaller.
Umupasala-*v*-To defame; slander; insult; deride.
Umupo-*v*-To sit.
Umupo-*v*. *imp.*-Sat.
Umuriturit-*v*-To stammer; titter; stutter; hesitate.
Umurong-*v*-To recoil; fall back; retrograde; back; regress; backslide.
Umurong ang kabayo-*v*-To balk.
Umurong ñg marami-*v* To quaff.
Umusig-*v*-To investigate; inquire; examine; follow; register.
Umusos-*v*-To go down; descend.
Umutalutal-*v*-To stutter; stammer; haw; hesitate.
Una-*adv*.-Soon; early; first.
Una-*a*-First; primitive.
Unahan-*v*-To go first; preoccupy; preceed; lead; anticipate; expect; foresee.
Unahan-*n*-Front; lead; fore end; beginning.
Unan-*n*-Pillow.
Unang araw ñg buan sa langit-*n*-Neomenia; first night of the new moon.
Unano-*n*-Dwarf; pigmy; manakin.
Unatin-*v*-To stcatch, unfold; expand.
Unatin ang baluktot-*v* To straighten.
Unauna-*adv*.-First; principally; chiefly.
Uñga-*n*-Lowing; low.
Uñgal-*n*-Howl; cry of horror.
Uñgas-*a* Stupid; foolish; dull; ignorant; simple; idiotic.

Ungo-*n*-Monkey.
Ungong babaye-*u*-Female monkey.
Ungos-*n*-Sprout; shoot; anything that protrudes from another.
Unos-*n*-Tornado; tempest; storm; hurricane; heavy shower of rain.
Unosin-*v*-To storm.
Unouno-Stammer; stutter; stuttering; stammering.
Unsayanin-*a*-Rickety; chaffy; without resistance.
Untiunti-*adv*.-Slowly; little by little; by degrees; gradually.
Untian-*v*-To lessen; curtail; clip; decline; sink; decay.
Untog-*n*-Collision; encounter; blow; contusion.
Uod *n*-Worm; larva; larvae.
Upa-*n*-Wages; salary; pay; fee; recompence; stipend.
Upahan-*v*-To pay; recompence.
Upahan ñg araw-*n*-Daylaborer; journeyman.
Upak-*n*-Bark; peel; rind; crust; skin.
Upakan-*v*-To bark; peel; skin.
Upasala-*n* Insult; scorn; derision; defamation; slander; mockery.
Upa sa pagtawid-*n*-Bridge or ferry toll.
Upat-*a*-Bald; hairless; destitute.
Upat-*n*-Deceit; delusion; fraud.
Upatan-*v*-To deceive; defraud; delude; impose upon; leave bald.
Upaw-*a*-Bald headed; bald.
Upawin-*v*-To make bald.
Upo-*n*-Squash.
Upo-*n*-Seat; sitting.
Upuan-*n*-Chair; seat.
Uralian-*v*-To imbue; instigate; inspire; persuade; induce; incite; stimulate; urge.
Uraling masama-*n*-Temptation; enticement; incitement.
Uraing-*n*-Stake; cudgel; club.
Uria-*n*-Border; fringe.
Uriin-*n*-To assay; examine; look into.
Urongsulong-*a*-Undecided; irresolute.
Uroy-*inter*.-Get out; git.
Uroy-*n*-Mockery; scoff; jeer.
Uruñgan-*v*-To retrocede; take back; back.
Usa-*n*-Deer.
Usang babayi-*n*-Doe; roe.
Usang inahin-*n*-Doe; roe.
Usang lalaki-*n*-Hart; buck.
Usap-*n*-Dispute; litigation; lawsuit; contest; strife; dissent; contract.
Usbong-*n*-Sprout; shoot; sucker.
Usigi-*v*-To examine; investigate; persue; follow.
Usisa-*n*-Probation; examination.

19

Usisain-v-To examine; investigate. survey; inquire; inspect; scrutenize; probe scan; discern; espy.

Uso-n-Use; habit; custom; usage.

Usok-n-Smoke; vapor; steam.

Usós-n-Rupture; (of the scrotum.)

Utak-n-Brain.

Utak ñg buto-n-Marrow.

Utal-a-Stammering; stuttering, hesitating; tonguetied.

Utal-n-Stammering; stuterer.

Utang-n Debt; obligattion; duty.

Utas-a-Finished; closed; concluded.

Utasin-v-To finish; terminate; end; conclude; close; bring to an end.

Utayutay-adv.-Gently; softly; easily.

Utong-n-Nipple.

Utos-n-Law; order; command; rule; statute; precept; edict; injunction; mandate; errand; message; proclamation.

Utúsan-v-To send; convey; command; order; edict.

Utusan-v-To send; convey; command; order; edict,

Utusan-n-Servant; errandboy; messenger; porter.

Uupan-n-Chair; seat.

Uyam-n-Sarcasm; mockery; ridiculedisdain; decrial.

Uyamin-v-To mock; scoff; deride ridicule; scathe; make fun of.

V

Varnis-n-Varnish.

Vervo-n-Verb; predicate.

Verso-n-Verse.

Viage-n-Voyage; passage; journey; excursion.

Violeta-n-Violet.

Violin-n-Violin; fiddle.

Violinista-n-Violinist.

Virgen-n-Virgen.

Visagre-n-Hinge.

Visita-n-Visit; chapel;

Visitahin-v-To visit; examine.

Vocabulario-n-Vocabulary.

Volcan-n-Volcano.

Voluntarios-n-Volunteer.

Voto-n-Vote.

W

Wágas-a-Neat; pure; clean; clear; free; innocent; virtuous; genuine.

Wahiin-v-To tear; rend; lacerate; cut; wear out; break; fracture.

Wakal-n-Termination; end; conclusion; extremity; edge; border; extreme; limit; boundary; bounds.

Wakas-n-Extreme; extremity; end; limit; bound; boundary; edge; border; conclusion; termination.

Wala-n-Nothing; naught.

Wala-adv.-No; not; in on degree.

Wala-a-Distant; absent; not present.

Walang ala ala-a-Calm; free; tranquil; peaceful; having nothing to think about.

Walang asa-a-Desperate.

Walang asawa-a-Single; unmarried.

Walang asawa-n-Bachelor; old maid.

Walang awa-a-Heartless; cruel; ruthless; inclement; fell; inhuman; hardhearted; soulless.

Walang ayos-a-Disarranged; disorderly; slovenly; careless; filthy; confused; pellmell; immethodical; unclean; harum-scarum.

Walang bahid dumi-a-Clean; untouched; pure; neat; unmingled; innocent; virtuous; holy.

Walang bait-a-Thoughtless; imprudent.

Walang baro-a-Shirtless.

Walang basagulo-a-Peaceful; calm; serene.

Walang bayad-a-Gratis; free of cost; gratuitous.

Walang buhay-a-Lifeless; inanimate.

Walang buhok-a-Bald; baldheaded.

Walang daan-a-Impossible; impracticable.

Walang dalita-a-Painless; well.

Walang damdam-a-Insensible; well-without pain; painless.

Walang damit-a-Naked.

Walang dañgal-a-Infamous; vile; despicable; low; abject.

Walang dulo-a-Pointless.

Walang daya-a-Equitable.

Walang galang-a-Disrespectful; rude; impudent; morose; insolent; haughty; peevish, inattentive; thoughtless; lofty; discourteous.

Walang galang adv.-Peevishly; impudently; morosely; insolently; discourteously; thoughtlessly.

Walang galit a-Quiet; serene; calm; unmolested.

Walang gawa-n-Liesure.

Walang gulo-a-Silent; quiet; still; calm; tranquil; noiseless; loyal; constant; faithful.

Walang gulugud-a-Invertebrate.

Walang gusto-a-Loath; loth.

Walang halag-a-Cruel; heartless; hardhearted; inclement; incompassionate; inhuman; soulless.

Walang halaga-a-Worthless; trifling; vain; frivolous; mean; vulgar; empty; void; fruitless.

Walang halo-a-Pure; unmixed; unmingled; clean; neat; mere.

Walang hanap buhay-a-Destitute; helpless; without work or employment.

Walang handa-a-Extempore; informal.

Walang hangan-a-Boundless; endless; interminable; perpetual; everlasting; immortal; infinite; infinitive.

Walang hanganan-a-Unlimited; boundless; interminable; endless; everlasting; infinite; without end.

Walang hiya-a-Shameless; impudent; insolent; forward; disrespectful; obscene; petulant; without selfrespect.

Walang humpay-a-Continual; incessant; uninterrupted; continuous.

Walang ikababayad-a-Insolvent.

Walang ingat-a-Careless; incautious; heedless; reckless; forgetful; neglectful.

Walang interes-a-Impartial; uninterested; candid; just; loyal.

Walang kaba-a-Bold; intrepid; dauntless; valiant; firm; constant; serene.

Walang kabuluhan-a-Worthless; trifling; catchpenny; futile; addle; void; empty; incapable.

Walang kahulilip-a-Incomparable;matchless; singular; unequalled; unparalleled.

Walang kahulugan-a-Senseless; unmeaning; trifling; wortless; useless; foolish

Walang kalinga-a-Inattentive; careless; thoughtless; heedless; negligent; neglectful.

Walang kalulwa-a-Soulless; inanimate; lifeless.

Walang kamahalan-a-Insolent; impudent; haughty;vulgar;ordinary; shameless; ignorant; without; dignity.

Walang kapalaran-a Hapless; luckless.

Walang kapara-a-Matchless; special; unequalled; unparalleled; incomparable; particular; singular.

Walang kaparis-a-Singular; special; unequalled; unparalleled; matchless; particular; peerless.

Walang kapintasan-a-Immaculate; faultless; perfect.

Walang karapatan-a-Unjust; unjustifiable; unfit; unreasonable; without justice.

Walang kasama-a-Solitary; sole; only.

Walang kasama-adv.-A lone; solely.

Walang katapusan-a-Endless; interminable; immortal; without end; infinite.

Walang katawan-a-Bodiless; immaterial.

Walang katulad a-Unequalled; matchless; unparalleled; special; peerless; without comparison; incomparable.

Walang caya-a-Unable; incomparable; unfit; powerless.

Walang kibo-a-Silent; quiet; dumb.

Walang kimi-a-Free; disengaged; unembarrassed.

Walang kimot-a-Silent; quiet; undisturbed; dumb; motionless; noiseless.

Walang kinikilingan-a-Impartial; just; unprejudiced.

Walang kulang-a-Complete;entire;whole; integral;perfect; exact; right; finished; enough.

Walang labas sa matowid-a-Just;lawful; true; fair; truthful.

Walang laman a-Empty; addle; vacant; void.

Walang lasa-a-Tasteless; insipid; flat.

Walang lihim-a-Open; frank; clear; unreserved.

Walang likat-a-Perpetual; everlasting; continuous; continual; endless; erect.

Walang likit-a-Straight; erect; continuous.

Walang makakamukha-a-Matchless; incomparable; unparalleled, unequalled.

Walang mansa-a-Immaculate; spotless; pure.

Walang hanga at mula-a-Endless; eternal; without end.

Walang nag aampon-a Helpless; destitute.

Walang nagkukupkop-a-Helpless; destitute; solitary; lonely.

Walang nasa-a-Disinterested; not desirous.

Walang ngipin-a-Toothless.

Walang pagod-a- Indefatigable; unwearied.

Walang pagtitiis-a-Insufferable; intolerable.

Walang pakiramdam-a-Insensible;senseless; indifferent; shameless.

Walang palad-a-Unfortunate; unlucky; sad; hapless.

Walang pananampalataya-*a*-Incredulous, unbelievable.

Walang pangalawa-*a* Matchless, unparalleled, solitary, singular, unequalled

Walang pangdamdam-*a* Insensible; indifferent, shameless

Walang paniniwala *a*-Incredulous, unbelievable.

Walang pinag aralan-*a*-Coarse, rough, illbred, rustic, ignorant, abject, low

Walang puri-*a*-Infamous, vile, despicable, shameless

Walang sakit-*a* Hale, well

Walang sandata-*a*-Disarmed

Walang sapin *a* Barefoot

Walang sigla-*a* Infirm, lifeless, inactive, slow; weak

Walang sinelas-*a* Barefoot.

Walang sukal-*a* Clean, pure, free; neat, cleanly.

Walang taba *a*-Lean, meagre

Walang tahan-*a* Continual, endless, incessant, uninterrupted, continuous

Walang tahi-*a*-Seamless

Walang takot-*a*-Bold; fearless, intrepid, dauntless, audacious, valiant, plucky

Walang testamento *a*-Intestate

Walang tigil-*a*-Incessant; continual, uninterrupted .

Walang turing-*a*-Ungrateful, low, abject, mean, ignorant.

Walang tuto-*a*-Ignorant, dumb; silly, unlearned; foolish.

Walang ulo-*a*-Headless

Walang wasto-*a* Disarranged, confused, disorderly, simple, silly, artless

Wala sa horas-*a*-Unseasonable; untimely.

Wala sa capanahunan-*a*-Abortive, untimely.

Wala sinoman-*n*-Nobody, none,

Wala sinoman-*pro* Neither

-Walis-*n*-Broom, duster

Walisin-*v*-To sweep, dust

Walo-*n*-Eight

Walo-*a* Eight

Walong puo-*n*-Eighty

Walong puo *a*-Eighty

Wari-*n*-Reasoning, thought, idea, meditation

Wariwarin-*v*-To think, reason, meditate, recall to mind.

Watak *a*-Wide open, clear, separated

Watakwatak-*a* Wide; open, clear, separated; at or by intervals

Wawa-*n*-The mouth of a stream

Wika-*n* Language, idiom, discourse talk, lingo, dialect, conversation, converse

Wikain-*v*-To talk; converse; pronounce, speak, say, tell, discourse

Wikain labas sa matowid *v*-To lie, tell a falsehood

Wika ng Judio *n*-Hebrew

Wilig *n*-Sprinkling

Wiligan-*v*-To Sprinkle

Wisik-*n* Sprinkler.

Wisikan-*v*-To sprinkle; water, spray.

Y

Yabag-*n*-Footstep; tread; noise of a footstep.

Yagyag-*n*-Trot

Yacap-*n*-Hug; embrace.

Yacapin *v*-To hug, embrace, imbosom.

Yaman-*n*-Riches, mammon

Yaman-*adv*-Since, well; then, now that.

Yaman-*prep* Therefore.

Yamut-*n*-Disgust, abhorrence, molestation, displeasure, impatience, vexation, loathing, disturbance, chafe, disquiet, distaste

Yamuan *n*-Rasure, scrapings; filings, parings

Yamutin *v*-To disturb, displease, vex; molest; irritate, worry, bother, disgust.

Yangyangan-*n*-Place of stretching anything; stretcher.

Yanig-*n* Oscillation; vibration; shake, trembling; wave.

Yanigin *t* To wave, shake.

Yano-*a*-Average, regular, even, ordinary, mediocre, plain, flat, neither good nor bad

Yantas-*n*-Tire, felloe

Yaon-*pro*-That·

Yaon din *adv* Ditto, idem

Yapak *n*-Tread, footstep

Yari-*n*-Cut, shape, make, figure, work, form, fashion, termination, finish, ending

Yari *pro* This

Yarin *v*-To finish, close, terminate, end; do, make; effect.

Yasak-*n*-Desolation, break, destruction, tear.

Yasakin-*v*-To desolate, destroy, break; tear, lay waste

Yasyas *n*-Polish; planing.

Yasyasin *v*-To plane, smooth, polish

Yawe-*n*-Stopcock.

Yaya-*n* Invitation

Yayain-*v*-To invite, stand treat.

Yayamang- *prep* -Therefore, yet, since

Yayang-*adv* -Then; now then, now that,

Yajat-*n*-Extenuation, weakness; leanness, languidness

Yimot-*n*-Oakum, tow, tow cloth.

Ymari-*i*-To make, form, produce, cause, exist, be

Yuko-*n*-Bow, stoop, salutation, bend; inclination

Yukod-*v*-Salutation; bow, salute, nod; greeting

Yumagyag-*v*-To trot; jog, be in haste.

Yuinaing *v*-To tremble, vibrate, oscillate

Yumaman-*v*-To enrich; grow or become rich, thrive; prosper

Yumamot-*v*-To vex; disgust, displease; glut, pique, irk, molest; disturb, afflict, be displeased or vexed, anger, oppress

Yumi-*a*-Faded, withered, decayed

Yumim-*v*-To fade; wither, decay

Yumuko *v*-To bow; nod; bend, stoop

Yumukod *v*-To nod, bow; stoop, bend the head

Yumurak-*v*-To tread, trample, stamp.

Yungib-*n*-Cave, grotto, cellar, hole, cavern; haunt; pit

Yupi-*n*-Bend, fold; double

Yurak-*n*-Stamp; tramp

Yurakan-*i*-To tread, stamp; trample

Yusakin-*v*-To tread, trample, stamp

Yupin *v*-To fold; double; bend

MAÑGA PAÑGALAN

Adan-n-Adam.
Adelaida-n-Adelaide.
Aldriano-n-Adrian.
Alberta-n-Bertha.
Alberto-n-Albert.
Alejandra-n-Alexandra.
Alejandro-n-Alexander.
Alfonso-n-Alphonso.
Andrea-n-Andrea.
Andres-u-Adrew.
Angel-n-Angelo.
Angela-n-Angeline.
Ana-n-Anna.
Anselma-n-Selma.
Antonio n-Anthony.
Arturo-n-Arthur.
Agustin-n-Augustin.
Barbara-n-Barbara
Bartolome-n-Bartholomew.
Basilio-n-Basil.
Beatricia-n-Beatrice.
Benancia-n-Bernice.
Benjamin-n-Benjamin.
Bernaldo-n-Bernard.
Bibiano-n-Vivian.
Cain-n-Cain.
Canuto-n-Kenith.
Carlos-n-Carl-Charles.
Carlota-n-Charlotte.
Carolina-n-Caroline.
Catalina-n-Kathrine; Kate.
Cecilia-n-Sisilia.
Cristina-n-Chistiana.
Cristino-n-Chistian.
Clara-n-Clara.
Claro-n Clare.
Claudio-n-Claude.
Clementa-n-Ruth. ←
Conrado-n-Conrad.
Constantina-n-Constance.
Daniel-n-Daniel; Dan.
David-n-David.
Diego-n-Diego.
Dionicio-n-Dennis.
Dora-n-Dora.
Dorotea-n Dorothy.
Doroteo-n-Dorchester.
Eduardo-n-Edward.
Elena-n-Helen; Lena; Ellen.
Elias-n-Elias.
Emilia-n-Emily.
Emilio-n-Emil.
Engracia n-Grace.
Enoc-n-Enoch.
Enrique-n-Henry.
Enriquetta-n-Henrieta; Harriet.

Erman-n-Herman.
Eugenio-n-Eugene.
Eva-n-Eve.
Federico-n-Frederick.
Felix-n-Felix.
Fernando-n-Ferdinand.
Felipe-n-Phillip.
Flora-n-Flora.
Florencia-n-Florence.
Francisca-n-Francis.
Francisco-n-Frank.
Gabriel-n-Gabriel.
George-n-George.
Gerónima-n-Jeremy.
Gerónimo-n-Jeremiah; Jerome.
Gil-n-Gil.
Gregorio-n-Gregory.
Guillerma-n-Wilhelma.
Guillermo-n-William.
Herodes-n-Herod.
Herculano-n-Hercules.
Isac-n-Isaac.
Jacob-n-Jacob.
Jarme-n-James.
Job-n-Job.
José-n-Joseph.
Josepa-n-Josaphine.
Juan-n-John; Jonathan.
Juanita-n-Juniata.
Julia-n-Julia.
Julian-n-Julian.
Juliana-n-Juliana.
Julio-n-Julius.
Justo-n-Justus.
Laura-n-Laura.
León-n-Leon.
Leonardo-n-Leonard.
Leoncia-n-Leona.
Leoncio-n-Lionel.
Leonora-n-Leonoir.
Lorenzo-n-Lawrence.
Lucas-n-Luke; Lucas.
Lucia-n-Lucile; Lucy.
Luis-n-Lewis; Louis.
Luisa-n-Louisa.
Magdalena-n-Magdalene.
Magallanes-n-Magallan.
Manuel-n-Emanuel.
Marcelo-n-Marshall.
Marcelino-n-Marshall.
Marcos-n-Marcus; Mark.
Margarita-n-Margarita; Margery.
Maria-n Mary; Marie.
Mariana-n-Miriam.
Mariano-n-Marion.
Marta-n-Martha.

Martin-n-Martin.
Mateo n Matthew
Matias-n-Matthias
Mauricio n-Maurice
Melecio-n-Michael.
Meliton-n-Milton
Moises n-Moses
Nicolás-n Nicolas
Patricio-n Patrick.
Paula; Paulina n-Paulina
Paulino-n Paul
Pedro-n-Peter.
Rafael-n-Ralph
Raymundo n-Raymond
Rebeca-n Rebecca.
Ricardo-n-Richard
Roberto-n-Robert
Rosa-n-Rose, Rosa
Rosalia-n-Rosalind
Rufino n-Rufus
Ruperto-n-Rupert
Salome-n-Salome
Samuel n-Samuel

Sara n Sarah
Silvestre n-Silvester
Simeon-n-Simeon
Simon-Simeon
Sofia n-Sophia
Salomon n-Solomon
Susana n-Susanna
Teobaldo Theobald
Teodora-n-Theodora.
Teodoro-n-Theodore.
Timoteo-n-Timothy
Tobias-n Tobias.
Tomás-n Thomas,
Trinidad-n-Trinidad.
Vicente n-Vincent
Victor-n-Victor
Victoria-n-Victoria
Virginia-n-Virginia
Yreneo n Ira
Yiene-n-Irene.
Ysabel-n-Isabel
Ysayas-n-Isaiah
Zoilo n-Zoilus

MANGA BUAN.

Enero-n January
Febrero-n-February
Marzo-n-March
Abril-n-April.
Mayo n-May
Junio-u June.

Julio-u July
Agosto n-August
Septiembre-n-September
Octebre-n-October
Noviembre n-November,
Deciembre-n December

MANGA ARAW.

Lingo-n-Sunday
Lunes-n-Monday
Martes-n-Tuesday
Miercoles-n Wednesday

Jueves n Thursday.
Viernes-Friday.
Sábado-n-Saturday.

PROPER NAMES

Adelaide-n-Adelaida.
Adam-n-Adan.
Adrian-n-Adriano.
Albert-n-Alberto.
Alexander-n-Alejandro.
Alexandra-n-Alejandra.
Alphonso-n-Alfonso.
Andre-n-Andrés.
Andrea-n-Andrea.
Andrew-n-Andrés.
Angeline-n-Angela, Angelina.
Angelo-n-Angel.
Anna-n-Ana.
Anthony-n-Antonio.
Arthur-n-Arturo.
Augustin-n-Agustin.

Barbary-n-Bárbara.
Bartholomew-n-Bartolomé.
Basil-n-Basilio,
Beatrice-n-Beatricia.
Benjamin n-Benjamin
Bernard-n-Bernaldo.
Bernice-n-Benancia.
Bertha-n-Alberta.

Cain-n-Cain.
Carl-n-Carlos.
Caroline-n-Carolina.
Charles-n-Carlos.
Charlotte-n-Carlota.
Christian-n-Cristino.
Christiana-n-Cristina.
Clara-n-Clara.
Clare-n-Claro.
Claude-n-Claudio.
Conrad-n-Conrado.
Constance-n-Constancia.

Dan-n-Daniel.
Daniel-n-Daniel.
David-n-David.
Dennis-n-Dionicio.
Diego-n Diego.
Dora-n-Dorotea.
Dorchester-n-Deroteo.
Dorothy-n-Dorotea.

Edward-n-Eduardo.
Elias-n-Elias.
Ellen-n-Elena.
Emanuel-n-Manuel.
Emil-n-Emilio.
Emily-n-Emilia.
Enoch-n-Enoc.
Eugene-n-Eugenio.
Eva-n-Eva.
Felix-n-Felix.
Ferdinand n-Fernando.

Flora-n-Flora.
Florence-n-Florencia.
Francis-n-Francisca.
Frank n-Francisco.
Frederick-n-Féderico.
Gabriel n-Gabriel.
George-n-George.
Gil-n-Gil.
Grace-n-Engracia.
Gregory-n-Gregorio.
Harriet-n-Enriqueta.
Helen-n-Elena.
Henrietta-n-Enriqueta.
Henry-n-Enrique.
Hercules-n-Herculano.
Herman-n-Erman.
Herod-n-Herodes.
Ira-n-Yreneo.
Irene-n-Yrene.
Isaac-n-Isac.
Isabel-n-Ysabel.
Isaiah-n-Ysayas.
Jacob-n-Jacob.
James-n-Jaime.
Jeremiah n-Geronimo.
Jeremy-n-Geronima.
Job-n-Job.
John-n-Juan.
Johnathan n-Juan.
Joseph-n-Jose.
Josaphine-n-Josepa
Julia-n-Julia.
Julian-n-Julian.
Juliana-n-Juliana
Julius-n-Julio.
Juniata-n-Juanita.
Justus-n-Justicio; Justo.
Kathrine-n-Catalina.
Kenith-n-Canuto.
Laura-n-Laura.
Lawrence-n-Lorenzo.
Lena-n-Elena.
Lenoir-n-Leonora.
Leon-n-Leon.
Leonard-n-Leonardo.
Lewis-n-Luis.
Lionel-n-Leoncio.
Louis-n-Luis.
Louisa-n-Luisa.
Lucile n-Lucia.
Lucy-n-Lucia.
Magdalene-n-Magdalena.
Magellan-n-Magallanes.
Marshall-n-Marcelo.
Marcus-n-Marcos.
Margarette-n-Margarita.

20

Marie-n-Maria.
Marion-n-Mariano
Mark-n-Marcos.
Martha-n-Marta
Martin-n-Martin
Mary-n-Maria.
Matthew-n-Mateo.
Mathias-n-Matias
Maurice-n-Mauricio
Michael-n-Melicio.
Milton-n-Meliton
Moses-n-Moises
Nicolás-n-Nicolás
Patrick-n-Patricio.
Paul-n-Paulino.
Pauline-n-Paulina, Paula.
Peter-n-Pedro.
Phillip-n-Filipe.
Ralph-n-Rafael
Raymond n-Raymundo.
Rebecca-n-Rebeca
Richard-n-Ricardo.
Robert-n-Roberto.
Rosalind-n-Rosalia.
Rose-Rosa-n-Rosa.
Rufus-n-Rufino

Rupert-n-Ruperto.
Ruth-n-Clementa.
Salome-n-Salome.
Samuel-n-Samuel.
Sarah-n Sara.
Selma-n-Anselma.
Sisilia n-Cesilia.
Silvester-n-Silvestre
Simeon n-Simeon; Simon
Solomon-n-Solomon.
- Sophia-n-Sofía.
Susanna-n-Susana.
Theobald-n-Teobaldo.
Theodora-n-Teodora.
Theodore-n-Teodoro
Thomas-n-Tomas
Tobias-n-Tobias.
Trinidad-n-Trinidad
Victor-n-Victor
Victoria-n-Victoria.
Vincent-n-Vicente
Virginia-n-Virginia
Vivian-n-Bibiano.
Wilhelma-n-Guillerma
William-n-Guillermo.
Zoilus-n-Zoilo.

Months of the year

January-n-Enero.
February-n-Febrero.
March-n-Marzo.
April n-Abril.
May-n-Mayo.
June-n-Junio.

July-n-Julio
August-n-Agosto.
September-n-Septiembre.
October-n-Octubre.
November-n-Noviembre.
December-n-Diciembre.

Days of the week

Sunday n-Lingo
Monday n-Lunes.
Tuesday-n-Martes
Wednesday-n-Miercoles.

Thursday-n-Jueves.
Friday-n-Viernes.
Saturday-n-Sábado.

A

A-*a*-Isang, sang.
Aback-*adv*.-Sa likod; sa gawing likod.
Abacus-*n*-Kasangkapan pangbilang
Abaft-*adv* -Sa gawing likod, sa gawing huli.
Abandon-*v*-Umalis, maiwan lumayo, pabayaan; tampuhan.
Abandonment-*n*-Pag iiwan; pag alis; kapabayaan, kawalan ng̃ kalinga.
Abase-*v*-Magpahamak, ibaba ang loob ng̃ kapwa.
Abate-*v*-Bumaba, humimpil, lumubay; umigi, guminhawa.
Abbet-*n*-Convento.
Abbot-*n*-Amo ng̃ convento.
Abbreviate-*v*-Iklan.
Abbreviation-*n*-Pag iikli.
Abcess-*n*-Pigsa; bagá, bukol na mananá.
Abdicate-*v*-Ibigay sa iba ang kaharian; umalis sa pagkahari.
Abdication *n*-Ang pagaalis sa pagkahari
Abdomen-*n*-Tian, tiyan.
Abdominal-*a*-Nauukol sa tiyan.
Abduct-*v* Itanan, agawin, iagaw.
Abduction *n*-Pagtanan, pag agaw.
Abed *adv* -Nakahiga, nasasa hihigan
Abet-*v*-Kalongin; kumalong.
Abettor-*n*-Taga pagkalong.

Abeyance-*n*-Pag aasahan, pag aantay.
Abhor-*v*-Masuklam sa kapwa, magalit; kamuluan, mapoot, mamuhi, yumamot
Abhorrence-*n*-Dumal, kasuklaman; muhi, suklam ng̃ loob sa kapwa, yamot.
Abide-*v*-Tumira, maghinto, magluat; dalumatin; damotin; batakin; dalitain, magtiis, umayon,
Ability-*n*-Kaya, kapangyarihan, kasanayan, bisa, karunungan, katalinuhan, lakas, talas ng̃ isip, pag iisip
Abject-*a* Hamak, mababa, malait, walang dang̃al; walang pinag aralan.
Abjure-*v* Talikuran, makaila, mag renuncia
Ablaze-*adv* -Naniningas
Able-*a* Makaya; sanay, may kaya, matalino, marunong bihasa
Ablution-*n*-Ang pag lilinis.
Aboard-*adv* -Nasa sasakyan; nakasakay sa sasakyan
Abode *n*-Tirahan; bahay, tahanan, pamamahay
Abolish-*v* Lipulin, alisin, burahin, antalahin, pawiin.
Abolition-*n*-Pagkalipol, paglilipol.
Abominable *a*-Nakahihiya, hamak, masama, kahiyahiya.

Abominate-v-Magpahamak; hamakin.
Abomination - n - Pagpahamak; kahamakan.
Aboriginal-a-Caunaunahan; unang.
Aborigines-n Ang mğa unang tawo na tumira sa isang lugar.
Abortion-n-Pangangaanak labas sa panahon; pagkakunan.
Abortive-a Labas sa panahon; walang kabuluhan.
Abound-v-Sumagana; masagana.
About-adv.-Malapit; saan; dako; sa palibid; sa paligid.
About-prep.-Nang; ayon; dahil sa, sa.
Above-prep.-Hingil sa; tangi sa; mataas pa sa.
Above-adv.-Sa itaas; sa ibabaw.
Above mentioned-a-Nabangit; nasabing.
Abreast-adv.-Sa tabi; katabi. sa tagilid.
Abridge-v-Iklian; liitan; magbawas; sumalin; awasan.
Abridgement-n-Pag ikli; pagkaliit; pagbabawas; salin.
Abroad-adv.-Sa tanyag; sa labas ng bahay; hayag.
Abrupt-a-Bigla; golpe.
Abscond-v-Tekasin; manekas; tumekas.
Absconder-n-Manenekas.
Absence-n-Pagkawala; kawalan.
Absent-a-Wala.
Absent-v-Umalis; lumayo; lumayas.
Absentee-n Ang umalis na; ang hindi humarap.
Absolute-a-Totoong; tunay; makapangyayari.
Absolution-n-Patawad; pag papatawad.
Absolve-v-Patawarin.
Absorb-v-Higupin; humigop; humitit.
Absorption-n-Higop; hitit.
Abstain-v-Magtiis; tiisin.
Abstaining-a-Matitiisin.
Abstemious-a-Matitiisin; mapagpigil; mahinahon.
Abstinence-n-Pagtiis; kasiyahan; kasukatan.
Abstinent-a-Mapagtiis; mapagpasiya.
Abstract-v-Hugutin; bunutin; hiwalayin; ialis.
Abstract-n-Kasulatan.
Abstracted-a-Nakahiwalay; nakabukod; wala sa isip.
Abstraction-n-Pagkahiwalay; hiwalay; hugot; bunot.
Abstruse-a-Malalim; mahirap talastasin; malabo.
Absurd-a-Makatatawa; walang kabuluhan; walang casaysayan.
Absurdity-n-Kamangmangan; kaululan.
Abundance -n-Kasaganaan; karamihan; kahustuhan; kasukatan.

Abundant-a-Sagana; husto; marami; masagana.
Abundantly-adv.-Malabis; masagana.
Abuse-v-Lampastanğanin; alimurahan; lumait; laitan; pamihasanin; paslanğin; salantain; alipustain; murahin.
Abuse-n-Lapastanğan; paglait; pagaalimura; katampalasanan; dowahagi; pagmumura; kalapastanğanan.
Abusive-a-Tampalasan; bastos; masama.
Abusiveness -n - Kalapastanğanan; pagalimura.
Abut-v-Magpisan; umabot; lumapit.
Abutment-n-Pader na bato.
Abysmal-a-Malalim na totoo; walang pusod ó puit.
Abyss-n-Lugal na totoong malalim.
Academic-Academical a-Nauukol sa academia.
Academy-n-Academia.
Accede-v-Pumayag; umabot; abutin; kamtan.
Acelerate-v-Tumulin; lumiksi.
Acceleration-n-Tulin; katulinan; liksi; kaliksihan.
Accent-n-Accento; lakas.
Accent-v-Ilagay ng accento ó lakás.
Accentuate-v-Ilakas.
Accentuation-n-Pagkalagay ng accento.
Accept-v Tangapin; tumangap; damotin.
Acceptable-a-Dapat tangapin; marapat tangapin; matatangap; nakalulugod.
Acceptance-n-Pagtangap.
Acceptation-n-Ang pagtatangap; kahulugan.
Access-n-Pag abot; pag lapit.
Accessible-a-Makakaabot; makakamtan.
Accession-n-Pag abot; pagkamtan; pagkamit.
Accident-n-Ang nangyari na hindi sinasadya; nagcacataon; pagkabalatong; sakuna.
Accidental-a-Hindi sinasadya; nagkataon; hindi tinatalaga; mataonan.
Acclaim-v-Purihin; parangalin.
Acclaim-n-Pagpupuri.
Acclamation-n-Pagpupuri.
Acclivity-n-Tibag; akyatan; tirik.
Accomodate-v-Magbigay loob; makibagay; magkasundo.
Accomodating-a-Mapagbigay loob; mapagtiis.
Accomodation-n Pagkasunduan.
Accompany-v-Sumama; isama; sumabay; ihatid; maghatid.
Accomplice-n-Ang kasáma sa paggawa; kamiyaw; kasáma; katulong.
Accomplish v-Tapusin; yariin; totohanin.
Accomplished-a-Yari; natapos na.

Accomplishment n-Pagkayari, pangyayari; katapusan

Accomptant-n Taga bilang

Accord-n-Kasulatan, salitaan, pagkasunduan.

Accord v-Pumayag, umayon, mag-kasundo.

Accordance-n-Salitaan, pagkasunduan

Accordant-a-Nagkakaayon.

According-a-Ayon; nauukol.

According to law-Naayon sa matowid

Accordion-n-Cordion

Accost-v-Ilapit, lumapit, bumati'

Account-n-Balak, saysay, turing, salaysay, kasaysayan, kuenta

Account-v-Salaysayin, balakin; saysayin, magturing.

Accountable-a-Masasagutin, taga panagot

Accountant-n-Taga bilang ng kuarta

Accounter v-Ibigay ng kailangan.

Accouterments-n-Manga kasangkapan ng sundalo

Accredit-v-Ibigay ng katowiran o kapangyarihan; pumayag.

Accredited a-Balitang; bantog.

Accrue-v Magdagdag; lumaki.

Accumulate-v-Magipon; bumunton, umipon; lumaki

Accumalation n-Pag iipon, dagdag, pagsasámasáma

Accurate-a-Kawanlan ng mali, dunong.

Accurse-v-Sumpain, sumumpa, manumpa; magtungayaw, tungayawin.

Accursed-a-Hamak, malait

Accusation n-Bintang, sumbong, paratang.

Accusative-a-Dapat sumbungin

Accusable-a-Dapat isumbong

Accuse-v Isumbong, sumbungin, bintangin, paratangan, magsumbong, magparatang, magbigay sala

Accustom-v-Mamihasa, bihasahin; pamaratihin; hiratihan, gamitin.

Accustomed-a-Hirati, bihasa, datihan; palagi

Ace-n-Alas

Acerbity-n-Kasaklapan.

Ache-v-Sumakit, humapdi; humapis, magdamdam.

Ache-n-Sakit, damdam, hapdi; antak. dalamhati, hapis; kirot.

Achieve-v-Gawin; tapusin

Achievement-n-Pagyayari, tapos.

Acid-n-Aksido.

Acid-a-Maasim.

Acidity-n-Asim kaasiman

Acknowledge-v-Sumagot, tumugon.

Acknowledgement-v-Sagot, tugon

Acme-n-Panduli. Lataastaasan, luzon

Acorn-n-Bunga ng kahoy na tinatawag (acorn).

Acoustic-a-Nauukol sa dinig

Acoustics-n-Karunungan sa pandinig.

Acquaint-v-Kilalanin.

Acquaintance-n-Kakilala; kilala, pagkikilala; pagpapakilala.

Acquiesce-v Makiayon, pumayag.

Acquiescence-n-Pakikiayon pagkapayag, pagkaayon

Acquire-v-Makinabang; magkamtan; magkaroon, pumulot, pulutin.

Acquirement-n-Pagkamit, pagkakaroon, pagabot

Acquisition-n-Pagkakamtan; tubo, pakinabang

Acquisitive a-Mahilig sa tubo.

Acquittal-n-Pagpatawad

Acquittance-n-Tawad, recibo

Acie-n-Pirasong lupa na may 123 baras at tatlong dankal ang haba at 49 ½ ng baras ang lapad

Acrid-a-Mapait, maasim; naninigid

Acrimony-n-Kapaitan, hanghang.

Acrimonious-a-Mapait, masaklap.

Acrobat-n-Tawong malakas at sanay.

Acrobatic-a-Malakas at sanay.

Across-prep -Sa kabila, nakahalang.

Acooss-adv -Sa ibayo, pahalang

Acrostic-n-Bugtong na may isang salitang nakatago.

Act-n-Kilos, gawa, bawat isa ng manga bahagi ng teatro.

Act-v-Kumilos, gumawa; magkomediante

Act like a child-v-Kumilos parang bata, magbinata

Action-n-Kilos, gawa, asal

Actor-n-Komediante

Actress-n-Komedianteng babayi

Active-a-Maliksi, buhay, harumpak; masigap, masigla, madali, mabisa; bihasa, matalas.

Activeness-n-Kaliksihan, agap, kasipagan; kabihasanan, sigla, liksi

Activity-n-Liksi, agap, sipag; kasipagan; kaliksihan, sikap, bisa, katulinan, sigla.

Actual-a-Kasalukuyan, tunay.

Actually-adv.-Kasalukuyan tunay.

Actuate-v-Ipakilos, iudyok.

Acute a-Matulis, matalino; matalas

Acuteness-n-Katulisan; katalasan

Adage n-Patnugot; salita nangaling sa kanunuan.

Adapt-r-Ikama, gamitin, ikapit.

Adaptable-a-Mabagay, bagay.

Adaptation-n-Paggagamit, pagkama.

Add v-Dagdagan; bilugin ipatong; patungan, magsuma, magdugtong, mag-

Adder-n-Alupong
Addible-Addable-a-Makasnsuma
Addict-v-Gumamit na lagi.
Addition n-Sumar; pagdaragdag; karagdagan; dagdag, dugtong, pagbuti; pamakpak.
Additional-a-Nakadagdag pa.
Addle-a-Bugok; walang kabulahan, walang laman.
Addle-v-Bumulok.
Address-v-Magsalita, batin.
Address-n-Sermon, pagsasaysay, discurso, kinatitirahan, pagbuti
Adduce-v-Ilitaw; iharap; ipakita.
Adept-a-Bihasa, sanay, marunong; matalas
Adept-n-Tawong marunong at sanay.
Adequate-a-Husto, sukat, sapat; bagay; sagana
Adhere-v-Sumama; dumikit, magpisan, sumapit, pumisan
Adherence-n-Pagdidikit, pagkapisan, pagsapit.
Adherency-n-Pagdidikit, pagkapisan; pagsapit
Adherent-a-Nakadikit
Adhesion-n-Pagdidikit
Adhesive-a-Nakadikit.
Adieu-n-Paalam.
Adipose-a-Puro taba
Adjacent-a-Malapit, katabi, hindi malayo.
Adjective-n-Adjectivo
Adjectively-adv-Parang adjectivo
Adjoin-v-Ipisan, isama, magdugtong.
Adjourn-v-Tumapos, tumigil ang kapisanan.
Adjournment-n-Pagtitigil ng kapisanan
Adjudge-v-Mag hatol, hatulan
Adjudicate-v-Humatol, hatulan
Adjudication-n-Paghahatol
Adjunct-a-Makadugtong.
Adjuration-n-Panalangin, panumpa.
Adjure-v-Manumpa, ipanumpa
Adjust v-Ayosin, husayin, banatin, igayak, ihanda, maghusay.
Adjustable-a-Makakaayos.
Adjustment-n-Pagkakaayos, pagkakahusay; katotohanan.
Adjutant-n-Ayudante
Administer-v-Kumalinga, mamahala, suyuin, manuyo
Administration-n-Pamamahala, pagpupúno
Administrator-n-Ang namamahala, taga bantay ng ari ng iba, ó kapwa.
Administratrix-n-Ang babaying namamahala sa ari ng kapwa.
Admirable-a Katakataka, dapat purihin, mainam.

Admiral-n-Admirante, puno ng mga sasakyan de guerra.
Admiration-n-Pagkapuri, mangha, pagtataka, pagmamangha; panğingilalas;
Admire-v-Purihin, ipagpuri, mamangha; manğingilalas; magtaka.
Admissible-a Dapat tangapin, matatangap.
Admission-n-Pahintulot' pagpasok
Admit v-Ipasok, ipahintulot; magbigay daan, magkaloob, tumangap
Admittance n-Pahintulot, tulot pagpasok
Admix v-Ihalo, ilahok
Admixture-n-Halo lahok
Admonish v-Aralan, panğusapan; sisihin, sumaad, bumala; magpasiya, payuhin
Admonition-n-Babala, payo, pasiya pagpasisi
Ado n-Gulo, hirap
Adobe-n-Ladrillo na natuyo sa araw lamang
Adopt-v-Gamitin
Adoption-v-Paggagamit
Adore-v-Gumiliw; lumigaw, gihwin, ligawin, umibig, ibigin.
Adorable-a-Dapat giliwin, dapat ibigin.
Adoration-n-Paggiliw, pagibig.
Adorn v Gayakan, igayak, pamutihin; magalingin; gumayak
Adornment-n-Gayak; hiyas; pamuti.
Adrift a-Nakalutang
Adrift-adv-Nakalutang
Adroit-a-Matalas, tuso, sanay.
Adulation-n-Pagpalayaw Paglalangis ng dila
Adulatory-a-Nauukol sa pagpapalayaw
Adult-a Matanda, may edad
Adult-n-Tawong husto na ang laki.
Adulterate-a-May halo
Adultery-n-Pakikiapid
Advance-v-Sumulong; magtuloy, lumapit
Advance-n-Sulong, paglalapit; pagtuloy.
Advancement-n-Pagbuti, pagsulong, paggaling, paglalapit.
Advantage-n-Pakinabang, tubo, luta, l atamasan.
Advantage-v-Makinabang
Advantageous a-Pakikinabanğan; makikinabang.
Advent-n-Ang nagyari na, nagkakataon.
Adventure-n-Ang hindi sinasadya ang nagkakataon.
Adventure-v-Magkataon
Adventurous a Matapang, mangahas
Adverb n Adverbio.
Adverbial-a-Nauukol sa adverbio.
Adversary-n-Kalaban, katalo.

Adverse-a-Laban; malaban
Adversity-n-Kasalatan kahirapan.
Advertise-v-Ipahayag, ipabalita.
Advertisement-n-Babala, pahayag balita
Advise-n-Aral, babala, pañgunğusap, payo, inaaralan, pagpayo.
Advise-v-Aralan, payuhan, sumaad, pañgusapan, ipanğusap, umaral.
Advisable-a-Dapat sundin
Advisedly-adv.-Dapat sundusunduin
Avisory a Marapat sumunod.
Advocate-n-Ang taga pamagitan
Advocate-v-Mamagitan; lumaban, kupkupin
Adz or adze-n-Dahas
Aerial-n-Nauukol sa hanğin
Aesthetic-a-Nauukol sa lasa
Aesthetics-n-Lasa; lasap.
Aether-n Etero.
Afar-adv -Sa malayo.
Affability-n-Saya, kasayahan, lugod; kaluguran
Affable a-Maamong loob, malambot na ngali; nakalulugod masaya, palagay.
Affableness-n-Saya, lugod, kasayahan, kaluguran.
Affair-n-Gawa.
Affect-v-Magkonowari, ibahin, maukol.
Affectation-n-Pagkokonowari, kaibhan, kaukulan, daya.
Affected-a-Nakadadaya
Affecting-a-Nauukol sa.
Affection-n-Pag ibig, pagakwili, paggiliw
Affectionate-a-Magiliw, mairog, mairugin, masintahin, taos sa loob, magandang loob, dapat ibigin, maramdamin.
Affidavit-n-Kasulatan na ipinanumpa.
Affiliate-v-Isama, gamitin.
Affiliation-n-Pagsasama, pag gagamit.
Affinity-n-Pagkakamaganak dahil sa pag aasawa
Affirm-v-Tibayin; tumutol, tumibay, manibay
Affirmation-n-Pagpapatotoo, pagtibayan.
Affirmative-a-Sinasaysay.
Affirmative n-Kasaysayan
Affix-v-Idugtong sa dulo
Affix-n-Dugtong sa dulo.
Afflict-v-Habagin, hapisin, pasakitan, yamutin, yumamot, humapis, mahapis
Affliction-n-Damdam, lumbay, pighati, kahirapan, kasakitan, hambal; hinagpis; alipusta
Affluence-n-Kayamanan, kasaganaan.
Affluent a-Mayaman; sagana; husto.
Afford-n-Ibigay, pumayag
Affray-n-Away, pagsasagupa, laban; pagpapamook; takapan, babag.

Affray-v-Takutin, labanin
Affright-n-Takot
Affright-v-Takutin
Affront-n-Kamurahan, kapalibhasaan, paglapastanğan, pagaalipusta.
Affront-v-Murahin, lapastanğanin, alipustain, hiyain.
Afghan-a-Nauukol sa Afghanistan.
Afghan-n-Taga Afghanistan.
Afield-adv.-Sa parang ó bukid
Afire-a-Nalilinğas; naliliab.
Afire-adv.-Nakaliliñgas.
Afloat-adv -Nakalutang, langoy, lumulutang.
Afoot adv. Nakaladlad, palakad.
Afore adv -Nauna, nabanğit, sinundan.
Aforesaid-a-Nasabing, nasabi na, nabangit, nauran na
Aforementioned-a-Nabangit, nasabing, nauran na.
Aforetime-adv -Nauna sa panahon
Afraid-a-Natatakot, matakot
Afresh adv.-Uli; panibago
Aft-adv -Sa gawing likod
After-adv -Pagkatapos, su hulihan, sa huli.
After-prep.-Pagka; pagkatapos
After-a-Sumunod; nakasunod, huling.
Aftermath-n-Hapon, pagkatanghali.
Afternoon-n-Hapon.
Afterward-adv.-Pagkatapos, pagka; sa hulihan
Afterwards adv -Pagkatapos, pagka, sa hulihan; sa huli, saka.
Again-adv -Uli, nuli, ulit
Against-prep -Sa harap; laban sa; balintuna, laban kay.
Agate-n-Isang metal na mararami ang kulay
Age-n Gulang; edad, panahon, kapanahunan; katandaan, laon.
Age-v-Tumanda, lumaon, lumipas.
Aged-a Matanda, magulang; laon.
Agency-n-Oficina nğ isang katiwala, pag kakatiwala
Agent-n-Katiwala, encargado
Agglomerate-v-Pumisanpisan sa isang bola.
Aggrandize-v-Dagdagan, idagdag, lumaki, lumalo; magpalaki, pagdilagin.
Aggrandizement-n-Pagpalaki; pagdaragdag.
Aggravate-v-Pasamain, hamakin; yamutin pagalitin
Aggravation-n-Tukso, kahamakan
Aggregate-v-Umabot, abotin, dumagdag, idagdag pumisan
Aggregate-a-Bilog, buo nakapisan
Aggregate-n-Buo; kabilugan, pagsasama, kalahatan.

Aggregation-*n*-Pagsasama, pagpipisan, kalahatan

Aggression-*n*-Pag laban; pag aalsa.

Aggressive-*a*-Matapang, mangahas

Aggressor-*n*-Ang lumalaban, unang lumaban

Aggrieve-*v*-Magpahirap; saktan, pahirapin

Aghast *a*-Kakilakilabot, nakataka

Aghast-*adv*.-Nakamamangha, kakilakilabot

Agile *a*-Maliksi, masigla, magaan, maagap.

Agitate-*v*-Sulsulin, udyokin, tuksuhin

Agitation-*n*-Sulsol; gulo, udyok.

Agitator *n*-Ang sumulsol, mangugulo.

Ago-*adv*.-Nakaraan na; lipas

Agoing *adv*-Pagalaw, lumalakad.

Agonize-*v*-Pahirapin, tuksohin, sumakit na lubha, maghingalo

Agony-*n*-Hirap, hingalo, sakit.

Agree-*v*-Magkaisa, umayon, pumayag; tumango, pahintulutin, ipahintulot

Agreeable-*a*-Mabagay, makalulugod, nakangiti, matatawanin, makatatawa.

Agreeably-*adv*.-Kawiliwili; kalugodlugod

Agreement - *n* - Kasulatan, pinagkasunduan, salitaan, tipanan trato, pinagusapan, pagkaisa, pagkakaayon.

Agriculture-*n*-Agricultura, pagsasaka

Agriculturist-*n*-Magsasaka.

Aground-*adv*.-Nakasayad sa lupa.

Ague *n*-Ngiki

Ah-*inter*-Abá.

Ahá-*adv*-Aha; aroy,

Ahead-*adv*-Nauna, sa una, sa harap, sa dulo

Aid-*v*-Tulungin, amponin; abuluyan, saklolohan, gumibik, kupkupin; tangkilikin.

Aid-*n*-Tulong, andukha, abuloy, paghibik, saklolo, tangkilik; pagaabuloy, manunulong

Ail-*v*-Magkasakit, magdamdam

Ail-*n*-Sakit, damdam.

Aim-*n*-Tudla; punta

Aim *v*-Tudlain, puntahin.

Aimless-*a*-Walang dulo, pabaya.

Air *n* Hangin, kahambugan.

Air-*v*-Ibilad, iyangyang, patuyuin sa hangin.

Airily-*adv*-Magaan, masaya

Airiness-*n*-Saya, kasayahan; gaan ng katawan

Airing-*n* Pasial, pagpapahangin.

Airy-*a*-Parang hangin; magaan, naunkol sa hangin

Antight-*a*-Di makapasok ang hangin

Aisle-*n*-Sulambi, daan sa pag itan ng dalawang taludtod unpuan ó banko.

Ajar *adv*-Nakalukas ng kaunti

Akimbo-*a*-Baluktot, nakabaluktot.

Akin *a* Kamaganak sa dugo, kamukha

Alabaster-*n*-Bicarbonato de cal

Alacrity *n* Liksi, kaliksihan, tulin, agap,

Al amode-*adv*-Ayon o sunod sa ugali, sunod sa uso

Alarm-*n*-Gulat, gulo, takot, babala, balitang masama

Alarm clock-*n*-Relos na pangising

Alarm-*v* Gulatin, takutin, guluhin

Alas *inter*-Sayang, kaawa.

Albatios-*n* Ibon sa dagat

Albiet-*adv*-Bagaman, datapua, yamang.

Albiet-*prep*-Datapuat; bagaman.

Albino-*n*-Bata na maputi ang buhok.

Album-*n*-Libro na kinalalagyan ng mga larawan o sulat

Albumen-*n*-Ang puti ng itlog

Alcohol-*n*-Alak na 36

Alcoholic-*a* May halong alak

Alcove *n*-Lugar na tago sa isang silid.

Alderman-*n*-Consejal

Ale-*n*-Alak.

Alee-*adv*-Sa gilid ng sasakyan na walang hangin.

Alert-*a*-Maliksi, maagap; buhay

Algebra *n* Algebra

Alias-*n*-Bansag, pamagat

Alibi-*n*-Ibang lugar.

Alien-*a*-Buhat sa ibang lupa; iba.

Alien-*n*-Tawong taga ibang lupa

Alienate-*v*-Sirain ang mabuting kaugalian, ilipat ang pagibig, lumayo.

Alienation-*n*-Paglipat ng pagibig, kaululan

Alight-*v*-Umibis

Alike *adv* -Magkaparis, magkamukha; kawanki, kawangis, kamukha.

Aliment-*n* Pagkain

Alimental-*a*-Nauukol sa pagkain, may sustancia

Alimentary-*a*-Nauukol sa pagkain; may sustancia

Alimony-*n*-Pagsusustento, salaping na mauui sa asawang babaye kung nataboy sa kaniyang asawa.

Aliquot-*a*-Makakahati na walang labis.

Alive-*a*-Buhay, maliksi, mabuhay.

All-*a*-Lahat, lahat lahat, pulos.

All-*n*-Ang kalahatan.

All *adv*.-Lahatlahat

Allay-*v*-Patahimikin, payapain, tumahi mik, pumayapa, umigi.

Allegation-*n*-Palagay, pagkalagay.

Allege-*v*-Magpalagay, magsabi, sabihin

Allegoric-*a*-Tinatalinghaga.

Allegorical-*a*-Tinatalinghaga

Allegory-*n* Talinghaga.

21

Alleviate-*v*-Gaanan; umigi; pahimpilin; humimpil.

Alleviation-*n*-Pag iigi; paghihimpil.

Alley-*n*-Daang makipot; paraan; paso.

Alliance-*n*-Pagkapisan; pagkasama; pag kakalakip.

Alligator-*n*-Buaya.

All-night-*adv*.-Magdamag; damag.

Allot-*v*-Ibigay; ikalat; ipagkaloob.

Allotment-*n*-Pagbibigay; pagkalat.

Allow-*v*-Pahintulutin; pumayag; pabayaan; magbigay loob; magbigay daan.

Allowable-*a*-Dapat pahintulutan.

Allowance-*n*-Pagkapayag; pagpapahintulot; dahilan; pagdadahilan.

Alloy-*n*-Halo; lahok.

Alloy-*v*-Ihalo; ilahok.

All Saints day-*n*-Kaluluwa.

All souls Day *n*-Undas; kaluluwa.

Allspice-*n*-Bunga ñg paminta.

Al-lude-*n*-Ibangit.

Al-lure-*n*-Dayain; gahisin.

Al-luring-*a*-Nakahahalina.

Al-lurement-*n*-Pagdadaya; paggagahis.

Al-lusion-*n*-Pagkabangit.

Al-lusive-*n*-Nauukol sa bangit.

Ally-*v*-Isama; ilakip; magpisan.

Al-ly-*n*-Katulong; kapisan; kasama.

Almanac-*n*-Almanaque.

Almighty-*a*-Makapangyayari.

Amighty-*n*-Ang May-kapal; Bathala.

Almost-*adv*.-Halos; malapit; malapit na malapit; kumulang sa.

Alms-*n*-Limos.

Almshouse-*n*-Bahay na tinitirahan ñg mga pulubi.

Aloft-*adv*.-Sa itaas.

Alone-*a*-Bugtong; nagiisa; nabubukod; walang kasama; natatañgi.

Alone-*adv*.-Lamang; natatañgi; walang kasama.

Along-*adv*.-Kasama sa gawi.

Alongside-*adv*.-Sa tabi kasiping.

Aloof-*adv*.-Buhat sa malayo; nabubukod; nakabukod.

Aloof-*prep*.-Nakabukod sa; buhat sa.

Aloud *adv*.-Malakas.

Alphabet-*n*-Alfabeto; mga titik na ginagamit sa isang salita.

Alphabetic-*a*-Nauukol sa mga titik; sumusunod sa mga titik.

Alphabetical-*a*-Nauukol sa mga titik; sumusunod; sa mga titik.

Already-*adv*.-Ñgayon na.

Also-*adv*.-Naman; gayon din; din; rin; man; gayon.

Altar-*n*-Altar.

Alter-*v*-Ibahin; baguhin; magbago; ilipat; bumago.

Alterable-*a*-Makakaiba; umubrang ibahin ó baguhin.

Alterant-*a*-Nakakaiba.

Alteration-*v*-Pagkaiba; pagbabago.

Altercate-*n*-Umaway; makipagtalo.

Altercation-*n*-Away pagtatalo; pagaaway.

Alternate-*v*-Humalili.

Alternate-*n*-Kahalili.

Alternate-*a*-Sunodsunod.

Alternation-*n*-Pagkahalili.

Alternative-*v*-Makapipili.

Alternative-*n*-Pagkapili sa dalawang bagay.

Although-*conj*.-Datapua; baga man.

Altitude-*n*-Taas.

Alto-*n*-Voces ñg babaying kumakanta ñg mababa.

Altogether-*adv*.-Sabaysabay; lahatlahat.

Alum-*n*-Tawas.

Alway-Always-*adv*.-Lági; sa boong panahon; parati; towitowi na; lagi na; magkailan man.

Am-*r*-Ay; may.

Amain-*adv* -Biglangbigla; malakas.

Amalgam-*n*-Halo ñg mga metal.

Amalgamate-*v*-Ihalo ang azogue sa ibang metal.

Amalgamation-*n*-Ang paghahalo nang azogue sa ibang metal.

Amanuensis-*n*-Taga sulat ñg idinidikta; ñg iba.

Amass-*v*-Ipunin; tipunin; samsamin.

Amatuer-*n*-Ang hindi pa lubhang sanay.

Amaze-*v*-Magpamangha; gitlahin.

Amaze-*n*-Gitla; mangha.

Amazement-*n*-Mangha; taka; pagtataka; pangiñgilalas.

Amazon-*n*-Babaying malakas at may ugaling lalaki.

Ambassador-*n*-Katiwala ñg isang Gobierno sa ibang lupa.

Ambassadress-*n*-Ang asawa ñg ambassador.

Ambiguous-*a*-Mararami ang kahulugan.

Ambiguity-*n*-Pagkarami ñg mga kahulugan.

Ambition-*n* Sipag; nais; pita.

Ambitious-*a*-Masipag; mapita.

Amble-*v*-Lumakad; magpasial.

Ambulance-*n*-Ambulansa.

Ambulatory-*a*-Makalalakad.

Ambuscade-*n*-Harañgin; pagharang.

Ambuscade-*v*-Harañgin; sabatin.

Ambush-*r*-Harang.

Ambush-*v*-Harañgin; sabatin; sumaklaw.

Ameliorate-*v*-Butihin; bumuti.

Amelioration-*n*-Pagbubuti.

Amen-*adv*.-Siya nawa.

Amen-n-Ang siya nawa.

Amenable-a-Mananagotin; makapaparusa

Amend-v-Baguhin, ibahin.

Amendatory-a-Makaiiba; makababago.

Amendment-n-Dagdag, pagkabuti.

Amends-n-Ganti.

Amenity-n Kagandahan ng loob, kagalangan.

American n-Tawong taga America, Americano.

American-n-Nauukol sa America.

Americanism-n-Ang pagkagusto sa America.

Americanize-v-Gawin parang America, Gawin parang Americano.

Amiable a-Magsusunuran; mairog, mairogin; dapat ibigin.

Amiability-n-Kabutihan ng loob; kainaman ng asal.

Amicable-a-Masusunurin; tahimik, magkakaibigan, mabait, mabini

Amicability-n-Kabutihan ng ugali ó loob; kabaitan, kabinian.

Amid-Amidst-prep.-Sa pagitan.

Amiss-a-Mali.

Amiss-adv.-Hindi tama, may sala

Amity n-Pagkakaibigan.

Ammonia-n-Espiritu de amonia.

Ammunition-n-Mga kartucho ó bala ng baril.

Amnesty-n-Pagkakalimot, patawad.

Amnesty-v-Patawarin.

Among-Amongst-prep -Sa pagitan

Amorous-a-Mahilig sa pagibig, magiliw, maningas ang loob.

Amount-v-Umabot; abutin, sumapit; magkahalaga.

Amount-n-Halaga, kalahatan; kabuoan.

Amphitheatre-n-Teatro.

Ample-a-Maluang, husto; sapat, sagana; aliwalas, malawak

Amplify-v-Habaan, laparan, gawing husto, luangan.

Amplitude n-Kalakihan, kahustuhan; kasaganaan.

Amputate-v-Putlin, pugotin

Amputation-n-Pagpuputol; pagpugot.

Amuck-a-Pabaya, walang ingat.

Amuse-v-Giliwin, lituhin, mag aliw; magpasaya, sumaya.

Amusement-n-Kasayahan, aliwan, saya; paglilibang, libang, pag aaliw.

An-a-Isang, isa, sang.

Anaconda-n-Sawá.

Anaesthesia n-Kawalan ng damdam.

Anaesthetic-n-Gamot na pangpatulog.

Anal-a-Nauukol sa tumbong .

Analagous-a Kamukha, nagkakahawig.

Analogy-n-Pagkakahawig.

Analysis-n-Pagsasaysay; salaysay

Analyst-n-Ang nagsasaysay.

Analytic-Analytical-c-Nauukol sa Kasaysayan

Analyze-v-Saysayin; magsaysay, salaysayin.

Anarch-n-Ang autor ng kataksilan laban sa Gobierno.

Anarchist-n Ang lumalaban sa Gobierno.

Anarchy-n-Ang kataksilan laban sa Gobierno; Pag aalsa.

Anastrophe-n-Pagkabaliktad ng dating ayos ó kahusayan.

Anatomic-Anatomical a-Nauukol sa katawan ó sa paghihiwa ng katawan.

Anatomist-n-Ang marunong tungkol sa katawan.

Anatomize-v-Siyasatin ang katawan.

Anatomy-n-Ang karunungan tungkol sa katawan.

Ancestor-n-Nuno, kanunuan, pinagbuhatan; pinangalingan. (nauukol sa tawo).

Ancestral-a-Nauukol sa kanunuan.

Ancestry-n-Kanunuan.

Anchor-n-Sinepete, kasangkapan na gigamit sa pagpundo ng sasakyan.

Anchor-v-Sumadsad; pumundo dumoeng.

Anchorage-n-Doongan, punduhan

Anchored-a-Nakapundo, nakasadsad.

Anchovy-n-Halobaybay

Ancient-a-Matanda, luma, unang, laon.

Ancient-a Unang tawo.

And-conj.-At, saka.

Anecdote-n-Aral na patnugot.

Anew-adv.-Pambago; bago, uh, muli; uht.

Angel-n-Angel.

Angelic-a-Parang angel; mukhang angel; nauukol sa angel

Anger-n-Galit, kasamaan ng loob, kapootan, pagkagalit, sama ng loob.

Anger-v-Pagalitan. yamotin, magpagalit.

Angle-n-Sulok; liko, gawing labas ng panulukan

Angle-v-Mangisda, magbinwit.

Angler-n-Ang nagbibinwit.

Angrily-adv -Magalit, pagalit,

Angry-a-Galit, nagagalit, masama ang loob.

Anguish-n-Kahirapan, hapis, hirap; sakit, dalita, dawis, hambal, hinagpis, pighati, lumbay.

Angular-a-Maraming panulukan, mapanulukan.

Angularity-n-Karamihan ng mga panulukan.

Angularly-adv -Mapanulukan

Anil-n-Tinang azul nangagaling sa India

Anmal-*n*-Hayop
Animate-*i*-Buhayin, paliksihin, pagilasin
Animate-*a*-Buhay, maliksi
Animated-*a* Buhay, maliksing maliksi
Animation-*n*-Pagpaliksi
Animosity *n* Galit.
Ankle-*n*-Kasukasuan
Anklet-*n* Sankap na i-inusuot sa ka-sukosnan
Annals-*n*-Mĝa kasaysayan tungkol sa historia
Anneal-*v*-Painitin at pagkatapos ay palamigin sa tubig, timplahin
Annex-*v* Dugtungin
Annex-*n*-Dugtong karugtong
Annexed-*a*-Nakadugtong, kasama
Annexation-*n*-Pagkakarugtong
Annihilate *a*-Lipulin.
Annihilation-*v*-Paglipol, pagpapalipol
Anniversary-*a*-Taon taon
Anniversary-*n*-Kapistahan
Announce-*i*-Magbalita, magsabi, ipaha-yag, magpahayag, ibalita, magbigay alam, tumawag; tawagin ipaunawa
Announcement *n*-Balita, pahayag; tawag babala, paunawa
Annoy-*v*-Yamutin, pagalitin, payamutin, pasuklamin
Annoy-*n*-Pighati, galit, yamot
Annoyance *n*-Pagpagalit, yamot, suklam galit, kayamutan
Annual-*a* Mangyayari sa taon taon
Annual-*n*-Ang nangyayari sa taon taon
Annually-*adv*-Sa taon taon
Annuity-*n*-Salaping tinatangap sa taon taon
Annul-*i*-Pawalan ang kabuluhan
Annular-Annulary-*a*-Nauukol sa sing-sing ó buklod.
Annunciate-*v*-Ipahayag, ipaunawa.
Annunciation-*n* Pahayag, pagpapaha-yag, paunawa, pagpapaunawa
Annus *n*-Tumbong
Anodyne *n*-Gamot na pangpaigi nĝ sakit.
Anoint *v*-Buhusan ó pahiran nĝ langis
Anomalism-*n*-Ang kawalan nĝ pagsunod sa regla
Anomalistic-Anomalistical *a*-Hindi su-musunod sa anomang regla.
Anomaly-*n*-Pag lihis sa regla
Anon-*adv*-Agad, mayamia, sa ibang pa-nahon noong, muli
Anonimous-*a*-Di nakikilala, walang pirma.
Another *a*-Iba, isa pa.
Answer-*n*-Sagot, tugon, pag-sasagot, tutol, kasagutan
Answer-*v*-Sagutin, tumugon, sumagot, tumutol

Answerable-*a*-Masasagutin, makasasa got
Ant-*n* Langam
Ant eater-*n*-Hayop na kumakain nang langam
Antagonism-*n*-Pag lalaban, pagtatalo, laban, talo, away, salang-sang
Antagonist-*n*-Kalaban, katalo
Antagonize *v*-Lumaban, magtalo, suma-langsang
Antarctic *a*-Antaitico
Antecedent-*a*-Nauna, unang
Antecedent-*n*-Ang nasasa una
Antedate-*n*-Unang fecha o bilang nĝ panahon
Antedate *v*-Ilagay nang fechang naka-iaan
Antediluvian *a*-Nauuna sa pag lubog nĝ sang kalibutan sa panahon ni Noah
Antediluvian-*n*-Ang tawong nabuhay nauna sa paglubog nĝ mundo
Antelope-*n*-Isang hayop sa iamo na kamukha nĝ usa
Antemeridian-*a*-Sa umaga
Antenuptial-*a*-Nauuna sa kasal
Antepaschal-*a*-Nauukol sa kuaresma
Anterior-*a* Sinusundan, nauna
Anthem-*n*-Kanta sa simbahan
Anthropoid-*a*-Mukhang tawo, makaka hawig sa tawo
Anthropoid *n*-Ungong malaki.
Anthropology-*n*-Ang karunungan tung-kol sa sariling katawan
Antic *n*-Kilos; kilos na nakakatawa
Antic-*v*-Kumilos nĝ nakakatawa.
Antichrist-*n*-Ang ayaw sumampalataya sa Dios
Antichristian *a*-Nauukol sa Antichristi
Anticipate *v*-Iagap, ipagpauna, iunahan, umuna, kilalanin maagap.
Anticipation-*n*-Agap, pag aasahan
Antidote *n*-Gamot na panlaban sa ka-mandag.
Antipathy-*n*-Pighati, kapighatian, kasuk-laman, suklam, galit
Antipathetic-*a*-Mapighati, masuklam
Antipode-*n*-Ang tawong tumitira sa ka-bila nĝ mundo
Antiquarian-*a*-Nauukol sa unang pañahon.
Antiquated-*a*-Luma, matanda, malaon.
Antique *a*-Luma, matanda, malaon
Antique-*n*-Anomang bagay na lumang luma ó matanda
Antiquity-*n*-Laon, katandaan
Antiseptic-*a*-Laban sa bulok
Antiseptic-*n*-Gamot na panlaban sa ka-bulukan
Antler *n*-Sungay nĝ usa

Anvil-*n*-Palihan
Anxious-*a* Balisa, masikap
Any-*a*-Ilang, manga
Anybody-*n* Sinoman
Apace *adv* -Matulin; bigla, pabigla,
Apart *adv* -Nakabukod, nakahiwalay.
Apartment-*n*-Silid
Apathetic-*a*-Walang damdam
Apathy-*n* Kawalan ng damdam.
Ape-*n*-Bakulaw, ungong malaki
Ape-*v* Gumagad, gagarin.
Aperture-*n* Butas
Apex-*n*-Dulo '
Apiary-*n*-Lugar ng magalaga ng manga
  pokyutan
Apiece-*adv* Balang isa
Apish-*a* Mukhang ungo, parang ungo
Apod-*n*-Hayop na walang paa
Apodal-*a*-Walang paa, nauukol sa ha-
  yop na walang paa
Apologetic-Apologetical-*a*-Nauukol s a
  paghingi ng patawad
Apologist-*n* Ang humihingi ng tawad.
Apologize-*v*-Humingi ang tawad, mag-
  dahilan, tumangkakal.
Apologue-*n*- ! alinhaga
Apology-*n*-Dahilan, tangkakal, paghi-
  ngi ng tawad, pagdadahilan
Apoplexy-*n*-Hipan ng hangin.
Aport *adv* -Sa gawing kaliwa
Apostasy-*n*-Pagtatalikod sa dating pana-
  nampalataya.
Apostle *n*-Apostoles
Apostleship-*n*-Ang pagka apostoles
Apostolic-Apostolical-*a*-Nauukol sa Apos-
  toles, Apostolico
Apostrophe-*n*-Kurlit na ginagamit sa
  lugai na may laktaw ng isang titik.
Apostrophize-*v*-Ilagay ng kurlit
Apothecary-*n*-Ang marunong ilahok ó
  gumawa ng mga gamot
Appall-*v*-Takutin.
Apparatus-*n*-Kasangkapan
Apparel-*n*-Manga damit
Apparel-*v*-Isuot ang damit
Apparent-*a*-Maliwanag, makakikita.
Apparently-*adv* -Maliwanag, tila
Apparition-*n* Pagsipot, pag litaw
Appeal-*n*-Panalangin, daing, pakiusap,
  luhog
Appeal-*v*-Dumaing, manalangin, ipaki-
  usap, iluhog
Appear-*v*-Lumitaw; sumipot, sumilang,
  sumikat; suminaw; matagpuan.
Appearance-*n*-Hitsura, pagsipot, pagsi-
  kat, tabas, tingin sa labas, palitaw.
Appease-*v*-Humimpil, magpatahimik; pa-
  tahimikin, pumayapa, tumahimik.
Appendix-*n*-Ang nakadugtong
Appertain-*v*-Maukol, marapat, matungkol

Appetite *n*-Ang pagkagusto sa pag. kain
Appetize-*v*-Magbigay lasa
Applaud *v*-Ipagdiwang, purihin
Applause-*n*-Pagdiwang, pagpupuri
Apple-*n*-Mansanas
Appliance *n* Kasangkapan; pag gamit
Applicable-*a*-Bagay, akma
Applicant-*n* Ang humihingi ng distino
  ó trabajo
Application *n*-Paglihingi ng distino ó
  trabajo
Apply-*v*-Gamitin, ikapit, ikama, guma-
  mit
Appoint-*v* -Maglagay; pilin
Appointee-*n*-Ang nakalagay sa katung-
  kulan.
Appointment-*n*-Distino, katungkulan
Apportion-*v*-Ipamahagi, ipamudmod, ha-
  tiin
Apportionment-*n*-Paghahati, pamama-
  hagi
Apposite-*a*-Bagay, akma, karapatan.
Apposition-*n*-Paglaban, laban, dagdag,
Appraise-*v*-Halagahan, ilagay ang ha-
  laga, lagyan ng halaga, tasahan
Appraisal-*n*-Pagtatasa, paglalagay ang
  halaga
Appraisement-*n*-Paglalagay ng halaga;
  katasahan, paghahalaga.
Appreciable-*a* Dapat mahalin
Appreciate-*v*-Igalang, magalingin, ma-
  halin, maibigan
Appreciation-*n* Paggalang, pagmamahal
Apprehend-*v*-Hulihin; dakipin idakip.
Apprehender-*n*-Ang dumakip, taga huli.
Apprehension-*n*-Hiraya, akalang mali.
Apprehensive-*a* Maguniguniin
Apprentice-*n*-Ang nagaaral ng hanap-
  buhay ó katungkulan
Apprentice-*v*-Aralan
Apprenticeship-*n*-Pag aaral
Apprise-*v* Ibalita, ipahayag
Approach-*v* Lumapit sumapit, ilapit;
Approach-*n*-Daan sa paglapit, paglapit.
Approachable-*a*-Makakalapit
Approbation-*n*-Pahintulot.
Approbative *a*-Makapapahintulot
Approbatory-*a*-Mapahintulotan
Appropriate *v*-Ariin, umari, lupigin,
  umankin; ankinin; kaniyahin.
Appropriate-*a*-Bagay, akma.
Appropriation-*n*-Pagkalupig, pagaankin,
  pagbubukod ng anoman
Approve-*v*-Pahintulotin magpatotoo, ma-
  galingin
Approval-*n* Pahintulot, katotohanan.
Approximate-*v*-Dumulog; ilapit
Approximate *a*-Malapit.
Approximation-*n* Paglapit; katasahan;
  pagkakalapat

Appertenance-*n*-Pagkaukol.

Apprcot-*n*-Bunğang kahoy na kamukha nğ mansanas.

April-*n*-Abril.

Apron-*n*-Topise

Apropos-*a*-Bagay; mabagay, akma.

Apt-*a*-Bagay, akma; dapat, marapat, kasia, sukat, sapat; nauukol, ukol.

Aptitude-*n*-Kabagayan; kasanayan; kasukatan, kaya.

Aqua-*n*-Tubig

Aquarium-*n*-Estanke. na kinalalagyan nğ manğa isda ó hayop sa tubig.

Aquatic-*a*-Nauukol sa tubig.

Aqueduct-*n*-Sangka.

Aqueous-*a*-Parang tubig.

Aquiline-*a*-Nauukol sa aguila.

Arab-*n*-Taga Arabia.

Arabic-*a*-Nauukol sa Arabia.

Arabic-*n*-Wika nğ taga Arabia.

Arable *a*-Dapat ararohin.

Arbiter-*n*-Hukom

Arbitrary-*a*-Mabagsik; masunğit, mabanğis; matigas ang ulo

Arbitrate-*v*-Pakingan at magpasiya.

Arbitration *n*-Pagkasunduan.

Arbor-*n*-Kahoyan

Arboreous-*a*-Nauukol sa mğa kahoy.

Arborescent-*a*-Mukhang kahoy.

Arc-*n*-Balanğaw, arco.

Arcade-*n*-Mğa arcong nakasunosunod.

Arcanum-*n*-Lihim.

Arch *n*-Arco; hubog.

Arch-*v*-Humubog, gumawa nğ arco

Arch-*a*-Kaunaunahan, puno, malaki sa lahat

Arched *a*-Balantok; hubog

Archaic-*a*-Nalaon, luma.

Archangel-*n*-Angel na kataastaasan.

Archbishop-*n*-Arsobispo.

Archdeacon-*n*-Puno sa simbahan at mababa lamang sa arsobispo.

Archer *n*-Ang nagpapana.

Archery-*n*-Ang pagpapana.

Archipelago-*n*-Kapuluan.

Architect-*n*-Ang gumawa nğ plano ng bahay.

Architectural-*a*-Nauukol sa paggawa nğ bahay.

Architecture-*n*-Ang karunuñgan sa paggawa nğ bahay.

Archives-*n*-Mğa sulat nğ isang Gobieno.

Archway-*n*-Daan sa ilalim nğ arco.

Arctic *a*-Nauukol sa Hilagaan.

Ardent-*a*-Maninğas; mainit; maalab.

Ardor-*n*-Init, kaninğasan; ninğas

Ardurous-*a* Matibay, maninğas; mainit, malakas; batibot, masunğit.

Are-*v*-Ay.

Are-*n*-Isang sukat na lupa na may isang daan metros quadrados.

Area-*n*-Laki nğ isang lupa.

Arena-*n*-Lugar na pinag labanan.

Argal *n*-Tartaro.

Argent-*a*-Makintab, makinis.

Argentiferous-*a*-May halong pilak.

Argil *n*-Lupang ginagamit sa pag gagawa nğ tapayan.

Argillaceous-Argillous-*a*-May halong lupa.

Argol-*n*-Tartaro.

Argue-*v*-Magmatuiran; manğatowiran; makipagtalo. salitain, taltalan

Argument-*n*-Pagmamatuiran, taltalan; pagtalo, pinag usapan; katowiran

Argumentative-*a*-Nauukol - sa pagtatalo o panğatowiran.

Arid-*a*-Tuyo, karat.

Aridity-Aaidness-*n*-Pagkatuyo.

Aright-*adv*.-Tama.

Arise-*v*-Magbanğon, tumindig, bumanğon, magmula; magbuhat, umaliñgasaw.

Aristocrat *n*-Tawong mataas ó dakila.

Aristocratic-*a*-Mataas, dakila.

Arithmetic *n*-Aritmética.

Arithmetical-*a*-Nauukol sa aritmética.

Arithmetician-*n*-Ang marunong ang aritmetica.

Ark-*n*-Bangkang malaki at may bubunğan.

Arm-*n*-Baraso, bisik

Armament-*n*-Kasangkapan panlaban.

Armful *n*-Pangko.

Armhole-*n*-Kilikili, subo.

Armistice-*n*-Pagpapahinğa nğ labanan.

Armlet-*n*-Munting baraso.

Armor *n*-Ang bakal na nakalagay sa mğa tabi nğ sasakyang panlaban.

Armory-*n*-Gawaan nğ mğa kasangkapang panglaban, taguan nğ armas.

Armpit-*n*-Kilikili.

Arms-*n*-Armas; mğa sandata.

Army-*n*-Hukbo

Arnica-*n*-Arnica.

Aroma-*n*-Amoy.

Aromatic *a*-Mabanğo.

Around-*adv*.-Sa palıgıd, sa palibid, sa palibot, malapit

Around *prep*.-sa palıgıd, sa palibot, sa palibid

Arouse-*t*-Sulsulan, buhayin, hamunin.

Arow-*adv*.-Nakakahusay.

Arraign-*v*-Iharap sa Juez, ó sa hukom.

Arraignment-*n*-Pagpaharap sa hukom ó juez.

Arrange-*v*-Husayin, ayusin, ihanda, areglahin, igayak; magayos; iligpit.

Arrangement-*n*-Pagkakaayos,ayos;husay

Arrant-a-Masama; hamak.
Array-n-Husay, ayos.
Array-v-Ayusin husayin.
Arrear-Arrears Arrearage-v-Kakulangan, utang
Arrest-v-Ibilango; abalahin; ilagay sa bilanguan.
Arrest-n-Abala; pagkabilango
Arrival-n-Pagdating, pagdatal.
Arrive-v-Dumating, dumulog, lumapit; pumantay; sumapit, umabot; abutin.
Arrogance-n-Kapulaluan, kahambugan; kataasan
Arrogant-a-Hambog; palalo, mapaghangin.
Arrogate-v-Ankinin; kanyahin; lupigin.
Arrow-n-Pana.
Arsenal-n-Gawaan at taguhan ng mga kasangkapan ng hukbo
Arson-n-Pagsisigan ng ari ng may ari.
Art-n-Arte; karunungan.
Arterial-n-Nauukol sa ugat.
Artery-n-Ugat ng dugo
Artful-a-Tuso; matalas.
Article-n-Bagay, pangkat.
Article-r-Pumangkat.
Articular-a Nauukol sa kasukasuan.
Articulate-v Sabihin, wikain.
Articulately-adv -Isaisa
Articulation-n-Pagsasabi; pagwiwika.
Artifice-n-Lálang;
Artificer-n-Taga gawa; trabajador.
Artificial-a Ginawa lamang, hindi dati.
Artillery-n-Artilleria.
Artisan-n-Machanico, mangagawa.
Artist-n-Artista.
Artless-a-Banayad; mababang loob; muang, walang wasto.
As-adv -Gayon, din; rin, naman; man; kasing. paano
As yet adv -Bagaman.
Ascend v-Tumaas; umakyat, pumanhik, sumalunga, umahon, sumampa.
Ascendant-a Paahon.
Ascedency-n-Pagaahon, pagpaahon pagakyat, pagtataas.
Ascension-n-Pagaayat; pagaahon.
Ascent-n-Pagahon, pagpanhik.
Ascertain-v-Kilalanin; talastasin, siyasatin, tantuin, pasiyasatin.
Ascribe-v-Ilagay, ipalagay.
Ascription-n-Pakalagay.
Ash-n-Kahoy na maputi, malambot at matibay.
Ashamed-a-Nahihiya.
Ashen-a-Maabo.
Ashes-n-Abo.
Ashore-adv.-Nasasa baybay dagat; nasa pangpang, •
Ashy-a-Kulay abo.

Aside adv.-Sa tabi.
Asinine-a-Mukhang ó ugaling jumento.
Ask-v-Magtanong, itanong; ipakiusap; tumanong; manalangin.
Askant-Askance-a-Pahalang
Askew-adv.-Pahalang.
Aslant-adv.-Pahalang
Asleep-adv.-Natutulog.
Aslope-adv -Pababa; paliwas
Asp-n-Alupong.
Aspect-n-Hitsura; bikas; lagay; mukha; tabas.
Asperity-n-Higpit; kasungitan; kabagsikan, sukal ng loob; sama ng loob; kapaitan; kasamaan ng lasa.
Asperse-v-Pintasin; pumintas.
Aspersion-n Pintas.
Asphyxia-Asphyxy-n-Kalagayan parang patay; pagkalagay parang patay.
Aspirant-n-Ang may nasa, may gusto.
Aspirate-v-Itunog parang kung may kasamang h.
Aspiration-n-Nasa; pita, asa.
Aspire-v-Magpita; asahan.
Ass-n-Ulol; jumente
Assail-v-Mangloob, bungain, daluhungin, dumaluhong, gulatin; labanin
Assailant-n-Ang bumanga; ang dumaluhong; ang lumalaban.
Aassassin-n-Ang nakamatay; pumatay
Assassinate-v-Pumatay sa kapwa.
Assassination-n-Pagkapatay
Assault-n-Lusob, labanan; pag lusob, paghandulong, daluhong banga
Assault-v-Lumusob, lumaban, mangloob; dumaluhong; bumanga, bangain.
Assay-n-Tikim; pagtitikman.
Assay-v-Tikiman; uriin, maginasid namabuti ang metal
Assemblage-n-Kapisanan ng mga tawo.
Assemble-v-Magtipon.
Assembly-n-Kapisanan; tipan; katipunan, samahan.
Assent-n-pagkapayag.
Assent-v-Pumayag, umayon.
Assert-v-Sabihin; magsabi, alalayan; matumpakan
Assertion-n-Sabi; alalay; pagpatotoo, paniniwala.
Assertor-n-Ang nag aalalay; nagsabi; nagbalita
Assess v-Halagahan; tasahan.
Assessment-n-Paghalaga, halaga.
Assessor-n-Ang tumatasa
Assets-n-Ang yaman ng sarili.
Asseverate v-Magsabi ng formal
Asseveration a Pagsasabi ng totoo.
Assiduous-a-Masikap; makalinga
Assiduity -n- Pagkakalinga, sikap, sipag.

Assign-v-Ilagay, idistino maglagay, sa lugar, tadhanan, ibigay ng katungkulan

Assign n-Tadhana, talaan. ,

Assignable a-Makapagtadhanan, matatalaan.

Assignee-n-Ang nagtatadhan ó nagtatala.

Assigner-Assignor-n-Ang · nagtatadhan ó nagtatala

Assignment-n Pagkalagay sa distino, pagkatadhanan pagtatala.

Assimilate-t-Iparis, imukha, itulad, tularan, magkawangis

Assimilation-n-Pagkakaparis; pagkakatulad, pagkakawangis

Assist-v-Tumulong, tulungin, abuluyin, umabuloy, gumibik, ampunin, umampon, lubukan, andukham

Assistance n-Ampon, tulong, abuloy; andukha, gibik, katulong, tangkakal.

Assistant-a-Pangalawang

Assistant-n-Ayudante, katulong, pangalawa

Associate-v-Ipisan; isama kamiyawin; pumisan; magsangayon; sumama; sumamib

Associate a-Kasamang

Associate-n-Katulong, kaulayaw, kasama, kaiamay, kaalakbay, abay.

Association-n-Pagsasama; pagpipisan, pagkapisan, pagkaalay.

Assort-t-Hiwalayin, ibukod.

Assortment-n-Paghihiwalay, pagbubukod, manga sarisaring bagay na nakakapisan. ·

Assuage-v-Bantuan, palubayin

Assuasive-a-Palambotlambot

Assume t-Gamitin; magpalagay

Assumption n-Pagkapalagay, palagay.

Assurance n-Patotohanan, patunayan, pangako.

Assure-v-Magpatotoo.

Assuredly-adv.-Totoongtotoo.

Aster-n Bulaklak na marikit at mabango ang amoy.

Astern-adv -Sa gawing likod, sa likod.

Asteroid-n-Kometang munti.

Asteroid n-Hika.

Astonish-v-Gitlahin, magpatulala; gulatin, hangalin, tulalain

Astonishing a-Kagitlagitla, nakamamangha.

Astonishment-n-Mangha; gitla, gulat.

Astound v-Imangha; magpamangha.

Astraddle-adv.-Pahalang.

Astral-a-Naunkol sa bituin.

Astray-adv.-Nakawala.

Astride-adv.-Nakasaysay

Astrologer-n-Ang humuhula ang mangyayari dahil sa bituin.

Astronomer-n-Ang nagaaral ng bituin.

Astronomoy-n Ang karunungan sa manga bituin

Astute-a-Bihasa, tuso, marunong

Asunder-adv -Nakasabog, nakahiwalay.

Asylum-n-Bahay ng manga ulol, auspicio

At-prep -Sa

Ate-v imp -Kumain

Atheism-n-Ang pagkaayaw sumampalataya sa P. Bathala.

Atheist-n-Ang ayaw sumampalataya sa P Bathala

Athirst-a-Nauuhaw, mapita, maasahan.

Athlete-n-Tawong malakas at sanay

Athletic-a-Naunkol sa tawong malakas at sanay, inalakas at sanay.

Athwart-adi -Pahalang.

Atlantic-n-Atlantico

Atlas-n-Kapisanan ng manga mapa sa isang libro.

Atmosphere-n-Hangin.

Atmospheric- Atmospherical a-Nauukol sa hangin, mahangin

Atoll v-Gantihin, magtis, bawin

Atom-n-Puasong, muntingmunti

Atomic-Atomical-a-Muntingmunti

Atomize-v-Pirasuhin nang finongpino gawin ng parang alikabok.

Atone-t-Magtis, gantihin, bawin.

Atonement-n-Pag gaganti, pagtitis.

Atop-adv.-Sa ibabaw, sa itaas.

Atrocious a-Katakot takot, kakilakilabot; bastos

Atrocity-n-Kabastosan, kawalanghiyaan.

Attach-v-Idugtong; mahalin

Attachment-n-Dugtong; sangla, pagibig.

Attack v Labanin, bangain; bumanga; makipag lamas; lumusob, harangin, magbangay

Attack-n-Pag aalsa, pgg laban, banga; laban, lunas, dalusong; dalusong.

Attain-v-Magkaroon, umabot, abutin, magkamitgn, kamtan, datnin.

Attainable a-Makakaabot, maabot, makakamtan; sukat makamtan.

Attainment-n-Pag aabot, pagkakamtan

Attempt-v-Tikman, mulaan, pamulain.

Attempt n-Tikhim; pagtitikman; paglihisay.

Attend-v-Dalawin; dumalaw; sumama; magingat, ingatin; mamahala, manuod.

Attendance-n-Pagiingat; paghilingkod; · panunuod

Attendant n-Alila.

Attention-n-Ingat, sipag, pagkakalinga.

Attentive-a-Maingat mahinhin: makalinga; maanyo; mapagbigay loob.

Attenuate-v Awasan ang taba, pahinahin

Attest-*v*-Sumaksi; magsabi ñg katotohanan.

Attestation-Pagkasaksi; pagsasabi nang katotohanan

Attic-*n*-Ang loob ñg bubuñgan.

Attire *v*-Magbihis, isuot.

Attitude-*n*-Tayo; lagay, hilig; kiling.

Attorney-*n*-Katiwala, abogado, taga kanlong.

Attract-*v*-Hikayatin, humikayat.

Attract by deceit-*v*-Mañgati

Attraction-*n*-Paghalina, panghinang; panghikayat.

Attractive-*a*-Mawili; nakahahalina, mapanghalina, mapanghikayat

Attribute-*v*-Magparatang magpalagay.

Attribution-*n*-Pagparatang, pagsumbong, pagpalagay.

Attributive-*a*-Mapaparatañgin

Auburn-*n* Kulay kayumanging mura

Auction-*n*-Almoneda.

Auctioneer-*n*-Ang may katungkulang mag almoneda

Auctioneer-*v*-Mag almoneda.

Audacious-*a*-Matapang, mañgahas; walang takot; tampalasan, walang hiya

Audacity-*n*-Pañgahas, tapang katampapalasanan.

Audible-*a*-Makaririnig.

Audience-*n*-Ang mañga nanunuod.

Audit-*v* Isulat ó ilista sa libro Siyasatin ang nakasulat sa libro.

Audit-*n*-Pagsisiyasat ñg mañga libro.

Auditor-*n*-Ang dumirig, taga siyasat ñg mañga libro

Auditory-*n*-Ang mañga nanunuod

Auger-*n*-Balibol, bariena; pangbutas.

Aught-*n*-Wala, walang anoman

Augment-*v*-Dagdagan kumapal; lumaki; ipaibabaw, dumami, damihan, patuñgan, salopinlin, palakhin.

Augment-*n*-Patong, dagdag, tubo,

Augmentation-*n*-Patong, dagdag: pagdaragdag, pagtutubo, pagpalaki;

Augur-*n*-Pangbutas; barrena

Augur-*v* barrenahin, butasin

Augury-*n*-Hula.

August *a*-Mainam, dakila, marañgal.

August-*n*-Agosto.

Agustness-*n*-Kadakilaan, karañgalan, kainaman.

Aunt-*n*-Ale.

Aural-*a*-Nauukol sa taiñga

Aurich-*n*-Taiñga

Auricular-*a*-Nauukol sa taiñga

Aurist-*n*-Mangagamot ñg taiñga.

Aurora-*n*-Madaling araw.

Auspicious-*a*-Makakabuti ang hula

Austere-*a*-Mabagsik; masuñgit

Austerity-*n*-Kabagsikan, kasuñgitan.

Authentic-*a*-Totoo, tama, tunay.

Authenticate-*v*-Magsabi ó ibigay ñg katotohanan.

Authentication-*n*-Pagbibigay ó pagsasabi ñg katotohanan.

Authenticity-*n*-Ang katotohan.

Author-*n*-Ang gumagawa; mang gagawa; autor, may gawa

Authoress-*n*-Ang babaying autor.

Authoritative *a*-Makapangyayari; may kapangyarihan.

Authority-*n*-Kapangyarihan; pahintulot; bisa.

Authorization-*n*-Pahintulot.

Authorize-*v* Pahintulutin; ibigay ñg kapangyarihan.

Authorship-*n*-Ang kalagayan autor.

Autobiography-*n*-Ang pagsusulat nang sariling kabuhayan.

Autocrat-*n*-Hari.

Autocratic-Autocratical-*a*-Nauukol sa hari, mabagsik, masuñgit

Autograph-*n*-Ang sulat ñg sarili.

Autographic-Autographical-*a*-Nauukol sa sulat ñg sarili.

Automatic-Automatical-*a*-Talagang sumusunod na walang magturo

Autonomy-*n*-Ang kapangyarihan ó katowiran na magogobierno sa sarili.

Autopsy-*n* Pag uusisa ñg dahilan ñg kamatayan.

Autumn-*n*-Tag araw

Autumnal-*a*-Nauukol sa tagaraw.

Auxiliar-Auxiliary-*a* Nakatulong

Auxiliary *n*-Katulong.

Avail *v* Ganapin; gumanap.

Avail-*n*-Pag ganap.

Available-*a*-Makaganap.

Avalanche-*n*-Tibag ñg busilak

Avarice-*n*-Kamkani, karamutan, sakim; kasakiman, kaingitan, ingit.

Avaricious-*a*-Masakim; matakaw; kuripot, maramot.

Avast-*inter*-Lumayas; layas.

Avaunt-*inter*-Layas; sulong; maalis

Avenge-*v*-Gantihin

Avenue-*n*-Pasialan, Carsadang mahaba at may tanim na mga punong kahoy sa dalawang tabi

Aver-*v* Patunayin, patotohanan; sabihin saysayin.

Average-*a*-Karaniwan; katatagan.

Average-*v*-Ilagay sa katatagan.

Average *n*-Katatagan.

Averse *a*-Ayaw; laban.

Aversion-*n*-Suklam nang loob; dumal; pighati; kasuklaman; tanim sa loob. Pagtataninm gatit.

Avert-*v*-Lihisan; ilayo, pigilin ang anoman upang huag mangyari.

22

Aviary-n-Lugar ng̃ mag alaga ng̃ mg̃a ibon.

Avidity-n-Nasang mahigpit.

Avocation-n-Hanap buhay.

Avoid-v-Lihisan, umilag; mahulagpos; ilagan

Avoidable-a-Dapat ilagan, mailagan.

Avoidance-n-Pag ilag, paliwas.

Avouch;v-Magsabi; saysayin.

Avow-v-Manumpa, magpatunay.

Avowal-n-Katibayan ng̃ salitaan, panumpa.

Avowedly-adv-Sadya, tinalaga.

Await-v-Hintayin, antayin, mag antay.

Awake-v-Gisiñgin gumising.

Awake-a-Buhay ang loob, gising, matalas ang isip.

Awaken-v-Gisiñgin, gumising, buhayin

Award-n-Premio; ganting palad.

Award-v-Magbigay ng̃ premio ó ganting palad.

Aware-a-Maiñgat,

Away-adv.-Malayo, sa labas ó malayo.

Awe-n-Mangha, gitla

Awe-v-Imangha. gitlain

Awful-a-Makapañgiñgilabot; kasindak-sindak, nakasisindak, dapat katakutan

Aweather-adv-Sa gawi ng̃ hañgin.

Awhile-adv.-Samantala.

Awkward-a-Bastos, di mainam

Awkwardness-n-Kawalan ng̃ ganda ng̃ kilos, kabastosan

Awl-n-Panduio

Awn-n-Tabing

Awning-n-Tabing; kulandong

Awoke-v. imp Nagising, ginising

Awry-a adv.-Masamang hitsura.

Ax-Axe-n-Palakol.

Axial-a-Nauukol sa palakol

Axiom-n-Patnugot, punong aral.

Axis-n-Likiran, ikiran.

Axle-Axletree-n-Lalikan; ikirah

Ay-Aye-adv -Oo.

Azore-a-Azul

Azure-n-Azul.

B

Baa n-Iyak ng̃ tupa.

Baa-v-Umiyak ng̃ tupa

Babble-v-Masalita ng̃ kaululan.

Babble-n-Salita na walang kabuluhan.

Babbler-n-Ang nagsasalita ng̃ walang kabuluhan.

Babe-n-Bata, sangol, nilalang.

Baboon-n-Ungong malaki.

Baby-n-Bata; sangol

Baby-a-Nauukol sa bata ó sa sangol.

Baby-hood-n-Panahon nang pagkabata; kalagayan bata

Babyish-a-Parang bata

Bachelor-n-Bagong tawong may edad, lalaking may edad at wala pang asawa.

Back-n-Likod.

Back-a-Sa gawing likod.

Back-v-Umurongang kabayo, tumalikod

Backbite-v-Sumitsit, magalibugha, magalimura.

Backbiting-n-Pagaalimura; sitsit; pagaalibugha.

Backbone-n-Gulugod.

Background-n-Lupa sa licuran.

Backhanded-a-Pasaliwa.

Backside-n-Ang likod

Backslide-v-Umurong tumalikod

Backward-Backwards-adv.-Nakaharap ang likod, sa gawing likod, sa panahon nakaraan, nakasasama.

Backward-a-Sa likod, nahihiya

Backwardness-n-Kaduagan, pagyuyukod, hiya, kaduagan

Backwoods-n-Gubat

Backwoodsman-n-Tawong gubat.

Bacon-n-Tosino

Bad-a-Masama; mahalay, bastos, walang kabuluhan.

Bad-Bade-v. imp -Inanyaya; ipinag utos

Badge-n-Tanda

Badger-v-Tuksuhin.

Badinage-n-Tukso.

Badly-adv.-Sa masamang paraan, nakasasama; papaano.

Badness-n-Kasamaan.

Baffle v Abalahin, talunin.

Bag n-Bayong saco, supot.

Bagging-n-Kayong ipinagagawang bayong.

Bagasse-v-Bagaso

Baggage-n-Ang baul ng̃ damit na dinala sa viage.

Bail-n Katibayan, panagutan.

Bail-n-Tangnan, panghimas.

Bail-v-Ibigay ng̃ katibayan, managot

Bail-v-Manglimas; maglimas.

Bailiff-n-Katiwala ó kahalili ng̃ sheriff.

Bairn-a-Bata.

Bait-n-Panghuli

Bait-v-Ilagay ng̃ panghuli.

Bake-v-Ihawin, magihaw; iluto sa hurno.

Bakery-n-Panaderia, gawaan ng̃ tinapay.

Balance-n-Timbang, pakaway, panimbang, ang natitirang utang utang o

Balance-v-Timbañgin, matimbang; tumimbang, magtnas.
Balcony-n-Balcon
Bald-a-Panot upat, uban
Bald-head-Baldpate-n-Tawong panot.
Baldheaded-a-Upat; panot
Balderdash-n-Lahok na walang kabuluhan.
Bale n-Bigkis, pamigkis.
Bale-i-Ibigkis, magbigkis
Bale-n-Kahirapan; kasalatan;
Baleful-a-Mahirap; salat.
Balk-n Abala; hinto; urong
Balk-v-Huag arniohin, huminto nğ pabigla, umurong
Balky-a-Palaurongan.
Ball n-Bola; anomang bagay na mabilog.
Ball-v-Gumawa nğ bola, maging bola
Ball-n-Sayawan
Ballad-n-Kanta; awit.
Ballast-n-Pangbigat na nalulan sa sasakyan.
Ballast-i-Ilulan nğ panbigat
Balloon-n-Globo nğ hangin na mainit.
Ballot-n-Voto; pagvovoto.
Ballot-v-Magboto.
Balm-n-Pabañgo
Balm-v-Pabañgohin.
Balmoral-n-Sapatos na mataas.
Balmay-a-Mabañgo.
Basam-n-Balsamo.
Baluster-n-Barandilhas, gabay.
Balustrade-n-Gabay.
Bamboo-n-Kawayan, buho; bucaue,
Bamboozle v-Hibuin, dayain
Ban-n-Hayag, hayag nğ kasal.
Ban-v-Tuñgayawin; ipagbawal, magbawal.
Banana-n-Saging
Band-n-Tali, bigkis; pamigkis, sintaron
Band-i-Talian, ibigkis
Band-n-Banda.
Bandage-n-Pamigkis, balot.
Bandage-i-Ipamigkis; balutin
Bandanna-n-Panyong mapula.
Bandbox-n-Lalagyan nğ sombrero
Bandit-n-Túlisan.
Bandy-n-Banda (Isang laro)
Bandy-v-Magbanda.
Bandylegged a-Mabilog ang binti.
Bane-n-Kamandag, kasamaan
Baneful-a-May kamandag, masama
Bang-v-Paluin
Bang-n-Palo; lagpak, putok
Bang-n-Mğa kulot malapit sa noo
Bang-v-Gupitin ang buntot nğ kabayo.
Bang-Bangue-n-Gamot na may halong kamandag.
Bangle-n-Pulcera.

Bainsh-v-Itapon ang may sala sa ibang lupa ó lugar, ipadistierro
Banishment-n-Pagpapanawin, pagpapaalis; pagdidistierro; pagkatapon nğ may sala sa ibang lupa ó lugar.
Banister-n-Barandillas, gabay.
Banjo-n-Banduria.
Bank-n-Pangpang; tabi nğ ilog, tibagan.
Bank-v-Magpilapil.
Bank-n-Pilapil.
Bank-n-Bangko
Bank-v-Ilagay nğ salapi sa bangko.
Banker-n-Ang may ari nğ bangko
Banking-n-Katungkulan nğ may bangko.
Bankrupt-n-Ang hindi makakabayad nğ kanyang utang.
Bankrupt-a-Hindi makakabayad ang utang
Bankrupt-v-Ubusin ang salapi ó puhunan na kailañgan sa isang negocio ó sa pañgañgalakal, tunawin.
Bankruptcy-n-Kalagayan na hindi makakabayad ang utang.
Banner-n Bandila, bandera
Banns-n-Pahayag nğ kasal, tawag sa simbahan nğ mğa may ibig mag asawa.
Banquet-n-Piging, pista, kainan
Banquet v-Pigiñgin, ipiging, magpiging.
Bantam-n-Manok na nangaling sa Javia.
Banter-n-Biro, tukso
Banter-v-Biruin; tuksuhin.
Bantling-n-Batang munti; sangol.
Baptism-n-Pagbibinyag, pagkabinyag.
Baptismal-a-Nauukol sa pagbibinyag.
Baptist-n-Ang nagbibinyag.
Baptize-v-Magbinyag, binyagin; buminyag.
Bar-n-Bara; kapisanan nğ mğa abogado.
Bar-v-Barahin; iwaksi, ifuera; ibukod,
Barb-n-Balbas
Barb-n-Tinik nğ kawad.
Barbarian-n-Tawong salbahi; salbahi, tawong hindi marunong.
Barbarian-a-Nauukol sa salbahi.
Barbaric-a-Salbahi
Barbarity-n-Kasalbahihan.
Barbarous-a-Salbahi,
Barber-n-Mangugupit, mang ahit
Bard-n-Poeta
Bare a-Walang damit ó takip; hubo, hubad.
Bare-v-Ahsin ang takip, maghubo, mag hubad
Barefaced-a-Walang hiya
Barefoot-a-Walang sinelas; hubo ang paa, walang sapin.
Barely-a-halos hindi, laman
Bargain-n-Pinagkasunduan; kasulatan.
Bargain v-Magusap.

Barge-*n*-Kasko
Baritone-*n*-Voces ng̃ lalaki na kung kumanta ay alang̃anin
Bark-*n*-Balat ng̃ kahoy
Bark-*v*-Alisan ng̃ balat; upakin; kumakaw, talupan
Bark-*n*-Tahul
Bark-*v*-Tumahul
Bark-Barque-*n*-Sasakyan na may tatlong palo at layag.
Barley-*n*-Sebada
Barm-*n*-Labadura.
Barmy-*a*-May halong lavadura.
Barn-*n*-Caballeriza; bahay ng̃ hayop.
Barnacle-*n*-Talaan na dumidikit sa mg̃a bato at sasakyan
Barometer-*n*-Kasangkapang panghula ng̃ panahon.
Barouche-*n*-Carruage.
Barque-*n* Sasakyan na may tatlong palo at tatlong layag
Barrack-*n*-Cuartel, balankas.
Barrack-*v*-Tumira sa cuartel.
Barrel-*n* Bariles
Barrel-*v*-Ilagay ó isilid sa bariles.
Barren-*a*-Tuyo; tuyot, karat,di mamung̃a
Barren-*n*-Karat na lupa, lugar na ilang.
Barricade-*n*-Kutang munti.
Barricade-*v*-Magkuta, ilagay ng̃ kuta
Barrier-*n*-Pangharang; abala.
Barrister-*n*-Abogado
Barrom-*n*-Tindahan ng̃ alak.
Barrow-*n*-Kareton, na may isang gulong; lamang
Barrow-*n*-Baboy na kinapon.
Barrow-*n* Gulod
Barter *n*-Palit
Barrytone-*n*-Voces na alang̃anin.
Barytone-*a*-Alang̃anin ay voces.
Basalt-*n*-Batong matigas
Base *a*-Masama, mababa; hamak; mahalay.
Base-*n*-Fondo, paa
Base-*v* Ilagay sa fondo ó paa.
Baseball-*n*-Besbol.
Basement-*n*-Silong.
Baseness-*n*-Kahamakan; kahalayan
Bashaw-*n*-Maginoo sa turkia.
Bashful-*a*-Nahihiya
Bashfulness-*n*-Kahimpakhimpakan; hinhin; kahihiyasn: hiya; karuagan, kimpot.
Basin-*n*-Palangana.
Basis-*n*-Pinagmulaan, pinagbuhatan.
Bask-*v*-Magbilad; ibilad.
Basket-*n*-Batulang; bakol; bugsok, buslo; kaing.
Bass-*n*-Voces na mababa
Bass-*a*-Mababa ang voces.
Bass viol-*n*-Viola.
Baste *v*-Ihilbana.

Basting-*n*-Hilbana,
Bat-*n* Bayakan, paniki.
Bat-*n*-Pumalo.
Bat-*v*-Pumalo.
Batch-*n* Hang̃o.
Bath-*n*-Liguan pahligo, pagpapaligo.
Bathe-*v*-Mahgo, paliguan.
Bathe-*n*-Ligo.
Batsman-*n*-Ang pumapalo.
Battalion-*n*-Isang bahagi ng̃ hukbo na may apat na daan sundalo.
Batten-*v*-Patabain, yumaman
Batten-*v*-Tapalin.
Batten-*n*-Tablang makipot, panapal.
Batter-*v*-Pitpitin
Batter-*n*-Pinagbatihan
Batter *n*-Ang pumapalo.
Battery *n*-Kuta na may kanyon, isang companiang sundalong artilleria.
Batting-*n*-Ang pagpalo.
Battle-*n*-Pag laban; labanán, pag aaway.
Bauble-*n*-Bagay na walang halaga.
Bawl-*v*-Sumigaw, umiyak ng̃ malakas
Bawl *n*-Sigaw, hiyaw, iyak na malakas
Bay-*n*-Baraso ng̃ dagat
Bay-*a*-Mapula
Bay-*n*-Tahol.
Bay-*v* tumahol.
Bayonet-*n*-Bayneta
Bayonet-*v*-Saksakin ng̃ bayneta.
Bayou-*n*-Baraso ng̃ dagat
Bayrum-*n*-Rum y quinina
Bazaar-Bazar-*n*-Basar.
Be-*v*-Ay, mag; yari, magka
Beach-*n*-Baybay dagat,
Beach-*v*-Ilagay sa baybay dagat
Beacon-*n*-Siga na pananda
Bead-*n*-Batong munti na may butas
Bead-*v* Ituhog ang kuntas
Beadle-*n*-Utusan na taga tawag nang hukom.
Beagle-*n*-Asong munti na ginagamit sa pang̃ang̃aso.
Beak-*n*-Tuka.
Beaked-*a*-May tuka.
Beaker-*n*-Tabo
Beam-*n*-Kilo, ana man pinga (*of aplow*) Kabayo ng̃ araco.
Beam-*v*-Maningning, lumitaw, kumintab, ipalitaw.
Bean-*n*-Sitaw; patani
Bear-*v*-Tiisin; magtiis.
Bear-*n*-Oso
Bear-*v*-Ibaba ang halaga.
Bearable *a* Makatitiis.
Beard-*n*-Balbas.
Beard-*v*-Batakin ang balbas
Bearing-*n*-Kilos; asal; ugali.
Beast-*n*-Hayop.
Beastly-*a*-Bastos; parang hayop.

Beat-*n*-Palo; suko.
Beat-*v*-Pumalo, paluin, hampasin, da-gukan.
Beat-*v*-Lampasin, lusutin.
Beauteous-*a*-Maganda mainam marikit.
Beautiful *a*-Maganda, marikit, mainam
Beautify-*v*-Parikitan; gumanda; pagandahin; painamin
Beauty-*n*-Ganda; kainaman; karikitan, dikit; ganda, dilag, inam
Becalm-*v*-Humimpil; tumahimik; lumubay.
Became-*v. imp* -Nakabagay; naging
Because-*conj* -Sapagka't.
Bechance-*v*-Magkataon, mangyari.
Beck-*n*-Kaway, bati.
Beck-*v*-Kawayin; batiin
Beck-*n*-Sapa
Beckon-*v* Kawayin
Become-*v*-Mabagay, maging, maoui.
Becoming *a*-Bagay, akina
Bed-*n* Hihigan; tinutulugan, catre
Bed-*v*-Ilagay sa hihigan
Bedaub-*v*-Kulapulan, pahiran nğ putic
Bedclothes-*n*-Manğa damit nğ hihigan.
Bedew-*v*-Humamog
Bedfellow-*n*-Kasiping sa hihigan.
Bedim-*v*-Lumabo, labuin, dumilim.
Bedlam-*n*-Bahay na tinirahan nğ mğa ulol; gulo, kaguluhan.
Bedlam-*a*-Ulol.
Bedlamite-*n*-Ulol.
Bedrid-Bedridden-*a*-Ang hindi makababangon; ang nakafirme sa hihigan.
Bedroom-*n*-Silid na tulugan, tinutulugan.
Bedsheet-*n* Kumot na linso
Bedstead-*n*-Hihigan
Bedtime-*n*-Oras na dapat matulog.
Bee-*n*-Kumuino pukyutan.
Beech-*n*-Punong kahoy na tumutubo sa America.
Beef-*n*-Laman nğ baca ó calabaw
Beefsteak-*n*-Isang hiwa na manipis nğ laman nğ baca ó calabaw.
Beehive-*n*-Bahay pukyutan.
Beeline-*n*-Matowid na guhit
Been-*v. imp. & p p.*-Naging; nagka
Beeswax-*n*-Kalaba
Beetle-*v*-Pukpok na kahoy
Beetle-*v*-Pukpokin nğ pukpok na kahoy
Beetle-*n*-Bicho
Beeve-*n* Baca
Befall-*v*-Mangyari; magkataon.
Befit-*v* Maging bagay
Before-*prep*.-Nauna, umuna
Before-*adv*.-Muna, nauna
Beforehand-*adv*.-Naman.
Befoul-*v*-Bumulok, bulukin,

Befriend-*v*-Kupkupin,· tulunğin.
Beg-*v*-Magpalimos; pakiusapan; makiusap; sumamo; manalanğin; huminği.
Began-*v. imp* -Pinamulaan; nagmula.
Beget-*v*-Magkaroon, magkamtan.
Beggar-*n*-Pulubi; tawong walang hanap buhay at nagpapalimos, nagpapalimos.
Beggar-*v*-Magpahirap; upatin
Beggarly-*a*-Parang pulubi.
Beggary-*n*-Kalagayan nagpapalimos; pag papalimos
Begging-*n*-Pagpapalimos, pahinuhod
Begin-*v*-Magmula, pamulaan, banhain; pasimulaan, magbuhat; mulain; bumalong sumipot, magpasimuno.
Beginner-*n*-Bagong nag aaral.
Beginning-*n*-Pinagmulan, pinangalinğan, pamulan, pinagbuhatan; pamula.
Begone-*inter*.-Layas; alis.
Begot-Begotten-*v. imp.p p* -Nangyari, nag karoon, nagkamtan; kinamtan
Beguile-*v*-Aliwin, paalindugan.
Begun-*v. p p*.-Pinasimula
Behalf-*n* Pakinabang, interes.
Behave-*v*-Tumunğo, sumunod sa mabuting kaugalian.
Behavior-*n*-Kilos; tunğo, kaugalian.
Behead-*v*-Pugutin ang ulo, magpugot, pugutin.
Beheld-*v imp* -Nakita; nakakita
Behest-*n*-Utos.
Behind *adv*.-Sa likod; sa huli.
Behind-*prep*.-Sa huli, sa likod.
Behindhand-*a*-Huli.
Behold-*v*-Makita, makakita, tanawin, tuminğin.
Beholden-*a*-Kailanğan
Behoove-*v*-Matungkol, maukol.
Being-*n*-Tawo
Belabor-*v*-Paluin, hampasin.
Belate-*v*-Luatin; magluat.
Belay-*v*-Magluat
Belch-*v*-Duminghal; dumilhay.
Belch-*n*-Dilhay; dinghal
Beldam-Beldame-*n*-Impo, nunong babayi; matanda at panğit na babayi.
Belenguer-*v*-Ipaligid nğ hukbo.
Belie-*v*-Mag alibugha, sumitsit nğ ma sama.
Belief-*n*-Paniniwala, pananampalataya; sampalataya, religion
Believe-*v*-Maniwala; sumampalataya; sampalatayanin, hinagap.
Believable-*a*-Paniniwalaan, dapat maniwala.
Belittle-*v*-Pintasin; untian
Bell-*n*-Compana.
Bell-*v*-Ilagay nğ compana,

Bell clapper-*n*-Bayag ñg compana, panugtpg ñg compana.

Belle-*n*-Dalagang maganda.

Bellicose-*a*-Mapagbasagulo.

Belligerent-*a*-May gustong lumaban, ibig lumaban.

Belligerent-*n*-Ang may gustong lumaban.

Bellow-*n*-Sumigaw; humiyaw, umiyak ñg malakas.

Bellow-*n*-Sigaw; iyak; hiyaw.

Bellows-*n*-Balulusan, hungkoy

Belly-*n*-Tian; tiyan.

Bellyband-*n*-Pamigkis ñg tiyan

Belong-*v*-Matungkol; maukol

Beloved-*p* *p*-Iniibig; ginigiliw.

Beloved-*a*-Ginigiliw, giliw, iniibig, iniirog

Below-*adv*. Sa ilalim, sa ibaba

Belt-*n*-Pamigkis, bigkis, sintoron

Belt-*v* Bigkisin

Bemoan-*v*-Dumaing

Bench-*n*-Banko

Bend-*v*-Hubugin, humubog, balukturin, bumaluktot; yupiin; humintok hutukin.

Bend-*n*-Hubog, kibal; pagkabaluktot, yupi, tungo, kabaluktutan.

Beneath-*adv*-Sa ilalim, sa ibaba.

Beneath-*prep*.-Sa ilalim.

Benediction-*n*-Bendicion

Benefaction *n*-Kaloob, pakinabang.

Benefactor-*n*-Ang gumawa ñg mabuti sa kapua niya

Benefactor-*n*-Ang babaying gumawa ñg mabuti sa Kapwa niya.

Beneficence-*n*-Kagandahan ñg loob

Beneficent-*a*-Maganda ang loob; mapakinabañgan; may pakii abang.

Beneficial-*a*-Mapakinabañgan

Beneficiary-*a*-Mapakinabañgan.

Benefit-*n*-Pakinabang, tubo, kabutihan, galing.

Benefit-*v*-Tumubo, pakinabañgan, makinabang; bumuti.

Benevolence-*n*-Kagandahan ñg loob; kamahalan ñg ugali

Benevolent-*a*-Maganda ang loob; magandang loob, maawin.

Benight-*v*-Gumabi; gabihin.

Benign-*a*-Magandang loob, maamo

Benignant-*a*-Magandang loob, maamo.

Benignity-*n*-Kagandahan ñg loob

Bent-*v*. *imp* & *p* *p*-Hinubog; nakahubog, binaluktot.

Benumb-*v*-Mañgimay; pañgimayin; ina-,ñgumay, maimanhid.

Bequeath-*v*-Magpamana.

Bequest-*n*-Pagbibigay.

Bereave-*v*-Salatin; masalat.

Bereavement-*n*-Kasalatan.

Berg *n* Bundok ñg hielo.

Berry-*n*-Bungang munti.

Berth-*n*-Tinutulugan sa sasakyan ó tren.

Beseech-*v*-Ipakiusap; mamanikluhod; manalañgin, dumaing

Beseem-*v*-Maging, maging bagay

Beset-*v*-Ipaligid, pilitin; harañgin

Beside-*prep*-Bukod pa sa, bukod sa; kundi.

Besides-*adv*-Sa tabi, nakabubukod sa; mahigit pa

Besides-*prep*-Bukod pa, kundi.

Besiege-*v*-Ipaligiran ñg sundalo ang isang bayan at huag palabasin ang tawo ó ipasok ang mña pagkain.

Besmear-*v*-Kulapulan; pahiran ó puniin ñg putik

Besot-*v*-Mag lasing.

Besought-*v*. *p* *p*-ipinakiusap; namanikluhod dinaing.

Bespatter-*v*-Patilansikan, mansahin marumhan, tilansikan

Bespeak-*v*-Mamagitan, ipakita

Best-*a* Kabutibutihan.

Best-*n*-Ang kabutibutihan.

Best *adv*.-Kabutibutihang.

Be-stir-*v*-Magmadali, maghapht.

Bestow-*v*-Ibigay, ipagkaloob

Bestrew-*v*-Isabog, ikalat; Ipawalat

Bestride-*v* Ihakbang, umupo na nakacruz ang binti

Bet-*n*-Pusta; taya, pagpusta.

Bet-*v*-Magpusta, tumaya; magtaya; pumusta

Betake-*v*-Maukol.

Bethink-*v*-Alalahanin.

Betime-Betimes-*adv*-Sa mabuting panahon; agad; madali.

Betoken-*v* *imp*-Naukol; nakankol

Betook:-*v*. *imp*.-Naukol.

Betray-*v*-Ihayag ang hindi dapat, tumaksil sa capwa.

Betroth-*v*-Ipakasal

Betrothal-Betrothment-*n*-Kasal

Better-Bettor-*n*-Ang nagpupusta

Better *a*-Lalong mabuti, mabuti pa

Better-*n*-Ang lalong mabuti

Better-*adv*-Mabuti pa.

Better-*v*-Butihin, gumaling.

Betterment-*n*-Pagpapabuti.

Between-Betwixt-*prep*.-Sa pagitan

Bevel-*n*-Halang.

Bevel-*a*-Halang.

Bevel-*v*-Ipahalang

Beverage-*n*-Inomin.

Bevy *n*-Kapisanan ñg mañga ibon.

Bewail *v*-Dumaing; manañgis

Beware *v*-Mag iñgat iñgatin.

Beware-*inter*.-Tigil.

Bewilder-*v*-Gulubin; gitlahin.

Bewilderment-n-Ang paggugulo ñg isip, gulo ñg isip.

Bewitch-v-Kulamin, mangkulam.

Feyond-adv.-Sa ibayo malayo pa.

Beyond-prep-Sa ibayo

Bias-n-Joint.

Bias adv.-Pahalang.

Bias-v-Pahalangin; halangin.

Bib-n-Pangibabaw ñg damit ñg bata

Bible-n-Biblia.

Biblical-a-Nauukul sa biblia.

Bibulous-a-Mabutasbutas.

Bicker-v-Magtalò; magusap, magaway.

Bicycle n-Bicicleta.

Bid-n-Tawad; turing.

Bid-v-Tumawad; magturing.

Bidder-n-Ang tumawad.

Bidding n-Pagtatawad

Bide-v-Tumira, magtiis.

Biennial-a-Dalawa dalawang taon; nangyayari sa towing makalawang taon.

Biennial-n-Ang nangyayari sa towing dalawang taon.

Biennially-adv-Sa towing dalawang taon

Bier-n-Kalanda

Big-a-Malaki

Bigness-n-Kalakihan.

Bigamist-n-Ang tawong may dalawang asawa, ang nag aasawa sa dalawa.

Bigamy-n-Ang pagaasawa sa dalawa.

Biggin-n-Gorra ñg bata.

Bight n-Sulok.

Bigot-n-Ang tawong na umiisip na nasa kaniya ang lahat ñg katowiran at sa iba ang lahat ñg mali.

Bigoted-a-Matigas ang ulo, magdaraya

Bigotry-n-Katigasan ñg ulo.

Bile-n-Apdo.

Biliary a-Nauukol sa apdo.

Bill-n-Tuka.

Bill-v-Tukain

Bill-n-Listahan ñg anoman.

Bill-v-Maglista

Bill-n-Kasulatan

Billet-n-Sulat na maikli

Billet-v-Patuloyin ang manga sundalo sa bahay ñg manga paisano,

Billetdoux-n-Sulat na paninta.

Billiard-a-Naukuol sa billiar

Billiards-n-Billiar.

Billiard cue-n-Panudlok

Billion-n-Isang libong angawangaw

Billion-a Sang libong angawangawng.

Billow-n-Malaking alon

Billy-n-Palo ñg policia

Bin-n-Taguan ó sisiglan ñg palay ó trigo

Binary-a-Nakahalo sa dalawa.

Binate-a-Duble; dalawa.

Bind-v-Talian; higpitan; magkalawas; pigilan; pagipitan.

Bind-n-Tali.

Bindery-n-Gawaan ñg libro.

Binding-n-Yari ng libro, pagbalot.

Binnacle-n Kahon na kinalalagyan ñg gujon ñg sasakyan.

Biography-n-Historia ñg sariling buhay.

Biographer-n-Ang sumulat ñg historia ñg sariling buhay.

Biographic-Aiographical-a-Nauukol sa historia ñg sariling buhay.

Biped n-Tawo. Ang hayop na may dalawang paa lamang.

Bird n Ibon.

Bird v-Hulihin ó barilin ang manga ibon; mangati

Birdseye-a-Nakita buhat sa itaas.

Birth-n-Panganganak, kapanganakan, pagsipot

Birthday-n-Araw ñg kapangapakan.

Birthday-a-Nauukol sa araw ñg kapanganakan.

Birthplace-n-Lugar ñg panganganak, bayang tinubunuan.

Birthright-n-Katowiran na nagbuhat sa kapanganakan.

Biscuit-n-Bisquit.

Bisect-v-Biakin, dalawahin; hatiin

Bisection-n-Paghahati, pagdadalawahin, pagbibiak

Bishop-n-Obispo

Bit-n-Pangatngat, pirasong munti.

Bit-v-Ilagay ñg pangatngat sa bibig.

Bit-v-imp -Kinagat.

Bitch-n-Asong babayi.

Bite-n-Kagat.

Bite-v Kumagat, kagatin.

Bitter-a Mapait, masaklap.

Bitterness-n-Kapaitan, kasaklapan.

Bivalve n Talaan, tahong.

Bivouac-n-Bantay ñg isang hukbo.

Biweekly-a-Balang dalawang lingo

Biweekly adv -Sa towing dalawang lingo.

Biweekly-n-Pahayagan na lumilitaw sa towing makalawang lingo

Blab-v-Madiwara; sumitsit; magbungangaan, magtaltalan

Blab-n-Bunganga taltalan

Black-a-Maitim; itim, mapanglaw; walang awa, mabangis.

Black-n-Ang itim, kaitiman

Black-v-Paitiman.

Blackamoor-n-Negro

Blackant-n-Kutitb.

Blackball-n-Huag ihalal

Blackbird-n-Martinez, ibon na maitim,

Blackboard-n-Pisarang malaki,

Blacken-v-Umitim, paitiman, padilimin
Blackguard-v-Mag alibugha; magmura, magahpusta, alipustain, murahin
Blackguard-n-Tawong pala alipusta, tawong hamak.
Blackguard-a-Hamak, masama
Blacking-n-Panitim
Blacklead-n-Tingang itim.
Blackness-n-Kaitiman, kadiliman
Blacksmith-n-Panday.
Bladder-n-Pantog.
Blade-n-Talim; dahon
Blain-n-Sugat.
Blame-v-Bintangin, magbigay sala, sisihin sumbungin; magparatang
Blame-n-Sala; kasalanan
Blameless-a-Walang kasalanan.
Blanch-v-Mamutla.
Bland-a-Malambot
Blank-a-Walang sulat.
Blank-n-Papel na walang sulat.
Blanket-n-Kumot.
Blanket-v-Magkumot.
Blarney-n-Salitang makadadaya.
Blarney-v-Magsalita ng nakadadaya.
Blaspheme-v-Tumungayaw; sumpain; manunipa.
Blasphemy-n-Tungayaw, sumpa, himawa.
Blast-n-Putok na panibag
Blast-v-Putukan.
Blatant-a-Magulo.
Blaze-n-Liab, lingas, lagablab, apoy
Blaze-v-Magliab, lumagalab, masunog, maglingas
Bleach-v-Mamuti.
Bleak-a-Malamig, malunkot; mapanglaw.
Blear-v-Lumabo at pumula ang mata.
Blear eyed-a-Dirain
Bleat-n-Iyak ng tupa.
Bleat-v-Umiyak ang tupa, umiyak paiang tupa
Bleed-v-Dumugo
Blemish-n-Dungis; batik, mansa.
Blemish-v-Mamansa, dumungis; dungisin.
Blench-v-Umurong; tumakot
Blend-v-Ihalo, ilahok.
Blended-a-Nakalahok; nakahalo, buhaghag; may halo, may lahok
Bless-v-Hulugin ang gracia ng Dios.
Blessed-a-Mapalad, malwalhati.
Blessing-n-Gracia ng Dios, Kapalaran.
Blest-a-Masaya
Blet-n-Pagkabulok ng bunga dahil sa kahinugan.
Blight-v-Sirain
Blight-n-Sira, pagkabutod. kasiraan.
Blind-a-Bulag.

Blind-v-Bulagin.
Blind-n-Ang bulag
Blindfold-v-Takpanin ang mata.
Blinfold-a-Natatakpan ang mata
Blindness-n-Kabulaanan, kabulagan.
Blink-v-Pumikit, ilagay, ibukod
Blink-n-Pikit, silip.
Blinker-n-Panakip ng mata ng kabayo.
Bliss-n-Sayá; kasayahan; kaluguran
- Blissful-a-Masaya, matuwa, maligaya.
Blister-n-Lintos
Blister-v-Lumintos.
Blithe-a-Makinis; mainam.
Blithesome-a Makinis.
Bloat-v-Mamaga.
Block-n-Tangkalag.
Block-v-Abalahin, ilagay ng tangkalag
Blockade-n-Pagsasara ng bibig ng bahia upang hindi makalalabas at makapapasok ang manga sasakyan.
Blockade-v-Isara ng labasan ng bahia
Blockhead-n-Tawong hindi marunong
Blond-Blonde-a-Maganda, maputi ang balat at maganda
Blond-n-Tawong maputi at maganda ang balat.
Blood-n-Dugó.
Blood colored-a-Kulay dugo.
Bloodheat-n-Init na paris ang init ng katawan ó dugo
Bloodless-a-Walang dugo.
Bloodshed-n-Kamatayan, patayan
Bloodshot-a-Mapula ang mata.
Bloodsucker-n-Linta.
Bloodthirsty-a-Walang awa, mabangis, walang habag, dumudugo.
Bloodvessel-n-Ugat ng dugo
Bloody-a-Madugo, dugodnguan, dumudugo
Bloody-v-Dumugo, pahiran ng dugo.
Bloom-n-Bumula, bumulaklak.
Blossom-n-Bulaklak.
Blossom-v-Bumulaklak
Blot-n-Mansa, dungis; dumi.
Blot-v-Dungisin, mansahin, marumhan.
Blotch-n-Mansa.
Blotch-v-Mansahin.
Blotter-n-Sicante, pandampé.
Blouse-n-Barong pang ibabaw.
Blow-v-Umihip; ihipan; hipan, humihip,
Blow-v Ihip
Blow-n-Sumbi, bugbog, tampi, dagok, suntok, bungo, salpok.
Blow-v-Bumuka.
Blow-n-Bulaklak
Blower n-Taga ihip
Blown-v. p. p.-Nakaihip.
Blown-a-Hambog; mayabang
Blowpipe-n-Pangihip.
Blowse-n-Barong pang-ibabaw,

Blowze-n-Babaying mataba at mapula ang mukha.

Blowzy a-Magaspang; bastos.

Blubber-n-Taba ng isdang malaki.

Blubber-v-Umiyak; pumangit dahil sa pagiiyak.

Bludgeon-n-Palong maikli; palo.

Blue-a-Azul.

Blue-n-Kulay azul.

Blue-v-Tinain ng azul.

Blues-n-Kalungkutan; Kapanglawan.

Bluff-a-Maluag.

Bluff-n Batong matirik at malaki.

Bluff-v-Takutin.

Blunder-n-Mali; pagkakamali.

Blunder-v-Mamali.

Blunderbuss-n-Baril na maiksi at malaki ang butas.

Blunt-a-Pudpod; salsal ang dulo.

Blunt-v-Pulpolin; salsalin; pudpuran.

Blur-v-Palabuin; lumabo.

Blur-n-Mansa.

Blurt-v-Sabihin ng pabigla at malakas.

Blush-n-Pamumula ng muc-ha.

Blush-v-Mamula ang muc-ha.

Bluster-v-Maggulo; magalit; magsalita ng malakas at hambog.

Bluster n-Kahambugan; kayabangan.

Boa-a-Sawá.

Boar-n-Baboy na lalaki.

Board-n-Tabla.

Board-v-Ilagay ng tabla; ilatag ng tabla.

Board-v-Tumuloy; sumuno; manuluyan;

Boarding n-Pagsusuno; pagtutuloy.

Boarding house n Tuluyan.

Boast-n-Hambog; kahambugan; kahanginan; kayabangan; yabang.

Boast-v-Maghambog; maghangin; mamansa.

Boastful-a-Hambog, maparangalan; mapaghangin; mayabang.

Boat-n-Bangka; banka.

Boat-v-Mamanka.

Boatman-n-Bangkero.

Boatswaim-n-Ang puno na namamahala sa mga banka ng isang sasakyan.

Bob-v-Kilusin ng pabigla.

Bob-v-Kumilos ng pabigla.

Bobbin-n-Ikiran.

Bobbinet-n-Puntas.

Bobtail-n-Maikling buntot.

Bobwhite-n-Pugo.

Bodiless-a-Walang katawan.

Bodily-a-Nauukol sa katawan.

Bodkin-n-Kasangkapan pangbutas.

Body-n-Katawan

Body-v-Ibigay ng hitsura.

Bog-n-Burak kaburakan; banlik.

Bogg'e-v-Gawin ng pabigla; gawin ng pabastos.

Bogus-a-Howad; hindi totoo; falso.

Boil-v-Kumulo; maluto; lutuin; kuluin; magpakulo; ihalabos.

Boil-n-Kulo; pagkukulo.

Boiler-n-Pobia.

Boisterous-a-Malikot; maharot; magalaw; mapang gulo.

Bold-a-Matapang; walang kaba; marahas.

Boldness-n-Tapang; katapangan; tining ng loob; kapangahasan; sigla: dahas; kawalan ng takot.

Bole-n-Ang puno ng kahoy.

Bole-n-Isang sukat ó panukat.

Bole-n-Pusali na ginagamit sa pag gagawa ng tapayan.

Bolster-n-Tungkod; tukod.

Bolster-v-Itungkod; itukod.

Bolt-n-Tornillo na may ulo.

Bolt-v-Magsabi ng pabigla; bithayin; ibukod.

Bomb-n-Bomba.

Bombard-v-Ihagis ng bomba; barilin ng kanyon.

Bombshell-n-Bala ng kanyon.

Ponbon-n-Matamis.

Bond-n-Katibayan; panali; panagat.

Bond-v-Tibayan ng panali ó panagot.

Bond-a-Kulong; preso.

Bondage-n-Pagkapreso; kalagayan alipin.

Bondmaid n-Aliping babayi.

Bondman-n-Alipin.

Bondsman-n-Taga panagot.

Bone-n Buto.

Bone-v-Alisin ang buto.

Bonfire-n-Sigá.

Bonne-n-Ang pagaalaga sa isang bata taga alaga ng bata; taga iwi.

Bonnet-n-Tukarol.

Bonny-a-Maganda; masaya; maligaya.

Bonnyclabber-n-Gatas; na malapot.

Bonus-n-Ganting palad.

Bony-a-Mabuto; butuhan.

Booby-n-Ulol; bubo.

Book-n-Libro.

Book v-Ilagay sa libro.

Bookbinder-n-Taga gawa ng libro; ang gumagawa ng libro.

Bookbindery-n-Tahian at balatan ng libro.

Bookcase-n-Lalagyan ng mga libro.

Bookish-a-Masipag magaral.

Book keeper-n-Tenedor de libro.

Book keepiing-n-Ang pagtatanda sa libro.

Bookseller-n-Ang nagtitinda ng mga libro.

Bookworm-n-Ang tawong walang gawa kundi bumasa sa manga libro; ang maraming nabasa sa libro.

23

Boom-*n*-Palo nğ sasakyan na lumampas sa dulo nğ cable ó tanikala na nakakahalang sa labasan nğ ilog
Boom-*n*-Sigaw na malakas.
Boom-*v*-Sumigaw nğ malakas
Boon-*n*-Kaloob, favor; kapalaran.
Boon-*a*-Masaya, masagana
Boor-*n*-Tawong mahirap
Boorish-*a*-Bastos, magaspang
Boost-*v*-Buhatin, tulungin
Boot-*n*-Patong, gamot.
Boot-*i*-Makinabang, ipatong, tumubo
Boot-*n*-Bota
Boot-*v*-Sipain, isuot nğ bota
Booth-*n*-Tiakad; peria
Bootjack *n*-Kasangkapan pangpaalis nğ sapatos.
Bootless-*a*-Walang sapatos walang kabuluhan, di pakikinabangan
Booty-*n*-Ang ninakaw.
Borax-*n*-Sal de sosa
Border-*n* Gilid; tabi, wakal, wakas, baybay, dagdag, gasa; hanga, hangahan
Border-*v*-Umabot sa gilid, abutan ang gilid.
Bordering-*a*-Nakakahanga.
Bore-*v*-Butasin, balibulin, barenahin
Bore-*n*-Butas; tawong ikinayayamot.
Borough-*n*-Bayan.
Borrow-*v*-Manghiram, hiramin; sumandali
Bosh-*n*-Kaululan.
Bosom-*n*-Dibdib, puso
Boss-*n*-Amo, panğinoon, puno, jeffe
Boss *v*-Mamahala, magpuno; magjeffe.
Botany-*n*-Karunungan tungkol sa mğa gulay; kahoy, at bulaklak.
Botch-*n*-Pamamaga, mansa, gawa na hindi tama.
Botch-*v*-Mansahin, gawin nğ pabastos
Both-*a*-Dalawa; kapwa.
Both-*pro* -Ang dalawa; kapwa
Bother-*i*-Yamutin, abalahin, yumamot; umabala
Bother-*n*-Yamot, abala, hirap; pagal
Botheration-*n*-Abala, yamot, kayamutan
Bots-Botts *n*-Bulati sa lalamunan, bituka, at sikmura nğ kabayo.
Bottle-*v*-Bote.
Bottle-*v*-Ilagay ó isilid sa Bote.
Bottom *a*-Ang sa ilalim.
Bottom-*n*-Pusot, puit, ang ibaba
Bottomless *a* Walang pusot, di matarok.
Boudoir-*n*-Silid nğ babayi.
Bough-Malaking sanğa
Bought *v*-*imp*. Binili; namili
Bouillon *n*-Sabaw
Boulder *n*-Batong malaki.

Boulevard-*n*-Carsadang maluang.
Bounce-*n*-Udlot.
Bounce-*v*-Udlotin, umudlot
Bouncer-*n*-Bagay na malaki, tawong sinunğaling.
Bouncing-*a*-Malakas, malaki.
Bound-*n*-Hanga, wakal, wakas, udlot, lundag; lukso.
Bound-*v*-Ilagay nğ manğa hanga
Bound-*v*-Lumundag, umudlot, lumukso.
Bound *v imp & p p* -Tinali, nakitali
Boundary-*n* Hangahan, hanga, wakal; wakas, danay, hibaybay, katapusan
Bounden-*a*-Dapat gawin
Boundless-*a*-Walang hanga
Bounteous-*a*-Sagana, inaganda ang loob.
Bountiful-*a*-Masagana, husto
Bounty-*n*-Pabuya, ganting palad
Bouquet-*n*-Tali nğ manğa bulaklak
Bourn-Bourne-*n*-Sapang munti.
Bout-*n*-Talo, away, laban
Bovine-*a*-Nauukol sa balang lalaki otoro.
Bow-*v*-Batin, yumuko, iyuko, sumuko
Bow-*n*-Yuko, bati; tanğo
Bow *n*-Anomang bagay na baluktot
Bowed *a*-Balantok, baluktot
Bowel-*n*-Isaw, bituka
Bowel-*v*-Alisan ang manğa bituka
Bower-*n*-Bahay na munti sa halamanan na walang dingding at may mğa uupuan sa loob.
Bower-*n* Ang bumati, ang yumuko
Bowknot-*n*-Tali na mainam.
Bowl *n*-Mangkok
Bowlder-*n*-Botong malaki
Bowlegged *a*-Mabilog ang binti.
Bowline-*n*-Lubid nğ layag
Box-*n*-Kahon; kaha.
Box *n*-Sumbi, sampal, palo, tampal.
Box-*v*-Ilagay ó isilid sa kahon, ikahon.
Box-*v*-Sampalin, magboxing.
Boxer-*n*-Ang marunong magboxing.
Boxing-*n*-Boxing
Boy-*n* Batang lalaki
Boyish-*a*-May ugaling batang lalaki.
Brace-*n*-Pareja, tungkod, dipa, dalawa.
Brace-*v*-Itungkod
Bracelet-*n*-Pulsera.
Bracket-*n*-Tungkod
Bracket-*v*-Itungkod.
Brakish-*a*-Maalat
Brad *n*-Pakong maikli, pakong malit at walang ulo.
Brag *v*-Magyabang, maghambog maghanğin
Brag *n*-Kahambugan, kayabanğan, kahanğinan.
Brag-*a*-Mahambog, hambog mayabang
Braggart-*n*-Tawong hambog ó mayabang.

Braggartism-n-Kahambugan; kayaba-
ñgan; kahañginan.
Braid-n-Trintas.
Braid-v-Trintasin; mamirintas.
Brain-n-Utak; sa ulo.
Brake-n Pangpigil.
Brakeman-n-Taga pigil,
Brakish-a-Tapsim; maalat; maasim.
Bramble-n-Kaugoygoyan na may tinik.
Bran-n-Darak.
Branch-n-Sañga.
Branch-a-Kasañga.
Branch-v-Magsañga,
Brand-n-Tanda; marka; tatak; tala; ka-
sangkapang pang lagay ñg tanda.
Brand-v-Tandaan; markahin; ilagay ñg
tanda; tatakan; talaan;
Branding-n-Pag lalagay ñg tanda; pa-
nananda; pananaktak.
Brandish-v-Kawayin; pagpagin; ipag-
pag.
Brandish-n-Kaway; pagpag.
Brandnew-a-Bagongbago.
Brandy-n-Alak.
Brant-n-Gansang ramo; bibi; itik.
Brash-a-Marupok; mainit ang ulo; ma-
butlig.
Brash-n-Butlig.
Brasier-Brazier-n-Ang marunong guma-
wa ñg mga kasangkapan ñg tansong
dilaw.
Brass-n-Tansong dilaw.
Brassy-a-Parang tanso; may halong
tanso.
Brat-n-Batang hamak.
Bravado-n-Tawong hambog.
Brave-a-Matapang; mañgahas bayani;
marahas; marikit.
Brave-n-Tawong matapang.
Bravery-n-Katapañgan; dahas; kapañga-
hasan; tining ñg loob.
Bravo-n-Tulisán na matapang.
Bravo-inter.-Mabuti; tapang.
Brawl-n-Gulo; talo; away; usap.
Brawl-v-Makipagtalo; mag usap.
Brawn-n-Lakas; kalakasan.
Brawny-a-Malakas.
Bray-v-Durugin; dikdikin.
Bray-v-Pumutok.
Pray-n-Iyak ñg kabayong mula.
Bray-v-Umiyak ang mula.
Brazen-a-May halong tanso; bastos.
Breach-n-Puang; sira; puit ñg baril.
Breach-v-Pumutok.
Bread-n-Tinapay.
Breadth-n-Luang; lapad; kapalaran;
kaluagan.
Break-v-Basagin; sirain; tipuin; biakin;
lapakin; bumasag; masira, tumipo;
lumagok; lagutin; masayang.

Break-n-Basag; sira; tipo; lagot; kasi-
raan; puang.
Breaker-n-Ang maninira; maninira.
Breakfast-n-Agahan.
Breakfast-v-Kumain ang agahan.
Breakneck-n-Lugar na matirik.
Breakneck-a-Matulin na matulin.
Breakwater-n-Harañgan ñg tubig.
Breast-n-Dibdib; loob ñg dibdib.
Breast-v-Salubuñgan; lumaban; huma-
rap.
Breastbone-n-Buto ñg dibdib.
Breastpin-n-Alfiler.
Breastwork-n-Kuta.
Breathe-n-Ang hininga.
Breathe-v-Huminga.
Breathing-n-Paghihininga.
Breathless-a-Walang hinga.
Bred-v. imp. &p. p.-Nagalaga.
Breech-n-Puit.
Breech-v-Ibigay ñg salawal.
Breeches-n-Salawal.
Breeching-n-Salawalin.
Breed-n-Magiwi; magalaga.
Breed-n-Lahi
Breeding-n-Kagalañgan; kaugalian; asal;
galang; turo; dunong; karunuñgan;
kagalinñgan; inam ñg kilos; pinaga-
ralan.
Breeder-n-Taga alaga.
Beeze-n-Hanğin; amihan; habagat
Brent-n-Gansang lalaki.
Brethern-n-Magkakapatid.
Brett-n-Carruageng mahaba.
Breve-n-Nota ñg musica.
Brevet-n-Kalagayang mataas pero wa
lang dagdag ang sueldo.
Brevity-n-Kaiklian.
Brew-v-Ilahok.
Brew-v-Gumawa ñg servesa.
Brew-n-Lahok.
Brewery-n Gawaan ñg servesa.
Brewhouse-n-Gawaan ñg servesa.
Brewing-n-Pag gagawa ñg servesa.
Bribe-n-Suhol.
Bribe-v-Suhulin; suhulan.
Bribery-n-Suhol; pagsusuhol.
Bricabrac-n-Manğa sangkap na munti
ang halaga.
Brick-n-Lario; ladrillo.
Brick-v-Ilagay ñg lario.
Brickbat-n-Pirasong lario.
Brick kiln-n-Gawaan ñg ladrillos ó lario.
Bricklayer-n-Kantero.
Brickmaker-n-Ang gumagawa ñg lario.
Bridal-a-Nauukol sa kasal.
Bride-n-Mapañgasawa.
Bridegroom-n-Lalaking bagong kasal.
Bridesmaid-n-Babaying abay sa kasal.
Bridge-n-Tulay.

Bridge-v-Ilagay ng̃ tulay; gumawa ng̃ tulay
Bridle n-Cabesada
Bridle-v-Pigilin
Brief-a-Maikli.
Briefly-adv-Agad, mayamia
Brier-Briar-n-Tinik.
Briery-a-Matinik
Brig-n-Sasakyan na may lamang dalawang palo
Brigade-n-Tatlong regimentong sundalo
Brigand-n Tulisang, masamang tawo, tawong suitik.
Bright-a-Makintab; maningning; mahwanag, makisap; malinaw, malinis.
Brighten-v Lumiwanag, liwanagan, pakintabin; pakinisin.
Brightness-n-Kaliwanagan, kisap; kinang, kintab; kinis, dilag.
Brilliance n-Ningning, kisap, dilag.
Brilliancy-n-Kisap; ningning, dilag
Brilliant-a-Makinis; maningning, makisap, makinang, makintab.
Brilliant-n-Brilliante.
Brim n-Gilid; gasa; tagiliran
Brim-v-Punuin; pumuno hangang sa gilid
Brimful-a-Puno hangang sa gilid
Brimstone-n-Batong Matigas
Brindel-Brindeled-a Batikbatik.
Brindle n-Batik
Brine-n-Patis, tasik.
Brine-z-Asinan
Bring-v-Dalhin, magdala, ilapit.
Briny-a-Maasim
Brisk-a-Malikisi, magdala, masaya.
Brisket n-Dibdib ng̃ hayop
Bristle-n-Tutsang
Bristle-v-Tumutsang.
Bristle-v-Tumindig ang tutsang.
Bristly-a-Matutsang.
British-a-Nauukol sa Inglaterra.
British-n-Ang tawo sa Inglaterra.
Briton-n-Tawong Ingles, Ingles.
Brittle-a-Marupok, lahang̃in, malutong, bitakin
Broach-n Aspile; kasangkapang matulis
Broach-v-Butasing; ipahayag.
Broad-a-Malapad, maluang.
Broadax-n-Palataw na malapad ang talim.
Broadcast n Pagsasabog.
Broadcast-a-Masabog
Broadcast-adv-Pasabog
Broadcloth-n Kayo parang merino.
Broaden-v-Luang̃in, luminang.
Broadside-n-Tagiliran
Broadsword-n-Sabat na malapad at ma talim.
Progan-n-Sapatos na magaspang.

Brogue-n Salitang utal
Broil v-Lutuin sa baga
Broke-v imp -Sinira, sumira
Broken-v-Basag; sira
Brokenhearted-a-Malunkot na malunkot, malumbay.
Broker-n-Katiwala, negociante
Broma-n Pagkain.
Bronchial-a-Nauukol sa bága.
Bronchic-a Nauukol sa bága
Broncho-n-Kabayong Americano na munti at matigas ang ulo.
Bronze-n-Lahok ng̃ mang̃a metal na tila tansong pula.
Brooch-n-Alfiler sa dibdib
Brood-n-Akay
Brood-v-Takpanin ng̃ itlog ó akay; mag isipisip, magwariwari
Brook n-Saloysoy, ilog na munti, sapa.
Brook-v-Magtiis, matiisin.
Broom-n-Walis lawis
Broomstick-n Tangnan ng̃ walis
Broth-n-Sabaw
Brother n-Kapatid na lalaki.
Brotherhood-n-Ang pagkakapatid, katipunan.
Brother-in-law-n Bayaw; siaho.
Brotherly-a-Parangkapatid
Brougham-n-Carruage
Brow-n-Noo
Browbeat-v-Takutin ang kapwa sa salita lamang
Brown-a-Kayumangi.
Brown n-Kulay kayumangi.
Brown-v-Tinain ng̃ kayumangi.
brownish a-Kulay trigo, kayumanguing mura
Bruise n-Bugbog.
Bruise v-Bugbugin, bumugbog
Bruiser-n-Tawong bastos at malakas
Brunette-n-Babaye na hindi maputing maputi
Brunt-n Alsa, Lakas ng̃ isang suntok, untog
Brush-n-Walis na munti; escoba.
Brush-v-Escobahin; lawisin.
Brushwood-n-Kaugoygoyan.
Brusque-a-Magaspang.
Brutal-a-Bastos walang awa, parang hayop, hindi marunong maawa.
Brutality-n-Kawalang ng̃ awa, kabastosan, kahalayan; kahayupan, kabagsikan
Brute-n-Hayop; tawong bastos
Bryony-n-Lipay.
Bubble-n-Bula
Bubble-v-Bumula, bumukal, humining, sumilakbo, bumulubok
Buccaneer-n-Tulisan dagat.
Buck-n Usang lalaki, negro.

luck-v-Sumuwail; umurong.
lucket-n-Timba; baldi; panimba.
uckle-n-Hibilla.
uckle-v-Hibillahin.
uckle-v-Humubog; bumaluktot.
uckram-n-Sukob.
uckshot-n-Per de gones.
uckskin-n-Katad ng̃ tupa ó usá.
ud-n-Buka.
ud-v-Bumuka; isabak.
udge-v-Gumalaw.
udget-n-Ang Bayong at ang laman.
uff-n-Katad na ipinagamot sa langis.
nffalo-n-Kalabaw.
luffoon-n-Bubo; payaso.
luffoon-Buffonish-a-Matuwa.
uffoonery-n-Biro; katuwaan.
ng-n-Surot.
uggy-a-Masurot.
uggy-n-Karruageng munti.
ugle-n-Corneta.
ugler-n-Ang corneta.
uild-v-Itayo, gumawa; gawin.
uild-n-Yari ng̃ isang bahay; paraan sa
  pagtatayo.
uilding-n-Bahay.
ulb-n-Bukba.
ulb-v-Mamaga; lumake.
ulbous-a-Mabukba.
ulge-n-Hubog sa labas.
ulge-v-Humubog sa labas.
ulk-n-Laki.
ulky-a-Malaki.
ull-n-Toro; bakang lalaki.
ull-a-Malaki; mabagsik; mabañgis.
ulldose-v-Takotin sa salita lamang.
ullet-n-Bala.
ulletin-n-Pahayag.
ull frog-n-Palaka.
ullion-n-Ginto ó pilak na hindi pa.
ullock-n-Bulo.
ulls eye-n-Gitna ng̃ targeta.
ully-n-Tawong hambog at masama.
ully-v-Maghambog; Inmampastañganin.
ulwark-n-Maliit na kuta.
umblebee-n-Bubuyog.
amp-n-Umumpog; uutogin.
ump-v-Umpog; untog.
umper-n-Panumpog.
umpkin-n-Tawong bastos; hamak ó
  ulol; tawong bukid.
umptious-a-Mañgahas.
un-Bunn-n-Pandesal.
unch-n-Buig-n-Kiwan.
unch-v-Bumuig; isama.
unchy-a-May buig; mabuig.
und-n-Katipunan.
undle-n-Bigkis; balot.
undle-v-Ibigkis; ibalot; balutan; bigkisan.

Bung-n-Tapón; pasak.
Bunghole-n-Butas ng̃ bariles.
Bungle-v-Gawin na kung papaano.
Bungling-a-Bigla.
Bunk-n-Hihigan; catre.
Bunk-v-Mahiga sa hihigan; tumira sa.
Bunker-n-Lalagyan ng̃ uling.
Bunting-n-Kayong pangayak.
Bunyon-n-Pamamaga ng̃ daliri ng̃ paa.
Buoy-n-Tanda na lumutang sa ibabaw
  ng̃ tubig at tinaturo kung saan dapat
  magdaan ang mañga sasakyan.
Buoy-v-Palutañgin.
Buoyancy-n-Gaan.
Bouyant-a-Magaan; masaya.
Burden-n-Timbang; bigat; gawa; kahi-
  rapan; kapagalan.
Burden-v-Ipatrabohin ng̃ mabigat.
Burdensome-a-Mabigat;mahirap;matindi.
Burdock-n-Mores.
Bureau-n-Aparador; officina.
Burg-n-Nayon.
Burgess-n-Hukom sa nayon
Burgher-n-Ang tumitira sa nayon.
Burglar-n-Magnanakaw.
Burglarize-v-Gumapang; magnakaw; na-
  kawin sa bahay.
Burial-n-Paglilibing; baunan.
Burin-n-Kasangkapan ng̃ platero.
Burlesque-n-Katuwaan.
Burlesque-a-Matuwa.
Burly-a-Malakas; malaki.
Burn-n-Sapa; saluysoy.
Burn-n-Sunog; paso, silab; paltos.
Burn-v-Sunugin; silabin; sigan; papag-
  pasain; maglingas; magliab; mapaso;
  masunog.
Burner-n-Manunog; tagasunog.
Burning-a-Mainit.
Burning-n-Pagsunog; pagliab; paglingas;
  pagsilab.
Burnish-v-Bulihin; pakintabin.
Burnish-n-Buli.
Burnt-v p. p.-Nasunog; nakasunog.
Burro-n-Jumento.
Burrow-v-Nayon; Hukay ng̃ hayop.
Burrow-v-Hukayin ang lupa; humukay
  sa lupa.
Burst-v-Pumutok; sumabog.
Burst-v-Magputok.
Burst-n-Putok.
Burthen-n-Bigat; hirap; kahirapan.
Burthen-v-Bigatan; mahirapan.
Bury-v-Ilibing; ibaon; humukay.
Bush-n-Ugoygoy.
Bush-v-Magsañga.
Bushel-n-Cabán.
Bushy-a-Masañga; malago.
Busily-v-Masipag.
Busk-v-Iayos. ihan-la.

Busom-*n*-Loob ñg dibdib.
Buss-*n*-Halik
Buss *v*-Humalik, halikin
Bust *n*-Larawan ñg ulo at balikat.
Bustle-*n*-Kadalian, kasipagan, haplitan.
Bustle-*v*-Maghaplit, magmadali
Busy *a*-Masipag, may ginagawa
Busy-*v*-Sumipag; maghaplit
But-*conj*-Bagkus, nĝunit; datapua; yamang.
But-*adv*.-Yamang, bagkus
But-*n*-Hanga
Butcher-*n*-Mangigilit
Butcher-*v*-Patayin ang hayop
Bucherkñife-*n*-Cuchillong malaki
Butchery-*n* Pagpatay, kamatayan
Butler-*n*-Tagaiñgat ñg mĝa alak at pagkain
Butt-*n*-Malaking bariles
Butt *v*-Idugtong.
Butt end-*n*-Dulong malaki, puit.
Butter-*n*-Mantiquilla
Butter-*v*-Ipahiran ñg mantiquilla.
Butterfly-*n*-Paroparo
Buttermilk-*n*-Gatas na walang laknip

Buttery-*a*-May mantiquilla
Buttock *n*-Baywang, pigi
Button *n*-Butones
Button *v*-Magbutones
Button hole-*n*-Uhales
Lutiess-*n*-Haliging bato na pangpatibay sa bahay
Buxom-*a*-Mataba, malakas, masaya.
Buy *v*-Bumili; mamili
Buyer-*n*-Ang namimili.
Buzz-*n*-Haging, Haginit
Buzz-*v*-Humaging
By-*prep*-Sa sakay.
By *adv*-Sa tabi, malapit sa
By-Bye-*n*-Paalam
By-end-*n*-Sariling interes.
By gone-*a*-Nakaraan
By gone-*n*-Anomang bagay na nakaraan.
By-law-*n*-Ordenanza, utos.
By-name-*n*-Bansag.
By-name-*v*-Bansagin
Bypath-*n*-Landas na tago.
Byroad-*n*-Daan na tago
Bystander-*n*-Ang nanunuod.
Byway-*n*-Daan na tago
Byword-*n* Karaniwang salita, talinhaga

C

Cab-*n* Carromata.
Cabal-*n*-Kapisanan ñg tawo; katipunan.
Cabal *v*-Magakala.
Cabbage-*n*-Repolio.
Cabbage-*i*-Umitin; umumit
Cabin-*n*-Salong, kubo.
Cabinet-*n*-Aparador
Cabinet ma er *n*-Ang gumagawa nang mĝa aparador
Cable-*n*-Kable.
Cable *v*-Magtelegrama
Cable-gram-*n*-Telegrama, Hatid Kawad
Caboose *n*-Coche.
Cacao-*n*-Cacao, Puno ñg cacao.
Cackle-*v*-Tumilaok.
Cackle-*n*-Talaok
Cad-*n*-Tawong bastos
Cadaver-*n*-Bangkay, Burol
Cadaverous *a*-Parang patay; maputlá; mukhang patay.
Caddish *a*-Bastos, hamak, palalo.
Caddy-*ñ*-Maliit na sisiglan ñg cha
Cadence *n*-Pagkaayon ñg voees sa pag sasalita
Cadet-*n*-Ang nag aaral ñg magpuno sa hukbo.
Cafe-*n*-Restaurant, fonda, karihan
Cage-*n*-Jaula, kulungan ñg ibon.
Cage-*v*-Ilagay sa jaula.

Cairn-*n*-Bunton ñg bato
Caisson-*n*-Sisiglan ñg bala ñg kanyon, lalagyan ñg bala ñg kanyon
Caitiff *n*-Tawong hamak ó bastos.
Caitiff-*a*-Masama, hamak bastos
Cajole *v*-Palayawin
Cajolery-*n*-Pagpapalayaw
Cake-*n*-Mamon, bara
Cake-*v*-Tumigas, maging matigas
Calamitous-*a*-Mahirap, mahapis; masakit, masakuna.
Calaboose-*n*-Bilango, calaboso
Calamity-*n*-Sakuna, kahapisan; kahirapan, kapahamakan; kasakitan, kasiraan ñg puri
Calash-*n*-Carruage na umubrang ahsin ang itaas
Calcareous-*a*-Parang apog, may halong apog.
Calcimine-*n*-Pamalitada
Calcimine-*i*-Pumalitada
Calculate *v*-Balakin, kuentahin, bilañgin; tasahin, bumilang
Calculation-*n*-Bilang; kuenta, balak; katasahan, kabilugan
Calculator-*n*-Taga bilang, ang gumagawa ñg kuenta
Calculous-*a* Parang bato.
Calculous *n* Bato sa loob ñg pantog,

Caldron-n-Kawa katiñgan.

Calendar-n-Calendario, almanake.

Calf-n-Bulo

Caliber n-Laki

Calico-n-Cita, sita

Calipers n-Panukat nang mga bagay na mabilog.

Calisthenics-n-Ejercicio; Pagsanay

Calix n Balat nğ bulaklak.

Calk n Pasakin; tasakin.

Calk-n-Pasak, tasak

Call-v-Tumawag, tawağin, dapitin, magvisita, visitahin, dumalaw

Caller-n-Ang magvisita, Tagatawag

Calling n-Tawag, hanap buhay.

Calligraphy-n-Sulat na mainam

Callosity-n-Kalipakan

Callous-n-Lipak

Callous-a-Malipak

Callow-a-Walang balahibo

Calm-n-Kawalan nğ hanğin.

Calm-a-Tahimik, walang gulo, payapa, mahinahon.

Calm-v-Katahimikan, humimpil, tumahimik, pahimpilin, palubayin, payapain; itiwasay, pumayapa

Calmness-n-Katahimikan, kapalagayan; kapayapaan; kapanatagan.

Caloric-n-Taginit, panahon nğ init.

Calorific-a-Mainit; nauukol sa init.

Calumniate-v-Bintanğin; magbingtang.

Calumniation-n-Bintang; pagbibintang.

Calumniator-n-Ang nagbintang, hindi tama, masama, falso

Calumniatory-a-Falso, hindi tama; sinunğaling

Calumny-n-Paratang na falso, alibugha

Calve-v-Manğanak, (nauukol sa kalabau ó baka

Calyx-n-Manğa dahon sa labas nğ bulaklak.

Cambric-n-Cambray,

Came-v. imp -Dumating

Camel-n-Camelo.

Camera-n-Kasangkapan sa pagkuha nğ retrato

Camp-n-Lugar nğ pagpabinğa nğ hukbo, pahinğahan nğ hukbo.

Camp-v-Magpabinğa

Campaign-n-Panahon nğ pag lalaban nğ hukbo

Camphor-n-Alcampor.

Camphorate-v-Ilagay nğ alcampoi

Can-v-Maka, umubra.

Can n-Lata

Canal-n-Sangka, padaluyan nğ tubig; sangkang patubigan

Canard-n-Daya, hibo.

Canary-n-Ibon na munti at azul ang kulay.

Cancel-v-Lipulin, burahin, umayaw.

Cancellaton-n Pagbura; paglipol.

Cancer-n-Pigsa.

Cancerous-a-aNuukol sa pigsa.

Cancriform-a-May hitsurang alimanğo; hitsurang alimanğo

Cande-labrum-n-Lalagyan nang candila, candilero.

Candid a-Tunay totoo, ganap. mabait; tapat ang loob, walang labas sa matowid

Candidacy-n-Pagkacandidato.

Candidate-n-Candidato

Candidature n-Pagkacandidato

Candidly-adv -Tunay, totoo, tapat

Candle n Candila.

Candle-stick-n-Tirikan nğ candila, candilero

Candle-light-n-Ilaw nğ candila.

Candor-n Katapatan ó katibayan nang loob.

Candy-n-Matamis

Cane-n-Cawayan; baston, tungkod.

Cane-v-Hampasin nğ baston

Cane brake n-Tubuhan.

Canine-a-Parang aso, nauukol sa aso.

Canister-n-Bala nğ kanyon na kung lui magpak ay sasabog.

Canker-n-Gibik nğ suso; pamamato nğ suso.

Canker-v-Gumibik ang suso; mamato ang suso

Cannel coal n-Uling na maitim at matigas

Cannibal-n-Ilongot, ang tawong kumakain ang kapwa.

Cannibalism-n-Kasalbahian, pagkasalbahi, pagkakain nğ kapwang tawo

Cannon-n-Kanyon.

Cannonade-v-Kumanyon,

Cannonade-n-Pagpuputok nğ kanyon.

Cannon ball-n-Bala nğ kanyon.

Cannon shot-n-Putok nğ kanyon

Cannot-Walang kaya, di maka

Canoe-n-Bangka

Canoe-v-Mamangka

Canon-n-Utos, regla

Canonic-Canonical-a-Nauukol sa regla ó utos

Canonize-v-Ilagay sa pagkasanto ang namatay.

Canopy-n Tabing, baldokan.

Canopy v-Itabing, ilagay nğ tabing.

Cant-v-Kumanta, mag awit.

Cant-n-Salita na nakakahawig sa kanta labas nğ sulok

Canteloup-Canteloupe-n-Munting melon.

Cantata-n-Poema na may halo ang mğa, kanta.

Canteen-n Tindahan; lalagyan nğ tubig.

Canter-n Takbo.

Canter-v-Tumakbo
Canticle-n-Ang kanta ni Salomon.
Canton flannel-n-Frenela
Canvas-n-Balindang
Canvas-back-n-Patong dagat
Canvass-v-Siyasatin; humanap ng voto
Canvass n-Siyasat; paghanap ng voto.
Cap-n-Tukarol, gorro
Cap-v-Tuptopin, takpan, tapusin
Capable-a May kaya, bihasa, mabait, sanay; sapat.
Capacious-a-Maaliwalas, maluag, maluang, malaki
Capacity-n-Kalaparan, sukat; takal, laki.
Cap-a-pie-adv -Mag buhat sa ulo hangang sa paa.
Caparison-n-Kasangkapan ng cabayo.
Caparison-v-Gayakin.
Cape-n-Kapa.
Caper-v-Maglikot; maglundagan
Caper-n-Likot, lundag
Capillary-a Parang buhok
Capital-a-Nauukol sa buhay ó ulo Primero sa halaga; mainam; marikit
Capital-n-Capital; mauscula
Capital-n-Puhunan.
Capitalist-n-Ang may puhunan, ang namumuhunan.
Capitalize-v-Mamuhunan
Capital letter-n-Letrang mauscula
Capitation-n-Pagpugot
Capitol-n-Bahay ng gobierno
Capitulate-v-Sumuko
Capitulation-n-Pagsuko
Capon-n-Kapon.
Caprice-n-Ligaya, inam; pagkaibig
Capricious a-Mainam; maligaya.
Capsicum-n-Paminta.
Capsize-v-Itaub, tumaub
Capsize-i-Pagtataub
Capsular-Capsulary-a-Hitsurang capsula, nauukol sa capsula.
Capsule-n-Capsula.
Captain-n-Kapitan, puno.
Captaincy-n-Pagka' apitan, kalagayan kapitan.
Caption n-Pandulo
Captious a-Makapipintas; mapintasin
Captive n-Preso, ang nakulong
Captivate-i-Bihagin, bumihag, pasul uin.
Captivity-n-Pagkapreso, pagkabihag.
Captor-n-Ang bumihag
Capture-v-Bihagin, bumihag, samsamin, dakpin
Capture-n-Pagl abihag, pagkuha; pagsamsam; pagbihag
Car-n-Karo, bagol.
Carabine-n Baril na maikli
Caracole-v-Gulungin.
Caramel-n Caramelitos

Carat-n-Timbang ng ginto
Caravansary-n-Tulutan.
Carbine-n-Baril na maikli.
Carbolic-a-Carbolico
Carbon-n-Uling.
Carbonaceous-a-May halong uling
Carboy-n-Damajuana
Carbuncle-n Pigsa.
Carcass-n-Bangkay.
Card-n-Suklay ng balahibo
Card-n-Sulat na maikli, Pirasong carton na may nakasulat ang ngalan, baraha.
Card-v-Suklayin ang balahibo.
Card board-n-Carton.
Cardia-n-Puso
Cardiac-a-Nauukol sa puso
Cardialgia-Cardialgy-n-Sakit ng puso
Cardinal-a-Unang, mahalagang.
Cardinal-n-Cardinal
Care-n-Ingat, pagkakalinga, pagiingat, pamamahala; kahirapan.
Care-v-Ingatin, pamahalaan, mamahala.
Careful-a-Maingat, maalaga, makalinga; mapagsunod.
Careless-a-Pabaya, walang ingat; mabagal, walang kalinga, walang ayos
Carelessness-n Kapabayaan, kaligtaan; katamaran, kabagalan, kawalan ng ayos.
Careen-v-Humilig; humapay.
Career-n-Carrera, palakad, hanapbuhay
Career-v-Lumakad ng matulin'
Caress-v Alindugin, palayawin.
Caress-n-Alindog, anis, palayaw
Careworn-a-Pagod, mahirap, mapagal.
Cargo-n-Pamamahala, ang nilulan
Caribou-n-Kalabaw.
Caricature-n-Retratong mapapatawa
Caricature-i-Gumawa nang retratong falso
Caricaturist-n-Ang gumawa ng retratong falso
Carl-n-Tawong mala' as; tawong bastos
Carman-n-Cochero.
Carminative-n-Carminativo.
Carnage-n-Laman ó carne ng tawo ó hayop na patay, kamatayan.
Carnal-n-Mataba, malaman.
Carnation-n Carnación
Carnation-a-Mapulapula.
Carnival-n-Karnaval.
Carniverous-a-Makakain ng karne.
Carol-n-Kanta; Awit
Carol-i-Kumanta; Mag awit.
Carousal-n-Kalikutag, ingay, kaguluhan, kaingayan, biroan.
Carouse-i-Uminom at magkagulo
Carouse-n-Ang pag inom at pag gugulo.
Carp v-Pintasin

Carp-n-Bumbuan.
Carpenter-n-Anluague.
Carpentry-n-Pag aanluague.
Carper-n-Ang pumipintas.
Carpet-n-Kayong makapal na nakalatag sa sahig.
Carpet-bag-n-Saco de noche.
Carriage-n-Carruage; pagdadala.
Carrier-n-Tagadala; ang nagdadala; taga pasan.
Carrion-n-Carneng nabubulok.
Carrom-n-Carom.
Carry-v-Magdala; pasanin; dalhin.
Cart-n-Bagol; careton.
Cart-v-Dalhin; ilagay sa bagol.
Cartage-n-Pag lululan sa bagol.
Carter-n-Cochero.
Cartilage-n-Butong malambot.
Cartilageous-a-Nauukol sa butong malambot.
Cartridge-n-Cartucho; punlo.
Carve-v-Guhitin; hiwain.
Carving-n-Ang pagguhit; paghiwa.
Cascade n-Talonan ng tubig.
Case-n-Bahay; lalagyan.
Case-v-Isilid sa lalagyan.
Case-n-Usap; ang nangyayari.
Caseous-a-Parang queso.
Cash-n-Salapi; kuarta.
Cash-v-Ipamalit ng kuarta.
Cash book-n-Librong tandaan ng pagpasok at pag labas ng kuarta sa caja.
Cashier-n-Tenedor de libros.
Cashier-v-Ialis sa katungkulan.
Casing-n-Takip; kahon; lalagyan.
Cask-n-Bariles.
Casket-n-Ataul.
Casque-n-Bariles.
Cassimere n-Kayo de lana.
Cassock-n-Hábito.
Cast-v-Hagis; pukol; balibag; tapon; pagpukol; pagtapon; pagtudla.
Cast-v-Ipukol; ibalibag; itapon; ihagis.
Casta way-v-Tawong hamak.
Casta way-a-Hamak; walang kabuluhan.
Caste-v-Kapisanan ng tawo; lahi.
Caster-v-Gulong ng mga kasangkapan ng bahay.
Castigate-v-Parusahin; paluin; hampasin.
Casting v-Pagbububo; ang binubo.
Castle-v-Kuta; bahay na mainam at matibay.
Castor-v-Sombrero.
Castor oil-v-Aceite de castor.
Castrel-v-Lawin.
Casual-a-Hindi sinasadya; mataonan.
Casual-v-Sundalong walang distino.

Casualty-v-Ang nagkakataon; pangya yari; ang hindi sinadya.
Cat-n-Pusa.
Catacomb-n-Lugar ng tipunin ang mga buto ng nangamatay.
Catalepsy-n-Kalagayan parang patay.
Cataleptic-a-Nauukol sa himatay.'
Catalogue n-Tandaan.
Catalogue-v-Ilagay sa tandaan; ilista ó isulat sa tandaan.
Catamaran-n-Sasakyan na may dalawang katawan.
Catamount-n-Hayop na mabangis na nakakahawig sa tigre.
Cataplasm-n-Tapal.
Catapult-n-Panghagis na mga bato at pana.
Cataract-n-Talon ng tubig; (malaki).
Catarrh-n-Sipon.
Catarrhal-a-Nauukol sa sipon-
Catastrophe-n-Sakuna.
Catawba-n-Alak.
Catboat-n-Bangka.
Catch-v-Hulihin; humuli; umabot; abutin; dakpin; habulin; humabol; kunin.
Catch-n-Ang nahuli; ang hinuli'
Catching-n-Paghuhuli.
Catch penny-a-Walang kabuluhan.
Catchup-Catsup-n-Sarsa.
Catechise-v-Magturo sa pagtatanong.
Catechism-n-Catecismo.
Category-n-Lagay; kalagayan.
Categorical-a-Nauukol sa lagay; totoo.
Cater-v-Maghanda nang pagkain; maghanda.
Caterpillar-n-Uod; higad.
Catfish-n-Kanduli.
Catgut-n-Pisi ng bituka.
Cathartic-n-Purga.
Cathartic-a-Nauukol sa purga.
Cathedral-n-Katidral.
Catholic-a-Katolico.
Catholic-n-Ang sumasampalataya sa religiong catolico.
Catholicism-Catholicity-n-Pananampalataya sa religiong catolico.
Catholicize-v-Pilitin ng magiging catolico.
Catkin-n-Tinik.
Catmint-Catnip-n-Kabling.
Catsup-n-Sarsa.
Cattle-n-Manada ng baka; mga baka.
Caucus-n-Kapulongan ng mga partida.
Caucus-v-Magtipon ng partida.
Caudal-a-Nauukol sa buntot.
Caudate-a-May buntot.
Caudle-n-Inumin ng mainit para nang may sakit.
Caught-v. imp. & p.p.-Hinuli; nakahuli.

24

Caul-n-Panakıp nğ ulo.

Cause-n-Pınagmulan; pinagbuhatan, pı-, nangalınğan, dahilan, katowıran, katampatan.

Cause-v-Yumarı, ibıgay nğ pinagbuhatan ó pınagmulan.

Causeless-n Walang dahilan.

Cause way-Causey-n-Daan na mataas

Caustic-a-Mapapasuhan.

Caustic-n-Gamot na pangpaso

Cauter-n-Bakal na maınıt na pamaso

Cauterize-v-Pasuhın

Cautery-n-Pagpaso.

Caution-n-Inğat, siyasat, bait, unahan.

Caution-v-Umabala; magbıgay alam

Cautionary-a-Nauukol sa inğat.

Cautious-a-Dala, maınğat, mapagmasıd; mahinahon

Cavalcade-n-Procession nğ mğa tawong nakasakay sa kabayo.

Cavalier-n-Ang nakasakay sa kabayo.

Cavalier-a Masaya

Cavalry-n-Kaballıria

Cave-n-Yunğib, lunğa, lonğib, tibag.

Cave-v-Tıbagin, ıtıbag; tumıbag.

Cavern-n-Yunğıb; lonğib, lunğa.

Cavernous-a-Nauukol sa yunğıb, mayunğib

Cavıl-n-Dahilan na walang kabuluhan

Cavıl-v-Magbigay nğ dahilan na walang kabuluhan

Caviler-n Ang nagbigay nğ dahilan na walang kabuluhan.

Cavity-n Hukay, ukıt, butas.

Caw-v-Magwaka

Caw-n-Wak

Cayenne-n-Paımınton.

Cayman-n-Buaya.

Cease-v-Tumigıl, humımpıl, tumahan

Ceaseless-a-Walang tahan.

Cedar n Kahoy na malaınbot at mapula

Cede-v-Magbıgay; ibigay; ipagkaloob, pumayag.

Ceil-v Maglagay nğ kisame.

Ciling-n-Kısame

Celebrate-v-Magdıwang, ipagpista, magfiesta

Celebrated-a-Bantog, balita, bunyi; bayanı, mabantog

Celebrity-n-Bantog, kabayanihan.

Celebration-n Dıwang pista.

Celebrator-n-Ang nagdıdiwang.

Celerity-n-Katulınan; kadalıan; liksı; tulin

Celery-n-Kinsay

Celestial-a Nauukol sa insik.

Celestial-n Insık.

Celibacy-n-Kalagayan na walang asawa, pagkabagongtawo

Cell-n-Hadlang, butas

Cellar-n-Lunğa, lonğıb, yunğib

Cellular-a-May maraming butas, butas-, butas

Cement-n-Cınento

Cement-v-Ilagay ó pahıran nğ cımento

Cemetary-n-Pantion.

Censer-n-Incensario

Censor-n-Taga pıntas. ang pumıpıntas: mamimıntas

Censorious-a-Mapıntasin; pala pintasin.

Census-n-Censo; kabilanğan nğ manğa tawo sa ısang lugar.

Cent-n-Baria; cuarta.

Cental-n Isang daang lıbra.

Centenarian-a-Nauukol sa ısang daang, taon.

Centenarian-n Tawo na may ısang daan taon nğ gulang.

Centenary-n Luat nğ ısang daan taon

Centenary-a-Nauukol sa ısang daan taon; may isang daan taon

Centenial-a-Nauukol sa isang daan taon

Centenial-n-Pagdıwang sa katapusan nğ isang daan taon.

Center-n-Gıtna, ubod; kaıbuturan, laot, kaloobloobán

Center-v-Ipagıtna, pırmihin.

Centesımal-a-Icaısangdaang bahagı.

Centıgrade-a-May isang daang grado.

Centıgram-n-Centigramo.

Centiliter-n-Centılıtro

Centımeter-n-Centimetro

Centiped-n-Uod na may maraming paa.

Centıpede-n-Uod na may maraming paa

Central-a Sa gitna, nauukol sa gıtna.

Centralize-v-Ipagıtna.

Centric-a Gıtna.

Centrical-a-Gıtna

Centrifugal-a-Nakakaalis sa gitna

Centripetal-a-Nakakalapıt sa gıtna.

Centuple-a-Isang daang duble

Centuple-v-Dublihın nang ısang daang veces.

Century-n-Luat nğ isang daang taon.

Ceramic-a-Nauukal sa mğa tapayan

Ceramics-n-Karununğan sa pag gagawa nğ mğa tapayan.

Cereal a Nauukol sa mğa mais, palay, trigo, etc.

Cereal-n-Maiz, palay, trıgo, etc.

Ceremonial-a-Nauukol sa ceremonıo

Ceremonial n-Ceremonio.

Ceremonious-a-Nauukol sa ceremonio, dakıla; ayon sa kaugalian.

Ceremony-n-Ceremonıo, kaugalian; kaasalan.

Certain-a-Totoo; tunay.

Certainly adv.-Tunay, totoong.

Certainty-n-Katunayan, katotohanan.

Certificate-*n*-Titulo, katotohanan.

Certificate-*v*-Patotohanin.

Certification *n* Pagpapatotoo, pagpapatibay.

Certify-*v*-Sumaksi.

Certitude *n*-Katotohanan

Cervical-*a*-Nauukol sa liig.

Cervine-*a* Nauukol sa usa

Cessation-*n* Paghinto; paghimpil; tapos, paglubay.

Cession-*n*-Suko.

Chafe-*v*-Yumamot, yamutin

Chafe-*n*-Yan ot; alipunga

Chaff-*n*-Darak; gilig, uban.

Chaff-*v*-Tuksuhin

Chaffy-*a* Unsayanin.

Chagrin-*v*-Pighati, hiya, yamot.

Chain-*n*-Tanikala, kadena.

Chain-*v*-Talian ng tanikala.

Chair-*n*-Upuan; silla

Chairman-*n* Presidente, ang namumuno sa isang katipunan.

Chaise-*n*-Karromata.

Chaldron-*n*-Takal ng uling na may pitongpuong aroba.

Chalice-*n*-Calis, kupon.

Chalk *n*-Yeso; lupang puti

Chalk-*v*-Guhitin ó pahiran ng yeso

Chalky-*a*-Parang yeso.

Chalk line-*n*-Pitik.

Challenge-*n*-Hamon, dayo, bala, dayuhan

Challenge *v*-Humamon, hamunin, dayuhin.

Chamber-*n*-Kuarto, silid.

Chamber-*v*-Ilagay 'sa silid

Chamberlain-*n*-Puno sa bahay nang gobierno.

Chamber-maid-*n*-Alila sa bahay.

Chameleon-*n*-Butiki,

Champ-*v*-Ngumasab.

Champagne-*n*-Champagne

Champaign-*n*-Lupang maluang at patag.

Champaign-*a*-Patag; maluang, malawak

Champion-*n*-Puno, tawong bayani.

Champion-*v*-Lumaban, kupkopin

Chance *n*-Kapalaran, palad

Chance-*v*-Ilagay sa kapalaran.

Chance-*a*-Nagkataon.

Chancel *n*-Lugar nangaltar sa simbahan

Chancellor-*n*-Hukom,

Chandelier-*n*-Lalagyan ng kinki, aranya.

Chandler-*n*-Ang magtitinda ng candila; mangagawa ng candila

Chandlery-*n*-Tindahan ng candila.

Change-*v*-Baguhin, palitan, halinhan, ibahin; ipamalit, bumago, humalili; magpalit, sukhan.

Change-*n*-Sukh; palit, pagkabago; kaibhan, halili.

Changeable Changeful *a*-Hindi firme.

Channel-*n*-Agos ng tubig, pusod nang ilog.

Chant-*v* Mag awit; magkanta.

Chant-*n*-Awit; kanta, dalit.

Chanticleer-*n*-Manok.

Chaos *n* Gulo.

Chaotic *a*-Magulo.

Chap-*n*-Alipunga.

Chap-*n*-Panga; sihang; lalaki; batang lalaki.

Chaparral-*n*-Kaugoygoyan

Chapeau-*n* Sombrero, sambalilo.

Chapel-*n* Visita

Chaperon-*n*-Ang matandang babayi na taga ingat sa mga dalaga na nasa isang funcion

Chaperon-*v*-Ingatan ng matandang babayi ang mga dalaga.

Chapfallen-*a*-Malungkot, nahihiya

Chaplain-*n*-Capillan, Pari nang manga sundalo

Chaplet *n* Rosario

Chapman-*n*-Tawong mangangalakal.

Chaps-*n*-Bibig

Chapter-*n*-Pangkat.

Chapter-*v*-Magpangkat.

Char-*v*-Sunugin

Character-*n*-Kaugalian, ugali, asal, kaasalan

Characteristic-*a*-Gawing, nauukol.

Characteristic-*n*-Kaugalian

Characterize-*v*-Saysayin, magsaysay.

Charcoal-*n*-Uling.

Charge-*v*-Ipagbilin; huningi

Charge-*n*-Ilingi, gasta, gugol, halaga, bilin, tagobilin; parating; bintang

Chargeable-*a*-Dapat humingi ang bayad

Charger-*n*-Kabayo ng sundalo.

Charitable-*a*-Maawain, maluang ang loob, magandang loob.

Charity-*n*-Limos.

Charlatan-*n*-Ang nagsasalita ng walang kabuluban

Charm-*n*-Panghalina; panghinayang, pagtataka; puko.

Charm-*v*-Patakanin, pasukuin.

Charming-*a*-Mainam, dakila.

Charnel-*a*-May lulan ng mga bankay.

Charnel house *n*-Libing, pantion; bahay na ikinalalagyan ng mga bangkay.

Chart-*n*-Mapa

Chart-*v*-Gumawa ng mapa.

Charter-*n*-Pahintulot ng gobierno; kasulatan

Charter-*v*-Upahan

Chary-*a*-Maingat, maimot.

Chase-*v*-Habulin, mang-aso, humabol.

Chase *n* Paghabol, pangangaso.

Chaser-*n*-Ang humahabol

Chasm *n* Bangin, sa'uy-oy.

Chaste-a-Mahinahon, wagas, dalisay, mabini, mahinhin.

Chasteness-n-Kabinian, kalinisan, kapurihan.

Chasten-v-Dalisayin· linisin

Chastening n-Pagdadalisay; pag lilinis

Chastity-n-Kabinian, kapurihan; kalinisan; timtim, katimtiman.

Chastise-v-Hampasin, paluin, parusahin; magparusa.

Chastizement-n-Parusa; hampas, palo

Chat-n Salitaan; salita, usap.

Chat-v-Magsalitaan; makipagusap.

Chateau-n-Bahay sa parang.

Chattel-n-Bagay; kasangkapan

Chatter-v-Magsalita ng matulin.

Chatter-n-Salita

Chatterbox n-Tawong masalita.

Chatty-a-Masalita.

Cheap-v-Mura, hamak.

Cheapness-n-Kamurahan

Cheapen-v-Bawasan ng halaga

Cheat-n-Tekas, daya, patibong hibo, tawong magdaraya; tawong suitik, paghibo, Manunuba

Cheat-v-Hibuin; dayain, tumekas, tekasin, manuba; ankinin

Check-n-Pigil, billete

Check-v-Pigilin; punigil, ampatin; pahintoin, awatin

Cheek-n-Pisngi

Cheer-n-Sigaw ng tuwa.

Cheer-v Sumigaw dahil sa tuwa.

Cheer-v-Bigyan lakas

Cheerful-a-Masaya, maligaya; nakalulugod, nakatutuwa, matuwa.

Cheerless-a-Malunkot, mapanglaw.

Cheese-n-Queso

Cheesy-a-Parang queso

Chemise-n Camison.

Chemist-n-Kemista

Cheque-n-Cheque

Cherish-n-Palayawin, ingatin.

Cheroot-n-Tabaco

Cherry-n-Ceresa.

Cherry-a-Mapula

Cherub n-Sangol, batang maganda.

Cherubic Cherubical-a-Nauukol sa batang maganda.

Chest-n Kaban; baul

Chestnut-n Castaño.

Chevalier-n-Tawong sumasakay sa kabayo.

Chew v-Nguyain, ngumuya

Chick n-Sisiw.

Chicken-n-Manok

Chicken-hearted-a-Duag, mahina ang loob, matatakutin.

Chicken pox-n Bulutong tubig.

Chide-v-Gasaan; tuksuhin.

Chief-a-Unang, malaki, primerong.

Chief-n-Puno, singkad

Chiefly-adv ·Nauna

Chieftain-n-Puno

Chaignon-n-Pusod

Chilblain n-Alipunga.

Child-n-Bata

Childhood-n-Pagkabata, kasangulan.

Childish-a-Parang bata, ugaling bata.

Childless-a-Walang anak.

Childlike-a-Parang bata, ugaling bata.

Chill-n-Ngiki

Chill-v-Ngumiki

Chilly-a-Malamig na kaunti; malamiglamig.

Chime-n-Tugtog ng compana

Chime-v-Tumugtog ang compana.

Chimerical-a-Maguniguniin

Chimney-n Palabasan ng asó, dapugan na labasán ng asó

Chimpanzee-n-Ungong malaki

Chin-n-Baba.

China n China.

Chinch-n-Surot

Chin cough-n-Ubong malakas.

Chine-n-Gulugod

Chinese a-Nauukol sa Insik

Chinese-n-Insik; tawong insik.

Chinese-n-Wika ng Insik.

Chink-n-Bitak, lamat, lahang.

Chink-v Bitakin, lahangin; lumahang.

Chintz n Sita.

Chip-n Tatal, pingas

Chip-v-Pingasin, tatalin

Chips-n-Pinagtatalan

Chirp n-Siap.

Chirp v-Sumiap

Chirrup n-Siap.

Chirrup-v-Sumiap.

Chisel-n-Pait; lukob.

Chisel-v-Magpait, maglukob, lukubin·

Chit-n Batang munti, supling

Chit chat-n-Salita.

Chivalric-a-Mabuting loob, nauukol sa kaginoohan

Chivalrous-a-Mabuti ang loob, maginóo, maganda ang loob.

Chivalry-n Pagkaginoo

Chive-n-Sibuyas na munti.

Chloroform-n-Cloroformo

Chloroform-v-Patulugin sa Cloroformo.

Chock-v-Talian

Chock-adv-Puno, lubos; punongpuno.

Chocolate-n Sikolate

Choice n-Hirang, pili; lugod; pagpili, pamimili.

Choice a Hirang; mainam

Choir-n Coro.

Choke-v-Inisin, uminis.

Choler-*n*-Galit.
Cholera-*n*-Colera.
Choler-*n*-Apdo.
Choleric-*a*-Nauukol sa galit.
Choleric-*a*-Nauukol sa apdo.
Cholera morbus-*n*-Colera morbo: colerin.
Choose-*v*-Ihalal: piliin; pumili; humirang; hirañgin; humalaw; maghalal; lisanin.
Chop-*v*-Putolin; tadtarin; palakolin.
Chop-*n*-Putol; pagpuputol; tadtad.
Chop-*n*-Bifstek.
Chop stick-*n*-Cubiertos ñg mañga Insik.
Choral-*a*-Nauukol sa coro.
Chord-*n*-Kuerdas.
Chord-*v*-Ilagay ñg kuerdas.
Chore-*n* Munting trabajo.
Chorister-*n*-Cantador.
Chorus-*n*-Kapisanan ñg mañga cantadores.
Chose-*v. imp.*-Pinili; pumili.
Chosen-*v. p. p.*-Pinili na; nakapili na.
Chowder-*n*-Pagkasahog ñg pagkain.
Chowder-*v*-Lutuin ñg sahogsahog.
Christ-*n*-Cristo.
Christen-*v*-Binyagin; buminyag; magbinyag.
Christendom-*n*-Lupain ñg mañga binyagan.
Christian-*n*-Binyagan; ang bininyagan.
Christian-*a*-Nauukol sa pagbibinyag.
Christianity-*n*-Pagkabinyagan.
Christianize-*v*-Binyagin; magbinyag.
Christmas-*n*-Pasco.
Chromatic-*a*-Nauukol sa mañga kulay.
Chrome-*n*-Metal na maputi at matigas.
Chronic-*a*-Nauukol sa panahon.
Chronicle-*n*-Tandaan ñg mañga bagay na nangyari sa iba,t, ibang panahon.
Chronicle-*v*-Listahin ñg mañga nangyari saiba,t, ibang panahon.
Chronometer-*n*-Relos ó Orasan na mabuti.
Chub-*n*-Halobaybay.
Chubby-*a*-Pandak; mataba.
Chuck-*v*-Sumiap.
Chuck-*n*-Siap.
Chuckle *n*-Tawa.
Chum-*n*-Kaulayaw; kalaguyo; kaibigan.
Chum-*v*-Magkalaguyo; magkaulayaw.
Chunk-*n*-Piraso.
Chunky-*a*-Mataba: pandak.
Church-*n*-Simbahan.
Church man-*n*-Tawong simbahan.
Churchwarden-*n*-Piscal ñg simbahan.
Churchyard-*n*-Patio.
Churl-*n*-Tawong bastos at may masamang kaugalian.
Churlish-*a*-Maramot at bastos.
Churn-*v*-Pagpagin; galawin.
Cider-*n*-Katás ñg mansanas: alak.

Cigar-*n*-Tabaco.
Cigarette-*n*-Cigarrillo.
Cilia-*n*-Pilikmata.
Ciliary-*a*-Nauukol sa pilikmata.
Cinder-*n*-Uling; Abo.
Cinnamon-*n* Canela.
Cion-*n*-Supling.
Cipher-*n*-Zero.
Cipher-*v*-Kuentahin; magkuenta.
Circle-*n* Bilog; kabilugan.
Circle-*v*-Paligirin; pumaligid.
Circlet-*n*-Munting bilog.
Circuit-*n*-Palibid; bilog; palibot; paligid.
Circuit-*v*-Pumaligid; pumalibot; pumalibid.
Circuitous-*a*-Mabilog; palikoliko; pasuotsuot.
Circular-*a*-Mabilog.
Circular-*n*-Pahayag ñg isang bagay.
Circularity-*n*-Kabilugan.
Circulate-*v*-Ikalat; ipamalat.
Circulation-*n*-Ang pagkakalat.
Circumference-*n*-Paligid; palibid; kabi lugan.
Circumflex-*n*-Kurlit.
Circumflex-*a*-Nauukol sa kurlit.
Circumlocution-*n*-Salitang baliktad.
Circum navigate-*v*-Paligiring ang mundo; pumaligid sa mundo.
Circum navigation-*n*-Pagpapaligid ñg mundo.
Circum polar-*a*-Malapit sa hilagaan ñg mundo.
Circumscribe-*v*-Kulungin; paligirin ñg guhit.
Circumscription-*n*-Guhit sa labas ñg anomang bagay ó lugar.
Circumspect-*a*-Mabait marunong: mahinahon; banayad: mahinhin.
Circumspection-*n*-Kahinhinan; bait; tuto; dunong; karunuñgan; hinahon.
Circumstance-*n*-Ang Nangyari.
Circumstancial-*a*-Nauukol sa mañga bagay.
Circumvent-*v*-Manalo sa pagdadaya; magbalatkayo.
Circumvention-*n*-Pagdaraya; pananalo sa pagdaraya; daya.
Circus-*n*-Circo.
Cis atlantic-*a*-Sa gawi rito ñg dagat na atlantico.
Cistern-*n*-Balon.
Citadel-*n*-Kuta ñg bayan.
Cite-*v*-Sabihin; saysayin; magsaysay; magsabi; magpahayag; pahayagin.
Citation-*n*-Pagsabi; pahayag.
Citenzen-*n*-Tawong bayan.
Citric-*a*-Nauukol sa kundol ó dayap.
Citron-*n*-Kundol.
City-*n*-Bayan na malaki; malaking bayan.

Cives-n-Bawang.

Civic-a-Nauukol sa paisano.

Civil-a-Masuyo; mabait; magalang.

Civilian-n-Paisano.

Civility-n-Anyo; suyo; galang; hinhin; kilos na mainam; handog.

Civilization-n-Dunong; kalagayan marunong.

Civilize-v-Turuan.

Civilized-a-Marunong; may dunong.

Clabber-n-Paglalapot ng gatas.

Clabber-v-Lumapot.

Clack-v-Ngumasab.

Clack-n-Ngasab.

Clad-v. imp. & p. p.-Nakasuot; sinuot.

Claim-v-Humingi; ariin.

Claim-n-Hingi.

Claimant-n-Ang humihingi.

Clam-n-Talaan.

Clamber-v-Umakyat.

Clammy-a-Maputik; parang ubog.

Clamor-v-Guluhin; maggulo; umugong; sumigaw; humiyaw.

Clamor-n-Gulo; ingay; ugong; kalabog; hiyaw; kaguluhan; kaingayan.

Clamorous-a-Maingay; magulo.

Clamp-n-Panipit.

Clamp-v-Ipitin.

Clan-n-Lahi.

Clansman-n-Balang tawo, ng isang lahi.

Clandestine-a-Lihim; tago.

Clandestination-n-Lihim.

Clang-v-Tumunog.

Clang-n-Tunog.

Clangor-n-Gulo; ingay.

Clangorous-a-Magulo.

Clank-n-Tunog.

Clank-v-Tumunog.

Clap-v-Tumagupak; tagupakin.

Clap-n-Tagupak.

Claptrap-n-Hibo; daya.

Claptrap-a-Nakadadaya; nakahihibo.

Claret-n-Tinto.

Clarify-v-Towirin; husayin; liwanagin; dalisayin; lumiwanag.

Clarinet-Clarionet-n-Clarinete.

Clarion-n-Trumpeta.

Clash-v-Umumpog; bumungo.

Clash-n-Bungo; banga; umpog; untog.

Clasp-v-Humawak; hawakin.

Clasp-n-Hawak.

Class-n-Clase; hinlog; lahi.

Class-v-Ilagay sa grado.

Classic-n-Gawa na mainam.

Classic-Classical-a-Nauukol sa pagaaral.

Classification-n-Paglalagay sa grado.

Classify-v-Ilagay sa grado ó sa karampatan.

Classmate-n-Kasama sa pagaaral.

Clatter-v-Kumalog.

Clatter-n-Kalog.

Clause-n-Pangkat.

Clavicle-n-Buto ng liig.

Claw-v-Kuko ng paa ng hayop ó ibon.

Claw-v-Umukyabit.

Clay-n-Pusali.

Clay-v-Pahiran ng pusali.

Clayey-a-May halong pusali; nauukol sa pusali.

Clean-a-Malinis; wagas; walang halo; maselang; hawan; taganás; maayos.

Clean-adv.-Wagas; walang halo; walang sukal.

Clean-v-Linisin; maglinis; kayasin; kintalin; pakalinisin; ayusin.

Cleanliness-n-Kalinisan; kakinisan; kalinawan.

Cleanly-adv.-Malinis; walang halo; maselang.

Cleanse-v-Dalisayin; linisin; pakalinisin.

Clear-a-Puro; tunay; totoo; maliwanag; hawan; hayag; di malabo.

Clear-a-Malinis; watak; maaliwalas.

Clear-adv.-Wagas; walang halo; malinis; aliwalas.

Clear-v-Liwanagin; dalisayin; linisin.

Clear-n-Lugar na walang kahoy sa gubat.

Clearance-n-Pag lilinis.

Clearing-n-Lugar na malinis.

Clearness-n-Liwanag; kaliwanagan; kalinawan.

Cleat-n-Tablang makitid.

Cleavage n-Pagbibiak.

Cleave-v-Lahangin; biakin.

Cleaver-n-Palataw.

Cleft-n-Bitak; lahang.

Cleft-a-Mabiak.

Clematis-n-Lipay na may bulaklak.

Clement-a-Maawain.

Clemency-n-Awa; habag; kaawaan.

Clergy-n-Kapisanan ng mga pari.

Clergy man-n-Pastor.

Cleric-n-Taga sulat; pari.

Cleric-Clerical-a-Nauukol sa pari; nauukol sa taga sulat.

Clerk-n-Escribiente; taga sulat; ang nagtitinda; tindera.

Clever-a-Bihasa; marunong; ganap; mabait.

Cleverness-n-Karunungan; dunong.

Clew-n-Bola ng pisi.

Click-v-Pumalatak.

Click-n-Palatak.

Client-n-Ang kinalong ng abogado.

Cliff-n-Batong matárik.

Climate-n-Clima.

Climax-n-Dulo; pandulo.

Climb-n-Umakyat; umahon.

Clime-n-Clima.
Clinch-v-Silsilin.
Clinch-n-Silsil.
Cling-v-Sumabit; dumikit.
Clink-v-Umalalad.
Clink-n-Alala.
Clinker-n-Abo ñg uling.
Clip-v-Bawasan; awasan; untian; gupitin; hiwain.
Clip-n-Gupit hiwa.
Clipper-n-Ang gumugupit.
Clipping-n-Paggugupit.
Clipping-n-Pinag gupitan.
Clique-n-Kapisanan.
Cloak-n-Damit na pang ibabaw.
Cloak-v-Isuot ñg pang ibabaw.
Clock-n-Relos; orasan.
Clock work-n-Makina ñg relos.
Clod-n-Tingkal.
Clod-v-Tumingkal.
Cloddy-a-Matingkal.
Clod hopper-n-Tawong bastos; tawong parang; tawong hamak.
Clog-n-Abala.
Clog-v-Abalahin.
Cloggy-a-Makakaabala.
Close-v-Tapusin; isara; yariin; utasin; tumapos; sadhan.
Close-a-Tipi; masinsin; maramot; matipid kuripot; mahigpit; gipit.
Close-adv.-Malapit; makipot; makitid.
Close-n-Tapos; katapusan.
Closed-a-Utas.
Closely-adv.-Malapit na malapit.
Closeness-n-Lapit; kalapitan; kakitiran; kasikipan; kagipitan; kakiputan kasinsinan.
Closet-n-Silid na kinalalagyan ñg mga damit.
Clot-n-Patak ñg dugo.
Cloth-n-Kayo.
Clothe-v-Isuot ñg damit.
Clothes-n-Mañga damit.
Clothing-n-Damit.
Cloud-n-Ulap; alapaap.
Cloud-v-Dumihan; labuan; padilimin.
Cloudless-a-Walang ulap; maliwanag.
Cloudy-a-Maulap; may ulap; malabo.
Clout-n-Tutop; pakong munti at walang ulo;
Clout-v-Tutupan.
Clove-n-Buñga ñg paminta.
Cloven-a-Biniak nabiak.
Clover-n-Damo.
Clown-n-Bobo.
Clownish-a-Parang bobo.
Cloy-v-Mabusog; yumamot.
Club-n-Palo; tungkod pumalo.
Club-v-Paluin; pumalo; paluin nang tungkod.

Club foot-n-Pilay ang isang paá.
Clue-n-Guni; tanda.
Clump-n-Bunton na walang hitsura.
Clumsy-a-Bastos; mabagal.
Clung-v. p. p.-Nakadikit; dinikit; sinabit; nakasabit.
Cluster-n-Piling.
Cluster-v-Pumiling.
Clutch-n-Hawak.
Clutch-v-Hawakan; humawak.
Coach-n-Coche.
Coach-v-Magturo.
Coachman-n-Cochero.
Coadjutor-n-Ang lalaking tumutulong sa iba.
Coadjutrix-n-Ang babaying tumutulong sa iba.
Coal-n-Uling.
Coal-v-Ilagay ñg uling; punuin nang uling.
Coalesce-v-Ihalo; ilakip; ilangkap;isama; sumama; humalo.
Coalition-n-Pagkakalapat; pagkakalakip; pagkakapisan.
Coal pit-n-Hukayan ñg uling.
Coarse-a-Magaspang; bastos; hañgal; walang pinag aralan.
Coarseness-n-Kabastusan; kapal.
Coast-n-Baybay dagat.
Coast-v-Lumayag malapit sa baybay dagat.
Coaster-n-Sasakyan na hindi lumayo sa baybay dagat.
Coat-n-Baro.
Coat-v-Ilagay sa baro.
Coax-v-Palayawin; alindugin; paamoin; manuya; magdiladila.
Coaxing-n-Pag lalayaw; pag aalindog; pagdidiladila.
Cob-n-Busal.
Cobble-Cobble stone-n-Batong munti.
Cobble-v-Tutupan ñg magaspang.
Cobbler-n-Taga tutop.
Cobra de capello-n-Tankaiba.
Cobweb-n-Bahay gagamba.
Cochineal-n-Tinang mapula.
Cock-n-Manok; yawi.
Cockade-n-Buhol sa sombrero
Cockle-n-Talaan.
Cockney-n-Taga bayan ñg Londres.
Cock pit-n-Sabuñgan; gallera.
Cockroach-n-Ipis.
Cocks comb-n-Tuktok ñg manok.
Cock swain-n-Ang umuugit sa sasakyan.
Cocoa-n-Cacao.
Cocoa-n-Punong cacao.
Cocoa palm-n-Punong niog.
Cocoanut-n-Niog.
Cocoon-n-Bahay ñg uod.
Cod-n-Bakalaw.

Coddle-v-Palayawin.
Code-n-Kapisanan nğ mañga atos nang gobierno
Codger-n-Tawong maramot
Codicil-n-Sulat na kasama sa testamento
Codify-v-Ilagay sa codigo.
Coefficient-n-Katulong
Coequal-a-Kapantay
Coerce-v-Pilitin; hibuin; dayain.
Coercion n-Pagpilit, hibo, daya
Coercive-a-Makapipiht.
Coeval-n-Kalaban, katalo.
Coffee-n-Kape.
Coffee pot-n-kapetera.
Coffer-n-Kaban, ataul, baul.
Coffin-n-Ataul.
Cog-v-Hibuin
Cog-i-Hibo, Ñğipin nğ gulong.
Cogency-n-Kalakasan
Cogent a-Malakas, di makalalaban.
Cogitate-v-Magwariwari, magbulaybulayin, magwari, magisipisip
Cogitation n-Pagwawariwari, wari; pagbubulaybulayin; pagiisipisip.
Cognac-n-Coñat.
Cognate-a-Kambal, kambal.
Cognation-n-Pagkakamaganak
Cognition-n-Alam, pagkakaalam.
Cognizable-a-Magkakaalam.
Congnizance-n-Pagkakaalam, alam, pagkikilala
Cognize-i-Malaman, makialam
Cognomen-n-Apellido
Cog wheel-n-Gulong na may nğipin.
Cohere-v-Dumikit
Coherence-Coherency-n-Pagdidikit
Coherent a-Makadikit.
Cohort-n-Pulutong nğ sundalo.
Coil-v-Ikirin
Coil-n-Ikit, bilog.
Coin-n Salapi; kuarta.
Coin-v-Gumawa nğ salapi
Coinage-n-Salapi; paggagawa nğ salapi.
Coincide v-Umayon, makiayon; makiisa; umayos.
Coincidence-n-Ang nangyari sa isang panahon, ang pagkayaring sabay.
Coincident-a-Nauukol sa isang panahon.
Coir-n-Bunot nğ niog ó mansana.
Coke n-Uling nğ metal.
Coke-v Gumawa nğ uling.
Colander-n-Salaan,
Cold-a-Malamig, maginaw.
Cold-n-Lamig, ginaw.
Coldness-n-kalamigan; kaginawan.
Cole-n Gulay parang repollo.
Cole wort-n Repollo na malambot ang ulo.
Colic-n-Kabag, apad.

Cohcky-n-Kinakabagan
Collapse-v-Lumagpak, masira
Collar-n-Liig, cuello
Collar-i-Isuot ang cuello, hawakan sa liig.
Collation-n-Pagtatapat, minindal.
Colleague-n-Kasama, kasabay
Collect-v-Iponin, samsamin, tipunin; magsamsam, magtipon; ikama, magtipon, magsamasama. pumisan.
Collect-n-Dasal na maikli.
Collected-a-Naipon, nasamsam; buo ang loob
Collector-n-Manininğil; taga paninğil.
Collection n-Panininğil, pagsamsam, pagtitipon, pag ipon
Collective-a-Sinkad; magkakasabay.
Collectively-adv.-Sabaysabay, samasama.
College-n-Colegio
Collegian-n-Ang nagaaral sa colegio
Collegiate-a-Nauukol sa colegio
Collegiate-n-Ang nagaaral sa colegio
Collide-i-Ibungo; bumungo; umumpog, magumpugan, umuntog.
Colher n-Ang maguuling, maninibag.
Collier-n-Sasakyan na may lulang uling.
Colliery-n-Tibagan nğ uling
Colhsion-n-Umpog, untog, bungo
Colloquial-a-Nauukol sa salita.
Colloquialism-n-Karaniwang pananalita.
Colloquy-n Pananalita; salitaan
Collusive-a-Nauukol sa salitaang lihim.
Cologne-n-Pabanğo
Colonel n Koronel, puno .nğ isang regimientong sundalo.
Colonelcy-Colonelship-n-Kalagayan koronel.
Colinist-n-Colonista.
Colony-n-Colonia
Colonnade-n-Taludtod nğ mğa haligi.
Color-n-Kulay, color.
Color-v-Tinain.
Coloring-n-Color, pagtitina.
Colored a-May kulay; makulay.
Colossal-a-Totoong malaki
Colossus n Larawan na totoong malaki.
Colt n Potro
Coltish-a-Nauukol sa potro, parang potro
Colter-n-Sudsod.
Column-n Haligi
Columnar a-May maraming haligi.
Coma-n Coma.
Comate-a-Mabuhok.
Comb n-Suklay
Comb-(of a chicken)-Tuktok nğ manok.
Comb-v-Suklayin, magsuklay.
Combat-i-Magaway, umaway, lumaban. magbanğay, lumusob, bumaka; magbaka.

Combat-*n*-Digma; pagbabaka; labanan; laban; pag-aaway.
Combatant-*a*-Nauukol sa digma.
Combatant-*n*-Mandirigma; ang lumalaban; ang nagbabaka.
Combative-*a*-Masungit; mabagsik.
Combination-*v*-Pagkakalapat; pagkakapisan; pakakasama.
Combine-*v*-Isama; ilapat.
Combustible-*a*-Madaling maglilingas.
Combustible-*n*-Ano mang bagay na madaling maglilingas.
Combustion-*n*-Lingas; sunog; paglingas.
Come-*v*-Dumating; lumapit; mangaling.
Come up-*v*-Pumanhik; Umahon.
Comedian-*n*-Kumediante.
Comedy-*n*-Kasayahan; komedia.
Comely-*a*-Maganda.
Comeliness-*n*-Kagandahan.
Comet-*n*-Cometa.
Cometery-Cometic-*a*-Nauukol sa kometa.
Comfort *n*-Aliw; tuwa.
Comfort-*v*-Aliwin; matuwa.
Comfortable-*a*-Nakakaaliw; nakalulugod; magaling.
Comforter-*n*-Kumot.
Comfortless-*a*-Walang kaginhawahan; walang aliw; hindi maaliw.
Comic-Comical-*a*-Masaya; mapagpatawa.
Comicality-Comicalness-*n*-Kasayahan.
Coming-*a*-Darating.
Coming-*n*-Pagdating; pagdatal.
Comma-*n*-Kurlit.
Command-*n*-Utos; pamumuno; kapangyarihan; katungkulan; pamamahala.
Command-*v*-Magutos; maghari; mamuno.
Commandant-*n*-Puno.
Commander-*n*-Puno.
Commandment-*n*-Utos.
Commemorate-*v*-Magdiwang,
Commemoration-*n*-Pagdiwang.
Commence-*v*-Mulaan; buhatin; magmula; pasimulan; magsipamula.
Commencement-*n*-Pasimula; pinagbuhatan; pinagmulaan ,
Commend-*v*-Purihin; igalang.
Commendable-*a*-Dapat purihin; dapat mahalin; dapat ipagtagubilin.
Commendation-*n*-Pagpupuri.
Commensurate-*a*-Parisukat.
Commensurate-*v*-Husayin; ayusin, parisukatin.
Comment-*v*-Saysayin sa pintas.
Comment-*n*-Pintas; kasaysayan.
Commentary-*n*-Kahulugan; kasaysayan; salaysay.
Commentater-*n*-Ang nagsasaysay.
Commentator-*n*-Ang nagsasaysay.
Commerce-*n*-Pangangalakal.
Commercial-*a*-Nauukol sa pangangalakal

Commiserate-*v*-Maawain.
Commiseration-*n*-Awa; habag.
Commission-*n*-Bilin; katungkulan.
Commission-*v*-Ibigay ng katungkulan; ipagbilin.
Commit-*v*-Isangla; sanglain; gawin.
Commitment-*n*-Sangla; pagsasangla.
Committee-*n*-Kapisanan ng tawo.
Commodious-*a*-Maaliwalas; maluang malaki; maluag.
Commodity-*n*-Kalakal.
Commodore-*n*-Puno ng mga sasakyan na pandirigma.
Common-*a*-Karaniwan; gawi.
Common-*n*-Solar; plaza.
Commoner *n*-Karaniwang tawo.
Commonly-*adv*-Gawing; karaniwang.
Common-place-*a*-Karaniwan.
Common-place-*n*-Karaniwang sagot ó tugon; karaniwang tutol.
Common-wealth-*n*-Isang nacion; sang katawohan; manga tawo nang isang nacion.
Common-weal-*n*-Isang nacion; sang katawohan; manga tawo nang isang nacion.
Commune-*v*-Magsalitaan.
Communicant-*n*-Ang tawong nakikinabang.
Communicate-*v*-Magsabi; magbigay alam; sabihin ipahayag.
Communication-*n*-Pahayag; balita; sulat; salita.
Communicative-*a*-May gustong magsalita.
Communion-*n*-Comunion.
Community-*n*-Kapisanan ng tawo.
Commute-*v*-Palitan; pumalit.
Commutation-*n*-Kapalit; palit.
Compact-*a*-Malaki; masinsin; siksik; tipi.
Compact-*v*-Higpitin; ipitin.
Compact-*n*-Salitaan; trato.
Compactness-*n*-Katibayan; kasinsinan.
Companion-*n*-Abay; kasama; kaalakbay; kalaguyo; kalihim; kasabay; kansap.
Companionable-*a*-Mainam makisama.
Companion-ship-*n*-Pagkakasama.
Company-*n*-Tropa; compañia; kaalakbay; kasabay; kasama; pagkakatipon; katipunan; kapisanan.
Comparable-*a*-Makakaharap.
Comparative-*a*-Di pa siguro.
Compare-*v*-Iharap; sukatin; magparis; taruhin; itulot.
Comparison-*n*-Pag tatapat; pag harap; pagsukat.
Compart-*v*-Hatiin; hiwalayin.
Compartment-*n*-Kuarto; silid; isang bahagi.
Compass-*n*-Aguhon.

25

Compass ι-Pumaligid.
Compassion-n-Awa; habag; kahinahina-
yang, hinagpis.
Compassionate-a-Maawain, maawa, ha-
bag, mahabag
Compassionate v-Maawa, habagin.
Compel-v-Pilitin, higpitan
Compend-n-Kasaysayan, sulat na ma-
ikli.
Compendious a-Maikli.
Compendium-n-Tandaan.
Compensate-v-Bayaran; magbayad, upa-
hin, umupa; tamtaman, upahan.
Compensation-n-Bayad; upa; kagam-
pan; ganti.
Compete-v-Lumaban, labanin.
Competence-n-Kabagayan; kaya, kasu
katan
Competency-n-Kaya; kasukatan, kaba-
gayan.
Competent-a-Makaya, bagay, akma.
Competition n-Paglaban, pagtatalo.
Competitive-a-Nauukol sa paglaban
Competitor-r-Kaagaw, kaaway, kalaban,
katalo.
Compilation n-Pag gagawa nang anoman.
Compile-v-Tipunin, gawin.
Complacence-n-Saya; wili; kasayahan
Complacency-n-Saya, wili; kasayahan.
Complacent-a-Masaya, masunurin
Complain v-Dumaing, magdaing, mag-
damdam; maghimutok, managhoy.
Complainant-n-Ang dumadaing
Complaint-n-Daing, sumbong, taghoy;
hinanakit, damdam; karamdaman.
Complement-n-Kahustuhan, kasukatan.
Complete-a-Lubos, husto, puno, ganap;
lipos, sakdal puspos, sinkad, sawa;
walang kulang
Complete-v-Tapusin, ganapin, idaos;
hustuhin
Completeness-n-Kayarian lubos, sidhi
Completion-n-Kayarian, sidhi
Complex-a-Pasuotsuot; hindi; mahiwa-
nag, mahirap tarukin; magulo
Complexion-n-Kulay at hitsura nang
mukha.
Compliance-n-Pagtupad, handog, suyo,
paglinkod; kapakumbabaan.
Compliant-a-Mapaglinkod, mapagbigay
loob, malambot ang ugali, masunu-
rin; masaya ang loob, masuyo
Complicate-v-Guluhin, pilipitin
Complicate-a-Magulo, pasuotsuot
Complication-n-Kaguluhan; kapilipitan,
gulo.
Compliment-n-Pakumusta, pabilin; bi
yaya, bilin, kumusta.
Compliment v-Purihin, galangin.
Complimental a Mapuri.

Complimentary-a-Mapuri.
Comply-v-Tumupad, tuparin; umayon;
magbigay loob, pahinuhod; sumunod,
umayos
Component a-Nakatulong.
Component-n-Bahagi
Comport-v-Dalitain, dalitaan; dalumatin;
damutin
Compose-v-Isulat; gumawa ng sulat.
Composed-a-Buo ang loob, tahimik.
Composedly-adv.-Tahimik
Composer n-Ang gumagawa ng sulat.
Composite-n-May isang bahagi.
Composition-n-Halo; lahok, ang sinulat
ng sarili.
Compost-n-Dumi ng hayop
Composure-n-Katahimikan.
Compound v-Haluhin, lahokin; ilahok.
Compound-a-Nakakahalo, nakakalaho.
Compound-n-Halo, lahok.
Comprehend-v-Tarukin ng isip, umin-
tindi, dingin, mawatasan, duminig,
tantuin, abutin ng isip
Comprehension-n-Pang intindi, dunong
Comprehensive-a-Maabot ng isip
Compress-ι-Tipiin; pai-pikin, ipitin.
Compress-n-Tipi; pangpaikpik.
Compressed-a-Paikpik, tipi
Compression n Pagpapaikpik
Comprise-v-Ilahok, ilangkap, maglaman
Compromise-n-Sahtaan, pagkakasundu-
an, pinagkasunduan
Compromise-v-Magkasundo.
Comptroller-n-Puno.
Compulsion-n-Pagpilit.
Compulsory-a-Mapilitan.
Compulsive-a-Mapilitan
Compunction-n-Hiya.
Computation n-Bilang, kabilugan.
Compute-v-Bilangin, bumilang.
Comrade-n-Kaulayaw; kasama, kaibigan,
kalaguyo; kasabay.
Con-ι-Magwariwari, magisipisip
Concave-a-Malukong
Concave-n-Hubog, hukay.
Concavity-n-Kahumbakan.
Conceal-v-Itago, tumago, magtago, ibaon,
iligpit, lumigpit, ikalong, kumalong,
ilihim, itaan
Concealed-v p p -Tinago
Concealment n-Pagtatago, pagkalong-
pagtatakpan.
Concede-v-Pumayag; umayon, sumunod,
magbigay; magkaloob; sumuko.
Conceit-n-Yabang; hambog, kayabangan;
kahambugan, kapalaluan
Conceited-a-Mayabang, hambog
Conceive v-Akalain, isipin, unawin
Conceivable a-Maabot ng isip, madaling
maintindihan.

Concentrate-v-Ipagitna; isama.

Concentration-n-Pagpapagitna; pagsasamasama.

Conception-n-Aha; dilidili; banta.

Concern-v-Maukol; marapat; matugkol; ipagmasakit

Concern-n-Sakit; dalamhati; imbot hañgad; lumbay.

Concerning-prep.-Tungkol sa; nauukol sa.

Concert-v-Magkaisa; umayon; husayin.

Concert-n-Pagkakasunduan.

Concertina-n-Concertina.

Concession-n-Pagpayag; pagsuko.

Concierge-n-Concierge.

Conciliate-v-Pagkasunduan; magkasundo

Conciliation-n-Pagkakasundo.

Conciliatory-a-Nauukol sa'pagkakasundo.

Conclude-v-Tapusin; yariin; utasin; mautas; tumapos.

Conclusion-n-Tapos; yari; dulo; pandulo; pagtatapos; pang wakas; katapusan.

Conclusive-a-Pang wakas.

Concoct-v-Ihalo; ilahok.

Concord-n-Salitaan; pinagkasunduan.

Concordance-n-Salitaan; pag kakasun duan.

Concordant-a-Nagkakaayon.

Concourse-n-Pag galaw; kilos; bunton ñg tawo.

Concrete-a-Nakakapisan.

Concrete-n-Pagkakapisan ñg mga bagaybagay; halo; ñg bato at cimiento.

Concrete-v-Isamsam; pumisan.

Concretion-n-Pagsasamsam.

Concubine-n-Kaagulo; kalunya.

Concur-v-Umabuloy; magkaisa; umayon.

Concurrence-n-Abuloy; pag kakasundo; pinagkasunduan; salitaan.

Concurrent-a-Nauukol sa salitaan ó abuloy.

Concussion-n-Putok

Condemn-v Bigyan sala; humatol; sumentencia.

Condemnable-a-Dapat pintasin.

Condemnation-n-Pagbibigay sala.

Condensation-n-Paglalapot; sinsin.

Condense-v-Lumapot; cinsinan; palapuputin; suminsin.

Condescend-v-Bigyang loob; magbigay loob; umaayon; sumunod; dalitain.

Condescension-n-Pagbibigay loob.

Condign-a-Dapat nararapat, aqma.

Condignness-n-Karapatan.

Condiment-n-Karampatan.

Condition-n-Lagay; kalagayan; kabagayan; pagkakalagay; kalidad.

Condition-v-Magsalitaan.

Conditional-a-May condiciones.

Condole-v-Maawain; habagin.

Condolence-n-Habag; awa; hinayang.

Condone-v-Patawarin.

Conduce-v-Ihatid; ihilig; maghatid.

Conducible-a-Mahilig.

Conduct-v-Maghatid; akayin; dalhinihatid; saklawin.

Conduct-n Kilos; anyo; gawa; lakad.

Conductor-n-Tagahatid; taga dala.

Conduit-n-Tubo ñg grifo.

Cone-n-Cono.

Confection-n-Manga matamis.

Confectioner-n-Taga gawa nang manga matamis.

Confectionery-n-Manga matamis.

Confederacy-n-Kapisanan.

Confederate-a-Nakikisama.

Confederate-n-Kalihim; kaulayaw.

Confederate-v-Isama; pumisan.

Confederation-n-Kapisanan.

Confer-v-Ipagkaloob.

Conference-n-Pañguñgusapan.

Confess-v-Magcompisal.

Confession-n-Compisal.

Confessional-n-Compisionario.

Confessional-a-Nauukol sa pananampalataya.

Confidant n-Kalihim; kaunuran.

Confide-v-Ipagkatiwala.

Confidence-n-Katapatan ñg loob; liksi; tapang; kabuoan ñg loob.

Confident-a-Buo ang loob; matapang mapalagay ang loob.

Confidential-a-Malihim; palihim; mahinahon; nalilihim.

Confidentially-adv.-Palihim.

Confine-n-Hanga.

Confine-v-Kuluñgin; bawasan; awasan; padilimin.

Confinement-n-Pakulong; pagkabihag.

Confirm-v-Tibayan; tumangkilik; tumulong; patotohanin.

Confirmation-n-Pagpapatotoo; tibay ñg anoman; pagpapatibay.

Confirmative-a-Matitibayan.

Confirmatory-a-Matitibayan.

Confiscate-v-Kunin ñg gobierno.

Confiscation-n-Pagkakuha ñg gobierno

Conflagration-n-Sunog.

Conflict-n-Talo; laban; away.

Conflict-v-Lumaban; guluhin.

Confluence-n-Bunton ñg tawo.

Conform-v-Umayon; ibagay; imukha.

Conformable-a-Kumukha; kaparis.

Conformation-n-Pagkakasunduan; pinagkasunduan.

Conformity-n-Kasukatan; pagkakaisa; pagkakapisan; pagkakawañgis; pagkaugnay; tañgo.

Confound-v-Guluhin.

Confounded-a-Gulo; magulo.

Confront-v-Iharap; humarap.

Confuse v-Lumabo, gumulo, guluhin.
Confused-a-Magulo, walang ayos.
Confusion-n-Kaguluhan, kahihiyaan, kaliluhan; ligalig; pagkahito.
Confutation-n-Kaayawang pumayag.
Confute-v-Manalo sa pañguñgusap, patahimikin.
Congeal-v-Mamuo.
Congenial a-Magkaparis, kamukha, kaparis, makibagay.
Congeniality-n-Pagkakamukha.
Congenital-a Buhat ipinañganak, bu' at sa pañgañganak
Conger n-Palos.
Conger eel-n-Palos
Congest-v Samsamin; iponin
Congestion-n-Pagsasamsam; pagiipon
Conglomerate-v-Maipon, umipon
Conglomerate-a-Nakapiling
Conglomeration-n-Pagiipon
Congratulate-v-Purihin, panuyoin
Congratulation n-Panuyo
Congratulatory-a-Panunuyo
Congregate-v-Pumisan, tuimpon; lumakip; lumagom
Congregation-n Katipunan; tipon, kapisanan, pagpupulo, pagtitipon;lupong
Congregational a Nauukol sa pulong ó tipon ó katipunan
ongress-n-Congreso
Congressional-a-Nauukol sa congreso
Congruence-n-Kabagayan, pagkakasunduan.
ongruency n-Pagkakasunduan
Congruent-a Masunurin
ongruity-n-Pagkakasunduan
ongruous a-Masunurin.
onic a-Parang cono.
onical a-Parang cono.
onjectural-a-Hindi pa siguro.
onjecture-n-Hinala, sapantaha, hula; tumbak, bintang
onjecture-v-Maghinala humula; sumapantaha.
onjoin-v-Igawgaw; ihalo; ilakip, isama.
onjoint-a-Nakakapisan, nakakasama
onjugal-a Nauukol sa kasal.
onjugate-v-Ibahin ñg kahulugan ñg isang verbo
onjugate a-Nakakapisan
onjunct-a Kalapit, katabi
onjunction n-Conjuncion, pagkakalapat; pagkakapisan, pagkakalakip; paguugnay.
onjunctive-a-Nauukol sa pagkakapisan, nakakalapat, nakakapisan
onjunctor-n-Pagsasama
onjure-v Tumawa, panumpain.
onnate-a-Kambal
onnect-v-Isama, ilapat; idugtong.

Connection-n-Kadugtong, pagkakalapat, pagkakaugpong kaukulan.
Connive-v-Huag makita ang mali
Connoisseur-n-Taga pintas
Connubial-a-Nauukol sa kasal.
Conquer-v-Manalo, isakop, magpasuko
Conquerable-a-Malalaluan.
Conquest-n-Pananalo
Consanguineous a-Kadugo.
Consanguinity-n-Kadugo.
Conscience-n-Isip; loob
Conscientious a-Ayon sa isip
Conscious-a-May isip, may pangdamdam
Conscript-a-Nakalista, nakatanda
Conscript-n-Sundalo
Conscription-n Paglilista.
Consecrate-v-Benditahin; ipanagano, lalay, magalay; itaan.
Consecrate-a-Maalay
Consecration-n Pagaalay, panagano
Consecutive a-Sunodsunod
Consent-n-Pahintulot.
Consent-v-Ipahintulot, tulutin; tumañgo.
Consequence n-Bigat, kahulugan; dulo.
Consequent-a-Nakakasunod.
Consequent n-Pandulo.
Consequential a-Sumunod
Consequently adv -Dahil dito
Conservation-n Pagluluat; luat, tagal
Conservative-a-Matibay, di mabubulok
Conservator n-Taga kalong, ang lumalaban, para sa iba
Conserve-n-Conservas, matamis.
Consider-v-Akalain; bulaybulayin, isipin; magisipisip kilalaning mabuti, magwari, magwariwari.
Considerable-a-Marami ñg kaunti
Considerate-a-Mabait, mapagwari; mahinhin, mahinahon.
Consideration-n-Dahilan, katamtaman, katampatan, katowiran.
Consign-v-Ipagkaloob
Consignment-n-Pagpapadala.
Consist-v-Magkaroon
Consistence-n-Kalagayan; katibayan.
Consistency-n-Kalagayan; katibayan.
Consistent-a-Masinsin, matatag.
Consolation n-Aliw; kaaliwan, pag aliw.
Consolatory-a-Maaliw.
Console v-Aliwin
Consolidate-v-Isama, ilakip.
Consolidation-n-Pagsasama
Consonant-n-Consonante
Consort-n-Kasama; asawa
Consort-t-Magsama.
Conspicuous a-Bunyi, bantog, litaw, mahlwanag.
Conspiracy-n Hibo isip na masama
Conspirator-n-Ang umisip; gumawa ñg masama.

Conspire-*v*-Isipin ñg masama; dayain.

Conspirer-*n*-Ang umisip gumawa ñg masama.

Constable-*n*-Policia; constable.

Constancy-*n*-Katiyagaan; tibay ñg loob; katibayan uğ loob; katamanan; pananalig.

Constant-*a*-Tiaga; matibay; matitiis; matiyaga; firme ang loob; patag; walang gulo; hindi mababago.

Consternation-*n*-Takot; gulat; gulo.

Constipate-*v*-Sumipon.

Costipation-*n*-Sipon.

Constituency-*n*-Kapisanan ñg manga nagvovoto.

Constitution-*n*-Constitución.

Constitutional-*a*-Ayon sa utos; matowid; tama; walang laban sa utos.

Constitutionality-*n*-Pagkakaayon sa constitución.

Constrain-*v*- Pigilin.

Constraint-*n*-Pagpigil.

Constrict-*v*-Talian; isama.

Constriction-*n*-Pagtatali; paghigpit.

Construct-*v*-Gumawa; gawin; itoyo; magtayo.

Construction-*n*-Paggagawa; pagtatayo.

Construe-*v*-Ipatalastas; ituro.

Consul-*n*-Consul.

Consulate-*n*-Officina ñg consul.

Consulship-*n*-Kalagayang consul.

Consult-*v*-Sumangunit; magtanong.

Consu'tation-*n*-Pagsasanguni.

Consume-*v*-Ubusin; lamunin; lusawin; gamitin.

Consummate-*v*-Tapusin.

Consummately-*a*-Matatapos.

Consummation-*n*-Tapos.

Consumption-*n*-Pag ubos; pag gagamit.

Consumptive-*n*-Tawong natutuyo.

Contact-*n*-Hipo; sagi; salubong.

Contage-*v*-Makahawa.

Contagion-*n*-Pagkakahawa.

Contagious-*a*-Makakahawa.

Contain-*v*-Magkaroon; magkaugat; magkalaman; malulan; may.

Contaminate-*v*-Mansahin; bulukin.

Contamination-*n*-Pagkakamansa.

Contemn-*v*-Murahin; hamakin.

Contemplate-*v*-Bulaybulayin; wari wariin mag isip isipin; nilayin.

Contemplation-*n*-Pag wawariwari; pagalaala; pagdilidili.

Contemplative-*a*-Mapag wariwari; mapag isip; isipin.

Contemporaneous-*a*-Makasabay.

Contemporary-*n*-Kasabay; kapanahon.

Contempt-*n*-Pintas; kawalan nang galang kaalimurahan; pag lait; pagpahamak.

Contemptible-*a*-Hamak; mababa; malait; masama.

Contemtuous-*a*-Mapaglait.

Contend-*v*-Lumaban; umaway; bumabag; humamon; ipagmatowid; pumilit.

Content-*n*-Tuwa; katahimikan; galak; kasayahan.

Content-*a*-Masaya; natutuwa; malugod.

Content-*v*-Matuwa.

Contention-*n*-Pagtatalo; talo; laban.

Contentious-*a*-Nakakahilig sa laban; mapagpatalo; mapagbasagulo.

Contentment-*n*-Katuwaan; kasayahan.

Contest-*v*-Umaway; lumaban; magtalo; magusap.

Contest-*n*-Talo; usap; away; buno.

Contestation-*n*-Pakli; tugon; sagot.

Contestable-*a*-Matatalo.

Contestant-*n*-Ang nakikipagtalo.

Context-*n*-Mğa pangkat ñg sermon.

Contiguity-*n*-Lapit; lakip; paguugnay; pagkalakip.

Contiguous-*a*-Malapit; katabi.

Continence-*n*-Hinahon; bait; katahimikan; kabaitan.

Continency-*n*-Bait; hinahon; kabaitan; katahimikan.

Contingence-*n*-Palad; kapalaran.

Continency-*n*-Palad; kapalaran.

Contingent-*a*-Nag ataon; hindi sinasadya; hindi tinatalaga.

Continent-*n*-Mahinahon; tahimik; mabait

Continent-*n*-Continente.

Continental-*a*-Nauukol sa continente.

Contingent-*n*-Pulutong ñg mğa sundalo.

Continual-*a*-Walang tigil; walang likat; walang humpay; walang tahan.

Continuance-*n*-Laon; pagtutuloy; pagtatagal; kapanayan.

Continuation-*n*-Pagtutuloy; pagtatagal, kapanayan.

Continued-*a*-Tuloytuloy; sunodsunod.

Continue-*v*-Sumunod; ipatuloy; mamalagi; magtuloy; ituloy.

Continuity-*n*-Pagtutuloy.

Continuous-*a*-Walang tigil; walang humpay; walang tahan; lagi; panay; nagkakadugtong dugtong.

Contort-*v*-Pilipitin.

Contortion-*n*-Pagpipilipit.

Contour-*n*-Hanga.

Contraband-*a*-Laban sa utos nang gobierno.

Contract-*n*-Kumuntrato; mag salitaan; magkasunod; magtrato.

Contract-*v*-Salitaan; pinagkasunduan; tipan; trato; kasulatan.

Contracted-*a*-May bawas; may hanga.

Contraction-*n*-Pangunğurong; bawas; pagurong.

Contractor-*n*-Ang may salitaan; ang pumapakyaw ng ano man.

Contradict-*v*-Magkaila; itatua; labagin; tumangi; isalangsang sumumbang; ipagkait; tumalikod.

Contradiction-*n*-Pagtatalikod; pagkakaila; paglabag; tatua; pagkait.

Coutradictory-*a*-Sowail; matigas ang ulo.

Contrariwise-*adv*.-Pabaliktad; sa kalaban; pabalik; pasalungat.

Contrary-*a*-Salungat; sowail; matigas ang ulo; pabaliktad.

Contrast-*v*-Salangsangin.

Contrast *n*-Salangsang.

Contravene-*v*-Lumaban; sumalangsang; sumoway.

Contravention-*n*-Salangsang; paglaban; pagkakaila; pagsoway.

Contribute-*v*-Magambag; umambag; umabuloy.

Contribution-*n*-Ambag; abuloy.

Contrite-*a*-Malungkot; malumbay.

Contriteness-*n*-Kalungkutan; lumibay.

Contrition-*n*-Kalungkutan; kalumbayan.

Contrivance-*n*-Kasangkapan.

Contrive-*v*-Akalain; isipin kumatha.

Control-*n*-Kapangyarihan; kapal; pamamahala.

Control-*v*-Mamahala; supilin.

Controller-*n*-Ang namamahala; ang may kapangyarihan.

Controversial-*a*-Nauukol sa basagulo.

Controversy-*n*-Basagula; pagtatalo.

Controvert-*v*-Makipagtalo; magtalo.

Controvertible *a*-Hilig sa basagulo.

Contumaceous-*a* Matigas ang ulo.

Contumacy-*n*-Katigasan ng ulo higpit; kasungitan.

Contumelious-*a*-Hamak; bastos; tampalasan.

Contumely-*n*-Kahamakan; kabastusan; tampalasan.

Contuse *v*-Bugbogin; dikdikin; mamuho ang dugo.

Contusion-*n*-Bugbog; pamumuo ng dugo.

Conundrum-*n* Bugtong.

Convalesce-*v*-Mangaling sa sakit; gumaling sa sakit.

Convalescence-*n*-Pag galing sa sakit.

Convalescent-*a*-Nagpapalakas.

Convalescent-*n*-Ang tawong bagong galing sa sakit.

Convene-*v*-Magtipon; pumisan.

Convenience *n* Katapatan; kabagayan.

Convenient-*a*-Ginhawa; bagay; akma; agpang; tama; maayos; mabuti; dapat.

Convent-*n*-Konvento.

Conventual-*a*-Nauukol sa konvento.

Convention-*n*-Tipanan; pulong; katipunan.

Conventional-*a*-Makikiayon; bagay.

Converge-*v*-Lumapit sa isang dulo.

Convergence-*n*-Paglalapit sa isang dulo; paglalapit ng dalawang bagay.

Conversant-*a*-Marunong; magsalita.

Conversation *n*-Salita; pag-usap; wika.

Conversational-*a*-Nauukol sa salitaan.

Converse *v*-Magsalitaan; wikain; magumpok; mangusap.

Converse-*n* Salita, wika.

Conversion-*n* Pagiiba ng pananampalataya.

Convert-*v*-Baguhin; ibahin; binyagin.

Convert-*n*-Bagong binyagan.

Convertible-*a* Madaling baguhin; madaling mabago.

Convex-*a*-Umbok ang gitna; kukob; mataas ang gitna.

Convex-*n*-Kukob.

Convey-*v*-Dalhin; ihatid; maghatid; isama; sumama; akayin; iakay.

Conveyance *n*-Paghahatid; kasangkapang pandala.

Convict-*v*-Magbigay sala.

Convict-*n*-Ang may kasalanan; ang nakukulong sa bilango; ang nabibilango; ang nagkasala.

Conviction-*n*-Pagbigay sala.

Convince-*v*-Liwanagin; pilitin.

Convivial *a*-Masaya; maligaya; malugod.

Conviviality-*n*-Kasayahan; kaluguran; kaligayahan.

Convoke-*v*-Tawagin; sunduin; tumawag sa marami.

Convocation-*n*-Pagtitipon; pulong.

Convolve-*v*-Ikirin.

Convoy-*v*-Ihatid; maghatid.

Convoy-*n*-Tulong; kumboy.

Convulse-*v*-Pumulikat.

Convulsion-*n*-Pulikat.

Cony-*n*-Conejo.

Coo-*v*-Sumiap.

Cook-*n*-Tagaluto; cocinero.

Cook-*v*-Lutuin; magluto; magkosina.

Cookery-*n*-Pag luluto ng pagkain.

Cooky-*n*-Mamon; hupia.

Cool-*a*-Malamig; sariwa.

Cool-*v*-Magpalamig; lumamig.

Coolie-*n*-Taga pasan.

Coolness-*n*-Kalamigan.

Cooly-*n*-Taga pasan; trabajador.

Cool-*n* Kalamigan.

Coop-*n*-Kulungan ng manok; tangkal.

Coop-*v*-Ilagay sa kulungan.

Co-oper-*n*-Ang gumagawa ng bariles; taga gawa ng bariles.

Cooperate-*v*-Tulungin; sumabay sa trabajo; tumulong.

Co-operation-*n*-Pagtutulong.
Co-operator-*n*-Ang tumutulong.
Co-ordinate-*a*-Magkaisa ang taas ng katungkulan.
Co-ordinate-*v*-Makaisa.
Co-ordination-*n*-Pagkakaisa.
Coot-*n*-Ulol, tawong mangmang.
Copartner-*n*-Kalaguyo; kaulayaw.
Cope-*n*-Habito ng pari.
Cope-*v*-Lumaban; magtalo; subukin.
Copier-*n*-Taga salin.
Coping-*n*-Ibabaw ng pader.
Copious-*a*-Marami; maluang; malaki.
Copiously-*adv*.-Masagana.
Copper-*n*-Baria; tansong pula.
Copper-*v*-Ibalot ng tanso; ilubog sa tanso.
Copse-*n*-Kaugoygoyan.
Copulative-*n*-Conjunción.
Copy-*n*-Tulad salin; howad; pasunod.
Copy-*v*-Howaran; tularin; tumulad; gagarin; gumagad.
Copyier-Copyist-*n*-Taga sulat.
Coquet-*n*-Kalakero; babayingsalawahang loob.
Cord-*n* Lubid; pisi.
Cord-*v*-Talian ng pisi.
Cordage *n* Mga lubid at pisi.
Cadate-*a*-Hitsurang puso.
Cordial-*a*-Tapat na loob.
Cordiality-*n*-Katapangan ng loob.
Core-*n*-Ubod; puso.
Core-*v*-Alisan ng ubod ó puso.
Cork-*n*-Tapon; tasok.
Cork-*v*-Ilagay ng tapon; tasakin.
Cork screw-*n*-Pang alis ng tapon; tirabuson.
Corn-*n*-Mais.
Corn-*v*-Asnan; magpaksiw.
Corn cob-*n*-Busal ng mais.
Corner-*n*-Sulok; panulukan.
Corner-*v*-Ilagay sa sulok: gipitin.
Cornered-*a*-Nakasulok.
Cornet-*n*-Cornetin.
Cornice-*n*-Gilid ng pader.
Corn knife-*n*-Itak, pisaw.
Corn shuck-*n*-Balat ng mais.
Corn stalk-*n*-Puno ng mais.
Corn starch-*n*-Almirol.
Corol-Corolla-*n*-Loob ng bulaklak.
Corona-*n*-Corona.
Coronary-*a*-Hitsurang corona.
Coronation-*n*-Pagpuputong ng corona.
Coroner-*n*-Taga siyasat sa patay.
Coronet-*n*-Putong.
Corporal-*n*-Kabo.
Corporal-*a*-Nauukol sa katawan.
Corporate-*a*-Samasama.
Corporation-*n*-Kapisanan ng mga mangangalakal.

Corporeal-*a*-May katawan.
Corps-*n*-Hukbo.
Corpse-*n*-Bangkay; burol.
Corpulent-*a*-Mataba; malakas; malaki; makipal; may katawan.
Corpulence-*n*-Katabaan.
Corpulency-*n*-Katabaan.
Correct-*a*-Tama; totoo.
Correct-*v*-Towirin; correhin; husayin; aralan magmatuwid.
Correction-*n*-Pagaayos; paghusay; pagaaralan.
Correspond-*v*-Umayon; matugkol gumanting loob; magsusulatan.
Correspondence-*n*-Pagkakaayon pagsusulatan; kaukulan; pagka'aakma.
Correspondent-*n*-Katugon; ang sumusulat.
Correspondent-*a*-Maukol; tungkol; ayon.
Corresponding-*a*-Karampatan.
Corridor-*n*-Salas.
Corroborate-*v*-Tumankilik; umayon; sumaksi; magkaisa.
Corroboration-*n*-Tankilik; pagtitibayan, saksi; pagkakaisa sa salitaan.
Corrode-*v*-Kumalawang.
Corrosion-*n* Kalawang.
Corrosive-*a*-Makakalawangin.
Corrugate-*v*-Kutunin; kunutin.
Corrupt-*v*-Mabulok; bulukin; dumhan; dumumi; sasamáin; sumamá. bumulok.
Corrupt *a*-Bulok; marumi; madungis; masama.
Corruptible *a*-Marumi; mabulok.
Corruption-*n*-Baho; dungis; kabulukan; pagkabulok.
Corruptive-*a*-Nakakabulok.
Corsair-*n*-Tulisan dagat.
Coruscate-*v*-Kumintab; kumisap.
Coruscation-*n*-Kintab; kisap; kislap.
Corvine-*a*-Nauukol sa wak.
Cosmetic-*n*-Blankete; cosmetico.
Cosmopolitan-*n*-Tawong la ad; tawong walang bahay na pirme.
Cosmos-*n*-Sangkalibutan; sang katawohan.
Cost-*v*-Mahalaga; magkahalaga.
Cost-*n*-Halaga; gasta.
Costal *a*-Nauukol sa tadyang.
Costly-*a*-Mahalaga; mahal.
Costume-*n*-Damit.
Costumer-*n*-Ang nagtitinda ng damit.
Cot-*n*-Bahay na munti; kubo.
Cot-Cott-*n*-Hihigan na munti.
Contemporary-*n* Kapanahon; kaalakbay.
Coterie-*n*-Kapisanan; katipunan.
Cotillion-*n*-Rigudon.
Cottage-*n*-Bahay na munti; barong barong.

Cotter-*n*-Susi.
Cotton-*n*-Bulak.
Couch-*n*-Sandalan; hiligan; hihigan na munti.
Cough-*v*-Umubo; tumikhim.
Cough-*n*-Ubo; tikhim.
Could-*v*-Maka.
Coulter-*n*-Sudsod.
Council-*n*-Consejo.
Councilman-*n*-Concejal.
Counsel-*n*-Hatol; pasiya.
Counsel-*v*-Aralan; magpasiya.
Count-*n*-Bilang; Kabilangan.
Count-*v*-Bumilang.
Countenance-*n*-Mukha; pagmumukha.
Countenance-*v*-Pumayag; ipahintulot; pabayaan; Hayaan.
Counter-*n*-Panbilang.
Counter-*a*-Kalaban; laban.
Cunteract-*v*-Lumaban.
Connteraction-*n*-Timbang; katimbang.
Counterfeit-*n*-Howad; tulad; katalad; kahuwad.
Connterfeit-*a*-Howad; konowari; falso; hindi tunay.
Counterfeit-*v*-Howaran; parisan; gagarin; gumagad.
Counter-mand-*v*-Baguhin ang utos.
Counter-pane-*n*-Kumot.
Counter-part-*n*-Kabiak.
Counter-poise-*v*-Tumimbang.
Counter-poise-*n*-Katimbang.
Counter-sign-*n*-Hodyat; hodyatan.
Counter-sign-*v*-Pumirma.
Countess-*n*-Asawa nğ visconde.
Counting-house-*n*-Banko.
Countless-*a*-Di makabilang.
Country-*n*-Parang; bukid; kabukiran.
Country-*a*-Nauukol sa parang ó bukid.
Country-man-*n*-Taga bu id; kababayan.
Country-woman-*n*-Babaying taga bukid.
County-*n* Lalawigan.
Couple-*n*-Ang dalawa; paris.
Couple-*v*-Isama, kumasal; ikasal.
Coupling-*n*-Panali.
Courage-*n*-Tapang; bisa; dahas; lakas loob; sigla; pagkabayani.
Courageous-*a*-Matapang; malakas ang loob; buo ang loob; marahas; bayani.
Courier-*n*-Taga dala nğ telegrama.
Course-*n*-Paraan; daan; takbo.
Course-*v*-Pumaraan; tumakbo dumaan.
Courser-*n*-Manğanğaso; kabayong matulin.
Court-*n*-Juzgado; hukuman.
Court-*v*-Lumigaw; luningkod; manuyo.
Courteous-*a*-Magalang; bihasa; marunong makipag kapwa tawo.
Courtesy-*n*-Galang; yuko; yukod.
Courtesy-*v*-Yumuko; gumalang.

Court house-*n*-Bahay nğ juzgado.
Courtly-*a*-Magalang; nauukol sa juzgado.
Court-martial-*n*-Juzgadong militar.
Cout-plaster-*n*-Patko.
Court-ship-*n*-Pagligaw; paglilingkod.
Cousin-*n*-Pinsan.
Cove-*n*-Yunğib; lalaki.
Covenant-*n*-Salitaan.
Covenant-*v*-Magsalitaan; magtipanan.
Cover-*v*-Tutupan; takpanin; atipan; balutin; itakip.
Cover-*n*-Tutop; balot; tungtong; tapal; karang takip.
Covering-*n*-Balot; karang takip.
Covert-*a*-Natakpan.
Covert-*n*-Lugal na tago.
Coverlet-*n*-Kumot; na mantil.
Covet-*v*-Magnasa; maingit.
Covetous-*a*-Maingitan; maramot; masakim.
Covetousness-*n*-Kasakiman; karamutan, kahalayan; kaingitan.
Covey-*n*-Akay nğ ibong.
Cow-*n*-Baka.
Cow-*v*-Takutin; tumakot
Coward-*a*-Duag; mahina ang loob; matatakutin.
Coward-*n*-Duag
Cowardice-*n*-Karuagan; pagkaduag.
Cowardly-*a*-Duag; maduag; matata utin mahina ang loob.
Cower-*v*-Tumakot.
Cow herd-*n*-Ang nagpapastol; pastol.
Cow hide-*n*-Balat nğ baka.
Cowl-*n*-Tukarol nğ pari.
Coy-*a*-Nahihiya; mahihiyain.
Cozen-*v*-Dayain; manuyo.
Cozy-*a*-Mainam; maganda.
Crab-*n* Alimanğo; talangka; alimasag.
Crabbed-*a*-Masunğit;mabagsik;maramot.
Crack-*v*-Pumutok; lumahang; lahanğin; baliin; lamatin.
Crack-*n*-Ugong; putok; lahang; lamat; basag; bali.
Crack-*a*-Sanay; marunong; makinis; mainam.
Cracker-*n*-Galleta.
Crackle-*v*-Humaging; lumagutok; lumagitik.
Crackle-*n*-Lagitik; lagutok; langitnğit.
Cradle-*n*-Duyan.
Cradle-*v*-Ilagay sa duyan; iduyan.
Craft-*n*-Talas; katalasan; katusuhan; lansi; katalinuhan.
Crafty-*a*-Matalas; tuso; suitik.
Crag-*n*-Batong mataas at matarik.
Cragged-*a*-Mabato; hindi patag.
Craggy-*a*-Mabato; hindi patag.
Cram-*v*-Siksikin; isiksik.
Cramp-*n*-Pulikat; manhid; apad.

Cramp-v-Pumulikat; mamanhid.
Crane-n-Tagak; grua; kamaboy.
Cranium-n-Bao nğ ulo.
Crank-n-Puluhan.
Cranky-a-Masuñgit; mabagsik.
Cranny-n Litak; sulok.
Crape-n-Kayong manipis at maitim; kayong panluksa.
Crash-n-Bungo; lagpak; kalog; umpog.
Crash-v-Bunungo; lumagpak; kumalog; durugin.
Crate-n-Kahon; kaing; loelang; buslo.
Crater-n-Bibig ó butas nğ volcan.
Cravat-n-Corbata.
Crave n-Magnasa; maingit; sumamo; manalañgin; dumaing.
Craving-n-Ingit; nasa; pita.
Craven-a-Duag; maduag; mahina ang loob.
Craw-n-Balunbalunan.
Crawl-v-Gumapang.
Crawl-n-Pag-gapang.
Crawl-n-Kuluñgan nğ isda; baklad.
Crawfish-n-Alimasag.
Crayon-n-Yeso.
Craze-v-Maging ulol; maulol.
Craze-n-Uso; ugali; kaugalian; modo.
Crazy-a-Ulol; baliw; sira ang isip.
Crazyman-n-Tawong ulol; tawong sira ang isip; ulol.
Creak-v-Umalitiit; lumañgitñgit.
Creak-n-Alitiit; lañgitñgit.
Cream-n-Laknip.
Creamy-a-Malaknip.
Craziness-n-Kaululan; kasiraan nğ isip; pagkaulol.
Crease-n-Bakas nğ tiklop.
Crease-v-Bakasin sa pagtiklop.
Create-v-Lumalang; magsangol.
Creation-n-Kapal; lalang; paglalang.
Creator-n-Ang may kapal.
Creature-n-Nilalang; sangol; hayop.
Credence-n-Pananampalataya; paniniwala.
Credent-a-Pananampalatayanin.
Credential-n-Titulo.
Credible-a-Dapat maniwala; tapat ang loob.
Credit-n-Pautang; pananampalataya; paniniwala.
Credit-v-Pautañgin; sumampalataya; maniwala; magbigay puri.
Creditor-n-Ang nagpapautang; pinagkautañgan.
Credulous-a-Dapat maniwala.
Credulity-n-Sampalataya; pananampalaya; paniniwala.
Creed-n-Pananampalataya sa Dios.
Creek-n-Ilog; sapa.
Creel-n-Buslo.

Creep-v-Gumapang.
Creeping-n-Paggapang.
Creeper-n-Ang gumagapang.
Cremate-v-Sunugin nğ bangkay.
Cremation-n-Pagsunog nğ bankay.
Crept-v-imp. & p. p.-Gumapang.
Cresent-n-Paglaki nang buan; bagong buan.
Crest-n-Tuktok.
Crest-v-Ilagay nğ tuktok.
Crested-a-May; puaot; may tuktok.
Crestfallen-a-Malungkot; nahihiya.
Cretaceous-a-May halong yeso.
Crevasse-n-Baris; saluysoy; sungoy.
Crevice-n-Baris; saluysoy; sungoy.
Crew-n-Ang mğa tawong nagtatrabajo sa isang sasakyan.
Crew-v. imp.-Tumalaok.
Crewel-n-Torcilla.
Crib-n-Bithay; kakanan nğ hayop labañgan.
Crib-v-Bithayin; magbithay.
Cribbing-n-Pagkulong; pag-umit.
Cribbage-n-Laro nğ baraha.
Cribble-n-Bithay.
Cribble-v-Magbithay; bithayin.
Crick-n-Manhid nğ liig.
Cricket-n-Paklong.
Cried-v. imp. p. p.-Umiyak; nakaiyak.
Crier-n-Taga tawag.
Crime-n-Kasalanan; sala.
Criminal-a-Laban sa utos.
Criminal-n-Ang may kasalanan; ang nagkasala.
Criminality-n-Gawang masama; kasalanan; kasamaan, kataksilan.
Criminate-v-Magbigay sala paratañgin; bintañgin.
Crimp-n-Kuton; pilegas.
Crimp-v-Kutonin; pilegasin.
Crimson-n-Pula.
Crimson-a-Mapula.
Crimson-v-Pulain.
Cringe-v-Umurong.
Cringe-n-Urong.
Crinkle-v-Kutonin.
Crinkle-n-Kuton.
Crisis-n-Pandulo; hanga; taning na pa nahon.
Crisp-a-Kulot.
Crisp-r-Kulotin; kutonin.
Criterion-n-Katotohanan.
Critic-n-Ang pumipintas; taga pintas.
Critical-a-Ganap; mabigat.
Criticize-v-Pintasin; kutyain; pulaan.
Crochet-v-Magganchillo; gumanchillo.
Crock-n-Tapayan; kamaw.
Crock-a-Uling.
Crock-v-Umuling.
Crockery-n-Mangʌ tapayan.

26

·ocodile *n*-Buaya.

·oft-*n*-Pitak na lupa; Munting bukid.

·one-*n*-Matandang babayi.

·ony-*n*-Kaulayaw; kalaguyo; kaunuran.

·ook-*n*-Bukot; hubog.

·ook-*v*-Bukotin; hubugin; baluktotin.

·ooked-*a*-Hubog; baluktot; pasuotsuot.

·op-*n*-Balunbalunan.

·op-*n*-Ani; inani; pagani.

·op-*v*-Putlin ang dulo; kumain ng damu.

·osier-*n*-Tungkod ng Arsobispo.

·oss-*n*-Krus; bigat; dalamhati; kasakitan.

·oss-*a*-Masungit; mabagsik.

·oss-*v*-Kumabila; tumawid.

·oss bar-*n*-Anoman.

·oss bow-*n*-Pana.

·oss examine-*v*-Tanongin ng saksi.

·oss-eyed-*a*-Duling

·oss grained-*a*-Masungit.

·ossing-*n*-Krus;

·ossly-*adv*.-Pasungit,

·ossness-*n*-Kasungitan.

·oss-question-*v*-Tanongin ng saksi.

·ossroad-*n*-Salubungan ng daan; krus ng carsada,

·oss-timber-*n*-Anoman; balikilan.

·oss way-*n*-Krus ng daan ó lansangan.

·osswise-*adv*.-Pahalang.

·otch-*n*-Sabak.

·otchet-*v*-Gumanchillo.

·ouch-*v*-Yumuko.

·oup-*n*-Likuran; gawing likod.

·ow-*n*-Wak; awak; talaok.

·ow-*v*-Tumalaok.

·owbar-*n*-Bareta.

·owd-*n*-Bunton ng tawo; kakapalan ng tawo.

·owd-*v*-Kumapal ng tawo; tumulak.

·own-*n*-Korona; putong; kaharian.

·own-*v*-Putungan ng korona; koronahin; tapusin.

·ucial-*a*-Hitsurang krus.

·ucible-*n*-Pangpatunaw ng medico.

·ucifix-*n*-Larawan ni Jesu-Cristo na nakapako sa krus.

·ucifixion-*n*-Pagpayako sa krus.

·ociform-*a*-Hitsurang krus.

·ucify-*v*-Ipako sa krus.

·ude-*a*-Maasim; hilaw.

·udeness-*n*-Asim; kahilawan.

·udity-*n*-Kaasiman; asim; kahilawan.

·uel-*a*-Walang awa; ganid; walang habag; mabangis; mabagsik; malupit.

·uelly-*adv*.-Kalupitlupit.

·uelty-*n*-Kawalan ng awa; kabangisan; kabagsikan; kasamaan kalupitan.

·uet-*n*-Lalagyan ng suka.

·uise-*n*-Lakad sa dagat.

Cruise-*v*-Lumayag sa dagat.

Cruiser-*n* Sasakyan pandirigma.

Cruller-*n*-Mamon na nakaluto sa mantika

Crumb-*n* Pindot ng tinapay; pirasong munti.

Crumb-*v*-Pumiraso; pirasohin ng munti.

Crumple-*v*-Kusotin; kutonin.

Crunch-*v*-Ngumasab.

Crunch-*n*-Ngasab; sabsab.

Crupper-*n*-Baticola.

Crusade-*n*-Lakad ng hukbo.

Cruse-*n*-Tasa; bote.

Cruset-*n*-Pangpatunaw ng platero.

Crush-*v*-Inisin; uminis; inisin; dikdikin; durugin;

Crush-*n*-Dikdik; durog; bunton.

Crust-*n*-Upak; balat.

Crusty-*a*-Mabalat; maupak.

Crutch-*n*-Tunkod.

Cry-*n*-Sigaw; iyak; tangis.

Cry-*v*-Tumangis; umiyak; sumigaw.

Cry of danger-*n*-Hulhol.

Crypt-*n*-Libing sa ilalim ng simbahan.

Criptogram-*n*-Zero; tanda;

Cryptograph-*n*-Zero; tanda

Crystal-*a*-Parang bubog.

Crystal-*n*-Bubog.

Crystaline-*a*-Parang bubog.

Crystalize-*v*-Maging bubog.

Cub-*n*-Munting oso; bagong nagaaral ng katungkulan; batang bastos.

Cube-*n*-Kubo; tangkalag.

Cubic-*a*-Nauukol sa kubo.

Cubeb-*n*-Cigarrillo ng bunga ng paminta.

Cubit-*n*-Ang haba ng baraso buhat sa siko hangang sa dulo ng malaking manggpang.

Cucumber-*n*-Pepino.

Cud-*n*-Ang ningunguya ng baka.

Cuddle-*v*-Sumiping ng malapit.

Cudgel-*n*-Pumalo, palo; kahoy.

Cudgel-*v*-Paluin; kahoyin; orangin.

Cue-*n*-Buntot ng insik.

Cuff-*n*-Sampal; tampal; tampi.

Cuff-*v*-Sampalin; tampalín.

Cuisine-*n*-Kosina.

Culinery-*n*-Nauukol sa kosina.

Cull-*v*-Iwaksi, ihiwalay.

Cullender-*n*-Salaan.

Cully-*n*-Tawong mahina ang isip.

Culm-*n*-Puno ng mais.

Culminate-*v*-Abutan ng kataastaasang lugar ó grado.

Culpa-*n*-Kasalanan; sala.

Culpable-*a*-May kasalanan; dapat parusahan.

Culprit-*n*-Ang may kasalanan.

Cultivate-*v*-Baghagin; linangin ng lupa; magsaka.

Cultivation-*n*-Pagsasaka; paglinang.

Cultivator-n-Ang nagsasaka; magsasaka.
Culture-n-Karunuñgan.
Culture-v-magturo.
Culvert-n-Imbornal; sangka sa ilalim ñg lansañgan.
Cumber v-Bumigat; tumagal.
Cumbersome-a-Mabigat; matindi.
Cumbrance-n-Abala.
Cumbrous-a-Mabigat; malaki.
Cumulate-v-Mag ipon; bumunton.
Cunning-a-Tuso; bihasa; matalas; madiwara; suitik.
Cunning-n-Karunuñgan; katusuhan; katalasan.
Cup-n-Tasa; kopa.
Cup bearer-n-Taga abot ñg tasa sa isang función.
Cupboard-n Lalagyan ñg mga pagkain.
Cupidity-n-Nais; ingit; kaingitan; kasakiman; karamutan.
Cur-n-Asong walang kabuluhan.
Currish-a-Bastos; hamak.
Curable-a-Magagaliñgin.
Curate-n-Cura.
Curative-a-Makakagaling.
Curator-n-Puno taga pamahala.
Curb-v-Pigilan; pumigil.
Curb-n-Pigil.
Curb stone-n-Bato sa tabi ñg lansañgan.
Curd-v-Lumapot.
Curdle-v-Lumapot.
Cure-n-Gamot; kagamutan; pag gagamot.
Cure-v-Gamutin; gumamot; pagaliñgin.
Curfew-n-Tugtog ñg compana sa alas nueve.
Curiosity-n-Kadiwaraan; nasang makialam.
Curious-a-Madiwara; masinop.
Curl-v-Kulutin; balisurin; pilipitin.
Curl-n-Kulot.
Cur-mudgeon-n-Tawong bastos.
Currant-n-Pasteles.
Current-a-Lumalakad.
Current-n-Agos ñg tubig; kaagusan.
Curry-v-Linisin ñg kabayo.
Curry-comb-n-Panlinis ñg kabayo.
Curse-v-Sumpain; manumpa; murahin; tuñgayawin.
Curse-n-Tuñgayaw; sumpa.
Cursed-a-Hamak; malupit.
Cursory-a-Bigla; madali; pabaya.
Curt-a-Maikli.
Curtail-v-Untian, abalahin; iklian; putlin ñg buntot; magtipiran.
Curtain-n-Tabing.
Curtain-v-Ilagay ñg tabing.
Curtsy-n-Bati; yuko.

Curtsy-v-Bumati; yumuko.
Curvate-a-Baluktot.
Curvation-n-Pagkabaluktot; kakubaan.
Curvature-n Kakubaan.
Curve-n-Yuko; hubog; kabaluktutan.
Curve-a-Baluktot.
Curve-v-Yumuko; hubugin; baluktutin; bumaluktot; lumubog.
Curbity-n-Kabaluktutan.
Cushion-n-Upuan na malambót.
Cuspid-n-Pañgil.
Cuspidal-a-Matulis ang dulo.
Cuspidate-v-Tulisan.
Cuspidor-n-Luraan.
Custard-n-Chiflan.
Custodian-n-Ang nagbabantay; taga bantay.
Custody-n-Tanod; bantay; pagkabantay.
Custom-n-Kaugalian; ugali; uso; modo; gawi; anyo; asal; kaasalan.
Customary-a-Karaniwan; magawi; kaugalian.
Customer-n-Kasuki.
Custom-house-n-Aduana.
Cut-v-Hiwain; tigpasin; putulin; gilitin; hiwasin.
Cut-n-Hiwa; gilit; putol; tigpas; yari hitsura.
Cutaneous-a-Nauukol sa balat ñg tawo.
Cute-a-Tuso; matalas; maganda.
Cuticle-n-Balok.
Cutlass-n-Hapak.
Cutler-n-Ang nagtitinda ñg mga lanceta, gunting at iba pang kasankapang panghiwa.
Cutlery-n-Manga kasangkapang panghiwa.
Cutter-n-Mangigilit; taga hiwa.
Cut throat-n-Ang natay sa kapwa; ang nakamatay.
Cutting-n-Pag gilit; paghiwa; pag gupit.
Cut worm-n-Uod.
Cycle-n-Bicicleta.
Cycler-Cyclist-n-Ang sumasakay sa bicicleta.
Cyclone-n-Bagyo.
Cylinder-n-Bilog; kaidkuran.
Cylindric-Cylindrical-a-Mabilog.
Cymbal-n-Piang.
Cynic-n-Tawong masuñgit.
Cynic-Cynical-a-Masuñgit.
Cynicism-n-Kasuñgitan.
Czar-n-Hari sa Ruso.
Czarina-n-Asawa ñg Hari sa Ruso.
Czarowitz-n-Pañganay na anak na lalaki ñg hari sa Ruso.

D

Dab-n-Tawong sanay, hampas na magaan
Dab-v-Hampasin ñg magaan
Dabble-v-Basain.
Daft-a-Ulol; loco; siia ang isip.
Dagger-n-Puñal, panaksak.
Daily-a-Araw araw
Daily-n-Pahayagan na lumitaw sa araw araw
Dainty-a-Mainam; malasa
Dainty-n-Bagay na mainam.
Dairy-n-Bahay lalagyan ñg gatas
Dale n-Parang
Dally v-Magluat, tumagal
Dam-n-Salopilan, harañgan ñg tubig
Dam-a-Salopilin.
Dam-v-Harañgin ang tubig.
Damage-n-Kasiraan, sira; pagkasira.
Damage-v-Sirain
Damask-n-Damasko.
Dame-n-Babaying puno sa isang familia ó escuelahan.
Damn-r-Ihulog ang kapowa sa infierno
Damp-a-Basá; halumigmig; lamig
Damp-n-Basá, lamig.
Dampen-v-Basain, basabasain.
Damper-n-Panharang ñg asô.
Damsel-n-Binibini; babaying ginoo.
Dance-v-Sumayaw; magsayaw.
Dance-n-Sayawan sayaw
Dancer-n-Mananayaw.
Dandle-v-Palayawin, iwiin
Dandruff-n-Balakubak.
Dandy-n-Tawong hambog.
Danger-n-Panganib, kapanganiban.
Dangerous-a-Mapanganib, may panganib
Dangle-v-Isabit; sumabit, sabitin
Dapper-a-Munti at maliksi
Dare-v-Mangahas; ipangahas.
Dare-n-Pangahas, paslang
Dark-a-Madilim, malabo, maitim
Dark-n-Dilim; itim.
Darken-v-Umitim, dumilim; dumhan, dungisan; labuan, lumabo.
Darkness n-Kadiliman, kapanglawan.
Darling a-Minamahal, pinalayaw.
Darling-n-Ang minamahal.
Darn-v-Sursihan.
Darn-n-Sursi
Dart-n-Palaso, suligi, sibat.
Dart-v-Ihagis ñg palaso; itulag.
Dash-n-Takbo
Dash-v-Ihagis ñg malakas.
Dastard-n-Karuagan; duag
Dastard-a-Duag.
Dastardly-a-Maduag; mahina ang loob

Date-n-Bilang ñg panahon, fecha.
Date-v-Ilagay ñg fecha.
Daub-v-Dumhan, dungisin, mansahin.
Daub-n-Dungis, dumi
Daughter n-Anak na babayi.
Daughter-in-law-n-Manugang babayi
Daunt-i-Supilin; takutin.
Dauntless-a-Walang takot, m a t a p a n g, hindi marunong matakot
Dawdle-v-Sayañgin ang panahon
Dawn n Madaling araw, liwayway.
Dawn-a-Lumiwanag sa umaga.
Day-n-Araw, kaarawan
Day-before-yesterday-Kamakalawa.
Day break n-Madaling araw
Day-laborer-n-Ang nagpapaupa sa maghapon, mangañgaraw.
Day light-n-Liwanag ñg araw
Day spring-n Madaling araw, pinagmulaan; pinangaliñgan..
Day time-n-Panahon ñg araw buhat sa madaling araw hangang sa dilim.
Daze-v-Tumulig, masilaw
Dazzle-v-Makasilaw, sumilaw, patak̃ain.
Dead-a-Patay, walang buhay, namatay.
Dead-adv -Patay
Dead-n-Ang nangamatay
Deaden-v-Patayin.
Deaf-a-Bingi
Deafen-v-Bingihin: mamingi.
Deaf-mute-n-Tawong bingi, at pipe
Deal-n-Pangangalakal
Deal-v-Mangalakal, magtinda.
Dealer-n-Mangangalakal
Dealing-n-Pangangalakal.
Dean-n Puno sa katidral
Dear-a-Inuibig, mahal, minamahal, iniirog, irog.
Dear-n-Iniirog; palayaw, ang iniibig.
Dear-adv -Mahal.
Dearth-n-Kawalan, kakulañgan
Death-n-Kamatayan, pagkamatay.
Deathless-a-Walang kamatayan.
Deathly-a-Makakamatay
Death-bed n-Huling oras ñg buhay, hiñgalo; kamatayan
Debar-v-Ibukod; iwaksi
Debase i-Hamakin, bawasan
Debasement-n-Pagkahamak, pagbawas.
Debate-v-Ipagmatowiran, magmatowid.
Debate-n-Pagmamatowiran.
Debauch-v-Maglasing, maghilo, bumulok.
Debauch-n-Ang labis.
Debauchery-n-Paglalasing; pagkabulok.
Debilitate-v-Mangayayat; humina.

Debility-n-Kahinaan; latá; pangangaya-
yat; hina.
Debit-n-Utang.
Debit-v-Fautangin.
Debonair-a-Magalang; mapagbigay loob.
Debris-n-Pinagpilian; kasukalan.
Debt-n-Utang.
Debtor-n-Ang may utang; ang nagka-
utang.
Debut-n-Primerong litaw.
Decade-n-Luat ng sampuong taon.
Decadence-n-Pagkabawas; pagkabulok.
Decadency-n-Pagkabawas; pagkabulok.
Decaliter-n-Takal na may sampuong;
litro.
Decalogue-n-Ang sampuong utos ng
Dios.
Decameter-n-Layo ng sampuong metro.
Decamp-v-Tumakas; umalis.
Decant-v-Ibuhos.
Decanter-n-Lalagyan ng mga alak.
Decapitate-v-Pugutin; magpugot.
Decapitation-n-Pagpugot.
Decay-v-Bumulok; lumipol; sumira.
Decay-n-Pagkasira; pagkabulok.
Decease-n-Pagalis; pagkamatay.
Decease-v-Mamatay.
Deceit-n-Daya; hibo; patibong; kasi-
nungalingan; panunuba; paghibo.
Deceitful-a-Magdaraya; daya; nakadaya;
manuba.
Deceive-v-Hibuin; dayain; magdaya;
magsinungaling; magbulaan; manekas.
December-n-Diciembre.
Decency-n-Kabaitan; timtim; kamahalan;
kabinian; kahinhinan; kahusayan.
Decennary-n-Luat ng sampuong taon.
Decennial-a-Nauukol sa luat ng sam-
puong taon.
Decent-a-Matimtim; magalang; maginoo;
mabait; mabini.
Deception-n-Daya; hibo; kasinungali-
ngan.
Deceptive-a-Makakadaya.
Decide-v-Magbigay hatol; hatulan; hu-
matol; magtika.
Decided-a-Buo ang loob.
Decimal-n-Bahagi; decimal.
Decimal-a-Nauukol sa decimal.
Decimal fractions-n-Quebrados; decima-
les.
Decipher-v-Hanapin ng kahulugan; ihu-
log; saysayin.
Decision-n-Hatol; tigas ng loob; kahu-
oan ng loob; pasiya.
Decisive-a-Totoo; huli.
Deck-n-Sahig ng sasakyan; balasa.
Deck-v-Bihisin; takpanin.
Declaim-v-Magtalumpati; magsalita sa
marami; manalangin.

Declamation-n-Pagsasalita sa marami.
Declare-v-Sabihin; ipahayag; ipakilala;
ipatalastas; salaysayin; saysayin;
bumalak.
Declaration-n-Kasaysayan; salaysay
pahayag; pagpapatalastas.
Declension-n-Pagbawas; paguunti.
Decline-v-Bumawas; umunti; umayaw;
tumangi.
Decline-n-Paghupa; pagbawas; paguunti.
Declination-n-Paghuhupa; pagbabawas;
paguunti.
Declevity-n-Dahilig na lupa; dalisdis;
lupang matarik; tibagan.
Decoct-v-Haluin; ihalo; ilahok.
Decolor-v-Alisin ang kulay; putiin.
Decolorize-v-Putiin.
Decompose-v-Bumulok.
Decomposition-n-Pagbulok.
Decorate-v-Gayakin; pagandahin; pai-
namin.
Decorated-n-Tagagayak; anggumagayak.
Decoration-n-Paggayak; paghanda.
Decorative-a-Nakagagayak.
Decorous-a-Mahinhin; mahinahon; ma-
bait; maginoo.
Decorum-n-Kabaitan; kahinhinan; ka-
mahalan; kalinisan.
Decoy-v-Hibuin; dayain.
Decoy-n-Hibo; pangati.
Decrease-v-Bumawas; umunti; umikli;
lumiit.
Decrease-n-Pagbawas; pag uunti.
Decree-n-Utos; pasiya.
Decree-v-Mag utos.
Decrepid-a-Ulianin; mahina; matanda.
Decrepitude-n-Katandaan; kahinaan; pag
kahukluban.
Decrial-n-Uyam; pintas; alibugha.
Decry-v-Mag alibugha; halayin; kut-
yain.
Dedicate-v-Mag alay; ialay; ipanagano.
Dedication-n-Pag alay; alay.
Dedicator-n-Ang nag aalay.
Deduce-v-Hanguin; hugutin; awasan.
Deduct-v-Awasan; bawasan; untian; ku-
langin.
Deduction-n-Pagbawas.
Deed-n-Gawa; titulo.
Deed-v-Ibigay ng titulo.
Deem-v-Mag isip; magwari.
Deep-a-Malalim.
Deep-adv,-Malalin.
Deep-n-Laot.
Deepen-v-Ipalalim; palaliman.
Deer-n-Usa.
Deface-v-Sirain; sirain ang mukha.
Defamatory-a-Maninira ng puri.
Defamation-n-Panira nang puri; upa-
sala.

Defame-v-Murahın; mag alımuı a, umupasala, kutyain
Default n-Daya, tekas
Default-v-Manekas, dayaın, kanıyahın
Defaulter-n-Manenekas.
Defeat-ı-Pasukuın, talonın, supılın
Defeat-n-Talo, suko
Defect-n-Kakulañgan; kulang, pıntas, kapıntasan; malı, sala, kasalanan
Defection-n-Kamalian, kakulañgan.
Defective-a-Dı yarı, hindı ganap, kulang.
Defence n Saklolo, tulong, ampon tankılık
Defend-v-Tulungın, tumulong, kanlongın; kupkupın; ıpagtangol, tumankılık, amponın
Defendant-n-Ang kınakanlong, ang tınatangol
Defense-n-Kanlong, tankılık, tulong; saklolo, pagtatagumpay, tagumpay.
Defenceless-Defenseless-a-Walang magaampon
Defer-ı-Antalahin, bımbingın, maantala; ıpagpaluat.
Deference-n-Antala, abala, galang
Deferential-a-Magalang
Defiance-n-Kapangahasan, hamon
Defiant-a-Mañgahas
Deficience-Deficiency-n-Kakulañgan, kawalan.
Deficient-a-Kulang
Deficit-n-Kakulañgan, kulang.
Defile-n-Landas.
Defile-ı-Bumulok; sumira, dungisan
Defilement-n-Pagkabulok, pagkasıra
Define-v-Saysayin; salaysayın; ıhulog.
Definite-a-Fırme, totoo
Definition-n-Kahulugan, kasaysayan.
Deflect-v-Ihko lumıko
Deflection-n-Paglıko
Deflexure-n-Paglıko.
Defoliation-n-Paglalaglag ng dahon
Deform-v-Pumangıt ang hitsura
Deformity-n-Pagkapangıt ng hitsura.
Defraud-v-Manekas, manuba, dayaın, kanıyahın.
Defray-v-Abuluyan, umabuloy; amponin.
Deft a-Bagay; marunong; sanay
Defunct-a-Patay, walang buhay
Defy-ı-Lumaban, hamanın; humamon
Degeneracy-n-Pagkahamak
Degenerate a Hamak; mababa, walang kabuluhan
Degenerate v-Humamak, bumaba
Degredation-n-Pagkahamak; pagkababa
Degrade-v Sumıra; sıruin humamak.
Degraded a-Hamak; mababa ang pagkatawo.

Deign-v-Pumayag, pagıng dapat.
Deject-v-Humamak, maglungkot
Dejected-a-Aba, hamak, hapıs, mahapıs kulang palad
Dejection-n-Pagkahamak; lungkot; ka kulangan ng palad
Delay-n-Abala, antala, pigil; pagluat
Delay-ı-Umabala; antalahin
Delectable-a-Maaliw, magıliw; malugod masaya.
Delectation-n-Saya, lugod, alıw
Delegate-n-Kahalili, katıwala, kapalıt.
Delegate-ı-Ipagkatiwala, humalılı, mag katiwala
Delegation n-Kapısanan.
Deleterious-a-Makasisira, masama.
Delf-n-Mañga tapayan.
Deliberate-ı-Sadyaın; magwarı; mag ısıpısıp
Deliberately-adv -Tinalaga, sınadya.
Deliberation n-Pagwarı, sadya
Delicacy-n-Kabutıhan, kaınaman, kalan butan, lambot kakınısan.
Delicate-a-Banayad, malambot; manıpıs marupok, maselang
Delicious-a-Masarap, malasa, kaalıwalıw kalugodlugod.
Delight-n-Tuwa; alıw, ınam, lugod, lusap katuwaan; lıgaya.
Delight-v-Manuya, maglugod, magsaya
Delighted a-Masuya, malugod, maalıw.
Delightful-a Kaalıwalıw; kalugodlugod kasayasaya.
Delineate-v Tumabas, padparin, say sayın
Delineation-n-Pagtabas
Delinquency-n-Pagsoway sa utos, ka kulangan, pagkakasala.
Delinquent-a-May kasalanan
Delinquent-n-Ang may kasalanan
Delirious-a-Ulol, sıra ang isip
Delirium n-Pagkasıra ng isip, pag kaulol.
Deliver v-Magdala, sagipin
Deliverance-n-Pagdadala; pagsagip; pag ligtas
Delivery n-Paghahatıd; pagdadala; pag sagip
Dell-n-Parang
Delta n-Labasan ng ılog.
Delude-v Upatın, dayain, hibuin.
Deluge-n-Apaw, lubog
Deluge-ı-Umapaw, ılubog.
Delusion-n-Pagupat, daya; hıbo, kası nungahıngan.
Delusive-a-Makakadaya, magdaraya
Delve-r-Humukay; tumarok.
Demagogue-n-Puno ng isang katıpunan
Demand-v-Humıngı, lumuhog

marcation-*n*-Hanga; hanganan.
mean-*v*-Gumawa.
meanor-*n*-Gawa; paguugali; ugali; palakad; asal; kilos.
mentate-*a*-Ulol; walang isip.
mented-*a*-Ulol; sira ang isip.
mentia-*n*-Kaululan; pagkaulol kasiraan ng isip.
merit-*n*-Pintas; gawa ó kilos na masama.
mijohn-*n*-Damajuana.
mise-*n*-Kamatayan.
mise-*v*-Magpamana.
molish-*n*-Lipolin; sirain; gibain; guluhin.
molition-*n*-Paglipol; pagsira; kasiraan.
mon-*n*-Demonio.
moniac-*a*-Nauukol sa demonio.
moniacal-*a*-Nauukol sa demonio.
monstrate-*v*-Ipakilala; ipakita; paliwanagan; ipatalastas.
monstration-*n*-Kilos; kasaysayan; pagpapakita.
monstrative-*a*-Sinasaysay.
monstrative-*n*-Kasaysayan.
moralization-*n*-Pagkasira ng mabuting kaugalian.
moralize-*v*-Sirain ng mabnting kaugalian.
mur-*v*-Sumalangsang; tumigil.
mur-*n*-Tigil.
mure-*a*-Mababang loob.
un-*n*-Yungib.
engue-*n*-Lumpo.
eniable-*a*-Maipagkakaila; mapagkaila.
enial-*n* Pagkakaila; pagkaayaw; pa hindi; kaayawan; pagkatangi.
enizen-*n*-Ang tumitira sa isang lugar.
nominate-*v*-Pamagatin; pumagat; magsaysay.
nominate-*a*-May ngalan.
nomination-*n*-Tawag; ngalan; pamagat; bansag.
note-*v*-Tandaan.
nounce-*v*-Magdenuncia; ipaglait; isumbong.
nse-*a*-Siksik; masinsin.
nsity-*n*-Kasiksikan; kasinsinan kapal, kadiliman.
nt-*n*-Ukit.
nt-*v*-Ukitin; umukit.
ntal-*a*-Nauukol sa ngipin.
ntist-*n* Mangagamot ng ngipin; dentista.
ntistry-*n*-Karunungan sa paggagamot ng ngipin.
ntoid-*a*-Hitsurang ngipin.
nudation-*n*-Paghubad.
nude-*v*-Hubaran; humubo; humubad; maghubo; maghubad; hubaran.

Deny *v*-Magkaila; tumangi. tangihan; huag ipagkaloob; ipang-ayaw.
Deodorize-*v*-Alisan ng amoy.
Depart-*v*-Umalis; lumakad; tumakas.
Departure-*n*-Pagalis; paglayas; pagtakas.
Department-*n*-Departamento.
Depend-*v*-Sumabit; mabitin; humilig.
Depict-*v*-Pintahin; ipinta; saysayin liwanagin.
Depicture-*n*-Pagliliwanag.
Depicture-*v*-Liwanagin; lumiwanag.
Deplorable-*a*-Kahambalhambal; kahapishapis; kalunoslunos.
Depopulate-*v*-Umalis ang manga tawo sa isang lugar.
Deplore-*v*-Magdamdam.
Deport-*v*-Ipaalis sa isang lugar.
Deportation-*n*-Pagpapanaw; pagdedestiero.
Deportment-*n*-Kilos; ugali.
Deposal-*n*-Pagpaalis sa katungkulan.
Depose-*v*-Ialis sa katungkulan.
Deposit-*v*-Ideposito; ilagay; ipagkatiwala; kilaga.
Deposit-*n*-Deposito; lalagyan.
Deposition-*n*-Pagdedeposito.
Depot-*n*-Deposito.
Depravation-*n*-Kabulukan; kahamakan.
Deprave-*v*-Humamak; pasamain.
Depraved-*a*-Paslit; masama; hamak.
Depravity-*n*-Kahamakan ligalig; pagkabulok.
Deprecate-*v*-Manalangin.
Deprecation-*n*-Panalangin.
Depreciate-*v*-Hamakin; bawasan ang halaga; halayin; laparan.
Depreciation-*n*-Pagalipusta; paghamak.
Depreciatory-*a*-Mapakahamak.
Depredate-*v*-Nakawin; manduit.
Depredation-*n*-Panduduit.
Depress-*v*-Hamakin; inisin; tumumal.
Depression-*n*-Pagiinis.
Depressive-*a*-Hatumal.
Deprivation-*n*-Kawalan; pagkawala.
Deprive-*v*-Alisan ang kailangan; iwala.
Depth-*n*-Lalim; kalaliman.
Deputation-*n*-Kahalili; katiwala.
Deputy-*n*-Katiwala; kahalili.
Derail-*v*-Umalis sa railes.
Derange-*v*-Sirain ang ayos.
Derangement-*n*-Pagkasira ng ayos.
Dereliction-*n*-Pag-iiwan.
Deride-*v*-Umupasala; uyamin; libakin.
Derision-*n*-Upasala; uyam; libak.
Derisive-*a*-Mauyam.
Derive-*v*-Hanguin sa iba.
Derivation-*n*-Pagkuha sa iba.
Derivative-*n*-Salita na nangaling sa ibang wika.
Derive-*v*-Kunin sa.

Derm-*n*-Balat.
Derogate-*v* Pawalan ñg kabuluhan
Derogate-*a*-Sira, may bawas
Derogation-*n*-Pagbawas.
Descend-*v*-Lumusong, manaog, bumaba, bumawas.
Descendant-*n*-Anak; lahi, hinlog, inapo.
Descendent-*a*-Mangaling sa.
Descension-*n*-Pagpanaog, paglusong
Descent-*n*-Paglusong, lusong
Describe-*v*-Liwanagan saysayin; sabihin ñg maliwanag.
Description-*n*-Kasaysayan; pagsasaysay.
Descry-*v*-Tanawin; tumanaw
Desecrate-*v*-Sirain, sumpain, tumuñgayaw
Desecration-*n* Pagtutuñgayaw, tuñgayaw. sumpa; pagpasira.
Desert-*v*-Magtanan
Desertion-*n*-Pagtatanan.
Désert-*n*-Lugal na ilang, ilang
Désert *a*-Ilang, karat
Deserter-*n*-Sumdalong nagtanan.
Deserve-*v*-Magkaroon ñg karampatan, paging dapat.
Deservedly-*adv*-Nararapat.
Deserving-*a*-Nararapat.
Des habille-*a*-Walang ayos ang pagbibihis
Desiccate-*v*-Tuyuin; matuyo
Desiccation-*n*-Pagtutuyo.
Desiderate-*v*-Magkailañgan, magkaroon ñg kailañgan.
Desiderative-*a*-May nasa; mapipitain.
Design-*v*-Guhitin akalain; isipin; gawin.
Design-*n*-Plano, guhit, tika, akala, banta; pag gagawa.
Designedly *adv*-Tinalaga, sinadya, kinusa
Designing-*a*-Nakahihibo
Designate-*v*-Ituro, sabihin,
Designation-*n*-Pagtuturo, pagsasabi, pili; tuñgo.
Desirable-*a*-Maibigan, nasain
Desire-*v*-Magnasa; nasain, magpita, umibig, humañgad
Desire-*n*-Nasa; ibig, gusto, nais
Desirous-*a*-Magnanasain· maiibigan, mapaguasa, mapagpita, mapagha ñgad.
Desist-*v* Huminto; maghinto, tumigil; humimpil; magtahan
Desk-*n*-Kupitre
Desolate-*a*-Mapanglaw; ilang.
Desolate-*v*-Lipulin gibain. sirain.
Desolation-*n*-Pagyasak, kasiraan
Despair-*v*-Mawala ñg pag asa humina ang loob.

Despatch-*v*-Ipadala, tapusin.
Despatch-*n*-Telegrama, hatid kawad.
Desperado-*n*-Tulisán, magnanakaw.
Desperate-*a*-Walang asa.
Desperation-*n*-Pagkawala ñg pagaasa.
Despicable-*a*-Hamak; walang puri, madiri, mahalay, malait, masama.
Despise-*v*-Yamutin, yumamot, masuklam
Despite *n* Galit, tanim sa loob
Despite-*prep*-Masque
Despiteful-*a*-Masama, hamak.
Despoil *v*-Sirain, lansagin; gibain.
Despoliation-*n*-Pagkasira; paglansag
Despond-*v*-Humina ang loob, mawala ang pagaasahan
Despondency-*n*-Kawalan nang pagaasa; paghina ñg loob.
Despondent *a*-Walang ipagaasahan, malungkot
Despot-*n*-Punong mabaksik, haring, mabagsik
Despotic-*a*-Mabagsik, mabañgis; masama.
Despotism-*n*-Kabagsikan, kabañgisan
Dessert-*n*-Himagas.
Destination-*n*-Destino, pag uukol, kaukulan, taan.
Destine-*v*-Ipadistino, idistino
Destiny-*n*-Distino.
Destitute-*a*-Walang hanap buhay; salat; walang mag aampon, dukha
Destitution-*n*-Kasalatan, kahamakan, kadukhaan
Destroy-*v*-Sirain; basagin gibain, lansagin, igiba.
Destructible-*a*-Makasisira.
Destruction-*n*-Kasiraan; pagkalipol, pag kalugso.
Destructive-*a*-Makasisira
Detach-*v*-Ibukod, tangalin, tumangal
Detachment-*n* Destactamento, pagtangal; pagbukod.
Detail *n*-Kasaysayan.
Detail-*v*-Magsaysay.
Detain-*v*-Pigilin, magluat, pihitin
Detect-*v*-Tuklasin; tagpuan; makita, usisain, siyasatin.
Detection-*n*-Pag uusisa; siyasat.
Detective-*a*-Nauukol sa secreta
Detective-*n*-Policia secreta; policiang lihim
Detention-*n*-Pagluat; pagpigil, abala
Deter-*v*-Umabala, pigilin
Deteriorate-*v*-Sumama, bumigat ang sakit ó karamdaman, sumira; lumipas
Deterioration-*n*-Pagsasamá, pagkasira.
Determination-*n*-Pasiya, kabuoan nang loob
Determine-*v*-Hatulan; magpasiya; bumuo

Determinate-*v*-Ilagay nḡ mḡa hanga; say-sayin.
Determined-*a*-Buo ang loob.
Detest-*v*-Suklamin; yumamot.
Detestable-*a*-Kalupitlupit; kusuklam-suklam; kalunoslunos; masuklam.
Detestation-*n*-Pagsusuklam; kulupitan; kasuklaman.
Dethrone-*v*-Talunin ang hari.
Dethonement-*n*-Pagtatalo sa hari.
Detour-*n*-Lumakad nḡ pasuotsuot.
Detract-*v*-Manumpa; tumunḡayaw; sumpain; alisin; bawasan.
Detraction-*n*-Pagalis; pagbawas; panumpa; pagsumpa; tunḡayaw.
Detriment-*n*-Abala; bagay na makasasamá.
Detrimental-*a*-Makasisira; makasasamá.
Devastate-*v*-Gubatin; sirain; lipulin.
Devastation-*n*-Kasiraan; paglilipol.
Develop-*v*-Bumuti; butihin; isulong.
Development-*n*-Pag sulong; pag kakabuti.
Devest-*v*-Alisin; hubdan; hubarin.
Deviate-*v*-Baguhin; ibain; ilipat; lumapat; bumago; huminkod.
Deviation-*n*-Pagkabago; kaibhan; hinkod.
Device-*n*-Kasangkapan.
Devil-*n*-Demonio.
Devil-*v*-Manukso; tuksohin.
Devilish-*a*-Parang demonio; nauukol sa demonio.
Deviltry-*n*-Kasamaan; gawa nang demonio.
Devious-*a*-Pasuot suot; pabaya; tamad.
Devise-*v*-Akalain; isipin; magpamana.
Devise-*n*-Mana; huling sulat nḡ nanḡamatay.
Division-*n*-Paghahati; paghihiwalay.
Devoid-*v*-Alisin; bawas.
Devoid-*n*-Walang laman; salat.
Devolve-*v*-Bumalik mauwi sa dati; mabinat.
Devolution-*n*-Pagbalik; pagsasauli.
Devote-*v*-Alayin; ialay.
Devoted-*a*-Masipag, tapat; naibig.
Devotion-*n*-Alay; pagtatapat nḡ loob.
Devotional-*a*-Nauukol sa pag aalay.
Devour-*v*-Lamunin.
Devout-*a*-Totoo; tapat; malinis.
Dew-*n*-Hamog.
Dew-*v*-Humamog.
Dew-Drop-*n*-Patak nḡ hamog.
Dewy-*a*-Mahamog.
Dexter-*a*-Nauukol sa kanan.
Dexterity-*n*-Kasanayan; katalasan; karununḡan.
Dexterous-*a*-Matalas; marunong; sanay; bihasa.

Dextrous-*a*-Sanay; marunong; matalas bihasa.
Diabetes-*n*-Sakit na madalas umihi ang may sakit.
Diablery-*n*-Kalikotan.
Diabolic-*a*-Nauukol sa demonio.
Diabolical-*a*-Nauukol sa demonio.
Diadem-*n*-Korona.
Diagram-*n*-Plano; guhit; tabas.
Dial-*n*-Mukha nḡ orasan.
Dialect-*n*-Salita nḡ mḡa tawong hindi marunong; dialecto.
Dialogue-*n*-Salitaan nḡ dalawa.
Diameter-*n*-Kagitnaan.
Diametric-*a*-Nauukol sa kagitnaan.
Diametrical-*a*-Nauukol sa kagitnaan.
Diamond-*n*-Diamante; brillante.
Diaper-*n*-Lampen.
Diaphragm-*n*-Balat sa pag itan nḡ dibdib at nḡ tiyan.
Diarrhea-*n*-Bululos; pag iilagan.
Diarrhoea-*a*-Pag iilagan; bululos.
Diary-*n*-Tandaan nḡ nangyayari sa araw araw.
Dia-tribe-*n*-Pagtatakapan.
Dibble-*n*-Panaksak.
Dice-*n*-Kubo na may bilang ang mḡa mukha.
Dicker-*n*-Kapalit; pagpalit; pagtuturing.
Dictate-*v*-Idicta.
Dictate-*n*-Utos.
Dictation-*n*-Pagdidicta.
Dictator-*n*-Ang nagdidicta; ang naguutos.
Dictatorial-*a*-Nauukol sa pagdidicta.
Diction-*n*-Wika; salita; pagpili nḡ salita.
Dictionary-*n*-Diccionario;
Did-*v*. *imp*.-Nangyari; gumawa; ginawa.
Didst-*v*. *imp*.-Ginawa; gumawa; nangyari.
Die-*v*-Mamatay; tumapos.
Die-*n*-Hulmahan.
Diet-*n*-Pagkain; dieta.
Diet-*v*-Magdieta.
Diety-*n*-Kadiosan; pagkadios.
Differ-*v*-Magkaiba.
Difference-*n*-Kaibhan; pagkakaiba.
Different-*a*-Iba; hindi kaparis ó katulad.
Difficult-*n*-Mahirap; magulo.
Difficulty-*n*-Kahirapan; kahigpitan.
Diffident-*a*-Ayaw sumanpalataya; matatakutin; ayaw maniwala.
Diffidence-*n*-Katakutan.
Diffuse-*v*-Ibubos; lumaki; isabog; ipahayag; ipatalastas.
Diffuse-*a*-Maluag; malawak.
Diffusion-*n*-Pagpaparami; karamihan; pagbubuhos

27

Dig-v-Hukayin: humukay.
Digest-v-Tumunaw ang kinain
Digest-n-Codigo, kapisanan ñg mañga utos
Digestible-a Mangyayaring matunaw sa sikmura.
Digestion-n-Pagtunaw ñg kinain.
Digit-n-Daliri isa.
Dignify-i-Ipagpuri. magalıñgin, purihin.
Dignity-n-Dañgal; puri, kamahalan, karañgalan, karapatan.
Digress-v-Lumiko; lumayo humiwalay
Digression-n-Pagbihiwalay; paghko
Dike-n-Pilapil, harañgan, ñg tubig
Dike-v-Magpilapil.
Dilapidate-v Sumira, sirain
Dilapidation-n-Pagkasira, sira
Dilate-v Bumuka, dumilat; lumaki
Dilation-n-Pagbuka; paglaki; pagdilat,
Dilatory-a-Pabaya, mabagal; tamad; huli
Diligence-n-Kasipagan, sipag.
Diligent-a-Masipag, maagap, mabisa, masigla, masikap
Dilute-i-Labnawin; lumabnaw, tunawin; tumunaw.
Dilute-i-Lusaw, malabnaw
Dilution-n-Pagtutunaw.
Dim-a-Madilim, malabo.
Dime-n-Sangbillion.
Dimension-n-Sukat, laki at lapad.
Diminish-v-Bumawas; umunti; umimpis; lumit; bawasan
Dimunition-n-Pagbawas; pagkulang; pagpaunti, pagpaliit.
Diminutive a-Nagpapaliit; nababawas.
Dimity-n-Kayong sita.
Dimple-n-Butas ñg pisñgi.
Din-n-Gulo, ugong.
Dine-v-Kumain.
Dingle-n-Parang munti na sa pagitan ñg dalawang bundok.
Dingy-a-Marumi, marungis, mapanglaw.
Dinner-n-Tanghalian.
Dint n-Ukit, lakas, kapangyarihan.
Dint-v-Ukitin.
Diocese-n Kapangyarihan ñg obispo.
Dip-v-Isawsaw, isisid, ilubog.
Dip-n-Lubog, sisid, ligo
Diploma-n Titulo.
Diplomacy-n-Salitaan ñg dalawang naciones; karunuñgan; katalasan.
Dipper-n-Tabo lumbo.
Dire-Direful-a-Katakottakot, kakilakilabot, masama.
Direct-a-Matowid walang liko
Direct-v-Tinagin, ulogin, akayin, ituñgo; mamahala.
Director-n-Ang namamahala.
Directory-a-Nakatuñgo.

Directress-n-Babaying marunong mamahala.
Direful-a-Katakottakot; kakilakilabot
Dirge-n-Dalit sa paghlibing
Dirk-n-Panaksak, puñal
Dirk-i-Isaksak.
Dirt-n-Dumi, duñgis, karumihan, kasukalan; kasalaulaan, lupa, putik.
Dirt-i-Dumhan, duñgisin
Dirty-v-Marumi; marungis, masukal, salahula; pañgit, malibag, may mansa.
Dirty-v-Dumhan, duñgisin
Dis able-a-Pilayinkapilay, kapilayan.
Dis ability-n-Pag.
Dis advantage-n-Lugi, kahirapan, kasiraan.
Dis advantageous-a-Mahirap makalulugi, nakasisira
Dis agree-i-Magkasira, huag umayon
Dis agreeable-a-Masamang ugali, masuñgit; makayayamot, nakababagot nakagagalit
Dis agreement-n-Pagkasira, pagkagalit; kasiraan
Dis allow-v-Huag ipahintulot
Dis annul-v-Pawalan ang kabuluhan.
Dis appear-v-Mawalan
Dis appearance n-Kawalan
Dis appoint-v-Magdaya, yumamot, kumulang, matalo.
Dis appointment-n-Kakulañgan kasiraan; pagkatalo
Dis approval n-Katangihan; paghaayaw.
Dis approve-v-Huag ipahintulot; pintasin; tumangi
Dis arm-v-Alisan ang mañga sandata
Dis armament-n-Pagtangol ñg mañga sandata.
Dis arrange-v-Sirain ang ayos; guluhin.
Dis aranged-a-Walang ayos; magulo
Dis arrangement n-Kawalan ñg ayos ó wasto.
Disaster n-Kahirapan; sakuna.
Disastrous-a-Masakuna; mahirap
Dis avow-v-Malimutan, huag malainan.
Disband-v-Tangalin ang mañga sandata ñg mañga sundalo
Disbelief-n Kawalan ñg pananampalataya.
Disvelieve-v-Huag maniwala ó sumampalataya.
Disburse-v-Magbayad gastahin.
Disbursement-n-Pag babayad, pag gagasta.
Disc-n-Bilog.
Discard-v Itapon, ialis; magdiscarte
Discard-n-Barahang panapon.
Discern-v-Tanawin, makita, tumingin.
Discerning a-Matalas, matalino, tuso.
Discernment-n Pagtatanaw

Discharge-v-Tumupad; bawasan; bitiwan; gumanap; ialis sa katungkulan.

Discharge-n-Pagkukumpli.

Disciple-n-Alagad; dicipulo.

Disciplinarian-a-Nauukol sa pagtupad ó sa gobierno.

Disciplinarian-n-Maestrong mabagsik; ó masungit.

Discipline-n-Disciplina; pagtupad sa kautusan.

Discipline-v-Aralan; magturo; turuan.

Disclaim-v-Magkaila; talikuran; huag kumilala; umayaw.

Dislaimer-n-Ang nagkakaila; ang tumalikod.

Disclose-v-Buksan; ilitaw; ipalitaw; pahayag; ihayag.

Disclosure-n-Pahayag; paglitaw.

Discolor-v-Kumupas.

Discoloration-n-Pagkupas.

Discolored-a-Kupas; maputla.

Discomfit-v-Manalo; talunin.

Discomfort-n-Kakulañgan nğ kaginhawahan; kahirapan.

Discomfort-v-Yumamot; humina ang loob; pagalitin.

Discommode-v-Abalahin; pagalitin.

Discompose-v-Sirain ang ayos; guluhin.

Discomposure-n-Galit; gulo.

Disconcert-v-Guluhin.

Disconnect-v-Tangalin; hiwalayin.

Disconnection-n-Pagkatangal tangal.

Disconsolate-a-Malungkot; salat; mahapis; mahapis.

Discontent-n-Yamot; sibañgot; galit.

Discontent-a-Galit; masama ang loob.

Discontent-v-Yumamot; magalit.

Discontented-a-Sowail; galit.

Discontinuance-n Pagtigil.

Discontinuation-n-Pagtigil.

Discontinue-v-Tumigil; pigilin.

Discord-n-Gulo; galit; pagkasira; kasiraan.

Discordance-n-Kaguluhan; kasiraan.

Discordancy-n-Pagkasira; kasiraan.

Discordant-a-Magulo; di maayos.

Discount-v-Bawasar; kulañgin.

Discount-n-Ang por cientc; pagbawas.

Discountenance-v-Huag ipahintulot.

Discourage-v-Pahinain ang loob.

Discouragement-n-Kahinaan nğ loob.

Discourse-n-Discurso; pagmamatowid; salitaan.

Discourse-v-Wikain; magmatowid.

Discourteous-a-Walang galang; tampalasan.

Discourteousness-n-Kawalan nğ galang; katampalasanan; paslang.

Discourtesy-n-Kawalan nğ galang katampalasanan.

Discover-v-Tuklasin; tumuklas; buksan; makita ang di pa nakita.

Discovery-n-Ang bagong tinuklas.

Discredit-n-Kawalan nğ paniniwala; kakulañgan nğ paniniwala.

Discredit-v-Huag maniwala.

Discreditable-a-Hamak; bastos.

Discreet-a-Mabait; tuso; matalas; marunong; matalino.

Discrepancy-n-Kakulañgan; kamalian; kaibhan.

Discrepant-a-Iba; kulang; mali.

Discrete-a-Nakabukod; malayo.

Discretion-n-Kabaitan; karunuñgan; katalasan.

Discriminate-v-Ibukod; hiwalayin.

Discrimination-n-Pagkabukod; paghihiwalay.

Discuss-v-Matagpuan; magmatowiran; magsalitaan.

Discussion-n-Pagmamatowiran.

Disdain-n-Uyam; tampalasan; kahambugan; kapalaluan.

Disdain-v-Maghambog; uyamin.

Disdainful-a-Palalo; hambog; mauyam.

Disease-n-Damdam; sakit.

Diseased-a-May sakit.

Disembark-v-Umibis; umahon.

Disembarkation-n-Pag ibis sa sasakyan.

Disembarrass-v-Hañguin sa kahiyahiya.

Disembody-v-Alisin sa katawan.

Disencumber-v-Hañguin sa kagipitan.

Disengage-v-Hañguin; iligtas.

Disengaged-a-Walang gawa.

Disentangle-v-Hañguin sa kaguluhan.

Disfavor-v-Huag ipahintulot.

Disfavor-n-Kakulañgan nğ galang.

Disfigure-v-Mansahin; pañgitin.

Disfigurement-n-Pagpapañgit.

Disfiguration-n-Pagpapañgit.

Disfranchise-v-Alisin ang pahintulot.

Disgorge-v-Sumuka; isauli; gantihin.

Disgrace-v-Pahamakin; ipahamak.

Disgrace-n-Kahamakan; kahiyahiyaan.

Disgraceful-a-Nakahihiya; nakadudusta; hamak.

Disguise-v-Ibahin ang hitsura; magbalatkayo.

Disguise-n-Pagkabalatkayo.

Disgust-v-Yumamot, yamutin; mamuhi; pasamain; sumama ang loob.

Disgust-n-Yamot; sama nğ loob; kapighatian; hapis; kadalamhatian; poot.

Disgusted-a-Hapis; nasusuklam.

Dish-n-Pingan.

Dish-v-Isandok.

Dishearten-v-Humina ang loob; tumakot.

Disheveled-a-Walang ayos; magulo; gusot.

Dishonest a-Mahalay; taksil; suitik.

Dishonesty-n-Kasuitikan, kabalayan, kataksilan
Dishonor-n-Kahamakan kahalayan kahihiyaan, kamurahan kasamaan
Dishonor-v-Mapapahiya, hiyain.
Dishonorable a-Nakadudusta, kahiyahiya, mahalay, suitik.
Disincline-v-Huag pumayag
Disinclination-n-Kawalan ñg gusto; kawalan ñg kahiliñgan
Disinfect-v-Suobin; sumuob, linisin
Disinfection-n-Kalinisan, puir.
Disinherit-t-Huag pamanahin.
Disintegrate-v-Tangalin, tumangal
Disintegration-n-Pagtatangal
Disinterested-a-Walang interes, walang nasa
Disjoin-v-Palinsarin, luminsad.
Disjoint-t-Palinsarin, luminsad
Disk-n-Bilog
Dislike-v-Yumamot: sumaina, masukla min
Dislike-n-Yamot,· kasuklaman, poot, suklam, kaajawan
Dislocate t-Palinsarin, luminsad, mawala sa lugar.
Dislocation n Pagpapalinsad.
Dislodge-v-Alisin sa lugar.
Dislodgment-n-Pagkawala sa lugar.
Disloyal-a-Malilo, masukab, lilo taksil, suitik
Disloyalty-n Kalilihan, kasukaban; kasuitikan
Dismal-a-Mapanglaw, malungkot, mahambal, malaipis
Dismantle-t-Hubaran, alisan ñg damit ó kasangkapan
Dismay-v-Pahinain ang loob, takotin, tumakot. humina ang loob.
Dismay-n-Kahinaan ñg loob, tukot
Dismember-v-Hatiin, hiwalayan, pirasuhin.
Dismemberment-n-Paghihiwalay ñg katawan.
Dismiss v-Itaboy; paalisin, palayasin, ipagtabuyan
Dismissal-n Pagtaboy, pagpaahs; pagpalayas
Dismount t-Umibis, lumusong
Disobedience-n Pagsowail, katigasan ñg ulo, alintana
Disobedient a-Sowail, matigas ang ulo, masowayin.
Disobey-v-Sumuway, mag alintana
Disoblige-v-Pagalitin, huag tumupad
Disobliging a-Makagagalit
Disorder-n-Gulo, kawalan ñg ayos ó wasto
Disorder-v Guluhin, sirain ang ayos.
Disorderly-a Magulo; pagulogulo· hindi mabait, bastos.

Disorganize-v-Guluhin, sirain ang ayos.
Disown-v-Huag kilalanin, huag kumilala, tahkuran, magkaila
Disparage-v-Hamakin, pintasin
Disparagement-n Pagpahamak, pintas, kapintasan
Disparity-n-Kaibhan ñg kalagayan o gulang
Dispassion n-Katahimikan
Dispassionate-a-Tahimik, walang gulo
Dispatch-t-Dahdalin, idaos, ipahatid, - tapusin; magpadala, magtapos
Dispatch-n-Telegrama, hatid kawad
Dispel-v-Isabog; palayasin, paalisin
Dispensable-a-Di kailañgan.
Dispensary-n Tindahan ñg gamot
Dispensation-n Paghahati, pagkalat, pagbigay.
Dispense-t-Ikalat, isabog.
Disperse-v-Isabog, sabugin, kalatin
Dispersion-n Pagkalat, pagsabog.
Dispirit-t-Takutin, pahinain ang loob
Displace-v-Ilayo sa lugar, baguhin ang lugar; ibukod.
Displacement-n-Pagbabago ñg lugar
Display-v-Ipakita, ipahalata, buksan
Display-n-Pagpapakita, kainaman.
Displease v-Pagalitin. pasamain ang loob
Displeasure-n-Yumot, galit, kawalan ñg gusto, dalamhati
Disposal-n-Paraan; pamamahala.
Dispose-v-Idaos, tapusin, ayusin, ikalat at ilagay sa lugar, humilig
Disposed a Nakahilig, natatalaga
Disposition-n-Ugali; ayos, kilos, bait, kalagayan; paraan.
Dispossess-v-Kaniyahin, angkinin
Dispossession-n-Pag aankin.
Disproof n Pagbigay nang kasinungaliñgan.
Disproportion-n-Kawalan sa sukat
Disproportion v-Gawin ñg hindi tama sa sukat
Disprove-v-Ibigay ñg kasinungaliñgan sa iba.
Disputable a-Makapagpapatalo
Disputant-n-Ang nag uusap, ang nakikipagtalo.
Disputation-n Pagmamatowiran, pag uusap, basagulo
Dispute v-Makipagtalo; magmatowiran, umaway, salangsañgin, mag usap
Dispute n-Pagtatalo; usap; pag mamatowiran, basagulo; aliñgasñgas.
Disqualification-n-Kakulañgan, pintas, kakulañgan ñg kaya
Disqualify-v Huag abutin ang grado, pintasin
Disquiet n-Kakulañgan ñg katahimikan; gulo.

Disquiet-v-Guluhin

Disquietude n-Gulo, kaguluhan.

Disquisition-n-Pagmamatowiran

Disregard-v-Huag mahalin, huag kaliñgayin; hamakin, halayin

Disregard-n Alintana, tampalasan

Disreputable-a Bastos; hamak, tampalasan.

Disrepute-n-Kahamakan, kahalayan; kabastusan

Disrespect-n Kawalan ñg galang; tampalasan; kabastusan.

Disrespect-v Huag kilalanin; huag sumunod

Disrespectful-a Bastos, tampalasan, walang galang, walang hiya, masama

Disrobe-i-Hubaran, alisan ang damit, maghubo at maghubad.

Disrupt a Sira, bulok, bali

Disrupt-c-Sirain, baliin, punitin

Disruption-n-Kasiraan.

Disrupture-n-Kasiraan.

Dissatisfaction-n-Kawalan ñg gusto, kasamaan ñg loob

Dissatisfy-v-Pagalitin; huag tumupad.

Dissect-v Pirasuhin; usisain.

Dissection-n-Pagpipiraso.

Dissemble-i-Magkonowari

Disseminate-v Isabog ang binhi

Dissemination-n-Pagsasabog ñg binhi

Dissension-n-Pagtatalo, basagulo gulo,

Dissent-v-Umayaw, huag sumunod, magkaiba,

Dissent-n Basagulo.

Dissentation-n-Pagmamatowiran

Dissimilar-a-Hindi kaparis; gansal, hindi kamukha ó katulad.

Dissimilarity-n-Pagkakaiba, kaibhan.

Dissimulate-i-Magkonowari

Dissimulation-n-Pagkakaiba kaibhan.

Dissipate i-Maglasing

Dissipation n Paglalasing

Dissolute a-Pabaya, talipandas, tamad

Dissolution n-Kapabayaan, kawalan ñg kalinga

Dissolve-v-Tumunaw tunawin

Dissonance-n-Pagkakasira ñg tugtog

Dissonant-a-Masama ang tunog.

Dissuade v-Pigilin, pasiyahin

Dissuasion-n-Pagpipiguil, pagpapasiya.

Distaff-n-Panulid.

Distance-n-Layo, pagitan; palugit, puing, kalat.

Distance v Ilayo, lumayo palayuin,

Distant a-Malayo, tangi,

Distaste n-Yamot, pighati

Distasteful-a-Makayayamot mapighati.

Distemper-v-Yamutin.

Distemper-n-Katigasan ñg ulo, sipon ñg kabayo.

Distend-v-Lumaki, humaba

Distention-n-Kahabaan, paghaba.

Distill-v-Alakin; gumawa ñg alak

Distillation n-Pag gagawa ñg alak.

Distellery-n-Gawaan ñg alak

Distinct-a-Maliwanag; bukod tañgi.

Distinction-n-Pamumukod, pangingiba; kaibhan, kamahalan

Distinguish-v-Kilalanin, mamukod; takdaan, saysayin.

Distinguishable-a-Maliwanag, madaling makikilala.

Distinguished-a-Balita; bunyi, bantog; bayani.

Distort-v Pilihin, pumilipit; pilipitin.

Distortion-n Pagpipilipit

Distract-v-Guluhin ang isip

Distracted-a-Ulol, gulo ang isip.

Distraction n-Kaguluhan ñg isip

Distress-n Hirap, pighati, sakit, kahirapan; kasakitan.

Distress-i-Pahirapin.

Distribute v Ipamahagi, kalatin, ikalat

Distribution-n-Paghati; pamamahagi; pamumudmod, pagkalat.

Distributive-a-Nakakasabog.

District-n-Danay, hanga, lugar, pagkat ñg bayan, nayon, distrito.

District-v-Ilagay ang hanga ñg mga danay ó nayon.

Distrust-v-Magagamagain ang loob; kumulang ang katapatan ñg loob.

Distrust-n Kakulañgan ñg katapatan ñg loob

Distrustful a-Mapañgambahin, kulang; confianza.

Disturb-v-Yamutin, bagabagahin, guluhin, pasuklamin ang loob, sabarin; tuksuhin, balisahin

Disturbance-n-Gulo; kaguluhan; yamot; kabalisahan.

Disunion-n-Paghihiwalay, pagkabukod.

Disunite-v-Bumukod, tangalin; ihiwalay.

Disuse n-Kawalan ñg paggamit.

Disuse v-Huag gamitin.

Ditch-n-Sangka

Ditch v-Gumawa ñg sangka.

Ditto-n-Ang nabangit na

Ditto-adv.-Paris ang dati; gayon din, naman, idem

Ditty-n Awit, dalit.

Diurnal-a-Arawaraw.

Dive-v-Sumisid

Dive-n-Sisid, hititan ñg apian

Diverge v-Humiwalay, lumayo.

Divergence-n-Paghihiwalay

Divergency-n-Paghihiwalay.

Divers-a-Marami, ilan

Diverse a-Iba,hindi kamukha,nakabukod

Diversification-n-Kaibhan

Diversify-v-Ibhan, baguhin

Diversion-n-Kaibhan; aliwan kasayahan, pagpapahinga; kutuwaan.

Diversity-n-Kaibhan

Divert-v-Lumiko, iliko; ahwin.

Diverting-a-Nakakaaliw

Divest-v-Hubaran, alisin, magbawal.

Divide-v-Hatiin, hiwalayin, itiwalay; bumahagi, humiwalay

Divider-n-Taga pamahagi.

Divination-n-Paghuhula, hula.

Divine-a-Nauukol sa langit.

Divine-n-Pari, pastor·

Divine-v-Humula, hulaan.

Divinity-n-Bathala, Dios

Division-n-Pamamahagi; paghihiwalay, pagbahati.

Divorce-n-Pagtaboy.

Divorce-v-Itaboy, ipagtabuyan, ihiwalay; ilayo.

Divulge-v-Ipahayag, ihayag; tuklasin; tumuklas sabihin.

Dizziness-n Pagkalula, pagkahilo.

Dizzy-a-Hilo, lula.

Do-v-Gawin; gumawa.

Docile-a-Maamo; banayad; masunurin

Docility-n-Kaamoan; kaanayaran

Dock-v-Putlin ang buntot,iklian,bawasan

Dock-v-Punduhan ng sasakyan kung hilinisin

Docket-n-Listahan.

Doctor n-Mangagamot.

Doctor-v-Gamutin.

Doctrine-n-Pananampalataya, doctrina, pagtuturo

Document n-Documento, kasulatan; katibayan

Documental a-Nauukol sa kasulatan.

Dodge v-Umilag, mawala.

Dodge n Hibo, daya.

Doe-n-Usang babayi, inahing usa.

Doer-n-Ang gumagawa.

Does-v-Gumagawa.

Doff-v-Maghubad, alisin.

Dog-n-Aso.

Dogfish-n-Pating na munti.

Dog-v-Sumunod ng pilit,

Dogged a-Matigas ang 'ulo, sowail.

Doggerel-a-Mababa at bastos, hamak.

Dogma-n-Pananampalataya, isip.

Dogmatic-a-Totoo; tunay

Dogmatical a-Totoo, tunay.

Doily n-Servilletang munti.

Doings-n-Manga ginagawa.

Dole-n-Daing, panaghoy.

Doleful a-Kahambalhambal; kahapishapis; mapanglaw; malungkot.

Doll-n Munika

Dollar-n-Dollar, piso.

Dolor-n-Sakit; hirap, dain; panaghoy.

Dolorous a-Mahirap, masakit.

Dolt-n-Ulol

Domain-n-Kapanghanian; nayon; lupain.

Domestic-n-Alila sa bahay.

Domestic-a-Nauukol sa sariling bahay; maamo.

Domesticate-v-Paamoin

Domesticity-n-Kaamoan.

Domicile-n-Tirahan; tahanan

Dominate-v-Supilin

Domination-n-Pagkasupil,

Domineer-v-Mamahala ng mabagsik

Dominion-n Lupain, lupa. nayon

Domino-n-Domino.

Don-v-Isuot.

Don-n-Maginoo

Donate-v-Magbigay; ipagkaloob, iambag

Donation-n-Bigay, caloob, ambag

Done-v. p p-Ginawa, nangyari na,

Donkey-n-Kabayong munti at mahaba ang tainga, ulol jumento.

Donor-n-Ang nagbigay

Doom-n-Hatol; kapalaran, pasiya.

Doom-v-Sumentencia humatol.

Dooms day n-Kaarawan ng paghahatol.

Door-n-Pinto, pintuan.

Door keeper-n-Ang namamahala sa isang bahay; taga bantay ng pinto.

Door way-n-Pintuan.

Dormant-a-Natutulog.

Dorsal-a-Nauukol sa likod.

Dose-n-Takal ng gamot, doses.

Dose-n-Magpainom ng gamot.

Dost-v-Gumawa.

Dot-n-Punto

Dot-n-Ilagay ang punto, puntuhan.

Dotage-n-Kaululan, pagkaukol.

Dotal-a-Nauukol sa panhik.

Dotard-n-Tawong matanda at mahina ang isip

Dote v-Umulol, humibang.

Doth-v-Gumawa.

Double-n-Yupi, tiklop.

Double-v-Yupiin, tiklupin, ulitin, dublihin.

Double a-Doble, ulit,

Doublet-n-Paris, pareja.

Doubly adv.-Doble

Doubt-n-Agamagam ang loob, pangamba.

Doubt-v-Mangamba, huag maniwala.

Doubtful-a-Againagam ng loob; hindi pa siguro.

Doubtless a Siguro, walang agamagam ng loob.

Dough n-Harinang, minasa para sa tinapay, minasa

Dough nut-n-Buchibuchi

Doughty a-Matapang mangahas.

Douse-v-Ihulog sa tubig.

Dove-n-Kalapati

Dove cot-*n*-Bahay nğ kalapati.
Dove cote-*n*-Bahay nğ kalapati.
Dove like-*a*-Maamo; magandang loob.
Dove tail-*n*-Pagnğinğipinğin at pagla-
    patan nğ kahoy.
Dove tail-*v*-Ilapat nğ mabuti.
Dowdy-*a*-Marunğis; salabula; marumi.
Dowdy-*n*-Tawong marunğis.
Dowel-*n*-Pakong kahoy.
Dowel-*v*-Ipako nğ pakong kahoy.
Dower-*n*-Kaloob; bigay; ang minana nğ
    asawang babayi nğ nanğamatay.
Down-*n*-Balahibong malambot.
Down-*adv*-Sa ibaba; sa gawing ibaba.
Down-*prep.*-Sa ibaba.
Down-*a*-Malungkot.
Down cast-*a*-Malungkot.
Down cast-*n*-Tinğin na malungkot.
Down fall-*n*-Pagkasira·
Down right-*a*-Tunay; totoo.
Down right-*adv.*-Sa gawing ibaba.
Down ward-Downwards-*adv.*-Sa gawing
    mababa.
Dowry-*n*-Bigay; kaloob; Yaman nğ asa-
    wang babayi.
Dowse-*v*-Isisid; ilubog.
Doze-*a*-Matulog.
Dozen-*n*-Labing dalawa; isang docena.
Dozen-*a*-Labingdalawa; isang docena.
Drab-*n*-Kayumangi.
Drab-*a*-Kayumanging,
Drable-*v*-Basahin; tigmakin.
Draft-*n*-Pagpili; cheke.
Draft-*v*-Guhitin ang banhay, paliin ang
    sundalo.
Drafts man-*n*-Taga gawa nğ plano ó ka-
    sulatan.
Drag-*v*-Hilahin; humila.
Drag-*n*-Paghihila· paragos
Draggle-*v*-Basahin at hilahin sa lupa.
Dragonfly-*n*-Gamogamo.
Dragon-*n*-Sundalong nakasakay sa kabayo
Dragoon-*v*-Pahirapin.
Drain-*v*-Tumita; patitiin.
Drain-*n*-Sangka.
Drainage-*n*-Pagtita.
Drake-*n*-Patong lala'ki: bibi.
Drama-*n*-Teatro.
Dramatic-*a*-Nauukol sa teatro.
Dramatical-*a*-Naunkol sa teatro.
Drank-*v.imp.*-Uminom; nakainom.
Drape-*v*-Takpanin nğ kayong itim.
Draper-*n*-Ang nagtitinda nğ kayo.
Drapery-*n*-Manğa kayo; katungkulan
    nğ nagtitinda.
Draught-*n*-Lagok; higop, pag-guhit nğ
    banhay; paghila;
Draught-*v*-Humula; hilahin; gumawa nğ
    plano.
Draw-*v*-Humila; iguhit.

Draw-*n*-Batak, hila; paghila.
Drawback-*n*-Pintas; abala.
Drawer-*n*-Kaja.
Drawing-*n*-Pag-guhit paghila.
Drawl-*v*-Magsalita nğ dahandahan.
Drawl-*n*-Pagsasalita nğ marahan.
Dray-*n*-Bagol.
Dread-*n*-Kaba; panğamba; takot, sindak.
Dread-*v*-Kumaba; tumakot.
Dread-*a*-Katakot-takot kasindak-sindak.
Dreadful-*a*-Kasindaksindak; katakot-ta-
    kot; masama; kagulatgulat; kakila-
    kilabot
Dream-*n*-Panaginip; panğarap.
Dream-*v*-Managinip, manğarap.
Dreamy-*a*-Mapagpanaginip.
Drear-*a*-Mapanglaw; malungkot;
Dreary-*a*-Mapanglaw; malungkot.
Dredge-*n*-Panhukay nğ lupa sa ilalim
    nğ ilog.
Dreg-*n*-Tira
Drench-*v*-Tigmakin, basahin.
Dress-*n*-Damit; bihisan.
Dress-*v*-Magbihis; isuot ang damit.
Dressy-*a*-Mainğat sa pagbibihis.
Dribble-*r*-Pumatak; tumalas.
Dribblet-*n*-Pirasong munti.
Dried-beef-*n*-Tapa; pindang.
Drier-*n*-Pangpatuyo,
Drift-*n*-Pagpasulong; paglutang kasama
    nğ agos; tungo.
Drift-*v*-Lumutang.
Drill-*n*-Pagsasanay; aral; pangbutas.
Drill-*v*-Aralan; magturo; butasin.
Drilling-*n*-Pagpaaral; pagturo.
Drink-*v*-Uminom; inomin,
Drink-*n*-Inomin.
Drip-*v*-Tumalas; pumatak.
Drip-*n*-Patak.
Dripping pan-*n*-Salay.
Drive-*v*-Pasulonğin; pilitin;   magmane-
    jar nğ kabayo; itulak;
Drizzle-*v*-Umambon.
Drizzle-*n*-Ambon.
Droll-*a*-Makatatawa, palabiro siste.
Droll-*n*-Tawong palabiro.
Drollery-*n*-Biro; katuwaan.
Drone-*n*-Tawong tamad.
Drone-*v*-Magpabaya.
Droop-*v*-Yumuko; lumanta.
Drop-*n*-Patak.
Drop-*v*-Lumagpak; malaglag; pumatak.
Dropsy-*n*-Sakit na manás.
Dross-*n*-Dumi; tae nğ bakal; tira.
Drossy-*a*-Marumi.
Drought-Drought-*n*-Tuyo; panahong sa-
    lat sa ulan.
Droughty-*a*-Matuyot; matutuyot.
Drove-*v. imp.*-Pinasulong.
Drove-*n*-Manada, kapisanan nğ hayop

Drover-*n*-Ang may ari nğ maraming baka.
Drowr-*v*-Lumunod; malunod
Drowse-*v* Magantokantokan.
Drowsiness-*n*-Antok.
Drowsy *a*-Nagaantok; inaantok.
Drub-*v*-Pumalo, paluin
Drubbing-*n*-Pagpapalo; paghahampas.
Drudge *v*-Pumagal; magtrabajo nğ malakas.
Drudge-*n*-Alipin sa trabajo.
Drudge *n* Gawa na mabigat.
Drug-*n*-Pangpatulog, gamot
Drug-*v*-Patulugin, painumin ang pangpatulog
Druggist *n*-Ang nagtitinda nğ gamot.
Drum-*n*-Tambol.
Drum-*v*-Magtambol.
Drum stick-*n*-Palo nğ tambol.
Drunk-*a*-Hilo; lasing, lanğo
Drunkard-*n*-Tawong palaging naglalasing
Drunken-*a*-Lanğo lasing
Dry-*a*-Tuyo
Dry-*v*-Tuyuin, ibilad, patuyuin
Dryly-*adv*-Patuyo
Dub-*v*-Magbansag; bansagin.
Dubious *a* Malabo
Duck-*n*-Pato; itik.
Duck-*v*-Isilid; ilubog
Duckling-*n* Patong munti, sisiw nğ pato, sisiw nğ itik
Duct-*n*-Sangka.
Ductile-*a* Masunurin, malambot.
Dudgeon *n*-Tangnan nğ puñal ó nğ panaksak
Due-*a*-Bagay, akma; marapat.
Due-*adv*-Totoo, tunay.
Due-*n*-Utang
Duel-*n*-Hamon
Duel *v*-Humamon
Duet *n* Kanta nğ dalawa.
Dug *v* *imp* & *p p*-Hmukay, humukay.
Duke-*n*-Duke.
Dukedom-*n*-Kalagayang duke
Dulcet-*n*-Mainam sa dinig.
Dull *a*-Maputol, mapudpod, dunğo; mahanğal, walang kabuluhan, torpe.
Dull-*v*-Purulin, pumurol, pudpurin.
Dullness-*n*-Kapurulan, kalabuan.
Duly-*a* Karampatan
Dumb *a* Pipe; walang tuto, hamak.
Dumb-bell *n* Peso.
Dummy-*n* Tawong pipe; larawan nğ tawo, sa teatro
Dummy-*a*-Tahimik, walang kibo.
Dump-*n*-Bual, kasukalan
Dump-*v*-Ibual itapon
Dumpy *a*-Pandak, at mataba.
Dun-*a*-Maitim ang kulay.
Dun-*v*-Maninğil, sinğilin.
Dun-*n*-panininğil.

Dunce-*n*-Ulul, bobo, tawong walang karununğan
Dung-*n*-Dumi, tae nğ hayop.
Dungeon-*n* Bilangong madilim.
Duo *n*-Dalawa
Duodesimal *n*-Ikalabing dalawang bahagi
Duodecimo *n*-Ang may labing dalawang dahon
Dupe-*v*-Davain, hibuin.
Duple-Duplex-*a*-Duble;
Duplicate *v*-Dubhhin, ulitin; parisan, tularan; dalawahin.
Duplicate-*n*-Salin, parisan, howad
Duplication-*n*-Pagkadnble.
Duplication-*n*-Pag aduble, kataksilan, kasulitkan
Durability-*n*-Tibay, tagal; pamamarati.
Durable-*a*-Hindi masisira, matagal; lagi.
Durance-*n*-Tagal, kahirapan.
Duration-*n*-Tagal, laon, pamamarati.
Duress-*n*-Kahirapan.
During-*prep*-Samantala
Durst-*v* *imp*-Pinanğanğahas.
Dusk-*a*-Madilim.
Dusk-*n*-Orasion
Dusky-*a*-Maitim; madilim
Dust-*n*-Alkabok alabok, gilik.
Dust-*v*-Alisin ang alikabok, paspasin; budburin nğ alikabok; dikdikin
Duster *n*-Walis.
Dustpan-*n*-Pungke.
Dusty-*a*-Maalikabok.
Dutch *a*-Nauukol sa Hollandesa.
Dutch-*n*-Hollandesa
Duteous-*a*-Masunurin.
Dutiable-*a*-May buis, dapat ibuis
Dutiful-*a*-Masunurin.
Duty-*n* Katungkulan, pamamahala; utang, buis nğ aduana
Dwarf-*n*-Unano.
Dwarf-*v*-Pandakin.
Dwell-*v*-Tumira, manahan; tumahan.
Dwelling-*n*-Bahay.
Dwindle-*v*-Bumawas; umunti.
Dye-*v*-Tinain, magtina.
Dye *n*-Tina.
Dyeing *n*-Pagtitina.
Dyer-*a*-Ang nagtitina.
Dying-*a*-Namamatay; naghihinğalo.
Dyke-*n* Pilapil.
Dynamite-*n*.Dinamita
Dynasty *n*-Kaharian; lahi nğ hari.
Dysentery-*n*-Iti; pagdudumi na may halong dugo.
Dyspepsia-*n*-Sakit nğ sikmura.
Dyspeptec *a*-Nauukol su sakit nang sikmura.
Dyspeptic-*a*-Ang may sakit nğ sikmura-

H

Each *a*-Balang, tuwi, bawat, bawat isa.
Each-*pro*-Balang isa
Eager-*a* Mainip, mapagnais.
Eagerness-*n*-Kainipan, nais, pita
Eagle *v*-Aguila
Eaglet *n* Aguilang munti.
Ear-*n* Tainga; puso ng mais.
Ear-*v*-Tumubo ang puso ng mais.
Earless-*a* Walang tainga
Early *a* Maaga, unang, agap, maagap.
Early-*adv*-Maaga.
Ear mark-*a* Tanda sa tainga.
Earn-*v*-Makita, kumita.
Earnest-*a*-Totoo, hindi biro, pormal
Earnest-*n*-Katotohanan; kapormalan
Earnings-*n*-Ang kinita ng isa
Ear ring-*n*-Hikaw.
Earth-*n*-Lupa, sang kalibutan
Earth-*v*-Ibaon sa lupa
Earthen-*a*-Bagay lupa, yari ng lupa, malupa
Earthliness-*n*-Kalupaan.
Earthly-*a*-Bagay lupa; nauukol sa lupa.
Earth quake *n*-Lindol.
Earth worm *n*-Bulati, nod
Earthy-*a*-Malupa; may halong lupa
Ease-*n*-Kaginhawahan, kaigihan, igi; kadalian, kalubayan.
Ease-*v*-Umigi; lumuag, lumubay, humimpil
East-*n*-Silanganan,
East *a*-Sa gawing silanganan.
East-*v*-Pumunta sa silanganan
Easter-*n* Kuaresma, paskong mahaba.
Easterly-*a*-Nangaling sa silanganan; sa gawing silanganan
Easterly-*adv*-Sa gawing silanganan
Eastern-*a*-Nasa silanganan; sa gawing silanganan
East ward *adv*-Sa gawing silanganan
Easy-*a*-Ginhawa, madali.
Eat-*v*-Kumain, *hoggishly* lumamon
Eatable-*a*-Makakain
Eatable-*n*-Pagkain
Eat dinner-*v*-Mananghali.
Eat supper-*v*-Humapon.
Eaves-*n*-Lambang, balisbisan
Eaves trough-*n*-Alulod
Eaves dropper-*n* Manunubok
Eavesdrop-*v*-Pakingan; ng palihim.
Ebb *n*-Pagkati ng tubig
Ebb *v* Kumati
Ebon-*a*-Parang ebono
Ebonize-*v* Itiman, umitim

Ebony-*n*-Ebono
Ebony-*a*-Yari ng ebono; maitim.
Eccentric *n* Mangaling sa gitna; hindi karaniwan; katuwa.
Ecclesiastic *a*-Nauukol sa simbahan.
Ecclesiastic-*n*-Pari; pastor.
Echo *n* Uliyaw; alingawngaw; aladalad
Echo-*v*-Umuliyaw, umalingawngaw.
Eclipse *n*-Pagdilim ng buan ó araw.
Eclipse-*v* Dumilim ang araw ó buan, lampasin.
Ecliptic *n*-Daan ng araw.
Economic-Economical-*a*-Tipid, matipid.
Economist-*n*-Ang tawong marunong magtipid.
Economize-*n*-Tipirin; tumipid, magtipiran.
Economy-*n*-Pagtitipid, katipiran.
Ecstasy-*n*-Saya na malabis.
Eddy-*n*-Tubig na tulog, uliuli.
Eddy-*v*-Umuliuli
Edentate-*n* Hayop na walang ngipin; kundi ang bagang
Edge *n*-Gilid, laylayan, wakal, wakas, baybay, dungot, gasa; hangang, tabi.
Edge *v* Lumapit sa gilid, gumawa ng gilid
Edged-*a*-Matalim
Edging-*n*-Gilid, tabi, puntas na makitid.
Edge ways-Edge wise-*adv*-Pagilid, sa gawing gilid
Edible-*a*-Makakain
Edict-*n*-Utos, kautusan.
Edification-*n* Pagtatayo; pagtuturo.
Edifice-*n* Bahay
Edify-*v*-Magtayo, gumawa, magturo.
Edit-*v*-Maglimbag.
Edition-*n*-Limbag, pinaglimbagan
Editor-*n*-Ang nagpapalimbag
Editorial-*a*-Nauukol sa pag lilimbag.
Editorial-*n* Ang sinulat nang nagpapalimbag.
Educate *v*-Turuan, magturo, palakhin ang isip
Education-*n* Galang, karunungan; dunong; aral.
Educational *a* Nauukol sa karunungan.
Educator-*n* Ang nagtuturo.
Educe-*v* Ipahtaw, hangin.
Eel-*n*-Palos
E'en-*adv*. Masque; hangang sa.
E'er-*adv*-Kailan man; sa ano mang panahon
Efface-*v*-Burahin, lipulin

28

Effect n-Ang nangyayari, kayarian; gawa

Effect-v-Maramay, idamay, yarin.

Effective-a-Kasalukuyan, mabisa, malakas, masidla.

Effectual-a Husto, sukat, totoo

Effeminacy-n-Karuagan, kahinaan ng loob.

Effeminate-a-Parang babayi, duag; mahina ang loob

Effervesce-i-Kumulo, bumula

Effervescence-n-Pangkakulo, kulo.

Effervescent-a-Kumukulo

Effete-a-Lipas, karat walang kabuluhan, gasgas

Efficacious-a-Malakas; mangyayari.

Efficiency-n-Pagyayari, kahustuhan.

Efficient-n-Husto, mangyayari.

Effigy-n-Larawan

Effort-n-Tikhim, subok.

Effrontry-n-Lampastangan, tampalasan.

Effulgence-n-Kahinawan, kahwanagan.

Effulgent-a-Mahnaw; mahwanag

Effuse-c-Ibuhos, ipalabas.

Effusion-n-Pagbuhos; pagpalabas.

Effusive-a-Mapagbuhos, bumukal.

Eft-n-Butiki.

Egg-n-Itlog

Egg-i-Iudyok, isulong.

Egg plant-n-Talong.

Egotism-n Kariputan; kasakiman, karamutan, kapalaluan.

Egregious-a-Lampas, katakataka

Egress-n-Pag labas, pag alis.

Egyptian-a-Nauukol sa taga Egipto.

Egyptian-n-Taga Egipto.

Eh-inter-Ano.

Eight-a-Walo.

Eight-n-Walo

Eighteen-a-Labing walo.

Eighteen-n-Labing walo.

Eighteenth-a-Ikalabing walong.

Eighteenth-n-Ikalabing walo

Eighth-a-Ikawalong

Eighth-n-Ikawalo.

Eighthly-adv Ikawalo.

Eightieh-a-Ikawalong puong

Eightieh-n-Ang ikawalong puo.

Eighty-a-Walong puong

Eighty-n-Walong puo.

Either-a-Alin

Either-pro -Alinman.

Either-conj.-Alin.

Ejaculate-i-Magsalita ng bigla.

Ejaculation-n Salitang bigla.

Eject-v-Itapon, ipalabas.

Ejection-n-Pagpalabas, pagtapon sa labas.

Ejectment-n Pagtapon sa labas pagpalabas.

Eke-v-Lumaki, magdaragdag.

Eke-adv.-Naman; gayon din

Elaborate a-Ayos, mainam, maganda

Elaborate-i-Ayusin tapusin ng mahusay,

Elapse-v-Lumipas, magdaan, macaraan.

Elastic-a-Parang goma.

Elastic n-Ligas.

Elate-a Mataas, masaya

Elate-v-Sumaya.

Elation-n-Saya; tuwa, kaluguran

Elbow-n-Siko.

Elder-n-Tawong matanda

Elder a-Lalong matanda, matanda pa

Elderly-a-Matanda.

Eldest-a-Matanda sa lahat, katandatandaan

Elect-a-Pinili, hinalal.

Elect-v-Humalal, pumih, ipalagay

Elect-n-Ang pinili

Election-n-Paghahalal, eleccion.

Electioneer-c-Tumulong sa isang candidato

Elective-a-May kapangyarihan pumili

Elector- i-Ang may katuwiran magvoto.

Electoral-a-Nauukol sa paghahalal.

Electric-a-Nauukol sa lintik

Electrical-a-Nauukol sa lintik.

Electricity-n-Lintik; kidlat.

Electrify-v-Buhayin.

Elegance-n-Inam; inam ng kilos; kainaman, karikitan, kagandahan

Elegant-a Mainam, makinis bihasa, maganda, dakila, marilag; magaling, halata, maayos

Element-n-Bahagi, parte; pinagmulaan,

Elemental a-Nauukol sa piraso, nauukol sa parte ó pinagmulan

Elementary-a-Primero, bago.

Elephant-n-Elepante

Elephantine-a-Malaki.

Elevate-v-Itaas, ibangon; padakilain.

Elevation-n Pagpapataas, kadakilaan

Elevator-n-Makinang pangpataas.

Eleven-a-Labing isa.

Eleven-n-Labing isa.

Eleventh-a-Ikalabingisang.

Eleventh n-Ang ikalabingisa

Elf-n-Duende.

Elfin-a-Nauukol sa duende

Elfin-n-Munting duende.

Elicit-v-Hanguin; ipalitaw

Eligible-a-Mararapat.

Elixir-n-Gamot na halohalo.

Elk-n-Malaking usa.

Ellipse-n-Talohaba

Ellipsis-n-Paglaktaw.

Elocution n-Pagsasalita, pagdidiscurso.

Elocutionary a Nauukol sa salita o sa discurso.

Elocutionist-*n*-Ang nagsasalita ó nag-didiscurso.

Elongate-*v*-Humaba, unatan.

Elongation-*n*-Paghaba; pagunat.

Elope-*v*-Magtanan.

Elopement-*n*-Pagtatanan.

Eloquence-*n*-Kainaman ng̃ pagsasalita.

Eloquent-*a*-Maaya, mainam magsalita.

Else-*a*-Iba.

Else-*pro*.- Iba.

Else-*adv* -Bukod sa rito

Else *conj* -Bukod sa ito.

Else where *adv*.-Sa ibang lugar

Elude-*v*-Umilag.

Eludible-*a*-Mailagin.

Elusion-*n*-Ilag, pagkailag.

Elusory-*a*-Makadadaya.

Elve *n*-Duende

Elvish-*a*-Naunkol sa duende

Emaciate-*v*-Pumayat, mang̃ang̃ayayat.

Emaciation-*n*-Pang̃ang̃ayayat

Emanate-*v*-Sumipot, bumukal, manga-ling

Emanation-*n*-Pagsipot; pagbukal.

Emancipate *v*-Pawalan ang alipin, mag-bigay ng̃ kalayaan.

Emancipation *n*-Pagbibigay nang kala-yaan

Emasculate-*v*-Kaponin.

Emasculate-*a*-Mahina, duag.

Embalm-*v*-Gamutin ang bangkay upang huag mabulok

Embank-*v*-Magpilapil.

Embankment-*n*-Pilapil.

Embarcation-*n* Pagsakay sa sasakyan

Embargo-*n*-Pagbawal ng̃ pag alis ng̃ isang sasakyan sa isang puerto

Embark-*v*-Ilulan; maglulan, isakay; su-makay

Embarrass-*v*-Hiyain

Embarrassment-*n*-Hiya.

Embed-*t* -Ilagay sa hihigan.

Embellish-*v*-Gumayak; gayakan, guman-da, pagandahin; pamutihan parikitan.

Embellishment-*n*-Pag gagayak, pagpa-paganda; gayak, pamuti.

Ember-*n*-Baga

Embezzle-*v*-Manekas, ankinin ang ini-lagak sa isa

Embezzlement *n*-Tekas, pag aankin ng̃ ari ng̃ iba.

Emblem-*n*-Tanda

Emblematic-*a*-Nauukol sa tanda.

Emblematical-*a*-Nauukol sa tanda.

Embodyment-*n*-Pag sasama sama; pag-ipon

Embody-*v*-Isama; iponin.

Embolden-*v*-Tumapang.

Emboss-*t* -Itampok, padilagin.

Embrace-*v*-Yumakap, yakapin; humag-kan.

Embrace-*n*-Yakap, hagkan.

Embracement-*n*-Pagyakap.

Embrocate-*v*-Pahiran ng̃ gamot, hilurin; hilutin

Ebrocation - *n* - Paghilot, pagpahit nang gamot

Embroider-*v*-Gumawa ng̃ puntas.

Emend-*v*-Ayusin, linisin.

Emendation-*n*-Paglinis ng̃ kasalanan

Emerge-*v*-Lumitaw.

Emergency-*n*-Ang nangyari na hindi sinasadya.

Emery-*n*-Liha.

Emetic-*n*-Gamot na pangpasuca.

Emetic-*a*-Nakasusuka

Emigrant-*n* Ang lumipat sa ibang lupa.

Emigrate-*v*-Lumipat sa ibang lupa.

Emigration-*n*-Paglipat sa ibang lupa

Eminence *n*-Kadakilaan, karilagan; ka-rang̃alan.

Eminency-*n* Karang̃alan; kadakilaan, karilagan.

Eminent-*a*-Dakila, marang̃al, makapang-yayari.

Emissary *n*-Kalihim

Emissary-*a*-Malihim.

Emission *n*-Pagpalabas, ang lumitaw sa isang panahon.

Emit-*v*-Iutos; ipalitaw, palabasin

Emmet-*n*-Langam

Emolliate-*v*-Lumambot; lambutin.

Emolient-*a*-Malalambutin.

Emolument-*n*-Pakinabang, tubo.

Emotion-*n*-Pakiramdam, damdam, ka-ramdaman, kaba

Emotional-*a*-Nauukol sa pakiramdam

Emperor-*n*-Emperador; hari.

Emphatic-*a*-Malakas

Empire-*n*-Emperio; kabarian

Employ-*v*-Gamitin, upahan.

Employ-*n*-Hanap buhay, katungkulan.

Employee-*n*-Ang nagtatrabajo.

Employment-*n*-Hanap buhay; katung-kulan

Emporium-*n*-Lugar ng̃ pang̃ang̃alakal, plaza; palinke

Empower-*v*-Ibigay nang kapangyarihan sa isa

Empress-*n*-Haring babayi.

Empty-*a* Walang laman, bugok; kalog, walang kabuluhan

Empty-*v*-Ibuhos, alisin ang laman, isa-lin

Emulate-*v*-Lumaban, pasukuin, lampasin

Emulation *n*-Hiling ng̃ loob.

Emulsion-*n* Gamot

Emulsive-*a*-Makalalambot

Enable-*v*-Magkaroon ng̃ kaya; makaya; n

Enact-v-Iutos, gumawa ñg leyes

Enactment-n Paggagawa·ñg mga utos

Enamor-v-Umibig ñg mahigpit.

Encamp-ı-Magpahinga ang hukbo.

Encampment-n-Pagpapahinga ñg hukbo

Encampment-n-Gayuma.

Encircle-v-Paligirin; ipaligid.

Enclose-v-Bakurin, magbakod, kulungin, ipaligid.

Enclosure n-Lugar sa loob ñg bakod, kural.

Encompass v-Paligirin

Encore-adv.-Ulit, muli.

Encore-inter -Ulit

Encore-n-Pagpuri; paghiñgi ñg ulit

Encounter-v-Sumalubong, umuntog, bumanga, sabatin

Encounter-n-Umpog; untog, salubong, banga, laban.

Encourage-v-Iudyok, ipabuya

Encouragement-n-Pagudyok.

Encroach v-Ankinin.

Encumber-v Abalahin; antalahin, umabala.

End-n-Dulo; tapos, katapusan; wakal, wakas; dungot; hanga, hangahan

End-v-Tapusin, tumapos, yariin; utasin, mamatay, humanga

Endanger-ı-Ihulog ó ilagay sa may panganib

Endear v Mahalin.

Endearment-n-Pagmamahal.

Endeavor-v-Tumikim, subukin.

Endeavor-n-Tikim; subok.

Ending-n-Utas,' katapusan; dulo; pagkayari.

Endless-a-Walang dulo, walang hanga, walang katapusan, walang mula at ˙hanga.

Endorse-v-Pirmahin; pumayag

Endow-v-Magpamana.

Endowment-n-Mana; karununãan, dunong

Endure-v-Magtiis, tiisin, mamalagi; lumagi, alalayan, batahin

Endurance n-Pagtitiis; pamamalagi.

Endways-Edwise adv -Patayo, pahalang.

Enemy-n-Kaalit, kalaban; katalo, kaaway.

Energy-n-Lakas loob; liksi; kasipagan.

Energetic-a-Malakas ang loob, maliksi, masipag

Enfeeble-v-Humina.

Enforce-ı-Pilitin, patapangin.

Enforcement n-Pagpilit.

Enfranchise-v-Hanguin sa kagipitan ó pag kaalipin, magbigay uano kala yaan

Engage-v-Itali, isama, luinaban, lahanin,

Engaged-a-May pañgako,

Engagement-n-Pañgako, dulog.

Engine n-Makina de vapor

Engineer-n-Makinista,taga sukatñglupa

Engineer-v-Mamahala.

Engineering-n-Karununãan sa makina.

English a-Englés

English n-Englés, taga Englaterra.

English-v-Ihulog sa wikang Englés.

Engrave-v-Idukit, lilukan, gumuhit.

Engraving-n Pagdukit, dukit

Engross-ı-Isalin ang sulat.

Engulf-v-Lamunin

Enhance-v-Tumaas;lumaki,magdaragdag

Enhancement-n-Paglaki, pagdaragdag.

Enigma n-Bugtong, talinhaga

Enigmatic-a-Malabo

Enjoin-ı-Ipagbilin, ipagmasákit. bumala, magbilin magbawal

Enjoy-v-Magustuhan, ibigin, umaliw; sumaya

Enjoyment-n Kasayahan, tuwa, kaaliwan.

Enlarge v-Lumaki, magpalaki; dumami, biklarin; habaan, humaba.

Enlargement-n Paglaki, pagdami

Enlighten v-Liwanagan, magilaw, magturo.

Enlightenment-n-Pag liwanag, pagturo

Enlist-v-Pumasok sa servicio

Enlistment-n Pagpasok sa servicio.

Enliven-ı-Buhayin, lumiksi

Enmity-n-Galit, sama ñg loob, tanim sa loob.

Enormous-a-Malaki ñg totoo, dakila; lubha. malabis

Enormity-n-Laki; kalakihan; kabigatan.

Enough-a-Husto, sukat, sawa

Enough-adv.-Sukat.

Enough n Kasukatan, kahustuhan.

Enquire-v-Magtanong. tanonãin, tumanong

Enquiry-n-Tanong.

Enrage-v-Pagalitin, magalit

Enrich-ı-Payamanin

Enroll-v-Listahin, pumirma.

Enrollment-n Pagpasok

Ensample-n-Halimbawa

Ensconce v-Itago, kanlonãin, kup'.upin

Enshrine v-Mahalin.

Enshroud-v-Balutin ñg sapot.

Ensign n Bandila.

Enslave v-Supilin; alipinin

Enslavement-n-Pagpaalipin.

Ensue v Sumunod, buntutan.

Ensue ı-Tibayin; tumibay.

Entangle-v-Guluhin.

Entanglement-n -Pagpapagulo

Entangling a-Mapagbasagulo.'

Enter-v-Pumasok, pasukin.

Enter the mind-v-Tarukin ñg isip.

Enter prise-*n*-Gawa; trabajo.
Enterprising-*a*-Buhay ang loob.
Entertain-*v*-Aliwin; lituhin; magpasaya.
Entertaining-*a*-Masaya; maaliw.
Entertainment-*n*-Pagpaaliw; kasayahan.
Enthrone-*v*-Ilagay sa trono.
Enthronement-*n*-Paglagay sa trono.
Enthusiasm-*n*-Pagkawili; interes.
Enthusiastic-*a*-May interes; buhay ang loob.
Entice-*v*-Tuksuhin.
Enticement-*n*-Tukso; uraling masama.
Entire-*a*-Lahat; buo; ganap; pulos.
Entirety-Entireness-*n*-Kalahatan; kabuoan.
Entitle-*v*-Marapatin.
Entomb-*v*-Ilibing.
Entrails *n*-Manĝa bituka; isaw.
Entrance-*n*-Pagpasok; pintuan.
Entrancé-*v*-Patulugin; tulugin.
Entrap-*v*-Hulihin; bitagin.
Entreat-*v*-Dumaing; manalanĝin; huminĝi; ipakiusap.
Entreaty-*n*-Pakiusap; luhog; daing.
Entree-*n*-Pagpasok.
Entrust-*v*-Ialok; ilagak.
Entry-*n*-Pagpasok; pintuan.
Enumerate-*v*-Bilanĝin; saysayin nang isa't isa.
Enumeration-*n*-Pagbilang; kabilanĝan.
Enunciate-*v*-Magpahayag; magsabi.
Enunciation *n*-Pagpahayag; pahayag; pagsasabi.
Envelop-*v*-Ibalot; balutin.
Envelop-Envelope-*n*-Balot nĝ sulat.
Envious-*a*-Maingit.
Environ-*v*-Ipaligid.
Environment-*n*-Pagpapatigid;kahilinĝan
Envoy-*n*-Taga bilin; taga utos; utusan; taga tupad.
Envy-*n*-Kaingitan; ingit; paninibugho.
Envy-*v*-Maingit; mainip.
Epicene-*a*-Nauukol sa lalaki at babayi.
Epidemic-*a*-Hayag; karaniwan.
Epidemic-*n*-Kasakitan.
Epidermis-*n*-Balat sa labas.
Epiphany-*n*-Pagsipot; litaw; pista nĝ tatlong Hari.
Episcopate-*n*-Kapisanan nĝ mĝa pari.
Episode *n*-Kasaysayan.
Epistle-*n*-Sulat.
Epistolar-*a* Nauukol sa sulat.
Epitaph-*n*-Karalula sa ibabaw nĝ libing.
Epitome-*n*-Maikling kasaysayan.
Epoch-*n*-Panahon; fecha.
Epsom salt-*n*-Magnesia calsinada.
Equable-*a*-Pantay at magkaparis; kawanki; katulad.

Equal-*a*-Impas; magkaisa; magkatulad; magkawanki.
Equal-*n*-Pagkatulad; pagkaisa.
Equal-*v*-Pantayin; tularan.
Equality *n*-Pagkakapantay; pagkakatulad; pagkakaisa; kasukatan.
Equalization-*n*-Pagkakapantay; pagtutulad.
Equalize-*v*-Pantayin; pumantay; parisan; tularin.
Equally-*adv.*-Naman; gayon din.
Equanimity-*n* Kapantayan; pagkakaisa.
Equator-*n*-Equador.
Equestrian-*a*-Nauukol sa kabayo.
Equestrian-*n*-Ang marunong sumakay sa kabayo.
Equiangular-*a*-Magkaparis ang mĝa sulok.
Equiangular-*a*-Magkaisa ang layo.
Equilateral-*a*-Magkaisa ang sukat nĝ mĝa gilid ó hanga.
Equilibrium-*n*-Timbang; tatag.
Equine-*a*-Nauukol sa kabayo.
Equinox-*n*-Panahon na magkasing haba ang araw at ang gabi.
Equip-*v*-Magbigay nĝ kailanĝan.
Equipage-*n* Pagbigay nang manĝa kailanĝan.
Equipment-*n*-Pagbibigay nĝ kailanĝan.
Equipoise-*n*-Timbang.
Equitable-*a*-Matowid;husto;walang daya
Equity-*n* Katotohanan; kabanayaran.
Equivalence-*n*-Katimbang; kasukat kapalit.
Equivalent-*a*-Magkasing halaga; magkaparis.
Equivocal-*a*-Nakakamali.
Equivocate-*v*-Mamali; lumihis; maligaw.
Equivocation-*n*-Kamalian; mali; paglihis; pagligaw.
Era-*n*-Panahon.
Eradicate-*v*-Labnutin; alisin; magbuhat sa ugat; bunutin.
Eradication-*n*-Pagbunot.
Erase-*v*-Burahin; pawiin.
Erasure-*a*-Bura; pagbuburan.
Ere-*adv.*-Nauna.
Ere-*prep.*-Nauna.
Erect-*a*-Matuwid; patayo; maayos.
Erect-*v*-Itayo; magtayo.
Erection-*n*-Pagtatayo.
Ere long *adv.*-Hindi maluluatan.
Err-*v*-Mamali; huag tumama; maligaw.
Errand-*n*-Utos; bilin; pasabi.
Errant-*a*-Pabaya; tamad.
Erratic-*a*-Palakadlakad; walang ayos.
Erratum-*n*-Mali sa sulat.
Erroneous-*a*-Nakamamali; may mali.
Error-*n*-Mali; kamalian; kabulaan.
Erudite-*a*-Marunong; may dunong.

Erudition *n*-Karununğan.
Eruption-*n*-Pagputok.
Erysipelas-*n*-Sakit nğ balat na na' akahawig sa bunğang araw.
Escapade *n*-Kalikutan, biro
Escape *v*-Makawala, umilag, makapulas
Escape-*n*-Pagkawala, pagkahgtas.
Eschew-*v*-Umilag.
Escort-*n*-Kumboy, bantay.
Escort-*v*-Ihatid, maghatid, sumama.
Escrotoire-*n*-Mesang sulatan
Esculent-*a* Makakain.
Esculent-*n*-Anomang bagay na kinain nğ tawo
Esophagus-*n*-Lalamunan.
Especial-*a*-Especial; bukod, nagiisa
Espousal-*n*-Kasal; pagagamit.
Espouse-*v*-Magasawa, kumasal, gamitin
Espy-*v*-Usisain, manubok
Essay-*n*-Tikim.
Essay-*v*-Tumikim.
Essence-*n*-Kaukulan, ubod, amoy.
Essential-*a*-Kailanğan
Essential-*n*-Ang kinakailanğan.
Establish-*v*-Magtayo, itayo, itatag, mag pundar.
Establishment-*n*-Pagtatag, bahay.
Estate-*n*-Ari, pagaari; lupa
Esteem-*v*-Galanğin, gumalang; mahalin.
Esteem-*n*-Galang, kamahalan, pagmamahal
Estimable-*a*-Dapat igalang; magalang; dapat mahalin.
Estimate-*v*-Taruhan; tasahan, maglagay, nğ halaga, kuentahin.
Estimate-*n*-Tasa, halaga
Estimation-*n*-Galang, pag gagalang, pagpuri.
Estrange-*v*-Lumayo, umilag.
Estrangement-*n*-Paglalayo, kailangan.
Etch-*v*-Gumuhit sa metal.
Etching-*n*-Guhit sa metal.
Eternal-*a*-Walang mula at hanğa.
Eternally-*adv.*-Sa buong panahon.
Ether-*n*-Etero
Etherial *a*-Magaan parang hanğin, nauukol sa lanğit.
Ethiop-*n*-Negro, tawong itim
Ethiopic-Ethiopian-*a*-Nauukol sa negro
Ethiopic-*n*-Wika nğ negro.
Etiquette-*n*-Galang, kainaman nğ kilos
Eucharist-*n*-Pakinabang, cumunion.
Eulogistic-*a*-Dapat purihin.
Eulogium-*n*-Pagpuri
Eulogize-*v*-Purihin.
Eulogy-*n*-Kasaysayan nğ pagpupuri
Euphonic-*a* Makikiayon sa tunog nğ voces.

Euphony-*n*-Ayos nğ tunog.
Europe-*n*-Europa
European-*a*-Nauukol sa Europa.
European-*u*-Taga Europa.
Evacuate-*v*-Umalis.
Evacuation-*n*-Pagalis
Evade-*v*-Umilag, lumayo.
Evanesce-*v*-Mawala.
Evanescence-*n*-Pagkawala.
Evangel-*n*-Mabuting balita, Santa Biblia
Evangelic-*a*-Nauukol sa Santa Biblia
Evangelical-*a*-Nauukol sa Santa Biblia.
Evangalist *n*-Pari na walang distino na firme
Evaporate-*v*-Suminğaw, Matuyo.
Evaporation-*n*-Pagtutuyo, pagsinğaw.
Evasion-*n*-Pagiilagan.
Evasive *a*-Manlagay, di mahwanag.
Eve-Even-*n*-Orasion.
Even *a*-Yano, pantay, patag, hangang; panay.
Even-*v*-Pantayin, pumantay
Even-*adv* -Bagaman, gayondin. pati.
Evening-*n*-Hapon, orasion, panayan
Event-*n*-Ang nangyari; Ang nagkakataon, pangyayari
Eventful-*a*-Maraming nangyayari.
Eventual-*a*-Tapus; sa katapusan
Ever-*adv* -Kailanman, sa anomang panahon, lagui
Ever-glade-*n*-Lawak.
Ever-lasting-*a*-Walang tapos, lagi; walang likat.
Ever-lasting *a*-Pagkakalagi
Ever-more *ad* -Lagi, palagi, walang tigil.
Every-*a*-Balang, bawat; pulos, tuwi
Every-body-*n*-Lahat nğ tawo
Every day-*a*-Araw-araw; balang araw.
Every-one-*n*-Lahat nğ tawo
Every-thing-*u*-Lahat nğ manğa bagay-bagay.
Every-where-*adv*-Sa lahat nğ lugar.
Eve-trough-*n* Alulod.
Evict-*v*-Alisin sa katungkulan
Eviction *n*-Pagpaalis sa katungkulan
Evidence-*n*-Subok katotohanan, pagsasaksi
Evidence-*v*-Ipakita, ipahalata.
Evident *a* Mahwanag; mahnaw; totoo, tunay; tapat.
Evil-*a*-Masama.
Evil-*n*-Kasamaan.
Evil-*adv*.-Kasamasama
Evince-*v*-Ipakita, ipahalata.
Evitable *a* Mailagan.
Evoke *r* Tawağin, tumawag.
Evolution-*n* Paglaki; tubo.
Evolve-*v*-Ilatag, hwanagan.

Ewe-n-Tupang babayi.
Ewer-n-Tapayan.
Exact-a-Husto; tama; sukat; ganap; walang kulang.
Exact-v-Huminĝi.
Exaction-n-Katowiran.
Exactitude-n-Katowiran.
Exaggerate-v-Ululan; dagdagan.
Exaggeration-n-Pagdaragdag. pagpalaki.
Exalt-v-Purihin.
Exaltation-n-Pagpupuri.
Examine-v-Umusig; usisain; siyasatin; ipaglisayin; magexamin.
Examination-n-Pagnusisa; siyasat; pagusig.
Example-n-Halimbawa; tularan; uliran; parisan; talinhaga.
Exasperate-v-Pagalitin.
Exasperation-n-Galit; poot.
Excavate-v.Hukayin, humukay.
Excavation-n-Hukay.
Exceed-v-Humigit; lumampas; lumabis; lumagpos; lumalo.
Exceeding-a-Lalo; mahiĝit.
Excel-v-Humigit; lumampas; lampasin.
Excellence-n-Danĝal; dunong puri; kamahalan; kaguinoohan; kalinisan.
Excellency-n-Kainaman; kaginoohan; karunungan.
Excellent-a-Mainam; bihasa; marunong; marilag; maranĝal; dakila; bunyi.
Excelsior-a-Mataas pa.
Except-v-Ibukod; itanĝi; mamukod.
Except-prep.-Bagkus; bukot; bukod sa liban.
Except-conj.-Bagkus; bukod; nĝuni; datapua.
Exception-n-Katanguihan; pamumukod.
Exceptional-a-Nakabukod; nagiisa.
Excess-n-Kalabisan; kalagposan labis; lagpos.
Excessive-v-Malabis; lagpos; lampas.
Exchange-v-Palitan; ipamalit; halinhan, humalili.
Exchange-n-Pagpalit; kahalili; kapalit.
Exchangeable-a- Makapapalit.
Excise-n-Buis.
Excise-v-Bumuis; magbayad ang buis.
Exciseman-n-Manininĝil nĝ buis.
Excision-n-Pagputol; paglipol.
Excite-v-Ibuya; indyok: udyukan; sulsulan.
Excitability-n-Kasiglahan.
Excitable-a-Masigla; Magulatin.
Excitement-n-Gulo; sigla; gulat; gitlá.
Exciting-a-Masigla; makagugulat.
Exclaim-v-Humiyaw; sumigaw.
Exclamation-n-Hiyaw sigaw.
Exclamatory-a-Makasisigaw.

Exclude-v-Huag isama; ibukod; ilayo; ifuera; ilabas.
Exclusion-n-Pagkabukod; kalayuan.
Exclusive-v-Nakabubukod.
Excommunicate-v-Ialis sa simbahan.
Excommunication-n-Pagpaalis sa sim bahan.
Excrement-n-Tae; dumi.
Excrete-v-Ibukod at itapon.
Excretion-n-Pagtapon.
Excruciate-v-Pahirapin; maghirap.
Excruciation-n Pagpapahirap.
Exculpate-v-Hanĝuin sa pagkakasala.
Exculpation-n-Pagpatawad sa kasalanan
Excursion-n-Lakad; viaje.
Excursive-a-Palakadlakad.
Exeuse-v-Patawarin.
Excuse-n-Dahilan; katowiran.
Execrate-v Manumpa; magtunĝayaw laitan, maglait.
Execration-n-Kalaitan; pagtutunĝayaw.
Execute-v-Bitayin; patayin; gawin; gu manap; ganapin; hustuhin; tumupad
Executer-n-Ang tumutupad.
Execution-n-Pagpugot; pagbitay; pag gagawa.
Executioner-n-Taga pugot; ang pumatay
Executive-a-Nauukol sa pagtupad.
Executor-n-Taga tupad; ang gumagawa
Executress-Executrix-n-Babaying alibas:
Exemplar-n-Halimbawa; tularan.
Exemplary-a-Dapat sumunod.
Exemplification-n-Halimbawa; pagliliwa nag.
Exemplify-v-Magbigay nĝ halimbawa
Exempt-v-Ilayo;patawarin;ibukod,iligta:
Exempt-v-Malaya; laya.
Exemption-n-Kalayaan; patawad.
Exercise-n-Sanay; gawa.
Exercise-v-Magsanay; gumawa.
Exert-v-Pilitin; pumilit; tumapang.
Exertion-n-Pilit; kapilitan.
Exhalation-n-Pagsinĝaw.
Exhale-v-Huminĝa.
Exhaust-v-Ubusin; umubus; tapusin.
Exhaust-a-Naubos.
Exhaustion-n-Pagubos.
Exhibit-v-Iharap; ipakita; itanghal.
Exhibit-n-Tanghalan.
Exhibition-n-Pagpapakita.
Exhilerate-v-Sumaya; pasayain; buhayir
Exhileration-n-Kasayahan; saya.
Exhort-v-Magpasaya; hulaan; aralan.
Exhortation-n-Aral; pasiya; hula.
Exhume-v-Hukayin muli.
Exhumation-n-Paghukay muli.
Exigence-Exigency-n-Kakailanĝan.
Exigent-a-Kailanĝan.
Exile-v-Idestiero; itapon ang may sala sa ibanĝ lupa.

Exile n-Tawong ipinadestiero

Exist-v-Magkaroon, maging.

Existence-n-Yari, paging; ang pagkakataon

Exit-n Palabasan, pintuan

Exodus-n-Pag alis, pag labas

Exonerate-v-Hanguin sa pagkakasala, patawarin.

Exoneration n-Pagpapatawad.

Exorbitant-a Malabis, mahal na mahal.

Exotic-a-Nangaling sa ibang lupa.

Expand-v-Lumaki, lumuang, umabot, idatay, umunat.

Expanse-n-Paglaki, laki; luang.

Expansion-n Paglaki

Expatiate-v-Lumaki; lumaki kung saan may gusto

Expatriate-v-Itapon sa ibang lupa.

Expatriation-n-Pagtapon sa ibang lupa

Expect-v-Asahan, umasa; magpita magantay

Expectance-Expectancy-n-Pagasa.

Expectant-a-May inasahan.

Expectorate-v-Lumura maglaway; dumahak

Expectoration-n Paglura, lura, paglaway; pagdahak; dahak

Expedience-n-Kadalian

Expedient-a-Madali, mapakinabangan.

Expedient-n-Kasangkapan.

Expedite-v-Tumulong; hawanan, ipadala

Expedition-n-Paglakad, viaje

Expeditious-a-Tuloytuloy, madali.

Expel-v-Ilabas; ifuera

Expend-v-Ubusin; gastahin, gumugol, gumasta, gasgasin, gamitin, gumasgas.

Expendible-a Sukat magasta

Expenditure-n-Paggagasta, pagubos.

Expense-n Gastos, halaga, gugol, paggasta

Expensive a-Mahalaga; mahal.

Experience-n-Sanay, kasanayan; dunong, karunungan, taho

Experience-v-Magsanay, matanto, matalastas, dumaan.

Experienced a-Sanay; marunong, biha-a; matalas.

Experiment-n-Pagsubok; subok

Experiment-v-Tumikman; usisain.

Expert-a-Matalas, marunong, bihasa, sanay

Expert-n-Tawong marunong ó matalas.

Expiate-v-Gantihin; gumamti.

Expiation-n-Paggaganti; ganti.

Expiration-n-Tapos; katapusan, dulo

Expire-v-Mamatay, tumapos. malagot ang hininga.

Explain-v Saysayin, , liwanagin, magsaysay, salaysayin, magturo ilathala.

Explanation-n-Kaliwanagan, kasaysayan salaysay.

Expletive a-Mapupuno

Expletive-n-Salitang ginagamit sa pagpuno

Explicit-a-Tunay, maliwanag.

Explode-v-Pumutok

Exploit-n Gawa.

Exploit-v-Gamitin.

Explore-v-Siyasatin, tuklasin

Exploration-n-Pagtuklas

Explosion-n-Pagputok

Explosive a Nauukol sa pagputok

Explosive-n-Anomang bagay na madaling puputok.

Export-v-Ipadala sa ibang lupa

Export-n-Ang mga bagay na ipinadala sa ibang lupa

Exportation-n-Pagpapadala ñg msñga bagaybagay sa ibang lupa.

Expose-v-Ibulid, ibulusok, ipalitaw paliwanagin

Exposition-n-Tangbalan

Expostulate-v Dumaing, managhoy.

Expostulation-n-Daing; taghoy

Exposure-n-Pagpakita.

Expound-v-Liwanagin, saysayin, salaysayin; ilathala; magsabi.

Express-v-Magpahayag, ipahayag, magsabi, sabihin.

Express-a-Maliwanag, tunay

Expression-n-Salita: wika.

Expulsion-n-Pagpaalis, pagpalabas.

Expunge-v-Burahin, lipulin

Exquisite-a-Mainam; maganda, marangal

Exseit-a-Napaliko

Extant-a-Napako.

Extempore-a-Walang handa.

Extend v-Biklarin, banatin, habaan, unatin

Extended-a-Banat, malnag mahaba.

Extension-n-Haba; luang, kaluagan.

Extensive-a-Malawak, maluag

Extent-n-Luang at lapad

Extenuate-v-Mañgayayat, pumayat.

Extenuated-a-Payat, inahina.

Extenuation n-Pañgañgayayat; kahinaan.

Exterior-n-Ang labas.

Exterioi-a-Labas

Exterminate-v Lipolin, patayin

Extermination n-Paglipol kamatayan.

External-a-Labas.

External-n Ang labas.

Extinct-a-Patay; walang buhay.

Extinction-n-a Kamatayan, pagpapatay

Extinguish v Lipulin; lumipol, patayin.

Extirpate-v-Bunutin; pitasin.
Extirpation-n-Pagbunot; pagpitas.
Extol-v-Ibunyi; purihin; itampok.
Extort-v-Pilitin; pumilit.
Extortionary-a-Mapilitin; mabagsik.
Extra-a-Nakabukod.
Extra-n-Bagay na nakabukod.
Extract-v-Alisin; hugutin; hanguin; kunin sa iba.
Extract-n-Anomang bagay na kinuha sa iba.
Extraction-n-Paghugot; paghango.
Extraordinary-a-Katakataka; kamanghamangha; bukodtañgi.
Extravagance-n-Pagkaburara.
Extravagant-a-Burara; mapagbigay.
Extreme-a-Huli; malabis; malubha dulo.
Extreme-n-Dulo; kaduluhan; katapusan.
Extremity-n-Dulo; wakal; wakas; duñgot; katapusan.
Extricate-v-Hanguin; alisin; kunin.

Extrication-n-Paghango; paghugot.
Exuberancy-n-Kalagpusan; kalabisan.
Exuberant-a-Malagpos; malabis.
Exult-v-Sumaya; maglugod.
Exultant-a-Malugod.
Exultation-n-Kasayahan.
Eye-n-Mata.
Eye-v-Tumiñgin.
Eye ball-n-Mata.
Eye brow-n-Kilay.
Eye glass-n-Salamin ñg mata.
Eye lash-n-Pilik mata.
Eye lid-n-Talukap ñg mata.
Eyeless-a-Walang mata.
Eye let-n-Matang munti.
Eye piece-n-Salamin ñg mata.
Eye sight-n-Tiñgin; paniñgin.
Eye tooth-n-Pañgil.
Eye witness-n-Saksing nakita ang nangyari.
Eurie-n-Pugad ñg lawin ó ñg aguila.

F

Fa-n-Fa.
Fable-n-Awit; kuento.
Fable-v-Magkuento; magsalita ñg kasinuñgalinñgan.
Fabric-n-Paggagawa ñg anoman.
Fabricate-v-Gumawa ñg anoman.
Fabrication-n-Paggagawa ñg anoman; kasinuñgalinñgan.
Fabulist-n-Ang taga sulat ñg mga kasinuñgalinñgan.
Fabulosity-n-Kabulaanan; kasinuñgalinñgan.
Fabulous-a-Hindi totoo; dakilangdakila; katakataka; konowari; kamanghamangha.
Facade-n-Harapan ñg bahay.
Face-n-Mukha; kita sa labas; harapan.
Face-v-Itihaya.
Faced-a-Tihaya.
Facet-n-Mukhang munti.
Facetious-a-Masaya; maalindog.
Facile-a-Ginhawa; madali; masunurin.
Facilitate-v-Hawanan; gamitin; ibigay.
Facilitation-n-Pag gagamit; kaginhawahan.
Facility-n-Kaginhawahan; kadalian.
Facination-n-Gayuma.
Facing-n-Mukha; aporo.
Facing-adv.-Nakatapat; nakaharap.
Facsimile-n-Salin; katulad; parisan.
Fact-n-Katotohanan; kilos; gawa.
Faction-n-Kapisanan; lahi; gulo; kaguluhan.
Factious-a-Magulo.

Factitious-a-Hindi totoo; konowari.
Factor-n-Katiwala; bahagi.
Factory-n-Gawaan.
Faculty-n-Kapangyarihan; karunuñgan.
Fad-n-Ugali; kaugalian; uso.
Fade-v-Kumupas; lumanta.
Faded-a-Kupas; yumi.
Fag-v-Pumagod; pumagal.
Fag-n-Alila.
Fag-end-n-Tirahan; ang natitira.
Fagot-n-Bigkis; kalawas.
Fagot-v-Ibigkis; magtali; kalawasin.
Fail-v-Mamatay; kumulang; bumawas; mawala.
Fail-n-Kakulañgan; kulang.
Failing-n-Kakulañgan; kahinaan; sakit;
Failure-n-Kakulañgan; sala.
Fain-a-Masaya; matuwa; malugod; bagay.
Fain-adv.-May malaking gusto.
Faint-a-Malata; mahina.
Faint-v-Manghimatay.
Faint-n-Himatay.
Fair-a-Marañgal; mãganda; mainam; akma; tama; walang interes ó daya.
Fair-adv.-Maakma.
Fair-n-Tanghalan; kapalaran.
Fairness-n-Dikit; ganda.
Fairy-n-Duende.
Fairy-a-Nauukol sa duende.
Faith-n-Pananampalataya; paniniwala; religion; katuparan sa pañgako.
Faithful-a-Tapat ang loob; tama.
Faithless-a-Sukab; suitik; taksil.
Falcon-n-Lawin.

29

Fall-v-Mahulog; lumagpak; malaglag; bumawas.

Fall-n-Lagpak; laglag, hulog, pagbawas, pagkabual

Fallacious-a-Magkasalanan, magdaraya, makahihibo.

Fallacy-n-Kasinungalingan; daya, hibo.

Fallen-a-Nalaglag, hamak; patay.

Fallible-a-Magkakasala.

Fallibility-n-Kahiligan sa pagkakasala

Fallow-a-Mapulapula.

Fallow n-Ararohin.

False a-Hindi tama; masama, hindi totoo, magdaraya, mapag banal banalan; sukab sinungaling falso.

False hood-n-Balatkayo,kasinungalingan

Falsify-v-Dayain; mag daraya, huwaran; humuwad, palsohin, magsinungaling

Falsity-n-Kabulaanan, kasinungalingan; daya.

Falter-v Mag utal, kumulang, maghinto.

Fame-n-Kabantugan, pagkabantog balita, bunyi, kabunyian, karangalan, lualhati.

Fame-v-Magbalita, ipagbantog.

Familiar-a-Sanay; karaniwan.

Familiar-n-Kasama, kalaguyo.

Familiarity-n-Kasanayan.

Familiarize v-Magsanay; mamalagi.

Family-n-Familia.

Famine-n-Gutom, kagutuman.

Famish-v-Magutom, gutumin, mamulubi, gumutom.

Famous a-Balita; bantog, bunyi; mabantog; dakila

Fan-a-Paypay; abanico.

Fan-v-Pumaypay.

Fanatic-a-Masigla.

Fanciful-a-Maguniguni.

Fancy-n-Ugali, isip; wari, guniguni; hilig ng loob; aha, banta.

Fancy v-Isipin, mag wari, maguniguni, akalain, bantain.

Fang-n-Pangil

Fantastic-a-Maguniguni; konowari.

Far-a-Malayo.

Far adv-Malayo.

Farce n-Konowa, kabiroan, bagay na hindi tama; kasamaan

Farcial a-Konowaring

Fare-v-Lumakad; maglakad; sumulong; bumuhay.

Fare-n-Halagang, ó kuartang, nagbayad sa pagpapahatid; upa; pagkain.

Fare well-inter.-Paalam.

Fare well n-Ang paalam.

Fare well-a-Huling

Farm-n-Bukid, lupang sinasaka.

Farm-v-Magsaka

Farmer-n Magsasaka.

Farming-n-Pagsasaka.

Farrier n-Ang nag babakal sa kabayo, mangagamot ng hayop.

Farrow-n-Manga biik na inakay nang inahing baboy

Farrow-v-Manganak ang inahing baboy.

Farther-a-Malayo.

Farther-adv.-Malayo pa, lalong malayo

Farthest a-Kalayo layoan

Fascinate-t-Manghalina.

Fascination-n-Panghalina.

Fashion-n-Asal, kaugalian, kayarian, tabas, yari.

Fashion-v-Gumawa, tabasin.

Fashionable-a-Mauso; kaugalian

Fast-a-Matibay, matulin; malakas, lagi.

Fast adv-Matulin.

Fast v-Huag kumain, magcolasion

Fasten-c-Ikabit, isabit, talian; ikawig

Fastening-n-Pagkakabit, tali.

Fastidious a-Hambog; mayabang

Fastness n-Katapatan ng loob, katibayan ng loob.

Fat a-Mataba.

Fat n-Taba

Fat-v-Patabain, tumaba.

Fatal a-Makamamatay.

Fatalism-n Kamatayan.

Fatality-n-Kamatayan.

Fate-n-Palad, kapalaran

Fated-a-Talaga

Father n-Ama, tata; tatay, tatang.

Father-v-Magama

Fatherhood n Kalagayan ama

Father in-law-n-Bienang lalaki.

Father land-v-Bayang tinutubuan.

Fatherless-a-Walang ama, ulila sa ama.

Fatherly-a-Parang ama

Fathom-n-Dipa.

Fathom v Tarukin, dipahin.

Fathomless a-Hindi matatarok, di matarok, di mahirip.

Fatigue-n Pagal, kapagalan; pagod, hirap, dalamhati.

Fatigue-v-Pumagal, pumagod; pagurin.

Fatten-v-Tumaba, patabain; magpataba.

Fatty-a Mataba.

Faucet-v-Grifo

Fault-n-Kasalanan, kakulangan, pintas; kapintasan; sala, kamalian; kasiraan; samá, kasamaan.

Faultless a-Walang pintas, makinis, walang kapintasan.

Faulty-a-May sala; di yari, may pintas.

Favor n-Tankilik; tulong, ampon, abuloy, pagkakalinga; biyaya.

Favor-v-Tumankilik, umampon, tumulong, abuluyan amponin, imukha, pumaris.

Favorable-a-Mabuti; maganap.
Favorite-a-Minamahal; layaw.
Favorite-n-Ang minamahal; kaulayaw.
Fawn-n-Munting usa.
Fawn-v-Purihin ng hindi totoo.
Fawn-n-Pagpupuri ng hindi totoo.
Fay-n-Duende.
Fay-v-Idugtong.
Fealty-n-Katapatan ng loob.
Fear-n-Takot; hinala.
Fear-v-Maghinala; tumakot-
Fearful-a Matatakotin; mapag hinala; mapangambahin; katakot takot; masama.
Fearless-a Matapang; walang takot; mangahas.
Feasible-a-Makagagawa;sukat mangyari.
Feast-n-Piging; bito; piesta; kapistahan; pagpipiging aglahi.
Feast-v-Magpiging; magbito; ipagpista; magalahi; pumista.
Feat-n-Gawa; yari; kagagawan.
Feather-n-Balahibo ng ibon.
Feather-v-Tumubo ang balahibo.
Feathery-a-Mabalahibo.
Feature-n-Yari; kayarian; hitsura; mukha.
February-n-Febrero.
Fed-v-Ipinakakain.
Federal-a-Nauukol; sa Federal.
Federal-n-Federal.
Federation-n-Kapisanang Federal.
Fee-u-Upa; ganti; bayad; kaupahan.
Fee-v-Upahan; magbayad; gantihin.
Feeble-a-Mahina.
Feebleness-n-Kahinaan; yayat.
Feed-v-Magpakain; pakanin; kumain.
Feed-n-Pagkain; kainan.
Feel-v-Hipuin; humipo; magdamdam; apuhapin; kapain; damdamin; indahin salatin.
Feel-n-Damdam; hipo; salat.
Feeling-n-Maramdamin.
Feeling-n-Pakiramdam; karamdaman.
Feet-n-Mga paá.
Feign-v-Magkonowari; magbalatkayo.
Feigned-a-Hindi totoo; mapagpaimbabaw; sukab.
Feint-n-Pagpapakonowari.
Felicitate-v-Sumaya; pasayahin; aliwin.
Felicitous-v-Maligaya; masaya; malugod.
Felicitation-n-Pagpapaligaya; kaaliwan.
Felicity-n-Ligaya; kaligayahan; kasayahan; kaaliwan.
Feline-a-Nauukol sa pusa.
Fell-v. imp.-Nahulog; lumagpak.
Fell-a-Masama; bastos; mabagsik; walang awa.
Fell-n-Balat ng hayop.
Fell-v-Magtagá ng kahoy.

Felloe-n-Kama.
Fellow-n-Tawo.
Fellow-feeling-n-Pagdamdam sa kapwa.
Fellow-ship-n-Pakikisama; kalaguyo; kalagayang kaibigan.
Felly-n-Kama.
Felon-n-Tawong suitik; Tawong taksil.
Felon-a-Suitik; taksil.
Felonious-a-Taksil; masuitik.
Felony-n-Kaliluhan; kasuitikan; kataksilan; kasamaan.
Felt-v. imp. & p. p.-Kinapa; hinipo; dinamdam.
Felt-n-Fieltro.
Female-n-Babayi.
Female-a-Nauukol sa babayi.
Feminine-a-Nauukol sa babayi.
Femoral-a-Nauukol sa bayawang.
Fen-n-Lawak.
Fence-n-Bakod; bakuran.
Fence-v-Magbakod; bakuran.
Fencing-a-Pagbabakod; kabakuran.
Fend-v-Iwaksi; lumaban.
Fender-n-Ang lumalaban.
Fennish-a-Malawak.
Ferine-a-Mailag; ramo; mabangis.
Ferment n-Pagkulo ng alak.
Ferment-v-Bumula ang alak.
Fermentation-n-Pagbubula ng alak.
Ferocious-a-Mabangis; masama; masungit.
Ferociousness-n-Kabagsikan;kabangisan.
Ferocity-n-Kabagsikan; kabangisan.
Ferret-v-Hanapin ng pilit.
Ferriage-n-Upa sa pagtatawid.
Ferric-a-Nauukol sa bakal.
Ferry-n-Tawiran.
Ferry man-n-Taga tawid.
Fertile-a-Mataba; mabunga; malago.
Fertileness-n-Katabaan ng lupa; kalagoan.
Fertility-n-Katabaan ng lupa.
Fertilize-v-Patabain ang lupa.
Ferule-n-Buklod; ikog.
Fervent-a-Maningas; mabisa; pusok na loob.
Fervid-a-Maningas; mainit ang loob.
Fervor-n-Kaningasan ng loob; kainitan.
Festal-a-Masaya; maligaya.
Fester-v-Magnana.
Fester-n-Sugat na nagnanana.
Festival-a-Masaya; nauukol sa pista.
Festival-n-Piging.
Festive-a-Nauukol sa piging; masaya; maligaya.
Festivity-n-Kasayahan; kaligayahan.
Fetch-v-Dalhin; magdala.
Fetch-n-Hibo; daya; biro.
Fete-n-Piging; kasayahan.
Fete v-Magpiging.

Fetid-a Mabaho; bulok
Fetlock-n-Balahibo ó buhok sa munika ng paá ng kabayo
Fetter-n-Pangapos ng paa
Fetter-v-Gapusin ang paa.
Feud-n-Galit, pagkakaaway.
Feudal-a-Nauukol sa galit
Fever-n-Lagnat
Feverish-a-Malalagnatin.
Few-a-Bihira, ilang.
Fiance-n-Ang may compromiso
Fiancee-n-Babaying may compromiso
Fiasco-n-Kakulangan
Fiat-n-Utos
Fib-v-Kasinnungalingan.
Fib-v-Magsinungalin.
Fiber-n-Hibla.
Fibrous-a-Mahibla.
Fibula n-Hebilla.
Fickle-a-Alisaga, walang firme, hindi matibay ang loob.
Fickleness-n-Kaalisagaan, kabulaanan, kasahwahan ng loob
Fictitious a Hindi totoo
Fiction-n Awit, balat kayo, kasinungalingan; katha.
Fiddle-n-Violin
Fiddle-v-Tumugtog sa violin.
Fiddle inter.-Hum
Fiddler-n-Ang tumutugtog sa violin, violinista
Fidelity-n-Katapatan ng loob
Fidget i-Maglikot, bumalisa.
Fidget-n-Kabalisahan, likot.
Fidgety-a-Malikot; balisa; mapakali; di mabait
Fie-inter.-Oroy
Fief n-Lupang kinamtan dahil sa pagseservicio
Field-n-Parang; bukid, pastulan
Field piece-n-Kanyon na may gulong.
Fiend-n-Demonio
Fiendish a-Parang demonio; nauukol sa demonio
Fierce-a Mabagsik; mabangis, gahasa
Fiery-a-Malingas, maningas, mahab; pusok na loob.
Fife-n-Pito.
Fife-v-Tumugtog sa pito.
Fifteen a-Labing lima
Fifteen-n-Labing lima
Fifteenth-a-Ikalabing lima.
Fifteenth-n-Ang ika labing lima.
Fifth a-Ikalima
Fifth-n-Ang ika lima
Fifthly-adv-Sa ikalima
Fiftieth-a-Ikalimangpuo.
Fiftieth n-Ang ikalimangpuo.
Fifty-n-Limangpuo.
Fifty-a Limang puo.

Fig-n-Higo
Fight-n-Away; banga, babag, bungo; labanan
Fight-v-Labanan, bumabag, umaway, awayin, labanin, babagin, humamon.
Figurative-a-Halimbawa
Figure-n-Numero, yari; kayarian.
Figure v-Kuentahin, magkuenta
Filament-n-Sumilid.
Filch-v-Umumit, umitin, nakawin
File-n-Kikil, taludtod, pagkakasunod-sunod.
File-v-Kikilin, kumikil.
Filial-a-Nauukol sa anak.
Filigree-n Sangkap ng ginto ó pilak
Filigree-a-Mainam; makinis
Filings-n-Pinag kikilan, yumauain.
Fill-i-Punuin pununo, bumusog, mamaulo, masandat.
Fill-n-Kabusogan, kahustuhan, pagkapuno, kasandatan.
Fillet-n-Munting bigkis, pirasong l arne na walang buto
Filly-n-Inahing kabayo.
Film-n-Balat na manipis
Filter-n-Salaan; pangpatalas
Filter-v-Tumalas, salain.
Filth-n-Karumihan, dumi, kasalaulaan; sukal; kasukalan; dungis
Filthiness-n-Karumihan, kasukalan
Filthy-a-Marumi; marungis; mahibag.
Filtrate-i-Tumalas
Fin-n-Palikpik.
Final-n-Tapos, katapusan, pandulo.
Final-a-Huling, katapustapusan.
Finality-n-Katapusan
Finale-n Katapusan
Finally-adv.-Sa katapusan
Finance-n-Kuaita ng bayan
Financial a-Nauukol sa kuaita
Financier-n-Ang humawak ng kuarta ng bayan.
Find-v-Humanap, hanapin; makita
Finding-n Paghanap, pagkain, paghatol
Fine a-Mainam, marikit, manipis, makinis; magaling, fino, maganda
Fine-n-Multa
Fine-v-Multahin, magmulta.
Finery-n-Dilag, kainaman, sangkap.
Finger-n-Daliri
Finger-v-Hipuin ng madalas
Finical-a-Tila mainam.
Finis-n-Tapos; katapusan, dulo.
Finish v-Tapusin, tapusin, utasin, yariin; ganapin, humanga, lutasin
Finish-n-Tapos, yari, hanga, kinis kinang, kintab
Finless a-Walang palikpik.
Finny-a May palikpik.

Fire-n-Sunog: apoy; sigá.
Fire-v-Sunugin; ilagay ng̃ apoy.
Fire arm-n-Baril.
Fire brand-n-Sulo.
Firefly-n-Alitaptap.
Fire man-n-Fogonero.
Fire place-n-Pinag aapuyan.
Fire proof-a-Di makasusunog.
Fireside-n-Tabi ng̃ pinag aapuyan.
Fire wood-n-Gatungan.
Fire work-n-Kuetes.
Firm-a-Matibay; tapat ang loob; lagi; malakas; matigas; matiis; matiyaga; matapang. hindi mababago.
Firm-n-Kapisanan.
Firmament-n-Lang̃it.
Firmness-n-Katibayan; katimtiman.
First-a-Unang; kaunahan.
First-adc.-Naunang.
First-born-n-Pang̃anay.
First-class-a-Primerong classe; kabutibutihan.
Firth-n-Baraso ng̃ dagat.
Fiscal-a-Nauukol sa kuarta ng̃ isang bayan.
Fiscal-n-Fiscal.
Fish-n-Isda.
Fish-v-Mang̃isda.
Fish bone-n-Tinik.
Fisher-n-Mang̃ing̃isda.
Fish corral-n-Baklad.
Fisher man-n Mang̃ing̃isda.
Fishery-n-Katungkulang mang̃isda.
Fish hawk-n-Limbas.
Fish hook-n-Kiba; tagá; kalawit.
Fishing-n-Pang̃ing̃isda.
Fish monger-n-Ang nagtitinda ng̃ isda.
Fish-net-n-Kitid; sakag; panti; lambat.
Fish spear-n-Salapang.
Fishy-a-May maraming isda.
Fissile-a-Baakin.
Fissure-n-Lahang; lamat; biak.
Fist-n-Ikom.
Fisticuff-n-Sampal ó suntok ng̃ kamay.
Fit-a-Bagay; ayos; dapat; akma. kasia; magagamit.
Fit-v-Ilapat; sukatin; ibagay; iakma.
Fit-n-Lapat; akma; pasma.
Fitful-a-Hindi panay; walang ayos.
Fitting-a-Bagay; akma.
Fitting-n-Paglapat; pagkakaakma.
Five-n-Lima.
Five-a-Limang.
Five fold-a-Limang duble.
Fix-v-Manatili; kumpunihin; ayusin.
Fix-n-Kagipitan.
Fixed-a-Matibay; manatili.
Fixedly-adc.-Matibay.
Fixture-n-Kasangkapan.
Fizz-v-Humaging; sumutsot.

Fizz-n-Hang̃in; suit.
Fizz-n-Suit; haging.
Fizzle-v-Sumuit; humaging; kumulang.
Fizzle-n-Kakulang̃an.
Flabby-a-Mataba.
Flag-n-Bandila; bandera.
Flag-v-Pigilin; humina.
Flagon-n-Lalagyan ng̃ alak.
Flagrant-a-Maning̃as; mainit; masama.
Flag ship-n-Sasakyan ng̃ almirante.
Flag staff-n-Palo ng̃ bandila.
Flail-n-Pambayo.
Flail-v-Magbayo.
Flake-n-Patak ng̃ busilak; suson.
Flambeau-n-Suló.
Flame-n-Ling̃as; kaning̃asan; liab.
Flame-v-Mag ling̃as; mag liab.
Flange-n-Gilid.
Flank-n-Gilid; tagiliran.
Flank-v-Tumayo sa galit.
Flannel-n-Frenela.
Flap-n-Tabing.
Flap-v-Galawin; sampalin; ilagpak.
Flap jack-n-Bibingka.
Flare-v-Lumiab; mag ling̃as.
Flare-n-Kaning̃asan; ning̃as; ling̃as liab.
Flash-v-Kumidlat.
Flash-n-Kidlat; kisap.
Flash-a-Makisap; makintab.
Flashy-a-Makinis; kintab.
Flask-n-Frasko.
Flat-a-Yano; patag; pantay.
Flat-n Lupang patag; isang grado ng̃ isang bahay.
Flatten-v-Patagin; salsalin; pulpulin.
Flatter-v-Tuyáin; manuya; magdiladila; purihin ng̃ hindi totoo.
Flattery-n-Pagpupuri ng̃ hindi totoo.
Flaunt-v-Isabog; ipakita.
Flautist-n-Flautista.
Flavor-n-Lasa; lasap.
Flavor-v-Magbigay lasa.
Flaw-n-Lahang; sala; pintas; lamat.
Flaw-v-Lumahang.
Flay-v-Bayuhin; magbayo.
Flea-n-Hanip; pulgas; kutong aso.
Fleam-n-Tulag.
Fleck-n-Mansa.
Fleck-v-Mansahin.
Flection-n-Paghubog.
Fled-v. imp. &p. p.-Nagtanan; tumakbo; nakatakbo.
Fledge-v-Tumubo ang balahibo.
Fledge-v-Tumubo ang balahibo.
Flee-v-Magtanan; tumakas; tumakbo.
Fleece-n-Balahibo ng̃ tupa.
Fleece-v-Manekas; dayain.
Fleecy-a-Mabalahibo.
Fleer-v-Alipustahin; uyamin; murahin.
Fleer-n-Uyam; alipusta.

Fleet-a-Matulin; maliksi.
Fleet-v-Magmadali; tumulin.
Fleet-n-Kapisanan ng mga sasakyan.
Flesh-n-Laman ng tawo, karne.
Flesh-v-Ipakain ng karne
Fleshy-a-Mataba, makalaman; malaman.
Flew-v. imp.-Lumipad; nakalipad.
Flex-v-Humubog
Flexible a-Malambot
Flexion-n-Paghubog.
Flicker-v-Pumisik
Flicker n-Pisik ng kandila.
Flier-n Ang lumilipad, ang nagtanan
Flight-n-Takbo; tanan, takas.
Flighty-a-Palipad lipad ang isip.
Flimsy-a-Di matibay.
Flinch-i-Umurong.
Flinders-n-Manga piraso
Fling v-Itapon; ipukol ihagis, ibalibag.
Fling n-Hagis, pukol. balibag
Flint-n-Batong matigas.
Flinty-a-Matigas na matigas
Flip-n-Pagkakahalo ng mga alak.
Flippancy-n-Kawalan ng galang
Flippant-a-Masalita; walang galang
Flipper-n-Palikpik.
Flirt-v-Magbiro, magsaliwahang loob
Flirt-n-Babaying salawahan.
Flit-v-Kumilos ng pabigla.
Flitch-n-Tosino ᴌ ꜱ. ᴊoᴄᴵᴍo
Flitter-n-Gulanit, piraso; basahan.
Float-n-Ano mang bagay na lumulutang
Float-v-Lumutang.
Flock n-Kapisanan; kawan.
Flock-v Umipon; pumisan.
Floe n-Agos ng hielo
Flog-v-Hampasin paluin.
Flood-n Baha, apaw
Flood-i-Umapaw, apawin, bumaha.
Floor-n-Sahig
Floor-i-Gumawa ang sahig.
Flooring-n-Tabla ng sahig
Flop v-Pumagpag, kumilos ng pabigla.
Floral-a-Nauukol sa bulaklak
Floret-n-Muting bulak'ak.
Florist-i-Ang nagtitinda ng bulaklak.
Florid-a-Makintab,mahiwanag ang kulay.
Floss-n-Sutlá
Flotage-n-Paglutang
Flotation-n-Pagpapalutang.
Flotilla n-Kapisanan ng mga sasakyang munti.
Flounce-v-Ibagis ang manga baraso at binti.
Flounce-n-Pilegas
Flounder-n-Kitang
Flounder-v-Kumilos; lumundaglundag.
Flour-n-Harina.
Flour-v-Budburan ang harina
Flourish v-Iwayway; tumubo lumaki.

Flourish-n Pagpag
Floury-a-Parang harina
Flout-v-Alipustain gagarin.
Flow-v-Umagos; bumaba.
Flow-n-Agos
Flower-n-Bulaklak.
Flower-i-Mamulaklak, mamunga
Flowery a-May maraming bulaklak.
Flown-v p p -Nakalipad na
Fluctuate-v-Bumawas; bumaba
Fluctuation-n-Pagbawas.
Flue-n Paasuhan.
Fluent-a Malangis ang salita, mainam magsalita, mainam manalita.
Fluency-n-Kainaman magsalita.
Fluid-a Tunaw, lusaw
Fluid-n-Anomang bagay na lusaw
Fluidity-n-Pagkatunaw
Flume-n-Daanan ng tubig
Flummery-n-Bagay na walang kabuluhan.
Flung-v. imp. & p. p -Hinagis; pinukol, binahbag
Flunky-n-Alila.
Flurry-n-Gulo
Flurry-v-Guluhin, gulatin.
Flush-v-Umapaw mamula ang mukha.
Flush-n-Apaw, pamumula ng mukha
Flush-a-Puno, pulos.
Fluster-v-Guluhin.
Fluster-n-Init, gulo
Flute-n-Flauta.
Flutist-n Flautista
Flutter-i-Kumilos na bigla, guluhin, tumibok
Flutter n-Tibok, kadalian, kaguluhan.
Fluttering-a-Pahkoliko.
Fluvial-a-Nauukol sa ilog
Flux-n-Dumi; tae.
Flux-v-Dumumi
Fly-v-Lumipad; maghparan.
Fly-n-Langaw.
Fly blown-a-Mabulok.
Fly trap-n-Panghuli ng langaw
Foal-n-Potrong bagong pinanganak
Foal-v-Manganak ang inahing kabayo
Foam n-Bula.
Foam-v Bumula.
Fob-v Kayrel.
Fob-i-Dayain.
Fodder-n-Pagkain ng hayop
Foe-n-Kalaban; kaaway; katalo.
Fog-n-Ambon.
Fog-v-Umambon; lumabo.
Foggage-n-Kugon.
Foggy-a-Balot ng ulap. maambon
Fogy-n-Tawong mapurol ang isip.
Foh-inter Oroy
Foible-n-Pintas, sala.
Foil-v-Abalahin; pigilin.
Fold-r-Tiklupin,lupiin,pilegasin;kutonin.

Fold-n Lupi, tiklop. pilegas.

Fol de rol-n-Kaululan.

Foliage n-Manga dahon ng kahoy

Foliate-a May dahon.

Folio-n-Dahon ng libro

Folk n-Manga towo

Follow-v-Sumunod, bumuntot

Following-n-Pag sunod, pagkakasunod sunod

Following-a-Sumusunod; kasunod

Folly-n-Kaululan, gawang hunghang; kabutingtingan

Foment-v-Itapal ang tubig na mainit.

Fomentation-n-Pagtatapal ng tubig na mainit.

Fond a-Mawiwili, maiibigin.

Fondle-v-Alindugin; pawihhin

Fondling-n-Ang minamahal

Font-n Bukalan.

Food-n-Pagkain, ikinabubuhay

Food-a-Makakain

Fool-n-Ulol, tawong tulig; kawalan ng isip

Fool-v-Ululin, biruin; tuligin.

Foolery-n-Kaululan, kabiruan

Fool hardy-a-Maulol; tulig, walang kabuluhan.

Foolish-a-Tulig, hunhang mangmang, walang isip, tungak, ungos.

Foolishness-n-Kaululan, kaungusan kamangmangan.

Fools cap-n-Papel de barba

Foot-n-Paá, panukat na may isang dangkal at kalahati ang haba.

Foot-v-Lumakad.

Footing-n-Lugar ng paá

Foot ball-n-Bolang malaki.

Foot fall-n-Yabag ng paá

Foot man-n-Sundalong la'kad

Foot note-n-Huling sabi.

Foot sore-a Pagod, mapagal.

Foot step-n-Bakas ng paá.

Foot way n-Landas

Fop-n-Tawong hunghang ó mangmang.

Foppery-n-Kaululan; kamangmangan; gawang hunghang

Foppish-a-Mangmang, muang

For-prep -Para sa, nang.

For-conj.-Para, sa, nang

Forage-n-Sakati.

Forage-v-Humanap at kumuha masque hindi kaniya

For as-much-conj -Sapagka't.

Foray-n-Panduduit.

Foray-v-Manduit.

For bade v. imp -Ipinagbawal

For bear-v-Tumigil, humimpil, tumangi, umayaw

For bearance-n-Tigil, paghimpil, katimtiman, hinahon, kahinhinan

For bid-v-Magbawal, ipagbawal.

For bidding a-Mapagbawal; malabo

Force n Lakas, katibayan; kalakasan, apilitan; pagpilit

Force-v-Gahisin, puersahin

Forcible-a-Malakas; mapilitin

Forceps n-Sipit

Ford-n-Batisan

Ford-v-Magtawid, bumatis.

Fore-a-Nauñang, na sa harap.

Fore-adv -Na sa harap

Fore and aft-Ang harap at likod

Fore bode-v imp -Ipinagbawal

Fare boding-n-Kaba ng dibdib, agamagam ng loob.

Fore cast-v-Humula, hulaan

Fore cast-n-Hula

Fore close-v-Magtuos, iwaksi.

Fore closure-n-Pag tutuos

Fore end-n Dulo sa una.

Fore father-n Kanunuan, magulang

Fore fend-v-Ilagin; umilag

Fore finger n-Hintuturo.

Fore go-v-Maiwan, bitiwan.

Fore ground-n Lupa sa harapan

Fore head-n-Noo

Foreign-a-Buhat sa ibang lupa

Foreigner-n-Taga ibang lupa.

Fore know-v-Maagap malainan.

Fore man-n-Taga pamahala, ang namamahala, tawong natatanoha

Fore mast-n-Palo sa una

Fore most-a-Kaunaunahan.

Fore noon n-Umaga

Fore rank-n Taludtod sa kaunahan, harapan

Fore sail-n-Layag sa una.

Fore see-v-Unahan, umagap; umuna

Fore show-v-Hulaan, ipakita

Forest-n-Gubat, kagubatan

Forester-n-Taga gubat

Forestry-n-Karunungan tungkol sa gubat

Fore stall-v-Unahan, asahan.

Fore taste-n-Tikim.

Fore taste-v-Asahan.

Fore tell-v-Hulaan, humula

Fore thought-n-Asa, hula.

Fore token-n-Tanda.

Fore tooth-n-Ngipin sa harap

Fore top-n-Buhok sa noo

For e ver-adv -Magpakailan man; walang hanga

Fore warn-v-Bumala, sabihin muna

Forfeit-n Prenda, multa.

Forfeit v-Magprenda

For gave-v. imp -Ipinatawad.

Forge-n-Pandayan, kalan.

Forge-v-Huwaran, tularan, palsohin

Forger-n-Ang pumalso sa sulat.

For get-v-Malimutan; pabayaan.

For getful a-Malilimutin, pabaya, wa-
lang ingat; maligtaan.
For give-c-Patawarin, magpatawad.
For giveness-n-Patawad; pagpapatawad
For giving-a-Makapag papatawad
For got-v imp.-Nalimutan
For gotten-v p.p -Nilimutan
Fork-n-Tinedor.
Fork-v-Humiwalay
For lorn-a-Malungkot, malumbay
Form-n-Hitsura; tayo; bikas.
Form-v-Gawin ang hitsura
Formal-a-Pormal
Formalist-n-Ang nagpopormal.
Formality-n-Kapormalan·
Formless-a-Walang hitsura.
Former-n-Ang unang, ang dati
Formerly-adv.-Sa una noong dati.
Formidable-a-Malakas; katakot takot
Formula-n-Regla; patnugot.
Formulation-n-Paggagawa ng reseta.
For sake-v Maiwan; umalis, huag gawin
For sooth adi-Totoo; tunay, sa katoto-
hanan
For swear-v-Manumpa ng kasinungali-
ngan.
Fort-n-Kuta.
Forte-n-Katowiran· dahilan
Forth-adv.-Sa gawing una
Forth-a-Ikaapat.
Forth-n-Ang ikaapat.
Forth coming-a-Darating
Forth with-adv -Dahil dito
Fortieth-a-Ikaapat na puo
Fortieth-n-Ang ikaapat na puo.
Fortification-n-Kuta
Fortify-v-Tibayin, gumawa ng kuta
Fortitude n-Tapang, tibay; tibay na loob,
lakas, tigas, lakas loob
Fort night-n Panahon ng dalawang lingo
Fort nightly-adv -Sa tuwing dalawang
lingo
Fortress-n Kuta
Fortuitous-a Hindi sinasadya, nagkaka-
taon; hindi tinalaga.
Fortuity-n-Kapalaran
Fortune-n-Yaman; kayamanan, kapala-
ran; pag aari.
Fortunate-a-Mapalad, mapalaran. ·
Forty-n-Apat na puo
Forty-a-Apat na puo.
Forum-n-Bahay ng hucuman
For ward-a-Mangahas.
For wards-adv.-Sa gawing harapan
For ward-i-Ipadala.
Foster-v-Pakanin; tumapang.
Fought-v. imp. & p p.-Lumaban, buma-
bag. umaway.
Foul-a-Mabulok.
Foul-i-Bumulok; bulukin

Foul-n-Gulo, umpog
Found-v imp. & p. p.-Pinulot, nakita;
nakapulot.
Found v-Itatag, itayo; magtayo, luma-
lang
Foundation-n-Tatayuan ng bahay
Founder n-Ang nagtatayo ng bahay.
Foundling n-Ulila sa ama at ina at
walang tinutuluyan.
Foundry-n-Bubuan.
Fount n Bukalan
Fountain-n-Bukalan.
Four-a-Apat·
Four-n-Apat.
Four fold-a-Apat na duble
Four footed-a-May apat na paá.
Four score-a-Walongpuo.
Fourteen-a-Labing apat.
Fourteen-n-Labiang apat.
Fourteenth-a-Ika labing apat.
Fourteenth-n-Ang ika labing apat
Fourth a-Ika apat
Fourth-n-Ang ika apat.
Fourthly-adi -Sa ika apat.
Fowl-n-Ibon.
Fowler-n Taga huli ng ibon.
Fox-n-Zorra
Fox-v-Maglasing
Foxy-a-Tuso, matalas
Fracas-n-Gulo, talo, usap
Fraction-n-Bahagi, quebrado
Fractious a-Mapootin, masungit, sowail
Fracture-n Bali; basag, lahang.
Fracture-v-Basagin, baliin, labangin
Fragile-a-Marupok.
Fragility-n Dupok, karupukan.
Fragment-n-Piraso, bahagi, kapiraso
Fragrance-Fragrancy -n- Amoy na maba-
ngo, kabangohan
Fragrant-a-Mabango; mainam ang amoy.
Frail n-Buslo, pangnan
Frail-a-Marupok, babasagin; mahina.
Frailty-n-Dupok; karupokan
Frame-n-Banhay
Frame-v-Magbanhay.
Frame work-n-Banhay
Franchise-n-Pahintulot ng gobierno.
Franchise-v-Ipahintulot; pumayag
Frangible-a-Marupok; dapok
Frank-a-Tapat ang loob; maliwanag
Frank-v-Ipadala ang sulat na walang
sello
Frank-n-Si Francisco
Frankin-cense-n-Adiyangaw.
Frankness-n-Katapatan, liwanag
Frantic-a-Baliw, galit na galit, ulol,
sira ang loob
Fraternal a-Nauukol sa pagkakapatid.
Fraternity-n-Pagkakapatid
Fraternize-v-Sumama parang kapatid.

Fratricide-n-Ang natay sa sariling ka-
patid.
Fraud-n-Daya: hibo; patibong; paraya.
Fraudulent-a-Magdaraya; suitik.
Fraught-a-Puno; may lnlan.
Fray-n-Pagtatalo; babag; laban; bangay;
bungo.
Fray-v-Gasgasin; kuskusin.
Freak-n-Sumpong.
Freckle-n-Mansa ng mukha.
Free-a-Timawa malaya; dalisay walang
tali.
Free-v-Timawain; iligtas; paluagin; ha-
nguin.
Free booter-n-Magnanakaw; manduduit.
Free born-a-Hindi alipin.
Freedman-n-Tawong malaya.
Freedom-n-Kalayaan.
Free man-n-Tawong malaya.
Free will-n-Sariling gusto; kusa.
Freeze-v-Maging hielo.
Freight-n-Ang nilulan.
Freight-v-Ilulan; lumulan.
French-a-Francois; nauukol sa Franceis.
French-n-Tawong Frances.
French man-n-Taga Frances.
Frenzy-n-Kaguluhan ng isip; galit.
Frequence-Frequency-n-Kadalasan; pa-
mamarati; pagkalagi.
Frequent-a-Madalas; towi; gamit.
Frequent-v-Madalas dalawin; magmada-
las; pamaratihin; mamalagi.
Frequently-adv.-Madalas.
Fresh-a-Sariwa; bago.
Freshen-v-Panariwain.
Freshet-n-Baha.
Fresh man-n-Ang bagong nag aaral,
Fresh water-n-Tubig na matabang.
Fret-v-Magtampo; magbalisa.
Fret-n-Tampo.
Friar-n-Fraile.
Frairy-n-Kapisanan ng mga Fraile.
Friction-n-Pagkuskos.
Friday-n-Viernes.
Fried-v. imp. & p. p.-Nakaluto; naka-
prito.
Friend-n-Kaulayaw. kalaguyo; kaibigan;
magkaibigan.
Friendless-a-Walang kaibigan.
Friendly-a-Maiibigan; magiliw.
Friend ship-n-Pagkakaibigan.
Fright-n-Takot; sindak; gulat ngimi.
Fright-v-Tumakot; magulat.
Frighten-v-Takutin; gulatin; manakot;
pukawin.
Frightful-a-Katakottakot; kakilakilabot;
kasindaksindak.
Frigid-a-Maginaw; malamig.
Frigidity-n-Ginaw; kalamigan; lamig.
Frigidness-n-Ginaw; kalamigan; lamig.

Frill-n-Pilegas.
Frill-v-Pilegasin.
Fringe-n-Uria; gilid; dagdag; borlas.
Frisk-v-Mag aliw; mag likot; maglu-
dag; tumakbo.
Frisk-n-Aliw; lundag.
Frisky-a-Maaliw; malugod.
Fritter-n-Buchebuche; maruya.
Fritter-v-Pirasohin.
Frivolous-a-Walang halaga; walang 1
buluhan.
Friz-Frizz-v-Kulutin ang buhok.
Frizzle-v-Kulotin.
Frizzly-a-Makulot; kulot.
Fro-adv.-Malayo; sa gawing likod nan
Frock-n-Kamisola.
Frog-n-Palaka; tugak.
Frolic-a-Masaya.
Frolic-n-Saya; kasayahan; lugod.
Frolic-v-Maglikot; mag lundag; tumakl
Frolic some-a-Masaya; malugod.
From-prep.-Buhat; nang; buhat sa; tar
Front-n-Harap; harapan; mukha.
Front-v-Tumapat; humarap.
Front-a-Harap; nasa harap.
Frost-n-Busilak.
Frost-v-Umulan ng busilak.
Frosty-a-Mabusilak.
Froth-n-Bula; subó.
Froth-v-Bumula.
Frothy-a-Mabula.
Frouzy-a-Mabulok.
Frow-n-Woman.
Froward-a-Matigas ang ulo; sowail.
Frown-n-Sibangot.
Frown-v-Makasibangot.
Frowsy-a-Sabog sabog; gusot ang buhc
Frozen-a-Hielo.
Fructification-n-Pagpapataba ng lupa
Fructify-v-Patabain ang lupa.
Frugal-a-Matipid; maramot.
Frugality-n-Pagtitipid; katipiran; ka
yahan; kahinhinan.
Fruit-n-Bunga.
Fruitage-n-Manga bunga.
Fruitful-a-Mabunga; malago; mataba.
Fruitfulness-n-Katabaan ng lupa.
Fruition-n-Paggagamit; kagamitan.
Fruitless-a-Walang bunga; karat.
Frustrate-v-Abalahin; supilin.
Frustrate-a-Walang kabuluhan.
Frustration-n-Pagpawala ng kabuluha
Fry-v-Prituhin; lutuin sa mantica.
Fry-n-Ano mang bagay na pinirito.
Fuddle-v-Palasingin; maglasing; luma
ang isip dahil sa alak.
Fudge-n-Kahambugan.
Fudge-v-Magsalita ng walang kabuluha
Fuel-n-Gatungan; uling.
Fugitive-a-Natatakbo; nakatago.

30

Fugitive-*n*-Ang nagtanan, tumekas
Fulcrum-*n*-Tungkod, panghuit; suhay.
Fulfill-*v*-Tumupad, gumanap
Fulfillment-*n*-Pagtupad
Full-*a*-Puno, lubos, puspos, sakdal, busog,
Full-*n*-Kabusugan, kasakdalan.
Full *adv*-Lubos, puspos.
Full-*v*-Punuin
Fullness *n*-Kasaganaan
Fulminate-*v*-Pumutok, kumulog.
Fulmination-*n*-Pagputok
Fulsome-*a*-Labis na labis, makasusuklamin, masusuklam.
Fumble-*v*-Biglain, gawin nang hindi tama.
Fume-*n*-Asô, usok
Fume *v*-Umasó, umusok
Fumigate-*v*-Isuob, sumuob; suobin.
Fumigation-*n*-Pagsuob.
Fumy-*a*-Maasô; mausok
Fun-*n*-Saya, tuwa, kasayahan, aliw.
Function-*n* Katungkulan.
Functionary-*n*-Ang may katungkulan
Fund-*n*-Pundo; puhunan; tinda.
Fund-*v*-Mamuhunan
Fundament-*n*-Tumbong
Fundamental-*a*-Unang.
Funeral *n* Paglibing
Funeral-*a*-Nauukol sa paglibing
Funereal-*a*-Nauukol sa paglibing.
Fungous-*a*-Buhaghag
Funk-*n*-Baho alingasaw.
Funk-*v*-Bumaho, umalingasaw.
Funnel-*n*-Paasuhan.
Funny-*a*-Masaya
Fur-*n*-Balat at balahibo ng hayop.
Furbish-*v*-Kiskisin, bulihin.

Furcate-*a*-May sanga
Furfur-*n*-Balakubak.
Furious-*v*-Baliw, galit na galit.
Furl-*v*-Ibalot; balutin.
Furlong-*n*-Layo ng 250 baras.
Furlough-*n*-Tulot, pahintulut.
Furnace-*n*-Apuyan
Furnish-*v*-Tulungin, ibigay ng kailangan.
Furniture-*n*-Manga kasangkapan sa bahay.
Furrow-*n*-Tudling, bakas, linang
Furrow *v* Itudling; tumudling, ibakas
Further-*adv*.-Malayo pa; sa gawi roon pa
Further-*a*-Dako roon.
Further-*v*-Pasulungin; isulong, tumulong.
Furtherance-*n*-Pagpasulong
Further more-*adv* -Bukod pa sa rito;lampas pa rito, mahigit pa
Further most-*a* Kalayo layoan
Furtive-*a*-Tuso; ninakaw
Fury-*n*-Galit.
Fuse-*i*-Tunawin, tumunaw.
Fusible-*a*-Maaling matunaw.
Fusion-*n*-Pagtunaw
Fuss-*n*-Gulo, talo, pagtatalo.
Fuss-*i*-Gumulo, magulo; magtalo
Fussy-*a*-Magulo
Fust-*n*-Amoy na masama.
Fusty-*a*-Maamag.
Futile-*a*-Walang kabuluhan.
Futility-*n*-Kawalang ng kabuluhan
Future *a*-Nauukol sa panahong darating, magiging.
Future-*n*-Panahon darating.
Futurity-*n*-Panahong darating,

G

Gab-*n*-Bibig, salita.
Gab *v*-Magsalita ng kaululan
Gabble-*v*-Magsalita ng walang kabuluhan.
Gabble *n*-Salitang walang kabuluhan.
Gad-*n*-Pasial.
Gad *v*-Gumala
Gad a-bout-*n*-Tawong mapagpasial
Gadder-*n*-Tawong mapagpasial.
Gad fly-*n*-Pangaw.
Gaff-*n*-Kalawit; panungkit.
Gaff-*v*-Sungkitin.
Gage-*n*-Katibayan.
Gage-*v*-Tibayin sa kasulatan.
Gage-*n*-Panukat.
Gage-*v*-Sukatin; manukat.
Gaiety-*n*-Kasayahan; saya.

Gaily-*adv* -Masaya, maaliwalw.
Gain-*n*-Pakinabang, tubo.
Gain-*v*-Tumubo, magtubo; manalo tamuhin, makinabang.
Gainsay-*v*-Talikuran, itatua, magkaila, tumahina.
Gait-*i*-Lakad; palakad.
Gaiter-*n* Takip ng bukongbukong
Gala-*n*-Piging; pista
Gale-*n*-Bagyo
Gall-*n*-Dagli, apdo; kapaitan, tampalasan.
Gall-*v*-Gumasgas.
Gallant-*a*-Magandang loob, mainam; maginoo, matapang.
Gallantry-*n*-Tapang, lakas; kagandahan ng kilos.

Galley-n-Kosina ng sasakyan.
Gallon-n-Galon.
Gallop-v-Tumakbo.
Gallop-n-Takbo.
Gallows-n-Bibitayin.
Galvanic-a-Nauukol sa galvanico.
Galvanize-v-Mag galvanizado.
Galvanized-a-Galvanizado.
Gamble-v-Mag sugal.
Gambler-n-Magsusugal; tawong mapag-sugal.
Gambol-n-Laro.
Gambol-v-Mag laro.
Gambrel-n-Paa ng kabayo.
Game-n-Laro; biro.
Game-a-Matapang.
Game-v-Magsugal; magsabong.
Gamin-n-Batang gala.
Gamster-n-Ang naglalaro; magsusugal.
Gander-n-Gansang barako.
Gang-n-Kapisanan ng tawo; bunton ng tawo.
Gan grene-n-Gangrena.
Gan grene-v-Bumulok ang sugat.
Gangrenous-a-May nana ó gangrena.
Gang way-n-Paraan; daan.
Gaol-n-Bilango; kalabuso.
Gap-n-Tipo; puang.
Gap-v-Tipuin; bingawin.
Gape-n-Hikab.
Gape-v-Maghikab.
Garb-v-Damit; hitsura; pananamit.
Garbage-n-Sukal; kasukalan.
Garble-v-Dikdikin; piliin.
Garden-n-Halamanan.
Garden-v-Maghalaman.
Gardener-n-Ang maghahalaman.
Gadening-n-Paghahalaman.
Gargle-v-Mugmogin.
Gargle-n-Mugmog.
Garish-a-Hambog; mayabang.
Garland-n-Koronang bulaklak.
Garlic-n-Bawang.
Garment-n-Damit; pananamit.
Garner-v-Ilagay ang palay sa bangan.
Garner-n-Bangan.
Garnish-v-Gayakin; pamutiin.
Garnish-n-Gayak; pamuti.
Garret-n-Loob ng bubungan.
Garrison-n-Manga sundalong nakadistino sa isang lugar.
Garrulous-a-Masalita; magulo.
Garrulousness-n-Kalagayang masalita.
Garter-n-Ligas; panali; tali.
Garter-v-Talian ng ligas.
Gas-n-Gas.
Gaseous-a-May kahalong gas.
Gash-v-Tumaga; tagain; hiwain; humiwa.
Gash-n-Taga; hiwa.
Gasp-v-Maghingalo.

Gasp-n-Hingalo.
Gastric-a-Nauukol sa sikmura.
Gate n-Trangkahan; trangka.
Gate way-n-Paraan; daan; trankahan.
Gather-v-Iponin; umani; anihin; iligpit; tumipon; magpisan; magtipon.
Gathering-n-Pagkatipon; katipunan; kapisanan.
Gaud-n-Sangkap na walang kabuluhan.
Gaudy-a-Mayabang; hambog.
Gauge-v-Takalin.
Gauge-n-Takal.
Gaunt-a-Payat.
Gauntlet-n-Guanta.
Gauze-a-Manipis; magaan.
Gauzy-a-Manipis; magaan.
Gave-v. imp.-Binigay; nagbigay.
Gavel-n-Talumpo.
Gawk-n-Ulol.
Gawk-v-Kumilos ng paulol.
Gawky-a-Bastos.
Gay-a-Masaya; malugod; natutuwa; makinis; maaliw.
Gayety-n-Tuwa; kasayahan; lugod; kaluguran; saya; katuwaan; kaligayahan.
Gaze-v-Tumingin; silayin.
Gaze-n-Tingin; masid; silay.
Gazette-n-Pahayagan.
Gear-n-Damit; kasangkapan.
Gear-v-Magbihis; isuot ang damit.
Geese-n-Manga gansa.
Gelatin-n Jelea.
Gelatinous-a-Malagkit.
Gem-n-Sangkap.
Gender-n-Kaibhan nang lalaki sa babayi.
Genealogical-a-Nauukol sa lahi.
General-n-General; puno ng hukbo.
General-a-Karaniwan; litaw; alam nang madla; hayag.
Generally-adv.-Sa karaniwan; hayag.
General ship-n-Kalagayang general; katungkulang general; pagkageneral.
Generate-v-Paramihin; gumawa; gawa.
Generation-n-Lahi.
Generator-n-Ang gumagawa.
Generosity-n-Kagandahan ng loob; kabutihan ng loob; kamahalan.
Generous-a-Magandang loob; mabuting loob; magaling; mapagaampon.
Genesis-n-Genesis.
Geniel-a-Maawain.
Genital-a-Nauukol; sa isang panahon ó sa isang lahi.
Genitive-a-Nauukol sa kalagayang lalaki ó sa kalagayang babayi.
Genitor-n-Tawong marunong at matalas.
Genteel-a-Magalang.
Gentile-n-Gentiles; ang hindi binyagan.

Gentile-*a*-Hindı binyagan.
Gentılıty-*n* Galang, kagalangan.
Gentle-*a*-Malambot na loob; mabait, banayad, maawaın
Gentle folk-*n*-Tawong maginoo
Gentleman-*n*-Tawong maginoo, ginoo
Gentlemanlıke-*a*-Parang ginoo, maginoo; mahal
Gentle manly-*a*-Mahal; magalang, maginoo.
Gentle woman-*n*-Bınıbinı
Gently-*a*-Anas, inot ınot, dahandahan, utay utay
Gentry-*n*-Manga tawo.
Genuıne *a*-Wagas, tunay, totoo; dalısay.
Geographıc *a*-Nauukol sa geografía.
Geography-*n*-Geografía
Gealogıcal-*a*-Nauukol sa bato.
Geometrıcal-*a*-Nauukol sa Geometrıa
Geometry-*n* Geometria.
Germ-*n*-Pınangalingan, pınagmulan; pınagbuhatan; bınhı.
German *n*-Taga Aleman.
Germane-*a*-Nauukol, bagay, akma
Germınate-*v*-Sumupling, magusbong.
Gestatıon-*n*-Pagkabuntıs.
Gesture-*n* Kaway ng camay
Gestıculate-*ı*-Kawayın, kumılos.
Get-*v*-Magkaroon, manalo, magaral; kamtan, magkamit.
Gewgaw-*n*-Bagay na walang kabuluhan
Geyser-*n*-Bukalan ng tubıg na mainıt
Ghastly-*a*-Parang patay; maputla, katakot takot.
Ghastly-*adv* -Katakot takot, kakılakılabot; maputla-putla.
Ghost-*n*-Nuno, gunıgunı, capre
Ghostly-*n*-Para ó nauukol sa nuno.
Ghoul-*n*-Demonıo.
Giant-*n* Gıganti, tawong, malakı
Giant-*a*-Malaking malakı.
Giantess *n*-Gıganting babayi.
Gibbet-*n*-Bibıtayan.
Gibbe*t*-*v*-Bıtayın, ıbitın sa hig.
Gibbon-*n* Ungong malakı at walang buntot.
Gibbous-*a*-Hubog
Gibe-*v*-Murahın, pintasın, alipustaın; uyamın.
Gibe-*n*-Alipusta, pıntas, uyam.
Giblets-*n*-Puso, atay at buche nang manok.
Giddy-*a*-Magaan ang ulo, malıliw
Gift-*n*-Bıgay, salubong; alay, kaloob; hayin
Gig *n*-Calesa, salapang
Gig-*v*-Salapangın ang isda.
Gigantıc *a* Malaking malaki.
Giggle-*v*-Tumawa.
Giggle-*n* Tawa.

Gild *v* Pahıran ng ginto; duraduhın.
Gill-*n*-Hasang
Gill *n*-Takal, gatang
Gim crack-*n*-Kasangkapan na walang kabuluhan; laroan
Gimblet-Gimlet-*n*-Balıbol.
Gimp-*n*-Trencıllas.
Gin-*n* Gınebra
Gingor-*n*-Luya.
Gingerly-*adv*.-Maınam, matatakotın
Gingham-*n*-Sıta: kayong sıta.
Gipsy *n* Hampas lupa, tawong walang tınıtırahan
Gird *v*-Bıgkisın, palıgirın.
Gird-*n* Pamıgkıs, sakıt; pıntas
Girdle-*n*-Pamıgkıs.
Girdle-*v*-Palıgirın, bigkısin.
Girl *n*-Batang babayı
Girl hood-*n*-Pagkabata ng babayi,
Girlısh-*a*-Nauukol sa batang babayı
Gırt *ı* *ımp* -Bınıgkıs.
Girth *n*-Ang bılog
Gıst-*n*-Pandulo, kahulugan
Give-*v*-Magbıgay, bıgyan, ıpagkaloob, tulutan
Giver *n*-Ang nagbıbıgay.
Gızzard-*n*-Balunbalunan
Glacıal-*a*-Nauukol sa hielo
Glacıer-*n*-Bundok ng hielo
Glad *a*-Tuwa, natutuwa, masaya; malugod, malıgaja, matuwa
Glad-*v*-Ahwın, pasayahın.
Gladden-*v*-Sumaya, pasayahın.
Glaır-*n*-Ang putı ng ıtlog.
Glaır-*v*-Ipahıd, pahıran
Glaıry *a* Nauukol sa puti ng ıtlog
Glance-*n*-Sılıp, tıngın; masıd, sılay; suhap
Glance-*v*-Silayin, sılıpın; suhapın; tumıngın.
Glanders-*n*-Sakıt ng hıg ng kabayo
Glare-*v*-Tumıngın ng masama.
Glare-*n*-Masamang tıngın.
Glass *n*-Crıstal, bubog, baso, kopa
Glassy *a*-Paı ang crıstal.
Gleam-*n*-Sınag
Gleam-*ı*-Lumıwanag
Glean *v*-Maghimalay.
Gleanings-*n*-Hımalay
Glebe-*n*-Lupang sımbahan.
Glee-*n*-Towa; saya, lugod
Gleeful-*a* Masayu, malugod, malıgaya.
Glıb *a* Malangıs, masalıta.
Glıde-*a* Dumapılas; madapılas
Glim-*n*-Ilaw ng kandıla.
Glımmer-*n*-Ilaw ng kandıla
Glımmer *v*-Kumıntab, maningmıng
Glımpse-*ı* Suhap, sılay.
Glısten *r* Kumıslap, kumıntab, kumıslıp; magnıngmıng

Glitter-v-Kumislap; kumisap; magningning.
Glitter-n-Kislap. kintab.
Glittering-a-Maningning; makislap.
Globe-n-Mundo; bilog; sangkalibutan.
Globular-a-Mabilog.
Gloaming-n-Orasion.
Gloom-n-Dilim; kapanglawan; lumbay; lungkot.
Gloom-v-Dumilim.
Gloomy-a-Mapanglaw; malungkot; madilim.
Glorification n-Kalualhatian.
Glorify-v-Malualhati.
Glorious-a-Malualhati.
Glory-n-Lualhati; kalualhatian; dañgal; karañgalan; ganti; kabantugan; puri; kabunyian; kamahalan.
Glory-v-Maglualhati; magparañgalan.
Gloss-n-Ningning; kintab; kislap; kinang; kinis.
Gloss-v-Kumintab; kumislap.
Glossy-a-Makintab; makislap; makinis; maluningning makinang.
Glottis-n-Lalamuuan.
Glove-n-Guantes.
Glow-v-Kumislap;kumisap;mag liwanag.
Glow-n-Kislap; ningning; liwanag.
Glow worm-n-Uod.
Glue-n-Pagkit; pandikit.
Glue-v-Idikit.
Glum-a-Madilim ang mukha.
Glume-n-Ipa.
Glut-v-Lamunin.
Glut-n-Kabusugan; kahustuhan abala.
Glutinous-a-Maganit.
Glutton-n-Tawong matakaw.
Gluttonous-a-Matakaw.
Gluttony-n-Kasibaar; katakawan.
Glycerine-n-Glicerina.
Gnarl-n-Kuton.
Gnarl-v-Umañgil; tumahol.
Gnash-v-Sumagpang.
Gnat-n-Pulgas.
Gnaw-v-Kagatin; kumain; ñgatñgatin.
Gnome-n-Nuno: unano.
Go-v-Pumaroon; pumunta; magpunta.
Goad-n-Panudlong; tudlong.
Goad-v-Tudluñgin.
Goal-n-Hanga; dulo; hanganan; hangahan; patay.
Goat-n-Kambing.
Goatee n-Balbas.
Goat herd-n-Ang nagpapastol.
Gobble-v-Lamunin; umiyak ang pavo.
Gobbler-n-Pavo; pavong barako.
Goblet-n-Baso; kopa.
Goblin-n-Tianak; duende.
Go-by-n-Kapabayaan. tañgi.
GOD-n-BATHALA; DIOS.

God child-n-Inaanak.
God daughter-n-Inanak. (babayi).
God dess-n-Babaying maganda.
God father-n-Inaama.
Godless-a-Walang Dios.
God like-a-Malualhati; parang Dios.
Godliness-n-Kalinisan ñg kalulua; kapurihan; puri; dikit; ganda.
Godly-a-Magalang; mapagdasal.
God mother-n-Iniina.
God send-n-Bahay na ipinagkaloob ñg P. Dios.
God son-n-Inaanak; (lalaki).
Goggles-n-Salamin sa mata.
Going-n-Pagparoon; pagpunta; pag alis.
Gold-n-Gintô.
Gold dust-n-Gabok ñg gintô.
Golden-a-May halong gintô; magintô.
Gold smith-n-Platero.
Gone-v. p. p.-Nakaalis; umalis na.
Gong-n-Kuliling.
Good-n-Mabuti; masunurin.
Good-n-Kabutihan; buti; kaamoan.
Good-adv.-Mabuti buti.
Good-by-Good-bye-n-Paalam.
Good-by-Good-bye-inter.-Paalam.
Goodly-a-Mabutibuti; mainam; malaki.
Good-natured-a-Masunurin; mabuti ang ugali.
Goodness-n-Kabutihan.
Good-tempered-a-Mabuti ang ugali masunurin·
Goody-goody-a-Mabuti.
Goose-n-Gansa.
Gore-n-Sesgo; dugong namuo.
Gore-v-Magsesgo; suagin.
Gorge-n-Saluysoy.
Gorge-v-Lamunin.
Gorgeous-a-Mainam; dakila; maganda.
Gorilla-a-Musang.
Gormand-n-Tawong matakaw.
Gormandize-v-Lamunin.
Gory-a-Madugo.
Gosling-n-Inakay ñg gansa.
Gospel-n-Biblia; passion.
Gossamer-n-Kalapiaw.
Gossip-n-Sitsit.
Gossip-v-Sumitsit.
Got-v. imp.-Nagkaroon kinamtan.
Gouge-n-Lukob.
Gouge-v-Lukubin.
Gourmand-n-Tawong matakaw.
Gout-n-Sakit ñg Bukongbukong.
Govern-v-Manuno; maghari; mamahala.
Governor-n-Hari; puno; gobernador.
Governess-n-Maestra.
Government-n-Pamumuno; paghahari; pamamahala; paggogobierno.
Governatorial-a-Nauukol sa gobierno.
Gown-n-Damit.

Grab-v-Dakutin, agawin.
Grab n-Agaw, dakot
Grace-n-Gracia; ganda ñg kilos, kainaman ñg ugali
Grace-v-Ihulog ang gracia.
Graceful-a-Maganda; marikit, makinis; mainam ang kilos
Graceless-a-Bastos, hamak.
Gracious-a-Magandang loob, mabuting ˙loob
Gradation n-Pagsulong ñg untiunti, pagayos, paghusay
Grade-v-Ayusin; ilagay sa grado.
Grade-n-Grado, lagay.
Gradual-a Untiunti
Graduate n-Ang bagong labas sa escuela.
Graduate v-Tumangap ang titulo, tapusin, ang carera.
Graduation-a-Paglabas sa escuela
Grain n Butil, binhi.
Grain v-Bumutil.
Gram-n-Gramo
Grammar-n-Gramatica
Grammarian n-Ang sumulat ñg gramatica.
Grammatical a-Nauukol sa gramatica; ayon sa gramatica.
Granary-n-Bañgan, tagnan ñg trigo, palay, at mais
Grand-a-Dakila, marañgal, maginoo; malaki, magalang, bantog, mahal, kagalang galang.
Grand child n-Apo, inapo
Grand daughter-n-Apong babayi
Grande-n-Tawong dakila; ó marañgal.
Grandeur-n-Kadakilaan, kalakihan, kainaman
Grand father-n-Nunong lalaki, ingko
Grandiloquence-n-Salitang marañgal; kainaman ñg pananalita.
Grandiloquent-a-Mainam manalita.
Grand mother n-Nunong babayi, impo
Grand sue-n-Ingkong
Grand son-n-Apong lalaki.
Grange-n-Ari ñg may lupa.
Granite-n-Batong mainam parang marmol.
Graniverous-a-Kumakain ñg palay.
Grant-v-Pumayag, ipahintulot, tulotin; magkaloob; magbigay.
Grant-n-I igay, kaloob
Grantee-n-Ang tumangap ñg kaloob.
Grantor-n-Ang nagbigay.
Granular a-Parang butil, mabutil.
Granule-n Butil
Granulous-a-Mabutil
Grape-n-Ubas
Grapery-n Halamanan ñg ubas.
Grape stone-n-Buto ñg ubas.
Grape vine-n-Lipay ñg ubas.

Graphic-a-Nauukol sa sulat
Graphite-n-Tinga
Grapple-a-Magbuno; bumuno
Grapple n Buno; sungaban.
Grasp-v-Hawakan, humawak; kunin, agawin, dampotin
Grasp-n-Hamak; dampot.
Grass hopper-n-Balang; lukso
Grassiness-n-Kalaguan ñg damo.
Grass-widow-n-Bao sa buhay. (baba-(yi)
Grass-widower-n-Bao sa buhay (lalaki)
Grassy-a Maramó
Grate-n-Ahtit
Grate-v-Umalitit ikudkod, kumayod; lumañgitnğit.
Grater-n-Kudkuran; panudkod
Grateful a-Marunong magutang na loob.
Gratification n-Ganti, biyaya; dulot, kaloob; alay; bayad; upa.
Gratify v-Gantihin, gumanti, magbigay loob, bigyang loob, ipabuya
Gratis-a-Walang bayad.
Gratitude n-Utang na loob
Gratuitous-a-Walang bayad
Gratuity-n Bigay, pagbigay, kawalan ñg bayad.
Gratulate-v-Batihin, bumati.
Gratulation-n-Pagbabati.
Gratulatory-a-Masaya.
Grave a-Porinal, mabigat; totoo, walang biro.
Grave-n-Libing, kabaon; libiñgan.
Gravel-n-Buhañgin na magaspang
Grave stone-n-Tumba ñg patay.
Grave yard-n-Pantion.
Gravitate v-Humiling, tumuntong.
Gravitation-n-Pagkahiling
Gravity-n-Tuntuñgan
Gravy-n-Sawsaw.
Gray a-Upat; mura, kayumangi.
Gray-n-Kulay na kayumangi
Gray beard n-Tawong matanda.
Gray headed a Mauban, maputi ang ulo.
Grayish-a-Kayumangi.
Graze-v-Magpastol
Grazing-n Pagpapastol
Grease n-Mantika, sebo.
Grease-v-Pahiran ñg sebo, pahiran ñg mantika
Greasy-a Mamantika, mataba, masebo; malagkit; malibag.
Great grand child-n-Apo sa tuhod.
Great-granddaughter-n Apo sa tuhod (babayi)
Great-grand father n-Ama ñg nuno.
Great-grand mother-n Ina ñg nuno.
Great-grand son n-Apo sa tuhod (lalaki)
Grebe-n-Pilepile
Grecian-n-Nauukol sa griego, Griego.

Greed-n-Kaingitan; nasa, katakawan; ka-
saktinian
Greedy-a-Matakaw, mapagnasa, masakim.
Greek-a-Nauukol sa taga Griego
Greek-n-Griego
Green-a-Verde, hilaw, sariwa mura
Green-n-Kulay verde
Green-c-Sumariwa.
Greenish-a-Verde; hilaw.
Green horn-n-Tawong hindi marunong,
bagong nagaaral.
Greet-v-Batin, yumuko; kumustahin.
Greeting n Bati, yuko, kumusta.
Grenadier-n-Sundalong lakat.
Grew-v imp -Tumubo, nakatubo.
Grey-a-Kayumangi
Griddle-n-Kawaling mababaw.
Gridiron-n-Ihawan
Grief-n-Dalita, lunkot; hambal, dawas,
lumbay, hapis, dalamhati, taghoy
Grieve-v-Damdamin; magdamdam, hu-
mapis; maglumbay, magdalita, ma-
naghoy
Grievance-n-Hapis, dalamhati; pighati;
daing; taghoy.
Grievous-a-Mahapis, agraviado. mapig-
.hati, malumbay.
Grill-v-Ihawin, magihaw.
Grim a-Mabagsik; madilim ang mukha
Grimace-n-Ngiwi; kibit.
Grimace-v-Kumibit, ngumiwi.
Grimalkin n-Pusang matanda.
Grime-n-Dungis, uling; dumi.
Grime-v-Dumungis; dumumi.
Grimy a-Marungis; marumi
Grin-v Ngumiti
Grin n-Ngiti
Grind v-Gumiling, muhhin, alihsin
Grinder-n-Ang gumiling, bagang.
Grind stone-n-Hasahan.
Grip-v-Hawakin; humawak
Grip n Hawak
Gripe-v-Hawakin ng mahigpit, maghi-
rap; sumakit ang tian.
Gripe-n-Hapis, hirap, hawak.
Grippe n-Sakit ng lalamunan
Grisly-a-Katakottakot, kakilakilabot.
Grist n-Mais na giniling
Gristle-n-Butong malambot.
Grit-n-Buhangin,tapang,kabuoan ng loob.
Grit-v-Gilingin; gumiling.
Gritty-a-Matapang
Grizzle n-Kayumangi
Grizzly-a-Kayumangi.
Groan-n-Hibik, Halinghing. ||
Groan n-Halinghing, hibik
Grocer-n-Ang nagtitinda ng manga
pagkain
Grocery-n-Tindahan nang manga pag-
kain.

Grog n-Alak.
Grogery-Grogshop-n-Tindahan ng alak.
Groin-n Sinapupunan, singit.
Groom n-Lalaking bagong kasal.
Groom-v-Magalaga sa kabayo
Grooms man-n-Abay ng lalaki sa kasal
Groove n Bakam; bakas.
Groove-v-Bakasin
Grope v-Apuhapin, damahin; kapain.
Gross a-Bastos, magaspang, masinsin,
mapurol, makapal, walang hiya.
Gross n-Bilang ng isangdaan at apat na
puo at apat, 144.
Grot Grotto-n-Yungib, lunga.
Grotesque a-Makatatawa
Ground v imp -Giniling.
Ground-n-Lupa, bukit
Groundless-v-Walang katowiran
Ground nut n-Muni
Ground work-n-Tatayuan ng bahay
Group-n-Grupo, bunton, katipunan.
Group-v-Ibunton, pumisan, tumipon
Grout-n-Mais ó bigas na durog, binlid
Grove-n-Kahoyan
Grovel-v-Gumapang sa lupa, humamak
Grow-v-Tumubo, tumaas, dumami, lu-
mago, sumilang
Growl-v-Umangil, dumabog, dumaing
Growl-n-Angil, dabog; daing.
Grown-v p p -Tumubo na, nakatubo
Growth-n-Tubo, paglaki.
Grub-v Hukayin, putulin sa ugat.
Grub-n-Uod
Grudge-n-Dula sa kapua; tanim sa kapua
Grudge-v-Dumula sa kapua
Gruel-n-Sabaw.
Gruff-a-Bastos
Grum-a-Tahimik, madilim ang mukha
Grumble-c-Bumulongbulong, dumabog,
dumaing; magdalamhati
Grunt n Gukgok.
Grunt-v-Gumukgok.
Guana-n-Bayawak.
Guano n-Dumi ng ibong dagat
Guarantee-c Tibayan, katibayan, tindi
Guarantee-v-Tibayin; tindigan, bigyang;
ng katibayan
Guaranty-n-Katibayan, tindi
Guard-v-Alagaan, bantayin; ingatin,
itago
Guard-n-Bantay, ingat, tanod, Ang nag-
aalaga
Guardedly-adv-Maingat
Guardian-n-Poder, taga ingat ang yaman
ng ulila
Guava-n-Bayabas
Gubernatorial-a-Nauukol sa gobernador.
Guess-v-Tumuring; tumama.
Guess-n-Turing, tama.
Guest-n-Visita, nanunuloy.

Guffaw-*n*-Halakhak; tawang malakas.
Guidance-*n*-Pagturo, pagakay
Guide-*v*-Akayin, ituro
Guide-*n*-Taga turo, taga akay
Guile-*n*-Hibo, daya
Guileful-*a*-Nakahihibo, magdaraya.
Guileless-*a*-Walang daya.
Guillotine *n*-Makinang pamugot ng ulo.
Guillotine-*v*-Pugutin ang ulo
Guilt-*n*-Kasalanan; sala
Guiltless-*a*-Walang kasalanan.
Guilty-*a*-May kasalanan
Guise-*n*-Hitsura; bikas
Guitar-*n*-Guitara
Gulch-*n*-Sungoy, saluysoy
Gulf-*n*-Baraso ng dagat loob
Gull-*v* Dayain, manekas, tekasin.
Gull-*n*-Daya, tekas
Gullet-*n*-Lalamunan.
Gullible-*a*-Makakadaya, madaling dayain
Gully-*n*-Sungoy saluysoy
Gully-*v*-Sumaluysoy.
Gulp-*v*-Lamunin
Gulp-*n*-Ang nilamon, anomang bagay na nilamon
Gum-*n*-Dagta, katas; goma.
Gum-*v*-Kumatas, lumapot
Gum-*n*-Gilagid ng ngipin
Gummy-*a*-Madagta; makatas
Gump-*n*-Ulol
Gumption-*n*-Katusuhan, talas

Gun-*n* Baril.
Gun-*v*-Mangaso.
Gunner-*n*-Ang marunong bumaril.
Gunning-*n*-Pangangaso
Gun powder-*n*-Pulvora ng baril.
Gun shot-*n*-Putok ng baril.
Gunsmith-*n*-Ang marunong maghuin poni ng baril
Gun stock-*n*-Tangnan ng baril
Gurgle-*v*-Mugmogin
Gurgle-*n*-Mugmog
Gush-*v*-Bumukal
Gush-*n*-Bukal
Gusset-*n*-Sukob.
Gust-*n*-Lasap, lasa, hipo ng hangin.
Gusto-*n*-Lasap, gusto.
Gusty-*a*-Mahangin.
Gut-*n*-Bituka, isaw.
Gut-*v*-Ahsan ang bituka
Gutta-percha-*n*-Goma parang adyangaw
Gutter-*n*-Sangka, alulod.
Gutter-*n*-Ilagay ang alulod
Guttural *a*-Nauukol sa lalamunan
Guy-*n* Lubid na pangpatibay
Guzzle-*v*-Uminom ng madalas
Gymnast-*n*-Gimnastico.
Gypsy-*n*-Hampaslupa
Gyrate-*n*-Uminog, umikit
Gyration *n*-Paikit, painog.
Gyratorv-*a* Pagikit, paginog
Gyve-*n*-Pangapos.
Gyve-*v*-Gapusin

H

Ha-Hah-*inter.*-Ha.
Habiliment *n*-Damit
Habit-*n*-Ugali; kaugalian, kagawian, pinagkaratihan
Habit-*v*-Tumira, tumahan, dalawin ng madalas.
Habitable *a*-Gawi, matitirahan
Habitat-*n*-Dating tirahan
Habitation-*n*-Tirahan, tahanan, hantungan.
Habitual-*a*-Lagi, lagi na.
Habituate *v*-Lumagi, mamalagi.
Habituation-*n*-Pamamalagi.
Hack-*v*-Tagain, hiwain, tadtarin
Hack *n*-Hiwa, tagá, tadtad
Hack-*n* Carruaging inupahan
Hack-*a*-Inupahan
Hackle-*v*-Suklayin ang sinulid ó bulak.
Hackle-*n*-Suklay ng sinulid ó bulak
Hackney-*a*-Kabayó.
Hackney-*a*-Karaniwan, inupahan
Had-*v*. imp *p*, *p*.-Nagkaroon.
Haft-*n*-Bitbitan, tangnan.

Hag *n*-Babaying masama at pangit
Haggard-*a*-Pagod, mahina.
Haggle-*v*-Magturing; tuksuhin
Haggling-*n*-Turing
Hail-*n*-Bugbog, bati
Hail-*inter* -Aba.
Hail-*v*-Umulan ng bubog, bumati, batiin magpugay.
Hail storm-*n*-Ulan ng bubog
Hair-*n*-Buhok, balahibo
Hair breadth-*a* Lapad ng isang buhok
Hair breadth-*n*-Ang lapad ng isang buhok
Hairless *a*-Walang buhok, panot; upat.
Hair pin-*n*-Ipit
Hair spring-*n*-Kuerdas na munti ng orasan
Hairy-*a* Mabuhok
Halcyon-*n*-Limbas.
Halcyon-*a* Tahimik, masaya
Hale-*a*-Malakas, walang sakit.
Hale-*v*-Hilahin
Half-*n* Kabiak, ang kalahati.

Half-a-Kalahati
Halfbreed n-Mestizo, mestiza.
Half brother-n-Kapatid sa ama ó sa ina.
Half caste n-Mestizo, mestiza.
Half penny n Isang kuarta
Half sister n-Kapatid ng̃ ama ó sa ina (babayi)
Half witted a Mahina ang isip.
Hall-n-Salas
alleluiah-Hallelujah-intei. Jesus, Ma-Hria v José
Hallo-n Sigaw na malakas. hoy.
Halloo v-Suunigaw na malakas.
Hallow-v-Sambahin
Hallucination-n Guniguni; daya.
Halo-n-Limbó.
Halt n-Tigil; hinto, kapilayan
Halt-v-Humantong, tumigil, huminto.
Halter-n-Mortigon.
Halter-v-Ilagay ang mortigon.
Halve-v-Hatiin. biakin; dalawahin.
Halves-n-Kabiak.
Halyard-n Lubid ng̃ layag.
Ham-n-Hamon.
Hamlet-n-Nayon
Hammer-n-Martillo, pukpok. pamukpok.
Hammer-v-Pukpokin, pumukpok.
Hammock n-Duyan.
Hamper-n-Buslo Kaing, abala
Hamper-v-Abalahin, ilagay sa buslo.
Ham string-n-Litid
Ham string-v-Litirin.
Hand-n-Kamay.
Hand-v-Iabot, umabot.
Hand breadth n-Dangkal
Hand cuff-n-Pangapos ng̃ kamay.
Hand cuff-r-Gapusin ang kamay.
Hand full n-Isang haya, dakot.
Handicap-n-Abala. palugit.
Handicap-v Palugitin
Handicraft-n-Katalasan. talas; lalang
Handily-a-Ginhawa, madali
Handiwork-n Ginawa ng̃ kamay
Handkerchief n-Panyo, birang.
Handle i -Ulugin; ugitin; lamasin; hipuin; inaglamas
Handle n-Tatangnan, bitbitan, tankay, puluhan.
Hand made-a-Yari ng̃ kamay
Hand maid Handmaiden n-Alilang babayi.
Hand saw -n-Lagaring munti.
Handsome-a-Maganda, marikit; mainam.
Hand spike-n-Pangsual.
Hand writing-n-Sulat kamay.
Handy-a-Matalas, sanay, marunong.
Hang-v-Bitayin; ibitin, ilaylay, isampay, isabit, sampayin; sabitin.
Hang-n-Sabit, pagsampay
Hanger-n-Sabitan sampayan.

Hanging n-Pagbitay.
Hangdog-n-Tawong hamak at bastos.
Hang dog-a-Hamak, bastos; mababa.
Hang man-v Verdugo; taga bitay sa may kasalanan.
Hank-n-Bigkis ng̃ sinulid
Hanker v-Mognasa, nasain, magpita.
Hankering-n-Nasa; pita.
Hap n-Kapalaran, palad.
Hap-v-Mapalaran; magkataon.
Hap hazard-a-Walang ayos
Hap hazard-n Kapalaran; ang pagkakataon palad.
Hapless-a Walang palad, sawing kapalaian; malungkot.
Haply-adv.-Marahil
Happen-v-Mangyari, magkataon.
Happiness-n-Kasayahan, lugod, kaluguran; kaligayahan, ligaya
Happy-a Masaya, maaliw, malugod, ma ligaya, mapagaglahi.
Harangue-n-Pang̃ung̃usap
Harangue-v Makipagusap; makiusap, magdiscurso.
Harass-v-Dowahaginin, yamutin; pagalitin.
Harbinger-n-Tanda.
Harbor-n Punduhan, ng̃ vapor ó sasakyan
Harbor-v-Ituloy, ikalong.
Hard-a-Matigas; malakas, batibot, masipag mahirap; hindi malambot, mabagsik; masung̃it.
Hard-adv.-Matigastigas
Harden-v-Tumigas.
Hard hearted-a-Walang awa, ganid.
Hardhood-n-Tapang; pang̃ahas.
Hardily-adv.-Mang̃ahas.
Hardness n-Katigasak.
Hard ship n-Kapagalan,kahirapan,pagal, hirap.
Hard ware-n-Mang̃a bagay sa bakal.
Hardy a-Malakas, matapang.
Hare -nConejo
Hare brained-a-Ulol; mahina ang isip
Hare lip-n-Hiwas
Harem-n-Kuarto ng̃ babayi.
Hark-v-Pakingan.
Harlot-n-Hitad; puta; patutot.
Harm-n-Sakit; hirap, kahirapan.
Harm-v-Pasakitin; sirain.
Harmful-a-Makakasira; masama
Harmless-a-Di makakasira, maamo.
Harmonic-n-Silendro.
Harmonium-n Silendro
Harness n-Guarniciones.
Harness v-Magsingkaw; singkawin
Harp-n-Arpa.
Harper-n-Ang marunong tumugtog sa arpa.

31

Harpoon-n-Salapang.

Harpoon-v-Salapangin.

Harpooner-n-Ang marunon gumawa ó ihagis ang salapang

Harrow-n-Paragos.

Harrow-v-Sabain

Harrowing-n-Pagparagos

Harry-t-Nakawin, magnakaw, manduit.

Harsh-a-Mabagsik, masungit

Harshuess-n-Kabagsikan, kasungitan.

Hart n-Usang lalaki, sungayan.

Harts horn-n Sungay ng usang lalaki

Harum-scarum-a-Paulol, papaano.

Harvest-n-Pagaani; paggapás, ani.

Harvest-v-Umani anihin, gapasin.

Harvester-n-Ang gumapas

Has-t-Mayroon.

Hash-n-Pagkain na sahogsahog.

Hash-v-Tadtarin.

Hasp-n-Seradura, kandaro.

Hast-c-Mayroon.

Htase-n-Kabiglaan, kadahan

Haste-Hasten-t Biglain, magmadali, tumakbo, maghaplit, haplitin

Hastines-n-Kadalian; kabiglaan.

Hasty-a-Bigla, madali

Hat-n-Sombrero, sambahlo

Hatch-t-Pumisa; humalimhim.

Hatch-n-Pagpisa, halimhim.

Hatchet-n Palataw

Hate-n-Galit, tanim sa loob.

Hate-v-Magalit

Hateful-a-Kalupitlupit, kasamasamá; kasuklamsuklam

Hatred-n-Tanim sa loob,galit, kalupitan

Haughty-a-Hambog, palalo, tampalasan, palamara, mayabang, mapagmayabang, mapagmarikit

Haughtiness-n Kahambugan, kapalaluan, katampalasanan.

Haul-t-Bumatak, hilahin, batakin.

Haul-n-Batak, hila.

Haul-n-Dayami

Haunch-n Pigi.

Haunt-v-Mamamalagi, lumagi

Haunt-n-Yungib, kagawian.

Have-t-Magkaroon, mangyari.

Haven n-Punduhan, lugar na walang kapanganiban.

Haversack-n-Dalaan ng pagkain.

Havoc n-Kasiraan, paghpol,

Haw-n-Pagkautal.

Haw-v-Umutal.

Hawk-n-Lawin.

Hawk-v-Dumahak.

Hawk-n Dahak

Hawk eyed-a-Matalas ang mata.

Hawser n-Malaking lubid.

Hay-n-Damung tuyo.

Hay cock-n-Talumpok.

Hayloft-n-Taguan ng damong tuyo.

Haymow-n-Taguan ng damong tuyo.

Hay rick n-Timbon

Hay stack-n-Mandala

Hazard-n-Kapalaran, palad, panganib

Hazard v-Ilagay sa panganib.

Hazardous-a-May panganib

Haze-n-Ambon.

Haze-v-Tuksuhin, manukso.

Haze-a Kayumangi.

Hazy-a Maulap, malabo, mapanglow

He-pro -Siya, (lalaki)

Head-n-Ulo, pandulo, pangulo, puno, ang namumuno

Head-v-Tumungo, itungó, mamuno.

Headache-n-Sakit ng ulo

Headdress-n-Damit sa ulo

Heading n-Pandulo

Headland-n-Dungot.

Headless-a-Walang ulo

Headlong-a-Papaano

Head piece n-Damit sa ulo

Head guarters n-Oficina,bahay nang puno

Heads man-n-Taga pamugot ng ulo ng may kasalanan

Head spring-n-Pinangalingan, bukalan.

Head stall n-Mortigon

Head strong-a-Matigas ang ulo

Head way-n-Lakad, tubo

Heady a-Sowail, matigas ang ulo

Heal-v-kumaling, pagalingin, gamutin loob, malalim

Health-n Kawalan ng sakit, galing.

Healthful-a-Mapagaling, mabuti sa katawan.

Healthy-a-Magaling, walang sakit, mahusay

Heap-n-Bunton.

Heap-t-Ibunton.

Hear-v-Dingin, maninig, duminig, makinig; manainga; pumakingan.

Hearing n-Dinig; panding, litis,paglitis

Hearken-v-Pakingan, manainga, batyagin, dingin, makinatyag

Hearsay-n-Satsit, alingawngaw, bahta,

Hearse n Cario.

Heart-n-Puso, ubod.

Heart felt-a-Buhat sa puso, tapat na loob, malalim

Hearth n-Pinaguapuyan, apuyan.

Heartless-a-Walang awa, mabagsik, walang habag, hindi marunong maawa.

Heartlessness-n-Kawalan ng awa ó ng habag.

Heart rending-a-Mabigat, malungkot na malungkot

Heart's-ease-n Katahimikau.

Hearty-a-Masaya, buhat sa puso.

Heat n-Init.

Heat-t-Painitin; idarang, uminit.

Heathen-n Tawo na hindi binyagan.

Heathen-*a*-Hindi binyagan
Heathenish-*a*-Nauukol sa hindi binyagan
Heave-*v*-Itaas, buhatin, magbuhat.
Heave-*n*-Pagbuhat.
Heaven-*n*-Langit
Heavenly-*a*-Para na sa langit, nauukol sa langit
Heaven ward-*adv*-Sa gawing langit
Heaver-*n*-Taga buhat
Heaviness-*n*-Kabigatan, bigat.
Heavy-*a*-Mabigat, malaki, matindi.
Hebrew-*n*-Judio; wika ng Judio
Hebrew-*a*-Judio, nauukol sa Judio
Hectic-*a*-Ayon sa utos
Hectic-*n*-Lagnat, tisis, tuyo.
Hector-*n*-Tawong bastos at hambog.
Hedge-*n*-Bakod.
Hedge-*v*-Magbakod kulungin.
Hedge row-*n*-Bakod.
Heed-*v*-Tumupad; magingat, alagaan ingatin, makinig.
Heed-*n*-Ingat, pagkakalinga
Heedful-*a*-Maingat, mahinhin, mabait
Heedless-*a*-Pabaya, walang ingat ó kalinga.
Heel-*v*-Sakong.
Heel-*v*-Yurakin ng sakong
Heft-*n*-Bigat, kabigatan
Heifer-*n*-Bulo ng baka ó kalabaw, bakang dumalaga.
Height-*n*-Tayog, mataas
Heighten-*v*-Itaas; palakihin.
Heinous-*a*-Katakot takot, kalupitlupit; bastos, hamak
Heir-*n*-Ang nagmamana, *(lalaki)*.
Heirdom *n*-Pagmamana
Heiress *n*-Ang nagmamana, *(babayi)*
Heirloom-*n*-Mana.
Held-*v* *imp & p* *p*-Hinawak, tinanganan
Hell-*n*-Infierno.
Hellish-*a*-Nauukol sa infierno, parang na sa infierno.
Helm-*n* Ugit ng sasakyan
Helms man-*n*-Ang umugit sa sasakyan.
Helmet-*n*-Capecete.
Help-*n*-Tulong, ampon, katulong, abuloy; paggibik, kupkop.
Help-*v*-Tumulong; amponin, kupkupin, gikban; abuluyan, umampon, gumibik.
Helpful-*a*-Makatutulong
Helpless-*a*-Walang katulong, dukha, walang hanapbuhay.
Help mate-*n*-Katulong, kasama
Help meet-*n*-Asawang babayi.
Helter shelter-*a*-Pasabogsabog.
Helve-*n*-Puluhan ng palakol.
Hem-*n*-Lupi.
Hem-*v*-Lupiin.

Hemisphere-*n*-Kalahating bilog.
Hemorrhage-*n*-Banguyngoy,
Hemp-*n*-Copra, abaka.
Hen-*n*-Inahin.
Hence-*adv*.-Dahil dito
Hence forth-Hencefrward *adv*.-Buhatngayon, magbuhat ngayon.
Hen coop-*n*-Kulungan ng manok
Her-*pro* *p*-Kaniya, niya.
Herald-*n*-Pahayagan.
Herald-*v*-Ipahayag, magbalita.
Herbage-*n*-Damu
Herculean-*a*-Malakas na lubha.
Herd-*v*-Manada
Herd-*v*-Magpastol.
Herds man-*n*-Ang nagpapastol.
Here *adv* -Dito dini
Here about-Hereabouts-*adv*.-Dito, dini; sa gawing dito
Here after-*adv* -Buhat ngayon.
Here after-*n*-Ang panahong darating.
Here at-*adv* -Dahilan dito.
Here by-*adv* -Dahilan dito
Hereditary-*a*-Nauukol sa mana
Here in-*adv* -Sa ito
Here of-*adv* -Buhat ngayon.
Here on *adv* -Dahilan dito.
Heresy-*n*-Mali sa pananampalataya.
Heretic-*n*-Ang namali sa pananampalataya
Hereto-Here unto-*adv* -Hangang ngayon.
Here tofore-*adv* -Hangang. ngayon
Here unto-*adv* -Hangang dito ó ngayon.
Here upon *adv*.-Dahilan dito.
Here with-*adv* -Dahil dito.
Hermetic-*a*-Nauukol sa kemico.
Hermit-*n*-Tawong ayaw sumama sa kapuang tawo
Hermitage-*n*-Bahay ng tawong kulung sa kusa
Hero-*n*-Tawong bayani, tawong matapang
Heroic-*a*-Matapang, bayani, bunyi.
Heroine-*n*-Babaying bayani
Heroism-*n*-Pagkabayani
Heron-*n*-Kamuboy.
Hers *pro* -Kaniya, niya; *(babayi)*.
Her self *pro* -Siya rin, *(babayi)*
Hesitate-*v*-Umutal umunouno.
Hesitation-*a*-Pag uutal; kautalan.
Heteroclite-*a*-Walang ayos.
Hew-*v*-Tagain; tumaga; putulin, putlin, magtaga
Hexagon-*n*-Plano na may anim na gilid
Hexangular-*a*-May anim sa sulok.
Hey-*inter*.-Oy.
Hibernal-*a*-Nauukol sa taglamig.
Hibernian-*n*-Irlanders.
Hiccough-*n*-Sinok.

Hiccough-*v*-Magsinok.
Hid-Hidden-*v* *imp & p. p.*-Tinago; natago.
Hidden-*a*-Lihim, patago, tago.
Hiddenly-*adv.*-Patago; palihim.
Hide-*v*-Magtago, itago, ilihim.
Hide-*n*-Balat, katad
Hideous-*a* Pañgit, kalait lait.
Hie-*v*-Magmadali.
Hieroglph-*n*-Sulat Egipto.
Higgle-*v*-Magturing, mañgatowiran
High-*a*-Mataas, dakila.
High *adv* -Itaas.
Higher *a*-Mataas pa, lalong dakila.
Highest-*a*-Kataastaasan
High-flown *a*-Hambog, palalo.
High-handed-*a*-Tampalasan
High land-*n*-Lupang mataas.
High lander-*n*-Taga bundok.
Highly-*adv.*-Totoong marami.
Highness *n*-Kataasan; taas.
High road-*n*-Lansañgan.
High-spirited *a*-Maliksi, mañgahas.
Hight-*n*-Taas, kataasan.
High way-*n* Carsada, lansañgan.
High wayman-*n*-Tulisan, magnanakaw.
Hilarious-*a*-Malikot; masaya; magulo.
Hilarity-*n*-Kasayahan; kalikutan.
Hill-*n*-libag, tugatog, gulod, pugpog
Hillock-*n* Pugpog; gulod.
Hilly-*a*-Mabundok
Hilt-*n*-Tangnan ñg sable ó puñal.
Him-*pro* -Siya *(lalaki)*.
Him self *pro.*-Siyaring *(lalaki)*.
Hind *n*-Likod, Likuran.
Hind-*a*-Likod
Hinder *ä*-Likod
Hinder-*v*-Abalahin; umabala.
Hinderance-*n*-Abala
Hinder most-*a*-Huli sa lahat, kahulihulihan.
Hind most-*a* Huli sa lahat, kahulihulihan
Hindoo-Hindu-*n*-Indio.
Hindustani-*n*-Wika ñg Indio.
Hindrance *n*-Abala.
Hinge *n*-Visagra.
Hinge *t*-Isabit ang visagra.
Hint-*v*-Isurot sa isip, sulsulan.
Hint-*n*-Sulsol
Hip-*n*-Pigi.
Hippodrome *n*-Circo
Hip shot-*a*-Hingkod, hiwid.
Hire-*v*-Upahan
Hire-*n*-Upa, bayad.
Hireling-*n*-Ang nagsusundalo dahil sa kuarta.
His-*pro.*-Kaniya *(lalaki)*.
Hiss-*n* Haging; Haginit
Hist *inter* -Huag.

Historian-*n*-Taga sulat ñg historia buhay.
Historie Historical *a*-Nauukol sa Histo ria
History-*n*-Historia.
Hit-*v* Hampasin, tumama, tamaan; pa luin.
Hit-*v*-Hampas; palo, tama.
Hitch-*v*-Magsingkaw, isingkaw; taha
Hitch *n*-Buhol; abala.
Hither-*adv* -Dini, dito.
Hither to *adv.* Hangang dito; hangan ñgayon
Hive-*n*-Bahay Pukyutan; butlig
Hive-*v*-Itago, ipunin
Hives-*n*-Butling.
Ho-Hoa-*inter* -Aba.
Hoar-*a*-Maputi, inauban.
Hoard-*n*-Anomang bagay na nakatago kayamauan.
Hoard-*v* Ipunin, itago.
Hoarfrost *n*-Hamong na maputi.
Hoarse-*a*-Mapaos, maalat.
Hoarseness-*n*-Paos
Hoary-*a*-Mauban, maputi ang buho
Hoax-*n*-Biro, uyam
Hoax-*v*-Biruin, magbiro
Hobble-*v*-Humingkod
Hobble *n*-Lakad na pilay
Hobby-Hobbyhorse *n*-Laroan na kabay
Hobgoblin-*n*-Demoniong munti.
Hod-*n*-Panghakot ñg ladrillos.
Hoe-*n* Asarol
Hoe-*v*-Asarolin; magasarol.
Hog-*n*-Baboy.
Hoggish *a*-Matakaw, salahula.
Hog pen-*n*-Kuluñgan ñg baboy.
Hoiden-*n*-Babaying mañgahas.
Hoiden-*a*-Tampalasan, bastos.
Hoist-*v*-Itaas, buhatin, taasan.
Hold *n*-Bawak, Tangnan.
Hold-*v*-Hawakin, humawak; mamalag tangnan, manatili.
Hole-*n*-Hukay; butas.
Holiday-*n*-Kaarawan ñg pista, kapi tahan.
Holiday-*a*-Masaya; maligaya
Holiness-*n*-Kabanalan; kasantosan.
Holland-*n* Hollanda
Hollow-Walang laman; kalog, kuyun pas.
Hollow-*n*-Hukay
Hollow-*v*-Ihukay, hukayin
Holster-*n* Lalagyan ñg rebolber.
Holy-*a*-Banal, lualhati, Santa.
Holy day-*n*-Araw ñg pista
Homage-*n*-Galang, paggalang
Home-*n*-Bahay na tinitirahan.
Home-*adv.*-Sa bahay.
Homeless-*a*-Walang tirahan.

Homely-*a* Pañgit; hindi maganda.
Homemade *a*-Yari sa bahay.
Homesick *a*-May gustong umuwi.
Homespun-*a*-Yari sa bahay.
Home stead *n*-Lupa ñg magsasaka.
Homeward *ada.*-Sa gawi ñg bahay.
Homicide-*n*-Ang natay sa kapowa.
Homilist-*n* Pari, pastor
Hommock-*n*-Gulod, pugpog.
Hone-*n* Hasaan, talaran.
Hone-*v*-Ihasa, Talarin.
Honest-*a*-Mahinhin; marilag; tapat ang loob; hindi magdaraya
Honesty-*n*-Katapatan ñg loob, karañgalan.
Honey-*n*-Pulot pokyutan.
Honey-*v* Maging pulot; mapulot.
Honey bee-*n* Pokyutan.
Honey comb-*n*-Kalaba.
Honey moon-*n*-Panahon ñg ligaya at sarap ñg bagong kasal, luna de miel.
Honor-*n*-Karañgalan, dilag, galang, puri.
Honor-*v*-Igalang; purihin; mahalin.
Honorable-*a*-Marañgal, bunyi, bayani, marilag, dakila
Hood-*n*-Kulambo
Hoodlum-*n*-Tawong hamak at bastos.
Hood wink-*v*-Dayain.
Hoof-*n*-Kuko ñg kabayo.
Hook-*n*-Tagá kalawit, panungkit, sabitan.
Hook-*v*-Kibitin; isabit, kalawitin, kumalawit
Hooked-*a*-Baluktot.
Hoop-*n*-Bilog, pamigkis ñg bariles.
Hoop-*v*-Ilagay sa bahay.
Hoot-*v*-Hiyawin, humiyaw.
Hoot-*n*-Hiyaw, sigaw.
Hop-*n* Kumandirit
Hop-*v*-Kandirit.
Hope-*n*-Asa, pagasa; pananalig.
Hope *v*-Umasa, asahan.
Hopeful-*a*-Ma-aasahan
Hopeless-*a*-Walang asa; walang pagasa.
Hopple-*n* Gapusin ang paa ñg hayop
Hopple-*n*-Pangapos ng paa ñg hayop
Horde *n* Bunton ñg tawo.
Horizontal *a*-Pahiga, nakahiga.
Lorn-*n*-Sungay
Horn-*v*-Suagin, manuag.
Horned *a*-May sungay
Hornet-*n*-Putakti
Horny-*a*-Masungay; parang sungay.
Horrible-*a*-Katakottakot, kakilakilabot; katakataka, kasindaksindak.
Horrid-*a*-Masama, pañgit, masuklam.
Horrific-*a*-Katakottakot, kakilakilabot, kasindaksindak.
Horrify-*v*-Takutin; gulatin.
Horror-*n*-Kilabot, takot.
Horse-*n*-Kabayo.

Horse-*v*-Ibigay ang kabayo; sumakay sa kabayo.
Horse back-*n*-Likod ñg kabayo.
Horse fly-*n*-Bañgaw
Horse hair-*n* Buhok ñg kabayo.
Horse laugh-*n*-Halak
Horseman-*n*-Ang marunong sumakay sa kabayo.
Horse play-*n*-Larong bastos
Horse shoo-*n*-Bakal ñg kabayo.
Horsewhip-*n* Latigo.
Horticulture-*n*-Paggagawa ñg halaman.
Horticulturist-*n*-Ang naghahalaman, maghahalaman
Hosanna-*n*-Josana.
Hose-*n*-Medias.
Hosier-*n*-Ang nagtitinda ñg medias.
Hosiery-*n*-Mañga medias.
Hospitable-*a*-Magandang ugali ó kaugalian, magalang.
Hospital-*n*-Ospital.
Hospitality *n*-Kainaman ñg ugali.
Host-*n*-Ang may bahay; may visita ang bunton ñg tawo
Hostess *n* Ang may bahay *(babayi)*.
Hostile-*a* Galit
Hostility-*n*-Galit, laban, away
Hostler-*n*-Ang nagaalaga sa kabayo.
Hot-*a*-Mainit, maningas.
Hot bed-*n*-Punlaan.
Hotel-*n* Bahay tuluyan.
Hot-head-*n* Tawong matigas ang ulo.
Hotly-*adv.*-Mabagsik; madali.
Hotness-*n*-Kainitan, gulo.
Hot spur *n*-Tawong mainit ang ulo.
Hough *n*-Bukongbukong.
Hound-*n*-Asong mataas at manipis ang katawan
Hound-*v*-Buntotin, pilitin.
Hour-*n*-Oras
Hourly *a*-Orasoras.
Hourly-*adv* -Sa orasoras.
House *n* Bahay, tirahan.
House-*v*-Ilagay sa bahay.
House-breaker-*n*-Magnanakaw.
House hold-*n*-Mañga tawo sa isang bahay
House keeper-*n*-Taga iñgat ang bahay, taga pamahala sa bahay,
House keeping-*n*-Pamamahala sa bahay.
House maid-*n* Alila sa bahay
House wife-*n*-Ina ñg isang familia.
Hove-*imp* -Tinaas, binangon.
Hovel-*n*-Kubo na walang kabuluhan.
Hover-*v*-Huag umalis
How-*adv.*-Paano, sa anong paraan; bakin
How-beit-*conj* -Datapuat.
However-How-so-ever-*adv.*-Sa anomang paraan
However-*conj* -Datapuat.

Howl-v-Tumahol, umangil, humulhol.
Howl-n-Tahol, angil, holhol, sigaw
Howler-n-Ang sumigaw.
Hub-n-Maso
Hubub-n-Gulong malaki; kaguluhan.
Huckster-n Maglalako
Hukster-v-Maglako
Huddle-v-Umipon
Huddle n-Ipon, bunton; gulo, kaguluhan
Hue-n-Hukay
Huff-n-Galit, poot: tawong hambog
Huff-r-Lumaki, humambog, magmaya-
bang
Hufiy a-Mapootin; hambog
Hug-n-Yakap, hagkan.
Hug-v-Humagkan; yumakap; yakapin,
Huge-a-Malaki, dakila.
Hulk-n Katawan ng sasakyan
Hull-n Katawan ng sasakyan, balat
Hull-v-Balatin.
Hum-n-Awit.
Hum-r-Mag awit.
Hum inter -Oroy
Human a-Nauukol sa tawo, maawin
Humane-a-Maawain
Humanity-n Sang katawohan.
Humanize-v-Maging tawo.
Humble-a-Mababa ang loob, tahimik.
Humble-v-Hiyain.
Humble bee-n-Kumumo
Humbug-n-Daya; kayabangan, kaham
bugan; tawong hambog ó magda-
raya.
Humbug-v-Dayain, magdaraya.
Humdrum a-Makayayamot.
Humid-a-Basa
Humidity-n-Pagkabasá
Humiliate-v-Hiyain; supilin
Humiliating-a Nakahihiya, nakadudusta.
Humiliation n-Hiya, pagkahiya.
Humility-n Kababaan ng loob, pagyuko
Humming-a-Humaging
Hummock-n-Gulod; pugpog
Humor-n Kaugalian; kilos
Humor-v-Palayawin; sumunod ang gus-
to ng kapwa
Humorist-a-Tawong mapagsiste.
Humorous-a-Masaya, maligaya, mal a-
tatawa
Hump n Kakubaan, kakubutan
Hump back-n Kubo
Hunch n-Kuko; tulak ng siko
Hunch v-Isiko, tulakin ng siko
Hunch back-n Tawong kuba.

I-pro -Ako.
Ice-n-Hielo.
Ice-v-Maging hielo

Hundred-n-Isangdaan.
Hundred-a-Isangdaan.
Hundredth-a-Ikaisangdaan.
Hundredth-n-Ang ika isangdaan.
Hung v imp & p p Sinabit; sinampay
binitbit nakasabit
Hunger-n-Gutom
Hunger-v-Magutom; mamulubi
Hungry-a-Nagugutom, magutom.
Hunk-n-Piraso
Hunks-n-Tawong masakim
Hunt v-Mangaso; humanap, hanapin.
Hunt-n-Paghanap, pangangaso
Hunter n-Mangangaso
Huntress-n-Mangangaso; (babayi).
Hunts man-n-Mangangaso
Hurdle-n-Bakod: pangharang
Hurl v Ihagis: ipukol
Hurl-n-Hagis, pukol
Hurricane-n-Unos
Hurriedly-adv -Biglangbigla
Hurry-n-Pagmamadali, kadalian.
Hurt-v-Babagin, saktan, sugatin; bug-
bogin
Hurt n-Sira, sakit, bugbog.
Hurtful-a-Masakit, makasisira: makasa-
sama.
Husband-n-Asawang lalaki
Husband-v-Magsaka
Husband man-n-Magsasaka; ang nagpa-
paupa sa araw araw
Husbandry n-Gawa: trabajo
Hush-v-Huag kumibo; patahimikin
Hush-n-Katahimikan, kawalan ng kibo
ó gulo
Husk-n Balat.
Husk-v-Balatin, alisin ang balat
Husky-a-Malakas, paos, mapaos.
Hussar n-Sundalong caballeria.
Hussy-n-Babaying tampalasan.
Hustle-v-Sumipag; maghaplit, magma-
dali
Hustle-n-Pagmamadali, kadalian, kasi-
sipagan.
Hut-n-Kubo.
Huzza-v-Ipagdiwang.
Hydrant-n-Grifo
Hymn n-Dalit na pagpupuri
Hymnal-a Nauukol sa dalit.
Hyphen-n-Gion, giyon.
Hypothecate-v-Isangla; magsangla
Hypothecation-n-Pagsangla
Hypothesis n Sapantaha, palagay
Hysteria-n-Hipan ng hangin.

I

Ice berg-n-Bundok ng hielo.
Icy-a-Malamig, mahielo.
Ichorous-a-Malalanaw

I'd *con* Ako'y nagkaroon
Idea-*n*-Wari, ang inisip,' akala; banta, haka, pakana
Ideal *a*-Sa isip lalang
Ideal-*n*-Halimbawa.
Idem *a*-Yaon din
Identical-*a*-Yaon din
Identification-*n*-Pagkakilala
Identify-*v*-Kilalanin, kumilala.
Identity-*n* Pagkakilala.
Idiocy *n*-Kalagayang ulol, kaululan.
Idiom-*n*-Wika, salita.
Idiomatic-*a*-Nauukol sa wika.
Idiot-*n*-Tawong maulol, ulol.
Idiotic-*a*-Maulol; tulingad; tulig.
Idle *a*-Tulala, walang trabajo, batugah, pagayon gayon, pabaya
Idle-*v*-Humayon gayon, pabayaan
Idleness-*n*-Katamaran; kapabayaan.
Idol-*n*-Anito, larawan.
Idolater-*n*-Ang sumasamba sa anito.
Idolatress *n*-Babaying sumasamba sa anito
Idolatrous-*a*-Nauukol sa anito.
Idolatry-*n*-Pagsasamba sa anito
Idolize-*v*-Ibigin ng malabis ó lubha.
I-*conj.*-Kung, kailan
Igneous *a* Nauukol sa apoy, nangaling sa apoy
Ignite-*v*-Sindihin maglingas.
Ignition-*n*-Pagsindi; paglingas.
Ignoble-*a* Kadusta dusta, hamak; masama.
Ignominious-*a*-Hamak, kadusta dusta
Ignominy-*n*-Kadustaan, kahamakan
Ignoramus-*n*-Ulol, tawong hindi marunong.
Ignorant *a*-Hindi marunong, ulol; mapurol ang isip, tulig, tulala, tulingad, ungas, walang tuto.
Ignore-*v*-Huag kilalanin.
Ill-*a*-Masakit
Ill *a* Masama
Illapse-*v*-Huag ituro
Ill-bred-*a*-Hamak, walang pinagaralan; bastos; magaspang.
Illegal-*a*-Laban sa utos, hindi ayon sa katowiran.
Illegality-*n*-Pagkalaban sa utos.
Illegible-*a* Di mabasá
Illegibility-*n*-Kalabuan
Ill-favored-*a*-Pangit.
Illiberal-*a*-Maramot, masakim
Illicit-*a*-Laban sa utos, lihis sa matowid
Illimitable-*a*-Walang hanga, walang ubos
Illiterate-*a*-Walang tuto, walang pinagaralan.
Ill-natured-*a*-Masamang kaugalian.

Illness-*n*-Sakit kasakitan.
Illogical-*a*-Walang tuto
Ill-starred *a*-Walang palad; sawing kapalaran
Illude-*v* Iudyok.
Illume *v*-Liwanagin, magilaw.
Illuminate-*v*-Liwanagin, magilaw.
Illumination-*n*-Pagpaliwanag, ilaw.
Illusion *n*-Akalang mali, hiraya.
Illusive-*a*-Makadadaya, konowari
Illustrate-*v*-Ipakita, liwanagin, ipakita.
Illustration-*n*-Kalinawan, kaliwanagan, pintura
Illustrative-*a*-Nauukol sa pag paliwanag
Illustrious-*a*-Bantog; bunyi, balita, marangal, dakila; marilag.
Image-*n*-Larawan.
Imagery-*n*-Pag gagawa ng larawan.
Imaginable-*a* Maguniguni, hindi totoo; sa isip lamang
Imaginary-*a*-Hindi totoo, sa isip, lamang
Imagination-*n*-Guniguni, kuro, dilidili
Imaginative-*a* Nangaling sa, guniguni
Imagine-*v* Gunigunihin, isipin, akalain, maghaka
Imbank-*v*-Magpilapil
Imbankment-*n*-Pilapil.
Imbecile *a* Mahina, tulala, mahina ang isip.
Imbecile *n*-Tawong mahina at tulala.
Imbecility-*n* Kalagayang tulala at mahina.
Imbed-*v*-Ilubog, ilagay sa
Imbibe-*v*-Uminom
Imbitter-*v*-Pagalitin
Imbosom-*v*-Yakapin, haghan.
Imbricate-*a*-Hubog, baluktot.
Imbrication-*n*-Pagkahubog, kabaluktotan.
Imbrown-*v*-Tinain
Imbrue-*v* Ibadbad ó tigmakin nang dugo.
Imbrute-*v*-Humayop, humamak
Imbue-*v*-Iudyok, ndyokan, ipabuya.
Imitable-*a* Dapat tularan.
Imitate-*v*-Tularan, huwarin, humuad, gagarin, gumagad
Imitation-*n*-Hagad; howad, pagtutulad, paghowad, parisan, salin.
Imitative-*a*-Hindi dati
Immaculate-*a*-Malinis, mapuri, maselang
Immaterial *a*-Walang kabuluhan: walang katowiran.
Immature-*n* Di pa tapos ó magulang, di pa panahon
Immeasurable-*a* Di masukatin, malaking malaki
Immediate-*a*-Karakaraka, tambing

Immediately-*adv.*-Pagdaka; karakaraka, tambing, ñgayon din; agad agad, sampo, pagkaraka.

Immemorial-*a*-Maluat na maluat.

Immense-*a* Malaki, walang hanga.

Immensity-*n*-Kalakihan.

Immerse-*v*-Ilubog.

Immersion-*n*-Paglubog

Immethodical-*a*-Walang ayos

Immigrant-*n*-Ang tawong lumipat sa ibang lupa at doon tumitira

Immigrate-*v*-Pumasok sa ibang lupa.

Immigration-*n* Pagpasok sa ibang lupa.

Imminent-*a* Malapit; mapañganib.

Imminence-*n*-Lapit, pañganib.

Immiscible-*a*-Di makakahalo

Immobility-*n*-Tibay, pagkapirme

Immoderate-*a*-Bastos hindi mabait: tampalasan; mapag lasing

Immodest-*a*-Bastos; salaula; malibog, walang hiya.

Immodesty-*n*-Kasalaulaan, kawalan ñg hiya, kalibugan

Immolate-*v*-Patayin at ialay sa Dios.

Immolation-*n*-Pag alay sa Dios.

Immortal-*a* Walang hangan, walang katapusan; di mamamatay.

Immotal-*a*-Masama; mahalay; malibog

Immortality-*n*-Kawalan ñg hanga, kawalan ñg tapos.

Immovable *a*-Di magalaw.

Immovability-*n*-Katibayan; kaluatan.

Immunity-*n* Tawad; patawad.

Immure-*r*-Kuluñgin.

Immutable-*a*-Di mababago.

Imp-*n*-Demoniong munti·

Impact-*v*-Ilapat

Impact-*n*-Umpog.

Impair-*v*-Sumira; humina.

Impale *v*-Itulag, ituhog sa sibat

Impalpable-*a*-Di mahipo, manipis na manipis; walang katawan

Impanel-*v*-Ihista.

Inparity-*n*-Kaibahan.

Impart-*r*-Sabihin, magsabi; magbalita, magbigay alam, ipahayag.

Impartial-*a*-Walang interes; walang kinikilinñan: walang tinitingnan

Impartiality-*n*-Kawalan nang interes kabanayaran; kabaitan sa pagtupad

Impassibility-*n*-Kawalan ñg daan.

Impassible *a*-Di makaraan.

Impassible-*a*-Walang damdam

Impassionate-*a*-Malaking damdam

Impassioned *a*-Maniñgas gulo ang isip.

Impassive-*a*-Walang damdam

Impatient-*a*-Balisa; mainip; muhiin

Impatience-*n*-Balisa; muhi; kainipan.

Impeach-*v*-Bintañgin; magbintang· mag

Impheacment-*n*-Pagbibigay sala, bintang, paratang

Impede-*v*-Abalahin, umabala; pigilin; pumigil

Impediment-*n*-Abala: kasiraan.

Impel-*v* Pilitin· tulakin, itulak

Impend-*v*-Maabala

Impenetrable-*a*-Di matagos; ó matarok, di makapasok

Impenitence-*n*-Katigasan ñg ulo

Impenitent-*a*-Matigas ang ulo

Imperative-*a*-Kailañgan, mapilitin, mataas.

Imperceptible-*a*-Di mahirip, di maramdamin.

Imperfect-*a*-Di yari; kulang may sala.

Imperfection-*n*-Kakulañgan, kalagayan na di pa yari, pintas.

Imperial-*a*-Nauukol sa hari.

Imperialism-*n*-Kapangyariham ñg hari.

Imperil-*v*-Ilagay sa pañganib

Imperious-*a*-Nauukol sa utos; kailañgan

Imperishable-*a*-Hindi nabubulok; maluluatan.

Impersonal-*a*-Hindi nauukol sa sarili.

Impersonate-*v*-Gagarin ang kapwa gumagad sa ibang tawo

Impersonation-*n*-Howad

Impertinence-*n*-Tampalasan, kawalan ñg galang.

Impertinent-*a*-Walang galang, tampalasan.

Imperturbability-*n*-Katahimikan.

Imperturbable-*a*-Di magagalit.

Impetuous-*a*-Maniñgas, malakas ang loob, mabigla; dalosdalos

Impetuosity-*n*-Kalakasan nang loob, kabiglaan

Impetus-*n*-Lakas

Impiety-*n* Kasamaan; kakulañgan ñg galang sa P Dios

Impinge-*v*-Mahulog, umumpog; umuntog; lumaban.

Impious-*a*-Masama,ayaw sumampalataya sa P. Dios

Implacable *a*-Di matatahimik; walang awa.

Implant-*v*-Magtanim, ibaon.

Implement-*n*-Kasangkapan

Implicate-*v*-Idamay, isama.

Implication-*n*-Pagdamay

Implicit *a*-Maniwalang lubos

Implore *v*-Dumaing, manalañgin; humiñgi, ipakiusap

Imploration-*n* Daing; panalañgin, hiñgi, pagdainy.

Imply *v* Sabihin, magbigay kahulugan.

Impolicy-*n*-Masamang halimbawa

Impolitic-a-Walang galang tampalasan.

Imporons a-Walang butas

Impoit v-Ipasok

Import-n-Kalakal na nangaling sa ibang lupa.

Importance-n-Tindi, kabigatan, kabuluhan.

Impoitant-a-Totoo, mabigat, pormal, kailangan.

Importation-n-Pagpasok sa ating lupa.

Importunate a-Kailangan

Importune-v-Manalangin, humingi ng pilit.

Importunity-n-Daing; hingi, panalangin

Impose-v-Davain, ilagay; ilugar.

Imposing-a-Magdaraya.

Imposition-n-Daya kasinungalingan

Impossibility-n-Kalagayan na hindi maari

Impossible-a-Di magagawa, di maari, hindi mangyayari.

Impost-n-Buis

Imposter-n-Tawong magdara.

Imposture-n-Kasinungalingan, daya.

Impotence-Impotency-n-Kawalan ng lakas, kahinaan

Impotent-a-Mahina, walang lakas.

Impotent n-Tawong mahina.

Impoverish-v-Maghirap.

Impracticable a-Di maari; hindi dapat gawin; mahirap gawin

Imprecate-v-Manungayaw, manumpa

Imprecation-n-Tungayaw, sumpa

Impregnable a Di makaraan, di mananalo

Impiegnate-v-Matigmak tigmakin

Impregnation-n-Pagtitigmak

Impress-v-Itatak taktakin

Impress-n-Tatak, taktak.

Impressible-a-Maramdamin

Impressive a-Mabigat, pormal

Impiint-v-Kintahn, ikintal

Imprint-n-Kintal; limbag.

Imprison-v-Ibilango.

Imprisonment-n-Pagbibilango

Improbability-n-Kalabuan.

Improbable-a-Marahil hindi.

Impromtu-adv.-Bigla pagkaraka.

Improper-a-Di bagay tampalasan

Impropriety n-Tampalasan

Improve v Bumuti, umigi, gumaling.

Improvement-n-Dagdag, pagigi; paglago, pagbubuti

Improvidence-n-Kapabayaan

Improvident a-Pabaya.

Imprudence-a Gawang hunghang, kakulangan ng bait

Imprudent-a-Walang bait, walang galang, walang hiya.

Impudence-n-Tampalasan, paslang, kawalan ng hiya, kawalan ng galang, kalapastanganan

Impudent-a-Walang hiya, tampalasan.

Impugn-v-Magsalangsang, lumaban

Impulse-n-Buya; pag uurali

Impulsion-n-Buya, pabuya, tulak.

Impulsive a Maningas; buhay ang loob

Impunity-n-Pag ligtas, pag adya

Impure-a-Mahalay, marumi, walang puri.

Impurity-n-Kahalayan, kawalan ng puri, kahibugan, karumihan

Imputation-n-Paratang, bintang

Impute-v-Magbintang; paratangin, magparatang, bintangin.

In-prep -Sa loob, nang, sa.

In-adv.-Sa loob

Inability-n Kakulangan, kawalan nang kaya, kamangmangan.

Inaccessible a-Di makararating.

Inaccurate-a-Mali; may mali, hindi tama.

Inaccuracy-n-Kamalian.

Inaction-n-Kawalan ng kilos

Inactive a Walang kilos, tahimik

Inactivity-n-Kawalan ng kilos

Inadequacy n Kakulangan.

Inadequate-a-Kulang; kapos, di sapat

Inadmissible-a-Hindi matatangap, dapat urungan

Inadvertence-Inadvertency-n Kapabayaan

Inadvertent-a-Pabaya

Inamorata n-Babayi, kalunya, bato.

Inamoiato-n-Lalaking lumiligaw, manininita

Inane-a-Walang laman, tuyo.

Inanimate-n-Walang buhay, walang kaluluwa

Inanition-Inanity-n-Kawalan ng laman.

Inapplicable-a Hindi magagamit.

Inapplication-n-Katamaran

Inappreciable-a-Di dapat galangin

Inapt-a-Di bagay, di akma.

Inappropriate-a-Di bagay.

Inaptitude-n Kalagayan na hindi bagay ó akma.

Inarticulate a-Hindi maliwanag, di masabi; utal.

Inas much-adv -Dahil dito.

Inattention-n-Kapabayaan; katamaian

Inattentive-a-Pabaya, tamad.

Inaudible-a-Di makarinig

Inaugurate-v-Ilagay sa katungkulan

Inauguration-n-Paglagay sa katungkulan

Inauspicious-a-Di bagay, masama at hilig, mahalay

Inbreathe-v-Huminga

Incage-v-Kulungin sa haula

Incalculable a-Di makabibilang.

Incandescence n-Kahwanagan; liwanag

32

Incandescent-a-Maputi dahil sa init, maliwanag; malinaw.
Incapability-n-Kakapusan. kakulañgan, kawalan ñg kaya
Incapable-a-Kulang, walang kaya; walang kabuluhan
Incapacitate-v-Alisin ang kaya.
Incapacity-n-Kakulañgan
Incarcerate-v-Ibilango; kuluñgin
Incarceration-n-Pagkulong, pagbibilango
Incarnate-a-May laman.
Incase-v-Ibalot, balutin.
Incautious a-Walang iñgat, pabaya.
Incendiary-n-Taga sunog; manununog
Incendiary-a-Nauukol sa sunog
Incense-v-Pasubuin ñg incenso.
Incense-n-Incenso
Incentive-n-Dahilan; udyok.
Inception-n-Pinagbuhatan; pinagmulaan.
Inceptive a-Nauukol sa pinagbuhatan
Incertitude-n-Agamagam ñg loob
Incessant-a-Walang lubay ó tigil, walang himpil.
Inch-n-Pulgada; dalawang dali
Inchoate a-Bago.
Inchoation-n-Pinagbuhatan, pinagmulaan.
Incidence-n-Pagkabalatong
Incident-n-Mabalatong.
Incidental-a-Kakaunti ang halaga
Incipient-a-Bago, una.
Incise-v-Hiwain, maghiwa, hiwasin.
Incised-a-Nakahiwa.
Incision-v-Hiwa.
Incisive-a-Makahihiwa, matulis, ma saklap
Incisor-n-Pañgil ñg aso.
Incite-v-Sulsulan, udyokan, ipabuya.
Incitement-n Udyok pabuya
Incivility-n-Katampalasanan, kawalan ñg galang
Inclemency-n-Kabagsikan, kawalan ñg awa; kasuñgitan.
Inclement-a-Walang awa; mabagsik; walang habag.
Incline-v-Humilig, humiling, ihapay, ihiñgil, ituñgo.
Incline-n-Dahilig na lupa, dahsdis.
Inclined a-Dahilig, nakahilig
Inclination-n-Hilig hiling; ugali; yuko, pagkahilig.
Inclose-v-Magbakod, bakuran; isama
Inclosure-n-Bakuran.
Include-v-Isama.
Inclusion n-Pagsama, paglahok
Inclusive-a-Kasama.
Incog-Incognito a Di nakikilala, nakabalatkayo.

Incoherent-a-Hindi maintindihan, ma labo
Incombustibility n-Kalagayan na hindi masusunog.
Incombustible-a-Hindi masusunog.
Income n-Ang kinita; upa; bayad, sahod
Incoming-a-Dumarating
Incomensurable-a-Walang katulad ó kapantay.
Incommode-v-Magmolestia, abalahin
Incommodious-a-Kulang, masikip.
Incommunicable-a Hindi makasasabi.
Incommunicative-a Ayaw magsabi, walang kibó.
Incomparable-a-Walang kaparis ó katulad, walang kahulilip
Incompatible-a-Sowail.
Incompetency-n-Kakulañgan ñg kaya
Incompetent-a-Walang kaya, hindi bagay.
Incomplete-a Kulang, kapos, hindi payari.
Incomprehensible-a-Hindi makaintindihan, hindi, matanto.
Inconceivable-a-Hindi matanto.
Inconclusive-a-Hindi pa tapos, ku lang
Incongruous-a-Hindi bagay, kulang.
Inconsequence-n-Kawalan ñg halaga.
Inconsequent a-Walang kabuluhan.
Inconsequential a-Walang halaga ó kabuluhan
Inconsiderable-a-Kakaunti, walang marami
Inconsiderate-a-Bigla, mali, pabaya
Inconsistency-n Gulo.
Inconsistent-a Sowail, magulo
Inconsolable a-Hindi humimpil.
Inconstancy-n-Kasaliwahan ñg loob, kaalisagaan, kataksilan, kasuitikan.
Inconstant-a-Saliwahan, alisaga, taksil
Incontestable-a-Di magkakaila.
Incontinency-n-Kalibugan, kabiglaan
Incontinent-a-Bigla; malibog, mababa ang isip
Incontinently adv -Pabigla; ñgayon-din
Incontrovertible a-Di magkakaila, totoo; walang kapintasan
Inconvenience n-Molestia; abala.
Inconvenient-a-Di karampatan, hindi mabagay, di bagay
Incorporate-a Guniguni
Incorporate-v-Puinisan, magtipon.
Incorporation-n-Pagpipisan ñg mañga mañgañgalakal.
Incorporeal-a-Walang katawan, guniguni
Incorrect a Hindi tama, mali; hiwas, talso.

Incorrigibility-n-kasamaan na hindi mababago
Incorrigible-a-Ayaw magbait, masama; di mabait.
Incorrigible-n-Tawong totoong masama
Incorrupt-a-Hindi nabulok, mahusay, mahnis
Incorruptibility-n-Kalagayan na hindi masisira.
Incorruptible a-Hindi masisira
Increase-v-Lumaki, tumubo, magdagdag; idagdag, dumami, kumapal; humigit.
Increase n-Dagdag; tubo, paglaki; pagdadami
Incredible-a-Di dapat maniwala.
Incredulous-a-Hindi naniwala; walang pananampalataya
Increment n-Dagdag; tubo, paglaki
Inculcate-v-Magturo.
Inculcation n-Pagtuturo.
Inculpate-v-Idamay, magparatang, magbintang, bintangin
Inculpation n-Bintang; paratang.
Incumbency-n-Paghiga, timbang, katungkulan.
Incumbent-a-Nakahiga; kailangan.
Incumbent-n-Ang nakahiga, ang may katungkulan
Incumber-v-Abalahin; pigilin
Incumbrance-n-Abala, pagpigil.
Incur-v-Marapatan, magkaroon; kamtan; magkamit
Incurable-a-Hindi magagaling
Incursion-n-Umpog, untog
Incurvate-a-Hubog, baluktot.
Incurvation-n-Pagbabaluktot, kabaluktotan
Indebt-v-Pautangin.
Indebted a-May utang
Indecency-n-Kabastosan, kahalayan, kalibugan, kasamaan
Indecent-a-Malibog; bastos, mahalay; masama, magaspang
Indecision-n Agamagam ng loob.
Indecisive-a-Hindi buo ang loob.
Indecorous-a-Bastos, tampalasan.
Indecorum-n-Kakulangan ng bait, kabastosan, katampalasanan
Indeed-apv-Totoo baga, totoo nga
Indefatigable-a-Walang pagod ó pagal, hindi marunong mapagod.
Indefensible a-Hindi makupkopin.
Indefinable-a-Hindi magsaysay; hindi masaysay
Indefinite-a-Malabo; walang hanga.
Indelible-a-Hindi mabubura
Indelicacy-n-Kabastosan, kasamaan ng ugali.
Indelicate-a-Masamang ugali, bastos.

Idemnification-n-Pagsasauli; pagganti, kabayaran.
Idemnify-v-Isauli.
Idemnify-v-Isauli, bayaran, gantihin
Idemnity n-Ganti; Katibayan; tawad.
Indent-v-Bingawin; Ukitin
Indent-n-Bingaw, ukit.
Indentation-n-Pagbingaw, pagukit.
Independence-n-Kalayaan, laya.
Independent-a-Malaya
Indescribable-a-Hindi masaysay.
Indestructible-a-Hindi masisira
Indeterminable-a-Hindi masaysay, hindi masabi
Index-n-Anoman bagay na tumuturo; hintuturo.
Index-v-Ilista
Indian-n-Indio.
Indian-a-Nauukol sa indio.
Indian corn-n-Mais
India rubber-n-Goma.
Indicate-v-Ituro, ibig sabihin, ipakita
Indication-n-Pagpakita, surot; hula, tanda.
Indicative-a-Tinuturo.
Indices-n Lista
Indict-v-Bintangin, magparatang
Indictment-n-Bintang, paratang
Indifference-n-Kawalan ng interes, kapabayaan
Indifferent a-Walang interes, pabaya, walang pakiramdam, batugan.
Indigent-a-Wualang hanapbuhay.
Indigestible a-Di matutunaw sa sikmura.
Indigestion n-Empatso, sakit na kinakabagan
Indignant-a-Galit, nagagalit.
Indignation n-Galit; poot
Indignity-n-Kahamakan, kabastosan, katampalasanan.
Indigo-n-Tayom, tina
Indigo plant-n-Tayom.
Indirect-a-Hindi matowid, hindi tapat; malabo.
Indirection-n-Pagdaraya.
Indiscreet-a-Pabaya; bigla walang bait.
Indiscrete-a-Masinsin, nakapisan.
Indiscretion-n-Kakulangan ng bait
Indiscriminate a-Walang ayos, magulo.
Indiscrimination-n-Kawalan ng interes, katapatan
Indespensible-a-Kailangan ng totoo ó ng mahigpit.
Indispose v-Sumira, magdaramdam.
Indisposed-a-May sakit.
Indisposition-n-Damdam; tamlay.
Indisputable-a-Hindi magkakaila.
Indissoluble-a-Di matutunaw
Indistinct-a-Malabo, mahina, utal.
Indite-v-Sumulat; diktahin.

Individual-a-Nagiisa; nakabukod; bugtong; tangi.
Individual-n-Tawo.
Individuality-n Pagkakaisa; pagkakasama.
Indivisible-a-Hindi makababahagi.
Indocile-a-Mapurol ang isip.
Indoctrinate-v-Magturo.
Indolence-n-Kapabayaan; katamaran; kakuparan.
ndolent-a-Tamad; pabaya.
ndomitable-a-Di susuko; matapang.
ndoor adv.-Sa loob ng bahay.
ndoor-n-Loob.
ndorse-v-Pirmahin.
ndorsement-n-Pagpirma; sulat sa likod ng isang kasulatan.
nduce-v-Ipabuya; pilitin; udyukan.
nducement-n-Pabuya; udyok.
nduct-v-Ipasok; dalhin; sa loob; ilagay sa katungkulan.
nductile-a-Maganit; hindi malambot; matigas at marupok.
nduction n-Pagpasok; pinagmulaan.
ndulge-v-Magbigay loob; pumayag.
ndulgence-n-Pagbigay loob.
ndulgent-a-Mapagbigay loob.
ndulgent-a-Matigas; mabagsik; walang awa.
ndurate-v-Tumigas; maging mabagsik.
nduration-n-Katigasan; kabagsikan.
ndustrial-a-Nauukol sa industria; nauukol sa nagtatrabajo.
ndustrious-a-Masipag; masikap.
ndustry-n-Trabajo; gawa; kasipagan; kasikapan; lalang.
nebriate-v-Maglasing; maglango.
nebriate-n-Tawong lasing ó lango.
nebriation-n-Kalasingan.
nebriety-n-Kalasingan.
neffective-a-Walang kabuluhan.
neffectual-a-Walang kabuluhan.
nefficacious-a-Walang kabuluhan.
nefficient-a-Kulang; pabaya.
nelegance-n-Kapangitan.
nelegant-n-Pangit; bastos; magaspang.
nelligibility-n-Kalagayang di maihahalal.
nelligible-a-Di maihahalal.
nequal-a-Hindi kaparis ó katulad; iba; hindi kawanki.
nequality n-Kakaibahan.
nert-a-Pabaya; tamad; mapurol ang isip.
nertness-n-Katamaran; kapabayaan; kapurulan ng isip.
nestimable-a-Lubhang mahalaga.
nevitable-a-Di maiilagan, mangyayari na walang sala.
nexcusable-a-Di dapat patawarin.

Inexhaustible-a-Hindi maubos.
Inexorable-a-Matigas ang ulo; buo ang loob; walang awa.
Inexpedience-n-Kasamaan.
Inexpedient-a Hindi bagay; wala sa panahon.
Inexperience-n-Kakulangan sa pagsanay; kawalan ng sanay.
Inexpressible-a Di makasasabi.
Inextricable-a-Hindi makahahango; gulong gulo.
Infallible-a-Tama; totoo; hindi mamamali.
Infamous-a-Walang dangal; hamak; masama; walang puri; katakot takot.
Infamy-n-Kapalibhasaan; kasamaan; kasiraan ng puri; kahamakan.
Infantile-a-Nauukol sa pagkabata.
Infant-n-Sangol; batang munti.
Infant-a-Nauukol sa bata.
Infantry-n-Sundalong lakad.
Infatuate-v-Hangalin; masira ang isip sa pagibig.
Infatuation-n-Kaululan; kahangalan.
Infect-v-Sumira; makahawa.
Infection-n-Hawa; pagkahawa.
Infectious-a-Nakakahawa.
Infelicitous-a-Hindi masaya; malungkot; mahapis.
Infelicity-n-Kalungkutan; kahapisan.
Infer-v-Awasan; magbigay kahulugan.
Inference-n-Kahulugan.
Inferior-a-Mababa; may pintas; kulang.
Inferior-n-Ang mababa sa iba.
Inferiority-n Kababaan sa iba.
Infernal a-Nauukol sa infierno.
Infertile-a-Karat; di mamunga.
Infertility-n-Kakaratan ng lupa.
Infest-v-Yamutin; pagalitin.
Infidel-a-Ayaw sumampalataya sa Dios.
Infidel-n-Ang ayaw sumampalataya sa Dios.
Infidelity-a-Kasukaban; kataksilan; kasuitikan.
Infinite-a-Walang hanga.
Infiniteness-n-Kawalan ng hanga.
Infinitesimal a-Lubhang munti.
Infinitive-a-Walang hanga.
Infinitude-n-Kawalan ng hanga.
Infirm-a-Hindi matibay; mahina.
Infirmary-n-Ospital.
Infirmity-n-Kahinaan; kapayatan.
Inflame-v-Mag lingas; mag liab; uminit.
Inflammable a-Madaling maglilingas mainit ang ulo.
Inflammation-n-Paglingas; pamumula ng balat; galit; kainitan ng ulo.
Inflammatory-a-Madaling masunog; taksil; mainit ang ulo.

Inflate-v-Punuin nang hañgin; mamantog.

Inflation-n-Pamamantog; pag lalagay ñg hañgin.

Inflect-v-Ibahin ang kahulugan; baguhin ang kahulugan.

Inflection-n-Pagbago ñg kahulugan.

Inffexibility-n-Katigasan; katibayan ñg loob.

Inflexible-a-Malakas; batibot; matigas ang loob.

Inflexion-n-Pagkabago ñg kahulugan.

Inflict-v-Gamitin na pilit; multahin.

Infliction-n-Multa; parusa.

Influence-n-Kapangyarihan.

Influence-v-Ihiling; itunĝo; ililig.

Influential-a-May kapangyarihan.

Influenza-n-Hika.

Influx-n-Pagpasok.

Infold-v-Balutin.

Inform v-Sabihin; ipagbalita; magbalita; magbigay alam; isumbong.

Information-n-Balita; alam; bala.

Informer-Informant-n-Ang nagsabi; ang sumumbong; manunubok; manunumbong.

Infraction-n-Sala; kasalanan.

Infrequency-n-Dalang; kadalañgan.

Infrequent-a-Madalang; hindi madalas; bihira.

Infringe-v-Magkasala.

Infringement-n-Kasalanan; sala.

Infuriate-v-Pagalitin.

Infuriate-a-Magagalit; galit.

Infuse-v-Isalin; ibuhos; ipabuya.

Infusion-n-Pagsalin; pabuya.

Ingenious-a-Matalas ang isip; matalino; marunong.

Ingenuity-n-Katalasan ñg isip.

Ingenuous-a-Malaya; dakila; marañgal.

Inglorious-a-Kahiyahiya; hamak; masama; mahalay.

Ingot-n-Bara ñg metal.

Ingrate-n-Tawong palamara ó hindi marunong ñg utang na loob.

Ingratiate-v-Magustuhan.

Ingratitude-n-Katampalasanan; kabastosan; kasuitikan; pag kapalamara.

Ingredient-n-Kalahok; kahalo.

Ingress-n-Pagpasok.

Ingression-n-Pagpasok.

Ingulf-v-Lamunin.

Inhabit-v-Tumira; manahan.

Inhabitable-a-Matatahanan.

Inhabitant-n-Ang tumitira sa isang lugar.

Inhale-v-Humiñga.

Inhalation-n-Paghiñga.

Inharmonic-a-Masama ang tunog.

Inhere-v-Dumikit; maukol; sa.

Inherent-a-Nangaling sa pinagmulaan.

Inherit-v-Magmana.

Inheritance-n-Mana; ari.

Inheritor-n-Ang nagmana.

Inhospitable-a-Hindi marunong makipagkapwa tawo.

Inhuman-a-Walang awa; walang habag; mabagsik; masuñgit; hindi tawo.

Inhumanity-n-Kabagsikan; kawalan ñg awa ó habag; kalupitan; kasuñgitan.

Inimical-a-Galit; malaban.

Inimitable-a-Hindi magagagad.

Iniquitous-a-Masama; makasalanan.

Iniquity-n-Kasamaan; gawang masama; kasalanan.

Initial-a-Unang; primero; walang pinangalinĝan.

Initial-n-Mañga letra ñg ñgalan.

Initiate-v-Magmula; magsimula; mulain.

Initiation-n-Pamumula; pamula.

Initiative-a-Naunkol sa primero.

Initiative-n-Pamulaan; pinagbuhatan.

Inject-v-Ihagis sa loob; ipasok.

Injection-n-Pagpasok.

Injudicious-a-Pabaya, bigla; hindi mabait.

Injunction-n-Utos.

Injure-v-Bugbugin; pahamakin; saktan; sirain; hamakin.

Injurious-a-Makasisira; masama.

Injury-n-Kasamaan; kasiraan; sakit.

Injustice-n-Kalapastañganan; kasiraan; kamalian; kawalan ñg justicia.

Ink-n-Tinta.

Ink-v-Pahiran nang tinta; lagyan nang tinta.

Ink stand-n-Lalagyan ñg tinta.

Inky-a-May tinta.

Inland-a-Malayo sa dagat.

Inland-n-Lupang malayo sa dagat.

Inlay-v-Maging bote.

Inlet-n-Daan sa pagpasok.

Inly-a-Loob.

Inly-adv. Sa loob.

Inmate-n-Ang tumitira sa isang bahay.

Inmost-a-Kaloob looban; kaibuturan.

Inn-n-Bahay na tinutuluyan; tuluyan.

Innate-a-Natural dati; talaga.

Inner-a-Sa loob; loob.

Inner most-a-Kaloob looban;kai buturan.

Innocence-n-Laya; kawalan ñg sala.

Innocent-a-Walang kasalanan; wagas; may puri.

Innocent-n-Ang tawong walang kasalanan; ang tawong may puri.

Innovate-v-Baguhin ang kaugalian.

Innoxious-a-May puri; malinis.

Innumerable-a-Di mabibilang.

Inoderous-a-Walang amoy.

Inoffensive-a-Tahimik; mabait; maamo.

Inofficial-*a*-Hindı oficial
Inoperative *a*-Mabagal
Inopportune-*a*-Wala sa sa panahon; dı bagay
Inordınate-*a* Lubha; lampas, malubha
Inorganıc-*a*-Walang buhay
Inquest *n*-Pagunsısa
Inquietude-*n*-Kaguluhan
Inquıre *v*-Umusıg, magtanong, tanungın, usisaın, siyasatın.
Inquıı y-*n*-Tanong, pagunsısa; sıyasat
Inquisition *n* Sıyasat, kadıwaraan; sınop
Inquisitive-*a*-Madıwaı̃a, masinop
Inquisitor-*n*-Ang nagtatanong
Inquisitorial-*a*-Madıwarang totoo.
Inroad-*n*-Pagpasok nğ sundalo
Insane *a*-Ulol; sıra ang ulo.
Insanıty-*n*-Kasiraan nğ ısıp.
Insatiable *a*-Dı mabubusog
Insatiety-*n*-Kalagayan na hindı mabubusog.
Inscrıbe-*v*-Isulat.
Inscription-*n*-Sulat
Inscrutable-*a*-Dı mahırap; hindi mahalata; dı matanto.
Insect-*n*-Hanıp
Insecure-*a*-Mahina, hindı matıbay.
Insecurıty-*n*-Kahınaan, kakulangan nğ tıbay.
Insensate-*a*-Walang daındam, tungak; mapurol ang isıp, walang dıwa
Insensıble *a*-Walang damdam, walang pakıramdam, walang dıwa
Inseparable-*a*-Dı makahıhıwalay
Insert-*v*-Ipasok
Insertion-*n*-Pagpasok
Inside-*adv* -Sa loob
Inside-*n*-Loob.
Insıduons-*a*-Matalas, tuso.
Insıght-*n* Tinğin sa loob, tarok nğ ısıp
Insıgnia-*n*-Tanda.
Insignificant-*a* Walang halaga
Insıncere-*a*-Lılo; taksil; suitık, hındı tapat ang loob
Insıncerıty-*n* Kahıluhan, kataksılan, kasuitikan
Insınuate-*v*-Magbıntang, magparatang
Insınuation-*n*-Bintang, paratang
Insipid-*a*-Walang lasa, matabang
Insıpidity *n*-Kakulangan nğ lasa.
Insıst-*v*-Pılıtın, pumılıt
Insnare-*v*-Hıbuin, dayain .
Insobrıety-*n* Kalasıngan
Insulate *v*-Ibılad; bıların.
Insolence *n*-Kalapastanğanan, tampalasan, panğahas; kapanğahasan; paslang; kawalan nğ galang
Insolent-*a*-Walang hiya, tampalasan, walang galang; talipandas; buhong.

Insoluble-*a*-Hındı matutunaw, di masaysay
Insolvency-*n*-Kalagayan na hindı makakabayad ang utang
Insolvent-*a*-Walang ıkababayad
In-so-much-*adı* -Dahılan dıto.
Inspect-*v*-Sıyasatın, usısaın, magmasıd, magınasdan, lumkalın
Inspection-*n* Pagsısıyasat, pagmasıd, pagunsisa.
Inspire-*v*-Umudyok, uralıan, damahin
Inspıration-*n*-Udyok, sumpong, ısıp
Inspırıt-*v*-Buhayın
Instable *a* Hındı matıbay, mahina
Install-*v*-Paupuan, ilagay sa katungkulan.
Instance-*n*-Halımbawa, hıraraan
Instance-*ı*-Maghalımbawa.
Instant-*n* Dalı, kısap mata.
Instant-*a*-Tambıng
Instantaneous-*a*-Agad, madalı, tambıng.
Instantly-*adv* -Pagkaraka, pagdaka, tambıng, nğayon dın.
Instate-*v*-Ilagay sa katungkulan.
Instead-*adv* Sa lugar nğ
Instep-*n*-Bubong nğ paa.
Instıgate-*v*-Sulsulan; udyukan; ısulong; ıudyok
Instigation-*n*-Sulsol, udyok.
Instıll-*v*-Isalin.
Instınct-*n*-Kılos na bıgla
Institute *v* Magtayo, itatag, lumalang
Instıtute-*n*-Instıtuto
Institution-*n*-Pag tatatag; pag tatayo
Instruct-*v*-Magtuıo; turnan; akayın
Instructor-*n*-Ang nagtuturo, maestro.
Instructress-*n*-Ang nag tuturo maestra.
Instruction-*n*-Pagtuturo.
Instrument-*n*-Kasangkapan, ınstrumento
Insubordınate-*v*-Lumaban, sumuay.
Insubordınation-*n*-Pagsuay; pag laban.
Insufferable-*a*-Hindi matıtıs
Insufficiency-*n*-Kakapusan kakulangan
Insufficient-*a* Kapos; kulang, di husto, dı sapat-
Insular-*a* Insular.
Insult-*v*-Lampastanğanın, murahın, laıtın, hıyaın; lunait, alımurahin; páslangın, magmura
Insult-*n*-Paslang, laıt, kalaıtan, alimuıa, sıphayo, kaalımurahan
Insuperable *a*-Dı madaıg.
Insupportable-*a*-Dı mıkatitıis.
Insurance-*n*-Katıbayan, sıguro.
Insure-*v*-Tıbayın; gawın ang katıbayan
Insurgent-*a* Naunkol sa ınsurecto ó sa taga labas
Insurgent-*n*-Ang lumalaban sa gobierno.

Insurmountable-a-Di matatalonin

Insurrection-n-Pag aalsa laban sa Gobierno

Intact-a-Buo; lubos

Intangible-a-Di maraindamin.

Integer n-Número

Integral-a-Walang kulang, buo, lubos.

Integral-n-Bilang, numero

Integrate v-Buoin, bilugin

Integrity n-Kabuoan, katibayan; katapatan ng loob

Intellect-n-Karunungan, bait, dunong.

Intellectual-a-Marunong, mabait, matalino; matalas.

Intelligence-n-Karunungan bait; dunong. kabaitan pangintindi

Intelligent-a-Marunong; mabait, matalas; matalino, may dunong

Intelligible-a-Madaling matalastas

Intemperance-n-Kalasingan

Intemperate-a-Mapag lasing, hilon go

Intend-v-Bantain, akalain, isipin

Intendant-n-Superintendente, puno

Intense-a-Masinsin; mabagsik, pormal, labis, lubha; matalas

Intent-n-Banta, ang inisip, ó makala.

Intention-n-Isip; akala, banta

Intentional a-Sinadya, tinalaga.

Inter-v-Ilibing.

Intercalation-n-Pakli, sabat.

Intercede-v-Mamagitan, ipakiusap, mamanhik

Intercept-v-Harangin; abalahin

Interception-n-Pagharang abala.

Intercession-n-Pamamagitan.

Intercessor-n-Taga mamagitan, pintakasi

Interchange-v-Magpalitan.

Interchange-n-Palitan

Interchangeable-a-Maipapalit

Intercourse-n-Kasulatan, sahtaan, salita

Interclude-v-Harangin, abalahin

Interdict-v-Ipagbawal; magbawal

Interdiction-n-Pagbawal.

Interest-n-Tubô, imbot, patubo, pakinabang, interes

Interest-v-Maimbot, magkaroon ng interes

Interested a-May interes

Interesting-a-Malibang, maalıw.

Interfere-v-Umabala, makialam, manghimasok; sabarin.

Interference-n-Abala; pakialam.

Interim-n-Interino, pagkasamantala.

Interior-n-Loob.

Interior-a-Na sa loob, loob

Interject-v-Ipasok, ipagitna, isalit.

Interjection-n-Pagpasok; pagsalit.

Interlace-v-Idugtong, ilapat, tahan

Interlard v Ihalo, ilahok

Interline-v Sumulat, sa pagitan nang guhit

Interlineation-n-Pagsulat sa pagitan ng mga guhit

Interlocution-n-Salitaan.

Interlocutor-n-Ang nagsasalita.

Interlope-v-Magtinda na walang licencia, makialam.

Interloper-n-Ang nakikialam.

Interlude-n-Puang.

Intermarry v-Maging kamaganak dahil sa kasal

Intermeddle-v-Makialam

Intermediate a Na sa pagitan.

Intermediary-a Nasa pagitan.

Interment-n-Paglibing.

Interminable-a-Walang hanga, walang katapusan.

Intermingle-v-Lumahok, ihalo.

Intermission-n-Likat, puang, pagpapanga

Intermit-v-Lumikat, magpahinga.

Intermitent-a-Tatahan at muling babalik

Intermix-v-Ilahok, ihalo

Internal-a-Na sa loob, loob

International-a-Alam nang lahat nang nacion.

Interpose-v-Mamanhik; mamagitan; bumala; ipagitna

Interposition-n-Pagpapagitna, pamamagitan.

Interpret-v-Ihulog; magsaysay, salaysayin.

Interpretation-n-Kahulugan, kasaysayan; salaysay

Interrogate-v-Itanong, magtanong.

Interrogation-n-Pagtatanong, tanong

Interrogative a-Nauukol, sa tanong

Interrogatory-n-Tanong

Interrupt-v-Umabala; sabarin; makialam, isabat, abalahin

Interruption-n-Abala, sabat, likat.

Intersect-v-Magkrus.

Intersection-n-Krus

Intersperse v-Ihalo, ikalat.

Interstice-n-Puang, likat

Interval-n Puang; pagitan.

Intervene-v-Mamagitan, makiusap, ipagitna.

Intervention n-Pamamagitan, pakiusap

Interview-n-Usap, pagtatanungan, salitaan

Interview-v-Magtanong, magusap.

Interweave-v-Lumahok; humalo

Intestate a-Walang testamento.

Intestine-n-Bituka, isaw
Intestinal-a-Nauukol sa bituka.
Intimate-a-Tapat na loob, taos ó taimtim ang loob.
Intimate-ι-Ipahalata; magsabi.
Intimation-n Pagpahalata, sabi
Intimidate-v-Takutin, gulatin
Intimidation-n-Takot.
Into-prep -Sa loob, sa
Intolerable-a-Di matitiis, di dapat tiisin .
Intolerance-n-Kabagsikan, kawalan ng pagtitiis
Intolerant-a Di makatitiis
Intomb-v-Ilibing
Intone v-Magdalit; magawit
Intoxicate-v-Maglasing, maglilo
Intoxication-n-Paglalasing, kalasingan.
Intractable-v Di masusunurin, masungit, mabagsik
Intransitive-a-Sarili.
Intrench-v-Gumawa ang trinchera.
Intrenchment-n-Trinchera
Intrepid-a-Matapang, mangahas; bayani, walang takot; walang kaba
Intrepidity-n-Tapang, katapatapangan; pagkabayani, kawalan ng takot.
Intricate-a-Pasuotsuot, gulo, malabo, mahirap gawin.
Intrigue n Salitaan na masama
Intrigue-ι Magsalitaan ng palihim.
Intrinsic-a Sa loob; totoo, kailangan.
Intruduce-v-Ipakilala, magpakilala
Introduction n-Pagpapakilala.
Intrude v-Makialam, abalahin, pumasok
Intrusion-n-Pakialam, abala.
Intrusive-a-Makikialaman
Intrust-v-lalok, ipagkatiwala.
Intuition-n-Katotohanan, isip na bigla.
Intwine-v Pilipitin, pumilipit
Ihundate ι-Umapaw, apawin; bumaha
Inundation-n-Baha, pagbaha; pagapaw.
Inure ι-Mamihasa, magawai, inamalagi.
Inutility-n-Kawalan ng kabuluhan
Invade-ι-Lumapit, at lumaban; pumasok sa ibang lupa at maglabanan.
Invalid-a-Walang kabuluhan, hindi umayon sa utos
Invalid-n-Tawong may sakit, ang may sakit.
Invalidate v-Pawalan ang kabuluhan.
Invaluable-a-Lubhang mahalaga.
Invariable-a-Hindi mababago
Invasion-n-Pagpasok ng sundalo sa ibang lupa
Invective a Maalipustain, malait
Invective-n-Alipusta, salitang malligat.
Inveigle v-Tuksuhin; udyukan.

Invent-ι-Tuklasin, umisip, isipin, kumatha, lalangin
Invention-n-Ang kinatha ó nilalang
Inventor-n-Ang kumatha ó lumalang
Inventory-n-Listahan ng manga bagay.
Inverse-a-Kalaban iba
Inversion n-Pagpatuad; pagkaiba.
Invert-ι-Ipatuad, ibalik
Invertebrate-a-Walang gulugod
Invertebrate n-Hayop na walang gulugod
Invest-ι-Lumaban, bumangay, hamonin
Investment-n-Paglalagay ng kuarta sa comercio.
Investigate-ι-Siyasatin, usisain
Investigation-n-Paguusisa; siyasat.
Inveterate-a-Matibay, matigas ang ulo, sowail
Invigorate-ι Buhayin, dahasin.
Invigoration-n-Paglalakas.
Invincible a Hindi masupil, di susuko
Inviolable-a-Malualhati
Inviolate a-Di nasira, buo pa; malinis
Invisible-a-Di makakita
Invite-v-Anyayahin, maganyaya
Invitation-n-Anyaya; hikayat
Invocate-n Manalangin; tumawag
Invocation-n Panalangin, tawag.
Invoice-v-Listahin ang manga bagay sa isang lugar ó sa isang tindahan
Invoice-n-Listahan ng manga bagay sa isang lugar ó tindahan
Invoke-v-Manalangin, tawagin.
Involuntary a-Wala sa loob
Involution-n-Pagtiklop, kaguluhan.
Involve ι-Balutin; itiklop.
Invulnerable a-Di masasaktan.
Inward-a Na sa loob
Inward-adv.-Sa gawing loob
Iracible-a-Magagalitin, mapootin
Irate a Galit, masama ang loob
Ire-n Galit; tanim saloob
Ireful-a Galit, magagalitin.
Iris-n-Bahag hari.
Irish-a-Nauukol sa Irlandes.
Irish-n-Tawong Irlandes
Irk v-Pumagod inuumot.
Irksome-a-Mayamutin
Iron n-Bakal.
Iron v Mamirinsa, bakalin
Ironics-ι onical-a-Masaklap.
Irony-n-Kasaklapan, tuyo
Irradiance-n Ningning; kainaman.
Irradiate-v Lumiwanag liwanagan
Irrational-a-Di ayon sa katowiran.
Irreconcilable-a-Hindi bubuti.
Irrecoverable-a Di makababawi.
Irredeemable-a-Hindi makababawi.
Irreducible-a Di babawasan,
Irrefutable-a-Di magkakaila

Irregular-a-Hindi karaniwan; iba,t, iba, di matowid
Irrelative a-Walang interes
Irrelevant-a Di bagay ó di akma
Irreligion n-Kakulangan nğ religion
Irreligious-a-Banday; walang religion.
Irremediable-a-Di magagaling, sira.
Irreparable-a Hindi magagaling, dimaiuuli
Irrepressible a-Di masupil
Irreproachable a-Di mapipintasin, walang pintas.
Irresistible-a-Di makakalaban.
Irresolute a-Alangan, urong sulong, salawahan, hindi firme.
Irrespective-a Walang pimpili.
Irresponsible-a-Walang isasagot; di kailangan managot.
Irretrievable-a-Di makakabawi.
Irreverence-n-Kakulangan nğ galang.
Irreverent-a-Walang galang
Irrevocable-a-Di mababago
Irrigate-v-Patubigin.
Irrigation-n-Pagpapatubig
Irritability-n-Yamot, poot.
Irritable-a-Mayamutin, mapootin; mahapdi.

Irritate-v-Yamutin; bagbagin; humapdi
Irritation-n Yamot; hapdi, poot.
Irruption-n-Butlig, pagputok
Is-i-Ay; may; mag
Island n-Pulo.
Isle-n-Pulo
Isolate-v-Ilayo sa iba; ibukod.
Isrealite-n Taga Israel
Issue-v-Ikalat; magmula, mangaling sa magbuhat
Issue n-Pangyayari; paglabas.
It pro -Siya, iyon, iyan, ito, ire
Italian-a Italiano
Italian-n Taga Italia
Italic a-Nauukol sa Italia
Itch v-Humapdi, kumirot, kumire.
Itch n Galis.
Item-n-Bagay.
Itemize-v Isulat nğ isaisa
Iterate-v-Uhtin, gawing muli
Iteration n-Pagulit.
Itinerant a-Paglakadlakad
Itinerant n-Tawong mapaglakad
Itinerate-v-Lumakad at magdiscurso.
Itself-pro -Iyondin; siyarin.
Ivory n-Marfil.
Ivy-n-Lipay.

J

Jabber n-Salita na walang kabuluhan.
Jabber-v-Magsalita nğ walangkabuluhan.
Jack-n-Bansag nğ nğalan ni Juan, Magdaragat, bandera; sota nğ baraha
Jackanapes-n-Ungo, tawong mahkot at hambog.
Jackass-n Jumento, tawong ulol
Jacket-n Baiong maikli
Jackknife n-Laseta
Jacobin n-Fraile Dominico
Jaculate-v-Itulag
Jade n Kabayong masama, babaying masungit.
Jade-v-Pumagal, pumagod
Jag-n-Bingaw; tinik; piraso.
Jagged-a-Magaspang
Jaguar n-Tigre Americano
Jail-n-Bilango; kalabuso
Jailer-n-Ang mamahala sa bilango
Jam n-Jelea.
Jam-v Ipitin, bugbogin, kumapal ang tawo
Jamb-n-Gilid nğ pinto.
Jangle v-Kumalasing; makipagtalo
Jangle-n Kalasing, pagtatalo
Janitor-n-Katiwala nğ bahay encargado, ang namamahala sa isang bahay.

Janty a Magaan; makinis, mainam
January-n-Enero
Japan n-Japon, pintang itim
Japan v-Pintahin nğ itim
Japanese-a-Nauukol sa Japon.
Japanese-n-Taga Japon, wika nğ Japon
Jar n-Jaro, saro
Jargon-n Salitang utal ó di maintindihan.
Jargon-n-Magsalita nğ hindi maliwanag.
Jaunt-v Magpasial.
Jaunt n-Pasial
Jaunty-a-Makinis, magaan, mainam
Javelin-n-Tulag; sibat
Jaw-n-Panğa
Jawbone-n-Sihang, panğa.
Jay-n-Tawong bukid
Jealous a Siloso, manğambahin, maiingitin
Jealousy-n-Panğimbubo; ingit; hinala, panğamba, alapaap nğ loob.
Jean-n-Kayong magaspang, gris
Jeer-v-Ujamin, tuksuhin, hiyawin
Jeer-n-Tukso, uyam; hiyaw.
Jehovah-n-Dios, bathala.
Jelly-n Jelea.

33 -.

Jeopardize-v-Ilagay sa panğanib.
Jeopardy-n-Panğanib
Jerk-v-Batakın, ihagis na pabıgla.
Jerk-n-Batak
Jerky-a-Dı panay.
Jest-n-Bıro; laro
Jest-v-Birum, magbıro
Jesuit n-Jesuita.
Jesuitic-a-Nauukol sa Jesuita.
Jet-n-Bukal
Jet-ı-Lumabas nğ pabigla
Jetty-n-Muella.
Jetty-a-Maıtim; itım.
Jew-n-Judıo
Jewel-n-Sangkap; brillante
Jeweler-n-Platero.
Jewish-a-Nauukol sa Judío
Jıb-ı-Umurong
Jibe v-Ibahın ang tuntunğan nğ sasakyan, magkasundo
Jıffy-n-Sangdalı.
Jıggle-ı-Galawin, gumalaw; kalogın.
Jilt-n-Babayıng salawahan ang loob
Jilt-v-Dayaın ó hıbuın sa pag ibıg.
Jıngle-v-Kumalasing, kumalog.
Jıngle-n-Kalasing, kalog
Job-n-Trabajo, gawa.
Jockey-v-Hıbuın, dayaın.
Jocose-a-Masaya; palabıro.
Jocoseness Jocosity-n-Kasayahan, bıro, kahbanğan
Jocular-a-Masaya; palabıro.
Jocularity-n-Kasayahan, kaligayahan, pag tatawa; kalibanğan, katuwaan.
Jog-ı-Sumagsag
Jog-n-Sagsag
Joggle v Kumalog, kalugin
Join-v-Idugtong, ıkama; ılangkap. ılapat, ısama, ıhalo,̄ ıgawgaw, pumısan
Joint-n-Hıwas, bias; samb; bukongbukong, kasukasukuan
Joint a Kasama.
Joint-v-Hıwasin, bıasın
Jointly-adr-Samasama, sabay sabay.
Joıst-n-Solero
Joke-n Biro aglahı, badya.
Joke-v-Magbıro, biroın; magbadya.
Jollıfıcatıon-n-Pagsasaya, kasayahan
Jollıty-Jollıness-n-Kasayahan, kaligayahan.
Jolly-a-Masaya, malgaya
Jolt-v-Umumpog; tumulak, umuntog.
Jolt-n Umpog, untog, tulak.
Jostle-v-Magumpog, bumanga; umuntog
Jostle-n-Umpog, untog; banga.
Jot-n-Pirasong munti, punto
Jot-v-Sumulat sa tandaan; isulat sa tandaan.
Jounce-v-Galaw in; umumpog

Jounce-n-Galaw; untog; umpog.
Journal n-Pahayagan, dahon.
Journey-n Lakad, vıaje,
Journey-v-Mag vıaje; lumakad, mag lakad
Journeyman-n-Trabajador, ang nag papaupa sa maghapon
Jovial-a-Masaya, malugod, maligaya, maamo ang loob
Jovıalıty-Jovıalness-n Kasayahan; kaligayahan
Jowl-n-Panğa, pısnğı, sıhang.
Joy-n-Kasayahan; kaligayahan, tuwa, kahbanğan; katuwaan
Joy-ı-Sumaya, malıgaya
Joyous Joyful-a-Masaya, natutnwa; mahbang, mapagpatawa, mapagsiste.
Joyless-a-Walang saya ó kasayahan; walang tuwa.
Joyfulness n-Kasayahan, kalıgayahan
Jubilant-a-Masaya; maligaya.
Jubılation-n-Kasayahan.
Jubılee-n-Kapistahan
Judaic-a-Nauukol sa mğa Judıo.
Judaism-n-Pananampalataya nğ manğa Judio.
Judge-n-Hukom, juez
Judge v-Humatol, hatulan.
Judgment-n-Hatol, pasıya, tuto, pag hatol; taros; bait, ısıp, akala
Jndicatıve-a-May kapangyarıng humatol
Judicial-a-Nauukol sa hukom
Judıcıary a-Nauukol sa hukom.
Judıcıous-a-Mabait; mahinhin; matalino, tahımık.
Jug-n Lalagyan, nğ manğa bagay na lusaw.
Juggle-v-Magsalamangka.
Juggle-n-Salamangka
Jugglery-n Pagsasalamangka.
Jugular-a-Nauukol sa lıg ó lalamunan
Juice-n Katas.
Juiceless n-Walang katas
Juicy-a-Makatas.
July-n-Julıo
Jumble-v-Haluin; guluhın
Jumble-n-Halo, kaguluhan
Jump-ı-Lumuudag, lumukso, magtalon, tumalon, laktawin.
Jump-n-Lukso, lundag, talon; laktaw.
Junctıon-n-Sanıb.
Juncture-n-Sanıb, dugtong
June-n-Junıo.
Jungle-n-Lasaw
Junior-a-Bata pa, bınata.
Juniorıty-n-Pagkabata.
Junk n-Manğa bagay na walang kabuluhan.

Junket-*n*-Mamon; matamis.
Junket-*v*-Magpiging.
Junta-*n*-Junta, katipunan, lupong
Junto-*n*-Katipunan
Juridic-Juridical-*a* Nauukol sa hucom.
Jurisdiction-*n*-Kapangyarihan; lupang
sinukuban; lupang sinakupan.
Jury *a*-Interino.
Just-*a*-Tapat, matowid; ayon sa kato-
wiran, batibot; husto; sukat.
Just-*adv.*-Sukat, husto.

Justice-*n*-Katowiran, katampatan, kasu-
katan; kahustuhan.
Justifiable-*a*-Dapat patawari; may ka-
towiran.
Justification-*n*-Katowiran.
Justify-*t*-Magbigay ng̃ katowiran.
Jut-*v*-Luminbutod; lumiko.
Jut-*n*-Liko
Juvenile-*a*-Binata.
Juvenile-*n* Bagong tawo, binata.
Juvenility-*n*-Pagkabata.

K

Kail *n* Repolio.
Kale-*n*-Repolio
Katydid-*n*-tipaklong.
Keel-*n*-Puit ng̃ sasakyan.
Keen-*a*-Matalas: matalino, tuso.
Keep-*v*-Alagaan, bantayin, ikalong,
ing̃atin
Keeping-*n*-Pagaalaga; pagiñgat
Keepsake-*n*-Kaloob, bigay; biyaya.
Keep secret-*v*-Huag sabihin.
Keg-*n*-Bariles na munti,
Ken *n*-Malaman, kilalanin; kumilala,
karunung̃an; tanawan, pagkikilala
Kennel-*n*-kubo ng̃ aso,
Kept-*v. imp & p p* Ining̃at; binantay.
Kerchief-*n*-Alampay, birang.
Kernel-*n*-Butil.
Kerosene-*n*-Gas.
Ketchup *n*-Katsup, sarsa.
Kettle *n* Kawali; kawa.
Kettle drum-*n*-Kaja.
Key-*n*-Susi.
Key-*v*-Susiin; isusi.
Key hole-*n*-Butas ng̃ susian.
Key stone-*n*-Batong pansara ng̃ arko.
Kick-*n*-Sipa, sikad
Kick-*v*-Isikad, sumikad, sipain.
Kid-*n*-Bata, tupang munti, kambing na
munti.
Kidnap-*v*-Bihagin, bumihag
Kidney *n*-Bato ng̃ katawan
Kill-*v*-Pumatay, patayin.
Killing-*n*-Patawan.
Kiln-*n*-Hurno.
Kilo Kilogram-*n*-Kilogramo; kilo
Kin *n*-Kamaganak
Kind-*n* Clase, lahi
Kind *n*-Mabuti ang loob, mabuti, ma-
pagpitagan
Kindergarten-*n*-Escuela nang̃ mg̃a ba-
ta
Kindle-*v*-Sunugin; sindihan; magsindi
Kindness-*n*-Kabutihan ng̃ loob, kabu-
tihan, pitagan; hinhin.

Kindred-*n*-Hinlog, mang̃a kamaganak;
kamaganakan
Kindred-*a*-Magkamaganak.
Kine-*n*-Baka.
King-*n*-Hari
Kingdom-*n*-Kaharian
Kingfisher-*n*-Lumbas.
Kingly-*a*-Parang hari
Kink-*n*-Kunot.
Kink-*v*-Kumunot
Kinky-*a*-Kumunot, makulot
Kinsfolk-*n*-Mang̃a kamaganak.
Kinsman-*n*-Kamaganak na lalaki
Kins woman-*n* Kamaganak na babayi
Kip-*n*-Katad ng̃ bulo.
Kirk-*n*-Sambahan.
Kirmess-*n*-Piging at pista.
Kismet *n*-Kapalaran
Kiss-*n*-Halik, hagkan.
Kiss-*v*-Humalik; halikin; humagkan.
Kit-*n*-Pusang munti, kuting.
Kitchen-*n* Kosina.
Kite-*n*-Buladol.
Kitten-*n*-Kuting
Knack-*n*-Tuto, karunung̃an, bait.
Knap-*n*-Dulo, dung̃ot
Knarl-*n*-Mata ng̃ kahoy.
Knave-*n*-Tawong masama; tawong ha-
mak ó mahalay.
Knavery-*n*-Gawang masama ó mahalay.
Knavish-*a*-Mahalay, masama
Knead-*v* Masahin, imaginasa.
Kneading-*n*-Pagmamasa.
Knee-*n*-Tuhod.
Knee cap-*n*-Bayugo.
Kneel-*v*-Lumuhod.
Knell-*n*-Tugtog ng̃ kampana.
Knelt-*v. imp & p p* -Nakaluhod, lumuhod.
Knew-*v imp* -Nalaman, kinilala
Knickerbockers-*n*-Salawal na putot.
Knickknack-*n*-Bagay na walang halaga.
Knife-*n*-Laseta, batavia.
Knife-*v*-Hiwain ng̃ laseta, saksakin;
Knit-*v*-Isama; gumanchillo.

Knitting-n-Paggaganchillo.
Knives-n-Mğa laseta ó batavia.
Knob n-Buhol, tanğan nğ pinto.
Knock-n-Tugtog, tuktok, bungo; dagok, katog
Knock-v-Tumuktok, bumungo, dagukan; kumatog
Knoll n-Tugatog, pugpog, gulod.
Knot-n-Buhol, tali, mulmol, talibugso
Knot-v-Buhulin, magbuhol, humulmol.
Knotted-a-Mabuhol
Knotty-a-Mabuhol.

Know-n-Malaman, kilalanin; matutuhan marawasan
Knowing a-Bihasa; marunong, matala tuso, matalino
Knowledge-n-Karununğan, dunong, t to, bait.
Knuckle-n Buko nğ kamay.
Knuckle-v-Sumuko
Knurly-a Magaspang
Kraal n Nayon; kulunğan nğ elepai te.
Kreosote-n-Kreosote

La n-La
Label-n-Tanda.
Label-v-Ilagay ang tanda.
Labial-a-Nauukol sa labi.
Labial-n-Salita nğ labi.
Labor-n-Trabajo, gawa
Labor-v-Magtrabajo, gumawa; pumagal
Laborer-n-Ang nagtatrabajo, ang gumagawa.
Laborious-a-Mahirap; matrabajo.
Laboratory-n-Labatorio
Labyrinth-n-Lugar nğ maraming landas.
Lace-n Puntas; panali
Lace-a-Tahan, ilagay ang puntas.
Lacerate-v Hiwain, pilasin, wahiin
Laceration-n-Paghiwa; pagwahi, hiwa; pilas.
Lache-n-Katamaran
Lachrymal-a-Nauukol sa luha.
Lachrymose-a-Maluha.
Lack-v-Kumulang.
Lack-n-Kakulanğan, kulang kakapusan, pagkulang.
Lacking n-Pagkulang.
Lacker-n-Varnis.
Lackey-n Ayudante.
Laconic-a-Maulol, loco.
Lacquer-n-Varnis.
Lacquer-v-Palitran nğ varnis, varnisin. magvarnis.
Lacrymal a-Nauukol sa luha.
Lactation-n Pagpasuso
Lacteal-a-Nauukol sa gatas
Lactean-Lacteons-a-Magatas.
Lactescent-a-Magatas
Lad-n-Batang lalaki.
Ladder n-Hagdanan
Lade-v-Ipasan, ilulan.
Lading-n Paglulan, pagpasan.
Ladle n-Sandak.
Ladle-v-Sandukin; magsandok.
Lady n Bmbini, babaying ginoo.

Lady like-a-Bimbini, mabait, mahi na ugali.
Lady love-n-Ang nililigawan, ang pin ngangasawa
Lady ship-n-Bimbini
Lag-a-Huling; katapusan
Lag-v-Magpabaya.
Laggard-n-Tawong tamad ó pabaya
Laggard-a-Tamad, mabagal, marahar huli
Lagoon n-Dagat dagatan.
Laid-v imp & p p-Nilagay; nakalaga
Lain-v p p-Nilagay; nakalagay.
Lair-n-Hihigan nğ hayop sa damo.
Lake n-Dagat dagatan.
Lamb n-Tupang munti
Lambkin-n-Tupang manti.
Lambent-a-Makintab, makisap
Lame-a-Pilay; mapilay, hiwid, hingko
Lame v Pilayin, pumilay, humingko hiwirin.
Lameness n-Kapilayan, pagkapilay.
Lament-v-Mananğis; dumaing, mana hoy, tumanğis.
Lament-n-Tanğis; daing; panaghoy, p nambitan.
Lamentable a-Mahabag, kaawaan
Lamentation n Daing, hibik, panamb tan, panaghoy.
Lamp-n-Ilawan, lampara; ilaw.
Lamp black-n-Uling.
Lamper eel-n-Palos.
Lampoon n-Uyam
Lance n Tulag, sibat.
Lance v-Sibatin, tulagin
Lancet-n-Lasetang panagra.
Lanch v Itulag, salapanğin
Land-n-Lupa.
Land v-Ilagay sa pangpang, isadsad
Landed a May maraming lupa.
Landing n Doonğan
Landlord n Ang may ari nğ hotel bahay panuluyan (lalaki).

League-v-Magtipan; magtipon; ilakip.
Leak-n Tulo; talas
Land lady-n-Ang may ari ñg hotel ó bahay panuluyan (babayi).
Land mark-n Muson.
Lane n-Daan
Language-n Wika, salita.
Languid-a-Mahina; malata, payat.
Languidness n Latá, kahinaan, kapayatan.
Languish-i-Lumata, humina pumayat.
Larguor-n-Latá, kapayatan, kahinaan.
Lank a-Payat, mataas
Lantern-n-Parol, laterna.
Lap-n-Kandungan, sinapupunan.
Lap-v-Dilain.
Lapel-n-Tiklop ng damit.
Lapse-i-Puang. likat; paglipas.
Lapse-v Lumikat, lumipas.
Lar board-n-Ang gawing kaliwa nang sasakyan
Larcency-n-Pagumit, pagnakaw
Lard-v Mantika
Lard-i-Mantikahin.
Larder-n-Banguera
Large a Malaki, dakila
Largeness-n-Laki, kalakihan
Lariat-n Silo ñg lubid.
Lark-n-Batobato, kabiruan.
Lark-v-Magbiro.
Larva-Larvea-n-Uod
Larnyx-n-Lalamunan.
Lash n-Latigo, pilikmata
Lash-v-Talian
Lass n Batang babayi.
Lassitude-n-Kahinaan,kapaguran;pagod.
Lasso n-Silo.
Lasso-v-Siluin
Last-a-Huling, kahulihulihan, katapusan.
Last v-Tumigas, tumagal.
Lasting-n-Matibay; di masisira; matagal.
Last-n-Lalan
Lastly adv.-Hulinghuli, sa kahulihuhan
Latch n-Kandaro.
Latch-v-Ikandaro
Latchet-n-Tali ñg sapatos.
Late-a-Bago; huling.
Late-adv -Tanghali, gabi na
Lately-adv.-Ñgayon lamang.
Latency-n-Kalabuan
Latent-a-Di makakita, malabo, tago.
Later-a-Mayamaya pa, huli pa
Latest-a Kabulihulihan.
Lather-n-Bula ñg sabon
Lather-v Magpahid ñg sabon
Latin-n-Latin
Latin-a-Nauukol sa latin.
Latitude-n-Layo sa hilagaan ó sa timugan.

Latter-a-Huli.
Laterly-adv.-Sa kahulihan.
Laud v-Purihin, magdiwang
Laud-n-Pagpuri; puri, lualhati
Laudable-a-Dapat purihin.
Laudation-n-Pagpuri
Laudatory-a-Dapat purihin.
Laugh-n-Tawa
Laugh-v-Tumawa
Laughable-a-Matatawanin; makatatawa, mapagpatawa.
Laughing-n-Tawa.
Launch-n Lancha, vaporsito.
Launch-v-Dumapilas; magmula
Launder-v-Maglaba;
Launderer-n-Maglalaba; labandero.
Laundress-n-Labandera.
Laundry-n-Palabahan.
Lavatory-a-Nauukol sa paglalaba.
Lave-v-Hugasin; maligo
Lavatory-n-Hilamusan; lavador.
Lavender-n-Kulay purpura
Laver-n-Batia.
Lavish-a Sagana: labis, mapagmamasa; burara.
Lavish-v Itapon; mag sabog; mag burara.
Law-n-Utos, ley.
Lawful-a-Ayon sa utos ó ley.
Lawfulness-n-Pagkakaayon sa katowian
Lawless-a-Laban sa ley ó utos
Lawn-n-Bakuran.
Lawsuit-n-Usap, pagtatalo, pag usap.
Lawyer-n-Abogado.
Lax a-Pabaya, tamad
Laxity-Laxness-n-Katamaran; kapabayaan
Lay-v imp.-Hiniga, nahiga.
Lay-v-Ihiga, ilagay
Lay-n-Kanta; awit.
Layer-n-Suson.
Laziness-n-Katamaran, kapabayaan, ligalig, kakuparan
Lazy-a-Tamad, pabaya, alisaga; batugan, mabagal, ayaw magtrabajo.
Lea-n-Bukid na pastulan.
Leach-n-Linta
Lead-v-Akayin, umakay; tamuhin, unahan.
Lead-n-Unahan; pamumuno.
Lead-n-Tinga.
Leaden-a-Tinga; may halong tinga.
Leader-n-Pañgulo, puno
Leaf-n-Dahon.
Leaf-v Lumago ang dahon.
Leaflet-n-Munting dahon.
Leafy a-Madahon.
League-n-Layo ñg isang oras ñg lakad, kapisanan, katipunan, tipan.

Leak-v-Tumulo; tumalas
Leakage-n-Tulo,· pagtulo.
Leaky-a-Larot.
Lean-v-Ihapay; ipahalang, ihiling. ·
Lean-a-Payat.
Lean-n-Laman
Lean to-n-Pakpak; sibi
Leap v-Lumundag; lumukso.
Leap-n-Lundag; lukso.
Learn-n-Magaral; matuto
Learned-a-Marunong, matalas; matali-no,t, bihasa
Learner n-Ang nagaral.
Learning-n-Karununga, paham; dunong.
Lease v-Ipabuis; bumuis
Lease-n Kasulatan tungkol sa pagbuis.
Leash-n-Panali, suga, tatlo.
Least-a Kauntiuntian.
Leather-n-Katad
Leather a-Yari ng katad.
Leathery-a-Parang katad.
Leave-i-Maiwan; tirahin, magtira, biti-wan, ipahintulot, umalis, pahintulotin.
Leave-n-Pahintulot, kapahintulotan.
Leaven-n-Lavadura
Leaves-n-Manga dahon ng kahoy
Leavings-n-Ang tinitira, Pinagpilian
Lecture-n-Discurso, pangungusap.
Lecture-v-Magdiscurso; pangusapin.
Led-v. imp.-& p p -Inakay.
Ledge-n-Paris.
Lee-n-Latak ng alak.
Leesh-n-Linta.
Leer-i-Tuminğin ng pabastos.
Leer-n-Tinğin na bastos.
Leeward-adv -Sa gawi na may hanğin.
Left-v. imp. & p p -Iniwan, tinira, uma lis.
Left-a-Kaliwang.
Left-n-Kaliwa.
Left hand-n-Kamay na kaliwa.
Left-handed-a-Sanay ang kamay na kaliwa.
Leg-n-Hita
Legacy-n-Mana.
Legal-a-Matowid; ayon sa utos ng Gobierno
Legalize v-Ilagay sa Katowiran.
Legality-n-Katowiran.
Legate-n-Pintakasi.
Legatee-n-Ang tumatangap ng mana.
Legator n-Ang nagpamana
Legend-n-Awit, kuento
Legendary-a-Nauukol sa awit.
Lager de main-n Salamangka.
Legible-a-Makababasa.
Legion-n-Hukbo, bunton ng tawo.
Legislate-v-Maglagda gumawa ng utos.
Legislative-a-Nauukol sa paglalagda.
Legislation-n-Paglagda.

Legislature-n-Katipunan ng manğa mag lalagda.
Legitimacy-n-Katunayan.
Legitimate a-Tunay, totoo.
Leisure-n-Kalibanğan, lugar, panahon na walang gawa
Leisure-a-Walang gawa.
Leisurely-n-Dahandahan.
Lemon n-Limon; dayap
- Lemonade n-Limonada
Lend-v-Magpahiram, pahiramin.
Length-n-Haba.
Lengthen-v-Habaan, unatin, banatin, batakin.
Length ways-adv -Pahaba.
Length wise-adv.-Pahaba.
Lengthy-a-Mahaba.
Lemency-n-Awa habag.
Lenient a-Mahabag, maawain.
Lenity-n-Awa, habag
Lent-v. imp. & p. p -Ipinahiram, nagpa-hiram.
Lent-n-Kuaresma
Leonine-a-Parang leon.
Leopard-n-Leopardo.
Leper-n-Lepra
Leprosy-n-Sakit na lepra; san lazaro.
Leprous-a-May sakit na lepra; nauukol sa Lepra.
Less-a-Kulang, kapos, liban.
Less-adv -Kapos, bukod pa.
Lessen v-Umunti; kumulang; bumawas, bawasan
Lesser n-Ang munti.
Lesson-n-Leccion, pinagaralan
Lessor-n-Ang nagpapaupa ng bahay.
Lest-conj -Baka sakali.
Let-v-Ipahintulot, pumayag, maiwan abalahin.
Let n-Abala.
Lethargic-a-Nagaantok, palaantok.
Lethargy-n-Antok
Letter-n-Sulat, letra, titik.
Letter-i-Letrahin, titikan, isulat.
Lettuce n-Litsuga
Levant-a-Nakatayo; nakatindig.
Levant i -Umalis, lumayas.
Levee-n-Panharang ng tubig
Level-a-Patag, pantay.
Level v-Patagin; pumatag
Level-n-Kapatagani kapantayan.
Lever-v-Panghikuat, panghuit, panğis-pike
Levity n-Gaan.
Levy-n Buis.
Levy v-Ipabuis
Lewd-a-Malibog, hamak; mahalay.
Lewdness n-Kalibugan, kahamakan, ka halayau.
Lexical-a-Nauukol sa salita, ó 'lexion-

Lexicographer-*n*-Ang gumagawa nğ diccionario.

Lexicography-*n*-Paggagawa nğ diccionario.

Lexicon-*n*-Diccionario.

Liable-*a*-Mahilng; mahanğad

Liar *n*-Tawong mapagsinunğaling

Libel-*n*-Pagwiwika nğ katampalasanan.

Liberal-*a*-Magandang loob; mapagampon sakapwa

Liberal *n*-Liberal.

Liberality-*n*-Kagandahan nğ loob, kalakhan nğ puso

Liberate *v*-Pawalan, patawarin; timawain, palayain-

Liberation-*n*-Pagkawala; pagpatawad, tawad,

Liberty-*n* Kalayaan, timawa; pahintulot.

Lice-*n*-Manğa kuto.

License *n*-Licencia, tulot

License-*v*-Ipahintulutin, tulutin, ibigay nğ licencia.

Lick-*v*-Dilaan

Lick-*a*-Pagdidilaan.

Lid-*n*-Tungtong; talob; takip; panakip.

Lie-*v*-Magsinunğaling.

Lie-*n*-Kasinunğalinğan

Lief *adv*-Nakahiling.

Liege-*n*-Nauukol sa buis.

Liege *n*-Mayari ó encargado nğ lupang buisan

Lien-*n*-Fianza; katibayan.

Lieu-*n*-Lugal, lugar

Lieutenancy-*n*-Kalagayan tiniente.

Lieutenant-*n*-Tiniente.

Life-*n*-Buhay, kabuhayan.

Lifeless *a*-Walang buhay, patay; payat, mabagal

Life like-*a*-Parang may buhay

Lift-*v*-Itaas, buhatin; damputin, ibanğon

Lift-*n*-Tulong, ampon, pagbuhat

Ligament *n*-Anat, litid.

Ligature-*n*-Pamigkis

Light-*n*-Apoy; ilaw, liwanag; araw.

Light-*a*-Magaan; maliwanag, maliksi, mabilis.

Light-*v*-Sindihan, magsindi.

Lighten-*v*-Bawasan; gaaning; gumaan; luminaw, lumiwanag, kumidlat.

Lightening *n*-Pagpapagaang, pagpalinaw, paghliwanag

Lightning-*n*-Kidlat nğ lintik, lintik.

Light-headed-*a*-Hilo, magaan ang ulo

Light-headedness *n*-Kagaanan nğ ulo, pagkahilo

Light-hearted *a*-Masaya, magaan ang loob

Light-minded-*a*-Magulo ang isip.

Lightness-*n*-Gaan, kagaanan; kaliksihan

Lights-*n*-Baga.

Ligneous-*a*-Yari nğ kahoy; parang kahoy.

Lignite-*n* Uling.

Like-*a*-Magkapaiis, kawanki; kaparis.

Like-*adv*-Paris; nğa, rin

Like-*v*-Umibig, ibigin, gihwin, gumiliw, magustuhan; maibigan

Liking-*n*-Nais, pita; gusto; nasa.

Likely-*adv*-Marahil.

Liken-*v*-Iparis, tumulad; itulad

Likeness-*n*-Kaparisan, tinğin sa labas, lagay; pagkakawanki.

Likewise-*adv*-Gayondin, naman.

Lilac-*n*-Lila.

Limb-*n*-Sanğa; hita ó baraso.

Limber-*a*-Malambot.

Limber-*i*-Lumambot.

Limbo *n*-Bilango

Lime-*n*-Apog

Lime *n*-Limon dayap.

Lime kiln-*n*-Gawaan nğ apog

Lime stone-*n*-Banton apugan

Limit *n* Hanga, hanganan; wakal, wakas; gihd, baybay, danay

Limit-*v*-Ilagay nğ hanga magtaan.

Limitation-*n*-Paghanga; paglalagay nğ hanga

Limitless-*a*-Walang hanga.

Limp-*n*-Hingkot, iko.

Limp-*v*-Humingkod, umiko.

Limp-*a*-Malambot.

Limpid-*a*-Malinaw maaninag, makintab, maliwanag

Limpidity-Limpidness-*n*- Kaliwanagan, liwanag, kintab, aninag.

Linch pin *n*-Tarugo; susi

Line *v*-Guhitin, gumuhit

Line-*n*-Lubid, rienda, guhit, taludtod

Lineage-*n*-Lahi; hinlog, kamaganakan kanunuan.

Lineal-*a*-Nauukol sa guhit.

Lineament-*n*-Hitsura.

Linear-*a*-Nauukol ó parang guhit.

Linen-*n*-Hinabing lino, linso, kayumangi

Linger-*v*-Lumuat, magluat, tumagal.

Lingering-*n* Paglulualan; luat, hinayang

Lingering-*a*-Mahinayang

Lingual *a*-Nauukol sa dila.

Linguist-*n*-Ang tawong marunong sa manğa wika.

Linament *n*-Gamot na pamahiran

Lining-*n*-Aporo.

Link-*n*-Silo

Link-*v*-Idugtong

Lint *n*-Pamigkis nğ sugat

Lion-*n*-Leon.

Lioness *n* Babaying leon, maling leon.

Lip *n*- Nğuso, labi
Lipothymy-*n*-Himatay.
Liquation-*n*-Pagtunaw.
Liquefraction-*n*-Pagtutunaw.
Liquefiable-*a*-Matutunaw; malusaw.
Liquid-*a*-Malabnaw.
Liquid *n*-Anomang bagay nalusaw
Liquidity-*n*-Kalabnawan, pagkalusaw
Liquidate-*v*-Huiniwalay, magbayad.
Liquidation *n*-Hiwalay; pagbayad.
Liquor-*n*-Alak.
Lisp-*v*-Umutal
Lisp-*n*-Kautalan
List-*n*-Listahan; tandaan.
List-*v*-Maglista; ilista, listahin
Listen-*v*-Batyagin, pakingan, duminig, maring, making
Listener-*n*-Ang nakikimatyag.
Listless-*a*-Pabaya, tamad; mahina
Lit-*t imp*-Sinindihan, tumuutong, siniga
Litany-*n*-Dasal, litania
Liter-Litre-*n*-Litre.
Literal-*a*-Ayon sa salita
Literary-*a*-Nauukol sa sulat ó sa libro.
Literature-*n*-Manğa libro, karunungan; dunong
Lithe-*a*-Malambot, maliksi.
Lithesome-*a*-Maliksi.
Lithograph-*v*-Magdibuho, isulat sa bato.
Litigant-*a*-Nauukol sa usap
Litigant-*n*-Ang nag uusap
Litigate-*v*-Mag usap
Litigation-*n*-Usap, talo.
Litter-*n*-Arag arag; kalanda
Litter-*v*-Guluhin.
Little-*a*-Munti; maliit, kaunti
Little-*n*-Kakaunti
Live-*v*-Bumuhay, tumira, tahanan
Live-*a*-Buhay; buhay ang loob, masaya
Livlihood-*n*-Hanapbuhay, ikinabubuhay.
Livelong-*a*-Sa habang buhay.
Lively-*a*-Maliksi, masigla, malikot, buhay ang loob.
Liveliness-*n*-Kaliksihan, sigla, liksi.
Lively-*adv.* Kasayásayá
Liver *n*-Atay
Lives-*n*-Mğa buhay.
Livid *a*-Mapula, kulay talong.
Living *a*-Buhay, mabuhay.
Living *n*-Kabuhayan, pagkabuhay.
Lizard *n*-Túko, butiki, bayawak.
Load-*n* Bigat; lulan.
Load *v*-Ilulan, ipasan; kargahin; maglulan
Loaf-*n*-Tinapay na malaki.
Loaf *v*-Mag a'isaga, magpabaya.
Loafer *n*-Hampa- lupa; tawong pabaya at tamad.
Loam-*n*-Lupang itim.

Loan *n*-Hiram, anomang bagay na ipinahiram
Loan-*v*-Magpahiram, pahiramin
Loath-*a*-Ayaw, walang, gusto
Loathe-*v*-Mamuhi, yumamot, masamain.
Loathful-*a*-Makayayamot, masuklamin
Loathing-*n*-Suklam, kasuklaman, yamot, kayamutan, dalamhati
Loathsome-*a*-Makayayamot, masusuklaman madiri, muhiin
Lobate-*a*-May nğipin
Lobby-*n*-Silid na munti.
Lobe-*n*-Tainğa.
Lobed-*a*-Parang tainğa.
Lobster-*n*-Hipon dagat.
Local-*a*-Nauukol sa isang lugar
Locality-*n*-Lugar.
Locate-*v*-Lumagay, hanapin.
Location-*n*-Lugar.
Loch-*n*-Danaw
Lock-*n*-Seradura
Lock-*v* Isara; isusi.
Locker-*n*-Baul; kaban
Locksmith-*n*-Ang gumagawa nğ seradura
Locket-*n*-Kayrel
Lockup-*n*-Bilango; kalabuso.
Locomotion *n* Kilos, galaw
Locomotive *n*-Makina nğ tren.
Locust-*n*-Balang, kuliglig.
Locution-*n*-Salita; panğunğusap.
Lode-*n* Daan nğ tubig,
Lodge-*n*-Bahay kubo.
Lodge-*v*-Magpalinğa.
Lodger-*n*-Ang sumusuno, ang tumitira sa bahay nğ kapiwa.
Lodging-*n*-Tuluyan, bahay.
Lofty-*a*-Mataas palalo, dakila mayabang
Log-*n*-Troso puno nğ kahoy, bordon.
Log-*v*-Magtaga at maglabas nğ mğa kahoy.
Logger head-*n*-Tawong mapurol ang isip, ulol.
Logic-*n*-Dunong, karunungan.
Logical-*a*-Marunong
Logician-*n*-Tawong marunong.
Logwood-*n*-Kahoy na mapula
Loin-*n*-Sinapupunan, singit, balakang
Loiter-*v* Magpabaya gumayongayon; mag alisaga.
Loiterer *n*-Tawong tamad ó pabaya.
Loll-*v*-Magpabaya.
Lone *a* Bugtong nagiisa.
Lonely-*a*-Mapanglaw, malungkot; walang kasama; nagiisa
Loneliness-*n* Kalungkutan; kapangla waan.
Lonesome-*a* Malungkot; mapanglaw
Long-*a*-Mahaba.

Long-v-Mainip, kainipan nais.
Longevity-n-Kahabaan ñg buhay
Long-lived-a Mahaba ang buhay.
Longshore a-Naunkol sa baybay dagat.
Long sighted a-Malinaw ang tiñgin; ó
   mata; matalas, matalino, tuso.
Long-suffering a-Matitiisin
Long-suffeiing n Pagtitiis
Long tongued a-Mahaba ang dila, masa-
   lita
Long ways adv -Pahaba
Long winded a Mahaba ang hininga; ma-
   lakas ang baga
Longwise a-Pahaba
Look-v-Tumiñgin, tanawin; tumanaw.
Look n-Tiñgin, hitsura, lagay.
Looking-glass n-Salamin.
Looks-n Hitsura
Look out-n-Bantay, tanod.
Loom n-Habihan
Loom-v-Sumipot, lumitaw.
Loon-n-Tawong masama
Loop-n Silo, buhol, bilog
Loop-v-Siluin.
Loop hole-n Butas sa kota
Loose a-Bugnos; maluag, lubag, tali
   pandas
Loose-v-Lumubag, lumuag
Loosen-v Luagin, kalagin; bumugnos.
Loot-n-Ang ninakaw
Loot v-Manduit, nakawin.
Lop-v-Putlin, putulin, iklian.
Lop a-Nakasabit
Lop eared-a-Mahaba ang taiñga.
Loquacious a-Masalita. masabi, matabil
Loquaciousness n-Kalagayang masalita.
Loquacity n-Pagsasalita ñg marami.
Lord-n-Dios; Bathala, Ang May kapal.
Lord-v-Ang namamahala
Lord-v-Mamahala
Lordly-a-Mataas; dakila,
Lore-n-Karunuñgan, dunong
Lorn-a-Iniwan
Lose-v-Mawala, iwala, iligaw, matalo,
   maligaw, malugi.
Loss n-Ang nawala; pagtalo, ang nata-
   lo, kawalan; lugi
Lost-a Nawala; natalo, naligaw
Lot-n-Kapalaran, pagkataon, solar; ba-
 - hagi; karamihan; dami.
Loth-a-Ayaw.
Lotion n-Gamot na pamahid.
Lottery-n-Loteria, rifa.
Loud-a-Malakas
Loud adv.-Malakas.
Lough n Danaw.
Lounge-v Magahisaga, magpabaya
Lounge-n-Sandalan; hiligan
Lounger-n-Tawong tamad ó tigagal
Louse a-Hanip, kuto.

Lousy-a-Makuto. kutuhin.
Lout-n-Tawong; ulol ó ligalig.
Loutish-a-Ulol; hindi marunong.
Lovable-a-Maiibigan.
Love n Pagibig, kaibigan, paglingkod;
   suyo, ligaw; pagsinta
Love-v-Sintahin; ibigin, umibig; sumin-
   ta, lumingkod; ligawin, lumigaw; su-
   muyo.
Loving-a-Maibigan
Loveless a-Walang umibig; di maibi-
   gan.
Lovelorn a-Naiwan ñg lumigaw.
Lovely a-Maganda, mainam
Lover n-Ang lumiligaw; ang sumisinta
   ó lumilingkod, manininta.
Low-a-Mababa, hamak, mababaw, pas-
   lit; walang pinagaralan.
Low-n-Iyak ñg baka; unga.
Low adv -Kadustadusta
Low-v-Umunga
Lowbred a-Hamak; mababa ó hamak
   ang pinangahñgan
Lower-a-Mababa pa.
Lower-v-Ibaba; ilusong, ibsan, umim-
   pis; yumuko
Lower most-a-Kababábabáan
Lowery-a-Maulap, mapanglaw; malung-
   kot.
Low land-n-Lupang mababa at patag.
Low-lived-a-Hamak, bastos.
Lowly a-Mababa
Lowness-n-Kababaan.
Low spirited-a-Mabagal, mahina ang
   loob, malungkot
Loyal a-Ayon sa katowiran; tapat ang
   loob.
Loyally-a-Tapat.
Loyalty-n-Katapatan ñg loob, pagkaayon
   sa katowiran.
Lubber n Tawong bastos ó hamak.
Lubricant-a-Malañgis.
Lubricant-n-Lañgis.
Lubricate-v-Lañgisin.
Lubricous-a-Madulas
Lucent-a-Maningning, makislap, maki-
   sap
Lucid a-Makintab, maningning, makis-
   lap, makisap
Luck-n-Kapalaran; palad.
Luckless-a-Walang kapalaran; sawing
   kapalaran
Lucky-a-Mapalat.
Lucrative-a-Pakikinabañgan; matubo;
Lucre-n-Pakinabang, kayamanan
Ludicrous a Matatawanin.
Lug-n-Taiñga.
Lug-v Dalhin, magdala,
Luggage-n-Baon, ang dinala sa viage.
Lugubrious-a-Malungkot

34

Lukewarm-a-Malakuko, malagamgam.
Lull-v-Tumahimik, tumigil
Lull-v-Tigil
Lullaby n-Awit.
Lumbago n-Sakit ng gulugod at balakang.
· Lumbar-a-Nauukol ó malapit sa balakang.
Lumber-n-Manga tabla, kahoy.
Lumber-v-Magkahoy
Lumberman-n-Mangangalakal ng kahoy; magkakahoy
Lumbering-n-Pangangahoy.
Luminary-a Nakaliliwanag.
Luminous-a-Maliwanag; maningning; nakaliliwanag
Lump-n-Bukol, tangkal.
Lump-v-Bumukol, magtangkal.
Lumpy-a Mantangkal; mabukol
Lunacy-Kaululan
Lunar-a-Nauukol sa buan
Lunatic-a-Ulol, loco, maulol
Lunatic-n-Ulol, tawong maulol.
Lunch-n-Minindal
Lunch-v-Magminindal
Luncheon-n Minindal
Lung-n-Bágá
Lunge-n-Tulak; saksak
Lunge-v-Itulak, isaksak.

Lurch-v-Kumilos
Lurch-n-Kilos na bigla
Lure-v-Hibuin, dayain.
Lure-n-Hibo, daya.
Lurid-a-Maputla, maputi,
Lurk v-Harangin humarang
Luscious-a-Masarap matamis
Lush-a Puno ng katas
Lust-n-Pita, nais, nasa, kalibugan kasalahulaan.
Lust-v-Magnasa.
Lustful-a-Malibog, mapagnasa
Luster-n-Ningning, kintab, kisap
Lustiness-n-Lakas, liksi.
Lustiate-v-Linisin, dilagin
Lustre-n-Ningning kintab, dilag.
Lusty-a-Malakas.
Luxuriance-n-Kalaguan; kasaganaan.
Luxuriant-a-Malago; masagana; mayabong
Luxuriate-v-Lumago, sumagana.
Luxury-n-Kasaganaan, kalaguan
Luxurious-a-Sagana, malago, husto.
Lymph-n-Bukalan ng tubig.
Lynch-v-Bibitayin
Lynx-eyed-a-Matalas ang mata.
Lyre n-Lira
Lyrest-n-Ang marunong tumugtog sa lira

M

Ma-n Ima, inang.
Ma'am-n-Binibini, babaying maginoo
Macadamize-v Lagyan ng batong durog sa lansangan
Mace-n-Tungkod, palo
Machine-n-Makina
Machinery-n Makina.
Machinist-n-Ang marunong magkumpuni sa makina.
Mackintosh-n-Capote.
Mad-a Galid; ulol, hunghang
Mad-v-Pagalitin.
Madam-n-Pabaying ginoo, binibini
Madcat-a Maharot, walang takot, mangahas.
Madden-v-Pagalitin.
Made-v imp. & p. p.-Ginawa, niyari
Mademoiselle-n-Dalaga, binibini
Madhouse-n-Auspicio.
Madly-adv -Paulol.
Madman-n-Ulol, tawong ulol.
Madness-n-Galit, kagalitan
Madonna-n-Larawan ng mahal na Virgen na si María.
Maelstrom n-Ulili.
Maestro-n-Maestro.

Magazine-n-Taguan ng manga bala at polvo
Magdalen n-Putangbumabait.
Maggot-n-Uod, tus
Maggoty-a-Manod, may tus.
Magi n-Mago.
Magic-n-Salamangka.
Magician-n-Mago.
Magisterial-a Nauukol sa maestro, may kapangyarihan
Magistracy n Katungkulang Juez ó hukom.
Magistrate-n-Hukom, juez
Magnanimity-n Kagandahan ng loob, magandang kalooban
Magnanimous a Maawain, mapagampon, magandang loob, magaling
Magnate-n-Tawong dakila at mayaman.
Magnesia-n-Magnesia
Magnet-n-Bato na may batobalani; panghinang.
Magnetic-Magnetical-a-May batobalani, mapaghinayang
Magnetize-v-Lagyan ng batobalani, pahinayangin
Magnifiable a-Magpalaki.

Magnific-a-Malaki; dakila; marangal; marilag.
Magnificence-n-Kadakilaan; karilagan.
Magnify-v-Magpalaki; dagdagan; ibunyi; itanyag; painamin; purihin.
Magnitude-n-Kalikahan; kadakilaan laki; karangalan.
Magpie-n-Martinez.
Mahogany-n-Narra; asana.
Maid-n-Dalaga; alilang; babayi.
Maiden-n-Dalaga.
Maiden a-Nauukol sa dalaga.
Maidenly-a-Parang dalaga.
Maidservant-n-Alilang babayi.
Mail-n-Correos.
Mail-v-Ilagay sa correo.
Maim-v-Pilayin; saktan; bugbugin.
Maim-n-Sakit; kapilayan; bugbog.
Main-n-Lakas.
Main-a-Unang; principal.
Mainland-n-Lupa malayo sa dagat.
Mainspring-n-Kuerdas ng orasan.
Mainstay-n-Katulong; kupkop.
Maintain-v-Batahin; tumagal; umalalay; ingatin; manatili; ipaglaan; ipagtangol.
Maintenance-n-Kupkop; abuloy; panana- tili; alalay.
Maize-n-Mais.
Majestic-a-Mataas; dakila; marangal.
Majesty-n-Kadakilaan; karangalan; ka- taasan.
Major-a-Malaki pa.
Major-n-Commandante.
Make-v-Gumawa; yaring; gawin.
Make-n-Yari; gawa; kayarian; pagkagawa.
Maker-n-Ang gumawa; mangagawa.
Make-believe-v-Magkonowari.
Make-believe-a-Hindi totoo; konowari.
Malady-n-Sakit.
Mal-apropos-a-Di bagay; di akma.
Malaria-n-Sakit ng lagnat at ngiki.
Malarial-Malarious-a-Nauukol sa lagnat at ngiki.
Malcontent-a-Mapagbasagulo; masukal ang loob; galit.
Male-a-Nauukol sa lalaki.
Male-n-Lalaki.
Malediction-n-Tungayaw; alipusta.
Malefactor-n-Ang nagkasala; tawong masama.
Malevolent-a-Masama; hamak.
Malfeasance-n-Kasamaan; pagkakasala.
Malice-n-Galit; kasamaan; gawang bas- tos ó hamak.
Malicious-a-Masama; bastos; hamak.
Malicioness-n-Kasamaan; kabastosan.
Malign-v-Palabintangan; masama.
Malign-v-Bintangin; tungayawin; ura- liin; alipustain.
Malignant-a-Masama; hamak.

Malignant-n-Tawong masama.
Malignity-n-Kasamaan, kabastosan.
Mall-n-Panbayo.
Mall-v-Magbayo; bayuhin.
Mallard-n-Patong malaki.
Malleable-a-Makunat.
Mallet-n-Panbayo.
Malpractice-n-Masamang pagsanay.
Malpractice-v-Magsanay ng kasamaan.
Malt-n-Palay na binabad sa tubig na mainit.
Maltreat-v-Lampastanganin; alipustain.
Maltreatment-n-Tampalasan; lampas- tanganan.
Mamma-n-Ima; inang.
Mammal-n-Hayop na malaki.
Mammon-n-Yaman; kayamanan.
Mammoth-a-Malakingmalaki.
Man-n-Lalaki; tawo.
Man-v-Mamahala.
Manacle-n-Pangapos ng kamay.
Manacle-v-Gapusin ang kamay.
Manage-v-Mamahala; ulogin; ipatnugot; galawin; palakarin.
Manageable-a-Madalin ulogin ò palakarin.
Management-n-Pamamahala; ulog; pala kad.
Mandate-n-Utos.
Mandatory-a-Nauukol sa utos.
Mandible-n-Sihang; panga.
Mandrel-n-Bara ng bakal.
Mane-n-Kiling.
Maneuver-n-Pagulog; palakad.
Maneuver-v-Ulogin; palakarin.
Mange-n-Galis.
Manger-n-Kakanan ng hayop.
Mangle-v-Bugbugin.
Mango-n-Manga.
Mangy-a-Magalis.
Man hood-n-Kalagayan lalaki.
Mania-n-Kaululan.
Maniac-n-Ulol.
Maniac-a-Nauukol sa ulol.
Manifest-a-Tunay; totoo; tanyag; mati- ning na loob; hindi mababago.
Manifest-v-Ilathala; ipakita; itanyag; ipahayag; ipatalastas; ipakilala; ipasabi.
Manifesto-Manifestation-n-Pakita; paha- yag; tangyag; alaala; pagtatalastas.
Manifold-a-Marami.
Manakin-n-Tawong pandak; unano.
Manipulate-v-Mamahala; ulogin.
Manipulation-n-Pamamahala.
Mankind-n-Lahat ng manga tawo.
Manlike-a-Parang lalaki.
Manner-n-Tayo; kilos; kaugalian; ugali; anyo; bikas; kagalangan.
Mannerism-n-Kilos na hambog; kaham- bugan.

Mannerly-*a*-Mapitagan, magalang.
Mannish-*a*-Parang lalaki.
Man-of-war-*n*-Vapor de guerra
Manse *n*-Bahay ñg pastor
Mansion-*n*-Bahay na malaki at mainam.
Manslaughter-*n*-Pakamatay sa . kapowa dahil sa pagdedefensa.
Mantel-*n*-Mantel, takip.
Mantilla-*a*-Pañalon.
Martyr-*n*-Martir.
Mantle *v*-Itakip, itakpan.
Mantuamaker-*n* Babaying mananahi
Manual *a*-Nauukol sa kamay, yari ñg kamay.
Manual-*n*-Librong munti
Manufacture-*n*-Paggawa; gawa.
Manufacture-*v*-Gumawa, gawa.
Manufactury-*n*-Gawaan
Manumission-*n*-Pagbigay ñg kalayaan sa alipin.
Manumit-*v*-Ibigay ñg kalayaan sa alipin
Manure-*n*-Dumi ñg hayop.
Manure-*v*-Patabain ang lupa
Manuscript-*a*-Sulat kamay
Manuscript-*n*-Sulat kamay.
Many-*a*-Marami.
Many-*n*-Karamihan.
Map-*n*-Mapa
Map-*v*-Gumawa ang mapa.
Mar-*v*-Sirain; labuin.
Mar-*n* Sira, kalabuan.
Marasmus-*n*-Tisis.
Maraud-*v*-Manduit.
Marble-*n*-Marmol. ·
Marble-*a*-Marmol
March-*n*-Marzo.
March-*n*-Lakad; paglakad.
March-*v*-Lumakad.
Marchioness-*n*-Asawa ñg maikis.
Mare-*n* Inahing kabayo
Margin-*n*-Gilid, gasa, hanga, ladlaran.
Marginal-*a*-Nauukol sa gilid ó ladla- ran.
Marguerite-*n*-Margarita
Marine-*a*-Nauukol sa dagat.
Marine-*n*-Sundalong dagat; marina.
Mariner-*n*-Magdaragat
Mariolatry-*a*-Pagsamba sa Mahal na Virgen.
Marital *a*-Nauukol sa asawa
Maritime-*a*-Nauukol sa dagat.
Mark-*n*-Guhit, tanda, marka; tala, sa Alemania ay kahati,
Mark-*v*-Tandaan, ilagay ñg tanda, gu- hitin.
Market-*n*-Baraka; palenke; tiangi
Market-*v*-Magbaraka, ipagbili sa Palin- ki. ·
Marline-*n*-Munting lubid
Marly-Marlaceous-*a*-May halong lupa.

Maroon-*n* Kayumangi
Marquis-*n*-Markis
Marquise-*n*-Asawa ñg markis
Marriage-*n*-Kasal, pagkakasal balayi
Marriageable *a* Umubrang magaasawa
Marrow *n*-Utak ñg buto
Marry-*v*-Ikasal, kumasal, magasawa
Marsh *n*-Lawak, lupang mababa at basa
Marshy-*a* Mabalaho malawak.
Marshal-*n*-Puno, polícia.
Marshal-*v*-Ayusin, mamuno.
Mart-*n*-Baraka, palinki, tiangi.
Marten-*n*-Martinez
Martial-*a*-Nauukol, sa militar.
Mantle-*n* Takip, pangibabaw.
Martyrdom-*n* Kamatayan ñg martir.
Marvel-*n*-Bagay na dakila, bagay na makamamangha
Marvel-*v* Magtaka, inamangha.
Marvelous *a*-Makamamangha, magaling na lubha.
Masculine-*a*-Masculino; nauukol sa lalaki
Mash-*n*-Pitpit.
Mash-*v*-Pitpitin
Mask-*n* Maska, panakip.
Mask-*v*-Itakpan, ilagay ang maska
Mason-*n*-Kantero; ang mag lalabra ñg bato
Masonry-*n*-Mañga kuta ó pader na bato
Masque-*n*-Maskara.
Masquerade-*n*-Sayawan; panakip.
Masquerade *v*-Magtago ang mukha
Mass-*n*-Kalahatan; kabilugan
Mass-*v*-Mag ipon, umipon.
Massacre-*n*-Kamatayan, patayan.
Massacre-*v*-Patayin; kamatayan.
Massive-*a*-Malaki, masinsin, may kata- wan.
Mast-*n* Palo ñg sasakyan.
Master-*n* Ginoo, puno, pañginoon; maes- tro.
Master-*v* Supilin.
Masterly-*a*-Nauukol sa pañginoon, mai- nam.
Masterpiece-*n*-Gawa na marañgal.
Mastery-*n* Pagpasupil, pananalo.
Masticate-*v*-Ñgumuya, ñguyain
Mastication *n*-Pañguñguya.
Mat-*n* Banig
Mat-*v* Gumawa ó gawin ang banig.
Match-*n*-Casafuego, katulad, kalaban.
Match *v*-Tularan, tumulad
Matchless-*a*-Walang katapat, walang ka- tulad ó kaparis.
Mate-*n*-Kasama, kalagujo
Mate-*v*-Parisan.
Material *a*-May katawan.
Material-*n*-Kasangkapan,
Maternal-*a*-Nauukol sa ina
Maternity-*n* Kalagayang ina.

Mathematic-a-Nauukol sa aritmetica.
Mathematical-a-Nauukol sa aritmética ó kuenta.
Matnemetician-n-Ang marunong magkuenta.
Mathematics-n-Mañga kuenta.
Matin-a-Nauukol sa umaga.
Matin-n-Dasal sa umaga.
Matinee-n-Komedia sa hapon.
Matress-n-Hihigan na malambot.
Matricide-n-Ang natay sa sariling ina.
Matriculate-v-Pumasok; pumirma.
Matriculation-n-Pagpasok; pagpirma.
Matrimonial-a-Nauukol sa kasal.
Matri nony-n-Kasal.
Matrix-n-Bahay bata.
Matron-n-Asawa; bao; ang namamahala sa bahay.
Matronal-a-Nauukol sa asawa ó sa bao.
Matronize-v-Mamahala.
Matter-n-Sakit; sustancia; kaukulan; nana.
Matter-v-Maukol.
Matting-n-Banig.
Mattock-n-Piko.
Mattress-n-Hihigan na malambot.
Matnrate-v-Pahinugin; huminog.
Maturation-n-Pahinog.
Mature-v-Huminog; gumulang.
Mature-a-Magulang; hinog; mabait; malasa; tahimik.
Maturity-n-Kahinugan; gulang; kapanahanan.
Maudlin-a-Maulol; halos lasing.
Maul-n-Pambayo.
Maul-v-Bayuhin; paluin.
Mausoleum-n-Libiñgang marilag.
Mauve-a-Kulay lila.
Mauve-n-Kulay lila.
Maw-n-Sikmura ñg hayop.
Maxilla-n-Sihang; pañga.
Maxillar-Maxillary-a-Nauukol sa sihang ó pañga.
Maxim-n-Punong aral; patnugot; kasabihan.
Maximum-n-Kalakilakihan.
Maximum-a-Kalakilakihan.
May-n-Mayo.
May v-Maka.
Maybe-adv.-Marahil; kung sakali.
Mayor-n-Presidente.
Mayoralty-n-Pagka presidente.
Maze-n-Kaguluhan; kalabuan; kawalan ñg ayos.
Maze v Patakahin.
Me-pro.-Ako.
Mead-n-Pulut at tubig.
Meadw-Meado-n-Parang.
Meagre-a-Walang taba; payat; mahina.
Meal-n-Harina; pagkain.

Mealtime-n-Panahon ñg kumain.
Mean-v-Saysayan; magsaysay; ipagintinde.
Mean-a-Hamak; dukha; masama; mabagsik.
Mean-n-Kagitnan.
Meander-n-Lakad; pasial.
Meander-v-Lakad ñg pasuot suot.
Meaning-n-Kahulugan; kasaysayan; salaysay.
Means-n-Yaman; kapangyarihan.
Meant v. imp. & p. p.-Ibig sabihin.
Mean time-Meanwhile-adv.-Samantala.
Mean time-Meanwhile-n-Sa panahong ito.
Measles-n-Tigdas.
Measly-a-May tigdas; tigdasin.
Measure-n-Sukat; panukat; takal.
Measure-v-Sukatin; sumukat; takalin.
Measureless-a-Walang takal ó sukat; walang hanga.
Measurement-n-Kasukatan; sukat; takal; pagtatakal.
Meat-n-Carne; ulam.
Mechanic-n-Mecánico.
Mechanical-a-Nauukol sa mecánico.
Mechanician-n-Mecánico.
Mechanics-n-Karununñgan sa pagmemecánico.
Mechanism-n-Kasangkapan ñg makina.
Medal-a-Medalla.
Medalic-a-Nauukol sa medalla.
Medallion-n-Medalla.
Meddle-v-Gumiit; makialam.
Meddlesome-a-Madiwara; mapakialaman.
Medial-a-Nauukol sa kalagitnaan.
Mediate-a-Kasiping; katabi.
Mediate-v-Mamagitan.
Mediation-n-Pamamagitan.
Mediator-n-Ang namamagitan; taga pamagitan.
Medical-a-Nauukol sa gamot.
Medicament-n-Gamot.
Medicate-v-Gamutin.
Medication-n-Pag gagamot.
Medicinal-a-Nauukol sa gamot.
Medicine-n-Gamot.
Mediocre-a-Karaniwan; yano.
Meditate-v-Mag wariwari; mag gunamgunam; magbulaybulayin; mag wari; mag isip isip; magnilaynilayin; gunamgunamin.
Meditation-n-Pagninilay; wari; pag wawari.
Meditating-a-Mapag wari.
Mediterranean-n-Mediteranio.
Medium-n-Kalagitnaan; gitna.
Medley-n-Kanta; awit.
Meed-n-Ganti.
Meek-a-Maamo; mabanayad; maamong loob.

Meekness-n-Kaamoan

Meet-v-Sumalubong, salubuñgin, pumulong, magtipon, masapong, umabot

Meet-n-Salubung, pagtipon

Meeting-n-Pulong; tipon, katipunan, lupon

Meetinghouse n-Bahay na pinagtitipunan

Melancholic-a-Malungkot, manimimdim.

Melancholy-a-Malungkot; malumbay.

Melancholy-n-Kalungkutan, kalumbayan, pighati

Melliorate-v-Pagalingin; butihin

Mellifeous-a-Mapulot

Mellifluent-Mellifluos a-Mapulot

Mellow-a-Malambot, malasa.

Mellow-v-Lumambot

Melodeon-n-Harmonica

Melodious-a-Mainam dingin

Melody n-Kanta, awit.

Melon-n-Melon, pakuan

Melt-v-Tunawin, tumunaw.

Melting-n-Pagtutunaw

Member-n-Kasali, kasama.

Membership-n-Pagkakasama.

Membrane-n-Balat na manipis

Memento-n-Alaala bigay

Memoir-n-Alaala, gunamgunam

Memorable-a-Maalaala, marangal.

Memorandum-n-Tandaan.

Memorial a-Maalaala.

Memorial-n-Dangal, alaala gunamgunam.

Memorize-v-Isaulo; cabesaduhin.

Memory-n-Alaala.

Men n-Mañga lalaki.

Menace-n-Pañganib

Menace-v-Umabala.

Mend-v-Baguhin, tutupan, iuli, husayin.

Mendacious-a-Mali; sinungaling

Mendacity-n-Kasinungalingan, kamalian.

Mendicancy-n Pagkapulubi

Mendicant-n-Mamulubi.

Mendicant-n-Pulubi.

Mendicity-n Pagkapulubi

Menial-a-Mababa, hamak; naunkol sa alila.

Menial-n-Alila

Mensal-a-Mangyayari sa buanbuan; buanbuan

Mensal-a-Nauukol sa lamesa.

Menses-n-Kapanahunan ñg babayi

Menstrual-a-Mangyayari sa buanbuan, nauukol sa panahon ñg babayi.

Menstruate-i -Mamanahon.

Menstruation-n-Pamamanahon

Mensurable a-Masusukatin.

Mensural a-Nauukol sa sukat.

Mensuration-n-Pagsusukat: pagtatakal.

Mental a-Sa ulo, hindi nasulat.

Mention-n-Pangt

Mention-n-Bangitin; alalahanin.

Mentor-n-Tawong murunong.

Mercantile-a-Nauukol sa pañgañgalakal

Mercenary-a-Inupahan, masakim.

Mercenary-n-Sundalong inupahan

Merchandise-n-Kalakal

Merchant-n-Mañgañgalakal.

Merchant-a-Nauukol sa pañgañgalakal.

-Merchantable-a-Mapagtinda

Merchantman-n-Sasakyan.

Merciful-a-Maawain, mahabagin.

Merciless-a-Walang awa, mabagsik

Mercurial-a-Maliksi, Nauukol sa azogue

Mercury-n-Azogue.

Mercy-n Awa, habag.

Mere-a-Malinis walang halo.

Mere-n-Hanga lawa.

Merge-v-Isama; ilubog.

Meridian-a Nauukol sa katanghalian

Meridian-n-Katanghalian

Merino-n-Merino

Merino-a-Merino

Merit-n-Katapatan;kabutihan, kaakmaan

Merit-v-Marapatin

Meritorious-a Magaling, dakila

Merriment-n-Kasayahan; tuwa, galak ligaya

Merry-a-Natutuwa, masaya; malugod.

Mesh-n-Mata ñg titid ó dala

Mesh-v-Humigit

Mess n-Pagkain sa lamesa

Message-n-Bilin, telegrama, hatid kawad

Messenger-n-Utusan.

Messiah-n-Jesu Cristo, Mesias

Mesieurs-n-Mañga ginoo.

Met-v-imp & p p-Sinalubong; sumalubong

Metal-n-Metal

Metallic-a-Nauukol sa metal; may halong metal.

Metamorphose-v-Ibahin; baguhin

Metaphor-n-Tularan

Mete-v-Sukatin, takalin

Mete-n-Sukat, takal; panukat

Meter-n-Metro

Methinks-v-Tila, sa akala ko

Method-n-Palakad, regla

Methodic-Methodical-a-Nauukol sa regla

Methodize-v-Ayusin, husayin.

Metric-Metrical-a Nauukol sa metrico

Metropolis-n-Bayang tinubuan, capital

Metropolitan-a-Metropolitano.

Metropolitan-n-Metropolitano

Mettle-n-Buhay ó liksi ñg loob, lakas loob

Mettlesome a-Malakas ang loob

Mew v-Ñgumiyaw.

Mew n-N

Mewl-v-Umiyak parang bata.
Mi-n-Mi.
Mice-n-Mañga dagá.
Microbe-n-Microbe.
Mid-a-Kalahati; gitna.
Midday-n-Tanghali; katanghalian.
Middle-n-Kagitnaan; kalahati; laot.
Middle-a-Ang sa gitna, nasa laot.
Middling-v-Katatagaan; alañganin;
Midge-n-Langaw na munti.
Midged-n-Unano; tawong munti.
Midland-a-Malayo sa dagat.
Midland-n-Lupang malayo sa dagat.
Midmost-a-Na sa gitna.
Midnight-a-Hating gabi.
Midnight-a-Hating gabi.
Midshipman-n-Punong mababa sa isang
  sasakyan.
Midships-adv.-Sa gitna ñg sasakyan.
Midst n-Gitna; laot.
Midst-adv.-Sa pagitan.
Mid way-n-Kalahati ñg daan.
Midway-adv.-Na sa kalahati ñg daan.
Midwife-n-Hilot.
Mien-n-Hitsura; kilos.
Miff-n-Galit; poot; kapootan.
Might-v-Maka; marahil.
Might-n-Lakas; kalakasan.
Mightily-adv.-Malakaslakas.
Mighty-a-Malakas.
Migrate-v-Pumunta ó magpunta sa
  ibang lugar,
Migration-n-Pagpunta sa ibang lugar.
Migratory-a-Palipatlipat.
Milch-a-Magatas; gatasan.
Mild-a-Maamo; mairog; tamhimik.
Mildew-n-Amag.
Mildew-v-Maamag.
Mildness-n-Kaamoan; katahimikan.
Mile-n-Milla,
Millitant-a-Nakakalaban.
Military-a-Nauukol sa hukbo ó sa
  militar.
Military-n-Militar; hukbo.
Militate-v-Lumaban.
Militia-n-Hukbo.
Milk-n-Gatas.
Milk-v-Gatasin; gumatas,
Milky-a-Magatas; may halong gatas.
Mill-n-Gilingan.
Mill-v-Dikdikin; gumiling; gilingin.
Milldam-n-Harañgan ñg tubig.
Millenial-a-Nauukol sa isang libong
  taon.
Millenary-n-Isang libong taon.
Miller-n-Ang mayari ñg gilingan.
Milliard-n-Isang libong añgawañgaw.
Milling-n-Paggiling.
Million-n-Isang añgawañgaw; añgaw.
Millionare-n-Tawong totoong mayaman.

Milt-n-Atay.
Mimic-a-Nakahawig; gumagad.
Mimic-v-Gumagad; gagarin; badyahin.
Mimic-n-Ang gumagad sa iba.
Mimicker-n-Ang bumadya; manbabadya.
Mimicry-n-Badya.
Miniatory-a-Maabala.
Mince-v-Tadtarin.
Mince meat-n-Carneng tinadtad.
Mind-n-Isip; bait, wari; kalooban akala;
  namman; tapang.
Mind-v-Magingat; iñgatin: bantayir;
  akalain.
Minded-v-Nakahiling.
Miudful-a-Mabait; maiñgat; masusunurin;
  matatandain.
Mine-pro.-Akin.
Mine-n-Mina.
Mine-v-Magmina.
Mineral-n-Mineral metal.
Mineral-a-Nauukol sa mineral.
Mingle-v-Ihalo; haluin; ilahok; salitin.
Miniature-n-Larawan na munti.
Minim-n Anomang bagay na munting-
  munti.
Minimize-v-Liitin; untian.
Mininum-n-Kauntiuntian.
Minion n-Alila.
Minish-a-Umunti; bumawas.
Minister-n-Pastor; alila; katiwala.
Minister-v-Magalila; magbigay ñg kai-
  lañgan,
Ministration-n-Pagbibigay ñg mañga
  kailañgan.
Minnow-n-Isang munti.
Minor-a-Munti.
Minor-n-Tawo na wala pa sa edad na
  karampatan.
Minority-n-Kauntian.
Minster-n-Simbahan ñg monasterio.
Mint-n-Gawaan ñg salapi.
Mint-v-Gumawa ñg salapi.
Minus-a-Kulang.
Minute-n-Minuto.
Minute-a-Muntingmunti.
Minute-v Tandaan.
Minx-n-Babaying mañgahas.
Miracle-n-Gawa ñg Dios.
Miraculous-a-Marañgal; kamanghamang-
  ba; katakataka; magaling na lubha.
Mire-n-Putik; burak; balaho; banlik;
  lusak.
Mire-v-Kaburakan.
Mire-v-Mabalaho sa putik.
Mirk-Mirky-a-Mapanglaw; madilim.
Mirk-n-Kadiliman; kapanglawan.
Mirror-n-Salamin.
Mirth-n-Kasayahan; tuwa; lugod; liga
  ya.
Mirthful-a-Masaya; natutuwa; malugod.

Miry-*a*-Mabalaho, maputık.

Misadventure *n*-Kasalatan; sakuna.

Misapply-*v*-Mamalı, sa paggamıt.

Misapplication *n* Kamalıan ṣa paggamit

Misapprehend-*v*-Maulınıg, mamalı sa pagdidinig

Misapprehension *n*-Kamalıan nang pag dınig

Misappropriate-*v*-Ankının

Misappropriation-*n*-Pagaankin.

Misbehave-*v*-Maglikot

Misbehavior-*n*-Kaharotan, kalıkutan

Miscalculate *v*-Mamali sa pagbılang

Miscalculation-*n*-Mali ṣa pagbilang.

Miscarriage-*n*-Pagkunan, agasan.

Miscarry-*ı*-Makunan, maagasan

Miscellaneous-*a*-Sarı-sarı.

Mischance-*n*-Sawıng kapalaran

Mischance-*v* Masawıng palad.

Mischief-*n*-Kalıkutan, samá.

Mischievous-*a*-Malıkot

Mischievousness *n*-Kalıkutan

Misconceive-*v*-Maulinigan

Misconception-*n*-Kaulınıgan

Misconduct-*n*-Kılos na masama

Misconduct-*v*-Mamahala ng̃ hındi tama

Misconstruct *v*-Saysayin ng̃ hındı tama, mamalı sa pag̃sasaysay

Misconstruction-*n*-Kamalıan sa pag saysay.

Misconstrue-*v*-Mamalı ṣa pagsasaysay.

Miscount-*v*-Mamalı sa pagbilang.

Miscount-*n*-Mali sa pagbilang

Miscreant-*n*-Tawong masamá.

Miscreant-*a*-Masamá hamak, bastos

Misdate-*v* Mamalı sa paglalagay ng̃ fecha

Misdate-*n*-Mali sa pag lalagay nang fecha.

Misdeed-*n*-Kılos na masama, kasalanan.

Misdemean-*ı*-Kumılos na masama, magkasala.

Misdemeanor-*n*-Sala, kasalanan

Misdirect-*v*-Ituro ng̃ hındı tama

Misdirection-*n*-Pagtuturo nang hındı tama.

Misdo-*ı* Gawin ng̃ hındı tama

Misdoer-*n*-Tawong may kasalanan

Miser-*n*-Tawong masakim ó maramot.

Miserly-*a*-Moramot, masakim

Miserable *a*-Malungkot hamak, aba

Misery *n* Kahirapan, hırap, kasalatan, kasaliwaan, karukhaan.

Misfit *a*-Dı bagay.

Misfortune-*n* Sawing kapalaian

Misfortunate *a*-Kulang palad, sawing palad.

Misgive-*ı*-Magduda, mag agam agam na loob

Misgiving-*n* Duda, agamagam na loob.

Misgotten-*a*-Falso ang pagkamit.

Misgovern-*ı*-Mamahala ó mamuno ng̃ masamá

Misgoverment-*n*-Pamamahala ng̃ falso ó masama

Misguidance *n*-Pagturo ng̃ hındı tama

Misguide-*ı*-Ituro sa hındı tama.

Mishap-*n*-Kakulang̃an ng̃ palad, kasalıwaan ng̃ kapalaran

Misinfoim-*v*-Ipatalastas ang hindı tama.

Misinterpret-*v*-Magkamali

Misinterpretation-*n*-Malı sa pagsasaysay.

Misjudge *v*-Mamalı, huag tamaan

Misjudgment-*n*-Malı, kamalıan.

Mismanage-*v*-Mamahala ng̃ masama ó falso

Mismanagement-*n*-Kapalsohan ng̃ pamamahala

Misname *ı*-Ibahın ang ng̃alan,

Misplace-*v* Ilagay sa hindı karampatan lugar.

Misplacement-*n*-I'aglalagay sa hındı karampatang lugar.

Mispronounce *v* Sabihin ng̃ pautal

Mispronunciation-*n*-Malı sa pagsabı.

Misrule-*v*-Mamahala ó magharı ng̃ dı ayon sa katowiran.

Misrule-*n*-Kabagsikan nang pag gogobierno.

Miss-*n*-Dalaga, bınıbini

Miss-*n*-Laktaw, malı.

Miss-*ı*-Ilaktaw, mawala sumala.

Miss, al-*n* Libro ng̃ misa.

Missend-*v*-Mamali sa pagpadala.

Misshapen-*a*-Masamang hıtsura

Missile-*n* Kasangkapang panghagıs

Mission-*n*-Bilın, dahılan

Missive-*n*-Sulat na maıklı, bilin

Misspend-*v*-Musawin ó isabog ang pagaarı

Misstatement *n*-Kamalian sa pagsasaysav.

Mist-*n*-Angı, ambon

Mist-*ı*-Umangı, umambon.

Mistaken *v*-Namali, mali.

Mistake-*v*-Mamali.

Mistake-*n* Malı, kamalian

Mistate-*v* Mamali sa pagsasaysay.

Mister *n*-Ginoo.

Mis treat-*v*-Lumapastang̃an

Mistress-*n*-Babaȳi kalunȳa

Mistrust-*n*-Duda.

Mistrust-*v*-Magduda

Mistrustful-*a* May duda.

Misty *a*-Maambon.

Misunderstand-*ı* Maulınigan;   mamalı, magdinig

Misunder standing-*n* Kaulinigan; galit; kagalitan, pagtatalo
Mis use-*ι*-Hamakin, salbahiin.
Mis use *n* Pagpahamak
Mite-*n*-Bagay na munti.
Miter *n*-Gorra ng̃ arsobispo
Miter *v*-Idugtong.
Mitigate-*v* Lumambot, maawa.
Mitigation-*n*-Awa; lambot
Mix *v* Ihalo, haluin, ilahok, ibahog
Mixture *n*-Kahalo, pag lahok, halo, lahok; pagkakahalo.
Mizzen-*a*-Kahulihulihan.
Mizzle *v*-Umambon; umangi
Mizzle *n* Ambon; angi
Moan-*ι* Humalinghing.
Moan-*n*-Halinghing
Moat *n* Sangka.
Mob-*n*-Bunton ng̃ tawo.
Mobile-*a*-Magalaw.
Mobility *n* Pag galaw, galaw.
Moccasin-*n*-Sapatos ó sinelas ng̃ Indio Americano
Mocha-*n*-Bayan sa Arabia
Mocha-*n*-Kafe nangaling sa Arabia.
Mock *ι*-Gagarin; gumagad, badyahin
Mock-*n* Badya; uyam
Mock-*a*-Mabadya, hindi totoo, konowari
Mockery-*n*-Pagbabadya, uyam; libak, npasala
Mode *n* Paraan; asal, hitsura; kaugalian; lagay: palakad.
Model *n* Halimbawa, huwaran, tularan
Moderate-*a*-Mabait; banayad, mahinahon.
Moderate *v*-Husayin, banayad.
Moderation-*n*-Kabanayaran, bait; kabaitan hinahon, tining na loob
Modern-*a* Bago, mura.
Modernize-*v*-Baguhin
Modest *a* Mabait, banayad, mabini, maingat.
Modesty-*n*-Bait, kabaitan, kabinian, timtim; kalinisan.
Modify-*v*-Baguhin, husayin
Modification *n*-Pagkabago; paghusay; kahusayan
Mohair-*n* Balahibo ng̃ kambing.
Moiety-*n*-Ang kalahati, kagitna
Moist-*a* Basa
Moisten-*v* Basain.
Moisture-*n* Hamog
Molar-*a*-Nauukol sa bagang
Molar-*n*-Bagang.
Molasses-*n* Pulot, inuyat.
Mold-*n*-Amag
Mold-*v*-Umamag.
Molding *n* Marko
Molder-*v*-Maging alikabok.
Moldy-*a*-Maamag
Mole-*v*-Humukay

Molest-*v*-Abalahin; umabala; magmolestia; muhiin; payamutin.
Molestation-*n*-Abala, muhi, yamot.
Mollification-*n*-Kalambutan.
Mollify-*v*-Lambutin; lumambot.
Molt-*r*-Malngas ang buhok.
Molten-*a*-Natunaw; lusaw; tunaw
Moment-*n*-Dali; kisap mata, bigat halaga.
Momentary-*a*-Hindi pirme.
Momentarily-*adv*.-Sa bawat isang dali.
Momento-*n*-Alaala.
Momentous-*a*-Mabigat, mahalaga
Momentum-*n*-Bilis; tulin; lakas
Monarch-*n*-Puno, hari; monarca.
Monarchal-*a*-Nauukol sa hari.
Monarchy-*n*-Kaharian.
Monastery-*n*-Convento
Monastic-*a*-Nauukol sa convento.
Monday-*n*-Lunes
Monetary-*a*-Nauukol sa salapi.
Mongol-Mongolian-*n*-Insik, hapon.
Mongolian-*a*-Nauukol sa Insik.
Monition-*n* Pang̃aral, babala.
Monitor-*n*-Ang nagtuturo.
Monk-*n*-Monje
Monkey-*n*-Ungo.
Monkey-*v*-Magbiro
Monogamy-*n*-Kasal; pagkakasal.
Monopolize-*v* Kunin ang lahat, ariin ang lahat.
Monotonous-*a*-Masasawa, masusuklaman.
Mon-soon-*n*-Bagyo
Monster *n*-Bagay na totoong malaki, Hayop
Monstrous-*a*-Katakot takot; kakilakilabot
Month-*n*-Buan
Monthly *a*-Buanbuan; balang buan.
Monthly-*n*-Pahayagan na lumitaw minsan sa bawat buan
Monthly-*adv*.-Sa buanbuan, buanan.
Monument-*n*-Monumento
Monumental-*a*-Nauukol sa monumento.
Moo *n*-Iyak ng̃ baka, ung̃a
Mood-*n*-Lagay ng̃ isip.
Moody-*a*-Mapootin
Moon-*n*-Buan sa lang̃it
Moon light-*n*-Liwanag ng̃ buan.
Moon shine-*n*-Sinag ng̃ buan.
Moor-*n*-Lawak, yaong taga Africa.
Moor-*v*-Sumayad ang sasakyan.
Mooring-*n*-Punduhan.
Moorland-*n*-Lupang malawak ó mabalaho
Moory-*a*-Malawak; mabalaho
Moot *v* Mang̃atowiran, magsalitaan
Moot-*n*-Pang̃ang̃atowiran.
Mop-*n*-Pang̃isis.
Mop *v*-Magisis.
Mope *v*-Magbaliv
Mopish-*a*-Baliw, tamad.

35

Moral-a-Nauukol sa kaugalian.
Moral-n-Talinhaga
Morality-n-Kalinisan; puri.
Morass-n Lawak
Morbid-a-Nakababagot; sira ang isip.
Mordant-a-Mapait, masaklap
More-a-Lampas, lubha, lalo.
More-adv. Lubhang, lalong
More over-adv -Bukod pa sa ito, bukód, lampas pa rito
Morn-Morning n-Umaga
Morn-Morning-a-Maaga.
Morocco-n-Katad na fino
Morose-a-Matigas ang ulo, masuñgit, bastos
Morphia-Morphine-n-Extracto de Apian.
Morrow-n-Samakalawa
Morsel-n-Pirasong munti.
Mortal-a-Masupil sa kamatayan; mag-kakamatay.
Mortal-n-Tawo
Mortar-n-Almires; dikdikan.
Mortgage-n-Sangla
Mortgage-v-Isangla.
Mortgage-v-Isangla
Mortification-n-Hiya, kapighatian.
Mortify-v-Mahiya, bagabagin
Mortise-n-Rabo
Mortise v-Magrabo.
Mosaic-n-Palamote.
Mosaic-a-Nauukol sa kay Moises.
Mosquito-n-Lamok.
Mosquito-net-n-Kulambo.
Moss-n-Lumot
Moss-v-Maglumot.
Mossiness n-Pagkalumot.
Mossy-a-Malumot
Most-a-Karamiramihan
Most-adv -Karamiramihan.
Mostly-adv.-Halos lahat.
Mote n-Pirasong munti.
Moth-n-Tañga
Moth eaten-a-May tañga
Mother-n-Ina.
Mother-a Natural, dati.
Mother hood n Pagkaina; kalagayan ina
Mother-in-law-n-Bienang babayi
Motherless a-Ulila sa ina
Motherly-a-Nauukol sa ina
Motherly-adv. Parang ina.
Motion-n-Kilos, galaw
Motion-v-Kawayin.
Motionless a-Walang kilos, walang kibo.
Motive-n-Dahilan, pinagmulaan, pinag-buhatan
Motley-a-Sarisaring kulay.
Mottle-v-Mamansa.
Motto n-Patnugot.
Mould-n-Marka
Mount-n-Bundok.

Mound-n-Pugpog, gulod
Mount-v-Umakyat, umahon; pumanhik, sumalungat.
Mounting-n Pagakyat
Mountain-n-Bundok.
Mountain-n-Nauukol sa bundok.
Mountaineer-n-Tawong taga bundok.
Mountainous-a-Mabundok.
Mourn-v Magluksa, tumañgis, manambitan, manañgis
Mournful-a-Malungkot, malumbay, ma-panglaw.
Mourning-n-Luksa; panambitan
Mouse n-Daga
Mouse-v-Hulihin ang daga.
Mouse hole-n-Butas na ginawa ñg daga.
Mouse trap n Panghuli ñg daga
Mouth-n-Bibig.
Mouth-v Ilagay sa bibig
Mouthful-n-Kagat.
Move-v-Kumilos, gumalaw baguhin; lumipat, galawin, kilusin, ilipat.
Movement-n-Kilos, galaw
Moving-n-Paggalaw, kilos.
Mow-n-Taguan ó sisiglan ñg dayami ó damung tuyo
Mow-v-Gapasin, guinapas.
Mower-n-Pangapas
Mr.-n-Ginoo
Mrs -n-Binibini
Much-a-Marami.
Much n-Karamihan
Much a Maraming
Mucilage-n-Pandikit, pagkit
Mucilaginous a-Pagkit; malagkit.
Muck-n-Pusali, putik, balaho
Mud-n-Putik, balaho, pusali, burak, banlik.
Mud-v-Pumutik, bumalaho.
Muddle v-Guluhin, labuin
Muddle-n-Gulo, kapurolan.
Muddy a-Mabalaho, maputik; mabuiak, mabanlik.
Muddy-v-Pumutik, labuin
Muffin-n-Torta.
Mug-n Tasa
Muggy-a Basa
Mulatto n-Mestizong negro
Mulch-n-Dayaming bulok.
Mulct n-Multa.
Mulct v Multahin; magmulta
Mule-n-Mula; kabayong mula
Muleteer-n Cochero ñg mula.
Mulish-a-Nauukol sa mula
Mullet n-Bumbuan
Multiped-n-Hayop na marami ang paa
Multiplication-n-Pagdadami, pagmumul-tiplicar, pagpaparami
Multiply-v-Magmultiplicar, paramihin
Multitude n-Kakapalan ñg tawo; bun-ton ng tawo.

Multitudinous a-Makapal; malaki.
Mum-a-Tahimik; walang kibo.
Mum-*inter*-Huag.
Mumble-v-Umimik
Mumble-n-Imik.
Mummy n-Bangkay ñg tawo na hindi mabubulok.
Mump-v-Umañgil; dumaing
Mumps-n-Baiki.
- Munch-v-Kumain, ñgujain.
Mundane a-Nauukol sa lupa
Municipal-a-Nauukol sa municipio
Municipality-n Municipio.
Munificence-n-Kagandang ñg loob
Munificent-a-Magandang kalooban
Munition-n-Kasangkapang panlaban.
Murder-n-Patayan; pag patay; matay
Murder-v-Pumatay; patayin.
Murderer-n-Ang nakamatay, ang natay sa kapwa
Murderess n-Babaying nakamatay
Murderous-n-Makamamatay.
Murky-a-Malabo, mapanlaw.
Murmur-n Imik, bulongbuloñgan, hinanakit, himutok; dabog.
Murmur-v-Dumabog; umimik; maghimutok
Muscle n-Lakas; litid
Muscular a-Malakas, malitid.
Muse-v-Magwariwari, magkuro, magdilidili, magisipisip
Muse-n-Pagkuro, wari; pagdidilidili.
Mush-n-Lugaw.
Music-n-Musica.
Musical-a-Nauukol sa musica.
Musician-n-Musico

Musket-n-Baril.
Musk-melon-n-Melon
Muslin-n-Freuela, muslina
Musquito-n-Lamok.
Muss-n-Gulo, kaguluhan.
Muss-v-Guluhin.
Must-a-Dapat, marapat
Mustache-n Balbas sa ñguso, bigote
Mustang-n-Kabayong munti at matigas ang ulo.
Mustard-n-Mustasa; kiluwa
Muster-n-Pagtipon ang sundalo.
Muster-n-Magtipon ang sundalo.
Mutable-a-Makapapalit
Musty-a-Maamag, amagin, laon.
Mutation-n-Pagpalit
Mute-a-Tahimik, walang kibo.
Mute n-Tawong pipe
Mutilate v-Sirain; pilayin
Mutilation-n-Pagsira, pagkapilay.
Mutinous-a-Ibig lumaban sa puno.
Mutiny-n-Pag aisa ñg mañga magdara gat laban sa kanilang puno.
Mutiny-v-Lumaban sa puno.
Mutter n-Imik
Mutter-v-Umimik
Mutton-n-Karne ñg tupa.
Mutual-a-Magkaayon, magkaisa.
Mutuality-n-Pagkakaayon.
Muzzle-n-Bibig ñg baka
My-*pro*-Akin, ko
Myriad-a-Isang laksa.
Myridom-n-Tawong bastos.
Myself-*pro*-Aking sarili; sarili ko.
Mysterious-a-Lihim, malalim.
Mystify-v-Ipalihim.
Myth-n-Kuento, awit.

N

Nab-v-Kunin, dampotin.
Nabob-n Tawong mayaman.
Nag n-Kabayo
Nag v-Tuksuhin;" manukso
Nail n-Pako.
Nail-v-Pumako; pakuin
Nailer-n-Ang mamamako
Naked-a-Hubad, hubo, walang damit
Name-n-Pañgalan ñgalan
Name-v-Magnğañgalang
Nameless-Walang pañgalang
Namely-*adv.*-Sunodsunod.
Namesake n-Kañgalang.
Nap-n Siesta, tulog sa tanghali
Nap-v-Magsiesta, matulog.
Nape n-Batcng
Napkin-n-Servilleta.
Narcotic-n-Pangpatulog.

Narrate-v-Magbalita; magsaysay, salaysayin, magsabi.
Narration n-Salaysay, balita, kuento
Narrative n-Balita; kuento; kasaysayan, salaysay.
Narrow-a-Makitid; makipot.
Narrow-v-Kumipot, kumitid.
Narrow-n-Kakiputan; kakitiran.
Nasal-a-Nauukol sa ilong, humal
Nastiness-n-Kasukalan, kasalahulaan; libag, duñgis; dumi; karumihan
Nasty-a-Marumi, maruñgis malibag, salahula
Natal-a-Nauukol sa kapañganakan
Nation-n-Sang katawohan; nacion
National-a-Nauukol sa sang katawohan, ó nacion.
Nationality-n-Pagkatawo.

Norse-n-Taga Norwega
Norman n-Taga Norwega.
Norseman-n-Taga Norwega
North n-Hilagaan.
North-a Hilaga.
North-v-Magpunta ó ipadala sa hilagaan.
Norther-n-Hañgin nangaling sa hilagaan, balas
Northerly a-Hilagaan
Northerly-adv Sa gawing hilaga
Northern-a Hilaga
Northener n-Taga hilaga
Northern most-a Malayo sa hilagaan
North ward-Northwards-adv -Sa gawing hilaga; patuñgo sa hilagaan
Northeast-n Habagat
Northeastern-a-Habagat
Nose-n-Ilong. ñguso
Nose-v-Makialam
Nose bleed n-Balangnyngñoy
Nostril-n-Butas nğ ilong.
Not-adv.-Hindi
Notable-a-Halata, mahalata.
Notably-adv.-Mahalata.
Notary-n-Notario.
Notch-n-Ukit, binğaw
Note-n-Sulat, tanda, nota
Note-v-Tandain; talastasin, halatain
Note book-n-Librong tandaan
Noted-a Bantog; bunyi, mabalita
Note worthy-a Dapat purihin
Nothing-n-Wala; walang ano man.
Nothing adv -Wala
Notice-n-Pahayag, paunawa.
Notice v-Humalata, magmasdan, pansin, makita
Noticeable a-Mapapansinin, mahalata
Notification-n Pahayag, balita, paunawa
Notifiy v-Ipatalastas, ipahayag, ibahta
Notion n-Akala, isip, ang inisip, wari, pagwawari, gunamgunam, pakana.
Notoriety-n Kabalitaan, kabantugan
Notorious a-Mabalita; bunyi.
Not with standing adv -Datapua't, nğu-ni't
Not with standing-prep -Datapua't; nğuni't.
Nought-n-Walang ano man.
Nought adv -Wala
Noun n-Nombre. sustantivo.
Nourish-v-Pakanin, magpalago.
Nourishment n-Pagkain, ikinabnbuhay.
Novel-a-Marilag, bago.
Novel n Novela, awit.'
Novelty-n-Pangingiba; kaibhan.
November n Noviembre.
Novice-n-Ang bagong nagaaral.

Now-adv -Nğayon.
Now a days-adv Sa panahon nğayon.
Now-and then-Maminsan minsan
Noway-Noways-adv -Sa anomang paraan ay hindi
No where-adv -Kahit saan
Noxious-a-Makasisira
Nozzle-n-Nğuso
Nucleate-a-Mabutil
Nucleus-n-Butil
Nude-a-Hubo, hubad, walang damit.
Nudge-n-Tulak
Nudge-v-Maniko, tulakin nğ siko.
Nudity-n-Kahubuan, kahubaran
Nugatory-a-Walang halaga ó kabuluhan
Nugget-n-Butil tingkal, pirasong metal na mahal
Nuisance-n-Kinasusuklaman.
Null-a-Walang, kabuluhan
Nullification-n-Kawalan nang kabuluhan
Nullify-v-Pawalan nğ kabuluhan
Numb a-Namamahid.
Numb-v-Mamamahid
Number-n-Bilang, número.
Number-v-Bumilang, bilangin
Numberless-a-Di mabilang.
Numeral-a Nauukol sa kabilanğan.
Numeral-n-Bilang, numero.
Numerable-a Makabibilang
Nunerally-adv -Ayon sa bilang
Numerate-v-Bumilang, bilanğin
Numeration-n Pagbilang, kabilanğan.
Numerator-n Taga bilang
Numeric-Numerical a-Nauukol sa bilang
Numerous a-Marami, makapal
Num skull-n-Ulol; tawong hindi marunong, tawong mapurol ang isip.
Nun-n-Monja.
Nuncupative Nuncupatory a-Di nakasulat, sinabi lamang.
Nunnery n Bahay nğ mğa monja
Nuptial a Nauukol sa kasal.
Nuptials n-Kasal, balayi
Nurse-n-Magsisiwa, taga iwi nğ bata
Nurse-v Magiwi.
Nursling n-Bata, sangol
Nurture n-Pagsisiwa;pag iwi, pag tuturo
Nurture-v-Mag iwi, magturo
Nut n-Bito
Nut-v Magbito
Nutant-a-Nakayuko.
Nut meg n Anis mascada.
Nutrient-a-May sustancia
Nutriment-n Sustancia
Nutritious-Nutritive-a-Nauukol sa pagkain, ikinabubuhay, mabuti.
Nut shell n Balat nğ buto.
Nymph-n-Duende, tianak; nuno.

O

Oakum-n-Yimot; gulot.
Oar-n-Gaod; sagwan.
Oar-v-Sumagwan; gumaod.
Oars man-n-Ang sumagwan ó gumaod.
Oath-n-Sumpa; tungayaw;
Obduracy-n-Katigasan ng ulo.
Obdurate-a-Matigas ang ulo; suwail,
Obdurateness-n-Katigasan ng ulo.
Obedience-n-Katuparan; kagalangan.
Obedient-a-Masusunurin; mapagbigay
    loob; magalang.
Obeisance-n-Katuparan; pagbibigay loob.
Obese-a-Mataba na lubha.
Obeseness-n-Kaabaan.
Obesity-n-Katabaan.
Obey-v-Sumunod; pintuhuin; tumalima;
    tumupad sa utos; sumunod.
Obfuscate-v-Padilimin.
Obit-n Kamatayan.
Obituary-n-Pahayag tungkol sa nanga-
    matay.
Obituary-a-Nauukol sa nangamatay.
Object-n-Patungo; dahilan; pakay; pi-
    nagusapan; salitaan.
Object-v-Lumaban; umayaw; isalang-
    sang; salungatin; huag pumayag.
Objection-n-Salangsangan; pintas; kaa-
    yawan.
Objectionable a-May pintas.
Objective-n-Dahilan; pinagtutunguhan.
Oblate-a-Pudpod
Oblation-n-Alay.
Obligate-v-Pilitin; pumilit.
Obligation-n-Katungkulan.
Obligatory-a-Kailangan.
Oblige-v-Pilitin; pigipitin.
Obliging-a-Masunurin; mahinhin.
Oblique-a-Mahalang; hiwas.
Oblique-v-Ipahalang; ihapay.
Obliquity-n-Pagkahapay; hiwas.
Obliterate-v-Lipulin; burahin; gibain.
Obliteration-n-Pagbura; kaburahan; ka-
    lipulan.
Oblivion-n-Kadiliman; pagkalimot.
Oblivious-a-Madilim; malilimutin.
Oblong-a-Talohaba.
Obloquy-n-Alibugha; alipusta.
Obnoxious-a-Makayayamot.
Obovate-a-Hitsurang itlog.
Obscene-a-Malibog; mahalay; marumi.
Obscenity-n-Kalibugan; kahalayan.
Obscuration-n-Kadiliman.
Obscure-a-Malabo; madilim: mapang-
    law.

Obscure-v-Padilimin; dumilim; lumabo;
    palabuin.
Obscureness-Obscurity-n-Kalabuan; di-
    lim; kadiliman.
Obsequeous-a-Mapaglingkuran.
Obsequy-n Responso.
Observance n-Masid; katuparan; pag-
    masid; paguusisa; kabaitan; bait.
Observant-a-Mapagmasid; mabait; mau-
    sisain.
Observation-n-Masid; pagmamasid; pag-
    uusisa.
Observatory-n-Observatorio.
Observe-v-Usisian; masirain; magmasid;
    magmasdan; malasin.
Observing-a-Mapagmasid.
Obsolete-a-Lipas; nakaraan; laon.
Obstacle-n-Abala, kaabalahan; kapinsa-
    lan; kahirapan; hirap.
Obstinate-a-Sowail; matigas ang ulo;
    masowayin.
Obstinacy n-Katigasan ng ulo.
Obstreperous-a-Magulo; malikot.
Obstruct-v-Abalahin; harangin; pasalin;
    pigilin; sadhan; pumigil.
Obstruction-n-Abala; harang; bood;
    kahirapan.
Obstructive-a-Mabood.
Obtain-v-Kamtan; abutin; magkamit;
    magkaroon; tamuhin.
Obtainable-a-Makaabot; sukat; kam-
    tan.
Obtrude-v-Makialam; sumabat.
Obtrusion-n-Pakialam.
Obtrusive-a-Mapakialam.
Obtuse-a-Mapurol; pulpol; salsal.
Obviate-v-Ilagan.
Obvious-a-Maliwanag; malinaw.
Occasion-n-Dahilan; panahon.
Occasional-a-Maminsanminsan.
Occident-n-Kalunuran; pag lubog.
Occidental-a-Gawing kalunuran.
Occiput-n-Likod ng ulo.
Occult-a-Tago; lihim; di nakikilala.
Occupant-n-Ang nakalugar.
Occupation-n-Gawa; hanap buhay.
Occupy-v-Makalugar; gamitin.
Occur-v-Mangyari; lumitaw; magmula;
    sumipot.
Occurrence-n-Pangyayari; pagsipot.
Ocean-n-Dagat.
Oceanic a-Nauukol sa dagat.
Octagon-n-Bagay na may walong panu-
    lukan.

Octagonal-*a*-Nauukol sa bagay na may walong panulukan
Octangular *a*-May walong panulukan
Octennial *a*-Nauukol sa luat ng̃ walong taon
October *n* Octubre
Octuple-*a*-Makawalong duble.
Ocular *a* Nauukol sa mata
Oculist *n*-Mangagamot ng̃ mata
Odd *a* Gansal, iba, walang kaparis
Oddity *n*-Kaibhan.
Odds-*n*-Patong, differencia
Ode *n* Verso, kanta awit
Odious-*a*-Magagalitin; nagagalit
Odium-*n* Galit, tanim na loob
Odor *n*-Amoy, pabang̃o
Odorous-Odoriferous *a*-Mabang̃o
O'er-*prep*-Sa ibabaw; sa itaas
O'er *adv*-Sa ibabaw, sa itaas
Of *prep*-Nang, sa, ni; sa cay nila
Off-*adv*-Malayo.
Off *prep*-Sa; di sa
Off *a* Kalayolayoan
Off-*inter*-Layas, alis
Offal *n*-Laman sa loob
Offend-*v*-Magkasala, pagalitin; yamutin, manampalasan
Offense *n* Sala, kasalanan, alipusta, kapaslang̃an; katampalasanan
Offensive *a* Hamak; masama, maahpusta
Offer-*n*-Alay, alok, panata, hayin.
Offer *v*-Ialok, ialay, maghayin
Offering-*n*-Pagalay, pagalok
Off hand *adv*-Ng̃ayon din, madali.
Office *n*-Oficina
Officer *n*-Puno; official
Officer-*i*-Mamuno
Official-*a*-Oficial.
Official-*n* Puno
Officiate-*v*-Mamuno,
Officious-*a*-Masipag masikap
Officiousness *n*-Kasipagan liasikapan
Offing-*n*-Laot ng̃ dagat; layo magbuhat sa pangpang
Offish-*a*-Maulol, loco
Off set *a*-Matimbang̃in; tumapat
Offspring-*n*-Lahi, mang̃a anak at mapo
Oft-Often *adv*-Madalas, towitowi na
Often times-Of times *adv*-Madalas
Oglle-*v*-Magmasdan, magmata.
Oh-*inter*-Aba, naku
Oil-*n* Gas, lang̃is
Oil *v*-Pahiran ng̃ lang̃is, lang̃isin.
Oil cloth-*n* Tapete
Oily-*a*-Malang̃is
Ointment-*n*-Ibuhos ang lang̃is sa ulo
Old-*a*-Matanda, laon, luma, magulang, ubanin dati.
Olden *a* Dating matandan.

Oldish *a* Matanda ng̃ kaunti
Old maid-*n* Dalagang matanda
Oleaster-*n*-Puno ng̃ olivas
Olfactory-*a*-Nauukol sa amoy
Olive-*n* Oliva
Omelet *n* Tinortas na itlog
Omen-*a*-Hula, tanda.
Omen *v*-Humula
Ominous-*a*-Nauukol sa hula ó tanda
Omit-*v*-Ilaktaw, laktawin, maiwan, malimutin ligtaan
Ommissible *a*-Makalilimot
Ommission-*n*-Laktaw, kalimutan.
Omnipotence-*n* Kapangyarihan, kakapalan
Omnipotent-*a* Makapal; makapangyayari; maalam ng̃ lahat
Omniscience-*n*-Karunungan sa lahat
Omniscient *a* Marunong sa lahat ng̃ mang̃a bagay
On-*prep*-Sa, sa ibabaw
Once-*adv*-Minsan At-once Ng̃ayon din.
One *n*-Isa
One-*a*-Isang
Oneness-*n*-Kaisahan
One by one *n*-Isaisa, isa,t,isa
Onerous-*a*-Sowail, mabigat, matigas ang ulo
Onion *n*-Cebuyas
Only-*a*-Bugtong
Only-*adv*-Lamang
Onset-*n* Pagmula; babag.
Onslaught *n* Babag, laban
Onward *a* Sumulongsulong
Onward-*adv* Sa gawing harap
Ooze-*v*-Putik, na malabnaw
Ooze-*v*-Tumalas, tumiin
Oozy-*a*-Maburak, malumot
Opacity-*n*-Kadiliman, kalabuan
Opal *n* Batong mahal
Opaque-*a*-Madilim, di maaninag
Opaqueness-*n*-Kalabuan, kadiliman
Ope-*a*-Bukas
Ope-*v*-Buksan, bumukas
Open-*a*-Bukas, maliwanag, maluang, watak, hayag, maaliwalas
Open *v*-Buksan, bumukas, luang̃in, liwanag̃in, lumuang
Opera-*n*-Opera
Operate *v*-Mamahala, ulugin, gawin, gumawa
Operator-*n*-Ang namamahala.
Operation *n* Gawa; pagulog
Operative *a*-Nauukol sa gawa
Opiate *n*-Gamot na may halong apian
Opine *v*-Sumapantaha, magakala
Opinion *n*-Akala, sapantaha.
Opium *n*-Apian
Opponent *n* Kaagaw, kalaban, katalo, kagalit.

Opponent-a-Kalaban; nakatapat.

Opportune-a-Sa mabuting panahon; bagay.

Opportuneness-n-Kapanahunan; panahon.

Opportunity-n-Kapanahunan; panahon.

Oppose-v-Lumaban; umaway; makipagtalo; nagtalo; sumuay; isalangsang; makipagaway; humamon.

Opposite-a-Katapat; harap; laban.

Opposite-n-Katapat; kalaban.

Opposition-n-Katapatan; away; laban; paglaban; pagsoway.

Oppress-v-Inisin; alipinin; magpahirap; pahirapan.

Oppression-n-Paginis; kahirapan.

Oppressive-a-Mabañgis; napakahirap.

Optative-a-Nauukol sa nais ó sa pita.

Optic-n-Mata.

Optic Optical-a-Nauukol sa tiñgin ó sa mata.

Optimist-n-Mangagamot nğ mata.

Option-n-Kapangyarihan humalal; pili; katowiran nğ bumili ó sa ipagbili.

Optional-a-Nakapipili.

Opulence-n-Yaman; kayamanan.

Opulent-a-Mayaman.

Or-conj.-Kung; ni; nila; ó.

Oracle-n-Tawong marunong.

Oral-n-Hindi nakasulat.

Orange-n-Dalandan; dalanghita.

Orange-a-Kulay dalandan.

Orang-outang-n-Bakulaw.

Oration-n-Sermon; luhog; panalañgin.

Orator-n-Ang marunong magsermon.

Oratory-n-Pagsesermon; pañgañgaral.

Orb-n-Bilog.

Orbed-a-Mabilog.

Orbit-n-Lakad nğ isang planeta.

Orchard-n-Halamanan.

Orchestra-n-Orkesta.

Ordain-v-Iayos; aynsin; itatag; ilagay sa katungkulan.

Ordeal-n-Subok na mahirap.

Order-n-Utos; kautusan; ayos; husay; pagkakawasto.

Order-v-Magutos; iutos; ayusin; husayin; mamuno.

Orderly-a-Maayos; mahusay; mabait.

Orderly-n-Sundalong utusan nğ puno.

Ordinal-a-Nauukol sa kahusayan.

Ordinance-n-Utos nğ Municipio.

Ordinary-a-Karaniwan; gawi; hirati; hayag.

Ordinary-n-Karaniwang bagay.

Ordination-n-Pagpili; paghalal; kautusan; pagutos.

Ordnance-n-Kasangkapan nğ bukbo.

Ore-n-Metal.

Organ-n-Harmonica.

Organic-Organical-a-Nauukol sa harmonica.

Organist-n-Taga tugtog sa harmonica.

Organize-v-Itayo; itatag; magpundar; arreglahin.

Organization-n-Pagtatayo; pagpundar.

Orient-n-Silañganan.

Orient-Oriental-a-Nauukol sa silañganan.

Oriental-n-Taga silañganan.

Orientate-v-Pumaroon sa silañganan.

Orifice-n-Bibig.

Origin-n-Pinagmulaan; pinagbuhatan; pinañgaliñgan.

Original-a-Dating; unang.

Original-n-Ang dati.

Origination-n-Pinagbuhatan; pinañgaliñgan; pinagmulaan.

Originally-adv.-Sa dati.

Originality-n-Datihan; kaunahan.

Orison-n-Orasion.

Ornament-n-Gayak; sangkap; pamuti; biyaya; hiyas.

Ornament-v-Gayakan; pamutiin; gumayak.

Ornamental-a-Maganda; mainam.

Ornamentation-n-Paggayak; pamuti.

Orphan-n-Ulila.

Orphan-a-Nauukol sa pagkaulila.

Orphanage-n-Kalagayan ulila.

Orthography-n-Pagsulat nğ mahusay.

Oscillate-v-Maningning; mañgatal; kumislap; kumintab.

Oscillation-n-Luningning; kisap; pagatal; ningning.

Ossification-n-Paging buto.

Ossify-v-Maging buto.

Ostent-n-Hitsura; bikas; pakita.

Ostensible-a-Maliwanag.

Ostentation-n-Kahambugan; pakpapakita.

Ostentatious-a-Hambog.

Ostler-n-Ang nagalaga sa kabayo.

Ostracea-n-Talaan.

Ostracize-v-Huag isama sa kapwang tawo.

Other-a-Iba.

Other-n-Ang iba; kasama.

Other wise-adv.-Kung hindi; sa ibang paraan.

Ottoman-a-Nauukol sa kaharian nğ Turko.

Ought-adv.-Dapat.

Ought-v-Dapat.

Ounce-n-Onza.

Our-pro.-Amin; atin; namin; natin.

Ours-pro.-Namin; natin.

Our self-pro.-Sarili namin; amin sarili; sarili natin; ating sarili.

Oust-v-Paalisin; alisin; palayasin.

Out-adv.-Sa labas; labas.

36

Out balance-v-Bumigat; lumampas.
Out bid-v-Tawarın ñg mataas sa ıba.
Out break n Pagalsa, alsa.
Out buildıng-n Bahay ó kamalig na na-
kabubukod.
Out cast-n-Tawong dı makikısama sa
ıba.
Out cast-a-Nakabukod, panapon.
Out come n-Pandulo, ang lumıtaw; ang
nangyarı
Out cry-n-Tunang, sigaw ñg maramı.
Out door-a-Nauukol sa labas nang ba-
yan.
Out doors-apv -Sa labas ñg bahay.
Outer-a-Labas.
Outer most-a-Kalayolayoan.
Out fit-n-Mañga kasamaan
Out go-v-Pumaroon sa ıbabaw, lumayo
Out go-n-Gastos
Out grow v-Lumampas ang paglakı.
Out growth-n-Pandulo
Out house n-Bahay na nakabukod
Out landısh-a-Katakataka
Out last-v-Tumagal sa ıba
Out law-u-Taga labas; tulısan. ,
Out lawry-n-Pagkatulisan
Out lay-Gastos, gugol.
Out let n Labasan.
Out line-n-Plano, banhay.
Out line-ı-Gawın ang plano.
Out lıve v-Bumuhay na mahaba sa ıba
Out look-n-Pakıta
Out lyıng a-Malayo.
Out post-n-Bantay na malayo sa hukbo
Outrage n-Kalapastanğanan, tampalasan,
kapalıbhasaan, paglaıt
Outrage-v-Gahisın, lapastanğanin, ma-
mıhasa; laıtın
Outrageous a-Katakot takot; bastos ma-
sama.
Out rıde-v-Sumakay nang matulın sa
ıba.
Outrıght-a-Tunay, totoong; hayag
Out run-v-Tumakbo ñg matulın sa ıba
Out saıl-v-Lumayag ñg matulın sa ıba
Out set-n-Pınagmulan, pamula.
Ont sıde-n Ang labas
Out sıde-a-Labas
Out skirt-n Gılid, hanga.
Out spread-v-Latagın; banatin
Out vıe-v-Humıgıt, mamukod
Out walk-v-Lumakad nang matulın sa
ıba.
Outward-Out wards-adv -Sa gawıng la-
bas
Out wear-v Tumagal sa ıba.   -
Out weigh-v-Bumigat sa iba
Out wit-v-Manalo sa talas ñg ısıp, daıgın
sa dunong.
Oval-n-Talohaba.

Oval-a-Talohaba
Ovate-Ovated-a-Hıtsurang ıtlog
Ovatıon n-Kapurıhan, pagpurı.
Oven-n-Hurno.
Over-adv -Sa ıtaas.
Over-a-Itaas, lampas, mahıgıt
Over-prep -Mahıgıt sa, sa.
Over abundance-n-Kalagpusan
Over abundant-a-Malagpos, labıs
Over awe-v-Takutin.
Over balance v-Ibual bumual.
Over balance n-Pagbual.
Over bear-v-Supılin
Over bearıng a-Palalo, tampalasan.   .
Over board-adv.-Na sa tubıg
Over cast-v-Labuın, tıklupin
Over coat n-Damıt na pangıbabaw
Over come-v-Daıgın, supilin
Over due a-Lampas sa panahon.
Over flow-v-Umapaw, bumaha.
Over flow n-Apaw, paglubog, pagapaw;
pagbaha, kalabısan
Over haul-v-Baguhın, kumpunıhin.
Over head-adv -Sa ıtaas
Over hear-v-Marinıg, dumınıg
Over joy-n-Kasayahan.
Over land-adv -Sa lupa ang daan.
Over look-v-Laktawın, ılaktaw, malımu-
tin
Over plus-n Kalabısan; kalagpusan, la-
bıs, lagpos
Over power v-Supılın, daigın
Over reach-v-Lumampas ang pagabot;
dayaın
Over rule-v-Supılın, daigın
Over see-v-Mamahala, mamuno
Over seer-n-Ang namamahala, kapatas.
Over set-v-Itaub; ıbual.
Over shoe-n-Sapatos na pang ıbabaw.
Over shoot-v-Huag tumama
Over sıght n-Malı, kamahan
Over spread-v-Ilatag, ıtakpan.
Overt a Malıwanag, palıtaw
Over take-v-Abutın, umabot, magkamıt;
datnın
Over throw-v-Ibual, talonın
Over throw-n Kahıtuhan; pagtatalunin.
Overture n Balak, alok.
Over turn-v Bumalıkuas, balıkuasın.
Over turn-n-Balıkuas, kalıtuhan.
Over ween-v-Maghambog
Over weigh-v-Lumampas ang bigat.
Over whelm v Supılın, patakahın.
Ovıform a Hıtsurang ıtlog
Owe-ı-Manğutang
Owl-n-Kuago
Owlet-n-Kuagong muntı
Owlısh-a-Parang kuago; nauukol sa
kuago.
Own-v-Arıın, umarı, magkaroon.

Own-*a*-Sariling.

Owner-*n*-Ang may ari; panginoon.

Owner ship-*n*-Pagkaari.

Ox-*n*-Bakang malaki na nakapon.

Oyster-*n*-Talaba.

P

Pabular-*a*-Nauukol sa pagkain.

Pabulum-*n*-Pagkain.

Pace-*n*-Hakbang; lakad; tulin.

Pace-*v*-Lakarin; hakbangin; lumakad.

Pacific-*a*-Tahimik.

Pacification-*n*-Katahimikan.

Pacify-*v*-Patahimikan; tumahimik.

Pack-*v*-Balutan; balot; bigkis; karga.

Pack-*n*-Balutin; ibalot; bigkisin; pasanin; ikahou isilid; magpasan.

Package *n*-Balutan.

Packer-*n*-Kargador; taga pasan.

Pad-*n*-Balutan ñg papel.

Pad-*v*-Sapinin.

Padding-*n*-Sapin.

Paddle-*n*-Gaod; sagwan.

Paddle-*v*-Gumaod; maglaro sa tubig.

Paddock-*n*-Pitak.

Paddy *n*-Pitak.

Padlock-*n*-Seradura.

Padlock-*v*-Ilagay ñg saradura; susuhin ñg seradura.

Padrone-*n*-Patron.

Pagan-*n*-Ang ayaw sumampalataya sa Panginoon Dios; tawong hindi binyagan.

Pagan-*a*-Nauukol sa hindi binyagan.

Paganish-*a*-Parang hindi binyagan.

Paganism-*n*-Kalagayang hindi binyagan.

Page-*n*-Mukha ñg dahon; pag ina; alila.

Page-*v*-Bilangin ang dahon.

Pagoda-*n*-Simbahan sa India, Japon at sa China.

Pail-*n*-Timba; baldi.

Pailful-*n*-Laman ñg baldi.

Pain-*n*-Sakit; bugbog; hirap; dalamhati; hapdi; hapis; kirot.

Pain-*v*-Sumakit; humapis. humapdi.

Painful-*a*-Masakit; mahapis; makirot; mahapdi.

Painless-*a*-Walang sakit ó damdam.

Pains-*n*-Ingat; kaingatan.

Pains taker-*n*-Tawong maingat.

Painstaking-*n*-Pag ingat.

Painstaking-*a*-Maingat.

Paint-*n*-Pinta.

Paint-*v*-Magpinta.

Pair-*n*-Paris.

Palace-*n*-Palacio; bahay ñg hari.

Palate-*n*-Lasap.

Palatable-*n*-Malasa; masarap.

Palatial-*a*-Nauukol sa bahay ñg hari; mainam; maganda.

Palaver-*n*-Salita.

Palaver-*v*-Magsalita.

Pale-*a*-Putla; maputla; kupas.

Pale-*v*-Mamutla; kumupas.

Pale-*n*-Tulos; hanga; bakod.

Paleness-*n*-Putla; kaputlaan.

Paleography-*n*-Ang dating paraan nang pagsulat.

Palestra-*n*-Pagbubuno.

Paletot-*n*-Damit na pang ibabaw.

Palfrey-*n*-Kabayong pangsakay.

Paling-*n*-Mañga tulos; hanga; bakod.

Palisade-*n*-Tulos na malaki: bakod ñg mga tulos na malaki.

Palisade-*v*-Magbakod ñg tulos na malaki.

Palish-*a*-Maputlaputla.

Pall-*n*-Damit na pang ibabaw.

Pall bearer-*n*-Taga pasan ñg kalanda.

Palliate-*v*-Ikanlong; itago; magbigay ñg dahilan.

Pallid-*a*-Maputla; mamutla.

Pallidness-Pallidity-*n*-Kaputlaan.

Pallor-*n*-Pagkaputla; kaputlaan.

Palm-*n*-Dangkal: ramos; balalaw.

Palm-*v*-Dangkalin.

Palm-*n*-Palad ñg kamay.

Palmate-*a*-Hitsurang kamay.

Palm Sunday-*n*-Lingo de ramos.

Palpable-*a*-Makararamdam sa hipo.

Palpitate-*v*-Tumibok; kumutog; kumaba.

Palpitation-*n*-Tibok kutog; kaba.

Palsy-*n*-Sakit na pasma.

Palsy-*v*-Mapasma.

Palsied-*a*-Pasmado.

Palter-*v*-Dayain; tumaksil; mamali; magbiro.

Paltriness-*n*-Karamutan; kasakiman.

Paltry-*a*-Maramot; masakim.

Pamper-*v*-Pakanin ñg husto; bumusog.

Pamphlet-*n*-Pampleta; munting libro.

Pan-*n*-Lalagyan ñg anoman.

Panacea-*n*-Gamot sa lahat nang mañga sakit.

Pancake-*n*-Bibinkang harina.

Pandemonium-*n*-Kaguluhan.

Pane-*n*-Cristal ñg bintana.

Panel-*n*-Balagi ñg pinto.

Pang-*n*-Gulat; kaba ñg dibdib.

Panic-*n*-Takot ñg marami.

Pannier-*n*-Batulang; bakol.

Pant-*n*-Hingal.

Pant-*v*-Huminñgal; humanñgos.

Pantaloon-n-Salawal.

Pantry-n-Silid nang manga pagkain; bangera.

Pap-n-Suso; pagkain na malambot para sa mga bata.

Papa-n-Tatang; tata; tatay; amang.

Papacy-n-Katungkalang papa.

Papal-a-Nauukol sa papa.

Papaw-n-Papaya.

Paper-n-Papel.

Paper-v-Ilagay ó idikit ng papel.

Papist-n-Katolico.

Papistic-Papistical-a-Nauukol sa Católico ó sa papa.

Par-n-Kapantayan ng halaha.

Parable-n-Talinhaga.

Parade-n-Procession.

Parade-v-Magprocession.

Paradise-n-Garden ni Adan; kasayahan.

Paragon-n-Halimbawa ng kabutihan.

Paragraph-n-Pangkat na maikli.

Paralell-a-Katabi; kasiping; pantay.

Paralysis-n-Pasma.

Paralytic-n-Ang may sakit na pasma.

Paralytic-Paralytical-a-Nauukol sa sakit ng pasma.

Paralyze-v-Mapasma.

Paramount-a-Kataastaasan; mataas sa lahat.

Parapet-n-Kuta.

Paraphrase-n-Kasaysayan.

Paraphrase-v-Ihulog sa ibang wika; magsaysay.

Parasite-n-Ang bumubuhay sa gugol ng iba.

Parasol-n-Payong.

Par boil-v-Kulain ng kaunti.

Parcel-n-Balutan; balot.

Parcel-v-Balutin; ibalot.

Parch-v-Ibusa.

Parchment-n-Katad ng tupa na ginayak sa pagsulat.

Pardon-n-Patawad; paglitos; pagkalag sa sala; pagpatawad.

Pardon-v-Kalagin sa sala; patawarin.

Pardonable-a-Dapat patawarin.

Pare-v-Talupan; balutan; bawasan; iklian.

Parent-n-Magulang; hinlog.

Parentage-n-Hinlog; pinaganakan.

Parental-a-Nauukol sa magulang.

Parish-n-Hukuman ng isang pari; lupang nasasakop ng kapangyarihan ng isang pari.

Parity-n-Kapantayan.

Park-n-Plaza; luneta.

Parlance-n-Salitaan.

Parley-n-Salitaan.

Parley r-Magsalitaan.

Parlor-n Silid na tinatawag ang loob.

Parochial-a-Nauukol sa paroquia; makitid; makipot; may hanga·

Parol-n-Salita ng bibig.

Parol-a-Nakasabi lamang.

Parole-n-Pangako.

Parole v-Patawarin; hanguin; iligtas; ibigay ng kalayaan.

Parricide-n Ang natay sa sariling amaó ina.

Parrot-n Loro.

Parry-v-Ilagan; umilag.

Parsimonious-a-Maramot; kuripot.

Parsimony-n-Kariputan; karamntan.

Parson-n-Pastor.

Parsonage-n-Bahay ng pastor.

Part-n-Bahagi; kapiraso; parte.

Part-v-Bahagiin; biakin; hiwalayin humiwalay; lumagot.

Par take-v-Sumali; kumain; kumuha.

Partial-a-Di buo; mababagi; mahilig may tinitignan.

Partiality-n-Kahiligan; kabilingan.

Participate-v-Sumali.

Participation-n-Pagkakasali.

Particle-n Piraso; kapiraso; kapirangot.

Particular-a-Bugtong; nakabukot; bantog.

Parting-n-Paghihiwalay.

Partisan-n-Kasali.

Partition-n-Paghihiwalay; dingding.

Partition-v Ilagay ang dingding.

Partly-adv-.Di buo.

Partner-n-Kasama; kaulayaw.

Partnership-n-Samahan.

Parturition-n-Panganganak.

Party-n-Samahan; katipunan; kapisanan.

Party-colored-Parti-colored-a-Sari sari ang kulay.

Parvenu-n-Tawong hambog ó palalo,

Pas-n-Hakbang; unahan.

Pascha-n-Kuresma.

Pass-v-Lumipas; makaraan; dumaan; mamatay.

Pass-n-Passes; pahintulot; hakbang; landas; paso.

Passable-n-Makararaan.

Passage-n Paraan; lakad.

Passenger-n-Ang sumasakay; ang lumalakad.

Passim-adv.-Dito at doon.

Passing-n-Pagdaan.

Passing-a-Makaraan.

Passion-Galit; pagkakagalit; kagalitan; tanim na loob.

Passion-n-Pasion.

Passionate-a-Mainit ang ulo.

Passive-a-Tahimik; maamo; matitiis.

Pass port-n-Pahintulot.

Past a Nakaraan; lipas.

Past n-Ang panahon nakaraan.

Paste-a-Pagkit; pandikit.

Paste-v-Idikit.
Paste board-n-Carton.
Pastil-Pastille-n-Pasteles
Pastime-n-Aliw, kaluguran, aliwan
Pastor n-Pastor, pari
Pastoral-a-Nauukol sa pastor
Pastorate Pastorship-n-Kalagayang pastor.
Pastry-n-Mañga mamon
Pasture v-Pastulan.
Pasture-v-Ipastol, magpastol
Pasturage-n Pastulan, pagpastol
Pasty-a Madikit; mapagkit.
Pat-a-Bagay, akma; ayon sa panahon
Pat adi -Sa mabuting panahon.
Pat n-Layaw.
Patch-n-Tutop, tagpi, dagdag
Patch-v-Tutupan; itagpi, hayumahin, husayin, kumpunihin
Patch work-n-Pagtutup; paghahayuma
Pate-n Bao ñg ulo.
Patella-n-Bayugo ñg tuhod
Patent-a-Mahiwanag; hayag, bukas
Paternal a-Nauukol sa ama.
Paternity-n-Hinlog, lahi, familia, kalagayang ama
Path-n Landas, daan
Pathless a-Walang landas.
Pathetic a Kaawa
Pathologist-n-Mangagamot.
Pathology-n-Karunuñgan sa mña sakit.
Path way-n-Landas, daan, paraan
Patient-a-Matitiisin
Patient-n-Ang may sakit.
Patience-n-Katitiisan, katimtiman ñg loob
Patriarch-n-Puno ñg isang familia, Tawong matanda.
Patrician a-Marañgal dakila
Patricide-n Ang namatay sa ama
Patrimonial a Nauukol sa mana
Patrimony n-Mana
Patriot-n-Patriota.
Patriotism-n-Pagibig sa lupang tinubuan.
Patrol-v-Magpatrulia, magbantay.
Patrol-n Bantay.
Patron n-Kasuki, pintakasi
Patronage n-Pagkakasuki, pagampon
Patroness n-Kabaying kasuki
Patronize-v-Sumuki, magkasuki.
Patten-n-Bakia
Patter-v-Pumatak
Patter-n Katapakan, pagpapatak
Pattern-n Huwaran; tularan, kahowad
Pattern-v-Humuwad, tumulad, tularin
Paucity-n-Kadalañgan, kautian.
Paunch-n Tiyan
Pauper n-Pulubi
Pauperism-n-Kalagayang pulubi

Pauperize v Lubug sa hirap.
Pause n-Hinto. utal kautalan
Pause v-Maghinto; magutal.
Pave v-Ilatag ang bato sa karsada.
Pavement-n-Latag ñg bato sa karsada.
Paw-n-Paa ñg hayop.
Pawn-v-Galawin, kurutin.
Pawn-n Sangla.
Pawn-v-Isangla
Pawnbroker-n-Ang mayari ñg bahay na sanglaan.
Pay n-Upa, bayad kaupahan; ikababayad.
Pay-v-Bayaran, magbayad, umupa, upahan.
Payee-n-Ang tumangap ang bayad ó upa
Payer-n-Taga bayad, ang magbabayad
Payment-n-Pagbayad, kabayaran, bayad, kaupahan, upa
Pea-n-Guisante
Peace-n-Katahimikan; kapanatagan, kapayapaan
Peaceable a-Tahimik, walang basagulo, payapa
Peaceful a-Tahimik, mabini, mahinahon, walang basagulo, payapa
Peach-n-Melocotones
Peach-v-Bintañgin, paratañgin.
Peak-n-Tuktok ñg bundok
Peal-n-Tunog na malakas
Peal v-Tugtugin ñg malakas
Peanut n-Muni
Pear-n-Peras
Pearl-n-Perlas
Pearly-a-Parang perlas
Peasant-n-Taga buked, tawong mahirap
Pease n-Guisante.
Pebble-n-Batong munti.
Pebbly-a-Mabato
Peck n-Tuka
Peck-v-Tumuka, tukain
Pectoral a-Nauukol sa dibdib ó sa sakit ñg dibdib
Peculate-v-Umitin, umumit, nakawin, magnakaw
Peculation n-Pagumit, pagnakaw
Peculator-a-Magnanakaw, mañguñgumit
Pecuniary-a-Nauukol sa salapi.
Pedagogue-n-Maestro.
Pedagogy-n-Karunuñgan sa pagtuturo.
Pedal-a Nauukol sa paa
Peddle-v-Ialok, maglako.
Peddler-n-Maglalako
Pedestal-n-Puno ñg haligi
Pedestrian-a-Nakalakad, lumalakad
Pedestrian-n-Tawong lakad
Pedestrianism-n-Paglalakad
Pedigree-n-Hinlog; lahi.
Peek-v-Sumilip.

Peek-n-Silip
Peel-v-Balatin, talupan, upakan
Peel-n-Balat, upak
Peep-v-Sumilip.
Peep-n Silip
Peeper-n-Sisiw.
Peer n-Sumilip.
Peer-n-Kasama, kaulayaw
Peerless-a-Walang kapantay ó kahulilip.
Peevish-a-Mapootin, magagalitin
Peg-n-Pakong kahoy
Peg-v-Ipako.
Pelf-n-Salapi, kayamanan
Pell-n-Balat
Pellet-n Bolang munti
Pellicle n-Balok
Pellmell-a-Walang ayos.
Pellucid-a-Maaninag
Pelt-n-Balat nğ hayop
Pelt-v-Batuhin, ipukol
Pelvic-a-Nauukol sa buto nğ bayawang.
Pelvis-n Buto nğ bayawang.
Pen-n Kulunğan.
Pen-v-Kulunğin, kumulong
Pen-n Pluma.
Penal a-Nauukol sa parusa
Penalty-n-Parusa
Penance-n-Katiisan
Pence-n-Dalawang kuarta, isang mala-
pad
Pencil-n-Lapis
Pencil v-Sumulat
Pend-v-Bumitbit, ikabit
Pendency-n Sabit, kabit
Pendent-a-Nakasabit, nakabitin
Pendulous a-Nakasabit; nakabitin
Pendulum-n-Paniktik nğ orasan
Penetrate-v-Tumagos, matarok.
Penetration-n-Tagos; tarok
Penitence-n Pagsisisi
Penitent-a Nakapagsisi
Penitent-n-Ang nagsisisi.
Penitential-a-Nauukol sa pagsisisi
Penitentiary-n Bilango
Pen knife n-Laseta.
Penman-n-Ang marunong sumulat
Penmanship-n-Sulat kamay
Penant-n-Bandera
Pennate-Pennated-a-May pakpak
Penniless-a-Mahirap, salat; walang
kuarta
Pennon n-Bandila, pakpak.
Pensile-a-Nakasabit, nakabitin.
Pensive-a-Palaisipin, mapag wari; ma-
lungkot.
Pent-v. imp. & p p.-Nakakulong.
Pentateuch-n-Ang mğa utos ni Moises.
Penthouse-n-Sibe; pakpak nğ bahay
Penult-n-Ang huli fuera caming isa.
Penumbra n-Pagdidilim nğ buan.

Penurious a-Maramot, madalang
Penury-n-Kahirapan, kakailanğan, kai-
gutan; karukhaan.
People n-Manğa tawo
People-v-Magkaroon nğ maraming tawo,
dumami ang mğa tawo
Pepper-n-Paminta
Pepper v-Ilagay ó ibudbuod ang pa-
minta.
Peppery a Maanghang,
Peradventure adv -Marahil
Perambulate-v-Lakarin, lumakad.
Perambulation-n-Lakad, paglalakad.
Perambulator-n-Ang lumakad
Perceive-v-Kapain, humalata, indahin,
intindihin, sumahod
Perceivable-a-Madaling maintindihan.
Percentage n-Por ciento
Perceptible a-Nahalata, litaw, maliwa-
nag
Perceptibility-n-Pakiramdam
Perceptive-a-Maramdamin
Perception-n-Pakiramdam; damdam, pa-
nğintindi
Perch n-Hapunan
Perch-v-Humapon
Perchance-a-Marahil
Percolate v-Salain
Percuss-v-Ilagpak, itupak
Percussion n-Lagpak; tagupak
Perdition-n-Lugi, kalipulan; kasiraan,
kamatayan
Peregrinate-v-Lumakad
Peregrination n-Lakad.
Peremtory-a-Totoo, tunay
Perennial a-Matagal maluat, walang
tigil ó likat, panay
Perfect-a-Lubos, puspos, walang kulang
dalisay, ganap, magaling, maganda.
Perfect-v-Tapusin, ganapin, gumanap,
tumapos, yariin.
Perfectibility-n-Kayarian; katapusan.
Perfectible a-Makatatapos.
Perfection-n-Kayarian, katapusan, ka-
ganapan
Perfidious-a-Taksil; sukab, suitik, lilo.
Perfidy-n-Kataksilan; kasuitikan, kalilu-
han, kasukaban.
Perforate-v-Butasin, tarukin, balibulin
Perforation-n-Pagbutas, pagkabutas bu-
tas
Perforce-adv.-Sa kakailanğan; sa lakas
Perform-v-Gumawa, tumupad, tuparin;
gawin
Performance-n-Kilos, teatro, acto.
Perfume-n-Pabanğo
Perfume-v-Pabanğohin, ilagay nğ paba-
nğo.
Perfumery-n-Pabanğo
Perhaps adv-Marahil, dili, sakali.

Peril-*n* Panganib.

Perilous-*a*-Mapanganib, may panganib.

Perimeter *n*-Paligid

Period-*n*-Panahon, luat, punto

Periodic-Periodical-*a* Nauukol sa panahon

Periphery *n*-Paligid.

Perish-*v*-Mamatay, lumipol

Perishable-*a*-Mamamatay

Perisome *n*-Balat ng hayop na walang gulugod.

Periwig-*n*-Buhok na postiso

Perjure-*v*-Manumpa ng kasinungalingan huag tumupad sa ipinanumpa

Perjury-*n*-Kasinungalingan

Permanence-Permanency-*n* Pananatili, pamamarati, katibayan, pagkalagi

Permament-*a* Lagi; matibay.

Permeable-*a* Makatatarok, matatarukin

Permeate *v*-Tarukin. .

Permissible-*a*-Maaring ipahintulot.

Permission *n* Tulot, kapahintulutan

Permit-*v*-Tulutan, ipahintulot, paraanin.

Permit-*n*-Tulot; pahintulot

Permissive *a*-Maaring ipahintulot.

Permutation-*n*-Kapalitan, pagpalit.

Permute *v* Ipamalit, palitan, pumalit

Pernicious-*a*-Masama, makasasama makasisira, makamamatay.

Perpendicular-*a* Patayo, tirik, nakatayo.

Perpendicular-*n* Tayo, tirik

Perpendicularity-*n*-Pagka tayo; katiri kan.

Perpetrate-*v*-Gumawa, gawin, magkasala.

Perpetration-*n*-Pag gagawa; gawa

Perpetrator-*n*-Ang gumawa

Perpetual-*a*-Walang hanga ó likat, lagi, pareti

Perpetuate-*v*-Gawing lagi, ipamalagi.

Perpetuation-*n*-Pagkalagi, pamamarati

Perpetuity-*n* Pamamarati, pamamalagi.

Perplex *v*-Guluhin ang isip

Perplexity *n*-Basagulo, gulo ng isip kalabuan, duwag

Persecute-*v*-Habulin, yamutin, pahirapan, sundin, ipagdowahagin.

Persecution-*n*-Kahirapan, dowahagi

Perseverance-*n*-Katiyagaan, kalakasan ng loob, katibayan ng loob

Persevere-*v*-Pilitin, magtagal; tumagal

Persist-*v*-Ipaglaon, lumagi, pilitin, pumilit

Persistence-Persistency-*n* Kapilitan, katiyagaan, pagpilit.

Persistent *a*-Nakapipilit; mapipilitin

Person-*n*-Tawo

Personage-*n*-Katawohan.

Personal-*a*-Nauukol sa tawo ó sarili

Personalty *n* Ari ng sarili

Personate-*v*-Gumagad sa iba, saysayin

Personify-*v*-Gagarin ang kapwa

Perspective *a*-Nauukol sa plano.

Perspective *n*-Tingin; plano

Perspire-*v*-Pumawis

Perspiration-*n*-pawis

Persuade-*v*-Iudyok, ihiling, pilitin, pumilit

Persuasible-*a*-Makapipilit

Persuasion-*n* Kapilitan, udyok

Pert *a*-Mangahas

Pertain-*v*-Maukol.

Pertinacious-*a*-Matigas ang ulo; matibay ang loob

Pertinacity-*n*-Kalakasan ng loob, kahigpitan, katigasan ng ulo

Pertinent-*a*-Akma, bagay, nauukol

Pertness-*n*-Pangahas.

Perturb-*v*-Sabarin, yamutin; tuksuhin, guluhin ang isip.

Perturbation-*n*-Kaguluhan nang isip, ligalig.

Perusal-*n*-Pag babása

Peruse-*v*-Bumasa ng patakbo, umusig, malasin

Perverse-*a*-Nakalihis, matigas ang ulo, masama

Perverseness-*n*-Katigasan ng ulo, pag kabalintuna

Perversity-*n*-Katigasan ng ulo, pagkabalintuna

Pervert-*v*-Iakay sa masama, pasamain

Pervious-*a*-Makapapasok, matatarukin.

Pest-*n*-Peste

Pester-*n*-Yamutin, sabarin

Pestiferous-*a*-Nauukol sa peste, makakahawa.

Pestilence-*n*-Peste.

Pestilent-*a*-Mahilig sa masama.

Pestle-*n*-Pandurog

Pet-*v*-Palaywin

Pet-*n*-Ang minamahal

Pet *a*-Minamahal

Petal-*n*-Dahon ng bulaklak.

Petit-*a*-Munti, walang kabuluhan; kuripot.

Petition-*n*-Panalangin, samo, daing

Petition-*v*-Manalangin; sumamo; dumaing

Petrification-*n* Pagiging bato

Petrify-*v*-Maging bato

Petroleum-*n*-Gas.

Petticoat *n* Naguas, enaguas.

Pettish *a*-Mapootin

Petty-*a* Munti, walang kabuluhan

Petulance-Petulancy *n* Kapootan, poot.

Petulant-*a* Mapootin

Pew-*n*-Upuan sa simbahan

Phalanx-*n*-Pulutong ng sundalo

Phantasm-*n*-Panaginip, guniguni

Phantom-*n*-Nuno, guniguni.

Pharisee-n-Fariseo.

Pharmacy-n Pag gagawa nang gamot, botica

Pharnyx-n-Ñgalanğala.

Phase n-Hitsura

Phenominal a-Kataka taka, kamangha mangha

Phial-n Boteng munti.

Philanthropic-Philanthropical-a-Mabuti o magandang loob

Philanthropy-n-Kagandahan nğ loob.

Philter-n-Gayuma.

Phiz n-Mukha

Phlegm-n-Kalagra,

Phlegmatic a Makalagra

Phonetic-a-Nauukol sa voces

Phonetics-n-Karununğan tungkol sa mañga tunog

Phonic-a-Nauukol sa tunog

Phonics-n-Karununğan tungkol sa mañga tunog

Phonographic a-Nauukol sa fonografo

Phonograph-n-Fonografo

Photograph-n-Retrato

Photograph-v-Kunin ang retrato.

Photography-n-Karunungan sa pagkuha nğ retrato

Phrase-n-Maikling kasaysayan

Phrenology n-Karununğan tungkol sa utak nğ ulo.

Phrensy-n-Kaululan.

Phthisic n-Tisis

Phthisical-a-May tisis

Phthisis-n-Tisis

Physic-n-Purga gamot

Physic-v Purgahin.

Physical-a-Nauukol sa catawan

Physician-n-Mangagamot

Physics n-Karununğan tungkol sa fisica

Physiognomy n-Hitsura, mukha.

Piano-Pianofortr-n-Piano.

Pianist-n-Pianista

Picayune-n-Sikolo

Pick-v-Pumulot, tukain, gayatin.

Pick-n-Tuka, piko

Pick ax-Pick axe-n Piko

Picket-n-Tungkod na matulis.

Pickle-n-Atsara

pick pocket-n-Manenekas

Picnic n-Kasayahan, kainan sa gubat.

Picnic-v-Magkainan sa gubat.

Pictorial-a-Nauukol sa mañga pintura

Picture-n-Pintura

Picture frame-n-Sanepa

Pie-n-Pastel

Pie bald-a-May maraming kulay

Piece n-Piraso, bahagi, kagyat, kapuaso, lapang.

Piece-v-Pirasohin, bahagin.

Piece meal-adv -Untiunti; dahandahan, pahintohinto

Pied-a-May maraming kulay mansado.

Piet-n-Pilar, haligi nğ bato.

Pierce-v-Tarukin butasin; tumagos.

Piety-n-Pagibig sa Bathala

Pigeon-n-Kalapati

Pig n-Baboy.

Piggish-a-Matakaw

Pig-headed-a-Matigas ang ulo

Pigment n Tina

Pigmy-n-Tawong pandak, unano.

Pike-n Pakong malaki

Pilaster-n-Haligi.

Pile-n-Bunton, haligi

Pile-v-Ibunton, punuin

Pilfer-v-Umitin, umumit

Pilgrim-n-Tawong mapaglakad.

Pilgrimage-n-Lakad

Pill-n-Pilduras

Pillage-v-Mangloob, gibain, manduit

Pillage-n-Panduduit

Pillar-n-Haligi, pilar.

Pillow-n-Unan.

Pillow-v-Mahiga sa unan

Pillow case-n-Punda nğ unan

Pilot-n-Ang umugit sa sasakyan

Pilot-v-Umugit, umakay, akayin.

Pimple n-Butlig

Pin-n-Aspili

Pin-v-Aspilihin

Pinafore-n-Camisola

Pincers-n-Sipit, panipit

Pinch-v-Kurutin, kumurot

Pinch-n-Kurot

Pinch beck-a-Hindi totoo, sinuñgaling

Pinchers-n-Sipit panipit

Pincushion n-Lalagyan nğ aspili.

Pine-v-Lumungkot, manimdim

Pine-n-Pina

Pine apple-n-Piña

Pinery-n-Gubat nğ pina

Pinion-n-Balahibo, pakpak, pangapos nğ baraso

Pinion-v-Gapusin

Pink-a-Mapulapula

Pink n-Saksak.

Pink-v-Butasin

Pinnacle-n-Lugar na mataas

Pint-n-Takalan nğ mañga bagay na lusaw.

Pintle-n-Aspiling munti

Pioneer n-Tawong lumipat sa bagong lupa

Pioneer-v-Umuna.

Pious a-Mapagdasal, banal

Pip-n-Sakit nğ manok, binhi.

Pip-v-Sumiap.

Pipe n-Kuako, tubo; flauta.

Pipe-v-Tumugtog sa flauta

Piquant-a-Masaklap; mapait;maanghang.
Pique-n-Galit; dalamhati; yamot;
Pique-v-Yamutin; pagalitin.
Piracy-n-Pagnanacaw sa dagat.
Pirate-n-Magnanakaw sa dagat; tulisang dagat.
Piratical-a-Nauukol sa tulisang dagat.
Piscatorial-a-Nauukol sa isda.
Piscivorous-a-Kumakain ng̃ isda.
Pistol-n-Revolber; pistola.
Pit n-Hukay; baunan; tibag.
Pit-v-Hukayin.
Pitch-n-Alketran; itsa.
Pitch-v-Magitsa; pahiran ng̃ alketran.
Pitch-dark-a-Madilim na madilim.
Pitcher-n-Pitchel.
Pitch fork-n-Panghakot ng̃ damung tuyo.
Pitchy-a-May halong alketran.
Piteous-a-Kahapishapis; malunos.
Pithy-a-Malambot ang loob.
Pitiable-a-Dapat nmawa.
Pitiful-a-Mahabagin; maawain.
Pitiless-v-Walang habag; walang awa; mabagsik; mabang̃is.
Pittance-n-Limos.
Pity-n-Habag; awa; hinagpis; hinayang.
Pity-v-Maawa; habagin.
Pivot-n-Ikiran.
Pivot-v-Umikit.
Placard-n-Pahayag; paunawa.
Placard-v-Ipahayag.
Place-n-Lugar; daan.
Place-v-Ilagay sa lugar; lagyan; lumagay; ayosin; maglagay.
Placid-a-Maamong loob; tahimik; walang gulo.
Plague-n-Peste.
Plague-v-Yamutin; payamutin.
Plaid-n-Sita.
Plain-a-Maliwanag; yano; aliwaswas; hayag.
Plain-n-Lupang patag.
Plaint-n-Daing: panalang̃in; panaghoy.
Plaintive-a-Malungkot; malumbay.
Plait-n-Kunot; suri.
Plait-v-Magsuri; magkunot; kunotin.
Plan-n-Anyo; katha; plano.
Plan-v-Isipin; kumatha.
Plane-n-Katam; pangkayas.
Plane-a-Yano; patag.
Plane-v-Katamin.
Planet-n-Planeta.
Planetary-a-Nauukol sa planeta.
Plank-n-Tablang makapal.
Plank-v-Ilatag ó takpanin ng̃ tablang makapal.
Plant-n-Punla.
Plant-v-Magtanim.
Plantain-n-Saging.

Plantation-n-Lupang sinasaka.
Planter-n-Manananim.
Plash-n-Labak; tilansik.
Plash-v-Tumilansik ang tubig.
Plashy-a-Malabak.
Plaster-n-Halo ng̃ apog at buhang̃in.
Plaster-v-Pahiran ng̃ apog.
Plat-n-Humabi.
Plat-n-Habi; kapirasong lupa.
Plate-n-Pingan; pirasong metal.
Plateau-n-Lupang mataas at patag.
Platform-n-Tablado; plataforma.
Platoon-n-Pulutong ng̃ sundalo.
Platter-n-Bandejada.
Plaudit-v-Pagpuri.
Plaudit-v-Purihin.
Plausible-a-Bagay; dapat purihin.
Play-n-Laro; teatro; acto.
Play-v-Maglalaro.
Player-n-Maglaro.
Play fellow-n-Kalaro.
Play mate-n-Kalaro.
Playful-a-Masaya; mapaglaro.
Play thing-n-Laroan.
Plea-n-Dahilan.
Plead-v-Manalang̃in; mamanhikluhod.
Please-v-Aliwin; magbigay lugod; palayawin.
Pleasantry-n-Kasayahan; kaligayahan; galak.
Pleasing-a-Maaliw; masaya; malugod; maligaya; kaaliwaliw; kalugodlugod; mairogin; nakalulugod.
Pleasant-a-Maaliw; masaya; maligaya; malugod; maaya.
Pleasure-n-Kasayahan; tawa; galak; handog; inam; kainaman; lasap; ligaya.
Pleat-n-Suri.
Pleat-v-Suriin.
Plebian-a-Hamak; mababa; karaniwan-
Plebian-n-Tawong hamak; tawong karaniwan.
Pled-v. imp. & p. p.-Namagitan; namanhikluhod; dumaing.
Pledge-n-Sanla.
Pledge-v-Isangla.
Plenary-a-Puno; .lubos.
Plentitude-n-Kasaganaan; karamihan.
Plenteous-Plentiful-a-Masagana; marami.
Plenty-n-Karamihan; kasaganaan.
Plenty-a-Sagana; marami.
Pleura-n-Loob ng̃ lalamunan.
Pleurisy-n-Sakit ng̃ lalamunan.
Plexiform-a-Hasuotsuot; magulo.
Pliable-a-Malambot; mahubugin.
Pliant-a-Malambot; mahubay.
Pliancy-n-Kalambutan.
Pliers-n-Sipit na munti.
Plight-n-Sangla; katibayan; kapang̃aniban; pang̃ako.

37

Plight-v-Isangla, magpañgako

Plod-v-Lumacad.

Plot-n-Lupang munti, isip na masama

Plot-v-Umisip.

Plough-n Araro; kasangkapang panlinang.

Plough-v-Ararohin· magararo, maglinang.

Plow n Araro; kasangkapan panlinang

Plow-v Ararohin, magararo, maglinang.

Plow boy-Plowman-n-Ang nagaararo

Plow share-n Sudsod

Pluck-n-Tapang, batak.

Pluck-v-Himulmulan.

Plucky-a-Matapang, mañgahas, walang takot -

Plug-n-Tasak, tapon; tasok.

Plug-v-Tasakin.

Plum n-Sineguelas.

Plumage n Balahibo ñg mga ibon.

Plumb-a-Patayo; tama.

Plumb-n-Hulog

Plumb-v-Towirin ang tayo ñg haligi

Plumb line-n Hulog

Plume-n-Tuktok

Plump-a-Malilog, mataba, may katawan

Plump-v-Lumaki; tumaba.

Plump-adv.-Ñgayon din, pagdaka

Plunder-n-Ang pagumit, ang inumit; umit

Plunder-v Nakawin manduit

Plunge-v-Sumisid; sumulong nang pa bigla.

Plunge-n-Sisid.

Pluperfect-a-Puspos, puno; walang pin tas, lubos.

Plural a-Mahigit sa isa

Plurality n-Kahigtan, karamihan.

Plus-a-Totoo; dapat idagdag.

Plush-n-Trespelo

Plutocrat-n-Ang may kapangyarihan dahil sa kanyang yaman

Pluvial-a-Nauukol sa ulan

Ply-v-Tanuñgin, pilitin, magtrabajo

Pneumatic-a-Mahañgin

Pneumonia-n-Sakit ñg baga

Pneumonic n-Gamot sa baga

Poach-n-Prituhin sa tubig, umitin; magnakaw.

Pock-n-Bulutong

Pock hole-Pock mark-n-Bulutong

Pocket-n-Bulsa

Pocket-v Ipamulsa, ilagay sa bulsa

Pocketbook-n-Lalagyan nang kuarta ó salapi

Pocket knife n-Laseta

Pocky-a-Mabulutong, bulutongo.

Pod-n-Bahay ñg binhi.

Pod-v-Tumaba, lumaki,

Poem-n-Tula,

Poet-n-Manunula

Poetess-n-Babaying manunula.

Poetic Poetical-a-Nauukol sa tula.

Poetry-n-Verso, tula

Poh-inter.-Oroy

Poignancy-n-Kapaitan; kaanghañgan.

Poignant-a-Maanghang; mapait.

Point-n-Dulo, tudla, tudlok; tulis; duñgot

Point-v-Ituro, itudla, tumudlok, tulisan.

Point blank-a-Matowid; maliwanag.

Pointed-a-Matulis

Pointer-n-Panturo.

Pointless-a-Walang dulo

Poise-n-Timbang, bigat

Poise v-Timbañgin

Poison-n-Lason, kamandag.

Poison-v-Lasunin, pakanin ñg kamandag

Poisonous-a-May lason, malason; may kamandag

Poke-n-Bayong, supot; mangas na maluang, tudlok.

Poke-v-Tudlukin; tumudlok.

Poker-n-Panudlok

Pole-n-Palo, haligi.

Polar-a-Mauukol sa hilagaan

Police-n-Policia

Police-v-Linisin; ayusin, husayin.

Police man-n-Policia.

Policy-n-Billete sa loteria.

Polish-v Bulihin; pakinisin, pakintabin, kintabin.

Polish n-Kinang, kintab; buli.

Polite-a-Magalang, mahinahon, masuyo, bihasa, matining na loob.

Politeness-n Galang; kagalañgan.

Politic-a Político.

Political-a Político

Politician-n-Ang marunong mag gobierno

Politics n-Karununñgan tungkol sa pag gogobierno

Polity-n Pag gogobierno

Polka n-Polka.

Poll-n-Padron; listahan ñg lahat ñg tawo sa isang lugar.

Pool-n Ilista ang lahat ñg tawo sa isang lugar.

Pollute-v-Dumhan, pañgitin, sirain.

Pollution-n-Dumi, kabulukan, pagka sira

Poltroon-n-Tawong duag.

Poltroon ery-n-Karuagan.

Polygamy-n-Pag aasawa sa marami

Polyglot-n-Ang marunong sa maraming wika

Pomade Pomatum-n-Cosmetico.

Pommel-n-Bukol

Pommel-v-Paluin.

Pomp-*n*-Gayak; handa; kainaman; kari-kitan.

Pompous-*a*-Maganda; mainam; marikit.

Pond-*n*-Labak.

Ponder-*v*-Magwari; magisipisip.

Ponderous-*a*-Malaki; mabigat.

Poinard-*n*-Panaksak.

Pontiff-*n*-Ang papa.

Pontifical-*a*-Nauukol sa papa.

Pontificate-*n*-Kalagayan ng̃ papa.

Pony-*n*-Kabayong munti.

Poodle-*n*-Asong munti at mahaba ang buhok.

Pooh-*inter.*-Oroy.

Pool-*n*-Labak.

Poop-*v*-Hampasin sa puit.

Poor-*a*-Mahirap; nasalat; dukha; payat.

Pop-*n*-Putok; soda.

Pop-*v*-Pumutok.

Pope-*n*-Ang papa.

Popedom-*n*-Katungkulan ng̃ papa.

Popery-*n*-Pananampalataya sa simbahan Católico.

Pop gun-*n*-Pasiblang.

Popinjay-*n*-Loro; tawong hambog.

Popish-*a*-Nauukol sa ó tinuro ng̃ papa.

Populace-*n*-Mang̃a tawo sa isong lugar.

Popular-*a*-Nauukol sa lahat ng̃ tawo bagay sa karamihan ng̃ tawo.

Populate-*v*-Dumami ang mg̃a tawo sa isang lugar.

Population-*n*-Mang̃a tawo sa isang lugar.

Populous-*a*-Matawo.

Porch-*n*-Sibi.

Porcine-*a*-Nauukol sa baboy.

Pore-*n*-Kilabot.

Pore-*v*-Magaral; magisip.

Pork-*n*-Carne ng̃ baboy.

Porker-*n*-Baboy.

Porous-*a*-Buhaghag; mabutas.

Porpoise-*n*-Pagong.

Port-*n*-Doong̃an; punduhan ng̃ sasak-yan.

Portable-*a*-Makadadala.

Portage-*n*-Pagdadala; halaga.

Portal-*n*-Pinto.

Portemonnaie-*n*-Lalagyan ng̃ salapi.

Portend-*v*-Humula.

Portent-*n*-Hula; tanda.

Porter-*n*-Utusan; kargador.

Porterage-*n*-Upa sa kargador.

Portfolio-*n*-Lalagyan ng̃ mg̃a papeles.

Porthole-*n*-Butas sa gilid ng̃ sasakyan.

Portiere-*n*-Tabing ng̃ pinto.

Portion-*n*-Bahagi; kapiraso.

Portion-*v*-Hiwalayin.

Portionless-*a*-Di mababahagi.

Portly-*a*-May katawan; mataba.

Portmanteau-*n*-Saco de noche.

Portrait-*n*-Retrato; larawan.

Portray-*v*-Gumawa nang larawan; say-sayin.

Portrayal-*n*-Pagsasaysay.

Portress-*n*-Babaying utusan.

Pose-*v*-Ayusin; ilagay sa lugar.

Pose-*n*-Kalagayan; tayo.

Poser-*n*-Bugtong.

Position-*n*-Lagay; lugar; tayo; kalagayan.

Positive-*a*-Totoo; tama; walang sala; tunay.

Positive-*n*-Katotohanan; katunayan.

Possess-*v*-Magkaroon; kamtan; magkamit.

Possession-*n*-Posession.

Possessor-*n*-Ang mayari.

Possibility-*n*-Bisa; kaya.

Possible-*a*-Mangyayari.

Post-*n*-Haligi; tukod; correo.

Post-*v*-Ilagay sa correo.

Postage-*n*-Bayad sa correo.

Postage stamp-*n*-Sello.

Postal-*a*-Nauukol sa correo.

Postdiluvial-*c*-Pagkatapos ng̃ panahon ni Noah.

Poster-*n*-Pahayag.

Posterior-*a*-Huli sa panahon; pagkatapos; huli; sa likod.

Posteriors-*n*-Bayawang ng̃ hayop.

Posterity-*n*-Inapo; lahi; kanunuan.

Postern-*n*-Pintuan sa likuran nang bahay.

Post haste-*n*-Kadalian.

Postman-*n*-Ang namamahala sa correo.

Postmark-*n*-Tanda na nakalagay sa sulat ng̃ malaman kung saan nangaling.

Postmaster-*n*-Ang namamahala sa correo.

Postmeridian-*a*-Sa hapon.

Post-mortem-*a*-Pagkanamatay.

Post-office-*n*-Oficina ng̃ correo.

Postpone-*v*-Ilayo; ilipat; lipatin.

Postponement-*n*-Paglipat sa panahon.

Postscript-*n*-Ang dugtong sa isang sulat.

Posture-*n*-Tayo.

Posy-*n* Bulaklak.

Pot-*n*-Palayok.

Pot-*v*-Isama.

Potash-*n*-Sosa.

Potato-*n*-Papas.

Potency-*n*-Kadakilaan; karilagan; kapangyarihan; kayamanan.

Potent-*a*-Mayaman; dakila; makapangyayari; marilag.

Potentate-*n*-Hari; ang makapangyayari.

Potential-*a*-Nauukol sa kapangyarihan.

Pother-*n*-Gulo; kaguluhan.

Potion-*n*-Gamot, lagok.
Potter-*n*-Magtatapayan
Potter-*v*-Gumawa ñg tapayan.
Pottery-*n*-Paggagawa ñg mġa tapayan
Pouch-*n*-Supot malaking tian.
Pouch-*v*-Ipamulsa, ipunin
Poultice-*n*-Tapal.
Poultice-*v*-Itapal.
Poultry-*n*-Manġa manok.
Pounce-*n*-Pulvo, kuko ñg ibon
Pounce-*v*-Hulihin.
Pound-*n* Libra
Pound-*v*-Durugin, bugbugin, dikdikin
Pour-*v*-Ibuhos; ibulusok.
Pout-*v*-Magtampo, ñgumuso
Pout-*n*-Nġuso, tampo.
Pouter-*n*-Ang nagtatampo.
Poverty-*n*-Kasalatan, kahirapan; dalita, karukhaan.
Powder-*n*-Pulvo; alabok; alikabok.
Powder-*v*-Dikdikin, durugin; budburin; ligisin.
Power-*n*-Kapangyarihan, kapal
Powerful-*a*-Malakas; makapangyayari; may kapal.
Powerless-*a*-Mahina, walang kapangyarihan.
Practicability-*n*-Cadalian gumawa.
Practicable-*a*-Madaling gumawa ginhawa
Practical-*a*-Mangyari, madaling magawa.
Practice-*n*-Kasanayan, paggamit, sanay
Practice-*v*-Magsanay, gamitin
Prairie-*n*-Lupang malaki' at patag.
Praise-*n*-Pagpuri, pagmamahal.
Praise *v*-Purihin; Mahalin.
Praiseworthy-*a*-Dapat purihin.
Prance-*n*-Lundag, lakad.
Prance-*v*-Lumakad ñg pahambog.
Prank-*n*-Biro, tukso
Prank-*v*-Gumayak
Prate-*v*-Magsalita nang walang kabuluhan.
Prate-*n*-Salita na walang kabuluhan.
Prattle-*n*-Salita na walang kabuluhan
Prattle *v*-Magsalita parang bata.
Pray-*v*-Magdasal, lumuhog
Prayer-*n*-Dasal, luhog, panalangin, daing
Prayer-*n*-Ang nagdadasal, towong mapagdasal
Prayer book-*n*-Librong dasalan.
Prayerful-*a*-Mapagdasal.
Preach-*v*-Magsermon; mangaral
Preacher-*n*-Ang nagsesermon
Preaching *n* Pagsesermon.
Prebend-*n*-Upa; bayad.
Precarious *a*-May panġanib.

Precaution-*n*-Inġat, kainġatan
Precautional *a*-Mainġat.
Precede *v*-Mauna, umuna.
Precedence *n*-Kaunahan.
Precedent-*n* Ang sinundan; halimbawa; tularan.
Precept-*n*-Utos, talunton
Preceptress-*n*-Babaying nag uutos.
Preceptor-*n*-Ang nag utos.
Preceptorial-*a*-Nauukol sa utos
Precinct *n* Bario, nayon
Precious-*a*-Mahal
Precipice-*n*-Kabubuliran, saluysoy
Precipitate-*v*-Biglain, dalidaliin, ibulusok, isugba
Precipitate-*a*-Bigla madali; dalosdalos, mabilis, matulin.
Precipitation-*n*-Kadalian, kabiglaan.
Precipitous-*a* Biglangbigla
Precise *a*-May hanga; tunay, totoo
Preclude-*v*-Ifuera, ibukod, iwaksi.
Preclusion-*n*-Pagkabukod, pagkawaksi.
Precocious-*a*-Manġahas.
Precocity-*n*-Kapanġahasan
Preconcert-*a*-Magsalitaan.
Preconcert-*n*-Salitaan.
Precursive-*a*-Mauna.
Precursor-*n*-Manunula.
Predecessor-*n*-Ang hinalinhan.
Predial-*a*-Malupa.
Predicable-*a*-Nauukol.
Predicament-*n* Kaguluhan ñg isip.
Predicate-*v* Magsabi
Predication-*n*-Pagsasabi.
Predict-*v*-Humula, hulaan.
Prediction-*n*-Hula.
Predilection-*n*-Pagmamahal ñg labis.
Preeminence-*n*-Kadakilaan, karilagan.
Preeminent-*a*-Dakila, mataas; maranġal.
Preface-*n*-Kasaysayan sa harapan ñg isang libro, tadhana, paunawa
Prefer-*v*-Mamili, pumili.
Preference-*n*-Kahilingan, kahilinġan, ang pinili.
Preferment-*n* Kapilian, kahilinġan.
Preferable-*a*-Dapat magalinġin.
Prefix-*n*-Dugtong sa una.
Pregnancy-*n* Kabuntisan.
Pregnant *a*-Buntis
Prehension-*n*-Pagkuha, pagdampot.
Prejudge-*v*-Hatulan nang hindi pa inu sisa.
Prejudgment-*n*-Paghatol ñg hindi pa inuusisa
Prejudicial-*a*-Makasisira.
Prelection-*n*-Sermon.
Premature *a*-Hindi pa panahon.
Prematurity-*n* Kaagapan
Premeditate-*v*-Mag wari ó wari warin muna.

Premeditation-*n*-Banta, wari
Premier-*a*-Uunang; mabuti; magaling.
Premium-*n*-Ganti, ganting palad, pabu-
ya; ganting loob
Prepare *v*-Gumayak, gayakan, maghan-
da, ipaglaan.
Preparation *n*-Gayak, handa, paghan-
dog
Preparative-*n*-Gayak; handa
Preparatory-*a*-Nakagayak.
Prepay-*v*-Magbayad muna.
Prepayment-*n*-Pagbabayad ng hindi pa
yari.
Preponderate-*v*-Bumigat sa iba
Prepositive-*a*-Nakalagay sa una
Prepossessing-*a*-Magandang loob; ma-
pagpapahalina
Preposterious *a*-Hindi tama, hambog
Prerogative-*n*-Katowiran.
Presage *n* Hula.
Prescribe-*i*-Magsabi; gumamot
Prescription-*n*-Gamot
Presence-*n*-Pagharap, harap
Present-*a*-Nakaharap, sa harap
Present-*n*-Ginaldo, bigay, salubong, bi-
yaya, regalo
Present-*v*-Magbigay, ibigay; magbigay
ng ginaldo, ipagkilala, iharap
Presentiment-*n*-Hinala.
Presently-*adv*-Bago, maya maya; pag-
daka
Preservation-*n*-Laon, tagal.
Preserve-*i*-Bantayin, gumawa ng con-
servas
Preserves-*n*-Conservas.
Preside-*v*-Mamuno, mamahala.
Presidency-*n*-Kalagayang presidente
President-*n*-Presidente
Presidential *a*-Nauukol sa presidente.
Presidentship-*n*-Katung kulang presi-
dente
Press-*i*-Hapitin, higpitan; ipitin, pili-
tin.
Press-*n*-Hapitan
Pressing-*a*-Kailangan
Pressure *n*-Hapit, kadahan; kakailangan
Presume-*v*-Sumapantaha, magsapantaha
Presumption-*n* Sapantaha, hinala, bin-
tang; kahambugan, kahanginan.
Presumptive-*a*-Marahil
Presumptuous-*a* Hambog, palalo.
Presuppose-*v*-Hakain
Presupposition-*n*-Haka.
Pretend-*v*-Magkonowari, magbalobalo.
Pretense-Pretence-*n*-Dahilan, pagkoko-
nowari, sapantaha.
Pretension-*n*-Dahilan, katowiran.
Pretentious-*a* Hambog, mayabang.
Preterit-*a*-Nakaraan, nangyari na.
Pretermit-*i*-Laktawin, maiwan.

Pretext-*n*-Dahilan; katowiran.
Pretty-*a* Maganda, marikit, mainam.
Prevail-*v* Pilitin; pumilit, supilin, mag-
kamit, kamtan; magkaroon.
Prevailing-*a* Malakas, karaniwan.
Prevalence-*n*-Kalakasan
Prevalent-*a*-Karaniwan, malakas
Prevaricate-*v*-Magsinungaling
Prevarication-*n*-Kasinungalingan.
Prevaricator-*n*-Tawong sinungaling.
Prevent-*i*-Sowain, abalahi, pigilin.
Prevention-*n*-Pagpigil, abala.
Preventive-*n*-Abala
Previous-*a*-Nauna.
Prey-*n*-Ang ninakaw
Prey-*v*-Nakawin.
Price-*n*-Halaga.
Price-*v*-Halagahan.
Priceless *a*-Mahal na lubha.
Prick-*n*-Duro.
Prick-*i*-Duruin.
Prickle-*n*-Hapdi
Prickle-*v*-Humapdi
Prickle-*a*-Mahapdi
Prickly heat-*n*-Bungang araw.
Pride-*n* Kapalaluan, kahambugan, ka-
tampalasanan, kayabangan.
Pride-*v*-Maghambog, magmayabang.
Priest *n*-Pari
Prig-*n*-Tawong mangahas.
Prig-*v*-Umitin, umumit.
Prigish-*a*-Hambog; palalo, mayabang.
Prim-*a*-Ayos, husay, mahusay.
Primary-*a*-Primero; naunang
Primate-*n*-Arsobispo
Prime-*a* Unang, mainam.
Primer *n*-Cartilla.
Primeval-*a*-Naunang; nauukol sa unang
panahon.
Primitive-*a*-Nauukol sa kaunahan.
Prince-*n*-Principe, anak ng hari.
Princess-*n*-Princessa, anak ng hari.
Princely-*a*-Parang principe; dakilang-
dakila.
Principal-*a*-Unang; totoong; tunay, ma-
ginoo.
Principal-*n*-Puno
Principality-*n* Kalagayang principe
Principally-*a*-Lalonglalo.
Principle *n*-Pamula; pinagbuhatan pa-
raan, pinagmulaan.
Print-*v*-Maglimbag; ikintal; kintalin.
Print-*n*-Bakas; limbag, guhit.
Printing *n*-Paglimbag.
Prior-*a*-Nauna
Prison-*n*-Bilango, kalabuso.
Prison-*v*-Kulungin; ilagay sa bilango,
ibilango.
Prisoner *n*-Preso.
Private-*a*-Nagiisa.

Privacy-n-Kaisahan; pagkaisa.
Private-n-Sundalong ultimo
Privateer n-Sasakyan ñg tulisan dagat.
Privation n Kakailañgan, kahirapan
Privilege-n-Pahintulot, kapahintulutan, tulot.
Privilege-v-Ipahintulot.
Privy a-Nauukol sa isang tawo lamang, lihim, hindi hayag.
Prize-n-Ganting palad, pabuha
Prize-v-Halagahan
Probable adv Marahil.
Probably-adv-Marahil
Probate-n-Katibayan ñg testamento
Probation-n-Tikhim, kasanayan, subok.
Probe-v-Usisain, siyasatin
Probity-n-Katapatan ñg loob
Problem n-Kuenta
Problematic-a-Nauukol sa kuenta
Probosis-n-Ilong ñg hayop
Proceed-v-Sumulong, magtuloy, bumalong, bumukal.
Proceedings-n Gawa; hatol
Proceeds-n-Tubo; pinagbilan.
Process-n Paraan, gawa.
Procession-n-Procession.
Proclaim-v-Tawagin tumawag, ipahayag; ihayag, ipatalastas
Proclamation-n-Pahayag, tawag, utos
Proclivity-n-Kabiligan; kahiliñgan.
Procrastinate-v-Ipagluatin.
Procrastination-n-Kaluatan; katagalan.
Procumbent-a-Nakadapa.
Procuration-n Pagkamit; pagkakamtan.
Procure-v Magkamit, isamsam, magkaroon; damahin
Procurement-n-Pagkamtan, pagkamit; pagsamsam.
Prodigal-a-Burara
Prodigal-n-Tawong burara.
Prodigality-n-Pagkaburara
Prodigious-a-Malaki na totoo, lubhang, malaki.
Produce-v-Gumawa, gawin, kathain; magkaroon, mamuñga.
Produce-n-Ang inani.
Product-n-Buñga, anomang bagay na yari.
Production-n-Paggagawa, gawa.
Productive-a Mataba
Profanation-n-Pagpaslang; kapaslañgan.
Profane a Banday; manunuñgayaw.
Profane v-Paslañgin; tuñgayawin.
Profanity n-Pagtutuñgayaw, kapaslañgan.
Profess v Magsabi, ipahayag.
Profession n Katungkulan
Professional a Sanay na lubha.
Professor n-Professor.
Proffer-v-Iabot; ialok; ialay.

Proffer n-Alok, balak.
Proficiency-n-Kasanayan; luta, karunuñgan
Proficient-a-Marunong sanay.
Proficient-n Tawong marunong at sanay.
Profile-n Larawan; retrato.
Profit n-Pakinabang, tubo.
Profit-v-Tumubo, pakinabañgin, maki nabang
Profitable a-May pakinabang, matubo, bagay; akma, pakinabañgan; mabuti
Profitless a-Walang tubo ó pakinabang.
Profligacy-n-Kasamaan, kasiraan
Profligate a-Masama, hamak; mahalay; walang hiya
Profound a Malalim
Profoundness-n-Lalim
Profundity-n-Kalaliman, lalim.
Profuse-a-Sagana, marami.
Profuseness-Profusion-n-Kasaganaan; karamihan.
Progenitor-n-Nuno, kanunuan.
Progeny n Angkan lahi; kamaganakan
Prognostic-n-Tanda, hula.
Prognosticate-v-Humula; hulaan.
Prognostication-n-Paghula.
Program-Programme-n-Babala sa madla
Progress-n-Pagbuti; pagsulong, kagaliñgan
Progression n-Pagsulong, galing.
Progressive-n-Mapagsulong; mabubuti.
Prohibit v-Magbawal, ipagbawal sowayin
Prohibition-n-Pagbawal; pagsoway.
Project n-Bala; balak, akala, anyo.
Project-v-Bumalak, akalain
Projectile-n-Bala ñg kanyon.
Projection-n-Liko
Prolific-a-Mamuñga
Prolix-a-Matagal, malaon, maluat, bagal, mabagal
Prolixity-Prolixness n-Katagalan; kalua tan, kabagalan.
Prolocutor-n-Taga pamagitan.
Prolong-v-Tumagal, itagal; luatan, humaba
Prolongation-n-Kaluatan, katagalan; pag tatagal, pagluluat
Promenade-n-Pasialan.
Promenade-v-Magpasial
Prominence Prominency-n-Kadakilaan; karilagan; kaginoohan.
Prominent-a-Dakila, marañgal; mataas; bantog bunyi.
Promiscuous-a-Walang ayos, halohalo hindi mahusay
Promise n-pañgako tipan, salitaan.
Promise-v-Mañgañgako; ipañgako.

Promontory-*n*-Lupang mataas at makitid

Promote-*v* Ipataas, umabuloy

Promotion-*n*-Pagpataas, abuloy.

Prompt-*a*-Maliksi, matulin; masipag; nakagayak; nakahanda

Prompt-*i*-Ibuho, isurot sa isip.

Premptitude-Promptness *n*- Kaliksihan, katulinan, kasipagan

Pione-*a*-Nadapa, nakadapa

Pronominal-*a*-Nauukol sa pronombre

Prong-*n*-Dulong matulis.

Pronoun *n*-Pronombre

Pronounce-*v* Wikain, Magsabi; sabihin

Pronunciamento-*n*-Pahayag, paunawa

Pronunciation-*n*-Kasaysayan; pagsasalaysay.

Proof-*n*-Katotohanan, katunayan.

Prop-*n*-Tukod; tungkod, abuloy.

Prop-*i*-Itukod; tungkod, umabuloy

Propagate-*v*-Maghasik, magpunla, paramihin

Propagation-*n*-Pagsulong; paghasik.

Propensity-*n* Kagawian ó kahilingan ng̃ loob.

Proper *a*-Akma, bagay; dapat; karampatan, maakma, nararapat.

Property-*n*-Lupa, ari, kayamanan.

Prophecy-*n*-Hula.

Prophesy-*v*-Humula, hulaan.

Prophet *n*-Manghuhula, mago

Prohetic-*a*-Nauukol sa hula

Propitious-*a*-Nakahawak

Propitiate-*i*-Patahimikin, pahimpilin.

Proportion *n*-Ayos

Proportion-*i*-Ayusin; hatiin; hiwalayin

Proportional-*a* Masiya, matamtaman

Proportional-*n*-Kasiyahan, katamtaman

Propose-*v*-Bumalak, ibalak, magturing, ialok

Proposal-*n*-Balak; turing

proposition-*n*-Turing, balak

propound *v*-Ialok; magsaysay

proprietor-*n*-Ang mayari

proprietress-*n*-Ang may ari babayi

propriety-*n*-Kabusayan, kaayusan, ayos

propulsion-*n*-Pagsulong; tulak

Propulsive *a*-Pasulong

Proscribe-*v*-Bintang̃in, ihulog sa infierno, magbigay sala

Proscription-*n*-Bintang, pagbibigay sala.

Prose-*n*-Karaniwang sulat.

Prosecute-*i*-Ihabla

Prosecution *n*-Paghabla, Bagong binyagan

Prosecutor-*n*-Ang naghahabla.

Prospect-*n*-Tanawan; ting̃in

Prospect-*v*-Usisain, tuming̃in.

Prospection-*n*-Paguusisa

Prospectus-*n*-Plano

Prosper-*v*-Gumaling, guminhawa.

Prosperity-*n*-Kaginhawahan, galing; kagaling̃an, kawalan ng̃ damdam

Prosperous-*a*-Magaling, masaya, mabuti

Prostitute-*v*-Magputa, magpatutot.

Prostitute-*n*-Hitad, puta; patutot.

Prostitution-*n*-Paghihitad, pagpuputa

Prostrate-*a*-Tihaya, nakahiga

Prostrate-*v*-Ihiga, itihaya; baliktarin

Prostration-*n*-Pagtitihaya· kalungkutan; kopanglawan

Protasis-*n*-Patnugot, punong aral.

Protect-*v*-Ikalong, kupkopin, tulung̃in, tumankilik, ipaglaban, bantayin; ipagsangalang, magtangol.

Protection-*n*-Kupkop tulong, andukha, ing̃at, bantay

Protector-*n*-Taga tangol, pintakasi, taga kalong.

Protege-*n*-Tawong na sa kapangyarihan ng̃ iba.

Protest-*v*-Dumaing, lumaban

Protest-*n*-Daing, paglaban

Protestant-*a*-Protestante.

Protestant-*n* Protestante.

Protestation-*n*-Daing

Protomartyr-*n* Kaunaunahan martir

Protract-*i*-Humaba, magluat; luatan, tumagal

Protracted-*n* Maluat, matagal

Protraction-*n*-Luat, haba; kahabaan, kaluatan tagal

Protrude-*v*-Sumipot, lumitaw, ilabas

Protuberance *n*-Liko, bukol.

Protuberant-*a*-Litaw, nakabukol.

Protuberate-*v*-Mamaga, bumukol

Protuberation-*n*-Pamamaga: bukol.

Proud *a*-Palalo, hambog, mayabang

Prove *v*-Damahin; siyasatin; ibigay ang katotohanan.

Provender-*n*-Pagkain ng̃ hayop.

Proverb *v*-Talinhaga, halimbawa; kasabihan kawikaan, kainkaan; patnugot.

Proverbial-*a*-Nauukol sa talinhaga

Provide-*v*-Ibigay ang kailang̃an, tumulong, bigyan ng̃ kailang̃an.

Provided-*conj* -Kung, sakali

Providence-*n*-Gayak, handog, handa.

Provident-*a*-Nakagayak, nakahanda

Province-*n*-Hukuman, lalawigan.

Provincial-*a*-Nauukol sa hukuman ó sa lalawigan

Provision-*n*-Paghanda; paggayak, mang̃a pagkain

Provision-*v*-Bumili ang mang̃a pagkain

Provisional *a*-Hangang hindi, interino

Proviso *n*-Condition; salitaan

Provocation *n*-Dahilan, katowiran, sul-sol.

Provoke-v-Humamon; hamuuin, yamútin; magsulsol, pagalitin, udyok.
Prow-n-Dulo ng sasakyan
Prowess-n Lakas, kalakasan.
Prowl-v-Gumapang.
Proximate-a-Kalapit, malapit, kasunod.
Proximity n-Kalapitan, pagkasunod
Proximo-n-Ang buang darating.
Prudence-n-Kabaitan, bait, dunong, karunungan, tuto, hinahon, kabanayaran, tumpak, taros, katalinuhan.
Prudent-a-Mahinahon, mabait, marunong, matumpak, maalam; bihasa, matalino; maingat, tahimik himanhiman
Prudential a-Marunong, nangaling sa kaiunungan, mabait.
Prune-v-Putin ang manga sanga nang kahoy.
Pry-v-Madiwara, usisain, mag usisa, magdiwara, itaas
Pry n Panghuit; kadiwaraan
Prying a Madiwara
Psalm-n-Salmo, kantang nauukol sa P D.
Psalmist-n-Ang sumulat ng mga kantang nauukol sa P Dios
Pseudonym n-Ngalan na hindi totoo
Pshaw inter Oroy, ba
Psyche-n-Kaluluwa; isip.
Psychic Psychical a-Nauukol sa kaluluwa
Public-a-Alam ng madla, hayag; karaniwan.
Public-n-Madla
Publicity-n-Pagkaká alam nang madla, alam, hayag
Publican-n-Maniningil, mayari nang hotel.
Publication-n-Pag limbag; tawag sa madla
Publish-v-Ipahayag, ipalastas, ilathala, ikalat
Pucker-n Nguso.
Pucker-v-Ngumuso
Puddle-n-Labak.
Puddle-v-Lumabak.
Pudgy-a Pandak at mataba
Puerile a Parang bata.
Puerility-n-Kalagayang bata.
Puff-n-Ihip ng hangin
Juff-v-Umihip; mamanas
Pug-v-Tasakin ng pusali.
Pugilism-n Suntukan.
Pugnaceous-a-Mapagbasagulo
Pugnose n-Ilong masapad
Pule-v-Sumiap
Puke-v-Sumuka, magsuka
Pull-v-Batakin, bumatak, biwasin, bumiwas, hilahin, humila.

Pull-n-Batak, hila, biwas
Pallet-n-Manok.
Pulley n-Kalooey
Pulmonic-Palmonary-a Nauukol sa baga
Pulmonic-n-Gamot sa baga
Pulpit-n-Pulpito, altar.
Pulsate-v-Pumukpok; tumibok, kumaba
Pulsation-n-Pukpok, tibok, kaba.
Pulse n Pulso
Pulse-v-Pumulso
Pulverization-n-Pagdurog; dikdikan.
Pulverize-v-Durugin, dikdikin
Pump-n-Bomba.
Pun-n-Bugtong, tukso.
Punch-n Suntok; surot
Punch-v-Suntukin, sumuntok, budlungin.
Puncheon-n-Pangbutas.
Punctual-a-Bagay, maagap, maliksi
Punctuality-n-Kaganapan; kaliksihan, kadalian
Puncture-n-Butas.
Puncture-v-Butasin
Pungency-n Kasaklapan; kapaitan.
Pungent-a-Masaklap mapait
Punish-v-Parusahin; hampasin
Punishable-a Dapat parusahin
Punishment-n-Parusa; dusa
Punster-n-Tawong mapagbiro
Puny a Mahina at munti.
Pup-n-Tuta.
Pupil-n-Ang nag aaral.
Pupilage n-Kalagayang nag aaral
Puppet n-Muneka.
Puppy-n-Tuta
Puppyish a-Parang tnta; mapootin
Pur v-Sumiap
Pur n-Siap
Pur blind-a-Balangaw.
Purchase-v-Bumili, mamili
Purchase-n-Ang pinamili.
Pure-a-Dalisay, malinis, banal, wagas, walang halo, tapat ang loob.
Purgation-n-Pagpurga
Purgative-a Makapagpurga
Purgative n-Purga.
Purgatory n-Purgatorio
Purgatory-a-Nauukol sa purgatorio
Purge v-Purgahin
Purge-n-Purga
Purification-n-Paglilinis, kalinisan
Purify-v-Linisin; dalisayin, kintalin
Purity-n-Kalinisan, kadalisayan, kamahalan kapurihan, puri
Purl-n-Borlas
Purl-v-Ilagay ang borlas
Purlieu-n Lugar na malapit.
Purlin-n Anoman.
Purloin-v-Umitin, umumit, nakawin, magnakaw.

Purple-*n*-Purpura
Purport-*n*-Kahulugan
Purport-*v* Magbigay kahulugan.
Purpose *n*-Akala, kahulugan, tungo
Purpose-*v*-Akalain, magbigay kahulugan
Purr-*v*-Ngumiaw
Purse-*n* Bulsa, bulsikot.
Purse-*v*-Ngumuso.
Purse-proud-*a*-Hambog dahil sa kayamanan
Pursuance-*n*-Pagkasunod.
Pursuant-*a* Ayon.
Pursue-*v*-Habulin humabol.
Pursuit *n*-Paghabol.
Pursy-*a*-Mataba at maikli ang hininga
Purulent *a*-May nana.
Purvey *v*-Ialok, maglako, magtinda.
Purview-*n*-Katawan ng isang larawan kapangyarihan.
Pus *n*-Nana, kabulukan ng sugat.
Push *v*-Tumulak, itulak, tulakin.
Push-*n*-Tulak; untog

Pusillanimity-*n* Karuagan
Pusillanimous *a*-Duag; dungo.
Puss-Pussy-*n*-Pusa, kuting
Pustule-*n*-Butlig
Pustular-*a*-Mabutlig.
Put-*v*-Ilagay, maglagay, lagyan; ihagis.
Put *n*-Hagis.
Putative-*a*-Nabahita.
Put off *v*-Ilayo.
Put out- -Ilabas, palabasin.
Putrefy-*v*-Bumulok, mabulok
Putrid-*a*-Bulok, mabulok
Putridity-Putridness-*n*-Kabulukan.
Puzzle *n*-Basagulo, bugtong.
Puzzle-*v* Magbugtong.
Pygmy-*n*-Unano.
Pygmy-*a*-Muntingmunti, unano.
Pyjama *n* Carsoncillos.
Pyriform-*a*-Hitsurang peras.
Pyrotechnics-*n*-Paggawa at paggamit ang kuetes
Python *n*-Sawa.

Quack-*n*-Iyak ng itik ó bibi
Quack *n*-Mangagamot na hindi nag aral.
Quack-*v*-Umiyak ang itik ó bibi
Quadragesima-*n* Koresma.
Quadragesimal-*a*-Nauukol sa koresmang mahaba
Quadrangle-*n*-Anomang bagay na may apat na sulok ó panulukan.
Quadrate-*a*-Parisukat
Quadrate-*n*-Parisukat
Quadratic-*a*-Nauukol sa parisukat.
Quadrennial *a*-Mangyayari minsan sa balang apat na taon.
Quadrilateral-*a*-May apat na gilid at apat na panulukan.
Quadrilateral *n*-Anomang bagay na may apat na gilid
Quadrille *n*-Rigodon.
Quadrillion *n*-Isang yutang angawangaw
Quadruped-*n* Hayop na may apat na paa.
Quadruped-*a*-May apat na paa.
Quadruple *a*-Aapat na duble.
Quadruple-*n*-Ang apat na duble.
Quadruple-*v*-Dublihin ng makaapat.
Quaere-*v*-Magtanong, tanungin.
Quaff-*v*-Uminom ng marami
Quagmire *n*-Lablab; lawak.
Quaggy-*a*-Malablab
Quail-*v* Manginginig.
Quail-*n*-Pugo.
Quaint-*a*-Di karaniwan, iba.
Quake-*v*-Manginig, uminig.

Quake-*n*-Inig, galaw.
Qualification-*n*-Pag abot sa grado.
Qualify-*v*-Umabot sa grado
Quality-*n*-Kalidad.
Qualm-*n*-Kahinaan, agam agam na loob.
Qualmish-*a*-Masakit ang sikmura
Quandary-*n*-Agam agam ng loob, kaguluhan ng isip
Quantity-*n*-Karamihan, dami.
Quarantine-*n*-Kuarentenas.
Quarrel-*n* Basagulo, talo usap.
Quarrel-*v*-Mag basagulo; makipagtalo, mag usap.
Quarrelsome-*a*-Mapag basagulo, palaaway.
Quarry-*n*-Pinaghukayan ng bato.
Quarry-*v*-Maghukay, mag tibag
Quart-*n*-Takal na may dalawang gatang ang laman.
Quarter-*n*-Kahati; ikaapat, na bahagi, luat ng tatlong buan.
Quarter-*v*-Apatin.
Quarterly-*a*-Balang tatlong buan.
Quash-*v*-Huimimpil, lumubay, durugin, inisin.
Quaver-*v*-Uminig; maningning.
Quaver-*n*-Inig, ningning
Quay-*n*-Muella.
Qrean *n* Babayi; batang babayi.
Queasy-*a* Masakit ang sikmura makilitiin
Queen-*n*-Haring babayi.
Queenly-*a*-Bagay sa haring babayi.

38

Queen consort-*n*-Asawa nğ hari.
Queen dowager *n*-Bao nğ hari
Queen mother-*n*-Ina nğ hari
Queen regent-*n* Haring babayi
Queer-*a*-Hindi karaniwan, iba
Queer-*n*-Kuartang masama
Quell-*v*-Tahimikin; supilin.
Quench-*v*-Patayin ang apoy ó sunog
Querist-*n*-Ang nagtatanong
Query-*n*-Tanong.
Query-*v*-Magtanong, tanungin.
Quest-*n*-Hanap, paghanap.
Question-*n*-Tanong.
Question-*v*-Magtanung; itanong
Questionable-*a*-Falso, hindi totoong malinis o mahusay
Questionless *a*-Malinis, totoo, tunay, dahsay, mahusay.
Queue-*n*-Buhok nğ insik
Quibble-*n*-Kailagan sa tanong
Quibble-*v*-Umilag sa tanong.
Quick-*a*-Matulin, maliksi, maagap.
Quick-*adv* -Madali
Quicken *v*-Tumulin, magmadali
Quicklime-*n*-Apog
Quick silver-Azogue.
Quid-*n*-Pirasong mascada.
Quiescent-*a*-Tahimik, walang kibo
Quiet-*a*-Tahimik, walang gulo, mabini, mabait; mahinahon.
Quiet-*n*-Katahimikan; pagpapahinğa, kapahinğahan.

Quiet-*v*-Tahimikin; magpahinğa.
Quietude-Quietness-*n* Katahimikan, pagpapahinğa
Quill-*n* Puno nğ balahibo nğ ibon.
Quilt-*n*-Kumot.
Quilt-*v*-Magkumot.
Quinine-*a*-Kinina
Quinquagesima-*a*-Ikalimangpuo.
Quinquangular-*a*-May limang panulukan
Quinquennial-*a*-Mangyayari minsan sa balang limang taon
Quinsy-*n* Sakit nğ lalamunan
Quintal-*n*-Kintal, isangdaan libra.
Quintuple *a* Dinuble nğ makalima.
Quip-*n*-Uyam, alibugha.
Quip-*v*-Magalibugha.
Quire-*n*-Dalawangpuo at apat na dahon nğ papel
Quirk-*n*-Kilos.
Quit-*v*-Maiwan; umalis, patawarin, bayaran.
Quite-*adv*.-Lubos puspos.
Quittance-*n*-Kabayaran
Quiver-*n*-Lalagyan nğ palaso
Quiver-*v*-Uminig.
Quiz-*v*-Magbugtong.
Quiz-*n*-Bugtong.
Quondam-*a*-Dating; unang.
Quota-*n*-Bahagi, parte.
Quote-*v*-Sabihin ang sinabi nğ iba
Quoth-*v*. *imp* -Sinabi, winika.
Quotidian-*a*-Mangyayari sa arawaraw

R

Rabbit-*n*-Conejo
Rabble-*n*-Bunton nğ tawo.
Rabid-*a*-Maulol, ulol, sira ang isip.
Race-*n*-Hinlog, lahi, pareja, takbuhan.
Race *n*-Tumakbo; magpareja.
Racer-*n*-Ang tumakbo, mananakbo
Raceme-*n*-Piling ó buig nğ bunğa o balaklak
Raciness-*n*-Lasa
Rack-*n* Lalagyan nğ pagkain nğ hayop, kakanan nğ hayop; kasiraan.
Rack-*v*-Ilagay sa kakanan.
Rack-*v*-Lumakad na matulin; banatin; pahirapan
Racket *n*-Gulo; kainğayan; inğay
Rackety *a*-Mainğay; magulo
Racy-*a*-Malasa, sariwa.
Radial-*a*-Nauukol sa kagitnaan
Radiance-*n*-Ningning, kintab, kakintaban; kisap, kislap.
Radiant *a* Maningnig, makintab, makisap.
Radiate-*v*-Kumislap, kumisap.

Radiate *a*-Maningning, makislap, makisap.
Radical-*a* Nauukol sa ugat ó sa pinagmulaan.
Radical-*n*-Dating salita.
Radically-*adv*.-Buhat sa pinagmulaan
Radicate *v*-Magtanim.
Radicel-*n* Munting ugat
Radish-*n*-Labanos.
Radius-*n*-Layo magbuhat ang gitna han gang sa gihid nğ bilog.
Radix-*n*-Pinagmulaan
Raffle-*n*-Rifa.
Raffle-*v*-Parifahin
Raft-*n* Balsa.
Raft *v*-Magbalsa.
Rafter-*n*-Balsero.
Rag *n*-Basahan, gulanit
Ragged *a*-Punit punit, punit.
Rage *n*-Galit, kagalitan, kapootan
Rage-*v*-Magalit.
Rail-*n*-Railes, barandillas, gabay
Rail-*v*-Magalibugha, uyamin; laitin.

Railing-n-Bakuran, bakod.
Railer n-Tawong tampalasan.
Raillery-n Katampalasanan; alibugha.
Railway-Railroad-n-Tren.
Raiment-n-Damit.
Rain-n-Ulan
Rain-v-Umnlan, umunos.
Rainbow-n-Bahaghari.
Rainy-a-Maulan.
Raise-v-Itaas, balilisin; buhatin, bumuhat, umalsa; damputin; ibangon; itayo
Raisin-n-Pasas
Rajah-n-Hari sa Persia
Rake-n-Pangkalaykay, pangalaykay.
Rake-v-Magkalaykay, kalaykayin
Rally-n-Katipunan.
Rally-v-Magtipon.
Ram-n Tupang lalaki
Ram-v-Umpugin, untugin
Ramble-n-Lakad na walang tuntungan.
Ramble-v-Lumakad na walang tuntungan.
Ramification-n-Pagsasanga.
Ramify-v-Magsanga, hiwalayin.
Rammish-a-Malansa; malibog.
Ramose-Ramous-a-Masanga, may maraming sanga.
Ramp-v-Lumundag; maglaro
Ramp-n Lundag, lukso
Rampage-n Kaharotan
Rampancy-n-Kaharotan
Rampant-a-Maharot; malikot na totoo.
Rampart-n-Kuta.
Rampart-v-Gawing ang kuta.
Ram rod-n-Baketa
Ran-v imp -Natakbo; tumakbo.
Ranch-n-Hacienda.
Ranch man-n-Ang mayari ng hacienda.
Ranchero n-Nagpapastol, ang tumitira sa hacienda
Rancho-n-Bahay ng manga nagpapastol.
Rancid-a-Malansa.
Rancidity-Rancidness-n-Lansa.
Rancor-n-Galit: tanim, na loob; poot
Rancorous-a-Magalit, nagagalit; mapagtanim na loob.
Random-n-Kilos na walang ayos
Random-a-Pagulogulo; walang ayos
Rang-v imp -Tumugtog; tinugtog.
Range-n-Taludtod, hilera, tayo
Range-v-Hilerahin; ituludtud
Ranger n-Tawong mapaglakad, ang namamahala sa lupa ng gobierno
Rank-n-Lagay; kalagayan, dangal· pagkaginoo.
Rank-v-Ilagay sa carampatang lugar.
Rank-a Malansa, lipas; luma, laon, mabulok.
Rankle-v-Maging magalit; maginit.
Ransack-v-Hanapin ng pilit

Ransom-n-Pagtubos; kuartang ibinayap sa pagtubos.
Ransom-v-Tubusin tumubos
Rant-v-Magsalita ng kaululan
Rant-n-Tawong ulol, tawong hambog.
Rap-n-Tugtog tuktok
Rap-v-Tumuktok, tumugtog
Rapacious-a-Mahiling sa pagnakaw, masakim-
Rapacity-Rapaciousness-n-Kahilingan sa pagnakaw, kasakiman.
Rape-v-Gahisin; agawin ang babayi, umagaw sa babayi, puersahin ang babayi.
Rape n-Paggahis, pagpupuersa, pagagaw ng babayi
Rapid-a-Mabilis; matulin.
Rapid-n-Agos na matulin.
Rapidity-Rapidness-n-Katulinan, bilis, kaliksihan.
Rapier-n-Sable, sandata
Rapist-n-Ang pumuersa sa babayi.
Rapt-v. imp & p. p -Inagaw; umagaw.
Rapt-a-Inagaw.
Rapture-n-Kawilian; kagustuhan
Rapturous-a-Mawili, makagusto
Rare-a-Bihira, bugtong, madalang, hilaw.
Rarefaction-n-Kalabnawan.
Rarefy-v-Labnawin, lumabnaw, buhaghagin, dumalang.
Rarity-n-Kadalangan, kalabnawan, pagkabugtong.
Rascal-n-Tawong masama, saragate.
Rascal-a-Masama; malikot.
Rascal-a-Masama; hamak; taksil.
Rascally-n-Kasuitikan; kataksilan.
Rase-v-Burahin; pantayin.
Rash-a-Bigla, magaspang.
Rash-n-Tigdas.
Rasher-n-Hiwa na manipis ng tosino.
Rasp-n Kikil na magaspang.
Rasp v-Kikiling; kumikil.
Rasure-n Kaburahan, pagpapantay.
Rat-n-Dagang malaki
Rate-v-Tasahan, halagahan.
Rate-n-Tulin, halaga.
Rather-adv-Bago; gusto pa;
Ratification-n Katibayan, tibayan.
Ratify-v-Tibayin; pumayag, uinayon
Ration-n-Kaukulan ng isang bagay sa iba
Ration-n-Pagkain, rasion.
Rational-a-May isip, mabait
Rationality-n-Katowiran; dahilan
Rationally-adv -Ayos sa katowiran.
Rattan-n-Yentok
Ratten-v-Nakawin ang kasangkapan.
Rattle-n-Kalatog; kalog; pangkalog
Rattle v-Kumalatog, kalogin, kumalog.
Rattoon-n Supling ng tubó.

Rattoon-v-Sumupling

Ravage-n Kasiraan; paggigiba.

Ravage v-Gibain, nakawin; sirain.

Ravager-n-Maninira

Rave-v-Masira ang isip, Magsalita ng kaululan, magbaliw.

Ravel v-Manutnot

Raven-n-Wak, awak.

Raven a Maitim.

Raven-v-Agawin; umagaw.

Ravenous-a-Matakaw

Ravenousness n-Katakawan.

Ravine n Saluysoy, sungoy, baris

Ravish-v-Agawin, puersahin, gahisin

Ravisher-n-Ang umagaw sa isang babayi

Ravishment-n-Pagagaw sa isang babayi, mamumuersa.

Raw-a-Hilaw, sariwa.

Raw boned-a-Payat

Raw hide-n-Latigo ng katad.

Ray-n-Sinag

Rayless-a-Walang sinag, madilim.

Raze-v-Lipulin, gibain, burahin.

Razor-n-Labasa

Razure-n-Pag gigiba; kalipulan

Reach-v-Umabot; abutin, dumating datnin, tamuhin. iabot, magkamit

Reach-n-Abot; dipa

React-v-Kumilos uli.

Read-v-Bumasa, basahin

Read-v. imp. & p p -Nakabasa, binasa.

Readable-a-Makababasa

Reading-n-Pagbasa.

Reader-n-Ang bumasa

Readily-adv -Maagap, madali, nakahanda.

Ready-a-Masipag; matalos; matulin, maagap, natatalaga.

Ready-adv.-Maagap, madali, nakahanda.

Ready-made-a-Yari na

Real-a-Tunay; totoo

Reality-n-Katotohanan; katunayan.

Realize-v-Totohanin, tumubo.

Realization n-Pagkatoto, pangyayari.

Really-adv.-Totoo ba; tunay kaya.

Realm-n-Kaharian.

Realty-n-Haring lupa

Ream-n-Bagkis ng papel na may apat na daan at walong puong dahon

Ream-v-Palakihin ang butas.

Reanimate-v Magpalakas, buhayin.

Reannex-v-Idugtong uli

Reap-v-Gapasin, gumapas, magani.

Reaper-n-Mangagapas

Reaping-hook-n Lilik

Reappear-v-Lumitaw ó sumipot uli

Reappearance-n-Paglitaw ó pagsipot muli.

Rear n-Likod; likuran.

Rear-a-Huling; likod,

Rear-v-Itaas, magalaga, palakihin.

Rear guard-n-Bantay sa huli.

Rear ward-n-Bantay sa huli.

Rear ward-adv -Sa gawing huli

Reason-n-Katowiran, dahilan, akala, isip, katha.

Reason-v-Magisip, isipin, magakala; mangatowiran; akalain, magsalita.

Reasonable a-Akma, tama sa katowiran.

Reasoning n-Pangangatowiran.

Reassure-n-Magpangako uli

Rebel-n-Ang lumalaban sa sarili niyang bandila

Rebel-v-Lumaban sa sariling bandila

Rebelhon-n-Pag alsa, pag laban sa sariling bandila.

Rebellious-a-Sowail, malabag.

Rebound-v-Umudlot, lumukso.

Rebuff-n-Pigil, tangi, pagkaayaw

Rebuff-v-Tangihan; tumangi; pigilin; umayaw.

Rebuild-v-Magtayo uli, itayo ng panibago

Rebuke-v-Parusahan, pasiyahan

Rebus-n-Bugtong

Rebut-v-Lumaban, sumalangsang

Recall-v-Maguhin, bawiin; tawagin

Recant-v-Magkaila; talikuran; tumahkod

Recantation-n Kaila, pagtatalikuran

Recapture-v-Bawiin ang manga sandatay masamsam ng kalaban.

Recede-v-Umurong, bumaba

Receipt-n-Recibo, pagtangap

Receipt-v-Magbigay ang recibo

Receivable-a-Dapat tangapin

Receive-v-Tangapin, tumangap, suma hod, sahuran

Receiver-n-Taga tangap.

Recency-n-Kasariwaan, pagkabago.

Recent-a-Bago; sariwa.

Recentness-n-Pagkago

Receptacle-n-Kasangkapan panahod.

Reception n-Pagtangap

Receptive-a-Nauukol sa pagtangap

Recess-n-Recreo, pagpahinga

Recess-v-Magpahinga.

Recession-n-Pagurong, pagsasauli

Recipe-n-Kasulatan tungkol sa pagga wa ng anoman.

Recipient-n-Taga tangap, ang tumangap

Recipient-a-Matatangapin

Reciprocal-a Nauukol sa kapwa.

Reciprocate-v-Humalili, maukol sa ka pwa, tumangap at magbigay.

Reciprocation-n-Paghahalili;

Recite-v-Saysayin, sabihin.

Recital-n-Kasabihan, pagsalaysay

Recitation-n-Pagsalaysay.

Reck-v-Magingat, mamahala; maukol

Reckless-a-Walang ingat, pabaya.

Reckon-ι-Magkaenta, bumilang
Reckoning n-Pagkuenta, kabilañgan.
Reclaim-v-Kunin uli.
Recline-ι-Humilig, sumandal
Recluse-a-Kinulong na kusa.
Recluse-n-Tawong ayaw sumama sa kapwa niya.
Recognition-n-Pagkikilala, pagkakáhalata
Recognizable-a-Makikilala
Recognize-v Makilala, halatain, kilalanin, tantuin.
Recoil-v-Umurong; umudlot.
Recoil-n-Urong, udlot.
Recollect-v-Tandaan, alalahanin
Re-collect-v-Sinğilin uli.
Recollection-n Alaala, pag aalaala
Recommence-v-Masimula uli
Recommend-v-Ipagbilin; ipagmasakit
Recommendation-n-Pagbilin, tagobilin.
Recommit-v-Gawin muli, sumala uli
Recompense n-Bayad, ganti pala, upa.
Recompense-v-Bayaran, upahan, magbayad, gantihin
Recompose-v-Gawin muli
Reconcile-v-Magkasundo, papagkasundain.
Reconciliation-n-Pagkakasundo
Recondite-a-Nakatago
Reconnoisance n-Paguusisa; siyasat.
Reconnoiter-v-Magusisa, usisain, subukin; manubok
Reconsider-v-Isiping muli
Reconstruct v-Magtayo muli, itayo ng panibago
Reconstruction-n-Pagtatayo ng panibago
Record-ι-Tandain; lumkalin, bangitin
Record-n-Tandaan
Recount-v Bilañin uli.
Recount-n-Muling pagbilang.
Recourse-n-Kasakdalan, pagdulog; paggamit.
Recover-ι-Bawiin; bumawi, magkamit uli
Recoverable-a-Makababawi.
Recovery-n Pagkabawi, paggaling.
Recreancy-n-Karuagan, kapalsohan, ka pabayaan
Recreant a-Duag, falso; pabaya
Re-create-v-Lalanğin uli
Recreate-v-Magaliw, maglugod
Recreation-n-Aliwan, pagaaliw
Recreative a-Makalulugod
Recriminate-v-Magbintang
Recrimination-n Pag bibintañgan
Recruit v Kumpunihin; punuin ang kakulañgan, lumakas, gumaling.
Recruit-n Sundalong bagong pasok
Rectification-n-Paghuhusay, pagtotowid.

Rectify-v-Towiring, husayin.
Rectilineal-a-Matowid ang guhit.
Rectitude-n-Katapatan ng loob.
Rector-n-Pastor, puno.
Rectory-n-Hucuman ng pari, bahay ng pastor ó pari.
Rectum-n-Tumbong
Recumbency-n-Sandalan, katamaran.
Recumbent-a-Nakasandal, nakahilig.
Recuperate-v-Lumakas; gumaling,
Recur-v-Umulit, bumalik uli.
Recurrence-n-Pag ulit
Recurrent-a-Maulit.
Recurvate-v-Lumiad; humubog.
Recurvation-n-Pag liliad
Recurvate-a-Nakaliad.
Red-a-Mapula
Red-n-Kulay na pula.
Redden-v-Pumula mamula
Reddish a-Mapulapula.
Redeem-v-Tubusin, tumubos, hanğin sa kagipitan.
Redemption-n-Pagtubos; katubusan
Red gum-n-Tigdas
Redness-n-Pula; kapulaan
Redolence-Redolency-n-Bañgo, kabanğohan
Redolent-a-Mabanğo
Redouble-v-Dublihing muli, tikluping muli
Redoutable-a-Matapang.
Redound-v-Lumago.
Redowa-n-Sayawan Parang ball
Re dress v-Magbihis, bihising muli.
Redress-v-Ayusin, husayin.
Redress n-Ganti.
Reduce-v-Bawasan, saysayin
Reducible-a-Mababawasan
Reduction-n-Pagbawas, bawas
Redundancy-n-Kalabisan
Redundant-a-Malabis.
Reed-n-Kugon
Reed organ-n-Armonica
Reef-n-Manğa bato sa ilalim ng tubig
Reef-v-Tiklupin ang layag
Reek-n-Aso, usok
Reek-n-Umuso, umasok
Reel-n-Gibang, ikiran, giray.
Reel-v-Magulak, ikirin, giniravgiray
Reenact-ι-Maglagda muli.
Reenaction-Peenactment-n-Pag lalagda muli
Reenforce-v-Palakasin, dagdaginid, agdag
Reenforcement-n-Pagdaragdag
Reenter v-Pumasok uli, muling pumasok.
Reestablish-v-Muling itayo, iuli.
Reestablishment-n-Muling pagtatayo.
Reeve-v-Isuot ang lubid sa kalooy
Refashion-v-Baguhin ang uso
Refer-v-Bangitin salaysayin; ibalita,

Referable-a-Umubrang bangitin
Referee-n-Sentensiador
Reference-n-Pagbangit.
Refine-r-Linisin, dalisayin
Refined a-Malinis; makinis, dalisay.
Refinement-n-Kalinisan, kadalisayan ·
Reflect-v-Gunigunihin; mag wari wari, mag isip isip.
Reflection-n Gunam gunam; pag wawariwari
Reflex-a-Nakaliad
Refold v-Tikluping muli
Reform-v-Husayin; ayusin, baguhin
Reform-n-Pagkabago.
Reformation-n-Pagbabago
Refract-v Hubugin, balin
Refraction-n-Pagkahubog, pagkabali.
Refractory-a-Baliktad
Refrain-v-Magtiis, tiisin, pigilin
Refrain-n-Kanta, awit
Refresh-v-Magpalamig, magpahangin, magpahinga
Refreshment-n-Pagpapahinga; inumin.
Refrigerant-a-Malamig
Refrigerant-n-Pangpalamig
Refrigerate v Palamigin.
Refrigerative-a-Malamig
Refrigerator-n-Lalagyan ng hielo.
Refuge-n-Kupkop; kalong
Refugee-n-Ang tumekas.
Refulgence-Refulgency-n Ningning, kintab; kislap, kisap
Refulgent a-Maningning, pakislap; makisap, maliwanag
Refund-v-Isauli
Refusal-n-Katangihan; pagkaayaw, kaayawan
Refuse-v-Tumangi, tangihan, umayaw, huag tangapin
Refuse-n-Bagay na walang kabuluhan; pinagpilian, kasukalan
Refuse-a Walang kabuluhan.
Refúte-v-Patotohanin
Regain-v-Bawiin; bumawi
Regal-a-Parang hari, Nauukol sa hari.
Regale-v-Magpiging
Regale-n-Piging
Regalement-n-Pagpapiging
Regalia-n-Ang nauukol sa kaharian, galon
Regality n Kaharian
Regard n-Alangalang, pagtingin.
Regard-v-Maukol, tumingin
Regardful a-Maingat.
Regardless-a Walang ingat.
Regency-n Katungkulang hari; pagkahari
Regeneracy n Muling pagsipot ó paggawa
Regenerate-v Muling gawin ó sumipot.

Regent-a-May kapangyarihan
Regent-n-Hari, puno
Regicide-n-Ang natay sa hari.
Regime-n-Panahon
Regimen-n-Paggogobierno ng mahusay.
Regiment-n-Regimento; kawal ng sundalo
Regimental-a-Nauukol sa regimiento.
Region-n-Lugar
Register-n-Registro.
Register-v-Isulat ang ngalang
Registrar-n-Taga ingat ang registro
Registration-n-Pagsulat ng ngalang sa registro.
Regnancy-n Kapangyarihan
Regnant a-May kapangyarihan
Regress-n-Pagbalik.
Regret-v-Magsisi
Regret-n-Pagsisisi.
Regretful-a-Masisisihan
Regular-a-Yano, karaniwan.
Regular-n-Sundalong regular
Regularity-n-Pagkakawasto, ayos.
Regulate-v-Ayusin; husayin, iayos
Regulation-n-Pagaayos, ayos husay
Rehearse-v-Magsanay, saysayin, ulitin
Rehearsal-n-Kasanayan; kasaysayan
Reign-n-Panahon ng pagkahari
Reign-v-Maghari.
Reimburse-v-Isauli ang kuartang ginesta
Rein-n-Rienda
Rein-v Pigilin.
Reinforce-v-Magbangkat, bangkatin, palakasin, idagdag
Reins n-Manga riendas
Reinstate-v-Ilagay uli sa dati
Reissue-v-Ikalat muli.
Reissue-n-Muling pagkalat
Reiterate-v-Sabihin uli; ulitin
Reiteration n-Pagsasabi uli, pagulit, pagsasabi ng panibago
Reject-v-Tangihan, tumangi, iwaksi, talikuran
Rejection-n-Pagtangi; pagkawaksi.
Rejoice-v-Sumaya magaliw
Rejoicing n-Kasayahan, aglahi, paglilibang.
Rejoin v-Muling magpisan ó pumisan.
Rejoinder n-Sagot, tugon
Rejuvenescence n-Pagbalik sa pagkabata
Rejuvenate-v-Bumalik sa pagkabata.
Relapse-n Binat
Relapse-v-Buminat, mabinat.
Relate v-Sabihin; magsabi; saysayin, magbalita; matungkol, maukol.
Relation n-Pagsasabi, kasaysayan; kamaganak
Relationship-n-Kamaganakan, kaukulan
Relative-a-Nauukol, tungkol

Relative-n-Kamaganak
Relator-n-Ang nagsabi ó nagbalita
Relax-v-Lumuag, luagin
Ralaxation n-Kaluagan, kaaliwan.
Relay-v-Muling ilatag
Release-v-Ilaya; hangin, magbigay ng kalayaan.
Release-n-Kalayaan.
Relegate v-Ialis, ipadistierro, palayasin
Relegation-n-Pagpapalayas
Relent-v-Maawa, mahabag
Relentless-a-Walang awa ó habag
Relevance-Relevancy-n Kaukulan
Relevant-a-Nauukol sa
Reliability-n Katotobanan, katapatan.
Reliable a-Totoo, tunay.
Reliance-n-Katibayan ng loob, katapatan ng loob.
Relict-n-Baong babayi.
Relief-n-Kahalili, kaginhawahan.
Relieve-v-Humalili, halinhan
Religion-n-Religion, pananampalataya.
Religious a-Banal; mapagdasal
Relinquishment-v-Bitiwan, maiwan
Relinquishment-n-Paghibitiw.
Relish-v-Lasapin, magkagusto, palinamnamin.
Relish-n-Gusto, lasap, lasa, tikim.
Reluctance-n-Kaayawan, kasalungatan
Reluctant-a-Salungat, sowail; ayaw.
Rely-v-Maniwala
Remain-v-Maiwan.
Remainder n-Ang natitira; pinagpilian kalabisan, lagpos
Remains n-Kalabisan, bangkay, buiol
Remark-v-Magsabi, matanto.
Remark-n Sabi; kasabihan, kasaysayan.
Remarkable a-Katakataka, kamangha mangha
Remediable-a-Magagamutin.
Remedial a-Magagamutin
Remedy-n-Gamot; kagamutan
Remedy-v-Gumamot; gamutin.
Remember-v-Alalahanin, tandain, maisipan
Remembrance-n-Alaala
Remind-v-Ipaalaala
Reminiscence-n-Alaala
Reminiscent-a-Maalaala.
Remiss-a-Pabaya; tamad, mabagal; walang ingat
Remission-n-Patawad.
Remit-v-Isauli, bitiwan, sumupil, awasan, patawarin, ipadala
Remittance-n Pagpapadala, pagpapatawad
Remittment-n Pagpapadala.
Remittent-a-Titigil at muling susulong
Remittor-n Ang nagpapadala.
Remnant-n-Retaso

Remodel-v Baguhin.
Remonstrance-n-Daing, luhog; dalita
Remonstrate-v-Dumaing, mapasiya.
Remorse-n-Hiya, pagkabalisa; lungkot
Remorseful-a-Nahihiya malungkot.
Remorseless a-Walang awa
Remote-a-Malayo
Removal v-Pagpaalis, paglipat
Remove-v-Ialis, ilipat; ibukod; ihiwalay
Remunerate-v-Bayaran, upahan, gantihin.
Remuneration-n-Pagbayad, kabayaran, bayad; upa, ganti.
Remunerative-a-May tubo ó pakinabang.
Renal-a-Nauukol sa lugar ng bato ng katawan.
Rencontre-v-Sumalubong, lumaban.
Rencounter-v Sumalubong, lumaban
Rend-v-Punitin, biakin.
Render-v-Isauli, ibigay, sumupil; ihulog sa ibang wika, mantikahin
Rendesvous-n-Hodyatan, gawi.
Rendition-n-Pagsupil, paggawa, suko.
Renegrade-n-Tawong taksil.
Renew-v-Baguhin, ulitin
Renewal-v l'agulit, pagkabago
Renewedly adv -Uliulit.
Renounce-v-Tumangi, tumangal, humiwalay, magrenuncia
Renovate-v-Linisin.
Renovation-n-Paglinis, pagkabago.
Renown-n-Balita, bantog; bunyi, kabantugan.
Renowned a-Balita; mabunyi, bayani; bantog
Rent-v. imp & p p.-Pinunit.
Rent-n-Upa.
Rent-v-Paupahan
Rent-n-Upa sa bahay
Renunciation-n-Pagtatagal, paghihiwalay, katangihan
Reorganization-n-Muling pagkaayos
Reorganize-v-Muling ayusin
Repair-v-Iuli, husayin, baguhin, tutupan.
Repair-n-Tutop, dagdag
Reparation-n-Paguli, pagbabago.
Repartee-n-Sagot; tugon, tutol
Repast n-Piging, pagkain
Repay v-Muling bayaran, bayaran uli, gantihin, isauli.
Repayment-n-Muling pagbabayad, bayad, ganti
Repeal-v Baguhin ang utos, pawalan ang kabuluhan.
Repeat-v-Ulitin, dumalas, sabihin nli
Repeat-n-Pagulit, muling pagsasabi
Repeatedly-adv.-Madalas, muunt, muli.
Repel-v-Lumaban, bumabag, itakwil, iwaksi.

Repent-ı-Magsısı, tiisin

Repentance n-Pagsısısı.

Repentant-a-Nagsısısı, mapagsısı

Repentant-n-Ang nagsısısı.

Repitition-n-Paguht.

Repine-v-Dumaing

Replace-v-Palıtan, ıuli, ılagay ulı sa lugar.

Replacement-n Paguli.

Replendısh-v-Punuin

Replete-a-Lubos, puno, puspos, walang kulang.

Repletion-n-Kabuoan, kasandatan, pag kapuno.

Replication-n-Sagot, tugon

Reply-ı-Sumagot, tumugon, sagutın

Reply-n Sagot, tugon; tutol

Report n-Palıta, putok, alam, repor, bulongbulonğan, kalatog, sabısabı.

Report-v-Magbigay alam; mag balita, ıbalıta.

Repose-v-Magpahınğa, huminto, humimlay

Repose-n-Pagpapahınğa, hınto

Repository-n-Kamalıg, taguan.

Repossess-v-Muling magkamıt

Reprehend v Sisihın.

Reprehensıble a-Dapat sisıhin

Reprehension n-Pag pasısi, panğusap, parusa

Represent-v-Magkatıwala

Representation-n-Pagkakatiwala

Representatıve-n-Pıntakasi, katıwala.

Repress v-Supilin.

Repression-n Pagsupıl

Reprıeve-v Palugitın.

Reprieve-n-Palugit

Reprimand-n Panğusap, pagpasısı.

Reprımand-v-Sisihın

Reprint v-Limbagın uli; muling maglımbag

Reprınt-n Muling pag lımbag.

Reprisal-n-Muling pagkuha

Reproach-v-Sisihın, murahın, tangıhan

Reproach-n-Pagsisısi; kamurahan, hıya

Reproachful a-Nakadudusta, hamak

Reproachless-a-Malinıs, mabuti

Reprobate a-Masama, hamak, pabaya

Reprobate-n Tawong masama

Reproduce v-Muling gawın, muling ıpalıtaw

Reproduction-n-Muling pag lıtaw

Reproof n-Panğusap

Reprove v Pıntasın, aralan, ipanğusapan

Reptant-a-Gumagapang.

Reptile n-Ahas, sawa, hayop na walang paa at pakpak.

Reptile-a-Gumagapang

Republic-n-Republica.

Republican a-Nauukol sa republica.

Republication-n-Muling paglımbag

Republish-v-Mulıng maglımbag, muling ipahayag

Repudiate-v-Talıkuran, tumangal, tan gihan

Repudiation-n-Katalikuran, katangıhan, pagkahıwalay

Repugnancy-n-Dımarim, suklam; kasu klaman.

Repugnant-a-Masusuklaman, marimarım

Repulse-ı-Lumaban, alısın

Repulse-n-Laban, paglaban

Repulsıón-n-Paglaban

Repulsıve-a-Nasusuklaman.

Repurchase v-Bumılı ulı

Reputable a-Dapat manıwala; dapat galınğin

Reputation n-Puri; danğal, kabantugan, mabutıng nğalan.

Repute-ı-Sabihin, ılagay sa katowıran.

Repute n-Lagay, kalagayan.

Request-n-Bılın, hınğı; luhog, pakiusap

Request-v-Lumuhog, manalanğin, makıusap, huminğı.

Requiem n-Dalıt.

Require-ı-Magkaılanğan; pilıtın

Requirement-n-Kakaılanğan

Requisite-a-Husto, kaılanğan

Requisite-n-Ang kaılanğan

Requisition-n-Ang kınakaılanğan

Requital-n-Ganti, bayad, parusa

Requite-ı-Gantihın, parusahın

Rescind-v-Putulın, putlın, pawalan nğ kabuluhan

Rescue-ı-Ilıgtas, sagipın, hanğuin.

Rescue-n-Pag lıgtas, kupkop; pagsasagıp

Research-ı-Usısaın ulı, sıyasatın ulı.

Research n Muling pagsisıyasat

Resemblance-n-Pagkakamukha, katulad

Resemble-v-Imukha, magkamukha; pumaris, tumulad.

Resent-v-Tampuhın, tumampo, magalıt magsalaghati

Resentment-a-Mapootın; tampuhın.

Resentment-n-Galit; salaghati; dalamhatı; yamot, tampo

Reservation-n Lihim; taan.

Reserve v-Itago, ıpaglaan, tirahın, magtira

Reserve n-Taan, hınahon

Reservedly-adv.-Palıhim

Reservoir-n-Lawa, labak

Reset v-Muling ilagay

Reside v Tumira, tumahan.

Residence n-Tirahan; tahanan; balıay

Resident n-Ang tumira sa ısang lugar.

Residual-a-Nauukol sa natira

Residue n-Tira, pınagpilian, kalabısan; lagpos

Residium-n Tira, pinagpilian, ang na-
titira; kalabisan.
Resign v-Tumangi, tumangal, umayaw,
magrenuncia; magtus
Resignation-n-Pagrerenuncia, pagtatan-
gal
Resigned-a-Mababang loob
Resin-n-Adiyangaw.
Resist v-Lumaban; bumabag, salungatin
Resistance n-Pag laban, pag labag
Resistless a-Mahina, di makalalaban
Resolute-a-Malakas ang loob, buo ang
loob, matibay; matatag.
Resolution-n-Kalakasan ng loob, kabuoan
ng loob, katibayan.
Resolve-n-Takdaan, pasiyahan, lumakas
loob.
Resolve n Takdaan, inisip, banta
Resonance n-Tunog, aladalad.
Resonant-a-Matunog
Resort-i-Gumawi; pumaroon
Resort-n-Gawi
Resound-v-Tumunog; umalalad
Resound-n-Tunog
Resource-n Pinangalingan, pinagmulaan
Respect-n-Galang, paggalang, pitagan,
kamahalan, pagpuri
Respect-i-Gumalang, galangin, pintu-
huin, pumintuho, magbigay puri; mau-
kol, matungkol
Respectability-n-Galang, kagalangan, pu-
ri, kamahalan, pagkaginoo.
Respectable-a-Magalang, ginoo, binibini,
mabini
Respectful-a Magalang, mapagpitagan.
Respecting-prep -Nauukol sa, tungkol
sa.
Respective-a-Karampatan, sarili.
Respell v-Titikin uli
Respirable-a-Mabuti sa paghinga.
Respiratory-a-Nauukol sa paghinga
Respiration-n-Hininga
Respire v-Huminga
Respite-n-Palugit
Respite-v-Palugitin.
Resplendent-a-Maningning, makisap, ma-
luningning; makislap
Respond-i-Sumagot, tumugon; tumutol,
matungkol
Respondent-n-Ang sumasagot, ang tu-
mutol
Response-n-Tugon, sagot, tutol.
Responsible a-Mananagutin, may ka-
tungkulang managot.
Rest-n-Pahinga, aliw; hinto, katahimi-
kan, kapahingahan, kapayapaan;
ang labis, ang natitira.
Rest-v-Magpahinga, maghinto, huminto,
humupa humimpil, tumahimik
Restaurant n-Karihan, restaurant.

Restitution-n-Pagsasauli.
Restive-a Balisa; malikot.
Restless-a-Malikot; balisa; magalaw.
Restlessness n-Kalikutan, pagkabalisa
Restoration-n-Pagsasauli.
Restore-v-Isauli, saulan.
Restrain-v-Pigilin, pumigil; higpitan, sa
watain, awatin.
Restraint-n-Pigil, kahigpitan; pag pi-
pigil
Restrict-v-Kulungin, ilagay ang hanga,
pigilin
Restriction-n-Pagkulong, paglalagay ng
manga hanga.
Result-n-Litaw, sagot, ang nangyayari,
ang lumitaw.
Result-v-Lumitaw, mangyari
Resume-v-Ituloy, kunin uli.
Resumption-n-Pagmumula ng muli.
Resurrection-n-Pagkabuhay ng muli;
muling pagkabuhay.
Resusticate-v-Buhayin uli
Resustication-n-Muling pagkabuhay.
Retail-v-Ipagbili ng untiunti.
Retail-n-Pagbili.
Retain-v-Bimbingin, lalamin, huag bi-
tiwan
Retainer-n-Lalam, bimbing.
Retaliate-v Gantihin, gumanti.
Retaliation-n-Ganti
Retard-v-Antalahin' pigilin, luatan,
magluat.
Retardation-n-Pagpigil; antala
Retention n-Pagkulong, antala
Retentive a-Maantalahin; maabala.
Reticence-n Kaayawan magsalita.
Reticent-n-Ayaw magsalita
Reticle-n Munting supot ó bayong.
Reticular a-Hitsurang kitid
Reticule-n Munting bayong.
Retina-n-Gitna ng mata.
Retinue n-Manga kasama; katulong.
Retire-v-Umurong, humiwalay; lumayo
Retirement-n-Pagurong; paglayas, ka-
tahimikan
Retiring-a-Nahihiya, tahimik.
Retort-v Sumagot, tumutol, tumugon.
Retort-n-Sagot, tugon, tutol.
Retrace-v-Guhitin, uli, bumalik.
Retract v-Baguhin ang salita, tumalikod,
talikuran, magkaila; umurong.
Retraction-n-Pag urong pagkakaila
Retreat-v-Umurong, lumayo.
Retreat n-Pag urong; pag layas. ihian;
panambitan
Retribution n-Bayad, ganti, upa.
Retrievable-a Makababawi
Retrieve-v-Bawiin, bumawi.
Retrocede-r-Bumalik sa dati, umurong,
sumama.

39

Retrocession-*n*-Pag balik sa dati, pag-urong
Retrograde *v*-Bumalik; umurong, suma-ma
Retrogression *n*-Pag urong; pagbalik
Retrospect-*v*-Lumingon, alalahanin.
Retrospect-*n*-Pag lingon; alaala.
Return-*v*-Bumalik, muling bumalik, isauli, saulan
Return-*n*-Pagbalik; pagsasauli
Reunion-*n*-Katipunan; pagtitipon· kapisanan.
Reunite-*v*-Pumisan uli, muling ilakip.
Reveal-*v*-Ipakita, ipasabi, ilitaw
Revel *n* Piging; Kasayahan, biro.
Revel-*v*-Magbiro, sumaya
Revelation-*n*-Pakita, pagpahayag
Revelry-*n*-Kasayahan, biroan; ingay; kaguluhan, kaingayan.
Revenge-*v*-Gantihin
Revenge-*n*-Ganti
Revengeful-*a* Ibig gantihin, ayaw patawarin.
Revenue *n*-Pakinabang, tubo; buis
Reverberate-*v*-Umalingawngaw, kumalasing.
Reverberation *n*-Alingawngaw
Revere-*v*-Galangin, gumalang, sambahin, pintuhuin.
Reverence-*v*-Galangin; pintuhuin
Reverence-*n*-Pintuho; galang, pitagan.
Reverend-*a*-Magalan; banal.
Reverent-*a*-Magalang, mababang loob
Reverential-*a*-Magalang, mapitagan
Reverie-*n*-Bulayan, wari, pagwawariwari.
Reversal-*n*-Kabaliktaran
Reverse-*v*-Baguhin, baliktarin, bawiin; talunin
Reverse-*n*-Pagkabaliktad.
Reverse-*a*-Baliktad, gusot, magulo.
Reversion-*n*-Pagkabaliktad.
Revert-*v*-Baliktarin, bumaliktad, bumalik.
Review-*v*-Muling magmasiran; siyasatin uli
Review-*n*-Muling paguusisa, repaso; pagulit
Revile-*v*-Murahin, alimurahin laitin, magalibugha
Revisal-*n*-Paggagawa ng panibago.
Revise-*v*-Baguhin, gawing panibago.
Revise *n*-Ikalawang burador
Revision-*n*-Pagkabago.
Revival-*n*-Pagbabago.
Revive-*v* Buhayin.
Revocation *n*-Pagurong.
Revoke *v*-Umurong, panrungan, pawalan ang kabuluhan.
Revolt-*v*-Magalsa, lumaban sa puno

Revolt-*n*-Paghihimagsik ng bayan laban sa kanilang puno
Revolution-*n*-Pagkakagulo
Revolutionary-*a*-Nauukol sa gulo
Revolutionize-*v*-Baguhin, ibahin.
Revolve-*v*-Umikit; uminog.
Revolver-*n*-Rebolber.
Revulsion *n* Kasuklaman.
Reward-*v*-Gantihin, bigyan ng ganting palá
Reward-*n*-Ganti, palá, bayad, pabuya.
Rheum *n*-Nana
Rheumatism-*n*-Rumatismo.
Rhyme *n*-Verso; tula.
Rhyme *v*-Tumula, magverso, manula.
Rhymster-*n*-Ang marunong magverso, manunula
Rib-*v*-Tadyang
Rib-*v*-Maglagay ng tadyang.
Ribbon-*n*-Liston; sintas
Rice-*n*-Palay, bigas.
Rich-*a*-Mayaman, masagana, masalapi.
Riches-*n*-Kayamanan, yaman.
Rick *n*-Mandala
Rickets-*n* Sakit ng buto
Rickety-*a*-Usayanin; mahina.
Rid-*v*-Alisin, palayasin
Riddance-*n*-Pagpalayas.
Ridden-*v p p.*-Nakasakay.
Riddle-*v*-Bugtong, bithay.
Riddle-*v*-Magbithay, bithayin
Ride *n*-Sumakay, sakayan, isakay
Ride-*n*-Sakay, pagsasakay.
Rider-*n* Ang sumasakay.
Ridge-*n*-Palupo
Ridicule-*v*-Bansagin, uyamin, tuksuhin, libakin
Ridicule-*n*-Uyam; libak
Ridiculous *a*-Makatatawa, matatawanin.
Rife-*a* Uso, sagana; marami
Riffraff *n*-Sukat manga tawong hamak.
Rifle-*v*-Nakawin, manduit
Rifle-*n* Rifle, baril
Rifler *n*-Manduduit
Rift-*n*-Lahang, bitak
Rift-*v* Lahangin, lumahang.
Rig-*v*-Sasakyan, kasangkapan
Rig-*v*-Magbihis; gayakan.
Rigging *n*-Manga damit.
Right *n*-Katowiran, katampatan, kabanayaran.
Right-*a* Hustong; matowid, ganap; walang kulang.
Right-*v*-Towiran, ganapin, gumanap; husayin, ayusin.
Righteous *a*-Banal; matowid; ayon sa katowiran
Rightful *a*-Ayon sa katowiran
Rigid-*a*-Batibot, matibay; mabagsik; masungit

Rigidity-Rigidness-n-Katibayan, tibay, kabagsikan; kasungitan
Rigmarole n-Salitang hunghang
Rigor-n-Kabagsikan; sidhi, kahigpitan
Rigorous-a-Mahigpit, mabagsik.
Rile v-Labuin.
Rily-a Malabo.
Rill-n-Sapa
Rim n Gilid; tabi
Rime-n-Lahang, bitak; baitang ng hagdanan
Rind n Balat, upak; talop
Rinderpest-n-Peste ng kalabaw
Ring-n-Singsing, buklod, bilog.
Ring v-Bilugin; balisusnin
Ring-n-Tunog
Ring-v Tumunog; tunugin
Ringleader-n-Puno
Ringlet-n-Sinsing na munti; kulot
Riot-n-Away, gulo ng marami, pagaalsa; tunang malaki.
Riot-v-Magalsa, gumulo ang marami
Riotous a-Magulo, palaaway·
Rip-n-Tastas
Rip-v-Tastasin, tumastas.
Ripe-a-Hinog, magulang
Ripen-v-Huminog; gumulang
Ripple-n-Munting alon.
Rise n-Pagbangon; pinangalingan, pinagmulaan, pagpapataas, taas.
Rise-v-Bumangon; tumaas
Risible-a-Makatatawa.
Risk-n-Kapalaran, kapanganiban
Risk-v-Ilagay sa kapalaran.
Risky-a May panganib
Rite-n-Sermon
Rival-a-Malaban; kalaban
Rival-n-Kalaban, katalo; katapat.
Rival v-Lumaban, magkatalo.
Rivalry-Rivalship-n-Pagkakatalo, paglaban.
Rive-v-Lahangin; lumahang; bitakin
River-n-Ilog
Rivet-n-Pakong maikli at makapal
Rivet-v Silsilin; baluktutin
Rivulet-n-Sapa.
Roach-n-Ipis.
Road-n Lansangan, daan, carsada
Roadstead-n-Punduhan.
Roam-v-Lumakad, gumala
Roan-a-Rosillo
Roan-n-Rosillo
Roar-v-Umangil, tumahol
Roar-n-Angil; tahol.
Roast-v-Ihawin, ibusa
Roast-n-Ihaw; paghusa
Roast-a-Naihaw, inihaw
Rob-v-Nakawin, harangin; magnakaw; umumit, umitin.

Robber-n Manloloob; manghaharang; magnanakaw; tulisan.
Robbery-n-Pangloob; pagnakaw, pagumit.
Robe-n Damit
Robe v-Isuot ang damit
Robust-a May katawan, mataba, balisaksakin, batibot, pisigan; maugat; malakas, malaki.
Rock-n-Bato, uga.
Rocket n Kuetes
Rock-v-Ugain; lagyan ang bato.
Rocky-a Mabato, mahina, masama
Rod-n-Pirasong bakal; panukat na may anim na baras ang haba.
Rode-v-Nakasakay, sumakay.
Rodent-a Mangatngat
Rodent-n-Hayop na mangangagat.
Roe-n Babaying usa, usang inahin.
Rogue n-Tawong masama; hampaslupa.
Roguery-n-Kasamaan
Roguish a-Palabiro; mapagbiro; masama.
Role-n Gawa ng komediante.
Roll-n-Bilog, balot,
Roll-v-Gumulong, gulungin, gumumon.
Rolling pin-n-Paralis
Roman-a-Nauukol sa Roma ó sa Romano.
Roman Catholic-n-Catalico Romano.
Romance-n-Kuento.
Romance-v-Magkuento
Romanesque-a-Nakakahawig sa Roma.
Romanism-n-Kaukulan sa Roma
Romanize-v-Gawin Catolico.
Romp-v-Maglaco magbiro
Romp-n-Laro
Rompish-a-Magulo, malikot, mapagpalaro.
Roof-n-Bubong, bubungan.
Roof-v-Lagyan ang bubungan.
Roofing-n-Kasangkapang ginamit sa bubungan.
Roofless a-Walang bubong.
Rookery-n-Bahay na malapit masira
Room-n-Silid; kuarto
Room-v-Tumira sa cuar-o.
Roominess-n-Kaluagan, kaluangan.
Roommate-n-Kasama sa kuarto.
Roomy a-Maluag, maluang
Roost-n-Hapunan
Roost-v-Humapon.
Rooster-n Manok
Root-n-Ugat; pinagmulan.
Root-v-Ngumuso.
Rootlet-n-Ugat na munti.
Rope-n-Lubid.
Rope-v-Talian ng lubid
Ropery-n-Gawaan ng lubid
Rope walk-n-Gawaan ng lubid.
Rosary-n-Rosario.

Rose-n-Rosas.
Rose-v. imp.-Nabangon, bumangon.
Roseate a-May maraming rosas.
Rose bud-n-Rosas na hindi pa bumuka.
Rose bush-n Puno ng rosas.
Rosin-n-Adyangaw, resina, patada
Roster-n Listahan.
Rosy-a-Kulay rosas
Rot-v Bumulok, bumugok, boogin, lapukin, dumapok
Rot-n-Kabulukan, kaboogin, lapok.
Rotary-a-Mabilog
Rotate-a-Sunodsunod
Rotate-v-Uminog, bumilog, humahli.
Rotation-n-Paghahalili, pag ikit
Rotten-a-Mabulok; bugok, latok
Rottenness n-Kabulukan, kahamakan
Rotund-a-Mabilog, lubos, puspos, pawang; buo.
Rotunda-n-Bilog; kabilugan
Rotundity-Rotundness n-Kabilugan
Rouge-a-Mapula
Rouge-n-Blankete
Rouge-v-Magblankete
Rough-a-Magaspang, bastos; walang pinag-aralan; makapal ang balat, hamak.
Rough-n-Tawong bastos.
Roughness-n-Kagaspangan, gaspang; kabastosan.
Round-a-Mabilog.
Round-n-Bilog.
Round-adv-Sa paligidligid.
Round-prep.-Sa paligid
Round-v-Bilugin.
Round about-a-Pasuotsuot, magulo
Round about-n-Tio vivo
Roundish-a-Mabilog.
Round-shouldered-a-Hubog ang balikat; kuba
Rouse-v-Udyukan, ipabuya, buhayin.
Rout-n-Supil; suko, yalo.
Rout-v Manalo, supilin, pasukin.
Route n-Daan.
Routine-n-Pagkasunodsunod.
Rove-v-Lumakad na walang tinutuntungan
Row-n-Taludtod, sulambi, talata, pagkakasunodsunod
Row-v-Gumaod, sumagwan
Row n-Gulo, basagulo
Rowdy-n-Tawong bastos at magulo
Rowdy-a-Bastos
Rowdyish a-Bastos
Rowdyism-n-Kabastosan.
Rowlock n-Lalagyan ng gaod ó sagwan.
Royal a-Marangal, dakila; nauukol sa hari.
Royalist n-Ang sumusunod sa utos ng hari.

Royalty n-Karangalan, kadakilaan, kaharian, tubo
Rub-t-Hilurin humilot, kusutin
Rub n-Hilot, kusot
Rubber-n-Goma
Rubbish-n-Kasukalan; pinag linisan.
Rubify v-Papagbagahin
Ruby-n Batong mahal
Ruby a-Mapula.
Rudder-n Ugit
Ruddy-a-Mapula, mamula
Rude-a-Bastos, bangingbangin. buhong, walang galang, tampalasan, talipandas.
Rudiment n-Pamula, pinagmulan
Rue-v-Magsisi
Rueful-a-Malungkot; mapanglaw
Ruff n Pelegas.
Ruff v-Pelegasin.
Ruffian-n-Tawong bastos, ang nakamatay
Ruffian-a-Masama, bastos
Ruffle-n-Pelegas.
Rug n-Banig.
Rugged-a-Malakas, mabanğinbanğin
Rugose-a Kunot kunot. kulubot
Ruin-n-Kasiraan; paghilipol, sira; lansag, pagkalansag, pagkasira.
Ruin-n-Sirain; lipulin, lansagin
Ruination-n-Pagkasira, pagkalansag; kasiraan.
Ruinous-a-Makasisira
Rule-n-Regla, utos, halimbawa, punong aral
Rule-v-Maghari; magpuno; mamuno
Ruler-n-Reglador, hari, puno.
Rum n-Alak.
Rumble v-Umugong
Ruminant-a- Nangunguya.
Ruminate-v-Nguyain.
Rumination-n Nanğunğuya.
Rummage-n-Paghanap
Rummage-v Hanapin ng pilit.
Rumor-n-Balita, alingawngaw, sabisabi.
Rumor-v-Magbalita, umalingawngaw.
Rump-n-Pigi, kalamnan
Rumple-v-Gumusot; gusutin.
Rumpus-n-Basagulo; gulo, pagtatalo
Run-v-Tumakbo
Run n Takbo.
Rung v p p Tinugtog
Rung-n-Baitang ng hagdanan
Runlet-n-Apa
Runner-n-Ang tumakbo.
Runt-n-Tawong pandak
Rupture-n-Pagkasira, pagputok
Rupture r-Sumira, puinutok.
Rural a-Nauukol sa bukid
Ruse n-Paraan, daya, hibo
Rush-r-Biglain; sumulong ng pabigla

Rush-n-Kabiglaan.
Rusk n Biskit
Russ-n-Ang taga Russo.
Russet-a-Mapulapula
Russian-n-Tawong taga Ruso.
Rust n-Kalawang
Rust-v-Kumalawang
Rustic-a-Taga bukid, magaspang; mabalat.
Rustic n-Tawong taga bukid ó parang.

Rusticate-v-Tumira sa bukid ó parang.
Rustication n-Pagtitira sa bukid.
Rusticity-n-Kagaspangan, kahunghangan
Rustle-v Kumaluskos
Rustle-n-Kaluskos.
Rusty-a Makalawang, kalawangin.
Rut-n-Bakas.
Ruth n-Awa.
Ruthless-a-Walang awa ó habag.

S

Saan-n-Tawong gubat.
Sabbath n-Panahon ng̃ pag papahing̃a, lingo
Sabatic-a Nauukol sa lingo.
Saber n Sable, sandata.
Sabot-n-Bakia.
Sabre-n-Sable.
Sac-n-Bayong
Saccharine-a Matamis
Sack-n-Payong; supot
Sack-v-Isilid sa bayong.
Sack cloth-n-Langotse
Sacker-n-Manduduit.
Sackful-n-Laman ng̃ bayong
Sacking-n-Langotse.
Sacrament-n-Sacramento
Sacramental-a-Naukol sa sacramento.
Sacred-a-Nauukol sa Bathala, inalay, banal.
Sacrifice-n Alay
Sacrifice v-Ialay.
Sacrilege-n Pagmura sa ng̃alan ng̃ Dios.
Sacrilegious a Ayaw sumamba sa Dios
Sad-a-Malungkot, mapanglaw, mahapis; mahambal; kahambalhambal.
Sadden v-Malungkot, pumanglaw; humapis, humambal
Sadness n-Kalungkutan; kapanglawan, hapis, kahapisan, hambal.
Saddle-n-Siya ng̃ kabayo
Saddle-v-Lagyan ng̃ sia sng kabayo.
Sad iron-n-Plancha.
Safe-a-Walang pang̃anib, tiwasay, mahusay.
Safe-n-Kaja ng̃ bakal
Safe guard-n-Bantay, katulong
Safe-keeping n Pag̃ing̃at
Safety-n-Katiwasayan, kahusayan, kawalan ng̃ pang̃anib.
Sag-v Humubog, bumaluktot
Sagacious-a-Matalas; tuso, matalino; marunong.
Sagaciousness n-Pagkatuso; katusuhan; katalinuhan, karunung̃an; dunong; katalasan; talas.

Sagacity-n-Talas, katalinuhan, katalasan, pagkatuso
Sagamore n-Puno sa mang̃a Indio sa America.
Sage n-Tawong marunong, mago
Sage-a-Marunong; matalas.
Sagittal-a-Parang pana.
Sago-n Sago
Said-v imp. & p p-Sinabi, nagsabi
Sail-n Layag.
Sail-v-Lumayag, layagin.
Sail boat-n-Bangka na may layag.
Sail cloth-n-Kayo na ginamit sa paggawa ng̃ layag
Sailer-n-Sasakyan na may layag
Sailor n-Magdaragat, marinero
Saint n-Santo
Saintliness-n-Kasantosan.
Sake-n-Dahilan, katowiran
Sal-n-Asin
Salaam-n-Bati, yukod
Salaam-v-Umukod, batiin, bumati.
Salable-a-Mabili
Salaeratus-n-Sal de sosa
Salam-n-Bati, yukod, yuko; pugay
Salam-v-Bumati, batin
Salary-n-Sahod, ang kinita; upa, bayad
Sale-n-Pagbibili, almoneda.
Saleable-a Mabili
Saleratus-n-Sal de sosa.
Sales man-n Ang nagtitinda.
Salient-a-Palundag, palukso
Saliferous-a-May kahalong asin; maalat.
Salify-v-Haluin ng̃ asin.
Saline-a-May kahalong asin.
Saline-n-Bukalan ng̃ asin.
Saliva-n-Laway.
Salival-Salivary-a-Malaway.
Sallow-a-Maputla
Sallowness n-Putla.
Sally-v-Lumabas ng̃ pabigla.
Sally-n-Pag labas, labas.
Salmon-n-Salmon.
Salon-n-Salas
Saloon-n-Salas

Salt-n Asin.
Salt a-Maasin.
Salt-v-Asinan; asnan
Saltish-a-Maasin
Salubrious-a-Makabubuti
Salubrity-n-Kabutihan ñg buhay
Salutary-a Magaling, mabuti
Salutation-n-Bati, yuko
Salute-n-Bati, yuko, pagbati, pugay.
Salute-v-Yumuko, bumati; magpugay,
    magbigay galang.
Salvage-n-Pagligtas ñg sasakyan
Salvation-n-Kalualhatian, pagligtas.
Salve-v-Gamot na pamahid sa sugat
Salver-n-Bandeja.
Salvo-n-Taan; dahilan.
Salvo-n-Pagputok ñg kanyon
Same-a-Yaon din, ñga, din, magkatulad
Sameness-n-Katulad pagkatulad, pagkakawangki.
Sample-n-Halimbawa, tikim, katulad
Sample-v-Tumikim, tikman.
Sanable-a-Makagagaling.
Sanative-a Makagagaling
Senatorium-n-Tinitirahan ñg manğa may
    sakit.
Sanctification-n-Gracia ñg Dios; kalooban ñg P Dios.
Sanctimonious-a-Banal, mapagdasal
Sanctimony-n Kabanalan.
Sanctify-v-Sambahin, ialay sa P Dios
Sanction-n-Pahintulot; tulot; kapayagan
Sanction-v-Pumayag, pahintulutin, ipahintulot.
Sanctuary-n-Lugar na laulhati.
Sanctum-n-Lugar na malualhati
Sand n-Buhanğin
Sand-v-Magbudbod ñg buhanğin.
Sandal-n-Sandalias, sinelas
Sand crab v-Alimango.
Sand paper n-Papel de lija
Sandwich-n-Dalawang pirasong tinapay
    na may isang hiwang carne sa gitna.
Sandy-a-Mabuhanğin.
Sane n-Buo ang isip, malinaw ang isip
Saneness-n-Kalinawan ñg isip
Sang-v. imd -Kumanta; magkanta.
Sang-froid-n-Katahimikan; kawalan ñg
    interes
Sanguiferous-a-May kahalong dugo.
Sanguification-n-Paggawa ñg dugo
Sanguinary-a-Dugodugoan; dumudugo.
Sanguine-a Mapula; kulay dugo; mani
    ñgas, maasshan.
Sanguineous-a-May maraming dugo, kulay dugo.
Sanies-n-Nanang malabnaw.

Sanitarium-n-Tinitirahan ñg mğa may
    sakit.
Sanitation-v-Sanidad
Sanity-n-Kalinawan ñg isip.
Sank-v imp -Nalunod, umanod,
Sap-n-Gata, katas; dagta.
Sap-v-Gumasgas, humina
Sapid a-Malasa, malasap.
Sapience-n-Karununğan, dunong; katahinuhan, katalasan; katusuan
Sapient-a-Marunong, matalas, matalas;
    tuso
Sapless a-Walang katas, walang gata
Sapling n-Munting kahoy.
Saponaceous-a-Parang sabon; masabon
Saponify-v-Maging sabon
Sappy-a-Madagta
Saracen n-Tawong taga Arabia
Saracenic-Seracenical-a-Nauukol sa Arabia
Sarcasm-n-Uyam, alipusta, birong masaklap.
Sarcastic-a-Mauyam, maalipusta
Sardine-n-Sardinas, halobaybay, tunsoy.
Sardonic-a-Mauyam
Sarsaparilla-n Sarsaparilla
Sash n-Pamigkis, pasamano
Sat-v. imp -Umupo, nakaupo
Satan-n-Satanas, ang demonio.
Satanic-Satanical-a-Nauukol sa demonio.
Satchel-n-Saco de noche.
Sate v-Mabusog
Satellite-n-Alila ñg tawong dakila
Satellite a Malapit, kasama, kalapit
Satiate v-Bumusog, busugin, magkasia,
    sandatin, buyain
Satiate a-Busog, puno
Satiation-Satiety-n-Kabusugan,   kabuyaan pagkasiya
Satin n-Kayong sutla na makintab
Satire n-Uyam
Satiric-Satirical-a-Mauyam
Satirize-v-Uyamin; magalibugha; alipustain
Satisfaction-n-Tuwa; aliw, bayad, lugod,
    galak, ganti, kabusugan; ikababayad
Satisfactory-a-Matuwa, husto, maaliw
Satisfy-v-Busugin; bayaran, gantihin
Saturate-v-Ibadbad; basahin
Saturation-n Pagbabasá; pagbabadbad
Saturday n-Sabado.
Sauce-n-Sarsa.
Sauce-v-Ilagay ñg sarsa.
Saucy-a-Mañgahas, matapang.
Sauer kraut-n-Repolio
Saunter-i -Magpasial.
Saunter-n-Pasial
Sausage-n-Soriso
Savage-n-Salbahi, tawong gubat.

Savage-a-Lubhang hunghang, salbahi.

Savageness-Savagery-n Kasalbahian.

Savant-n-Tawong marunong, mago

Save-v-Tubsin; iligtas; sagipin, gumibik; magtípon upunin.

Save-prep.-Bukod sa

Saving a-Maimot; hindi gastador, hindi buiara.

Saving-prep & conj -Bukod sa

Saving-n-Ang inipon.

Savior-n-Dios; Bathala, ang may kapal; ang mananakop.

Savor-n-Lasa

Savor-i-Lasahin, malasa.

Savory a-Malasa, masarap

Saw-v. imp -Nakita, kinita.

Saw-n-Lagari

Saw-v-Maglagari, lagarian

Sawdust-n-Pinaglagarian.

Sawmill-n-Makinang lagarian

Sawyer-n-Maglalagari.

Saxon-n Aleman

Say-v-Magsabi, sabihin; wikain, magwika, saysayin, magsaysay

Say-n Pagwiwika, pagsasabi, kasaysayan

Saying n-Patnugot, kasabihan

Scab-n-Langib

Scabbard-n-Baina.

Scabby-a-Malangib.

Scaffold-n-Bitbitayan; tablado,

Scald-v Banhan

Scald-n-Banh

Scald-a-Malangib

Scale n-Kiskis, kaliskis, panimbag.

Scale-v-Kaliskisin, alisin ang kaliskis

Scalp-v-Tuktok ng ulo

Scalp-v-Alisin ang tuktok ng ulo.

Scaly-a-May maraming kaliskis

Scamp n-Tawong masama

Scamper-i-Tumakas, tumakbo; maglaro

Scamper n-Takbo

Scan-v-Tumingin, siyasatin

Scandal-n Escandalo.

Scandalize-v-Hiyain ang kapwa, gumawa ng escandalo, mag escandalo

Scandalous-a-Masama, makahihiya; escandaloso.

Scant-a-Kulang, kakaunti; damot.

Scant-v-Ilagay ng hanga

Scantling-n Trocillo.

Scanty-a Salat; kaunti, kulang, tumal, maliit

Scape-v Tumekas, umalis; makawala

Scapegrace-n-Tawong masama

Scapula-n-Butong paypay.

Scar-n-Piklat, galos

Scarce a-Damot; tumal, madalang, salat; bihira

Scarce-adv -Halos wala, kagyat, halos, hindi.

Scarceness-Scarcity-n-Kadalangan, katumalan

Scare-v-Takutin, tumakot, bugawin, gulatin, gitlahin

Scare-n-Takot; gitla, gulat

Scarecrow-n-Pamaog, panakot, pamugaw

Scarf-n-Pamigkis.

Scarfskin-n-Balat sa ibabao.

Scarlatina-n-Escarlatina.

Scarlet-n-Mapula.

Scarlet-n-Pula

Scarletfever-n-Escarlatina

Scath-n-Kasiraan, sakit, kasakitan; ka saliwahang palad, sakuna, kasalatan

Scathe-v-Itapon, sirain, lipulin; saktan

Scatter-v-Isabog, ikalat; budburin; sabugin, sumabog, isambulat; sambula, tin., sabugan, ibudbod

Scatter-brain-n-Tawong mahina ang isip.

Scavenger-n-Taga linis ng dumi.

Scene-n-Tingin; acto.

Scent-i-Amoyin

Scent-n-Amoy.

Scepter-Sceptre-n-Tungkod ng hari, kapangyarihan ng hari.

Sceptic-n-Ang may duda

Sceptic-v-May duda

Schedule-n-Listahan, kasulatan.

Schedule-v-Ilista listahin

Scheik-n-Puno

Scheme-n-Katha, paraan. akala.

Scheme-v-Akalain, kathain

Schilling-n-Sicapat

Schism-n-Paghihiwalay.

Schnapps-n-Genebra

Scholar-n-Ang nagaaral, tawong marunong, mago, tinuturuan.

Scholarly-v-Marunong

Scholarship-n-Karunungan, pagaaral

Scholastic-a-Nauukol sa nagaaral ó sa escuelahan

School-n-Escuelahan

School-v-Ipagaralin, turuan, magturo

Schoolbook-n-Libro na ginagamit sa escuelahan

Schoolboy-n-Batang lalaki na nagaaral

Schoolfellow-n-Kasama sa escuelahan

Schoolgirl-n-Batang babayi na nagaaral

Schoolhouse-n-Bahay ng escuela

Schoolmaster-n-Maestro sa escuelahan, ang nagtuturo

Schoolmistress-n Maestra, babaying nagtuturo

Science n-Karunungan.

Scientific-a-Nauukol ea karunungan

Scientist-n-Tawong marunong; mago

Scintilla-n-Pirasong munti

Scintillant n-Maningning, maningas,

Scion-n-Suplng

Scissors-*v*-Gupitin; guntiñgin
Scissors-*n*-Gunting.
Scoff-*n*-Uyam, libak
Scoff-*v*-Uyamin; mañguyam; libakin, laitan, mangbadya
Scold-*v*-Sisihin; gasaan
Scold-*n*-Ang nagpapasisi
Sconce-*n*-Kuta, kubo, hadlang, bao ñg ulo
Scoop-*n* Sandok na malaki
Scoop-*v*-Sandokin; magsandok
Scope-*n*-Tudla
Scorch-*t*-Silabin, umangi
Score *n*-Tanda.
Score-*v*-Tandaan.
Scorn-*v*-Umupasala, uyamin, libakin, laitin
Scorn-*n*-Libak; uyam, upasala.
Scornful-*a*-Mauyam, maupasala; malibak
Scornfulness-*n* Kalaitan, kalibakan.
Scot-*n*-Tawong taga Escosia.
Scotch-*v*-Sugatin; saktan
Scotch-*n*-Sakit, sugat.
Scot-free-*a*-Walang bayad, walang sugat.
Scoundrel-*n*-Tawong hamak at masama.
Scoundrel-*a*-Masama; hamak, suitik taksil.
Scoundrelism-*n*-Kahamakan, kasuitikan, kataksilan.
Scour-*v*-Hilurin; ikuskos; kuskosin, kiskisin; maglinis, linisin.
Scourge-*n*-Palo, latigo; hampas; panghampas.
Scourge-*t*-Paluin; hampasin.
Scout-*v*-Tumangi, huag tangapin, manubok, subukin, tumiktik, tiktikan.
Scout-*n*-Tiktik, taga panubok, manunubok.
Scowl-*n*-Sibañgot.
Scowl-*v*-Makasibañgot, sumimañgot.
Scrabble-*v*-Agawin; magsungaban, isungab.
Scrabble-*n*-Pag aagaw, agawan; sungaban.
Scrag-*n*-Bagay na manipis ó payat
Scraggy-*a*-Payat; manipis
Scramble-*v*-Umagaw; agawin.
Scramble-*n*-Pag agaw, agawan
Scrap-*n*-Piraso
Scrape-*v*-Galusin; kaskasin; kuskusin, kalisan, umalitut.
Scrape-*n*-Galos, kaskas; kuskos
Scraper-*n*-Kudkuran; kaskasan, pangalos, pañgayod.
Scrapings-*n*-Pinagkaskasan.
Scratch-*v*-Kamutin; kumamot, umukyabit.
Scratch-*n*-Kamot; galos, ukyabit.
Scrawl-*n*-Sulat na hindi mainam

Scrawl-*t*-Sumulat ñg hindi mainam.
Scrawny-*a*-Payat,
Screak-*v*-Sumigaw, umalatiit.
Screak-*n*-Sigaw, ahtiit
Scream-*t*-Sumigaw; tumili.
Scream-*n*-Sigaw, tili.
Screach-*v*-Sumigaw, tumili.
Screach-*n*-Sigaw, tili.
Screen-*n*-Tabing, panabing, panambil
Screen-*v*-Kumalong, kalongin, tumabing.
Screw-*n*-Tornillo
Screw-driver-*n*-Pangpihit ñg tornillo.
Scribble-*v*-Sumulat ñg hindi mainam.
Scribble-*n*-Sulat na bastos.
Scribe-*n* Taga sulat
Scrimage-*n*-Laban, basagulo, talo.
Scrimp-*v*-Kulañgin, kumulang
Scrimp-*a*-Kulang
Scrip-*n*-Maikling sulat.
Scriptural-*a*-Nauukol sa Santa Escritura
Scripture-*n*-Santa Escritura
Scrivener-*n*-Taga sulat.
Scroll-*n*-Balutan ñg papel, listahan.
Scrotum-*n*-Supot ñg dalawang itlog.
Scrub-*v*-Magisisi, maglampaso
Scrub-*a*-Masama, karaniwan; hamak
Scrub-*n*-Tawong hamak.
Scrubby-*a*-Magaspang; bastos.
Scruff-*n*-Batok.
Scrunch-*t*-Ñgumasab
Scrupulous-*a*-Maiñgat, may duda.
Scrutinize-*t*-Siyasatin, usisain.
Scrutiny-*n*-Pagsisiyasat, pag uusisa,
Scud *v*-Kumilos ñg maliksi
Scuffle *n*-Sungaban, babag, kaiñgayan, buno
Scuffle-*v*-Magbuno, magsungaban, magmaiñgay.
Sculk *v*-Tumago, magtago, tumakas.
Scull-*n*-Gaod, saguan.
Scull-*t*-Gumaod, sumaguan.
Scullion-*n* Ahla sa kosina
Sculptor-*n*-Escultor
Sculptural-*a*-Nauukol sa escultura
Sculpture-*n* Escultura
Sculpture-*v*-Idukit
Scum-*n*-Subo, bula.
Scum-*t*-Salukan.
Scurf *n*-Buni, balagubak, lañgib
Scurfy-*a*-Mabalakubak, may buni
Scurfy-*v*-Umalis na madali, tumakbo.
Scurry-*n*-Biglang pagalis
Scurvy-*n*-Buni
Scurvy-*a*-Malañgib, may buni.
Scuttle-*v*-Tumakbo, magmadali
Scuttle *n*-Kadalian, pagmamadali, takbo.
Scythe-*n*-Lilik.
Sea-*n*-Dagat.
Sea board *n*-Baybay dagat.

Sea breeze *n*-Hanging nangaling sa da-
gat.
Sea coast *n* Baybay dagat
Sea coast-*a* Nauukol sa baybay dagat
Sea farer-*n*-Magdaragat
Sea hog-*n*-Pagong.
Seal *n*-Tanda, timbre
Seam-*n*-Dugtong, tahi
Seam-*v*-Tahiin
Sea man-*n*-Magdaragat,
Seamless *a*-Walang tahi
Seamstress-*n*-Mananahi
Sea port *n* Bayan na nilapitan ng manga
sasakyan.
Sear-*a* Tuyo malata, lanta
Sear *v* Matuyo, lumanta
Search-*v*-Hanapin, humanap, kapain,
siyasatin; usisain.
Search-*n* Paghanap
Sea shore-*n*-Baybay dagat.
Sea sick-*a* Lula; malula
Sea sickness-*n*-Sakit na lula.
Sea side-*n*-Baybay dagat
Season-*n*-Panahon, kapanahunan
Season-*v*-Pasarapin.
Seasonable-*a*-Ayon sa panahon
Seasoning *n*-Manga paminta at asin
Seat-*n* Upuan.
Seat-*v*-Umupo
Sea ward-*adv.*-Sa gawing dagat
Sea weed *n* Damo sa dagat
Secede-*v*-Umalig; humiwalay; lumayo
Secession-*n*-Paghihiwalay, pag alis
Seckel-*n* Peras na munti at matamis.
Seclude *v*-Itago; kulungin.
Seclusion-*n*-Pagtatago
Second-*a* Ikalawa; kasunod: isa
Second *n*-Kasama, ang ikalawa.
Second-*v*-Umayon
Secondary-*a* Ikalawang
Secondary-*n* Pangalawa.
Second hand-*a*-Hindi bago, nagamit na
Scondly *adv* -Sa ikalawang lugar
Second-rate *a* Ikalawang classe.
Secret-*n*-Lihim
Secret *a*-Nakatago; tinago, lihim
Secretary-*n* Taga sulat. kalihim
Secretaryship-*n*-Katungkulan kalihim.
Secrete-*v*-Itago, magtago, itaan.
Secretion-*n*-Pagtatago
Sect *n*-Lahi; hinlog
Sectarian *a*-Nauukol sa lahi ó hinlog
Section-*n*-Hiwa, parte, piraso, bahagi.
Secure *a*-Matibay; tiwasay, mahusay.
Secure-*v*-Higpitan; talian
Security-*n*-Katibayan; kapanatagan, ka-
siguruhan
Sedate *a*-Mabait, tahimik.
Sedateness *n* Katahimikan, kabaitan.
Sedative-*a*-Mapahimpil.

Sedentary-*a*-Palaging nakaupo
Sediment-*n*-Latak
Sedimentary-*a*-Nauukol sa latak.
Sedition-*n*-Gulo, paghihimagsik; pang-
hihimagsik laban sa puno ó gobierno
Seditious-*a*-Magulo; sowail, laksil
Seduce-*v*-Umapid, makiapid lumuyatan,
igahis
Seduction-*n*-Pakikiapid, apid; lamuyot.
Seducer-*n*-Ang nakikiapid.
Seductive-*a*-Mapanghalina
Sedulous-*a* Masipag.
See-*v*-Tumingin; makita, tanawin
Seed-*n*-Binhi, buto.
Seed-*v*-Tamnan, magtanim ng binhi.
Seedling-*n*-Punla
Seeds man-*n*-Ang nagtitinda ng binhi.
Seed time-*n*-Panahon ng pagtatanim.
Seedy-*a*-May maraming binhi, mabinhi,
uhanin, luma, laon.
Seek-*v*-Humanap, hanapin.
Seem-*v*-Maghitsurang, tumulad; maka-
hawig, humawig.
Seeming *a*-Tilang.
Seemingly-*adv* -Tila
Seemly-*a*-Bagay akma
Seen-*v*. *p p*-Nakakita, nakita; kinita,
tiningnan, tinanaw
Seer *n*-Ang nanunuod
See saw-*n*-Laro ng mga bata.
Seethe-*v*-Kumulo
Segment-*n*-Putol; parti; piraso
Segregate-*v*-Hiwalayin, partihin.
Segregation-*n*-Pag hihiwalay, kahiwala-
yan
Seine-*n*-Kitid, panti, lambat
Seismal-Seismic-*a*-Nauukol ó ginawa ng
lindol
Seize-*v* Hulihin, dakpin, kunin, dampu-
tin; hawakan ng mahigpit.
Seizure-*n*-Pagkuha, pagdampot, dakip,
dampot
Seldom-*adv.*-Madalang, bihira
Select-*a*-Hitang, malinamnam, pinili.
Select-*v*-Humirang; pumili, lisanin, hu
malaw
Selection-*n*-Pagpili; paghirang
Self-*a*-Sarili
Self abasement-*n*-Hiya, pagpahamak ng
sarili
Self conceit-*n*-Kahambugan, kapalaluan
Self defense-*n*-Pagtatangol sa sarili.
Self-denial-*n* Pagtitiis, katiisan
Self-esteem-*n*-Pagmamahal sa sarili.
Self-evident-*a*-Talagang maliwanag.
Self-government-*n*-Pag gogobierno sa
sarili.
Self-interest-*n*-Sariling interes
Selfish-*a*-Maingitin, maramot, kuripot;
masakim

40

Selfishness-n Kariputan, karamutan; pag
kakaingit
Self-love-n-Pag ibig sa sarili.
Self-made-a Ginawa ng sarili.
Self-possession-n-Katahimikan; kabaitan,
kabinian.
Self same-a-Yaon din, yaon nga
Self-seeking-a-Maramot
Self-sufficient-a-Hindi kailangan ng ka-
tulong; husto
Self-will-n-Katigasan ng ulo; lakas loob
Self-willed-a-Matigas ang nlo.
Sell v-Magtinda, magbili, ipagbili
Sell-n-Kabiruan, biro
Selvage selvedge-n-Gilid ng kayo
Selves-a-Sarili rin
Semblance-n-Hitsura, pagkakatulad
Semi annual-a-Nangyayari ng makalawa
sa taontaon.
Somi brebe n-Nota su musica.
Semi circle n-Kalahating bilog.
Semi colon-n-Punto y coma.
Semi diameter-n-Layo buhat sa ubod
hangang sa lasbas ng isangbilog.
Semi fluid a-Malapot pa, hindi malab-
naw.
Semi lunar-a-Hitsurang kalahati ng buan.
Semi monthly-a-Mangyayari ng makala-
wa sa buan buan.
Semi monthly-n-Ang nangyayari nang
makamakalawa sa buan buan.
Seminal-a Nauukol sa binhi
Seminary n-Colegia ng babayi.
Semi tone-n-Kalahating voces.
Semi weekly-a Mangyayari ng makama-
kalawa sa lingo lingo.
Senary-a-Nauukol sa anim
Senate-n-Kapisanan ng mga nag lalagda
sa America.
Send-v-Ipadala; sunduin, ipasundo, utu-
san; paroonin, magpadala.
Senescent-a-Tumatanda.
Senile-a-Nauukol sa katandaan
Senility-n Katandaan.
Senior-a Matanda sa lahat
Senior-n-Ang matanda sa lahat sa isang
lugar.
Seniority-n-Kalagayang matanda sa la-
hat
Sensation-n-Pagdaramdam;karamdaman
Sense-n-Bait; dunong, karunungan, isip,
kalooban.
Senseless a Walang damdam, walang ka-
hulugan; tulig
Sensible a Maramdaman mahalata; ina-
nipis
Sensitive a-Maramdamin, mahapdi; ma
nipis
Sensual a-Nauukol sa damdam, malibog,
hamak, malandi.

Sensuality-n-Kahbugan
Sent v. imp & p p.-Ipinadala
Sentence-n-Hatol, pasiya, sentencia.
Sentence-v-Hatulan, magpasiya
Sententious-a-May kahulugan, maikli
at masaklap.
Sentiment-n-Akala, pakiramdam, panag-
hoy
Sentinel-n-Bantay, tanod.
Sentry-n-Bantay, tanod
Sepal-n-Dahon ng bulaklak
Separable-a-Mangyayaring ihiwalay
Separate a-Iba; di kasama, tangi
Separate-v-Ihiwalay, hiwalayin, ibukod,
itangi; ilayo, lumayo; mamukod; tu-
miwalag.
Separation-n-Paghihiwalay; pamumu-
kod, pagtaboy.
Sepoy-v-Tawong taga India.
Sept-n Lahi
Septangle n Anomang bagay na may
pitong sulok
September-n-Setiembre
Septenary a-Nauukol sa pito
Septennial-a-Maginat ng pitong taon.
Septuagenarian-n-Ang tawo na may pi
tong puong taon ng gulang.
Septuagenary-a-Nauukol sa 6 mayroong
pitong puong taon
Septuple-a-Makapitong duble
Sepulcher-n-Baunan, libing, libingan.
Sepulcher-t-Ihbing
Sepulchral-a-Nauukol sa libing o sa ba-
unan
Sepulture n-Paglilibing
Sequel-n-Karugtong.
Sequence-n Karugtong
Sequent-n-Sumusunod
Sequester-v-Itago sa mav ari
Seraph-n-Angel
Seraphic a-Nauukol sa angel
Sere a-Tuyo, lata
Serenade-n-Serenata, barana
Serenade v Magseianata, magharana
Serene-a-Tahimik, maahwalas mabait
walang kaba
Serenity-Sereneness-n-Katahimikan, ka
tiwasayan
Serf n-Alipin, tahsuyo
Serfage-Serfdom-n-Pagkaalipin
Serge-n-Kayong de lana
Sergeancy-sergeantship- n -Pagkasaigen-
to.
Sergeant n Sargento
Series-n-Pagkakasunodsunod
Serious a-Pormal, totoo; tunay, maga-
lang
Sermon n-Sermon
Serous-a-Malabnaw.
Serpent-n-Ahas, alupong

Serpentine-n Nauukol sa ahas ó sa alupong
Seiried a Masinsin, makapal
Servant-n-Ahla, utusan, talisuyo.
Serve-v-Alindugin; inagsilbe, silbihan, maglingkuran.
Service-n-Servicio, alindog, lingkod; handog; kapagalan; pannyo.
Serviceable a-Magagamit; mapagkikinabanğan
Servile-a-Hamak, nauukol sa alila.
Servility-n-Kahamakan, pagkaalila
Servitude-n-Pagkaalila, pagkaalipin.
Session-n-Sesion; pagkakapulong.
Set-i-Ilagay; maglagay, naglagay.
Set a-Pirme matibay.
Set-n-Paglubog
Setoff-n-Sangkap
Setose-Setous-a Matutsang
Settee-n-Uupuan na mahaba.
Settle-n-Uupuan na mataas ang sandalan
Settle-i-Bayaran: payapain, tapusin, magtuos, tubsin; tumindi
Settlement n-Pagbabayad, pagtuos
Settlings-n-Latak tining
Setto-n-Laban, talo, babag, away
Seven-a-Pitong
Seven-n-Pito
Seven fold-a-Makapitong duble
Seventeen-a-Labing pitong.
Seventeen-n-Labing pito
Seventeenth-a-Ikalabing pito
Seventh-n-Ang ikalabing pito
Seventh-a-Ikapito.
Seventh-n Ang ikapito
Seventieth a Ikapitong puo.
Seventieth-n-Ang ikapitong puo.
Seventy-a Pitong puo
Seventy n Pitong puo
Sever-v-Ihiwalay, humiwalay; tumangal, tangalin.
Several-a-Ilang
Severally-adv -Ilangilan
Severance-n-Pagtatangal
Severe-a Mabagsik, mabanğis, masunğit.
Severeness-Severity-n-Kabagsikan, kasunğitan.
Sew-n Manahi; tumahi, tahiin
Sewer-n-Mananahi
Sewer-n-Sangka.
Sex-n Kaibhan nğ lalaki sa babayi.
Sexagenerian-n-Tawo na may anim na puong taon ang gulang.
Sexagenary-a-May anim na puong taon
Sextant-n-Ikaanim na bahagi nğ isang bilog
Sextuple a-Makapitong duble.
Sexual-a-Nauukol sa sexo.

Shabbiness-n-Kahamakan, pagkapunitpunit nğ damit.
Shabby-a-Lamuymoy; punitpunit ang damit, hamak
Shackle n-Pangapos.
Shackle-v-Gapnsin
Shad-n-Bumbuan, katkat.
Shade-n-Lilim; kalong.
Shade-v Ikalong, lumilim.
Shadow-n-Anino, lilim.
Shadow-v-Maanino, bumuntot
Shadowy-a-Maanino, makalilim
Shady a-Malilim
Shaft n-Tangnan, bitbitan, kasangkapang panlaban
Shagged-a-Magaspang.
Shah n-Hari sa Turkia
Shake-v-Pagpagin, yanigin; ipagpag, paspasin; pumaspas
Shake-n-Paspas, pagpag, yanig.
Shaker-n-Pamagpag; pamaspas
Shaky a-Mahina, hindi matibay
Shale-n-Balat.
Shall-v-Kailanğan.
Shallop-n-Bangka.
Shallow a-Mababaw.
Shallow-n-Lugar sa ilog na babaw.
Sham n Daya, hibo, kasinunğalinğan.
Sham a-Magdaraya, nakahihibo.
Sham-v-Magkonowari, hibuin, dayain.
Shamble v-Lumakad nğ pagiraygiray.
Shambles-n-Patayan.
Shame-n Hiya, kahiyahiyaan; kasiraan; pagsukot.
Shame-v-Hiyain.
Shame faced a Nahihiya
Shameful a-Kahiyahiya, mahihiyain nakadudusta
Shameless a-Walang hiya; tampalasan; walang kamahalan, bastos, mahbog, walang puri, mahalay.
Shank-n-Binti
Shant-v-Huag
Shanty n-Kubo.
Shape-n-Hitsura; tayo, bikas; yaii; anyo; kayarian
Shape-v-Tabasin; gawin ang hitsura
Shapeless-a Walang bikasbikas, walang hitsura.
Shapely-a-May hitsura.
Share n Parte, bahagi
Share-v-Hatiin, bumahagi, pumarte.
Shark-n Pating
Sharp a-Matulis, matalim; maasim
Sharp-n Tulos
Sharp v-Tulisan, tasahan
Sharpen-v Tasahan, tulisan; ihasa.
Sharper n-Tawong suitik, ó taksil, magdaraya
Sarpness-n-Katulisan; talim, tulis.

Sharp-set-a-Matakaw.
Shatter-v-Basagin, durugin,
Shave n-Ahit.
Shave v-Mangahit, ahitin.
Shaver-n-Mangangahit, batang lalaki
Shaving-n-Pinagkataman
Shawl-n-Panuelon
She-pro -Siya (babayi).
Sheaf-n-Haya; bigkis
Shear-v-Gupitin.
Shear-n Gunting.
Sheath n-Kalooban, baina
Sheathe-v-Ilagay sa baina ó kalooban
Sheabe n-Kaloob, kalo
Shed-n-Malugas ang buhok.
Shed-n-Kubo
Sheen-n-Niugning, kintab kisap
Sheep-n-Tupa
Sheep cot-Sheep cote Sheep fold-n-Kulungan ng̃ tupa
Sheepish-a-Mahihiyain, mukhang tupa
Sheep skin-n-Balat ng̃ tupa, titulo.
Sheer-a Mahwanag, malinis, walang halo, patayo.
Sheer-v-Lumiko; lumihis
Sheet n Dahon
Shelf-n-Hanga, paina.
Shell-n-Balat
Shell-v-Balatan, magbalat.
Shellac-n-Barnis.
Shell bark-n-Balat ng̃ kahoy.
Shelly-a-Mabalat.
Shell fish-a Tahong, halaan
Shelter-n Ampon; tankilik, kupkop.
Shelter-n Amponin; tumankilik; ikalong, magtangol.
Sheltie-n-Kabayo
Shelve-v-Ilagay sa pahina ó hanga.
Shepherd n-Ang nagpapastol sa mang̃a tupa
Shepherdess n-Babaying nagpapastol sa mg̃a tupa
Sherd n-Piraso
Sheriff-n-Sheriff.
Sherry-n-Alak na matapang.
Shetland pony-n-Kabayong munti.
Shew-v imp -Ipinakita
Shield-n-Kalasag.
Shield-v-Magtangol, tumankilik.
Shift-v-Galawin, gumalaw, lipatin
Shift n-Paglipat; paggalaw
Shiftless a Pabaya, tamad
Shifty-a-Masipag, magalawin.
Shilling-n Sikapat.
Shilly shally-adv.-Pagayongayon
Shilly shally-i -Gumayongayon.
Shily-adi -Mahihiyain
Shimmer-r-Kumintab, kumisap
Shimmer-n-Kintab, kisap; ningning
Shin-n-Lulod

Shin v-Umakyat
Shine-v-Kumisap; kumislap, kumintab; magningning.
Shine n-Kilos
Shiner-n-Tunsoy.
Shining a Makintab; maningning, makisap
Shinty-n-Gulo
Shiny-a-Maningning, makintab, makislap, makisap.
Ship-n-Sasakyan, daong
Ship-v-Ipadala, ibarka, ilulan sa daong ó sa sasakyan
Ship mate n-Kasama sa sasakyan.
Shipment-n-Ang mang̃a bagay na ipi naglulan ng̃ mayari
Shipper-n-Ang nagpapalulan sa sasakyan ó sa daong
Shipping-n-Paglulan.
Ship shape-a-Mahinis; maselang
Ship wreck n Pagkasira ang sasakyan.
Ship wrevk-v-Masira ang sasakyan
Ship wright n-Taga gawa ng̃ sasakyan.
Ship yard-n Gawaan ng sasakyan
Shire-n-Lalawigan
Shirk v-Huag tumupat, magkulang
Shirk-n-Ang kakulangan; sa pagtupad.
Shiri -n Suri, urong
Shirred a-Nakasuri.
Shirt n-Baro, camisa dentro
Shirtless-a-Walang baro, hubad.
Shiver n-Uminig, manginig.
Shiver-n-Inig, utal.
Shoal a Mababaw.
Shoat-n-Lichonin, buk
Shock-i-Umumpog, umuntog, bumungo
Shock-n-Umpog, untog, bungo.
Shocking-a-Kakilakilabot; nakapang̃ing̃ilabot.
Shod-v-Nagbakal, binakal.
Shoddy a-Masama, hindi mabuti.
Shoe-n Sapatos, bakal.
Shoe-v-Magbakal.
Shoe maker-n -Mangagawa ng̃ sapatos
Shone v. imp & p. p.-Kumisap, maning ning, kumintab.
Shook v. imp -Ipinagpag, ipinaspas
Shoot-v Ungos, supling, usbong, punla; sulol
Shoot-v Bumaril, un usLong sumupling.
Shop n-Tindahan
Shop v-Mamili
Shop keeper-n-Magtitinda, ang may tinda
Shore-n-Pangpang, baybay
Shoreless-a-Walang baybay ó pangpang walang hanga
Shorn-i p p-Ginupit
Short-a-Maikli, maiksi, damot, kulang, malit, maumid.

Short-*adv.*-Sumandali, bigla.
Shortage *n*-Kakulañgan.
Short coming-*n* Kakulañgan.
Shorten-*v*-Iklian, bawasan, padparin.
Shortening *n* Pagbawas
Short lived-*a* Maikli ang buhay.
Shortness-*n*-Kaiklian.
Short sighted *a* Bulinaw
Short-winded-*a* Maikli ang hininga.
Shot-*n*-Putok, perdegones.
Shot-*v* *imp.* & *p. p.*-Pinutok; binarik
Shote-*n*-Lichonin
Should-*v*-Dapat.
Shoulder-*n*-Balikat
Shoulder-*v*-Balikatin, ilagay sa balikat
Shoulder blade *n*-Butong paypay.
Shoulder strap *n* Galon
Shout-*n*-Sigaw, hiyaw
Shout *v*-Sumigaw, humiyaw
Shove-*v*-Itulak, tulakan, ipagtulak
Shove-*n*-Tulak
Shovel-*n*-Pala, pangsurong
Shovel *v*-Magsurong
Show *v* Ipakita, ipatanaw, iharap
Show-*n*-Kita, gayak, handa.
Shower *n*-Ulan, ungos
Shower-*v*-Umulan
Showery-*a*-Maulan
Showy-*a* Makintab, makisap
Shrew-*n*-Babaying bungangaan.
Shrewd *a*-Matalas, tuso, matalino; marunong.
Shrewish-*a* Nauukol sa bungangaan.
Shriek *n*-Tili
Shriek *v*-Tumili.
Shrift-*n*-Pangungumpisal
Shrill *a*-Matili.
Shrimp-*v*-Hipon
Shrink-*v*-Umurong, makuyumpisin
Shrink-*n*-Kuyumpis, pagurong.
Shrinkage-*n*-Pagurong.
Shrive-*v*-Tangapin ang kumpisal
Shrivel *v*-Umurong
Shroud-*n*-Balot na maputi.
Shroud-*v*-Balutin ng maputi
Shrub-*n*-Kaugoygoyan.
Shrubbery-*n*-Kaugoygoyan.
Shrubby-*a*-Makahoy.
Shrug-*v*-Kumilig.
Shrug-*n* Kilig
Shrunken *v* *p* *p*-Nakaurong; umurong na.
Shrunken *a* Nakaurong.
Shuck *n*-Balat.
Shuck-*v*-Balatin, magbalat
Shudder-*n*-Manginig sa takot.
Shudder-*n*-Panginginig sa takot
Shuffle-*v*-Suksukin; magsuksok.
Shuffle-*n*-Pagsuksok, suksok.
Shun-*v*-Umilag, lumayo

Shunt-*v*-Ilihis, iliko
Shut-*v*-Isara, ipuera.
Shut-*a*-Nakasara,
Shutter-*n*-Persiana, takip ng bintana.
Shy-*a*-Nahihiya; mahihiyain, mailag, duag, madaling takutin.
Shyness-*n*-Kimi, ilap; kimpot, hiya
Si-*n*-Si.
Sibilant *a* Mahaginit.
Sic *adv* -Sa ganito
Sick-*a* May sakit; masakit.
Sicken-*v*-Magkasakit
Sickish-*a*-May sakit ng kaunti.
Sickle *n*-Lilik
Sickly *n* Masakit.
Sickness-*n*-Sakit, kasakitan.
Side-*n* Gilid, tabi
Side-*v*-Nauukol sa gilid, ó sa tabi.
Side-*v*-Sumama sa isang partida
Side board-*n* Paninigalan.
Side ling-*adv.*-Pahaba.
Sidelong *adv* -Pahaba.
Sidelong-*a* Sa gilid
Side ways-Side wise-*a*-Patagilid
Sideral-Sidereal-*a* Nauukol sa bituin.
Sidle-*v*-Kumilos ng patagilid
Seige *n*-Pagkabikob.
Sienna-*n*-Pusali
Sierra-*n*-Pagkasunodsunod ng bundok
Sieve *n*-Agagan, bithay.
Sift-*v*-Bithayin, bumithay, magbithay.
Sigh-*v*-Magbunton hininga, humalinghing, bumunton hininga
Sigh-*n* Bunton hininga, halinghing
Sight-*n* Tingin, tanaw, pagkita.
Sight-*v* Tumingin; tanawin, tumanaw.
Sightless-*a*-Bulag
Sightly-*a* Maliwanag; mabuti sa tingin
Sign-*n*-Tanda
Sign-*v*-Pumirma, pirmahin, Ilagay ng tanda.
Signal-*n*-Tanda, kaway.
Signal-*v*-Tandain, kawayin; kumaway
Signature-*n*-Pirma, kintal
Signet-*n*-Latak
Significance-Significancy-*n*-Kasaysayan.
Significant-*a*-Masasaysay, may kahulugan
Signification-*n*-Kasaysayan, kahulugan.
Signify-*v*-Bigyan kahulugan.
Signor-*n*-Maginoo, señor
Signora *n* Señora. binibini.
Signorita *n*-Señorita, binibining dalaga
Silence-*n* Katahimikan, kawalan ng kibo
Silence-*n*-Huag kumibo, patahimikan.
Silent-*a*-Walang kibo, tahimik, pipe
Silk-*n*-Sutla.
Silken Silky-*a*-Masutla, parang sutla
Silk mercer-*n*-Ang nagtitinda, ng sulat
Silk-worm *n*-Uod na gumagawa ng sutla.

Sill-*n*-Pasamano; soleras

Silliness-*n* Kaululan; kamangmañgan, kawalan nğ tuto

Silly-*a*-Maulol, hunghang, mangmang, walang wasto ó tuto

Silt-*v*-Latak

Silt-*v*-Mapuno nğ latak.

Silver-*n*-Pilak

Silver *a* May halong pilak; yari nang pilak

Silver-*v*-Ilagay nğ pilak.

Silversmith-*n*-Platero

Silvery-*a*-May halong pilak; mapilak

Similar-*a* Kamukha, katulad, kawanki, kaisa, magkaisa, kapantay, magkaparis.

Similarity *n*-Pagkakawanki, pagkakamukha; kaisahan, pagkakaisa pagkakapantay.

Simile Similitude-*n*-Katulad; pagkawanki, pagkakamukha, pagkakapantay, pagkakaparis

Simmer-*v*-Kumulo.

Simoom-Simoon *n*-Bagyo

Simper *v*-Nğumiti.

Simper-*n*-Nğiti.

Simple *a*-Walang halo, malinis, banayad dalisay; muang, unğas.

Simpleness-Simplicity *n* Pag kadalisay; kadalisayan, kabanayaran, pagkamuang; kamangmañgan.

Simplification-*n*-Paglilinanag. kaliwanagan, paglililiwanag

Simplify-*v*-Liwanagan, dalisayin

Simulate-*v*-Huwarin; maghuad.

Simulate-*a*-Naghihibo, hindi totoo, konowari.

Simulation-*n*-Pagkokonowari

Simultaneous *a*-Sabaysabay, sabay, nangyaring sabay

Sin *n* Sala kasalanan

Sin-*v*-Sumala, magkasala; kumulang; sa kautusan.

Since *adv* -Buhat sa, kaya; mula sa

Since-*prep.*-Yamang, magmula sa

Since-*conj* -Yamang.

Sincere *a*-Tapat na loob, dalisay; malinis, ang loob

Sincereness Sincerity-*n*-Katapatan nğ loob.

Sinciput-*n*-Noo, harap nğ ulo

Sine *prep.*-Walang.

Sine cure *n*-Katungkulan na walang maraming gawa.

Sinew-*n*-Litid.

Sinewy-*a*-Malitid.

Sinful *a*-Masama, makasalanan.

Sinless *a*-Walang kasalanan, mabuti, malinis ang loob

Sing *v*-Kumanta, magkanta; mag awit; magdalit; umawit.

Singe-*v*-Salabin; idarang.

Singe *n* Salab, darang

Singer-*n*-Ang kumanta

Single-*a* Nag iisa, bugtong; tañği, bukod, iba

Single-*v*-Ibukod, hiwalay, hiwalayin

Single *n*-Isa

Singular *a*-Walang kahulilip, bugtong; walang katulad, lamang, nakabukod, walang pañğalawa

Singular-*n*-Isa

Singularity-*n*-Pagkakaisa, kaisahan, pag kakatanği

Sinister-*a* Masama, kaliwa, mali.

Sinistrous-*a*-Masama; nakahilig sa kaliwa

Sink-*v* Lumubog, umanod, umunti, bu mawas, ilubog

Sink-*n*-Sangka.

Sinless-*a*-Walang kasalanan.

Sinner-*n*-Ang nagkasala, ang makasalanan

Sinuate-*v*-Pumilipit, humubog.

Sinuous *a*-Mapilipitan, makunat

Sinuosity-*n*-Kabaluktutan; kapilipitan, kunat.

Sip-*v*-Higupin, humigop.

Sip-*n*-Higop,

Sir-*n*-Ginoo.

Sire-*n* Ama; lalaking hayop

Sire-*v*-Mañganak *(nauukol sa hayop)*

Sir name-*n*-Apellido

Sirup *n*-Pulot, katas nğ tubo

Sister *n*-Kapatid na babayi

Sister hood *n*-Kapisanan nğ manğa babayi.

Sister-in-law-*n*-Hipag

Sisterly-*a* Parang kapatid.

Sit-*v*-Umupo

Sitting *n*-Pagupo

Site-*n*-Lugar.

Situate-Situated-*a*-Nakalugar; nakalagay.

Situation-*n*-Lugar, tayo, kalagayan, katungkulan, hanap buhay

Six *a* Anim

Six *n*-Anim

Six fold-*a*-Anim na duble

Six pence-*n*-Sikolo

Sixteen *a* Labing anim

Sixteen-*n*-Labing anim.

Sixtenth *a*-Ikalabing aniin

Sixteenth-*n*-Ang ikalabing anim

Sixth-*a*-Ikaanim.

Sixth *n*-Ang ikaanim

Sixthly-*adv* -Sa ikaanim

Sixtieth *a*-Ikaanim na puo

Sixtieth *n*-Ang ikaanim na puo.

Sixty *a*-Anim na puo,

Sixty-*n*-Anim na puo.

Sizable-*a* Malaki
Size-*n*-Laki,
Size-*v*-Aynsin ayon sa kalakilian.
Sizing-*n*-Pagkit na malabnaw, pan-dikit.
Sizzle-*n*-Sulak
Sizzle-*v*-Mamuslak, sumulak
Skean *n*-Laceta
Skein-*n*-Labay.
Skeleton-*n* Mañga buto ñg tawo
Skeptic-*n*-Ang ayaw maniwala, ang ayaw sumampalataya sa Dios.
Sketch-*n*-Kasaysayan
Sketch *v* Saysayin
Skiff-*n*-Bangkang munti.
Skill-*n*-Dunong, katalasan, kabaitan karunuñgan; tuto, katalinuhan, tarok.
Skilled-Skilful-*a* Sanay; marunong, matalas, matalino
Skillet-*n*-Kawali
Skim-*v*-Salukan, sagapin
Skimmer-*n*-Panagap ñg bula.
Skin-*n* Balat, upak
Skin-*v*-Balatan, upakin
Skin-deep *a* Lalim ñg balat
Skin flint-*n*-Tawong masama, tawong suitik
Skinless-*a* Walang balat
Skinny-*a*-Payat, mabalat
Skip-*n*-Laktaw, lundag, kandirit.
Skip-*v*-Lumaktaw, laktawin, maglundag; kumandirit.
Skipper-*n* Puno sa sasakyan na munti
Skirmish-*v*-Lumaban.
Skirmish-*n*-Laban
Skirt-*n*-Saya.
Skirt-*v*-Pumaligid; paligirin
Skittish-*a* Magulatin, matatakutin.
Skulk-*v*-Matago, magtago, umilag
Skull-*n*-Buñgo, bao ñg ulo.
Sky-*n*-Lañgit.
Sky-blue-*a*-Azul parang lañgit.
Sky-high-*a* Magkasing taas ñg lañgit.
Sky larking-*n*-Pag lulundag, kasayahan
Sky light-*n*-Bintana sa bubuñgan
Sky rocket-*n*-Kuetes
Sky ward *adv* -Sa gawing lañgit
Slab-*n*-Tablang manipis
Slabber-*n* Laway
Slack Slacken-*v*-Lumuag: lumuang
Slack-*a*-Maluag, maluang.
Slack-*v*-Tunawin
Slag-*n*-Dumi.
Slake-*v*-Ilubog sa tubig, mamatay.
Slam-*v*-Itagupak, isara ñg malakas.
Slam *n*-Tagupak, palakpak
Slander-*v* Umupasala; murahin, magalibugha, magwika ñg masama.
Slander-*n*-Pagwiwika ñg masama; ali pusta; upasala, pagmumura, siphayo.

Slanderous-*a*-Maalipusta; maupasala; mapagmura.
Slang-*n*-Salitang bastos.
Slangy-*a*-Bastos ang salita
Slant-*i*-Ihapay, ihilig.
Slant-*n*-Hapay: hilig
Slanting-*a*-Mahapay, nakahilig.
Slap-*v*-Tumampal; tagupakin, sampalin, manampal, sumampal.
Slap *a*-Tapik: sampal; tampal.
Slap-*adv* -Madalingmadali
Slash-*v*-Hiwain, maghiwa, tagain.
Slash-*n*-Hiwa; taga
Slat *n*-Tablang makitid at manipis.
Slate-*n*-Pisara.
Slate-*v*-Isulat sa pisara
Slating-*n*-Tisa
Slattern-*n*-Babaying salaula
Slattern-*a* Salaula
Slatternly *a*-Salaula.
Slaughter-*n* Patayan
Slaughter-*v*-Patayin, pumatay
Slaughter house-*n*-Bahay patayan.
Slave-*n*-Alipin, tahsuyo
Slave *v*-Magtrabajo ñg maluat at masipag na walang bayad
Slave holder-*n*-Ang mayari ñg alipin
Slavery-*n*-Pagkaalipin
Slavish-*a*-Nauukol sa alipin.
Slaw-*n*-Repolhong ensalada
Slay-*v* Patayin- pumatay
Sleave-*n* Sutla
Sleave-*i*-Hiwalayin
Sleazy-*a*-Manipis
Sled-*n*-Careta
Sled-*v* Ilagay sa careta.
Sledge-*n*-Pukpok na malaki, panbuyo
Sleek-*a*-Makinis, makintab, tuso.
Sleep *n*-Tulog
Sleep-*v*-Matulog; tumulog.
Sleeper-*n*-Ang natutulog.
Sleepiness-*n*-Antok.
Sleepless *a*-Walang antok
Sleepy-*a* Nagaantok
Sleet-*n*-Bubog
Sleet-*v*-Umulan ñg bubog
Sleeve-*n* Mangas
Sleeveless *a*-Walang mangas
Sleight-*n*-Daya, karunuñgan, dunong, katalasan.
Slender-*a*-Payat; manipis
Slept *v*. imp & p p -Nakatulog, natulog
Slice-*n*-Hiwa, tigpas, kapiraso, lapang.
Slice-*v* Tigpasin, hiwain, pirasohin, gayatin, lapañgin
Slick-*a*-Makinis, madulas, tuso
Slick *v*-Pakinisin, padulasin
Slick-*n* Pait na malapad
Slide-*v* Dumulas, madapilas, hulagpos

Slide-n-Pagdudulas, pagdadapilas, dapilas, hulagpos
Slight-a-Kaunti.
Slight-n-Kakulañgan; kasalanan, sala
Slight-v Huag kalingayin, huag mahalin, huag tumupad sa katungkulan
Slily-adv -Matuso.
Slim-a-Payat, manipis
Slime-n-Uhog, burak, pusali.
Slimy-a-Mauhog, maburak; mabanlik, malumot
Sling-n-Paghagis.
Sling-v-Ihagis, hagisin.
Slink-v-Tumakas.
Slip v-Dumulas, hilagpos, madapilas
Slip-n Dulas, dapilas, hulagpos
Slipper n-Sinelas
Slippery-a Madulas.
Slip shod-adv -Pagayongayon.
Slip slop-n-Alak na masama
Slit-v-Hiwain; tastasin, sundutin
Slit-n-Hiwa, sundot.
Sliver-n Tinik, patpat
Sliver-v-Matinik.
Slobber-n Laway
Slobber v-Maglaway.
Sloop-of-war n-Sasakyan pandirigma.
Slop-n-Pinaghugasan.
Slop-v-Tumilansik, ibuhos
Slope n-Dahilig sa lupa, gulod.
Slope-v Ipahalang ipahilig.
Sloping-a-Dahilig, dilis, sandig.
Sloppiness-n-Kasalahulaan; putik, kaputikan
Sloppy-a-Salahula, basa, maputik.
Slot-n-Butas.
Sloth n-Katamaran, kakuparan, kapabayaan.
Slothful a-Tamad, pabaya, mahalantutay, mabagal, mapagbalantutay
Slouch-n Tawong pabaya ó salahula
Slouch-v-Mag pabaya, mapag balantutay.
Slough-n-Laog; kasukalan, baburakan
Sloughy-a Maburak.
Sloven-a Pabaya, salahula
Slovenliness-n-Kapabayaan, kabatuganan, karumihan.
Slow a-Dahan, mabagal, tumal, tunga; banayad, batugan, malawag; tanga
Slow-v-Dumahan, bumawas
Slowness-n Katumalan, kabatuganan, kahinayan; kabagalan
Slunge-n-Pusali, banlik burak.
Slue-v-Pihtin; pumilit
Slug-n-Tawong tamad
Slug v-Hampasin, suntukin.
Sluggard-n Tawong tamad.
Sluggish-a-Tamad, pabaya
Sluice-n Sangka; patulnyan ng tubig.
Slumber-v-Matulog.

Slumber-n-Tulog
Slump-v-Tumumal, bumawas.
Slung-v. imp & p p-Hinagis; pinukol, sinabit
Slunk-v imp & p p-Tumakas, natakas
Slur-v Lampastañganin
Slur-n-Tampalasan
Slush-n-Putik na malabnaw
Slut n Babaying salahula, babaying aso
Sly-a-Tuso, matalas; bihasa, ingtalino, saraguete
Slyly-adv -Matuso
Slyness-n-Katusuhan, pagkatuso; katalasan, katalinuhan
Smack-n-Lasa, lasap
Smack-v-Lasahin; lasapin
Small-a-Maliit, munti, kaunti.
Small-n-Kakaunti, kamurahan
Small pox-n-Sakit na bulutong, bulutong
Smart-v-Humapdi
Smart-n-Hapdi
Smart-v-Marunong, matalas, mahapdi, maganda.
Smash-v-Sirain, durugin, ipalagpak
Smash n-Sira, durog, lagpak.
Smatter v Magsalita ng walang kabuluhan.
Smattering-n-Kaunting karunungan.
Smear-v Pahiran; pumahid
Smear-n-Pahid.
Smell-n- Amoy, lansa
Smell-v-Amuyin; umamoy, malansa
Smelling-n-Pagaamoy, amoy
Smelt-v-Tunawin
Smelter n Hurno
Smerk-n-Ngiti
Smerk-v-Ngumiti
Smile-v-Ngumiti.
Smile-n-Ngiti
Smirch-v-Marumhan, dumhan
Smirch-n Dumi, mansa
Smirk-v-Ngumiti
Smirk-n-Ngiti
Smite-v-Hampasin, tumama
Smith-n-Panday
Smithy-n-Pandayan
Smock-n-Camison
Smoke-n-Aso, usok, paghihitit
Smoke-v-Humitit, umaso; mausok.
Smokeless a Walang usok ó aso
Smoke stack n Paasuhan
Smoky-a-Maaso; mausok
Smolder-Smoulder-v-Sumunog na walang ningas
Smooth a-Makinis, yano; mabuli, nakayasyas
Smooth v Pakinisin, kinisin, bulihin, yasyasin, kiskisin, pakintabin.
Smoothness n-Kakintaban, kakinisan
Smote-v. imp -Hinampas; tinamaan

Smother-v-Inisip, uninis •
Smother n Aso, inis.
Smoulder-v Sumunog na walang lingas.
Smudge-n-Siga na walang lingas
Smug-a-Maselang malinis
Smuggle v Dalhin ng palihim.
Smut n-Uling
Smutch n-Mansa dumi
Smutch-v-Mamansa dumumi
Smutty-a-Marumi, mahbog.
Snack n-Parte, bahagi, kapiraso.
Snaffle-n-Bibit
Snag n-Abala, buhol
Snail-n-Susó
Snail paced-a-Marahan na marahan
Snake-n-Ahas; alupong.
Snap-v Bahin, Kagatin ng pabigla, su-
magot ng masaklap.
Snappish a-Mahihg sa parkakagat
Snare-n Bitag, panghuli.
Snare-v-Bitagin, hulihin
Snarl-i-Umangil, dumabog.
Snarl-n-Angil, dabog.
Snatch v-Agawin, umagaw
Snatch n-Pagagaw.
Snath n-Hawakan ng lilik.
Sneak v-Tumakas
Sneak-n-Tawong hamak
Sneaking-a-Hamak; mababa
Sneer-v-Ipahamak; hamakin.
Sneer-n Pagpahamak
Sneeze-n Bahin
Sneeze-i-Magbahin
Snicker v-Tumawa ng palihim
Snicker-n-Tawa na lihim
Sniff v-Amoyin, suminghot
Sniff n-Amoy, singhot
Snigger-v-Tumawa ng palihim
Snigger n-Tawang lihim.
Snip-v-Gupitin, gumupit
Snip-n-Gupit
Snivel-v-Manangis
Snivel-v Nangis; tangis
Sniveler Sniveller n Ang mananangis.
Snob n Tawong hambog
Snobbish-a-Hambog.
Snooze-n Tulog
Snooze-v Matulog
Snore-n-Hilik
Snore-v-Maghilik, humilik
Snort n-Singa na malakas
Snort-v-Suminga ng malakas
Snot-n Uhog
Snout-n-Nguso, ilong
Snout-v-Ngumuso
Snow-n-Bubog, busilak
Snow flake n-Patak ng busilak
Snow storm-n Bagyo ng busilak.
Snow-white-a-Maputi parang busilak
Snowy-a-Mabusilak

Snub v-Paslangin, tampalasananin.
Snub-n-Tampalasan, paslang.
Snuff-n-Tabacong dinikdik.
Snuff v-Suminghot
Snuffle-v-Magsalita ng pahumal.
Snuffle-n Salitang humal.
Snug-a-Mainam, makitid.
Snuggle v-Magsiping, magpugad.
So adv.-Dahil dito, ganiri, ganito; at
ngayon, kasing, naman.
So conj -Kung sakali
Soak-i-Basahin, ibadbad.
Soap-n-Sabon.
Soap-a-Sabunan.
Soap bubble-n-Bula ng sabon.
Soap factory n Gawaan; ng sabon.
Soap maker n-Magsasabon.
Soap suds-n-Pinagsasabunan.
Soapy-a Masabon
Soar-v-Lumipad sa mataas.
Sob-n-Hibik, iyak, tangis
Sob-i-Manangis, tumangis, umiyak, hu-
mibik.
Sober-a Malinaw ang isip, hindi la-
sing
Sober-v-Gumaling sa pagkalasing
Sobriety-n Kasukatan
Sobriquet-n-Bansag
Sociable a-Mahihg sa pakikipagsama,
masaya, malugod
Sociable-n-Piging, diwang
Social-a-Mahilig; sa pakikipagsama-
masaya, marunong; makipagkapua,
tawo.
Society-n-Katipunan, kapisanan, pakiki-
sama.
Sock-n Medias.
Socket-n-Butas.
Sod-n Lupa na may tinubuang damo.
Soda n Soda; limonada.
Sodden a Nakulo, kinulo, mainit.
Sodium-n-Sosa
Safa-n-Hiligan, sandalan
Soforth-n Sa ganito
Soft a Malambot, anayad; buhaghag,
malagkit, malata.
Soften-i-Lumambot, lambutin, buhag
hagin, hagurin, hilutin, humilot; la-
masin, lamugin
Softly-adv -Utayutay, dahandahan, lunas
Softness-n-Kalambutan, kaanayaran ka-
dataan
Soggy-a Basa, buhaghag
Soil-n-Bukid, lupa, dumi; sukal.
Soil-v-Dumhan, dumumi, mansahin.
Soiree-n-Piging sa gabi
Sojourn-n Hinto, hantungan.
Sojourn-v-Humantong.
Sol n-Araw, ginto; sol
Solace-n Kaaliwan, lugod.

41

Solace-v-Aliwin
Solar-a-Nanukol sa araw.
Sold-v. imp & p p Ipinagbili, nagbili
Solder-n Panghinang, tinga
Solder-v-Hinangin, manghinang
Soldier-n-Sundalo, kawal
Soldier-v-Magsundalo.
Soldierly-a-Parang sundalo.
Soldiery n Pagsusundalo.
Sole-n Suelas ñg sapatos.
Sole v Ilagay ñg suelas.
Sole a Bugtong, nagiisa, walang kasama, tañging
Solely adv -Lamang, tañgi
Solemn-a-Pormal, dakila, magalang
Solemnity-n-Kapormalan, kadakilaan, galang
Solemnize-v-Purihin;magdiwang,ganapin.
Solicit v-Humiñgi, mamagitna, manalañgin
Solicitation-n-Daing, hiñgi, panalañgin; pamamagitan
Solicitor n-Ang namamagitan, taga hiñgi ó pamagitan.
Solicitous-a-Maingat; makaliñga, masikap.
Solicitude-n-Iñgat, kaliñga, pagkakaliñga.
Solid-a-Masinsin; matigas, buo at paikpik, tipi, matibay
Solid-n Ano mang bagay na malaman
Solidify-v-Patigasin.
Solidity-n-Kasinsinan; katibayan, tigas, tipi.
Solidly-adv -Matipi
Solidness-n-Kasinsinan, tigas, katigasan, pagkatipi, tipi
Soliloquize-v-Magsalita sa sarili
Soliloquy-n Pagsalita sa sarili.
Solitaire n Soltario
Solitary-a-Nagiisa; bugtong; walang kasama, natatañgi.
Solitude n Pagkaisa, kaisahan, pagkatañgi; katañgihan
Soluble a-Matutunaw, tunawin; madaling saysayin
Solus-a-Nagiisa, bugtong.
Solution n-Kasaysayan; kaliwanagan, pagtatangal.
Solven-v Saysayin, magsaysay; gawin.
Solvency-n Kalagayan makababayad ang utang
Solvent a Makababayad ang utang.
Solvent-n-Ang tawong makabayad ang kaniyang utang
Somber a Mapanglaw, malungkod
Some-a Ilang; mga ilan.
Some body-n-Sinoman.
Some how-adv -Sa anomang paraan.
Some one-n Sinoman,alinmang balang na.

Some thing-n-Anoman, anomang bagay
Some thing-adv -Kaunti'
Some time-n-Sa ilang panahon
Some time-adv -Noong panahon.
Some times adv -Maminsanminsan, manakanaka
Some what-adv -Mahigit kumulang
Some where-a Saan man
Somnambulism-n-Pag lalakad kung matulog.
Somnambulist n-Ang lumalakad ñg matulog.
Somnolence-Somnolency-n-Antok.
Somnolent-a-Nag aantok.
Son n-Anak na lalaki.
Sonant-a-Nauukol sa tunog, matunog.-
Sonant-n Voces, tunog
Sonata-n-Sonata
Song n Kanta, awit, dalit
Songster-n Ang lalaking marunong kumanta
Songstress n-Babaying palaging kumakanta.
Son in-law n-Manugang na lalaki
Sonnent n-Awit, dalit.
Sonorous-a-Mataginting, matunog
Son ship n-Kalagayang anak
Soon-adv.-Agad, agad agad, dagli, pagdaka, sa isang dali.
Soot-n-Uling, agiw
Soot-v Umagiw.
Sooth-n Katotohanan
Soothe-v-Tumahimik, sowayin
Sooth say-v-Maghula, hulaan, ihula.
Sooth sayer n-Manghuhula.
Sooth saying-n Paghuhula
Sooty a Maagiw, mauling
Sop-n Sawsaw.
Sop-v-Isawsaw,
Sophism n-Kamalian.
Sorcerer n Mankukulam.
Sorceress-n-Babaying mangkukulam
Soncery n-Pagkulam
Sordid a Mahalay; marumi; maramot
Sordidness n-Kahalayan, karumihan, kasalaulaan, kasukalan
Sore a Mahapdi, masakit.
Sore-n-Sugat
Sorghuin-n Pulot.
Sororicide n-Ang natay sa kapatid na babayi
Sorrel-n Castaño
Sorrow-n-Kalungkutan, lungkot, hapis; kahapisan; pighati
Sorrow v-Maglungkot, magdalamhati; humapis.
Sorrowful a-Malungkot, mapanglaw.
Sorry-a Malungkot, nagiisisi
Sort-n-Clase; lagay, grado.
Sort-v-Hiwalayin, ibukod, magbukot.

Sortie-*n*-Pag labas nğ hukbo
Soso *adv* -Katatagan
Sot-*n*-Tawong palaging lasing, lasengo.
Sottish-*a* Nauukol sa kalasingan
Souchong *n*-Cha na maitim
Sough-*n*-Haging, hagimit
Sough *v*-Humaging, humaginit
Sought *v* *imp* & *p* *p*-Hinanap
Soul *n* Kalulua.
Soulless *a* Walang kalulua
Sound-*n*-Tunog, tinig
Sound *v*-Tumunog, tuminig; tarukin; tumarok, kumalog, kumalasing, sukatin ang lalim nğ tubig, salatin.
Sound *a*-Tapat, matibay mahusay; walang pintas.
Soundings-*n*-Pagtatarok
Soup-*n*-Sopas, sabaw.
Sour *a*-Maasim.
Sour-*n*-Kaasiman
Sour-*v*-Umasim.
Source *n*-Pamulaan, pinagbuhatan, pinangalingan, pinagmulaan, ugat; binubukalan, bukal
Souse *n*-Tinunmes.
Souse-*i* Isawsaw
South-*n* Timog, timugan
South-*a*-Timugan,
South-*adv* -Sa gawing timog
South-*v* Ihko sa gawing timog.
Souther-*n* Bagvo nangaling sa timog
Southerner-*n* Taga timugan
Southing-*n* Kahiligan sa pagpunta sa timugan
Southion-*n* Taga timugan
South ward-Southward-*adv* -Sa gawing timugan.
Souvenir-*n*-Alaala, recuerdo
Sovergn-*n*-Hari, pirasong ginto na may halagang pfs 4 86
Sovergnity-*n*-Kaharian.
Sow-*n* Inahing baboy.
Sow *v* Budburin, magtanim, tamnan, hasikan, maghasik, isabog
Spa-*n*-Cebul, bukalan nğ tubig na may halong metal.
Space-*n*-Lugar, kalaparan; gitna; puang.
Space-*v* Lagyan nğ puang.
Spade *n* Pangsurong, pala.
Spade-*i*-Isurong.
Span-*n*-Dangkal
Span *v*-Dangkalin.
Spangle-*n* Sangkap.
Spaniard-*n* Kastila.
Spanish *a*-Nauukol sa kastila.
Spanish *n*-Kastila
Spanish *n*-Wikang kastila
Spank-*v*-Sampalin sa puit.
Spanker-*n*-Mananampal.
Span worm-*n*-Uod.

Spare-*v*-Patawarin
Spare *a*-Madalang; labis; bihira
Sparing *a*-Maimot.
Spark-*n*-Liab, lingas.
Spark *v*-Mag lingas.
Sparkle *n*-Inig, ningning; kintab.
Sparkle-*v* Kumintab, magningning
Sparkling-*a*-Maningning.
Sparrow-*n*-Maya
Sparse *a*-Madalang.
Spasm-*n*-Pasina, manliso, pulikat.
Spasmodic-Spasmodical-*a*-Di panay.
Spat-*v*-Nag lura, nag laway; niluran
Spatter-*v*-Tumilansik, tilansikan.
Spattering *n*-Pagpulandit, tilansik.
Spawn *i*-Mangitlog ang isda.
Spawn *n*-Pangingitlog nğ isda
Speak *v* Sabihin, magsabi, mag wika; wikain, magsalita.
Speaker-*n*-Ang mananalita.
Speaking *n*-Pagsasalita, pag wiwika.
Spear-*n*-Sibat, tulag, salapang.
Spear-*v*-Sibatin, itulag, salapangin.
Special *a*-Bukod, tangi.
Speciality-*n*-Bagay na nakabukod.
Specie-*n*-Salapi.
Species-*n*-Manğa classe
Specific *a* Tunay
Specific *n*-Gamot na panlanban sa sakit.
Specification-*n* Kasalitaan, salitaan trato.
Specify-*v* Sabihin nğ maliwanag
Specimen-*n*-Halimbawa
Specious-*a*-Maliwanag, masangkap.
Speck-*n*-Mansa
Speckle-*i*-Mansahin
Spectator-*n*-Nanunuod.
Specter-*n* Nuno
Spectral *a*-Nauukol sa nuno
Spectrum *n*-Sinag nğ araw.
Specular-*a*-Parang salamin
Speculate *v* Magwariwari, magbulaybulayin, magnegocio
Speculation-*n*-Pagnenegocio.
Speculative-Speculatory *a*-Nauukol sa negocio.
Sped *v* *imp* & *p* *p* -Tumulin, tumakbo; nakatakbo
Speech *n*-Salita, pamamalita, panğaral.
Speechless *a*-Walang kibo, pipe
Speed-*n*-Tulin, kabiglaan, kadalian.
Speed-*v*-Tumulin, magmadali.
Speedy-*a*-Matulin, madali; mabilis.
Spell *v*-Titikan
Spell-*n*-Panahon
Spell bound-*a* Namamangha.
Speller-*n*-Ang nag leletra
Spelling-*n*-Pagtititik.
Spelt-*v*. *imp*. & *p*. *p*.-Tinitik, niletra.
Spend-*v* Gumasta; gastahin.

Spend thrift n-Mananabog ñg pag aari, tawong,gastador, tawong burara
Spent-v imp. & p.p.-Ginasta.
Spermary-n-Itlog
Sphere n-Bilog
Spheric-Spherical-a-Mabilog.
Spherule-n-Munting bilog
Spice-n-Labul.
Spice-v-Labulin
Spicy-a-Maanghang, malasa.
Spicular-a-Parang palaso
Spiculate-v-Tulisan
Spider-n-Gagamba
Spider web-n-Bahay gagamba.
Spike-n-Pakong malaki
Spike v-Pumako, pakuin.
Spiked-a-Nakapako
Spikelet-n Pako
Spiky-a-Parang pako, mapako.
Spile-n-Haligi
Spill-v Lumiguak, maliguak.
Spill-n-Liguak
Spin i-Painugin, humabi.
Spinach-n-Gulay.
Spinal-a-Nauukol sa gulugod.
Spindle-n-Ulak, suliran
Spindle-v-Sumupling.
Spindle-legged-Spindle shanked-a-Mahaba ang binti at hita
Spine-n-Gulugod
Spinner n Manghahabi
Spinous a-Madawag; matinik.
Spinster-n-Dalagang matanda.
Spiny a-Matinik, madawag
Spiracle n Butas ñg ilong.
Spiral a Nauukol sa tore.
Spire n-Tore
Spirit-n-Kaluluwa, tianak, diwi
Spirit-v-Buhayin, sulsulan, bihagin
Spirited-a Mabuhay, buhay; matapang.
Spiritless-a-Mawalan ñg diwi, mabagal, batugan; malungkot.
Spiritous-a-Nauukol sa kaluluwa
Spiritual-a-Nauukol sa kaluluwa.
Spiritualize-v-Purihin.
Spirituelle-a-Parang kaluluwa, malinis; mapuri
Spirituous a-Parang kaluluwa; mapuri; malinis; maningas.
Spirit-v-Tumilansik, bumukal.
Spiry-a-Nauukol sa tore, mataas.
Spit-n Buga, lura, laway.
Spit-v-Bumuga,maglaway,lurain,maglura
Spite-n-Galit, tanim ñg loob.
Spite-v-Pagalitin
Spiteful-a Mapagtanim sa loob.
Spitfire n-Tawong mainit ang ulo.
Spittle n-Laway.
Spittoon-n-Luraan.
Splash-v-Tumilansik.

Splash-n-Tilansik
Splashy-a Matitilansikan
Splendid-a Makinis, mainam, dakila, maganda, marilag
Splendor-n-Kainaman, kadakilaan, karilagan kinang, liwanag, gayak, kamahalan
Splice v-Idugtong, magdugtong.
Splice-n Dugtong
Splint-n Bangkat.
Splint-v Bangkatin; ibangkat.
Splinter-n Tatal, patpat.
Splinter v-Lumahang, lumitak.
Split-v-Biakin, bumiak, litakin, sipakin
Split-n-Biak, sipak, litak.
Splurge n-Kahambugan
Splurge-v-Maghambog
Spoil-v-Sirain, mabulok, bumulok
Spoil-n-Ang mga bagay na sinamsam
Spoke-i imp-Nagsalita, sinabi, winika, nagwika
Spoke-n Rayos ó tukod, ñg gulong
Spoke v-Lagayin ñg rayos.
Spoken-v p p-Sinabi na,
Spoken-v p p.-Sinabi na; winika na; nagsalita na.
Spokes man n-Ang nagsasalita
Spoliate-v Nakawin, manduit
Spoliation-n Pagnanakaw; panduduit
Spoliator-n Magnanakaw, manduduit
Sponge-n Espongha
Sponge-v-Pahiran ó magpunas ñg espongha
Sgongy a Buhaghag, malambot
Sponsor-n Katibayan, kasiguruhan.
Spontaneous-a-Bukal sa loob
Spool-n-Ikiran
Spool v-Ilagay sa ikiran, ikirin
Spoon-n-Cuchara.
Spoonful-n-Laman ñg isang cuchara.
Spoor n Landas ñg hayop sa damo.
Sport n Kasayahan; kaluguran, aliw; kaaliwan, saya.
Sport-v Sumaya; maglibang, mag-aliw
Sportive-Sportful a-Masaya, malugod, maaliw
Sports man-n-Mangangaso.
Spot-n-Batik, daan, mansa
Spot-v-Hanapin, mansahin; batikin bumatik
Spotless-a-May puri, walang bahid dumi, malinis,
Spotty-a-May mansa
Spousal-n Kasal, pagkakasal
Spouse-n-Asawa
Spout-n-Alulod
Sprain-r-Pumilay
Sprain n-Pilay, kapilayan.
Sprawl-v-Umunat, dumapa,
Spray-n-Sañgang munti.

Spray-v-Diligin, magdilig.
Spread-t-Ilatag, idatay, iunat, kalupkupan
Spread-n-Datay, kumot, latag.
Sprig-n-Sañgang munti
Spright-n-Kaluluwa, nuno.
Sprightless a Mapurol, mabagal, tamad.
Sprightliness n-Kaliksihan, kasipagan
Sprightly-a-Maliksi, matulin, mayabong.
Spring-v-Lumundag, lumukso, bumukal
Spring-n-Bukalan; bukal, lundag, lukso.
Springe-n-Bitag
Springy-a Parang goma.
Sprinkle-t-Wiligin, diligin, wisikan, magdilig, magwisik, magwilig
Sprinkle-n-Wisik, dilig
Sprinkler-n-Pandilig, pangwisik.
Sprinkling-n-Pagdidilig, pagwiwisik.
Sprint-t-Tumakbo
Sprint-n-Takbo.
Sprite n-Tianak, duende
Sprout-n-Usbong; supling, sulol; punla
Sprout v-Magusbong, sumudling
Spruce-a-Mabuti, makinis, ayos, mahusay; malinis; mapagmarikit
Spruceness-n-Kalinisan, ayos
Sprung-v p p-Nakalundag; bumukal na
Spry-a-Maliksi, matulin, magaan, maagap.
Spue-v-Sumuka, magsuka
Spume-n-Bula subo
Spume t-Bumula.
Spumous-Spumy-a-Mabula, Nanukol sa bula
Spun-v imp & p p-Ipinainog, hinabi.
Spunk-n-Tapang, pangabas.
Spunky-a-Matapang: mangahas
Spur-n Babala, pabuyo.
Spur-t-Bumula, ipabuyo
Spurge-n-Gulay na may katas na maputi.
Spurious-a-Hindi totoo, falso
Spurn-t-Manikad, sicaran.
Spurt-n-Bumukal, tumilansik
Sputter-t-Pisik, pagpisik,
Sputter-t-Pumisik, magpisik.
Spy-n-Tiktik manunubok
Spy-v-Tiktikan, manubok, subukan, magmasiran, siyasatin.
Spy glass-n-Larga vista.
Squab-a-Mataba, makapal. pandak
Squabble-t-Magtalo, makipagtalo
Squabble n-Basagulo; pagtatalo; talo
Squadron-n-Escuadra.
Squalid-a Salahula, marumi.
Squalidness n-Kasalahulahan.
Squall-n-Bagyo sa dagat
Squally-a-Mabagyo
Squallor-n-Kasalahulahan, dumi, kasukalan, karumihan

Squander-v-Gumasta; gastahin; isabog; isambulat, sayañgin.
Square-n-Parisukat
Square-v-Parisukatin.
Squash n-Kalabasa, upo; tibyaya
Squash-v-Idiin; inisin.
Squashy-a-Malambot
Squat-t Tumingkayad, yumuko
Squat-a-Nakatingkayad, nakayuko.
Squat-n-Tingkayad; yuko.
Squawk-v Umiyak.
Squawk-n-Iyak
Squeak-v-Lumañgitñgit, umalititit,
Squeak n-Alitit, langitñgit.
Squeal-v-Umiyak, sumigaw.
Squeal-n Iyak; sigaw.
Squeamish-a Makayayamot
Squeeze-t-Higpitin, pigain; pindutin; pitisin; idiin.
Squib-n-Kuetes na munti.
Squint-a-Sulipat.
Squint-v-Magduling.
Squinteyed-a-Hiwas ang mata
Squirm-t-Kumilos.
Squirt-v-Papulanditin.
Squirt-n-Pulandit.
Stab-n-Saksak
Stab-v-Saksakin, sumaksak.
Stability-n-Katibayan, tibay; laon; luat.
Stable-n-Caballerisa
Stable-v-Ilagay sa caballerisa.
Stable-a-Matibay, maluat, matatagal.
Stack-n-Mandala
Stack-v-Magmandala.
Staff-n-Tungkod.
Stag-n-Usang lalaki.
Stag beetle-n Oyang
Stage-n-Entablado.
Stagger-v-Gumiraygiray, pumawidpawid, magulat, gitlahin.
Stagger-n-Giray.
Stagnancy-n-Lansa.
Stagnant-a Malansa; hindi malinis.
Stagnate-t-Malansa, lumansa.
Staid-v & p. p.-Naghinto, nakahinto.
Stain v-Tigmakin, tinain, dumhan mansahin.
Stain-n-Mansa, tigmak, tina, dumi
Stainless-v-Walang bahid dumi; malinis, maselang
Stair-n Hagdan, hagdanan.
Siair way-Stair case-n-Hagdanan.
Stake n-Uriang; tulos
Stake-v-Tulusin
Stale a-Maanta, malansa, lipas.
Stalk-n-Puno.
Stalk-t-Lumapit ñg palihim
Spall-n Hadlang
Stall-t-Ilagay sa hadlang
Stalliont-n Kabayong bulugan.

Stalwar Stalworth-a-Matapang,mangahas.

Stammer-x-Umutal.

Stammering-n-Kautalan, paguutal

Stamp-v Itatak, tumuntong; yurakin; yumurak, limbagin, imarka.

Stamp n Sello, yurak, tatak, yasak

Stampede-n-Takot ng maraming hayop.

Stampede-v-Tumakbo ang manada nang hayop

Stanch-a Matibay tapat ang loob

Stanch-i-Pigilin, pumigil

Stand-i Tumayo, tumindig.

Stand-n-Tindig, tayo, lagay.

Standard-n-Bandera Bandilla, bait

Standing-a-Patindig, ·nakatindig, nakatayo

Standing-n-Tayo, tindig, lagay,

Stanza-n Pangkat

Staple a-Matibay, matatagal, maglnat.

Star-n-Bituin

Star-v-Kumintab, maningning.

Starch-n-Almirol

Starch-v-Almirolan, mag almirol.

Stare-v-Tuminğin ng maluat

Stare-n-Tingin.

Stark-a-Matigas, malakas, makapangyayari, may kapangyarihan

Start-v-Ipagmulaan, umalis

Start n-Pamula, pag alis.

Startle v Gulatin.

Starvation-n-Kagutuman.

Starve-v-Magutom, masalat

State-n-Asal, lagay, kalagayan.

State a-Nauukol sa gobierno

State-v-Sabihin, magsabi.

Stated-a-Nasabing

Statement-n-Kasaysayan, pagsasabi

State house-n-Bahay ng gobierno

Stately-a-Dakila, marangal

Station-n-Estacion, lugar, kalagayan, lugar.

Station v-Idistino, ilagay sa lugar

Stationary-a Firme, matibay, hindi magagalaw

Stationer n-Taga tinda, ng· manga pepel

Stationery-n-Manga papel, tinta, at pluma.

Statuary-n-Mangagawa ng manga larawan; karunungan sa paggagawa ng manga larawan

Statue-n-Larawan, poon-

Statuette-n Munting larawan

Stature n-Bikas, tayo; taas ng katawan.

Status-n-Lagay.

Statute n-Utos

Statulory-a Ayon sa utos

Staunch a Matibay, tapat

Stave-v-Sirain, pumutok; ilayo

Stave off-v-Ilagin.

Stay-v-Humantong, magluat, huminto, pigilin

Stay-n-Tigil, hinto, hantong.

Stead-n-Lugar

Stead fast-a-Matibay ang loob, tapat ang loob

Steady-a-Panay, patag

Steady-v-Panayin, pigilin

Steady-n-Hiwa ng carne

Steal-v-Mangunğumit, magnakaw; nakawin, umitin.

Stealer-n-Mangunğumit, magnanakaw

Stealth-n-Pagnakaw, pangunğunmit; lihim

Stealthy-a-Dahandahan, palihim

Steam-n-Usok

Steam-v-Umusok

Steam boat-n-Sasakyan de vapor

Steam boiler-n-Caldera

Steam engine-n Makina de vapor.

Steamer-n-Vapor

Steam ship n-Vapor.

Steamy a-Mausok

Sted-n Lugal

Sted fast-a-Tapat ang loob; matibay

Steed-n-Kabayo

Steel n-Patalim.

Steel-v-Ipatalim, patalimin

Steely-a-Matalim

Steel yard-n-Panimbang.

Steep-a-Matarik

Steep-n-Lugar na matarik

Steep-v-Basahin, ibadbad

Steeple-n-Tore

Steer-v-Umugit sa sasakyan

Steer-n-Bakang lalaki na kinapon.

Steerage-n-Pag uugit sa sasakyan

Steers man-n-Ang umugit sa sasakyan.

Stellar Stellary-a-Naukol sa bituin.

Stellate-Stellated-a-Parang bituin

Stelliferous-a-Mabituin

Stelliform-a-Hitsurang bituin

Stellular-a-Parang bituin

Stem n Tangkay puno

Stem-v-Lumaban, pigilin; pumigil.

Stench n-Amoy lansa.

Stencil n Pananda

Stencil-v-Isulat, itanda

Step v-Humakbang

Step n-Hakbang, bayitang; baitang

Step brother n-Anak na lalaki ng amain ó ale sa pakinabang

Step daughter-n-Pamangkin sa pakina bang

Step father n Amain sa pakinabang

Step mother-n-Ale sa pakinabang.

Step sister-n-Anak na babayi ng amain o ale sa pakinabang

Step son n-Pamankin sa pakinabang

Sterile a-Karat

Sterility-*n*-Kakaratan.
Sterling-*v*-Totoo; tunay; malinis.
Stern-*a* Masungit; mahigpit.
Stern-*n*-Hulihang sasakyan.
Sternal-*a*-Nauukol sa buto ng dibdib.
Sternness-*n*-Kasungitan; kahigpitan.
Steve-*v*-Ilulan.
Stew-*n*-Gisa; laoya.
Stew-*v*-Gisain; igisa.
Steward-*n*-Ang puno ng mga alila
Stich-*n*-Taludtod; hilera
Stick-*n*-Patpat; palo; tungkod.
Stick-*v*-Dumikit; ikapit; idikit.
Sticky-*a*-Malagkit.
Stiff-*a*-Banat; matigas.
Stiffen-*v* Tumigas; manigas.
Stiffness-*n*-Katigasan; tigas.
Stifle-*n*-Siko.
Stifle-*v*-Inisin; umunis;patayin;pumatay; lipulin.
Stile-*n*-Hagdanan.
Stiletto-*n*-Panaksak.
Stiletto-*v* Saksakin.
Still-*a*-Tahimik; walang gulo.
Still-*v*-Patahimikin; tumahimik.
Still-*n* Gawaan ng alak.
Still-*adv*.-Bagaman; pa.
Stilly-*a*-Tahimik.
Stilt-*n*-Tiakiad
Stilt-*v*-Magtiakad.
Stimulant-*n*-Pangpalakas; pang udyok.
Stimulate-*v*-Udiokan; umudyod.
Stimulus-*n*-Pang udyok; panudlok.
Sting-*n*-Tinik; kagat nang bubuyog ó kamumo.
Sting-*v*-Kagatin; humapdi.
Stingy-*a*-Maramot; kuripot; masakim.
Stink-*v*-Umilingasaw; bumaho; umangis; bumantot.
Stink-*n*-Baho; alingasaw; amoy na malansa.
Stint-*v*-Pigilin; pumigil.
Stint-*n*-Hanga.
Stipend-*n*-Upa; ganti; bayad; sahod.
Stipulate-*v*-Sabihin; gumawa ng salitaan.
Stipulation-*n*-Salitaan.
Stipulator-*n*-Ang gumawa ng salitaan.
Stir-*v*-Gawgawin; guluhin; haluin; kalapsawin; kamiyawin.
Stir-*n*-Halo; gulo.
Stirrup-*n*-Estribo.
Stitch-*v*-Tusukin; tumusok; duruin.
Stitch-*n*-Tusok; tutos; duro ng karayom.
Stitchy-*a*-Matusok; matutos.
Stock-*n*-Puno; manga hayop.
Stock-*v*-Itago; iponin.
Stockade-*n*-Bakod nang manga tulos na malaki.
Stock company-*n*-Kapisanan ng mga mangangalakal.

Stock holder-*n*-Kabilang ng kapisanan.
Stock man-*n*-Magpapastol; mayari ng manga hayop.
Stock-still-*a*-Tahimik; firme.
Stocky-*a*-Pandak.
Stoke-*v*-Igatong.
Stoker-*n* Fogonero.
Stole-*v. imp.*-Ninakaw; inumit.
Stolen-*v. p. p.*-Ninakaw; inumit.
Stolid *a*-Mapurol ang isip.
Stolidity-Stolidness-*n*-Kapurulan ng isip.
Stomach-*n*-Sikmura; tokong.
Stomach-*v*-Ilagay sa sikmura.
Stomachic-*c*-Nauukol sa sikmura.
Stone-*n*-Bato.
Stone-*v* Batohin; puklin.
Stone-blind *a*-Bulag.
Stone coal-*n*-Uling na matigas.
Stone's cast-*n*-Pukol ng bato.
Stone's throw-*n*-Pukol ng bato.
Stone ware-*n*-Kasangkapang bato.
Stone work-*n*-Gawa sa bato.
Stony-*a*-Mabato; batobatohin.
Stood-*v. imp. & p. p.*-Tumindig; nakatindig.
Stook-*n*-Bunton ng mga haya.
Stool-*n*-Upuan na walang sandalan.
Stoop-*v*-Yumuko; tumingkayad.
Stoop-*n* Yuko; tingkayad.
Stop-*v* Pigilin; huminto; tumigil; humantong; magpahinga; pasakin.
Stop-*n*-Hinto; tigil; hantong.
Stop cock-*n*-Grifo.
Stoppage-*n*-Pagpigil.
Stopper-*n*-Tasok; pasak; tapon.
Stopper-*v*-Tasakin; ilagay ng tapon.
Stopple-*n*-Tasak; pasak.
Storage-*n*-Pag ipon.
Store-*v*-Itago; ipunin.
Store-*n*-Tindahan.
Store house-*n*-Kamalig; taguan.
Store rom-*n*-Taguan; bangan.
Storm-*n*-Unos; bagyo; sigwa.
Storm-*v*-Uumunos; bumagyo.
Stormy-*a*-Maunos; magulo; mabagyo; masigwa.
Story-*n*-Kuento.
Story-*v*-Magkuento; magsinuugaling.
Stoup-*n*-Panakal ó lalagyan ng tubig; benditahan.
Stout-*a*-Malakas; batibot; malaki; pisígan; magandang tikas.
Stout-*n*-Cervesang matapang.
Stove-*n*-Apuyan kalan.
Stow-*v*-Ibunton; itago.
Strabismus-*n*-Pagkaduling.
Straddle-*r*-Sakyan; sumakay.
Straggle-*v*-Lumakad nang pagayongayon.
Straight-*a*-Tapat; matowid; walang liko.
Straighten-*v*-Towirin; unatin..

Straight forward-a Mahwanag, matowid
Straightly-adv -Matowid, tapat.
Straightness n Katowiran, higpit; kata-
patan
Straight-out-a Mahwanag, tapat ang
loob
Straight way adv -Ñgayondin
Strain-v-Tumalas; salain, agagin
Strainer-n-Talaan, agagan l
Strait a-Makitid, mahigpit, mahirap,
masuñgit.
Strait-n-Kahirapan, kahigpitan
Straiten-v-Higpitin, pigilin, gipitin.
Strand-n-Baybay
Strand-v Sumadsad; sumayad.
Strange-a Katakataka, iba, buhat, sa
ibang lupa.
Stranger-n-Taga ibang lupa
Strangle-v-Uminis, inisin.
Strangulation-n-Paguinis
Strap n-Sinta, pamigkis, panali ñg ba-
lat; sinturon.
Strap-v-Hampasin ñg sinturon.
Strapping-a-Malakas.
Stratagem-n-Hibo,daya,paraan;balatkayo
Strategy-n-Paraan; daya, balatkayo
Straw-n-Dayami, ginikan, kugon.
Stray-v-Mahgaw, lumihis
Stray-a Gansal, nakahgaw.
Stray-n Hayop na nakawala.
Streak-n-Guhit
Streak-v-Guhitin, gumuhit.
Stream-n-Ilog
Stream-n-Ibuhos.
Streamer n-Tanda, bandera
Streamlet-n-Munting ilog, sapa.
Street-n Lansañgan, carsada.
Strength-n-Lakas; tibay; tigas, kalaka-
san, katibayan
Strengthen-v-Tumibay; tibayin, lumakas,
itambal; kapalin, palakasin.
Strenuous a-Masipag, maniñgas, mata-
pang
Stress n Lakas.
Stretch-v-Banatin, unatin; batakin, hu-
maba, humigit, umabot; idalay,
Stretch n-Tindi
Stretcher-n Tindihan
Strew-v imp -Kinalat; winisik.
Stricken i p. p-Tinaman
Strict-a Mahigpit, masungit; mabagsik
Strictness-n-Kahigpitan; kabagsikan, ka-
suñgitan.
Stricture-n-Pintas, kapintasan.
Stride-n Hakbang.
Stride-v-Humakbang, lumakad
Strife-n-Babag, laban, away; talo, pag-
papamook
Strike n-Tumuktok, dagukan; hampasin;
humampas, tumama, mamalo

Strike-n-Dagok, tuktok, hampas.
String-n-Sinulid, pisi, kuerdas
String-n-Tuhugin, kuerdasin
Stringed-a-May pisi
Stringer-n-Tuhog
Stringency-n-Kabagsikan, kasuñgitan.
Stringent-n-Mabagsik, masuñgit.
String halt-n-Hingkod
Strip-v-Alisin, ang takip, talupan, mag-
balat
Strip-n-Pirasong tabla na makitid, ta-
bla ñg lupa.
Stripe-n-Guhit
Stripe-v-Guhitin
Striping-n-Batang lalaki
Strive-v-Awayin, matikman, subukin,
lumaban, pumilit. pilitin
Stroke-n-Hampas, dagok, suntok
Stroke v-Hilutin, hilurin.
Stroll n Pasial, gala
Stroll-v-Gumala, magpasial.
Strong a-Malakas, tapat, balisaksakin;
batibot, mahtid, matibay, bayani, buo
Strong hold-n-Kuta
Strop n-Pirasong katad.
Strop-t-Ihasa sa katad
Strove v imp -Natikman, sinubok, pini
lit
Strow-v-Isabog, ikalat, kalatin
Struck-v imp & p p.-Hinampas, sinun-
tok; dinagok, tinamaan
Structure-n-Pagpatayo, pagpapagawa,
bahay.
Struggle v Bumabag, lumaban, umaway,
bumuno, pumipit, humamon, hamu-
nin
Struggle-n Talo, away, babag, laban,
buno, pagpapamook.
Stung-i imp & p p -Tinuhog
Strut-v-Lumakad nang pahambog, hu-
mambok.
Stub-n-Puno; tisod, upos, beha.
Stub-v-Matisod, bunutin, labnutin
Stubbed-a-Pandak, mapurol, mapupod.
Stubble-n-Pasiok
Stubborn-a-Matigas ang ulo, sowail
Stubbornness n-Katigasan ñg ulo, kaso-
wayan.
Stucco-v-Pahiran ñg apog
Stuck-v imp. & p p -Dinikit.
Stud n-Kilo
Student n-Ang nagaaral, estudiante.
Studied a Marunong.
Studio-n Estudio.
Studious-a-Masipag magaral.
Study-n Aral.
Study-v Magaral
Stuff n-Mañga bagay.
Stuff-n-Mamnalan, siksikan, isiksik, bu-
musog.

Stuffing-n-Ang laman.

Stumble-v-Matigod; tumipiaw; madapa.

Stumble-n-Tisod; tipiaw; dapa.

Stumbling-a-Tisurin;

Stump-n-Puno ñg kahoy; upos; beha.

Stump-a-Mataba; pandak.

Stun-v-Matulig; tuligin.

Stung-v. imp. & p. p.-Kinagat.

Stunk-v. p. p.-Bumaho.

Stunt-v-Pigilin ang pagpalaki.

Stupefaction-n-Pagkatulig; kaululan kahañgalan.

Stupefy-v-Tuligin; tulain; hañgalin; magpatulala.

Stupendous-a-Malaki ñg totoo; kamanghamangha.

Stupid-a-Tulig; ulol; mangmang; uñgas; hañgal; mapurol ang isip.

Stupidity-Stupidness-n-Kapurulan nang isip; kaunuran; kagaspañgan.

Stupor-n-Tulig; pagkatulig.

Sturdy-a-Malakas; matigas; matibay.

Stutter-v-Umutal; umuriturit; umunununo.

Stutter-n-Kautalan; pagkautal.

Stuttering-n-Paguutal; kautalan; amit; amil.

Sty-n-Guliti.

Style-n-Asal; uso; modo; gawi; kaugalian; ugali; yari.

Stylish-a-Marikit; mainam; mauso.

Suave-a-Suave; malambot.

Suavity-n-Kalambutan; giliw; kadataan; mahabag;

Subacid-a-Maasim ñg kaunti.

Subaltern-a-Mababa pa; kulang.

Subalternate a-Sunodsunod; mababa pa.

Subaqueous-a-Sa ilalim ñg tubig.

Subcutaneous-a-Sa ilalim ñg balat.

Subdivide-v-Hatiin at muli hatiin; ha tiin ang ipinagkahati na.

Subdue-v-Supilin; pasukin; sakupin.

Subject-n-Pinagusapan; pinagmulaan; ang nasa kapangyarihan ñg iba.

Subject a-Mahilig; may tali.

Subject-v-Supilin; pasukin; alipnin; sakupin.

Subjection-n-Paginis; pagkasupil; supil; pagsakop.

Subjective-a-Masupil.

Subjoin-v-Idugtong.

Subjugate-v-Supilin.

Subjugation-n-Pagpasupil.

Subjunction-n-Dugtong.

Sublimate-v-Tumaas ang kalagayan.

Sublime-a-Dakila: marañgal; bunyi.

Sublime-n-Kadakilaan; karañgalan; dañgal.

Sublime-v-Dakilain; parañgalin.

Sublimity-n-Karañgalan.

Sublinguar-a-Sa ilalim ñg dila.

Sublunar-Sublunary-a-Nasa ilalim ñg buan.

Submarine-a-Nasa ilalim ñg dagat.

Submerge-v-Ilubog; lumubog; ilunod; umanod; apawin.

Submergence-n-Paglubog; anod.

Submerse-Submersed-a-Nasa ilalim ñg tubig.

Submersion-n-Paglubog; anod.

Submission-n-Kapakumbabaan; pagsunod; pagsuko; pagkaayon; kalambutan ñg loob.

Submissive-a-Masusunurin; mababang loob; malambot ang ugali.

Submit-v-Sumuko; ipahintulot; pumayag; magbigay loob; sumunod; umayon.

Subordinate-a-Mababa pa.

Subordinate-n-Kababaan.

Subordinate-v-Ibaba; pahamakin.

Subordination-n-Pagsupil; pagsakop.

Suborn-v-Sumuhol; suhulan.

Subornation-n-Pagpasuhol; suhol.

Subscribe-v-Pumirma; pirmahin.

Subscription-n-Ambag; pagpirma;*

Subsequence-n-Pagkasuuod.

Subsequent-n-Sumusunod.

Subserve-v-Ipasulung; sulungin.

Subsidiary-a-Nauukol sa abuloy.

Subsidiary-n-Auxillar; katulong.

Subsidize-v-Abuluyan; magbayad nang buis.

Subsidy-n-Abuloy; katulong; pahintulot ñg gobierno.

Subsist-v-Mamalagi; tumagal; manatili.

Subsistence-n-Ikabubuhay; pagkabuhay;

Subsoil-n-Lupa na sa ilalim.

Substance-n-Sustancia laman.

Substantial-a-Matibay; di masisira.

Substantiality-n-Tibay; tagal; luat.

Substantiate-v-Totohanin; sumaksi.

Substantive-a-Malayo; matagal; matibay.

Substantive-n-Sustantivo.

Substitute-n-Kahalili; kapalit.

Substitute-v-Halinhan humalili; palitan; ipalit.

Substruction-n-Kinatatayuhan.

Substructure-n-Kinatatayuhan.

Subtend-v-Mapailalim; lumaban.

Subterfuge-n-Paraan; dahilan.

Subterranean-Subterraneous a Nasa ilalim; ñg lupa.

Subtile-a-Matibay; manipis; mainam; matalim; matalas; matalino.

Subtileness-n-Kanipisan; kainaman; katalasan; katalinuhan.

Subtilization-n-Pagpainaman.

Subtilize-v-Painamin.

Subtilty-n-Kanipisan; kainaman; katalasan.

42

Subtle-*a*-Manipis; matalas; matalino; tuso; taksil; suitik.
Subtly-*a*-Tuso; matalas.
Subtract-*v*-Awasan; bawasan; kunin; alisan.
Subtraction-*n*-Pagbawas; pagkuha.
Subtrahend-*n*-Ang binawas.
Suburb-*n*-Nayon; barrio.
Suburban-*a*-Naunkol sa barrio.
Subversion-*n*-Kalipulan; kasiraan, pagtatalonan.
Subvert-*c*-Lipulin; sirain; talonin.
Subway-*n*-Daan sa ilalim ng̃ lupa.
Succeed-*v*-Manalo; halinhan; sumunod; humalili; magtamasa; bumuti; magkamit; kamtan.
Success-*n*-Pananalo; pagsusunod; dulo; pagkamit, palad; kapalaran.
Successful-*a*-Mapalad; maginhawa.
Succession-*n*-Kahalili; pagbahalili.
Successive-*a*-Tuloytuloy; sunodsunod.
Successor-*n*-Kahalili; kasunod.
Succint-*a*-Masinsin; nakabigkis.
Succor-*v*-Iligtas; abuluyan; amponin; hang̃uin sa kagipitan; tumulong; gumibik; kupkopin; saklolohin.
Succor-*n*-Abuloy; ligtas; pagligtas; tulong; kupkop; ampon; saklolo.
Succotash-*n*-Mais sa lata.
Succulence Succulency-*n*-Sustancia.
Succulent-*a*-Masustancia.
Succumb-*v*-Sumuko; masupil.
Succussion-*n*-Untog; tulak.
Such-*a*-Gayon; ganyan.
Suck-*c*-Humitit; humigop; sumuso.
Suck-*n*-Hitit; higop.
Sucker-*n*-Usbong; supling.
Suckling-*n*-Hayop na hindi pa inawatan sa pagsususo.
Suckle-*v*-Pasusuhin.
Suction-*n*-Pagbitit.
Sudden-*a*-Bigla; biglangbigla; dalos; kaginsaginsa; pagdaka.
Suddenly-*adv.*-Kading̃atding̃at; kadalidali; kaginsakaginsa.
Sudoriferous-*a*-Nakapapawis; mapawis.
Sudorific-*a*-Mapawis; nakapapawis.
Sudorific-*n*-Gamot na pangpapawis.
Suds-*n*-Pinagsabunan.
Sue-*v*-Maghabla; sumunod.
Suet-*n*-Taba.
Suety-*a*-Mataba.
Suffer-*v*-Magtiis; tiisin; tumagal; batahin; tamuhin; magdalita, dalitain.
Sufferable-*a*-Makatitiis.
Sufferance-*n*-Katiisan; pagtitiis, tiaga; damdam; kasakitan, kahirapan.
Suffering-*n*-Kahirapan; kahapisan, kasakitan.
Suffice-*v*-Humusto; sumapat.

Sufficiency-*n*-Kahustuhan; kasapatan; kasiyahan; katapatan.
Sufficient-*a*-Husto; kasiya; sapat; katatagan; may kaya.
Suffix-*n*-Dugtong sa huli ng̃ isang salita.
Suffix-*v*-Idugtong.
Suffocate-*v*-Uminis; inisin.
Suffocation-*n*-Pag iinis; pag inis.
Suffrage-*n* Voto; voces.
Suffuse-*v*-Itakpan; tumakpan.
Suffusion-*n*-Pagtatakpan.
Sugar-*n*-Matamis; asukal.
Sugar-*v*-Haluin ng̃ matamis.
Sugar cane-*n*-Tubo.
Sugar mill-*n*-Kabiyawan.
Sugary-*a*-Matamis; may halong matamis.
Suggest-*v*-Isurot sa isip; sulsulan; ipaalaala.
Suggestion-*n*-Sulsol; paalaala.
Suicidal-*a*-Naunkol sa pagbibigti.
Suicide-*n*-Ang nagbigti.
Suicide-*v*-Mabigti.
Suit-*n*-Kasuotan; terno.
Suit-*v*-Bumagay; maakma; umayon; marapatin.
Suitable-*a*-Bagay; akma; nararapat; mabuti.
Suite-*n*-Kapisanan; bunton.
Suitor-*n*-Ang lumilingkod;ang lumiligaw.
Sulk-*v*-Magtampo; mapoot.
Sulk-*n*-Tampo; poot.
Sulks-*n*-Tampo; katampuhan.
Sulky-*a*-Matampuhin.
Sulky-*n*-Kalasin.
Sullen-*a* Galit; matigas ang ulo.
Sully-*v*-Mansahin.
Sulphate-*n*-Sulfato.
Sulphur-*n*-Sulfuro.
Sulphurate-*a*-Naunkol sa sulfuro.
Sulphurate-*v*-Lagyan ng̃ sulfuro.
Sulphureous-Sulphurous-*a*-May halong sulfuro.
Sulphury-*a*-May halong sulfuro.
Sultan-*n*-Hari sa turkia.
Sultry-*a*-Mainit.
Sum-*n*-Kabilugan; baguoan.
Sum-*v*-Bilugin; sumahin; buoin.
Summary-*a*-Maikli.
Summary-*n*-Sulat na maikli.
Summation-*n*-Kabilugan; kabuoan.
Summer-*n*-Taginit.
Summit-*n*-Dung̃ot; dulo. tuktok.
Summon-*v*-Tawagin; tumawag.
Summons-*n*-Tawag.
Sumptuosity-*n*-Kadakilaan, karang̃alan.
Sumptuous-*a* Marang̃al; dakila.
Sun-*n*-Araw.
Sun beam *n* Siuag ng̃ araw.
Sun burn *c*-Mamula ang balat dahil sa araw.

Sunday-n-Lingo.
Sunder-v-Ihiwalay; hiwalayin.
Sunder-n-Paghihiwalay.
Sun down-n-Paglubog ng̃ araw.
Sundries-n-Sitsiria; mang̃a bagay na
munti.
Sundry-a-Ilang; sarisaring.
Sun fish-n-Malakapas.
Sang-c. p. p.-Kumanta na; nakakanta.
Sunk-v. p. p.-Nilubog; nakalubog.
Sunken-a-Nakalubog.
Sunless-a-Walang araw.
Sun light-n-Ilaw ng̃ araw; liwanag ng̃
araw.
Sunny-a-Maaraw.
Sun rise-Sun rising-n-Pagsikat ng̃ araw.
Sun set-Sun setting-n-Pag lubog ng̃ araw.
Sun shine-n-Liwanag ng̃ araw; sikat ng̃
araw.
Sup-v-Humigop.
Sup-n-Higop; kaunti.
Superabound-v-Lumagpos; lumabis; su-
magana ng̃ malabis.
Superabundance-n-Kasaganaan; kalabi-
san; kalagpusan.
Superabundant-a-Malagpos; malabis.
Super add-v-Dagdagin.
Superannuate-v-Dagdagan ng̃ lakas.
Superb-a-Dakila; marang̃al; mainam na
malabis.
Supercede-v-Huag ipatuloy.
Supercilious-a-Hambog; palalo.
Superficial-a-Mapaibabaw; mababaw.
Superfine-a-Lubhang mainam.
Superfluity-n-Kalabisan; kalagpusan; ka-
yamuan; kasaganaan; kalaluan.
Superfluous-a-Malabis; malagpos.
Super human-a-Lampas sa kapangyari-
han ng̃ tawo.
Superincumbency-n-Pagkasandal sa iba.
Superincumbent-a-Nakasandal sa iba.
Superior-n-Kataastaasan.
Superior a-Mataas pa; lubhang dakila.
Superiority-n-Kadakilaan; kataasan; ka-
Lugtan; karang̃alan.
Superlative-a-Kataastaasan.
Superlative-n-Kataastaasang lagay.
Supernatural-a-Lampas sa kapangyari-
han mundo.
Supernumerary-a-Mahigit sa kailang̃an.
Supernumerary-n-Ang labis sa kaila-
ng̃an.
Superscribe-v-Pumirma sa itaas.
Superscription-n-Pirma sa itass.
Supersede-v-Humalili.
Supersedure-n-Kahalili.
Superstition-n-Guniguni; pamahian.
Superstitous-a-Maguniguni.
Supervise-v-Mamuno; mamahala.
SupervisionS-upervisal-n-Pamamahala.

Supervisor-n-Taga pamahala; puno.
Supervisory-a-Nauukol sa pamumuno.
Supination-n-Pagtitihaya ng̃ kamay.
Supine-a-Nakatihaya; matirik; tamad;
pabaya.
Supper-n-Hapunan.
Supperless-a-Walang hapunan.
Supolant-v-Halinhan; ialis.
Supple-a-Malambot; madaling mahubog.
Supplement-n-Kadugtong; katapusan.
Suppliance-n-Panalang̃in; luhog.
Suppliant-a-Mananalang̃in.
Supplicant-n-Ang nananalang̃in; ang du-
madaing.
Supplicate-v-Dumaing; manalang̃in; lu-
muhog.
Supplication-n-Daing; panalang̃in.
Supplicatory-a-Nauukol sa panalang̃in;
nauukol sa pagdaraing.
Supply-v-Magbigay ng̃ kinakailang̃an.
Support-v-Amponin; abuluyan; tulung̃an;
umampon; umabuloy; tumulong.
Support-n-Ampon; tangkilik; katulong.
Suppose-v-Sumapantaha; hakain; huma-
ka; maghinala; magpalagay; ipagpa-
lagay.
Supposition-Supposal-n-Sapantaha; pala-
gay; haka.
Suppress-v-Inisin; pigilin; daigin; ta-
lunin.
Suppression-n-Paginis; pagpigil; pagpa-
pasuko.
Suppurate-v-Magnana.
Suppuration-n-Pagnana.
Supramundane-a-Lampas sa kapangya-
rihan ng̃ mundo.
Supremacy-n-Kataasan; kapangyarihan.
Supreme-a-Kataas taasan; mataas sa la-
hat.
Sural-a-Nauukol sa binti.
Surcharge-v-Hulan ng̃ mabigat.
Surcingle-n-Pamigkis ng̃ siya.
Sure-a-Totoo; tunay; tapat; bagay; siguro;
matibay.
Sure-footed-a-Di matitisurin.
Surely-adv.-Siguro; oo nga; tunay.
Surety-n Katibayan; tibay.
Surf-n-Daluyong.
Surface-n-Balat; mukha; ibabaw.
Surfeit-v-Lampasan; kumain ng̃ dema-
siado.
Surfeit-n-Katakawan; kabusugan.
Surge-n-Alon na malaki.
Surge-v Umalon.
Surgeon-n-Mangagamot.
Surgery-n-Paggagamot; karunung̃an tung-
kol sa gamot.
Surgical-a-Nauukol sa mangagamot.
Surliness-n-Kapaslang̃an; katampalasa-
nan; kasung̃itan.

Surly-a-Mapaslang; mapanglaw.
Surmise-v-Sumapantaha; sapantahain; isipin; humalata.
Surmise-n-Sapantaha; halata.
Surmount-v-Daigin.
Surname-n-Apellido.
Surpass-v-Lampasin; lumampas; lumalo; daigin; humigit; lumagpos; manaig.
Surplice-n-Maputing habito nğ pari.
Surplus-n-Labis; kalabisan; kalagpusan.
Suprise-v-Gitlahin; gulatin; magitla; magulat; hanğalin; imangha.
Surprise-n-Gulat; gitla; mangha.
Surrender-v-Sumuko.
Surrender-n-Suko.
Surreptitious-a-Niyaring palihim.
Surrogate-v-Halinhan; humalili; palitan.
Surrogation-n-Paghahali; kahalili.
Surround-v-Pumaligid paligirin.
Survey-v-Usisain; lumkalin; sukatin ang lupa.
Survey-n-Pagunsisa; pagsukat nğ lupa.
Survive-v-Lampasin; lumampas.
Susceptible a-Makahilig.
Suspect-v-Magbintang; sumapantaha.
Suspect-n-Ang binintanğan.
Suspend-v-Ibitin; kabitin; isampay; itayo; magbigti.
Suspender-n-Sakbat.
Suspense-n-Panğamba.
Suspension-n-Pagpigil; pagkasabit; pagbitin.
Suspensory-v-Nakabitin.
Suspensory-n-Sabitan.
Suspicion-n-Hinala; alapaap ng loob; hinagap; sapantaha.
Suspicious-a-Maalapaap ang loob; dala; mahinagap; mapaghinala.
Sustain-v-Alalayin; batahin; ipaglaban; ipagsangalang; sumustento.
Sustenance-Sustentation n-1kinabubuhay; sustento.
Suter-n-Manğanğalakal sa mğa kawal nğ hukbo.
Suturn-n-Pananahi.
Swab-n-Pangisis.
Swab-v-Linisin; isisin.
Swaddle v-Pamigkisin.
Swag-v-Gumiray; umugoy; humubog.
Swag-n-Giray; ang ninakaw.
Swagger-v-Maghambog sa paglakad.
Swagger-n-Lakat na hambog.
Swain-n-Ang naninitang taga bukid.
Swale-n-Labak; lawak.
Swale-v-Tumunaw at mawala; silabin.
Swallow-n Higop; lagok.
Swallow-v-Higupin; lumagok; lamunin.

Swallow-n-Kumpapalis.
Swam-v. imp.-Luuanğoy na; nakalanğoy.
Swamp n-Kaburakan; laog; kabanlikan.
Swamp-v-Tumaob ang bangka.
Swampy-a-Mabalaho.
Swap-v-Palitin; pumalit.
Swap-n-Palit; kapalitan.
Sward n-Lupa.
Sware-v. imp.-Nanunpa; nagtunğayaw.
Swarm-n-Bunton.
Swarm-v-Bumunton.
Swarthy a-Maitin; kayu-mangi.
Swarthiness-n-Kayumangi; kaitiman.
Swash-v-Tumilansik; luniguak.
Swash-n-Liguak.
Swathe-v-Balutin.
Sway-v-Galawin; gumalaw.
Sway-n-Galaw.
Sweal-v-Tumunaw.
Swear-v-Manumpa; sumumpa; tumunğayaw. manunğayaw.
Sweat-v-Pumawis.
Sweat-n-Pawis.
Sweaty-a-Mapawis.
Sweep-v-Magwalis; maglawis.
Sweep-n-Lawis; walis.
Sweepings-n-Pinagwalisan; pinaglawisan.
Sweet-a-Matamis.
Sweet-n-Matamis.
Sweet bread-n-Tinapay na matamis.
Sweeten-v-Lagyan nğ matamis; patamisan; tumamis.
Sweetish-a-Matamistamis.
Sweet meat-n-Matamis.
Sweetness-n-Katamisan.
Swell-v-Mamaga; tumaas; lumaki; umalsa; lumago; dumami, kumapal; mamanas.
Swell-n-Mainam; dakila.
Swelling n-Pamamaga.
Swelter-v-Sumuko sa init.
Swept-v. imp. & p.p.-Niwalisan; nilawisan.
Swerve-v-Lumiko.
Swift-a-Magaan matulin; madali.
Swiftness-n-Katulinan, kadalian.
Swig-v-Uminom nğ malakas.
Swig-n-Higop na malaki.
Swill-v-Lamunin; maglasing.
Swill-n-Pagkain nğ baboy.
Swim-v-Maglanğoy; maglanğoy.
Swim-n-Ligo; langoy.
Swindle-v-Manekas; tumekas.
Swindle-n-Tekas.
Swindler n-Manenekas.
Swine-n-Manğa baboy.
Swine herd-n-Magpapastol nğ manğa baboy.

Swinish *a* Parang baboy, salaula
Swing-*v*-Ugoyin, umuga, ugain
Swing *n* Ugoy, uga; duyan
Swinge-*v*-Hampasin, parusahin.
Swinging-*a*-Malaki.
Swingle-*v*-Linisin sa hampas
Swinish *a* Parang baboy, salahula
Swiss *a*-Nauukol sa Suisa
Swiss-*n*-Taga Suisa
Switch-*v*-Ihko, ilipat
Swob *n*-Panglinis
Swob-*v*-Linisin
Swollen-*c. p p* Namaga, namanas, natambok.
Swoon-*v* Manghimatay, himimatayin
Swoon *n* Himatay
Swoop-*v*-Sungaban; kunin, agawin
Swop-*v*-Palitan, pumalit.
Swop *n*-Palit, kapalitan.
Sword *n* Espada
Sword fish *n*-Pagi.
Swore *v*-Nanungayaw, nanumpa
Swum-*c p p* -Lumangoy na, nakalangoy.
Swum-*v. p. p* -Nanga na, nakaduyan na

Syllable *n*-Silaba.
Sulph-*n*-Duende
Syphid-*n*-Munting duende
Symbol-*n* Kahulugan, tanda.
Symbolic Symbolical-*a* Nauukol sa tanda.
Symbolize-*v*-Tandain,ibigay ngkahulugan
Symmetrical-*a*-Maayos.
Symmetry-*n*-Ayos.
Sympathetic-Sympathetical-*a*-Mahabag, maawain.
Sympathize *v*-Mahabag, maawa
Sympathy-*n*-Awa, habag.
Symptom-*n*-Tanda.
Symptomic-Symptomical-*a*-Nauukol sa tanda.
Synagogue-*n*-Simbahan
Syneopate-*v* Bawasan ang letra.
Synonym *n*-Kahulugan, katulad.
Synopsis-*n*-Pagtingin
Syringe-*n*-Labatiba, hiringa.
Syringe-*v*-Labatibahin; hiringahin
Syrup-*n*-Pulot
System-*n* Sistema ayos. husay
Systemize *v*-Ayusin, husayin

T

Tab *n*-Puntas na makitid
Tabby-*n*-Pusa, dalagang matanda, bagay ng masitsit.
Tabernacle-*n* Tabernaculo; templo, simbahan.
Tabernacle *v*-Tumahan, tumira.
Table-*n*-Dulang, mesa
Tab e *v*-Ilagay sa mesa.
Table cloth *n*-Mantel ng mesa
Table-land-*n* Lupang patag at mataas
Table spoon-*n*-Cuchara
Table spoonful-*n*-Cucharada
Tablet-*n*-Munting mesa, mukha, tableta
Taboo-*n*-Pagbawal
Tabor-*n*-Tambol, caja
Taborat-*n*-Munting tambol
Taborine-*n* Pandereta
Tabouret-*n*-Upuan na walang sandalan, silleta
Tabular *a* Nauukol sa lamesa
Tabulate-*v*-Gawin parang isang dulang.
Tachygraphy *n*-Sulat na matulin
Tacit-*a*-Tahimik, walang kibo
Taciturn-*n*-Palaging tahimik.
Tack-*n* Pakong aspili
Tack-*v*-Ipako ng pakong aspili
Tackle *n*-Kasangkapan, manga luhid at kelooy.
Tackle *v*-Sungaban, sumungab.
Tact-*n*-Damdam, sanay, bait karunungan

Tactic-Tactical-*a*-Nauukol sa gawa nang hukbo ó ng mga pandirigma.
Tactics *n*-Pamamahala sa hukbo.
Tactile-*a*-Nauukol sa hipo
Taction-*n*-Hipo, kapa; hawa
Taffeta-Taffety-*n*-Sutlang makintab.
Taff rail *n*-Gawing likod ng sasakyan
Taffy-*n*-Matamis, inuyat, uyam
Tag-*n*-Tanda
Tag-*v*-Idugtong, isabit
Tail-*n* Buntot
Tailor *n*-Sastre
Tailoress-*n*-Modista, babaying mananahi.
Taint-*v*-Mansahin, malansa.
Taint-*n* Mansa; lansa.
Take-*v*-Kunin, kumuha, damputin, sumampot, tangapin, tumangap
Taking-*n*-Pagkuha, pagtangap
Take apart *v*-Tangalin, magtangal
Tale-*n*-Balita, kuento, kasaysayan
Tale bearer *n*-Tawong mapagsumbong, tawong palasumbungin
Tale bearing-*n*-Pagsumbong
Talent-*n* Katalasan ng isip, katusuhan, katalinuhan, dunong, karunungan.
Talented-*a*-Marunong, mapalad
Talipes-*n*-Kapilayan ng paa.
Talk *v* Mag-alita, inagwika, magsaysay; mag usap, kausapin.
Talk-*n*-Salita; pagsasalita; wika, pamamalita, kasaysayan.

Talkative-a-Masalita.
Tall-a-Mataas; matayog; matangkad.
Tallow-n-Pagkit.
Tallow-v-Pahiran ñg pagkit.
Tally-n-Tanda; kasama; katulad; biñgaw; tandaan.
Tally-v-Tandain.
Talon-n-Kuko ñg ibon.
Tamable-a-Madaling; maamo.
Tamarack-n-Sampalok.
Tamarind-n-Sampalok.
Tambour-n-Kaja.
Tambourine-n-Pandereta.
Tame-a-Maamo; maumak.
Tame-v-Umamo; paamuin; umakin.
Tamper-v-Makialam; galawin.
Tan-v-Gawin katad ang balat ñg hayop; mamula ang balat.
Tan-n-Kayumangi.
Tandem-adv.-Sunodsunod.
Tang n-Lasang mapakli; pakli; anghang; tunog.
Tangency-n-Dati; kasama.
Tangent-a-Nahipo; nakadayti.
Tangible-a-Makahihipo.
Tangle-v-Gulohin; gumulo; gusutin.
Tangle-n-Kaguluhan; gulo; gusot.
Tank-n-Lalagyan ñg tubig; estanka.
Tankard-n-Baso ñg alak na may takip.
Tannery-n-Gawaan ñg katad.
Tantalism-Tautalazation-n-Tukso.
Tantalize-v-Tuksuhin.
Tantamout-a-Magkaisa ang halaga.
Tantivy-a-Matulin; madali.
Tantrum-n-Kapootan; katampohan.
Tap-v-Hilurin; butasin.
Tap-n-Tuktok; butas.
Tape-n-Panali ñg kayo.
Tape line-n-Panukat.
Taper-n-Kandilang munti.
Taper-v-Lumiit.
Tapestry-n-Mañga tabing nang sutla at lana.
Tape worm-n-Bulati na mahaba.
Tapis-n-Mañga tabing na sutla at lana.
Tar-v-Magdaragat.
Tar-n-Alketran.
Tar-v-Pahiran ñg alketran.
Tarantula-n-Gagamba na malaki.
Tardy-a-Mabagal; huli; batugan; tamad; mabigat; marahan; maliwanag.
Tare-n-Pinagpilian; sukal.
Target-n-Targeta; tuntuñgan.
Tariff-n-Tarifa; buis.
Tarlatan-n-Kayong manipis na pinagamit sa saya.
Taru-n-Danaw sa bundok.
Tarnish-v-Mamansa.
Tarnish-n-Mansa.
Tarpaulin-n-Tarapal.

Tarry-v-Mag luat; maghinto; tumagal.
Tarry-n-Hinto; kaluatan; tagal.
Tarry-a-May halong alketran.
Tarsus-n-Bubong ñg paa.
Tart-n-Hupia na may laman.
Tart-a-Matapang; mapakli; maanghang.
Tartar-n-Latak na mapula.
Tartarean-Tartareous-a-Naunkol sa infierno.
Tartarus-n-Iufierno.
Tartness-n-Pakli; anghang.
Task-n-Trabajo; gawa; kapagalan; katungkulan; hanapbuhay.
Task v-Magbigay ñg trabajo; pahirapin.
Task master-n-Pañginoon;taga pamahala
Taste-v-Lasahin; tikman; lasapin; namnamin.
Taste-n-Lasa; lasap; namnam; tikim.
Tasteful-a-Malasa; malinamnam.
Tasteless-a-Walang lasa; matabang.
Tasty-a-Malasa; mainam; masarap; makinis.
Tater-v-Punitin; pumunit; magulanit.
Tattered-n-Punit; gulanit.
Tatter de mallion-n-Tawong sumusuot ñg damit na punit; hampaslupa.
Tatting-n-Puntas ñg sinulid.
Tattle-r-Sumumbong; magsumbong; bigkasin ang dila.
Tuttle-n-Salitang walan kabuluhan.
Tattoo-n-Tanda; marka.
Tattoo-v-Markahan; tandain.
Taught-v. imp. & p. p.-Nagturo; tumuro.
Taunt-v-Tuksuhin; payamutin.
Taunt-n-Tukso.
Taurine-a-Naunkol sa mañga baka.
Taurus-n-Bakang lalaki; mañga baka.
Taut-a-Mahigpit; nabanat; matibay.
Tavern-n-Bahay tuluyan.
Tawdry-a-Makulay; mura.
Tawny-a-Kayumangi.
Tax-n-Buis.
Tax-v-Magpabuis;bintañgin;magparatang
Taxable-a-Dapat ipabuis.
Taxation-n-Pagpapabuis.
Tea-n-Cha.
Tea cup n-Tasa ñg cha.
Teach-v-Magturo; turuan; ituro; pag aralan; magpaaral.
Teachable a-Makatuturo; maamo.
Teaching n-Pagtuturo.
Tea pot-n-Charera.
Tea spoon-n-Kutsarang munti.
Teal-n-Patong sa damo.
Team-n-Pareja ñg kabayo.
Teamster-n-Cochero.
Tear-n-Luha.
Tear-v-Punitin; pumunit; pilasin.
Tear n-Luha.
Tear-v-Punitin; pumunit; pilasin.

Tear n Punit pilas.
Tearful a-Maluha
Tearless-a-Walang luha
Tease v Tuksuhin, tumukso; manukso
Tease-n Manunukso, manbabadya
Teaser-n-Manunukso, manbabadya
Teat n-Suso
Techiness-n-Kapootan
Technic-Technical a-Nauukol sa manga katungkulan ó arte
Techy-a-Matampohin, mapopootin,
Tectonic a-Nauukol sa pag tayo nang bahay.
Ted v Bilarin ang damung sariwa.
Tedious-a Makayayamot, mayamutin, mabagal, maluat, makapapagod, makasunok
Tedium-n-Kayamutan, kabagalan, kabutingtingan.
Teem v Lumitaw, ihtaw, mamunga, ma nganak, sumagana
Teens-n-Manga taong ng gulang buhat sa labingisa hangang sa labing siam.
Teeth-n-Manga ngipin
Teeth-v-Tubuan ng ngipin
Tetotal a-Buo, lahat, lubos
Tetotally-adv-Lahat lahat, lubos
Tegument-n-Takip; panakip
Tegumentary-a-Nauukol sa takip
Telegram n Telegrama, hatid kawad
Telegraph n-Telegrama
Telegraph v-Mag telegrama, mag hatid kawad
Telegrapher-Telegraphist n-Telegrafista
Telegraphy n-Karunungan tungkol sa telegrama
Telephone-n-Telefono
Telephone v-Magtelefono
Telephonic-a-Nauukol sa telefono
Telescope-n-Largavista
Telescope-v-Ipaloob
Tell-v-Sabihin, magsabi, ipahayag; ibalita, magbalita, wikain, magwika, magsalita, magbigay alam
Teller-n-Ang nagsabi, ang nagbalita
Tell tale-n Tawong palasumbong, ang tawong hindi marunong ingatin ang lihim
Temerity-n-Karuagan, takot, kilabot
Temper-n-Timpla, isip, ugali.
Temper-v Timplahin.
Temperament n Kaugalian, kaasalan.
Temperance n-Katisan sa pag inom
Temperate-a-Mahinahon, katatagan, katamtaman
Temperature-n-Init ó lamig nang panahon
Tempest-n-Bagyo, unos
Tempestuous a-Mahagyo, magulo.
Temple-n-Templo, simbahan, pahispisan

Temporal a-Nauukol sa panahon
Temporary a Interino, hindi malulutaan, ngayon lamang
Temporize v Sumunod sa panahon.
Tampt-v Tuksuhin; manukso, damahin
Temptation n-Takso
Ten n Sampo
Ten a Sampuo.
Tenacious a-Mahigpit; maganit maramot, matigas ang ulo
Tenacity-Tenaciousness-n Katigasan ng ulo, kahigpitan, gamit
Tenancy-n Pagtitira sa isang bahay
Tenant-n-Ang tumira sa isang bahay
Tenant-v Tumira sa isang bahay
Tenantable v-Bigay ipaupahan
Tenantless a Walang tumira
Tenantry-n-Manga tawong tumitira sa bahay na inupahan
Tend v-Mag alaga, alagaan, tulungan; bantayin, magbantay, humilig.
Tendency-n Hiling kahilingan
Tender-n-Taga alaga, ang mamahala.
Tender v Ialok, iabot
Tender a Malambot, malata, maramdamin, mairog
Tender-n Lambot, loob
Tenderness n Kalambutan
Tenon n-Litid
Tendril n Lipay
Tenement-n Bahay na ipinaupahan.
Tenet-n Pananampalataya
Ten fold-a Makasampuong duble
Tenon-n Rabo
Tenon-v Magrabo
Tense n-Panahon ng verbo.
Tense-a Unat, banat
Tensile a Nauukol sa pag laki
Tension-n Pag unat, kaunatan.
Tent-n-Damara, torda
Tent-v-Tumira sa torda
Tentative a Nauukol sa subok
Tentative n-Subok.
Tenter-n Sampayan.
Tenter-v Isampay
Tenth a Ikasanpuong
Tenth-n-Ang kasampuo
Tenthly adv-Sa ikasampuo
Tenuity-n Kanipisan, kalabnawan, kadalangan
Tenuous-a-Manipis,malabnaw,madalang
Tepid-a-Malagamgam, malakuko
Tepidity-Tepidness-n-Pagkamalahininga
Term-n Kapanahunan, panahon, hanga.
Term-v Tumawag
Termagency n-Kaguluban kaingayan
Termagent n-Babaying magulo
Termagent a-Magulo, maingay
Terminable a-Makatatapos, dapat, tapusin, mangyaring matapos

Terminal-*a*-Tapos; katapusan.
Terminal-*n*-Kutapusan.
Terminate-*v*-Tapusin; tumapos; ubusin; umubos; yariin; mayari.
Teamination-*n*-Katapusan; tapos; pag-ubos; yari; kayarian.
Terminus-*n*-Tapos; katapusan.
Termite-*n*-Langam na maputi.
Ternary-*a*-Sumulong nğ tatlotatlo.
Terra *n*-Lupa.
Terra cotta-*n*-Lupang dilaw.
Terrace-*n*-Pilapil.
Terra firma-*n*-Lupang matigas..
Terrapin-*n*-Pagong.
Terrestrail-*a*-Nauukol sa lupa.
Terrible-*a*-Kakilakilabot; katakot takot; kasindak sindak.
Terrier-*n*-Asong munti at matapang.
Terrific-*a*-Malakas; nakadudulit; katakot takot; kakilakilabot.
Terrify-*v*-Takutin; manakot; manhilakbot.
Territorial-*a*-Nauukol sa lupa.
Territory-*n*-Lupain; nayon; hibaybay; lalawigan.
Terror-*n*-Sindak; takot.
Terrorize-*v*-Takutin.
Terse-*a*-Maikli; mahigpit.
Terseness-*n*-Kahigpitan; kaiklian.
Tertial-*a*-Ikatlo.
Tertian-*a*-Mangyayari sa balang tatlong araw.
Tertian-*n*-Sakit na humihimpil at bumabalik sa balang tatlong araw.
Tertiary-*a*-Ikatlong grado.
Test-*v*-Subukin; manubok.
Test-*n* Subok; katotohanan.
Testament-*n*-Testamento.
Testamental-*a*-Nauukol sa testamento.
Testamentary-*a*-Nauukol sa testamento.
Testate *a*-May iniwan nğ testamento.
Testator-*n*-Lalaking nangamatay na may iniwang isang testamento.
Testatrix-*n*-Babaying nangamatay na may iniwang isang testamento.
Testify-*v*-Sumaksi; patotohanin.
Testily-*adv*.-Masungit.
Testimonial-*n*-Katotohanan; saksi.
Testimony-*n*-Katotohanan; pag papatotoo.
Testy-*a*-Mapootin; masungit.
Tete á-tete-*n*-Salitaan nğ dalawa.
Tete-á-tete-*adv*.-Palihim.
Tether-*v*-Isuga.
Tether-*n*-Suga.
Tetragon *n* Paano na may apat na gilid at apat na sulok.
Tetter-*n* Buni.
Teutonic *a* Nauukol sa salitang Aleman.
Text-*n*-Pinagsalitaan; pinagusapan.

Text-book-*n*-Librong pinagaralan.
Textile-*a*-Nauukol sa paghahabi.
Texture-*n*-Kayo.
Thaler-*n*-Pisong Aleman.
Than-*conj*.-Kay sa; nang.
Thank *v*-Magpasalamat.
Thank-*n*-Pagpapasalamat.
Thankful-*a*-Marunong;magutang na loob.
Thankless-*a*-Hindi marunong magntang na loob; bastos.
Thans giving-*n*-Pagpapasalamat.
Thank worthy-*a* Dapat magpasalamat.
Thatch *n* Atip nğ kugon.
Thatch-*v*-Atipan nğ kugon.
Thaw-*v*-Tunawin; tumunaw.
Thaw-*n*-Tunaw; pagtutunaw.
The-*a*-Ang.
Theater-Theatre-*n*-Teatro; komediahan.
Theatric-Theatrical-*a*-Nauukol sa.
Theatricals-*n*-Komediahan.
Theca-*n*-Baina; lalagyan.
Thee *pro*.-Moiyo.
Theft-*n*-Pag umlit; pagnakaw.
Their *pro*.-Kanila; nila; sarili nila.
Them *pro*.-Nila; kanila.
Theme-*n*-Dulo; pinagsulatan.
Them selves-*n*-Sila rin; kanilang sarili.
Then *adv*.-Noong; niyon; kung gayon; nğ panahong yaon; saka; sa kahulihan; pagkatapos.
Then *conj* Dahil dito; kung gayon.
Thence *adv*.-Dahil dito; magbuhat doon; magbuhat noon.
Thence forth-*adv*.-Magbuhat noon.
Thence forward-*adv*.-Magbuhat noon.
Theorize-*v*-Mag wari.
Theory-*n*-Katha; isip; akala; paraan.
Therapeutic-Therapeutical-*a*-Nauukol sa pag gagamot.
There *adv*.-Doon; diyan; sa gawi roon.
There about-There abouts *adv*.-Sa dako roon; malapit doon.
There at-*adv*.-Doon; diyan; dahil dito.
There by-*adv*.-Dahilan doon; malapit doon.
There for-*adv*.-Dahilan doon.
There fore *adv*.-Gayon; dahilan doon.
There fore-*conj*.-Kaya; yayamang; dahil doon.
There from-*adv*.-Magbuhat yaon; magbuhat nito.
There in-*adv*.-Sa ito; sa lugar yaon.
There into-*adv*.-Sa lugar yaon.
There of-*adv*.-Nang ito.
There on-*adv*.-Sa ibabaw nito.
There to-*adv*.-Sa ito.
There nnto *adv*. Hangang doon.
There upon-*adv*.-Dahilan dito; agadagad; nğayon din.
There with-*adv*.-Bukod pa sa rito.

There withal-*adv* -Kasabay.
Thermal *a*-Nauukol sa init; mainit.
Thermometer *n*-Panukat ng init
Thermometric-Thermometrical-*a*-Nauukol sa panukat ng init.
These *pro* -Itong manga
Thew-*n* Lakas, litid
Thev-*p o* -Sila.
Thick-*a*-Makapal; malapot, masinsin, malabo mapurol, mabagal, batugan.
Thick-*n*-Kapal
Thick *adv* -Madalas, matulin madali.
Thicken *v*-Lumapot, kumapal, kapalan.
Thicket-*n*-Kaugoygoyan.
Thickness-*n*-Kakapalan, kalaputan, kasinsinan
Thick set-*a*-Mataba, makatawan
Thief-*n*-Magnanaka*v*; mangungumit.
Thieve *v*-Magnakaw, nakawin, manguimit, umilin
Thievery-*n*-Paknakaw.
Thievish-*a*-Nauukol sa pagnakaw, palanakaw, mahilig sa pagnanakaw
Thigh-*n*-Pigi, hita.
Thill-*n*-Baras.
Thimble-*n*-Didal
Thimbleful *n*-Laman ng isang didal
Thin-*a* Manipis, payat, malabnaw; magaan mahina; buhaghag
Thin-*adv* -Malabnaw, buhaghag
Thin-*v*-Labnawin; lumabnaw; pumayat; dumalang
Thine *m o* -Iyo, mo
Thing-*n* Bagay, kasangkapan.
Think-*v*-Mag isip, isipin; mag wari; maisipan; akalain, umisip, kumatha
Thinness *n* Kanipisan, kalabnawan; payat, kahinaan; kapayatang
Third *a*-Ikatlo
Third-*n* Ikatlo; ang ikatlong bahagi
Thirdly-*adv*.-Sa ikatlo
Thirst-*n*-Uhaw, nasa, pita, nais.
Thirst-*i* -Mauhaw, umuhaw, magnasa, magpita
Thirsty-*a*-Mauhaw
Thirteen-*n*-Labingtatlo.
Thirteen-*a*-Labingtatlo
Thirteenth-*a* Ikalabingtatlo
Thirtieth-*a* Ikatatlongpuo
Thirtieth-*n*-Ang ikatatlongpuo.
Thirty-*n*-Tatlongpuo
Thirty-*a*-Tatlongpuo.
This-*pro* -Ito, yari.
This *a* Ito; yaring
Thistle-*n*-Tinik
Thistly *a* Matinik.
Thither-*adv* -Doon, sa gawi roon, doon pa
Thither ward-*adv*.-Sa gawi roon
Thong-*n* Panali na Latad

Thoracic *a*-Nauukol sa lalamunan.
Thorax-*n*-Lalamunan.
Thorn-*n* Tinik.
Thorny-*a*-Matinik
Thorough-*a*-Di pabaya, lubos, puspos.
Thorough bred-*a*-Matapang, malikot
Thorough fare *n*-Lansangan, karsada; daan
Thoroughly *adv* -Lubos, yaringyari.
Thorough paced *a*-Lubos, puspos, tapos.
Those *pro* -Yaong manga
Thou *pro* -Ikaw
Though-*adv* -Kahiman, kung masque.
Though-*conj* -Kahitman; kahiman.
Thought-*n*-Isip, dili, akala, wari.
Thought-*v imp p & p* -Inisip, inakala.
Thoughtful-*a*-Mahinahon, maingat; mapagisip, mabait; mapagwariwari.
Thoughtless-*a*-Pabaya, walang isip, mapurol ang isip.
Thousand-*n*-Isang libo
Thousand *a*-Sanglibong.
Thousandth *a*-Ikasanglibong.
Thousandth *n*-Ikaisanglibo.
Thrall-*n*-Alipin, pagkaalipin
Thrall *v*-Alipinin, alipnan
Thralldom *n*-Pagkaalipin, kalagayan alipin.
Thrash-*v*-Gumiik, hampasin, paluin.
Thrasher-*n* Mangigiik
Thread *n* Sinulid.
Thread-*t*-Isnot ang sinulid sa mata ng karayom
Thread bare *a*-Kupas; lamuymoy, magu
lanit
Threat-*n*-Bala, hamon.
Threaten-*v*-Bumala, ipagbala, hamunin
Three-*n*-Tatlo.
Three-*a*-Tatlong.
Three fold-*a*-Tatlong duble.
Three penny-*a*-Mahirap, hamak, walang kabuluhan.
Three-score-*a*-Anim na puo.
Threody *n*-Dalit sa pag libing
Thresh-*v* Giikin; gumiik.
Thres hold-*n* Gilid, tabi, pasukan.
Threw-*v*-Hinagis, pinukol, binalibag.
Thrice *adv* Makatlo.
Thrift-*n*-Pagsulong; sipag; pakinabang, kasipagan.
Thriftless-*a*-Pabaya, tamad.
Thrifty *a*-Masipag.
Thrive-*v*-Sumulong; bumuti, guminhawa, dumami
Throat-*n*-Lig, lalamnnan.
Throb-*n* Pukpok; kaba
Throb *v*-Pumukpok; kumaba
Throe-*n*-Sakit na malabis.
Throne-*n*-Trono, upuan ng hari
Throne-*v*-Ilagay sa trono

Throng-n Bunton ng̃ tawo.

Throng-v-Kumapal ang tawo.

Throttle n-Lugar ng̃ lng

Throttle v Sakalin.

Through-prep Sa gitna ng̃.

Through-adv -Sa gitna.

Through out prep Samantalang.

Throw-v-Ihagis, humagis, ipukol, pukling; balibagin, bumalibag

Throw-n-Pukol. balibag; hagis.

Throw down-v Ihulog

Thrush n Sakit sa paa ng̃ hayop.

Thrust v-Itulak, tumulak; itudla, tudlain

Thud-n-Lagpak

Thug-n-Tawong bastos

Thum-n Hinlalaki

Thump n-Bungo untog, hampas

Thump v Hampasin, bumungo.

Thunder n Kulog

Thunder-v-Kumulog

Thunder bolt-n-Kidlat ng̃ lintik.

Thunder clap n-Kulog

Thunderous a-Parang kulog, matunog

Thunder shower-n-Ulan na may kasamang kulog.

Thunder storm-v Ulan na may kasamang kulog.

Thunder strike v Gitlahin; ipatakain, imangha

Thunder struck-a-Nagitla; namangha.

Thursday-n Jueves

Thus-adv.-Sa ganito, ganito, ganoon, ganyan gayon

Thwack-v-Hampasin.

Thwack-n-Hampas

Thwart a-Pahalang, nakahalang

Thwart-v-Ipahalang, abalahin.

Thy pro-Iyo, mo.

Thy self-pro-Ikaw rin, iyong sarili

Tiara-n-Krona ng̃ papa.

Tibia-n-Lulod.

Tibial-a-Nauukol sa lulod

Tick-n Hanip.

Tick-n-Taktak ng̃ arasan

Tick-v-Tumaktak, ilista.

Ticker-n-Arasan

Ticket-n-Billeta.

Ticket-v Magbigay ng̃ billete

Tickle-v-Kilitin

Ticklish-a-Makikilitin

Tidal a-Nauukol sa paglaki at pagkati ng̃ tubig.

Tidbit-n-Matamis.

Tide-n-Panahon; paglaki at pagkati ng̃ tubig; ilog, agos

Tide-v-Tumawid, sumama sa agos.

Tidily-adv -Maselang; malinis.

Tiding-n-Balita

Tidy-a-Malinis; maselang.

Tidy-n-Servilleta.

Tie-v-Talian; tumili, itali, ibuhol; bigkisin, magtali

Tie-n-Tali; buhol; pagkatali

Tier-n-Hilera, taludtod.

Tier-v Maghilera.

Tierce-n-Bariles na malaki.

Tiff-n Lagok ng̃ alak, poot, tampo

Tiger-n-Tigre

Tigress-n-Babaying tigre.

Tight a-Mahigpit, makipot; makitid, banat; salat; gipit.

Tighten v-Humigpit; higpitan

Tigrish a-Parang tigre.

Tike n-Tawong bukid .

Tile n-Tisa, hibinga

Tile v-Ilatag ang tisa.

Till n Lalagyan ng̃ kuarta ó salapi.

Till prep Hangang

Till-v Magsaka

Tillable-a-Lupang sakain

Tillage n-Pagsasaka.

Tiller-n-Magsasaka

Tiller n-Ugit ng̃ sasakyan

Tiller-n-Supling.

Tilt-v-Itikwas; ihapay.

Tilt n Pagkahapay, pagkatikwas.

Timber-n-Kahoy; kalap.

Timbrel-n-Kaja, tambol

Time-n Panahon, lugar; oras; laon, luat, kapanahunan; pagulit.

Time v-Sabihin ang panahon.

Timely-a Na sa sa panahon.

Timely adv -Sa mabuting panahon.

Time piece n-Orasan, relos

Time table-n Listahan ng̃ pagalis at pagdating ng̃ mg̃a tren

Timid a Duag, magulatin, dung̃o, gilalasin, matatakutin

Timidity-Timidness-n-Katakutan; karuagan, gulat

Timorous-a-Duag; dung̃o, magugulatin.

Timothy-n Timoteo

Tin-n-Sim, tingang puti lata

Tin-v-Balutin ng̃ tingang puti.

Tinner-Tinman-n-Mangagawa ng̃ lata

Tincture n-Mansa, kulay.

Tincture-v-Mansahin.

Tinder-n Gatong.

Tine-n-Ng̃ipin ng̃ tenedor.

Ting-n-Tunog ng̃ kompana.

Ting-v-Tugtugin ang kompana.

Tingo-n-Mansa; kulay.

Tinge-v-Mansahin.

Tingle-v-Humapdi; sumakit.

Tink-v-Tumunog, kumuliling

Tink-n-Tunog, kuliling

Tinker-n-Mangagawa.

Tinker v Gumawa.

Tinkle-n-Kuliling.

Tinkle-v-Kumuliling
Tinsel-n-Oropel.
Tint n Mansa.
Tint-v-Mansahin.
Tiny-a-Munting munti, maliit na maliit
Tip-n-Pabuya; dulo; dungot
Tip-v-Ipabuya
Tippet-n-Alampay.
Tipple-v-Mag lasing.
Tipple-n-Kalasingan.
Tippler-n-Tawong palalasing, tawong lasingo.
Tipsy-a-Hilo sa alak, lasing, lango.
Tipsily-adv-Palango lango
Tipsiness-n-Kalasingan, kahilohan
Tip toe-n-Lakad na patingkayad
Tip top-n-Kataastaasang dulo, dungot
Tip top-a-Mabuti sa lahat, kabutibutihan.
Tirade-n-Katampalasanan, kapaslangan, alipusta, alibugha.
Tire-n-Yentas.
Tire-i-Pumagod, pumagal, pagalin; pagurin
Tired-a-Pagod, mapagod, mapagal.
Tiredness-n-Kapagalan; kapaguran.
Tireless-a-Walang pagod; hindi marunong pumagod.
Tiresome-a-Nakapapagod; mahirap gawin, makasasawa, masusuya
Tissue-n-Ang hinabi.
Tit-n-Kabayong munti, kapiraso, pirangot
Titbit-n-Munting bagay; butingting
Tithe a-Ikasampong bahagi bahagi.
Titilate-v-Kilitiin, kumiliti.
Title n-Titulo.
Title-v-Bigyan ng titulo
Titter-v-Umurit urit, tumawa.
Titter-n-Urit, tawa.
Tittle-n-Kapirangot; pirasong munti.
Tittle-tattle-n-Salitang walang kabuluhan.
Tittle-tattle-v-Magsalita ng walang kabuluhan
Titularly-adv-Sa titulo lamang.
Titularly-a-May titulo; nauukol sa titulo
To-prep.-Sa, nang.
Toad-n-Palaka palakang kalapsoy.
Toad-eater-n-Hayop na kumakain ng palaka
Toady-a-Tawong mauyam
Toady-v-Uyamin
Toast-v-Tostahin; ihawin, ibusa; isangag
Toast-n-Tinapay na inihaw
Tobacco-n-Tabaco
Tobacco box-n-Lalagyan ng tabaco
Tobacconist-n-Mangangalakal ng tabaco

To day-adv.-Ngayong araw.
To-day-n-Ang araw nito.
Toddle-v-Lumakad parang bata.
Toddy-n-Halo ng alak at matamis.
To do n-Kilos, galaw, kadalian.
Toe n Daliri ng paa.
Toe v-Idayti ang daliri ng paa.
To gether-adv.-Sabaysabay; makasabay
Toil-n Gawa, hirap; bitag, panghuli.
Toil-v-Maghirap, pumagal, magtrabajo, gumawa
Toilsome-a-Mahirap; mabigat.
Toilet-n-Panabihan, paninigalan.
Token-n-Aalay, alaala; tanda.
Told-v. imp. & p. p -Sinabi na, winika na, nagsabi na
Tolerable-a-Makatitiis, matitiisin, katatagan; alanganin
Tolerance-n-Tiis, katiisan, pagtitis.
Tolerant a-Matitiisin, masunurin, mapagtiis
Tolerate-v-Tiisin; mag tiis; pumayag, umayon, dalitain.
Toleration-n-Pagtiis, katiisan.
Toll-v Tugtugin ang compana.
Toll-n-Buis upa sa pagtawid.
Toller-Tollman n-Maniningil ng buis.
Toll gatherer n-Maniningil ng buis.
Tomahawk n-Palataw.
Tomato n Kamates.
Tomb n-Libing, tumba nang patay; kabaong, libingan
Tombless a-Walang tumba.
Tomboy-n-Babayi na may ugaling lalaki.
Tomb stone-n-Tumba ng patay.
Tom cat-n-Pusang lalaki.
Tome-n-Libro; tomo
Tomfool n-Ulol
Tomfoolery-n-Kaululan.
To-morrow-adv.-Hangang bukas, bukas nga.
To-morrow-n Bukas.
Ton-n-Tonelada
Tone-n-Voces, tunog.
Tone v-Tumunog.
Toneless-a Walang tunog
Tongs n-Panipit, sipit.
Tongue-n-Dila
Tongueless-a-Walang dila; pipi; walang kibo.
Tongue-tie-n-Kautalan.
Tongue-tied a-Utal
Tonic n-Gamot na pangpalakas.
Tonic a-Nauukol sa tunog ó sa salita.
To-night a-Mayamayang gabi
To night-n-Ngayon gabi, itong gabi nito.
Tonnage-n-Lulan ng isang sasakyan.
Tonsil-n-Taguan ng laway.

Tonsile a-Makapuputol

Tonsor-n Barbero; mangugupit

Tonsorial-a-Nauukol sa mangugupit.

Tonsure-n-Paggupit . .

Too-adv.-Naman, din, rin, gayon din ·

Took-v imp -Kumuha, kinuha.

Tool-n-Kasangkapan.

Toot-n-Tugtog .

Toot-v-Tumugtog, tugtugin.

Tooth n-Ngipin

Tooth-v-Ngipinin, lalagyan ng ngipin

Tooth ache-n-Sakit ng ngipin.

Toothless-a-Walang ngipin, bungi, tipo.

Tooth pick-n-Panghininga.

Toothsome a-Masarap, malasa

Top-n-Dungot, dulo

Top-v-Tumaas; takpanin ang dulo, lumampas, lumagpos, alisin ang dulo

Topaz-n-Batong topas.

Tope-v-Maglasing. ·

Toper-n-Tawong palaging lasing

Top-heavy-a-Mabigat ang itaas

Topic-n-Pinag usapan ·

Topic-Topical-a-Nauukol sa lugal, may hanga, nauukol sa pinag usapan.

Top knot-n-Tuktok; pusot

Top most a-Kataastaasan

Topographer-n-Ang nagbigay alam tungkol sa isang lupain.

Topographic-Topographical-a-Nauukol sa isang lupain ó isang lugal

Topography-n-Kasaysayan tungkol sa isang pirasong lupa

Topple-i Mabual; bumual.

Top sail-n-Layag sa itaas

Topsy-turvy-a-Walang ayos, magulo

Torch n-Suló. ·

Torch bearer-n-Taga dala ng sulo.

Torch light-n-Ilaw ng suló

Tore-v imp -Pinunit, pumunit, mapunit, pinilas.

Torment n-Tukso; dalamhati; sakit, hirap, kahirapan

Torment-v-Pahirapin, tuksuhin, manukso. ·

Torn-v. p. p -Nakapilas, pinilas na, napunit na. ·

Tornado-n-Bagyo ·

Torpedo-n-Torpedo ·

Torpid-a-Dungo, tulig, mapurol ang isip.

Torpidity-Torpidness n-Pagkatulig, tulig, kadunguan, kapurnlan; isip

Torpor-n-Manhid, kapuiulan, kawalan ng kilos.

Torrefaction n Silab, pagsilag. ·

Torrefy v-Ibusa; silabin

Torrent n Ilog na malakas umagos

Torrid a-Mainit.

Torsion-n-Pilipit; kapilipitan.

Tortoise-n-Pagong. ·

Tortuous a Paliko liko, pasnot snot, baluktot

Torture n Kahirapan, kasakitan, hapis; pagpapasakit. ·

Torture v Pahirapin, saktan, hapisin

Toss n-Itsa, pagitsa

Toss v-Magitsa, itsain ·

Tot-n-Batang munti

Total-n-Kabilugan, kabuoan, kalahatan; suma.

Total a Lahat, buo, puno ·

Totality-n-Kalahatan, kabilugan, kabuoan.

Totally-adv -Lahat lahat ·

Totter-v Gumiraygiray ‚

Touch-v-Hipuin, kapain, humipo, tinagin, tuminag, maukol, banguin

Touch-n-Hipo, kapa, tinag, dayti.

Touching a Maawain, mahabag, naka dayti

Touchy-a-Mapootin, matampuhin.

Tough a-Maganit, bastos

Toughen v-Tomigas, patigasin.

Tour-n Lakad

Tour-v Lumakad; mag lakad.

Tourist-n-Ang lumalakad

Tournament-n-Laban tungkol sa karunungan; subukan.

Tourney-n Pagsusubukan

Touse-Touze v-Batakin, bumatak, pilasin, pumilas, pumunit, punitin

Tousle-v-Gusutin, guluhin

Tow v-Hilahin, akayin, hunila.

Tow n-Ang himihila

Towage n-Paghila.

Toward-Towards-prep -Sa dako, dapit sa, sa gawing

Toward-Towards adv -Malapit, nakahanda.

Towel-n-Towalia

Tower n-Tore

Tower-v-Lumampas sa taas

Town n Bayan.

Town ship-n Lupa nauukol sa nasasacop ng isang bayan. . ·

Towns man-n-Tawong taga bayan.

Toy-n-Laroan ,·

Toy-v-Maglaro, ipaglaroan.

Toy man-n Mangangalakal nang manga laroan

Trace-n-Tirante, guhit; bakas

Trace-v-Guhitin, sumunod.

Trachea-n Lalamunan

Track n-Bakas.

Track-v-Bumakas, sumunod sa bakas ·

Trackless-a-Walang bakas ó walang daan ó landas ·

Tract-n Pirasong lupa

Tractable-a-Masunurin, maamo.

Tractableness-Tractability n-Kaamoan; kaanayaran ng ugali.
Tractile a-Malarabot
Tractility-n-Kalambutan.
Traction n Hila
Tractive a-Mahinayang
Trade-n Panğanğalakal, palitan; negocio, comercio
Trade-n Panğanğalakal; magkalakal, pumalit, magpalitan
Trader n Manğanğalakal
Trade-mark-n-Tanda nğ kalakal.
Trades man-n-Manğanğalakal.
Tradition-n-Kuento.
Traditional-a Nauukol sa kuento.
Traduce-v-Hiyain, sirain ang puri nğ kapua, alipustain.
Traducer n-Maninira nğ puri nğ kapwa
Traffic n-Panğanğalakal.
Traffic-v-Manğalakal
Trafficker n-Manğanğalakal.
Tradegy-n-Kamatayan, sakuna
Tragic Tragical-a Nauukol sa kamatayan
Trail-n-Landas, bulaos
Trail v Sumunod, hilahin
Train-n-Tren
Train-v-Magturo, turuan, ituro.
Trained a-Bihasa, sanay.
Trait-n-Ugali, Kaugahan, asal.
Traitor-n-Tawong taksil ó suitik.
Traitoress n-Babaying taksil ó suitik, babaying sukab
Traitorous-a-Taksil, palamara, sukab
Traitress-n-Baba ying sukab ó taksil
Tram-n-Bagol.
Trammel-n-Bitag, panghuli, panggapos
Trammel v Hiluhin, gapusin.
Tramp n Hampaslupa, lakad; yurak
Tramp-v Maghampas lupa, lumakad, yurakin; yumurak, tumapak
Trample v-Yurakin, tumuntong, yumurak
Trance-n-Kalagayan parang patay.
Tranquil-a-Tahimik; walang gulo, mapalagay ang loob.
Tranquility-Tranquilness n Katahimikan timawa, payapa, kapayapaan; katiwasayan.
Tranquilize-Tranquillize-v Patahimikin, tumahimik, timawain, pumayapa, payapain.
Transact-v-Gawin, manğalakal
Transactment n Paggagawa.
Transactor n Mangagawa
Trans alpine a Sa kabila nğ bundok.
Trans atlantic a Sa kabila nğ dagat
Transcend v-Tumaas, lumampas, lampasin, humalimuyak
Transcendent-a-Maranğal, dakila, mataas
Transcribe v-Isahin.
Transcript n Salin

Transfer v-Ilipat, lipatin, maglipat; isalin.
Transfer-n-Pagpalit; paglipat.
Transferable-a-Makalilipat.
Transference-n Pag lipat.
Transfiguration n-Malikmata
Transfigure-v-Baguhin ang hitsura; magbalatkayo.
Transfix-v-Tuhugin.
Transform-v-Baguhin ang hitsura.
Transfuse-v-Isalin, ilipat.
Transfusion-n Pagsalin.
Transgress-v-Makasala.
Transgression-n-Sala, kasalanan.
Transgressor-n Ang may kasalanan
Transient a Hindi pirme, makaraan.
Transit-n Pagdaraan
Transition n Pagbabago
Transitive a Magdaraan
Transitory-a-Makararaan.
Translate-v Ihulog, saysayin, salaysayin.
Translation-n-Kahulugan; paghulog sa ibang wika; kasaysayan, salaysay
Translator-n-Ang marunong maghulog sa ibang wika
Transmarine-a-Sa kabilang ibayo nğ dagat.
Transmigrate-v Lumipat sa iba,t, ibang lupa.
Transmigration-n-Paglipat sa iba,t, ibang lupa.
Transmissible a-Makalilipat
Transmission-n Pag lipat.
Transmit-v-Dalhin, magdala; ipadala.
Transmittal-Transmittance-n Paglipat.
Transmutable a Makapapalit
Transmutation n-Pagbabago nğ hitsura
Transmute-v-Ibahin ang hitsura
Transparency-n-Aninag, pagkaaninag
Transparent-a-Maaninag
Transpicuous a-Maaninag.
Tranpierce-v-Itarok, butasin
Transpiration-n Hinğa.
Transpire-v-Mangyari.
Transplant-v-Ilipat ang tanim
Transplantation-n Paglipat nğ tanim
Transport-v Magdala, dalhin, alisin; lipulin.
Transportation-n Pagdadala, paglipol
Transpose-v-Halinan, ilipat.
Transposition-n-Paghahalih, paglipat.
Trans-ship-v-Isalin sa ibang sasakyan.
Transverse a-Baliktad; pahalang
Trap n-Hibo, bitag, panghuli, panunuba-
Trap-v-Humuli, manuba, hulihin, bi hagin.
Trapan-n-Hibo, daya; panghuli.
Trapan-v-Bihagin; hibuin, bitagin
Trappings-n-Manğa kasangkapan
Traps-n Manğa kasangkapan.

Trash-*n*-Sukal.
Trashy-*a*-Masukal.
Travel-*v*-Mag lakad; mag lakbay lakbayan.
Travel-*n*-Pag lakad; Jakad; viage; lakbay.
Traveler-Traveller-*n*-Ang nag lalakbay-lakbayan.
Traverse-*a*-Pahalang.
Traverse-*n*-Anomang bagay na nakahalang.
Traverse-*v*-Ipabalang; lakbayin.
Trawl-*n*-Kitid; panti.
Trawl-*v*-Mag kitid.
Tray-*n*-Bandeja.
Treacherous-*a*-Sukab; lilo; taksil.
Treacherously-*adv.*-Pasukab.
Treachery-*n*-Kasukaban; kataksilan; kasuitikan; kalilohan.
Treacle-*n*-Inuyat.
Tread-*v*-Yurakan; yumurak; tumuntong; yumapak; humakbang.
Tread-*n*-Yurak; yabag; tapak; tadyak; hakbang.
Treadle-*n*-Panyurak; pantadyak.
Tread mill-*n*-Gilingan na munti.
Treason-*n*-Kasukaban; kataksilan; kalilohan; pagtatalikod sa sariling bandila.
Treasonable-*a*-Taksil; sukab.
Treasure-*n*-Yaman; kayamanan.
Treasure-*v*-Mahalin; itago.
Treasurer-*n*-Taga ingat ng yaman; tesorero.
Treasury-*n*-Tesoreria.
Treat-*v*-Painumin; gamitin; gamutin; magdiscurso.
Treat-*n* Kasayahan; kaluguran.
Treatise-*n*-Kasulatan; pagsulat.
Treatment-*n*-Trato ng isa sa kapwa.
Treaty-*n*-Kasulatan; ng dalawang katawohan.
Treble-*a*-Tatlong duble.
Treble-*v*-Tatlohin ang duble; dublihing makatatlo.
Tree-*n*-Punong kahoy.
Tree-*v* Ipanhik sa kahoy.
Tree nail-*n*-Pakong kahoy.
Trellis-*n*-Palag; salang madalang.
Tremble-*v*-Manginig; kuminig.
Tremble-*n* Inig.
Trembling-*n*-Panginginig.
Tremendous-*a*-Malaking malaki.
Tremor-*n*-Inig.
Tremulous-*a*-Manginginig; matatakutin; mangangatal.
Trench-*n*-Hukay na mahaba; trinchera.
Trench-*v*-Humukay ng trinchera.
Trenchant-*a*-Matalim; masaklap; mabagsik; masungit.

Trencher-*n*-Taga; hukay; palaton nang kahoy; la mesa; pagkain.
Trend-*v*-Tumungo.
Trend-*v*-Tungo.
Trepan-*n*-Bitag; hibo; panghuli.
Trepan-*v*-Bitagin; hibuin.
Trepan-*a*-Manenekas.
Trepidation-*n*-Inig; takot; gulat.
Trespass-*v*-Magkasala; salangsangin; sumuway.
Trespass-*n*-Kasalanan; salangsangan; kasowayan.
Tress-*n*-Kulot ng buhok; trintas.
Trestle-*n*-Banhay; panukod.
Trot-*n*-Kalabisan.
Trevet-*n*-Upuan na may tatlong paa lamang.
Trey-*n*-Tatlo; *(nauukol sa baraha)*.
Triad-*n*-Kapisanan ng tatlo; trinidad.
Trial-*n*-Subok; pag litis; prueba.
Triangle-*n*-Anomang bagay na mayroong tatlong panulukan lamang.
Triangular-Triangled-*a*-May tatlong panulukan.
Tribe-*n*-Lahi; kapisanan; katipunan.
Tribulation-*n*-Kahirapan; dalamhati; hinagpis.
Tribunal-*n*-Bahay ng hukom; tribunal.
Tribune-*n*-Dating hukom sa bayan ng Roma.
Tributary-*a*-Nasasakop; mababa sa iba; hindi malaya.
Tribute-*n*-Buis; ambag.
Trice-*v*-Talian ng lubid.
Trice-*n*-Isang dali; dali; kisap mata.
Trick-*n*-Lalang; daya; panunuba.
Trick-*v*-Manuba; magdaraya; dayain.
Trickish-*a*-Mapagdaraya.
Trickster-*n*-Magdaraya; manunuba.
Tricky-*a*-Mapagdaraya.
Trickle-*v*-Tumalas.
Tricolor-*n*-Bandera ng manga Frances; tatlong kulay.
Tricuspid-*a*-May tatlong ngipin.
Tricycle-*n*-Kasangkapan na may tatlong gulong.
Trident-*n* Salapang na may tatlong tulis ó ngipin.
Trident-*a* May tatlong ngipin.
Tridentate-*n*-ridentated-*a*-May tatlong ngipin.
Triennial-*a* Mangyayari sa balang tatlong taon.
Trier-*n*-Manunubok.
Trifid-*a*-Nakatatlong bahagi.
Trifle-*n*-Bagay na munti ang halaga.
Trifle-*v*-Magbiro; biruin; huag totohanin.
Trifling-*a*-Magaan; walang halaga; walang kabulahan.

Trifoliate-a-May tatlong dahon.
Triform-a-May tatlong hitsura.
Trig a-Puspos; lubos; puno; mainam; maselang; malinis; makinis.
Trig-v-Pigilin.
Trigger-n-Pangpigil.
Trigon-n-Bagay na may tatlong sulok.
Trihedron-n-Bagay na may tatlong mukha.
Trilateral-a-May tatlong tabi ó gilid.
Trill-n-Inig ng voces.
Trillion-n-Isang libong angawangaw.
Trim-a-Malinis; ayos; husay.
Trim-v-Ayusin; huyasin; putlin ang sanga.
Trimmer-n-Taga ayos.
Trimming-n-Hiyas; sangkap.
Trinal-a-Nakatatlong duble.
Trine-a-Nakatatlong duble.
Trinitarian-a Nauukol sa trinidad.
Trinitarian-n-Manampalataya sa doctrina ni Santisima trinidad.
Trinitarianism-n-Pananampalataya sa Santisima Trinidad.
Trinity-n-Santisima Trininad; katipunan ng tatlo.
Trinket-n-Laseta; sangkap na munti.
Trinominal-a-May tatlong parte.
Trio-n-Tatlo.
Trip-n-Tisod; tipiaw; dapa; paglalakbay; paglakad.
Trip-v-Tumipiaw; tumisod; madapa; dumapa.
Tripe n-Tokong; bituka; isaw.
Tripetalous-a-May tatlong dahon) nauukol sa bulaklak).
Triple-a-Makatatlong duble.
Triple-v-Dublihin ng makatlo.
Triplet-n-Kapisanan ng tatlo.
Triplicate-a-May tatlong duble; triplicado.
Triplicate-n-Isa sa tatlo.
Triplication-n-Pagtataluhin.
Tripod-n-Tukod na may tatlong paa.
Tripping-n-Pagtitisod.
Tripping-a-Matisurin.
Trisect-v-Tatluhin.
Trisection-n-Pagtatatluhin.
Trite a-Luma; laon; gasgas: ulianin.
Triumph-n-Pananalo; pala; dangal; pagsupil.
Triumph-v-Manalo.
Triturate-v-Dikdikin; gumiling; durugin.
Trivet-n-Bagay na may tatlong paa.
Trivial-a-Munti ang halaga; walang halaga ó kabuluhan.
Triviality-n-Kawalan ng halaga.
Triweekly-a-Mangyayari makatatlo sa isang lingo.
Triweekly-n-Dahon ó pahayagan na lumitaw ng makatatlo sa isang lingo.

Troche-n-Tableta.
Trod-Trodden-v. imp. & p. p.-Niyurakan; tinapakan; niyurak.
Troll-v-Hilahin ang taga sa tubig; magbaliwas.
Troll-n-Galaw; kilos.
Trollop-n-Tawong tamad; tawong salaula; patutot; puta.
Trombone-n-Trombon.
Troop-n-Hukbo; bunton ng tawo; tropa
Troop-v-Lumakad; bumunton.
Trooper-n-Sundalong kaballeria; kabayo ng sundalo.
Trophy-n-Alaala ng isang labanan.
Trot-v-Sumagsag; yumagyag.
Trot-n-Sagsag; yagyag.
Trotter-n Kabayong mainam sumagsag.
Troth-n-Pananampalataya; katotohanan; katapatan ng loob.
Trouble-n-Kahirapan; abala; kabigatan; kasakitan; gulo.
Trouble-v-Abalahin; pahirapan; umabala; tuksuhin.
Troublesome-a-Magulo; mahirap; makayayamut; mayamutin.
Troublous-a-Mahirap; maraming abala; mabigat.
Trough-n-Labanan; sabsaban.
Trounce-v-Hampasin; paluin.
Troupe n-Kapisanan ng manga komediante.
Trousers-n-Salawal.
Trousseau-n-Traje de boda; damit na pangkasal.
Trow-v-Sumampalataya; sumapantaha.
Trowel-n-Cuchara.
Truant-a-Pabaya; tamad.
Truant-n-Tawong pabaya; tawong tamad.
Truce n-Pagpapahinga ng labanan.
Truck-n Gulong na munti; pangangalakal; manga bagay na munti.
Truck-v-Ilagay sa gulong; mangalakal.
Truckage-n-Pangangalakal.
Truckle-n-Gulong na munti.
Truckle-v-Umayon; pumayag; sumunod; sumuko.
Truck man-n-Mangangalakal; kargador.
Truculence-Truculency-n-Kasalbahian; kabagsikan; kabangisan.
Truculent-a-Mabangis; mabagsik; salbahi; bastos.
Trudge-v-Lumakad.
True-a-Tunay; totoo; tapat ang loob.
True-v-Ayusin; totohanin.
Truism-n Katotohanan.
Trump-n-Trumpo.
Trump-v-Lagyan ng trumpo.
Trumpery-n-Hibo; kahibuan; daya; kasinungalingan.
Trumpet-n-Trumpeta.

Trumpet-v-Ipahayag sa trumpeta; ipahayag; ipatalastas; tumunog.

Truncate-v-Putlin; pilayin.

Truncate-a-Putol; pilay.

Truncatión-n-Kapilayan, pagputol.

Truncheon-n-Tungkod.

Trundle-n-Gulong na munti.

Trundle-v-Gumulong; gulungin.

Trundle-bed-n-Hihigan na munti.

Trunk-n-Puno; katawan; baul; kaban.

Trunnel-n-Pakong kahoy.

Truss-n-Pamigkis.

Truss-v-Talian ng mahigpit.

Trust-n-Paghahabilin; pananampalataya; katapatan ng loob; pautang.

Trust-v-Pautangan; ipaghabilin.

Trustee-n-Ukol; katiwala; pintakasi·

Trustful-a-Maniniwalain tapat ang loob.

Trust worthy-a-Dapat maniwala; dapat ipaghabilin.

Trusty-a-Dapat maniwala; tapat ang loob.

Truth-n-Totoo; katotohanan.

Truthful-a-Walang labis at walang kulang; totoo; hindi sinungaling; totoo.

Try-v-Subukin; tantuin; tikman; manubok.

Trying-a-Makayayamot; mayamutin; mahirap.

Tub-n-Batia.

Tub-v-Ilagay sa batia.

Tube-n-Tubo.

Tuber-n-Tungo.

Tubercle-n Bukol.

Tuberculosis-n-Sakit ng baga.

Tuberose-a-Mabukol.

Tubing-n-Tubo.

Tubular a-Parang tubo.

Tubulate-a-Parang tubo.

Tubuliform-a-Hitsurang tubo.

Tuck-n-Tunog ng tambol; tiklop ng damit; urong; plegas.

Tuck-v-Urungin.

Tucker-v-Pumagal; pumagod; pagalin; pagurin.

Tuesday-n-Martes.

Tuft-n-Lambo; tali ng buhok ó damo.

Tufty-a-Malambo.

Tug-n-Batak; hila; biwas.

Tug-v-Tumatak; batakin; biwasin; humila; hilahin.

Tuition-n-Kuartang nagbabayad sa maestro.

Tumble-v-Bumual; mabual; ibual.

Tumble-n-Bual; pagkabual.

Tumefaction-n-Pamamaga; bukol; pigsa.

Tumefy-v-Mamaga; bumukol; pumigsa.

Tumid-a-Namaga; nakabukol.

Tumidity-Tumidness-n-Pamamaga.

Tumor-n-Bukol; pigsa.

Tumular-Tumulous-a-Nakabunton.

Tumult-n-Gulo; ingay; away; babag; pagkagulo ng madla.

Tumultuary-Tumultuous-a-Magulo; maingay; malikot; balisa; walang ayos.

Tun-n-Bariles na malaki.

Tune-n-Tunog; voces; tugtog.

Tune-v-Tumugtog; tumugtog; ayusin ang tunog ng kuerdas.

Tuneful-a-Matunog.

Tuneless-a-Walang tunog; walang ayos ang pagtugtog.

Tungsten-n-Metal na matigas at marupok.

Tunic-n-Baro.

Tunnel-n-Butas sa ilalim ng lupa; hukay sa bundok.

Tunnel-v-Humukay sa bundok; butasin ang bundok.

Turban-n-Tukarol.

Turbid-a-May latak; malabo; magulo; marumi.

Turbinate-a-Napapainog.

Turbine-n-Gulong na iniinog ng tubig.

Turbulence-n-Kalikotan; kaharutan; pagkabalisa.

Turbulent-a-Malikot; maharot; balisa.

Tureen-n-Lalagyan ng sopas; supera.

Turf-n-Lupa.

Turfy-a-Malupa.

Turgid-a-Namaga; namanas.

Turk-n-Turko.

Turkey-n-Pavo.

Turkey red a Kundiman.

Turkish-a-Nauukol sa turko.

Turkish-n-Wikang turko.

Turmoil-n-Gulo; kaguluhan.

Turn-v-Pihitin; pumihit; lumiko; pilihin; lumalik; lumingon.

Turn-n-Pagsimana; pagkit; liko; pihit; paghahalili.

Turning a-Paikitikit.

Turning n-Pagikit.

Turner-n-Manlalalik.

Turn coat-n Tawong tumalikod sa kaniyang bandera ó sa kaniyang manga kaibigan; tawong taksil ó lilo.

Turnip-n-Singkamas.

Turn key-n-Bantay sa bilango.

Turnout-n-Pagsipot; diwang.

Turnover-n-Pagkabual.

Turnpike-n-Lansangan; daan.

Turpitude-n-Kapurulan ng isip; kaululan; kahalayan; kasamaan; sama; kapangitan; kalupaan.

Turquoise-n-Pagong.

Turret-n-Torre na mababa sa ibabaw ng pandirigma.

Turtle-n-Pagong.

Turtle dove-n-Kalapati.

Tush-Tusk n-Pangil.

Tussle-*n*-Buno.
Tussle-*v*-Magbuno; lumaban.
Tut-*inter.*-Oroy.
Tutelage-*n*-Pagsasang galang; pag iiwi; pag iiñgat; pagtuturo.
Tutelar-Tutelary-*a*-Naunkol sa pag iiñgat ó sa pagtuturo.
Tutor-*n*-Taga turo; maestro; taga iñgat.
Tutor-*v*-Magturo; turnan; mamahala.
Twaddle-*v*-Magsalita nğ walang kabuluhan.
Twaddle-*n*-Salita na walang kabuluhan.
Twain-*n*-Ang dalawa.
Twain-*a*-Dalawa.
Twang *n*-Tunog nğ kuerdas.
Twang-*v*-Tumunog parang kuerdas.
Tweak-*v*-Pindutin; kurutin; pumindot; piralin.
Tweak-*n*-Pindot; kurot; piral.
Tweezers-*n*-Ipit; sipit; panipit.
Twelfth-*a*-Ika labiñg dalawa.
Twelfth-*n*-Ang ika labing dalawa.
Twelve *a*-Labing dalawa.
Twelve-*n*-Ang labingdalawa.
Twelvemonth-*n*-Taon.
Twentieth-*a*-Ikadalawangpuo.
Twentieth-*n*-Ang ikadalawangpuo.
Twenty-*a*-Dalawangpuo.
Twenty-*n*-Ang dalawangpuo.
Twice-*adv.*-Makalawa.
Twiddle-*v*-Hipuin; kapain.
Twig-*n*-Sanğang munti.
Twig-*v*-Malaman;maintindihan;manubok
Twilight-*n*-Liwayway.
Twilight-*v* Lumiwayway.
Twin-*n*-Kambal.
Twine-*n*-Pisi; pilipit.
Twine-*v*-Pumilipit.
Twinge-*n*-Batak; pindot; sakit; hapdi.
Twinge-*v*-Batakin; sumakit; pumindot; pindutin; humapdi.
Twinkle-*v*-Magningning; kumisap; mañginig.
Twinkle *n*-Ningning; kislap; kisap; inig.

Twinkling-*n*-Kisapmata; dali.
Twirl-*v*-Ikirin; umikit.
Twirl-*n*-Ikit.
Twist-*v*-Pumilipit; pilipitin; lubiring balisunsuñgin-
Twist-*n* Pilipit.
Twisted-*a*-Nakapilipit.
Twit-*v*-Biruin; tuksuhin.
Twitch-*v*-Bumatak; agawin; batakin.
Twitch-*n*-Batak.
Twitter-*n* Manunukso.
Twitter-*v*-Sumiap.
Twitter-*n*-Siap.
Two *a*-Dalawa.
Two-*n*-Ang dalawa.
Two-edged-*a*-May dalawang gilid; may dalawang talim.
Two-handed-*a*-May dalawang kamay.
Tymbal *n*-Kaja.
Type-*n*-Uliran;parisan;limbag;mañga litik na ginagamit sa limbagan; tulad; lahi.
Type writer-*n*-Makinillang sumulat.
Type writing-*n*-Paggamit nğ makinilla sa pagsulat.
Typhoid-*n*-Tifodea.
Typhoon-*n*-Sigwa; bagyo sa dagat.
Typhus *n*-Tifodea.
Typic-Typical-*a*-Naunkol sa titik.
Typify-*v*-Parisan.
Typographer-*n*-Taga limbag.
Typography-*n*-Paglimbag.
Tyrannic-Tyrannical-*a*-Nauukol sa haring mabagsik; mabagsik; walang awa; mabañgis; bañgin.
Tyrannicide-*n*-Ang natay sa haring mabagsik.
Tyrannize-*v*-Maghari nğ mabagsik.
Tyrannous-*a*-Mabagsik; mabañgis; bañgin; walang awa; walang habag.
Tyranny *n*-Kabagsikan; bañgis; panamahala nğ mabagsik.
Tyrant-*n*-Haring mabagsik.
Tyro-*n*-Bagong nagaaral.
Tzar-*n*-Hari sa Ruso.

U

Ubiquitary-Ubi,u itous-*a* Nakakaharap sa lahat nğ lugar.
Ubiquity-*n*-Pagkakaharap sa lahat nğ lugal
Udder-*n*-Puklo.
Udometer *n*-Panukat nğ ulan.
Ugly-*a*-Pañgit; hamak; bastos; nakasusuklam; nakaririmarim.
Ugliness-*n* Kapañgitan; kahamakan; kahalayan; kalibugan; kalupaan.
Ulcer-*n*-Sugat na may nana.
Ulcerate-*v*-Magnana; ang sugat.

Ulceration-*n*-Pagbubulok nğ sugat.
Ulcerous-*a* May nana.
Ullage-*n*-Kakulanğan sa pagpuno nğ bariles.
Ulster-*n*-Damit na pangibabaw.
Ulterior-*a*-Sa malayo; malayong; malayo pa; ibayo.
Ultimate *a* Huling; kahulihulihan.
Ultimatum-*n*-Huling utos nğ hukom; kahulihulihang pasiya ó salita nğ hari ó hukom.

44

Ultimo-a-Nakaraan lamang.

Ultra-a-Labis; lampas; lagpos;

Ultra-marine-a-Sa kabilang ibayo ñg dagat

Ultra montane-a-Na sa kabilang ibayo ñg bundok.

Ultra mundane-a-Na sa itaas ñg kapang-yarihan ñg mundo.

Umber-a-Maitim; kayumangi.

Umbilic-a-Nauukol sa pusod.

Umbilicus-n-Pusod ñg katawan.

Umbles-n-Mañga isaw at laman ñg usa.

Umbrage-n-Lilim; kaliliman; selos; agam-agam na loob.

Umbrageous-a-Malilim.

Umbrella-n-Payongna pangu-lan;payong.

Umpire-n-Taga hatol.

UUn-Wala.

Unable-a-Walang kaya.

Unabridged-a-Walang hanga.

Unacceptable-a-Di dapat tangapin.

Unaccountable-a-Di kailañgan sagotin; malihim.

Unadvisable-a-Di dapat.

Unalloyed-a-Walang halo.

Unamiable-a-Mapootin; di mabuting loob.

Unanimous-a-Magkaisa; walang kapin-tasan ñg lahat.

Unanimity-n-Pagkakaisa; pagkakaayos.

Unanswerable-a-Di makasasagot.

Unap-a-Di bagay.

Unassuming-a-Mahinahon; mabait.

Unavoidable-a-Di mailagin.

Unaware-a-Di nalalaman; pabaya.

Unawares-adv.-Bigla; hindi inisip muna; pagdaka.

Unbalanced-a-Di nakatimbang.

Unbecoming-a-Di bagay; masama bas-tos; hindi dapat.

Unbelief-n-Kakulañgan ñg pananampa-lataya.

Unbeliever-n-Ang ayaw sumampalataya.

Unbend-r-Towirin. alisin ang hubog.

Unbind-v-Kalagin; alisin ang tali.

Unborn-a-Hindi pa ipinaganak.

Unbounded-a-Walang hanga.

Unbreakable-a-Di mababasag;di masisira

Unbraid-v-Kalagin ang tinirintas.

Unbridle-v-Alisin ang kabesada; kalagin.

Unbroken-a-Di nasira; buo.

Unburden-v-Alisin ang bigat.

Uncalled-for-a-Hindi kailañgan.

Uncertain-a-Di pa totoo; may duda.

Uncertainty-n-Kabulaan; tayum.

Uncharitable-a-Walang awa: walang ha-bag; hindi marunong maawa.

Unchaste-a-Marumi; marungis; hindi ma-linis; malibog; mahalay.

Unchastity-n-Kalibugan; karumihan, dungis; kahalayan.

Unchristian-a-Hindi binyagan; di bagay sa bininyagan.

Uncivil-a-Di marunong gumalang; wa-lang galang.

Uncivilized-a-Salbahi; hindi marunong.

Uncle-n-Amain; tata; kapatid na lalaki; ñg ina ó ama.

Unclean-a-Marumi; salahula; marungis.

Uncleanliness-n-Kasalahulaan; karumi-han; dungis.

Uncomfortable-a-Balisa; di magaling sa katawan.

Uncommon-n-Di karaniwan; hindi hayag.

Uncompromising-a-Matigas ang ulo; ayaw umayon.

Unconcern-n-Kawalan ñg interes ó ka-liñga.

Unconcerned-a-Walang interes; hindi nakikialam.

Unconditional-a-Walang salitaan.

Unconscionable-a-Matigas ang ulo.

Unconscious-a-Walang damdam.

Unconstitutional-a-Hindi umayon sa mañga utos.

Uncontrollable-a-Di masupil.

Uncouth-a-Salahula.

Uncover-v-Alisin ang takip.

Unction-n-Pagdidilig ñg langis sa ulo.

Unctions-a-Mataba; malañgis; malagkit.

Undaunted-a-Walang takot; matapang.

Undeceive-v-Liwanagan; hañguin sa pagkahibo.

Undecided-a-Nagsasalawahan; saliwa-hang loob.

Undeniable-a-Di magkakaila; di mata-likuran.

Under-adv.-Nasasa ilalim.

Under-prep.-Sa ilalim.

Under-a-Ilalim.

Under brush-n-Kaugoygoyan.

Under clothes-n-Mañga damit sa loob.

Under do-c-Kumulang.

Under drain-n-Sangka sa ilalim nang lupa.

Under go-v-Magtiis; tiisin.

Undergraduate-n-Ang nagaaral na wala pang titulo.

Underground-a-Nasa sa ilalim ñg lupa.

Underground-adv.-Sa ilalim ñg lupa.

Undergrowth-n-Kasukalan na tumutubo sa gubat.

Underhand-a-Lihim; magdaraya.

Underhanded-a-Magdaraya. palihim; ma-lihim.

Underlay-v-Ilagay sa ilalim.

Underlie-v-Lumagay sa ilalim.

Underline-v-Guhitin sa ibaba.

Underlining-n-Pagguguhit sa ibaba.

Underling-n-Tawong hamak ó mababa ang kalagayan; tawong malungkot.

Undermine-v-Hukayin buhat sa ilalim.
Undermost-a-Ang napailalim na lahat.
Underneath-adv.-Sa ilalim.
Underneath-prep.-Nasa sa ilalim.
Underrate-v-Hamakin; halagahin ng mababa.
Underscore-v-Guhitin sa ibaba.
Undersell-v-Magbili ng mura pa kay sa iba.
Understand-v-Matalastas; talastasin; malaman; mawatasan; napakingan; duminig; mabatid; umintindi.
Understanding-n-Karunungan; dunong; watas; bait.
Undertake-v-Subukin; matikman; mulang; magsimula.
Undertaking-n-Gawa; paggagawa.
Undertone-n-Voces na mababa.
Undertook-v. imp.-Nagmula; inumpisa; sinubok.
Undervalue-v-Halagahan ng wala sa karapatan.
Underwent-v. imp.-Tiniis.
Underwood-n-Kaugoygoyan.
Underwrite-v-Pirmahin; sumulat sa ilalim ng ibang sulat.
Undeserving-a-Di marapatin; marawal; hamak; di dapat.
Undo-v-Baguhin; baliktarin.
Undoubted-a-Maliwanag; walang duda.
Undress-v-Maghubad; maghubo; ihubad; ihubo; hubaran; humubdan.
Undress-n-Pagkahubo; pagkahubad.
Undue-a-Di pa panahon.
Undulate-v-Umuga; umalonalon.
Undulation-n-Panginginig.
Unearth-v-Ipalitaw; ilitaw; tuklasin.
Unearthly-a-Hindi naukol sa lupa.
Uneasiness-n-Pagkabalisa; balisa; kalikutan.
Uneasy-a-Balisa; malikot.
Unequal-a-Hindi parejo ó kapantay; iba; bakat; hindi tama; hindi ayos.
Unequaled-a-Walang kaparis; walang katulad.
Unerring a-Walang sala; di magkasala.
Uneven-a-Hindi patag ó pantay.
Unexampled-a-Walang katulad; hindi sumnnod sa anomang halimbawa.
Unexceptionable-a-Walang kapintasan.
Unexpected a-Bigla; hindi tinalaga; hindi inisip muna.
Unfair-a-Di tama; daya; magdaraya.
Unfaithful-a-Taksil; lilo; suitik.
Unfasten-v-Kalagin; kumalag.
Unfathomable-a-Di matarok.
Unfavorable-a-Di mawiwili.
Unfeeling-a-Walang pakiramdam.
Unfilial-a-Di bagay sa bata; di bagay sa anak.

Unfinished-a-Di pa utas; di yari; kulang pa; hilaw.
Unfit-a-Di bagay; walang kaya.
Unfit-v-Mawala ng kaya ó kabagayan.
Unfold-v-Ilatag; magkatkat; banatin; unatin.
Unfortunate-a-Walang kapalaran; sawing kapalaran; buisit; masama.
Unforseen-a-Hindi sinadya; hindi tinalaga; hindi inisip muna.
Unfounded-a-Walang katowiran.
Unfriendly a-Di marunong magkaibigan; galit.
Unfruitful-a-Karat; baog.
Unfurl-v-Iladlad.
Unfurnish-v-Alisin ang kasangkapan.
Ungainly-a-Pangit; bastos; magaspang
Ungenerous-a-Kuripot; maramot; di maganda ang loob.
Unglued-a-Nabak bak.
Ungodly-a-Di binyagan; makasalanan; masama; laban sa utos ng P. Dios.
Ungovernable-a-Di masupil.
Ungraceful-a-Magaspang; bastos.
Ungracious-a-Walang galang; bastos; masamang ugali.
Ungrateful-a-Hindi marunong magutang na loob; buisit.
Ungent-n-Gamot na pangpahid sa sugat.
Ungula-n-Paa; kuko.
Ungulate n-Anomang hayop na may apat na paa.
Unhallow-v-Lumampastanganan sa ngalang ng P. Dios.
Unhallowed-a-Laban sa utos ng P. Dios.
Unhandy-a-Bastos ang gawa.
Unhappy-a-Di masaya; malungkot; malumbay; kulang palad.
Unhealthy-a-Makasisira sa katawan; may sakit.
Unhinge-v-Alisin ang visagra.
Unhitch-v-Kalagin.
Unholy-a-Laban sa utos ng P. Dios; makasalanan.
Unhorse-v-Mahulog sa kabayo.
Unhurt a-Walang sakit.
Unfoliate-a-May isang bulaklak lamang.
Uniform-a-Makakaakma; magkakaisa; nagkaparis; ayos; pantay.
Uniformity-n-Pagkakaisa; pagkakaayos; pagkakaayon.
Union-n-Pagkakalapit; kapisanan; katipunan.
Unintelligible-a-Hindi maintindihan; di matalastasin.
Uniped-a-May isang paa lamang.
Unique-a-Di karaniwan; bugtong.

Unison-*n*-Pagkakapisan; pagkakaisa; pagkakalakip.

Unisonance-*n*-Pagkakaisa; pagkakaayon.

Unisonant-*a*-Nakapipisan; magkakaisa.

Unit-*n*-Isa.

Unitarian-*n*-Ang sumampalataya sa P. Dios lamang at ayaw sa Anak at sa Espiritu Santo.

Unite-*v*-Pumisan; isama; idugtong; ilangkap; magsangayon; ibahog; idayti; ilakip; ikaling.

United-*a*-Nakakapisan; kasama; nakahalo; nagkakasama.

Unitedly-*adv.*-Sabaysabay; nakakalakip.

Unity-*n*-Pagkakaisa; pagkakaayon; pagkakapisan.

Univalve-*n*-Susó.

Universal-*a*-Maalam sa lahat; alam ng lahat; nakasasaklaw; karaniwan.

Universally-*adv.*-Kasali ang lahat; walang ipinwera.

Universe-*n*-Sangkalibutan; sangkatawohan; sandaigdigan.

Unjust-*a*-Hindi tama; hindi tapat ang loob; falso.

Unkind-*a*-Bastos; mabagsik hindi marunong maawa.

Unkindly-*v*-Mabagsik; bastos.

Unknown-*a*-Di nakikilala; di kilala.

Unlawful-*a*-Laban sa kautusan; libis sa katowiran.

Unlearn-*v*-Malimutan.

Unlearned-*a*-Ulol; walang tnto.

Unless-*conj.*-Kung hindi; kundi.

Unlike-*a*-Iba; hindi katulad; hindi kaparis.

Unlikely-*adv.*-Hindi siguro; walang kasiguruhan.

Unlimited-*a*-Walang hanga.

Unload-*v*-Ibisan ó ibsan ang nilulan.

Unlock-*v*-Buksan ang seradura.

Unloose-*v*-Luagin kalagin.

Unloosen-*v*-Kalagin; luagin; lumuag.

Unlucky-*a*-Walang kapalaran; kulaug palad; sawing kapalaran.

Unman-*v*-Humina ang loob.

Unmanly-*a*-Di parang lalaki.

Unmannerly-*a*-Masamang kilos; bastos; walang galang.

Unmeaning-*a*-Walang kahulugan.

Unmerciful-*a*-Walang awa; walang habag.

Unmeritable-*a*-Di marapatin.

Unmistakable-*a*-Walang sala; walang mali.

Unnatural-*a*-Di natural.

Unnecessary-*a*-Hindi kailangan.

Unneigborly-*a*-Di marunong makipagkapwa tawo.

Unnerve-*v*-Dumuag; humina; ang loob.

Unnumbered-*a*-Hindi nakabilang.

Unpack-*v*-Buksan ang balutan ó kahon at alisin ang laman.

Unpalatable-*a*-Walang lasa; matabaug, makasusnya; makasusunod.

Unparalleled-*a*-Walang katulad ó kaparis; gansal.

Unpin-*v*-Alisin ang aspili.

Unpleasant-*a*-Masusuklam; malungkot; masaklap.

Unpolished-*a*-Bastos; magaspang; mabalat.

Unprecedented-*a*-Walang nauna;primero.

Unprejudiced-*n*-Hindi nalugit.

Unpretending-*a*-Mahinahon; mabait; mabini.

Unprincipled-*a*-Walang kabanalan; hamak; taksil.

Unproductive-*a*-Hindi makikinabangan; di mamumunga; karat.

Unprofitable-*a*-walang pakinabang; walang tubo.

Unpromising-*a*-Di magaling; hamak.

Unqualified-*a*-Hindi umabot sa grado.

Unquestionable-*a*-Walang tanong; di maitatanong; toto; maliwanag.

Unquiet-*a*-Balisa; malikot; magulo.

Unravel-*v*-Tumustos.

Unready-*a*-Di pa nakagayak.

Unreal-*a*-Hindi totoo; sinungaling.

Unreasonable-*a*-Walang katowiran; matigas ang ulo.

Unreliable-*a*-Di dapat maniwala; walang kasiguruhan.

Unremitting-*a*-Walang lubay, walang patid.

Unreserved-*a*-Walang lihim; tapat ang loob,

Unrest-*n*-Pagkabalisa; kalikotan; kabalisahan; kawalan ng tulog; kagnluhan·

Unrestrained-*a*-Malaya; malnag; walang hanga.

Unrighteous-*a*-Masama; makasalanan; laban sa utos.

Unripe-*a*-Hilaw; sariwa; hindi pa magulang; mura.

Unroll-*v*-Banatin; unatin; ilatag.

Unruffled-*a*-Tahimik; walang gulit; makinis; hindi magusot.

Unsaddle-*v*-Humulog sa siya.

Unsafe-*a*-May pauganib.

Unsay-*v*-Baguhin ang salita.

Unscrew-*v*-Alisin ang tornillo.

Unscrupulous-*a*-Walang galang; bastos; sinungaling; hindi tapat ang loob.

Unseal-*v*-Bakbakin.

Unsearchable-*a*-Di mahahanapin.

Unseasonable-*a*-Wala sa panahon; labas sa panahon.

Unseat-*v*-Mahulog sa upuan.

Unseemly-*a*-Di bagay; di dapat.

Unseemly-*adv.*-Malibog.
Unseen-*a*-Hindi nakakita; hindi mahalata; hindi sinadya.
Unsettle-*v*-Gumalaw; galawin; gumulo.
Unsightly-*a*-Pañgit.
Unskillful-*a*-Hindi matalas; mapurol ang isip; hindi sanay.
Unsociable-*a*-Ayaw makipagkapwatawo.
Unsound-*a*-Di matibay; mahina; may sakit
Unsparing-*a*-Walang tawad.
Unstring-*c*-Alisin ang kuerdas.
Unsuccessful-*a*-Walang palad. kulang palad; malungkot; malumbay
Unsuitable-*a*-Di bagay.
Untangle-*v*-Ayusin; iayos.
Unthinking-*a*-Di maisipan; pabaya.
Untie-*v*-Mabugnos; ibugnos. kalagin; luagin ang tali.
Until-*prep.*-Hangang,
Until-*conj.*-Hangang.
Untimely-*a*-Wala sa panahon.
Untimely-*avd.*-Labas sa panahon.
Unto-*prep.*-Hangang.
Untold-*a*-Hindi pa sinabi.
Untouched-*a*-Dalisay; malinis; hindi nahipo.
Untoward-*a*-Pabaliktad.
Untowardly-*adv.*-Pabaliktad.
Untrue-*a*-Sinuñgaling; hindi totoo.
Untruth-*n*-Kasinuñgaliñgan.
Untwist-*v*-Tuwirin.
Unusual-*a*-Di karaniwan.
Unutterable-*a*-Di masabi.
Unvarnished-*a*-Walang varnis.
Unveil-*v*-Alisin ang takip.
Unwarrantable-*a*-Di dapat; walang karapatan.
Unwearied-*a*-Di pagod; walang pagod.
Unweave-*v*-Ilatag; tumastas; ang hinabi.
Unwell-*a*-Di magaling; may sakit; may karamdaman.
Unwholesome-*a*-Di magaling sa katawan; di bagay sa sikmura.
Unwieldy-*a*-Malaki; mahirap mamahala.
Unwilling-*a*-Ayaw; walang gusto.
Unwind-*v*-Luslosan; kidkirin.
Unwise-*a*-Hindi marunong; ulol.
Unwittingly-*adc.*-Wala sa loob.
Unwonted-*a*-Di karaniwan.
Unworthy-*a*-Marawal; hamak; walang karapatan.
Unwrap-*v*-Buksan ang balutan.
Unwritten-*a* Hindi nakasulat.
Unyoke-*v*-Kalagin.
Up-*ade.*-Sa itaas.
Up-*prep.*-Sa itaas.
Up-*n*-Taas.
Upbear-*v*-Itaas; lumaban,

Unbraid-*v*-Pintasin; parusahin; payohan; pasiyahan: murahin; alipustain.
Upheave-*v*-Tumaas.
Upheaval-*n*-Pagalsa.
Upheld-*v & p. p.*-Tinaas; sinustento; lumaban.
Uphill-*a*-Sa gawing itaas ñg bundok.
Uphold-*v*-Magsustento; lumaban; kumalong.
Upholster-*v*-Lagyan ñg sapin sa mañga kasangkapan..
Upland-*n*-Lupang mataas.
Uplift-*v*-Itaas; buhatin.
Upmost-*a*-Kataasan; mataas sa lahat; naipaibabaw sa lahat.
Upon-*prep.*-Sa ibabaw.
Upper-*a*-Ibabaw.
Upper-*n*-Ang nasasa ibabaw.
Upper-lip-*n*-Ñguso.
Upper most-*a*-Kataastaasan,
Uppish-*a*-Palalo; hambog.
Upraise-*v*-Itaas; buhatin.
Upright-*a*-Matowid; tapat; husto.
Upright-*adv.*-Patayo.
Upright-*n*-Haligi.
Uprise-*v*-Umalsa; lumaban.
Uproar-*n* Kaguluhan: kaiñgayan.
Uproarious-*a*-Magulo; maiñgay.
Uproot-*v*-Bunutin buhat sa ugat.
Upset-*v*-Ibual.
Upset-*n*-Pagkabual,
Upset-*a*-Nakatayo; fijo; halagang totoo buo ang loob.
Upshot-*n*-Dulo; ang nangyari.
Upside-*n*-Mukha sa itaas.
Upside down-*adv.*-Nakataob.
Upstart-*n*-Tawong palalo at hambog.
Upstart-*v*-Kumilos ñg pabigla.
Upward-Upwards-*adv.*-Sa gawing itaas.
Upward-*a*-Gawing itaas.
Urban-*a*-Nauukol sa bayan,
Urbane-*a*-Magalang; makinis. maganda; marunong makipagkapwatawo.
Urbanity-*n*-Galang mabuting pagungali; kabanalan.
Urchin-*n*-Batang lalaki.
Urge-*v*-Pilitin; pumilit; iudyok.
Urgency-*n*-Kakailañgan; kapilitan.
Urgent-*a*-Kailañgan.
Urinal-*n* Ihian.
Urinary-*a*-Nauukol sa ihi.
Urinary-*n*-Ihian.
Urinate-*v*-Manubig.
Urine-*n*-Ihi.
Urn-*n*-Vaso.
Us-*proi.*-Kami; tayo; amin; atin: amin; natin.
Use-*v*-Gamitin; tinagin.
Use-*n*-Paggamit; uso; kaugalian.
Usage-*n*-Paggamit; kaugalian; uso.

Useful-a-Magagamit; makikinabañgan;
  magagamitin; bagay.
Usefulness-n-Pakinabang; paggamit; ka-
  gamitan.
Useless-a-Di ginagamit; walang kabulu-
  han; walang kahulugan.
Usual-a-Karaniwan.
Usurp-v-Angkinin; lupigin; gagahin.
Usurpation-n-Pagaangkin; lupig; kalu-
  pigan.
Utensil-n-Kasangkapan.
Utility n-Paggamit; kagamitan; pakina-
  bang; kasaysayan; kahulugan.
Utilization-n-Pag-gamit; kagamitan.

Utilize-v-Gamitin.
Utmost-a-Kalayolayoan; kahulihulihan;
  kadulodulohan; kalakilakihan.
Utmost-n-Kaduluan; kalakihan; hanga.
Utter-a-Lubos; puspos; buo.
Utter-v-Magsabi; magsalita; sabihin.
Utter most-a-Kadulodulohan.
Uterrance-n-Kasabihan; salita; pagsabi;
  sabi.
Uveous-a-Parang uvas.
Uxorious-a-Masupil ó sumuko sa asa-
  wang babayi;
Uxoriousness-n-Pagsuko sa asawa.

Vacancy-n-Kawalan ñg laman; katama-
  ran; pagpapahiñga.
Vacant a-Walang laman; malaya; wa-
  lang ginagawa.
Vacate-c-Umalis; maiwan; pawalan ñg
  kabuluhan.
Vacation-n-Pagpapahiñga; paglilibang.
Vaccinate-v-Magtanim ñg bulutong.
Vaccinator-n-Magtatanim ñg bulutong.
Vaccination-n-Pagtatanim; ñg bulutong.
Vaccine-a-Nauukol sa baka.
Vacilate-v Gumiraygiray; gumalaw.
Vacillation-n-Giray; galaw; paggigiray-
  giray,
Vacuity-n-Kawalan ñg laman.
Vacuous-a-Walang laman.
Vacuum-n-Lugal na walang laman.
Vagabond-n-Hampaslupa.
Vagabond-a Hampaslupa,
Vagabondage-Vagabondery-Vagabon-
  dism n-Pagkahampaslupa.
Vagary-n-Paglipad ñg isip; nais; pita;
  nasa.
Vagrancy-n-Paghahampaslupa.
Vagrant-a-I abaya; hampaslupa.
Vagrant-n-Hampaslupa,
Vague-a-Malabo; di maliwanag; magulo;
  walang ayos; di siguro.
Vagueness n-Kalabuan.
Vail-n-Tabing; takip ñg mukha.
Vail-v-Maglagay ñg tabing; itakpan ang
  mukha.
Vain-a-Palalo; hambog.
Vainness-n-Kahambugan; kapalaluan.
Vain glorious-a-Palalongpalalo.
Vain glory-n-Kapalaluan; kahambugan;
  kayabañgan,
Vale-n-Parang.
Valediction n-Paalam.
Valedictory-n-Pagpapaalam.
Valedictory-a Nauukol sa paalam.

Valet-n-Alila ñg isang lalaki.
Valiant-a-Malakas. matapang; mañgahas;
  matinig na loob.
Valid-a-Matowid; ayon sa utos.
Validity-Validness-n-Katowiran; pagka-
  kaayon sa utos.
Valise-n-Saco de noche.
Valley-n-Bukid sa pagitan ñg dalawang
  bundok.
Valor-n-Bisa; tapang; katapañgan; ka-
  pañgasan; hinapang; kamahalan.
Valorous-a-Matapang; mañgahas.
Value-n-Halaga.
Value-v-Halagahan; tasahan; lagyan ñg
  halaga; mahalin.
Valuable-a-Mahalaga; may halaga.
Valuation-n-Halaga; katasahan.
Valueless-a-Walang halaga; walang ka-
  buluhan.
Vamp-n-Itaas ñg sapatos.
Vampire-n-Bayakan.
Van-n-Harapan ñg hukbo; bagol.
Vane-n-Kasangkapan na tinuturo kung
  saan nangaling ang hañgin.
Van guard-n-Bantay sa una.
Vanish-v-Mawala; kumupas; lumipol.
Vanity-n-Kapalaluan; kahambugan; ka-
  yabañgan.
Vanquish-v-Daigin; supilin; pasukuin.
Vanquishment-n-Pagpasuko; pagsupil.
Vantage-n-Pakinabang; tubo.
Vapid-a-Malansa; lipas; matabang; wa-
  lang lasa.
Vapor-n-Usok; vapor.
Vapor-v-Umusok.
Vaporize-c-Maging usok.
Variable-a-Hindi pirme; iba,t, iba.
Variableness-Variability-n-Kaibhan.
Variance-n-Kaibhan; pagtatalo; away;
  basagulo.
Variation n-Kaibhan.

Variegate-v-Mangiba,t, iba.
Variety-n-Sarisari; pagkakaiba.
Variola-n-Bulutong; sakit na bulutong.
Variolar-Variolous-a May bulutong.
Varioloid-a-Nauukol sa bulutong.
Varioloid-n-Bulutong tubig.
Various a-Sarisari; iba,t. iba.
Varlet-n-Tawong hamak at bastos.
Varnish n-Varnis.
Varnish-v-Magvarnis; pahiran ng varnis.
Vary-v-Magbago; bumago.
Vase n-Vaso.
Vaseline-n Vaselina.
Vassal-n-Alila; alipin.
Vassa-a-Nauukol sa alila ó sa alipin.
Vassalage-n-Pagkaalipin; pagkaalila.
Vast-a-Malaki; marami.
Vast-n-Lupang karat; lugal na walaug hanga.
Vastness-n- Kalakihan; karamuhan.
Vat-n-Kawa; kaang.
Vaticinate-c-Humula; manghula.
Vault-n-Yungib; libing; libingan; kabaon; lundag; lukso.
Vault-v-Lumundag; lumukso.
Vaunt v-Maghambog; magmayabang.
Vaunt-n-Kahambugan: kayabangan.
Veal-n-Carne ng bulo.
Vedette-n-Bantay.
Veer-v-Lumiko; ibahin ang tungtungan.
Vegetable-n-Gulay.
Vegetable-a-Magulay; nauukol sa gulay.
Vegetal a-Nauukol sa gulay.
Vegetarian-n-Ang tawong ayaw kumain ng karne.
Vegetate-v-Tumubo; lumaki; sumupling; pumunla.
Vegetation-n-Manga gulay.
Vehemence-Vehemency-n-Kalakasan; ka ningasan; lakas.
Vehement-a-Malakas; maningas.
Vehicle-n-Carromata; curruage; bagol.
Veil-n-Tabing takip ng mukha.
Veil-v-Itabing; itakpan.
Vein-n-Ugat.
Vein-v-Pumuno ng manga ugat.
Vellicate-v-Kumilos na bigla,
Velocity-n-Katulinan; kalakasan; tulin.
Vena-n-Ugat.
Venal-a-Makabibili; upahan.
Venary-a-Nauukol sa pangangaso.
Vend v-Magbili; magtinda.
Vendee-n-Ang mamili.
Vender-h-Ang nagbili; ang nag tinda.
Vendible-a-Umubrang ipagbibili.
Vendible-n-Anomang bagay na ipinagbibili.
Vendition-n-Pagbibili; pagtitinda.
Vendor-n-Ang nagtitinda.

Vendue-n-Almoneda.
Venerable a-Dapat igalang.
Venerate v-Igalang; galangin.
Veneration-n-Paggalang; kagalangan; galang; walanggalang.
Venerator-n-Ang gumagalang.
Venereal-a-Nauukol sa paklapid.
Venery-n-Pakiapid
Venery-n-Pangangaso.
Venesection-n-Pagbukas ng ugat upang madugo.
Vengeance-n-Ganti; higanti.
Vengeful-a-Mahiganti.
Venial-a-Dapat patawarin.
Venicon-n-Carne ng usa.
Venom-n-Kamandag; lason.
Venous-a-May kamandag; malason.
Vent-n-Butas; daan ng hangin.
Vent-v-Palabasin; magsabi.
Ventilate-v-Buksan ng pinto upang mag daan ang hangin.
Ventral-a-Nauukol satiyan.
Venture-n-Kapanganiban; kapalaran.
Venture-v-Ilagay sa kapalaran; mangahas.
Ventursome-a-Matapang; mangahas.
Venturous-a-Matapang.
Venue-n-Kapitbahay; lugal na pinagkayarian.
Veracious a-Di marunong magsinungalingan.
Veracity-n-Katotohanan.
Veranda-n-Veranda.
Verb-n-Verbo.
Verbal-a-Hindi nakasulat sinabi lamang.
Verbalism-n-Salita.
Verbally-adv.-Sa salita lamang.
Verbatim-adv.-Ayon sa salita.
Verbiage-n-Paggamit ng maraming salita. ngunit walang kabuluhan.
Verbose-a-Magsalita.
Verbosity-n-Karamihan ng salita.
Verdancy-n-Pagkasariwa; kamurahan.
Verdant-a-Sariwa; mura.
Verdict-n-Hatol; pasiya.
Verdure-n-Verde; kamurahan; kasariwaan.
Verge-n-Gilid; tabi.
Verge-v-Lumapit; lumusong,
Verification-n-Kasaksihan; pagkasaksi.
Verify-v-Patotohanin; sumaksi.
Verily-adv.-Totoo; tunay.
Verisimilar-a-Tila totoo; marahil.
Veritable-a-Totoo; tunay; tama.
Verity-n-Katotohanan.
Verjuice-n-Katas na maasim; kaasiman; anghang; kapaklian.
Vermicella-n-Fideos.
Vermicular-a-Nauukol sa bulati.
Vermiculate-a Hitsurang bulati.

Vermiculose-Vermiculous-*a*-May bulati.
Vermifuge-*n*-Gamot laban sa bulati; gamot sa bulati.
Vermillion-*n*-Pula.
Vermin-*n*-Hayop na malikot.
Vernacular-*a*-Nauukol sa lupang tinubuan.
Vernacular-*n*-Wika ng̃ isang tawo.
Vernal-*a*-Nauukol sa tagaraw; nauukol sa pagkabata.
Versatile-*a*-Makapipihit; mababago.
Verse-*n*-Verso; pangkat.
Versed-*a*-Marunong; sanay.
Versification-*n*-Paggagawa ng̃ verso.
Versify-*v* Gawin verso.
Version-*n*-Salaysay; kahulugan; kasaysayan.
Versus-*prerp.*-Laban kay.
Vertebra-*n*-Isang buto ng̃ gulugod.
Verterbral-Vertebrate-Vertebrated-*a*-May gulugod.
Vertex-*n*-Dulo; pandulo; kataasan.
Vertical-*a*-Patayo; nakatayo.
Vertigo *a*-Lilio; hilo.
Very-*adv.*-Totoong; tunay.
Vesica-*n*-Pantog.
Vesicate-*v*-Lumintos.
Vesication-*n*-Paglilintos.
Vesper-*n*-Bituin sa gabi.
Vespers-*n*-Orasion.
Vessel *n*-Vaso.
Vest-*n*-Chaleco.
Vest-*v*-Magbihis; bihisan; bigyan ng̃ kapangyarihan.
Vestal-*a*-Banal; maselang; malinis.
Vested-*a*-Nakabihis.
Vestige-*n*-Bakas; guhit; tanda.
Vestment-*n*-Damit; habito.
Vesture-*n*-Mang̃a damit.
Veteran-*a*-Sanay; dati.
Veteran-*n*-Tawong sanay.
Veterinarian-*n*-Mangagamot ng̃ hayop.
Veterinary-*a*-Nauukol sa paggamot sa mang̃a hayop.
Veto-*v*-Magbawal; umayaw; huag pumayag.
Vex-*v*-Abalahin; yamutin; sabarin.
Vexation-*n*-Yamot; tukso; abala.
Vexatious-*a*-Makayayamot; mayamutin; mapighati.
Via-*adv.*-Sa parang ng̃; sa gawi ng̃.
Viaduct-*n*-Tulay.
Vial-*n*-Boteng munti.
Viand-*n*-Pagkain.
Vibrate-*v*-Uminig; mang̃atal.
Vibration-*n*-Inig; pang̃ing̃inig; atal.
Vicar-*n*-Katulong; kahalili.
Vicarage-*n*-Bahay ng̃ kalihim.
Vice-*n*-Bisio; kasamaan; sala; kasalanan.
Vicinity-*n*-Lugal na malapit; paligid.

Vicious-*a*-Mabang̃is; mabagsik; masama.
Vicissitude-*n*-Pagkasunodsunod ng̃ paglipat.
Victim-*n*-Ang nahibo; ó dinaya.
Victimize-*v*-Tekasin; hibuin.
Victor-*n*-Ang nanalo.
Victory-*n*-Pananalo.
Victorious-*a*-Nanalo.
Victual-*n*-Pagkain.
Victual-*v*-Bigyan ng̃ pagkain.
Vide-*v*-Tingnan.
Videlicet-*a*-Sumusunod; ganiri.
Vidette-*n*-Bantay.
Vie-*v*-Lumaban; magtalo.
View-*n*-Tingin; tanaw; kita.
View-*v*-Tuming̃in; tanawin.
Vigesimal-*a*-Ikadalawangpuo.
Vigil-*n*-Bantay; pang̃at.
Vigilance-*n*-Paging̃at; pagkakaling̃a; bantay.
Vigilant-*a*-Maing̃at makaling̃a.
Vigor-*n*-Takas; kaliksihan; katibayan; tibay; bisa; kasapatan.
Vigorous-*a*-Matapang; malakas; matibay; mabisa; matigas; litiran; malitid; maugat.
Vile-*a*-Masama; hamak.
Vilification *n*-Pagaalipusta; pagmumura; pagpapahamak.
Vilify-*v*-Hamakin; murahin; alipustain; pasamain.
Villa-*n*-Tirahan ó tahanan sa parang.
Village-*n*-Nayon; bayan na munti.
Villain-*n*-Masamang tawo.
Villainous *a* Masama.
Villainy-*n*-Kasamaan.
Vindicate-*v*-Lumaban; magtulong.
Vindication-*n*-Paglaban; katulong.
Vindictive-*a*-Mahiganti.
Vine-*n*-Lipay.
Vinegar-*n*-Sukha.
Vine yard-*n*-Halamanan ng̃ uvas.
Vinous-*a*-Nauukol sa alak.
Vintner-*n*-Mang̃ang̃alakal ng̃ alak.
Viol-Viola-*n*-Viola; violin na malaki.
Violate-*v*-Magkasala; lumaban sa utos.
Violation-*n*-Pagkakasala; kasalanan.
Violator-*n*-Ang nagkasala.
Violence-*n*-Kalakasan.
Violent *a*-Malakas; gahasa.
Violet *n*-Violeta.
Violet-*a*-Kulay purpura.
Violin-*n* Violin.
Violinist-*n*-Violinista.
Viper *n*-Alupong.
Viperous *a* May kamandag; parang alupong.
Virago-*n*-Babaying malikot at mang̃ahas.
Virgen-*n*-Virgin; babaying banal.

Virgin-a-May puri; banal.
Virginity-n-Kabanalan; pagkadalaga.
Viridescent-a-Verde.
Virile-a-Parang lalaki; malakas.
Virtue-n-Kabanalan; virtud; puri; kala-
kasan; kapangyarihan.
Virtuousa-a-Banal; may puri; malinis;
maselang.
Virulence-n-Pagkakahawa.
Virulent-a-Makahahawa; may kamandag.
Virus-n-Nana na makahahawa.
Visage-n-Tiñgin; mukha; hitsura.
Vis-a-vis-adv.-Makakaharap.
Vis-a-vis-n-Visavis.
Viscera-n-Laman ñg tiyan.
Visceral-a-Nauukol sa mañga bituka.
Viscerate-v-Alisin ang laman ñg tiyan.
Viscid-a-Malagkit; madidikit.
Visconnt-n-Visconde.
Viscountess-n-Asawa ñg visconde.
Viscous-a-Malagkit; malumot.
Vise-n-Pañgipit.
Vise-v-Ipitin.
Visible-a-Makakikita.
Vision-n-Tiñgin; kita; pagtatanaw.
Visionary-a-Maguniguni; mapagwari.
Visit-n-Visita; dalaw; pagdadalaw.
Visit-v-Dalawin; magvisita.
Visitation-n-Pagdadalaw.
Visitor-n-Ang dumadalaw.
Vista-n-Tanaw.
Visual-a-Nauukol sa tiñgin.
Vital-a-Kailañgan na totoo.
Vitality-n-Kakailañgan ñg mahigpit.
Vitiate-v-Sirain.
Vitreous-a-Nauukol savaso.
Vitric-a-Parang cristal.
Vitrifaction-Vitrifacture-n-Paggagawa ñg
mañga bagay ñg cristal.
Vitrify-v-Maging cristal.
Vituperate-v-Murahin; magmura.
Vituperation-n-Kamurahau; pagmumura.
Vituperator-n-Ang nagmumura.
Vivacious-a-Masaya; buhay na loob.
Vivacity-n-Kasayahan; saya.
Vivid-a-Ayon sa buhay; buhay mala-
kas.
Vivify-v-Buhayin; pasipagin.
Vixen-n-Babaying mañgahas.
Vixenly-Vixenish-a-Masuñgit; mañgahas.
Vocable-n-Salita; ñgalaug.
Vocabulary-n-Vocabolario; listahan ñg
mañga salita.
Vocal-a-Nauukol sa voces,
Vocalist-n-Magdadalit.
Vocality-n-Pagdadalit.
Vocalize-v-Tunugin.
Vocation-n-Hanapbuhay; kahiligan.
Vociferate-v-Sumigaw; sigawin; hiya-
win.

Vociferation-n-Pagsisigaw; hiyaw.
Vociferous-a-Malakas; matunog.
Vogue-a-Kaugalian; uso; modo.
Voice-n-Voces.
Voice-v-Magsabi; sabihin.
Voiced-a-May voces; sinabi,
Voiceless-a-Walang voces.
Void-a-Walang halaga; walang kabulu-
han; walang laman.
Void-n-Lugal na walang anomang laman.
Void-v-Alisin ang laman.
Voidance-n-Kawalan ñg laman.
Volant-a-Nakalilipad; maliksi; matulin
masipag.
Volatile a-Masaya; saliwahang loob; ma-
daling sumiñgaw.
Volcanic-a-Nauukol sa volcan.
Volcano-n-Volcan.
Volley-n-Pagputok ng sabaysabay.
Volt-n-Panukat ñg lintik.
Voluble-a-Masalita.
Volume-n-Tomo; libro.
Voluminous-a-Malaki; may maraming
tomo; masagana.
Voluntariness-n-Pagkakaayon sa kahi-
liñgan.
Voluntary-a-Ayon sa kahiliñgan.
Volunteer-n-Voluntario.
Volunteer-v-Magprisinta.
Voluptuary-a-Masagana.
Vomit-v-Sumuka; magsuka; sukain.
Vomit-n-Suka; pagsusuka.
Vomition-n-Pagsusuka.
Vomitive-a-Makasusuka.
Vomitory-n-Pagsuka.
Voracious-a-Matakaw.
Voracity-Voraciousness-n-Katakawan.
Vortex-n-Uliuli; ipoipo.
Votary-a-May pañgako.
Vote-n-Voto.
Vote-v-Magvoto; ihalal.
Vouch-v-Mañgako.
Voucher-n-Recibo.
Vouchsafe-v-Paging dapat; pumayag;
ipagkaloob.
Vow-n-Numpa; pañgako.
Vow-v-Manumpa; mañgako.
Vowel-n-Vocal.
Vowel a-Vocal.
Voyage-n-Lakad; viage.
Voyage-v-Maglakad; magviage.
Vulcanian-a-Nauukol sa volcan,
Vulgar-a-Karaniwan; hayag; alam ñg
madla; hamak; mababa.
Vulgarness-n-Kahamakan; kababaan.
Vulgarity-n-Kahamakan; kababaan; ka-
halayan.
Vulnerable-a-Makasisira; umuubrang sa-
gutin.
Vulpine-a-Matalas; tuso.

45

W

Wabble-v-Gumiraygiray; uminig.
Wabble n Giray: paggigiraygiray; inig.
Wad-n-Takip.
Wad-v-Takpanin; itakpan.
Wadding n-Takip; panakip.
Waddle v-Lumakad na parang bata.
Wade-v-Pumatis; magbatis; lumakad sa tubig.
Wader-n-Ang bunatis.
Wafer n-Galletang manipis.
Waffle n Galletang manipis.
Waft-v-Lumutang lumipad; lumayag.
Wag v-Pumagpay; iwayway
Wag n-Pagpag: wayway; tawong masaya.
Wage-v-Lumaban; magpusta.
Wage-v-Lumaban; magpusta; kaupahan; upa; bayad.
Wager-v-Magpusta; pustahin; tumaya.
Wager-n-Pusta; taya.
Waggle-v-Pagpagin ang buntot; galawin; ang buntot.
Wagon-n Bagol.
Waif n-Batang walang tirahan; batang lansañgan.
Wail-n-Daing; hinagpos.
Wail-v-Dumaing.
Wainscot-n-Dingding na kahoy.
Waist-n-Bayawang.
Waist band-n-Pamigkis sa bayawang.
Waist coat-n-Chaleco.
Wait-v-Magantay; antayin.
Wait-n Pagaantay.
Waiter-n-Alila sa lamesa.
Waitress-n-Babaying alila sa lamesa.
Waive v Bitiwan; ifuera; maiwan.
Wake-n Bakas ñg sasakyan.
Wake-v Puyat; pagpuyat.
Wake-v-Gumising.
Wakeful-a-Magising; gising.
Waken-v-Gumising; gisiñgin.
Wale n-Latay ñg hampas; gubit.
Walk n-Lakad; pasial; gala; paglibot.
Walk-v-Magpasial; lumakad; gumala; lumibot.
Wall-n-Dingding; pader.
Wall-v-Gumawa ó ilagay ñg dingding ó pader.
Wallet-n-Bulsikot; lalagyan ñg kuarta ó salapi.
Wallop-v-Hampasin; paluin.
Waltz-n-Bal; sayaw.
Waltz v Sumayaw ñg bal; magsayaw.
Wan-a-Maputla; namutla; mahina.
Wand-n-Maikling tungkod.
Wander v Maglibot; lumibot.

Wandering-n-Paglibot.
Wane-v-Tumahimik; humimpil; lumubay; bumawas; humina.
Wane-n Pagbawas; kahinaan.
Wanness-n-Kaputlaan; kahinaan.
Want-n-Kakailañgan ibig; kakulañgan; gutom.
Want-v-Magkailañgan; maibigan; magnasa; magpita.
Wanting a-Kulang.
Wantion-a-Malaya; pagayongayon; matigas ang ulo; tampalasan.
Wanton-n-Tawong malubog.
Wanton-v-Magbaropaslupa; maglubog.
War-n Labanan; paglaban; digma; pagdirigma; pagbabaka.
War-v Lumaban; mabaka; magdirigma.
Warble-v-Kumanta.
Warble n-Kanta.
Ward-v-Bantayin; magbantay.
Ward-n-Silid; kuarta.
Warden-n-Taga iñgat; taga bantay; puno
Warder-n-Taga bantay; bantay.
Wardrobe-n-Mañga damit; lalagyan ñg damit.
Ware-v-Gumasgas; gamitin.
Ware-n-Kalakal.
Ware house-n-Kamalig.
War fare-n-Pagdirigma; paglalaban.
Warily adv.-Mailag.
Wariness n-Iñgat; ilag; kailagan.
Warlike-a-Bagay sa labanan; Nauukol sa pagdirigma.
Warm-a-Mainit; malagamgam; malakuko.
Warm-v-Painitin, uminit.
Warmth-n Init; kaniñgasan; kainitan.
Warn-v-Ibalita; magbigay alam; magbalita.
Warning n-Bala; babala; alam.
Warp-v-Baluktutin; bumaluktot.
Warp n-Kabaluktotan.
Warrant n-Tibayan; katibayan; demanda; kasulatan.
Warrant v-Tibayin; magdemanda; maging dapat.
Warrantable-a-May katowiran; naging dapat; karampatan.
Warranty-n-Kasulatan; pañgako.
Warrior-n-Sundalo; mandirigma.
Wart-n-Kulugo.
Warty-a Makalago.
Wary-a Maiñgat; mailag; mahinahon.
Was-v. imp.- Ay; naging; nagka.
Wash-v-Maglaba; labhan; maghugas; hugasin.

Wash *n*-Laba; paglalaba.

Washer-*n*-Makinang panlalaba; maglalaba.

Washer woman-*n*-Babaying maglalaba.

Wash stand-*n*-Hinawan ñg kamay; hilamusan.

Washy-*a*-Matubig; basa; mahina; payat; bu.

Wasp-*n*-Putakti.

Waspish-*a*-Nauukol sa putakti;mapootin.

Wast-*v.* *imp.*-Ay; naging.

Waste-*v*-Isabog; sayangin; gastahin sa walang kabuluhan.

Waste-*a*-Labis; sukal; nakasabog.

Waste-*n*-Kasukalan; kalabisan.

Watch-*n*-Orasan; relos na munti bantay; tanod.

Watch-*v*-Bantayin; magbantay; magiñgat; iñgatin talibaan.

Watchful-*a*-Masipag magbantay; mainğat; gising; maliksi.

Watch man-*n*-Bantay; taga igat.

Watch word-*n*-Hodyatan; tanod.

Water *n*-Tubig.

Water-*v*-Tubugin; diligan; magdilig; wisikan, sabuyan.

Watery *a*-Matubig; basa.

Water course-*n*-Daan ñg tubig.

Waterfall-*n*-Bulugan ñg tubig; paghulog ñg tubig.

Water fowl-*n*-Ibon na nawiwili sa tubig.

Water melon-*n* Pakuan.

Water proof-*a*-Di masisira sa tubig.

Water spout-*n*-Sigwa.

Water-tight-*a*-Di makapapasok ang tubig.

Waul-*v*-Umiyak.

Wave-*n*-Alon; daluyong; kaway.

Wave-*v* Kawayin; kumaway umalon; pumagpag; pagpagin.

Waveless-*a*-Walang alon.

Wavelet-*n*-Alon na munti; munting alon.

Waver-*v*-Gumiray; lumikoliko.

Wavering-*a*-Mahina; mabubual; hindi pirme.

Wavy-*a*-Maalon.

Wax-*n* Kalaba.

Wax-*v*-Pahiran ñg kalaba.

Waxen-Waxy-*a*-Makalaba; may halong kalaba.

Way-*n*-Daan; paraan; landas; layo; kahiligan; hangad.

Wayfarer-*n*-Tawong lakad.

Waylay-*v*-Harangin; humarang.

Wayside-*n*-Tabi ñg daan.

Wayward *a*-Pabaya; matigas ang ulo.

We-*n-pro.*-Kami; tayo.

Weak-*a*-Mahina; payat, marupok; malata; dapok; babasagin.

Weakly-*adv.*-Mahinahina.

Weaken-*v*-Hinain; humina; lumata.

Weakness-*n*-Kahinaan; lata.

Weal-*n*-Kalagayan mahusay; kahusayan.

Weal-*v*-Guhitin.

Wealth-*n*-Yaman; kayamanan.

Wealthy-*n*-Yaman; makuarta; masalapi.

Wean-*v*-Awatin sa pagsuso;huag pasusuin

Weapon-*n*-Kasangkapan ñg sundalo; kasangkapang panlaban.

Wear-*v*-Gamitin; isuot; gumasgas.

Wear *n*-Paggamit; kagamitang pagsuot; gasgas.

Weary-*a*-Pagod; mapagal; nahirapan.

Weary-*v* Pumagod; pumagal; yumamot.

Weather *n*-Panahon.

Weather-*v*-Tumagal sa kahirapan.

Weather cock *n*-Kasangkapang pangturo; ñg pinangaling ñg hangin.

Weave-*v*-Humabi; maglala; salahin;.

Weaver *n*-Manghahabi.

Weazen-*a*-Payat; mahina.

Web-*n*-Bahay gagamba.

Webbed-*a* Hindi makahiwalay ang mañga daliri ñg paa.

Wed-*v.* *imp.*-Kinasal; kumasal; nakasal; nagsawa; nagbalayi.

Wedding *n*-Kasal; balayi; pagkabalayi.

Wedge-*n* Sabat; kalang.

Wedge-*v* Sabatin.

Wed lock *n*-Kasal.

Wednesday-*n* Miercoles.

Weed-*n*-Damong magaspang.

Weedy-*a*-Maramo; masukal.

Week-*n*-Lingo.

Week day-*n* Mañga araw bukod sa lingo.

Weekly-*a*-Balang lingo; twing lingo.

Weekly-*adv.*-Sa lingolingo; lingolinguhan.

Weekly-*n*-Pahayagan na lumitaw minsan sa isang lingo.

Ween-*v*-Magisip; magwari.

Weep-*n*-Umiyak; magnangis; magluha; lumuha.

Weeping-*a*-Maluha; nananangis.

Weevil *n*-Bukbok; pangbutas.

Weigh-*v* Timbañgin; tumimbang; bigatin; bumigat.

Weight-*n* Bigat; timbang; kabigatan.

Weight-*v*-Pabigatan; patawin.

Weightless *a*-Walang bigat.

Weighty-*a*-Mabigat; malaki; mahalaga.

Weir-*n* Pangharang ñg tubig.

Weird-*a*-Nauukol sa mno.

Welcome-*a*-Masaya; mainam sa visita.

Welcome-*v*-Tangapin ang mañga visita.

Welcome *n* Pagtangap ñg visita.

Welcome-*v*-Tangapin ang visita; tumangap sa visita.

Weld-*n*-Hinang.

Weld-*v*-Hinañgin; maghinang.

Welfare-n-Kalagayan; kabutihan.
Welkin-n-Langit.
Well-n-Balon; bukalan.
Well-v-Buhos; umagos.
Well-a-Walang sakit; masaya.
Well-adv.-Mabuti; matowid; mahusay.
Well-being-n-Kalagayang walang sakit; kasayahan: kabutihan.
Well-born-a-Hindi nagbuhat sa masama.
Well-bred-a-Magalang; mabuting ugali.
Well-favored-a-Maganda.
Well-head-n-Bukalan; binukalan; pinangalinga; pinagbuhatan.
Well-nigh-adv.-Halos.
Well-spring-n-Bukalan; pinagbuhatan; pinangalingan.
We'll-Kami'y tayo'y.
Welt-n-Gilid; tabi.
Welt-v-Lagyan ng gilid.
Welter-v-Mahiga sa putik; lumublob.
Wen-n-Pigsa.
Wench-n-Babaying negra.
Wend-v-Pumaroon; sumunod.
Went-v. imp.-Naparoon; nagpunta.
Wept-v. imp. & p. p.-Umiyak na; nakaiyak.
Were-v. imp.-Ay; naging.
West-n-Ang kalunuran.
West-a-Kalunuran.
West-adv.-Sa gawing kalunuran.
Westerly-a-Sa kalunuran.
Westerly-adv.-Sa gawing kalunuran.
Western-a-Kalunuran.
West ward-West wards adv.-Sa gawing kalunuran.
Wet-a-Basa; natigmak.
Wet n-Pagkabasa.
Wet-v-Basain; bumasa; matigmak.
Wetness-n-Pagkabasa.
Whack-v-Hampasin.
Whack-n-Hampas.
Wharf-n-Muella.
What-pro.-Ano.
What-a-Anong.
What ever-pro.-Ano man; alin man.
What so ever-pro.-Ano man; alin man.
What so ever-a-Ano mang.
Wheat-n-Trigo.
Wheaten-a-Nauukol sa trigo.
Wheedle-v-Alindugin; amoin; palayawin; pawiliin.
Wheel-n-Gulong.
Wheel-v-Gulungin
Wheel wright-n-Mangagawa ng gulong.
Wheeze-v-Maghika.
Wheeze-n-Hika.
Wheezy-a-Mahika.
Whelk-n-Butlig.
Whelm-v-Supilin.

Whelp-n-Anak ng hayop; tuta; batang hamak.
When-adv.-Kailan; nang; niyong; noon.
When ever-When so ever-adv.-Kailan man.
Whence adv. Saan; kung saan; paano.
Whence so ever adv.-Magbuhat sa.
Where-adv.-Saan; saan banda; saan man.
Where about-Where abouts-adv.-Saan man; malapit sa.
Where abouts-n-Lugal kinalalagyan.
Where as-conj.-Dahil dito; yayamang; upang.
Where at adv.-Dahilan dito.
Where fore-adv.-Dahilan dito.
Where of-adv.-Nang ano.
Where on-adv.-Sa yaon
Where so ever adv.Saan saan; saan man.
Where to adv.-Sa lugal yaon.
Where upon-adv.-At ngayon.
Whet-v-Ihasa.
Whet-n-Paghahasa.
Whet stone-n-Asahan.
Whether-conj.-Kung.
Whey-n-Gatas na malabnaw.
Which pro.-Alin; kung alin.
Which ever-Which so ever-pro.-Alinman.
Whiff-n-Ihip; hitit.
Wiffle-v-Uminig; gumiraygiray.
Whiffle tree-n-Pansabit ng tiranti.
While-n-Panahon; dali.
While adv.-Samantalang.
While-v-Samantalahin.
Whilom-adv.-Dati; maminsanminsan.
Whilst-adv.-Samantala.
Whim-n-Sumpong; nais pita.
Whimper v-Umiyak; manangis.
Whimper-n-Iyak; nangis.
Whimsical-a-Mapootin; masumpungin.
Whine-v-Umiyak; dumaing; manangis.
Whine-n-Ningas; daing.
Whinny-v-Humuni ang kabayo.
Whinny-n-Huni ng kabayo.
Whip-n-Latigo.
Whip-v-Latiguhin; hampasin ng latigo.
Whir-n-Haging; haginit.
Whir-v-Humaging; bumaginit.
Whirl-v Umikit.
Whirl-n-Ikit; pagiikit.
Whirl pool-n-Uliuli
Whirl wind-n-Ipoipo; buhawi.
Whisk-v-Walisin.
Whisk-a-Walis; lawis.
Whisker-n-Balbas.
Whiskey-n-Wiske.
Whisper-v-Bumulong; magbulungan.
Whisper-n-Bulungan bulong.
Whist-inter.-Siit; tahan.
Whist a-Tahimik; walang kibo.
Whist-n-Tres y siete.

Whistle-v-Sumutsot; humaging; humaginit.
Whistle-n-Haginit; sutsut; panutsot.
Whit-n-Kakaunti.
White-a-Maputi.
White-n-Kulay puti; puti.
Whiten-v-Pumuti; putiin.
Whitish-a-Maputiputi.
White smith-n-Mangagawa ng la'a.
White wash-n-Halo ng apog at tubig.
White wash-c-Pahiran ng apog.
Whither-adv.-Saan; saan banda.
White so ever-adv. Saan man.
Witlow-n-Pamamaga ng mga daliri.
Whittle-v-Kayasin; kumayas; magkayas.
Whtle-n-Pagkayas.
Whiz-v Humaging; humaginit.
Whize-n-Haginit; haging.
Who-pro.-Sino; sinosino.
Who ever-pro.-Sino man.
Whole-a-Lahat; buo; ganap.
Whole n-Kalahatan; kabuoan.
Whole some-a-Makapagpapalakas; makagagaling sa katawan.
Wholly-adv.-Lahatlahat; buongbuo.
Whom-pro.-Sino man; alin man.
Whom so ever-pro.-Sino man.
Whoop-n-Sigaw; hiyaw.
Whoop-v Sumigaw; hiyawin.
Whose-pro.-Kanginong; kanikaninong.
Whose so ever-pro.- Kangino man kangikanino man.
Who so ever-pro.-Sino man.
Whur-n-Haging; haginit.
Whur-v-Humaging humaginit.
Why-adv.-Bakit; bakin; paano kaya ang dahilan.
Wick-n-Mitsa.
Wicked-a-Masama; malupit; hamak.
Wickedness-n Kasamaan; kalupitan.
Wicker-n-Sangan munti-
Wide-a-Maluag; maluang; malapad; maaliwalas; tiwangwang; madalang; malawak; watak.
Wide-adv.-Maluang; malapad.
Wideness-n-Kalaparan; lapad; luang.
Width n-Lapad; luang; kalaparan.
Widen-v-Lumapad; lumanang.
Widow-v-Baong babayi; babaying bao.
Widow-v-Magbao; maging bao.
Widower-n-Lalaking bao.
Widow hood-n-Kalagayan bao.
Wield-v-Mamahala; gamitin.
Wife n-Asawang babayi.
Wife hoop-n-Kalagayan may asawa.
Wig-n-Buhok.
Wiggle-v-Kumilos.
Wiggle-n-Kilos.
Wight-n-Tawo.
Wigwam-n-Bubo.

Wild-a-Mailap; mabangis; ramo; bangin tungak.
Wild-n-Gubat.
Wilder-v-Gumulo ang isip.
Wilderness-n-Gubat; kagubatan.
Wildness-n-Ilap.
Wile-n-Daya; hibo; lalang; lansi.
Will-n-Loob; isip, lakas loob.
Will v-Maibigan.
Willful-a-Matigas ang ulo: lakas loob.
Willfully-adv.-Tinalaga; sinadya.
Willing-a-Masusunurin,
Wilt-v-Lumanta; kumupas.
Wily-a-Tuso; magdaraya.
Wimble-n-Pangbutas-
Win-v-Manalo; magkamit.
Wince-v-Umurong; matakot.
Winch-n-Panghuit; pangikit.
Wind-n-Hangin.
Wind-v-Ikiran; umikit.
Windless-a Walang hangin.
Wind mill-n-Makinang ipinalalakad ng hangin.
Wind pipe-n-Lalamunan.
Window-n-Bintana.
Wine-n-Alak; tinto.
Wine glass-n-Kopa ng alak.
Wing-n-Pakpak.
Wing-v-Pilayin.
Winged-a-May pakpak.
Wingless a-Walang pakpak.
Wink-v-Kumindat; pumikit.
Wink-n-Kindad; pikit.
Winning-n-Panalunan.
Winning-a-Mananalo.
Winnow-v-Magpahangin.
Winsome-a-Maganda; masaya.
Winter-n-Taglamig.
Wintery-a-Malamig; maginaw.
Wipe-c-Pahiran; magpahid.
Wire-n-Kawad.
Wire-v-Lagyan ng kawad.
Wiry-v-Nauukol sa kawad; malakas; maliksi.
Wisdom-n-Karunungan; dunong; paham; kabihasahan; katalinuhan.
Wise-a-Marunong; tuso; matalas; matalino; bihasa.
Wise acre-n-Ulol.
Wish-v-Ibigin;magnasa;magpita;magnais
Wish-n-Ibig; nais; nasa; pita.
Wishful-a-Maibigan; mapagnasa; mapagpita.
Wisp-n-Munting bigkis.
Wistful-a-Maingat.
Wit-n-Lasa; lakas ng isip; katalasan katalinuhan.
Wit-v-Malaman; talastasin.
Witch-n-Babaying magkukulam.
Witch-v-Kulamin; mangkulam.

Witch craft-*n*-Mangkukulam.
With-*prep.*-Kasama ng; nang; sa; ni.
Withal *adv.*-Sabaysabay; naman; gayon din.
Withal-*prep.*-Kasama ng; nang; sa.
With draw-*r*-Magrenuncia; umurong; tumangi; itiwalay; lumayo.
With drawal-*n*-Pagurong; pagtangi; pagtangal.
Withe-*n*-Pamigkis.
Wither-*v*-Lumanta; kumupas.
Withers-*n*-Batok ng kabayo.
With hold-*v*-Ifuera; ibukod; huag sabihin; huag magsabi.
With in-*adv.*-Nasasa loob.
With in-*prep.*-Napapaloob.
With out-*adv.*-Wala.
With out-*prep.*-Sa labas; labas sa.
With stand-*v*-Tumagal;lumaban;labanin.
Wit ess-*a*-Ulol; mapurol ang isip.
Witness-*n*-Saksi; mannnuod.
Witness-*v*-Sumaksi; manuod.
Witling-*n*-Tawong hindi marunong.
Witty-*a*-Marunong; matalas; matalino.
Wive *v* Magasawa; makasal.
Wizard-*n*-Tawong marunong; mago.
Wizen-*a*-Payat; tuyo.
Woe-*n*-Kahirapan; sakuna; hirap.
Woe-begone-*a*-Nakakahapis.
Woeful-Woful *a* Kaawa; malungkot.
Wolf *n*-Lobo.
Wolfish-*a*-Nauukol sa lobo.
Wolves-*n*-Manga lobo.
Woman-*n*-Babayi.
Woman hood-*n*-Pagkababayi; kalagayan babayi.
Womanish *a* Parang babayi.
Woman kind-*n* Lahi ng babayi.
Womanly-*a* Parang babayi.
Womb *n*-Matriz; bahay bata.
Won-*v. imp.* & *p. p*-Nanalo; tinalo.
Wonder-*n*-Pamamangha; pagtataka.
Wonder *v*-Mamangha; magtaka.
Wonderful-*a*-Makamamangha; magtataka; magaling na lubha.
Wondrous-*a*-Makamamangha;magtataka.
Wont *v*-Hindi magawa.
Wont-*n*-Keugalian; paguugali.
Woo-*v*-Lumigaw; luminigkod; maglingkod.
Wooer-*n*-Ang naglilingkod.
Wood *n*-Kahoy; kalap.
Wood-*v*-Tumubo ang manga kahoy.
Woodbine-*n*-Bulaklak.
Wood cutter-*n*-Mananaga ng kahoy.
Wooded-*a*-Makahoy; may kahoy.
Wooden-*a*-Yari ng kahoy.
Wooden rattle *n*-Pagupak.
Woodland-*n*-Lupang gubat; gubat.
Woodland-*a*-Nauukol sa gubat.

Wood man-*n*-Tawong gubat; mangangaso; mananaga ng kahoy.
Woodsman-*n*-Tawong gubat; mananaga; mangangaso.
Wood work *n*-Sawa sa kahoy.
Wood y *a* Makahoy.
Wool-*n*-Balahibo ng tupa.
Woolen-*a*-De lana.
Woolens *n*-Manga damit na makapal.
Wolly-*a* Mabalahibo.
Word-*n*-Salita; wika; pangako.
Word-*v*-Magsalita; magsabi.
Wording-*n*-Pagsasalita.
Wordy-*a*-Masalita; may maraming salita.
Wore-*v. imp.*-Ginamit; sinuot; ginasgas.
Work *n* Trabajo; gawa; kapagalan.
Work-*v*-Magtrabajo; gumawa; pumagal.
Work box-*n*-Tumpiping munti.
Worker-*n*-Mangagawa; ang gumawa.
Work house *n*-Bilango.
Work man-*n*-Mangagawa.
Work manship-*n*-Paggagawa.
Work shop-*n* Gawaan.
World-*n* Sangkalibutan; lupa; mundo; sangkatawohan.
Worlding-*n* Tawong lupa.
Worldly *a*-Nauukol sa lupa; bagay lupa.
Worm-*n*-Uod; bulati.
Worm-*v*-Pumagal; pumagot.
Worm-eaten-*a*-May uod; may bukbok.
Worn-*v. imp.*-Ginamit; nakasuot.
Worry-*v*-Tuksuhin; yamutin; pagalitin.
Worry-*n*-Tukso; galit; yamot.
Worse *a*-Lalong masama; masama pa; lubhang masama.
Worse-*adv.*-Masama pa.
Worship-*n*-Pagsimba; pagsamba; paggalang.
Worship *v*-Magsamba; sambahin.
Worshipper-*n* Ang sumasamba.
Worshipful-*a* Dapat galangin; dapat purihin.
Worst *a* Kasamasamaan.
Worst-*n*-Ang masama sa lahat.
Worst-*v*-Supilin; pasukuin; manalo.
Worsted-*n*-Torcillo.
Worth *v*-Maging; marapatin.
Worth-*n*-Halaga.
Worth-*a*-May halaga.
Worthiness-*n*-Karampatan.
Worthless-*n*-Walang halaga; walang kabuluhan.
Worthy-*a*-Nararapat; marapatin.
Would-*v*-Kaya; ba.
Wound-*n*-Sugat; bugbog; hiwa; taga.
Wound-*v*-Sugatin; sumugat; bugbugin; bagbagin; hiwain.
Wound-*v. imp.* & *p. p.*-Inikid.
Wove *v. imp.*-Hinabi; humabi.
Woven *v. p. p.*-Hinabi na; nakahabi.

Wrangle-v-Magtalo; makipagtalo; magbasagulo; magusap.
Wrangle-n-Usap; talo; basagulo.
Wrap-v-Balutin; paluputin; magkidkid; ikirin; magulak.
Wrapper-n-Balot; balutan; lalagyan bahay
Wrath-n-Galit; tauim ng loob.
Wrathful-a-Magalit.
Wreak-v-Hapisin; gawin.
Wreath-n-Putong.
Wreath-v-Pamuton; putungin.
Wreck-v-Sirain.
Wreck-n-Pagkasira; kasiraan.
Wrench-n-Birador; pangpaikit.
Wrench-v-Pihitin; batakin.
Wrest-v-Agawin; pilipitin.
Wrestle-v-Magbuno; sumungab.
Wrestle-n-Bunuhan; buno; sungaban.
Wrestler-n-Ang marunong magbuno.
Wretch-n-Tawong masama; tawong hamak
Wretched-a-Hamak; masama; malungkot; mababa.
Wriggle-v-Kumilos; gumalaw.

Wright-n-Mangagawa.
Wring-v-Pilipitin.
Wrinkle-n-Kunot; kulubot.
Wrinkle-v-Kunumot; kulubutin; kunntin
Wrinkly-a-Makunot; makulubot.
Wrist-n-Kamaw; manika ng kamay.
Wrist band-n-Pamigkis sa kamay.
Writ-n-Sulat; kasulatan.
Write-v-Sumulat.
Writer-n-Taga sulat.
Writhe-v-Kumilos maghirap.
Writing-n-Kasulatan sulat.
Wrong-a-Hindi tama; mali.
Wrong-n-Kamalian.
Wrong-v-Sumuwail; saktan.
Wrongful-a-Masama; mamali.
Wrote-v imp.-Sinulat; sinulatan; sumulat.
Wroth-a-Galit; nakayayamot.
Wrought-v imp. & p. p.-Ginawa.
Wrung-v imp. & p. p.-Pinilipit.
Wry-a-Napilipit.
Wye-n-Ang titik Y.

X

Xanthic-a-Kulay dalanghita; madilaw.
Xiphoid-a-Hitsurang sandata.
Xylocarpous-a-Namumunga ng bungang

matigas.
Xyter-n-Kasangkapang ginamit ng mangamot upang kayasin ang manga buto.

Y

Yacht-n-Susakyan.
Yachting-n-Paglayag.
Yager-n-Sundalong lakad.
Yam-n-Kamoting dilaw
Yankee-n-Taga America.
Yap-v-Sumigaw; tumahol.
Yap-n-Sigaw; tahol.
Yard-n-Bakuran; bara.
Yard stick-n-Bara.
Yarn-n-Pisi na malambot; estambre.
Yataghan-n-Panaksak ng turko.
Yaup-v-Umiyak parang bata; sumigaw.
Yaup-n-Sigaw iyak.
Yawl-v-Umiyak sumigaw; umangil.
Yawn-v-Humikab; maghikab.
Yawn-n-Hikab; higab.
Ye-pro.-Ikaw; kayo.
Yea-adv.-Oo; oopo; tango.
Yea-n-Pagkaoopo.
Yean-v-Manganak.
Year-n-Taon.
Yearling-n-Hayop na may isang taon ang edad.
Yearly-adv.-Sa tuwing taon, sataon taon.

Yearn-v-Magnasa; magpita.
Yearning-n-Pita; nasa.
Yeast-n-Lavadura.
Yelk-n-Pula ng itlog.
Yell-v-Sumigaw.
Yell-n-Sigaw.
Yellow-a-Madilaw.
Yellow-n-Dilaw; kulay dilaw.
Yellow bird-n-Ibong na madilaw.
Yellow hammer-n-Ibong na madilaw ang dibdib.
Yellowish-a-Madilawdilaw.
Yellow jacket-n-Putakti.
Yelp-v-Umangil; sumigaw.
Yelp-n-Iyak; angil, sigaw.
Yerman-n-Tawong karaniwan.
Yerk-v-Batakin; bumatak.
Yerk-n-Batak.
Yes-adv.-Opo; oo.
Yester-a-Nauukol sa kahapon.
Yesterday-n-Kahapon.
Yesterday adv.-Kahapon.
Yet-adv.-Pa; man; yamang; gayonman,

Yet-*conj.*-Datapuat; nğunit; bagaman; yamang; baukod pa sa ito.
Yield-*v*-Pumayag; sumuko; umani.
Yield-*n*-Ani.
Yoke-*n*-Singkaw; pagkaalipin; kahirapan.
Yoke-*v*-Isingkaw; singkawin.
Yokefellow-Yokemate¸-*n*-Kasama.
Yolk-*n*-Pula nğ itlog
Yon-*a*-Iyan; iyon.
Yon-*adv.*-Diyan; doon.
Yonder-*a*-Iyan; iyon; yaon.
Yonder-*adv.*-Diyan; doon.
Yore *adv.*-Noong panahon.

You-*prop.*-Ikaw; kayó.
Young-*a*-Binata; bata pa; mura.
Young-*n*-Inakay; ang anak.
Youngish-*a*-Bata pa; hindi pa matanda.
Youngister-*n*-Bata; binata.
Your-*pro*-Iyo; inyo; mo; ninyo.
Your self-*pro*-Iyong sarili; sarili mo; ikaʍ rin.
Youth-*n*-Bata; bagongtawo.
Youthful-*a*-Bata pa; binata; di pa matanda.
Yule-*n*-Knaresma.
Ywis-*adv.*-Oo; totoo; tama; siguro; marahil.

Z

Zeal-*n*-Kasipagan; sipag; kaninğasan; kainitan nğ loob.
Zealot-*n*-Tawong masipag na lubha; tawong napakasipag.
Zealotry-*n* Kasipagan.
Zealous-*a*-Masipag; mainit ang loob; maninğas; manğahas.
Zenith-*n*-Kataastaasan lugal; pandulo.
Zephyr-*n*-Hanğin nangaling sa kalunuran.
Zero-*n*-Zero.

Zest-*n*-Kainitan; kaninğasan; kasipagan.
Zigzag-*adv.* Palikoliko; pasuotsuot.
Zigzag-*v*-Lumikoliko; lumakad nğ palikoliko.
Zinc-*n* Sim na malambot.
Zodiac-*n*-Daan nğ araw sa lanğit.
Zone *n*-Lugar; pamigkis.
Zounds-*inter*-Lintok.
Zygoma-*n* Sihang; panğa.
Zygomatic-*a*-Nauukol sa sihang ó sa panğa.

CPSIA information can be obtained at www.ICGtesting.com
Printed in the USA
BVOW06*1816240516

449353BV00008B/27/P